The Struggle for Human Rights

The Struggle for Human Rights

Essays in honour of Philip Alston

Edited by
NEHAL BHUTA
Professor of Public International Law, University of Edinburgh, UK
FLORIAN HOFFMANN
Professor of Law, Pontifícia Universidade Católica do Rio de Janeiro (PUC-Rio), Brazil
SARAH KNUCKEY
Clinical Professor of Law; Director, Human Rights Clinic and Human Rights Institute, Columbia Law School, USA
FRÉDÉRIC MÉGRET
Professor and Dawson Scholar, Faculty of Law, McGill University, Canada
MARGARET SATTERTHWAITE
Professor of Clinical Law, NYU School of Law, USA

OXFORD
UNIVERSITY PRESS

OXFORD
UNIVERSITY PRESS

Great Clarendon Street, Oxford, OX2 6DP,
United Kingdom

Oxford University Press is a department of the University of Oxford.
It furthers the University's objective of excellence in research, scholarship,
and education by publishing worldwide. Oxford is a registered trade mark of
Oxford University Press in the UK and in certain other countries

First Edition published in 2021

Impression: 3

Published in the United States of America by Oxford University Press
198 Madison Avenue, New York, NY 10016, United States of America

British Library Cataloguing in Publication Data

Data available

Library of Congress Control Number: 2021934435

ISBN 978–0–19–886806–4

DOI: 10.1093/oso/9780198868064.001.0001

Printed and bound by
CPI Group (UK) Ltd, Croydon, CR0 4YY

In memoriam Sally Engle Merry

Acknowledgements

This book has come together during extraordinary times. It would not have been possible without the constant encouragement and active contribution of many people beyond the editorial team. The first stepping stone, a workshop around the theme of the book held in 2019 was generously supported by New York University, Philip's professional home, and special thanks are due to Dean Trevor Morrison, Brianne Cuffe, Penelope Fernandes, Gabriel Rosenstein, and Lauren Stackpoole for making it possible, and for thus providing a crucial impetus for the book. Then, at Oxford University Press, we were fortunate to be accompanied in our venture by Merel Alstein with her customary encouragement and expert guidance as well as by Jordan Burke and Charlotte Holloway during editing and production, and by Libby Holcroft in relation to the cover design. Their responsiveness to and patience with the vagaries of transcontinental editing during a global pandemic was crucial to making this happen. In addition, Jemmy Erhiagonoma at McGill University provided excellent assistance with copyediting. Graphic artist Nathalie Jolivert graciously accepted our commission at short notice to provide the original artwork for the cover. Without their effort, this book would simply not have been possible. Finally, we are deeply grateful to the many of Philip's fellow travellers who, regardless of age, location, or professional pursuits, have answered our call to take part in this venture, be it as participants in the 2019 workshop, as authors to this collection, or both. Last, but not least, Gráinne de Búrca has been the one interlocutor without whose quiet complicity we could not even have started this project. To all of these collaborators our profound thanks; responsibility for any errors rests, of course, exclusively with us.

Nehal Bhuta
Florian Hoffmann
Sarah Knuckey
Frédéric Mégret
Margaret Satterthwaite
Edinburgh, Montreal, New York, Rio de Janeiro
January 2021

Contents

List of Contributors

Georges Abi-Saab, Graduate Institute of International Studies, Geneva

José E Alvarez, New York University School of Law, USA

Nehal Bhuta, Edinburgh Law School, The University of Edinburgh, UK

Hilary Charlesworth, Melbourne Law School, Australia

Obiora Chinedu Okafor, Osgoode Hall Law School, York University, Canada

Andrew Clapham, Graduate Institute of International and Development Studies, Geneva

Mac Darrow, Melbourne Law School, The University of Melbourne, Australia

Olivier De Schutter, University of Louvain, Belgium

Alicia Ely Yamin, Harvard Law School, USA

Sally Engle Merry †, New York University, USA

César Rodríguez-Garavito, NYU Law, USA

Thomas Hammarberg, Raoul Wallenberg Institute, University of Lund, Sweden and International Department of the Swedish Parliament, Sweden

Florian Hoffmann, Berlin DO School, Germany

Benedict Kingsbury, NYU Law, USA

Sarah Knuckey, Human Rights Institute, Columbia Law School, Columbia University, USA

Martti Koskenniemi, NYU Law, USA

Malcolm Langford, Faculty of Law, University of Oslo, Norway

Euan MacDonald, School of Law, University of Edinburgh, UK

Frédéric Mégret, Faculty of Law, McGill University, Canada

Rebecca Mignot-Mahdavi, Asser Institute, The Netherlands

Vitit Muntarbhorn, Faculty of Law, Chulalongkorn University, Thailand

Gerard Quinn, Raoul Wallenberg Institute, University of Lund, Sweden and University of Leeds, UK

Giorgia Sangiuolo, Centre of European Law, King's College London, UK

Margaret Satterthwaite, NYU Law, USA

Bruno Simma, Michigan Law, University of Michigan, USA

Henry J Steiner, Harvard Law School, USA

Hélène Tigroudja, Aix-Marseille University, France

John Tobin, Melbourne Law School, The University of Melbourne, Australia

Joseph H H Weiler, NYU Law, USA

List of Abbreviations

ACHR	American Convention on Human Rights
ACMW	ASEAN Committee on the Implementation of the ASEAN Declaration on the Protection and Promotion of the Rights of Migrant Workers
ACTIP	ASEAN Convention against Trafficking in Persons, especially Women and Children
ACWC	ASEAN Commission on the Rights of Women and Children
ADB	Asian Development Bank
AHRD	ASEAN Human Rights Declaration
AI	artificial intelligence
AICHR	ASEAN Intergovernmental Commission on Human Rights
AIIB	Asian Infrastructure Investment Bank
ANC	African National Congress
APA	ASEAN Plan of Action
ART	antiretroviral therapy
ASEAN	Association of South-East Asian Nations
BHR	business and human rights
BIT	bilateral investment treaty
BRI	Belt and Road Initiative
BRICS	Brazil, Russia, India, China, and South Africa
CEDAW	Committee on Elimination of Discrimination Against Women
CERD	Committee on Elimination of Racial Discrimination
CESCR	Committee on Economic, Social, and Cultural Rights
CIA	Central Intelligence Agency
CILC	Center for International Legal Cooperation
CJEU	Court of Justice of the European Union
COI	Commission of Inquiry
CRPD	Convention on the Rights of Persons with Disabilities
CSC	Correctional Service of Canada
CSOs	civil society organizations
CSR	corporate social responsibility
ECHR	European Convention on Human Rights
ECJ	European Court of Justice
ESC	economic, social, and cultural
ECtHR	European Court of Human Rights
EIB	European Investment Bank
ETOs	extraterritorial obligations
FFM	fact-finding mission
FLN	Front de Libérations Nationale
FPIC	free, prior, and informed consent
GNI	gross national income
GNP	gross national product
GONGOS	government-organized NGOs
HRBAs	human rights-based approaches
HRC	Human Rights Council
HRCAC	Human Rights Council Advisory Committee

IAHRC	Inter-American Human Rights Commission
IAHRS	Inter-American Human Rights System
ICC	International Criminal Court
ICCPR	International Covenant on Civil and Political Rights
ICERD	International Convention on the Elimination of All Forms of Racial Discrimination
ICESCR	International Covenant on Economic, Social and Cultural Rights
ICJ	International Court of Justice
ICRC	International Committee of the Red Cross
IFI	international financial institution
IHL	international humanitarian law
ILC	International Law Commission
ILO	International Labour Organization
IMF	International Monetary Fund
INCLO	International Network of Civil Liberties Organizations
IPCC	Intergovernmental Panel on Climate Change
ISC	Intelligence and Security Committee
ISDS	Investor–State Dispute Settlement
ISIS	Islamic State of Iraq and Syria
IPBES	Intergovernmental Science-Policy Platform on Biodiversity and Ecosystem Services
LDC	least-developed country
MDBs	multilateral development banks
MDGs	Millennium Development Goals
NGO	non-government organization
NHRIs	national human rights institutions
NIEO	New International Economic Order
NT	New Testament
NYU	New York University
OAS	Organization of American States
OHCHR	Office of the High Commissioner for Human Rights
PHC	primary health care
PLO	Palestine Liberation Organization
PPP	public–private partnership
R2P	Responsibility to Protect
RIA	Recognition, Institutionalization, and Accountability (framework)
SDGs	Sustainability Development Goals
SOMSWD	Senior Officials of the Ministries on Social Welfare and Development
SRHR	sexual and reproductive health and rights
TMBs	treaty monitoring bodies
TOR	Terms of Reference
TWAIL	Third World Approaches to International Law
UCMs	unilateral coercive measures
UNCTAD	UN Conference on Trade and Development
UNGPs	UN Guiding Principles on Business and Human Rights
UNHCR	UN High Commissioner for Refugees
UDHR	Universal Declaration of Human Rights
UNICEF	UN International Emergency Children's Fund
UN	United Nations
UPR	Universal Periodic Review
WJP	World Justice Project
WTO	World Trade Organization

Introduction

Nehal Bhuta, Florian Hoffmann, Sarah Knuckey, Frédéric Mégret, and Margaret Satterthwaite

This volume of essays goes to press in an era of faltering democratic institutions and practices, dramatically destructive climate events, collapsing economic growth, renewed attention to systemic racism and police brutality, global pandemics, and some of the most unequal distribution of income and wealth recorded in over a hundred years. These profound crises occur against the background of the collapse of long-standing assumptions that had structured politics and international relations. Even as the previous epoch-making political-economic settlement (whether we call it Keynesianism, Embedded Liberalism, Welfarism, or something else) comes dangerously unwound, it has come under renewed criticism for reproducing the legacies of colonialism, imperialism, and slavery, and for embedding the normative status of a concrete type of social persona: white, male, able-bodied, heterosexual. Can contemporary human rights laws and practices meet these and the many other challenges we face? Should the seventy-year project of legalizing human rights internationally be pushed further, paused, or rethought? This book attempts to generate questions about the status and goals of the human rights project, notably as it has come to be associated with the emblematic career of Philip Alston.

One productive starting point is that, even as the relationship of human rights to social and political change is everywhere shifting and contested, human rights remain the closest thing to a global *lingua franca* for representing, framing, labelling, and demanding redress for injustice and social suffering. As Sally Merry writes in her posthumously published essay in this book, organizations and groups—non-profits, social movements, and loose collectives—embrace the language of human rights in all regions of the globe, and have successfully used human rights to advance justice and accountability. The shared language of rights can be used to express and legitimate values, concerns, and needs, and can be an important organizing tool. Global movements—such as those led by indigenous peoples, peasants, workers, women, and people with disabilities—have organized to claim human rights and demand that their rights be recognized in law. The attention that can be garnered by claims of human rights violations can and has been used to label economic, political, and institutional structures as fundamentally unjust and inadequate. Formal human rights institutions can be used to spotlight abuse, focus attention on issues, serve as platforms for advocacy, and pressure governments to reform. They provide space for advocates to unite across borders, raise the profile of national struggles, and articulate their demands in new ways.

The exact place of human rights in international law and relations and in efforts to prevent abuses of power and advance social justice, however, has always been debated and critiqued. Human rights—whether as ideals, laws, modes of political action, or desirable objectives—have come under attack from a variety of horizons, and faced many longstanding and evolving internal and external challenges. The litany is a long one—human rights laws and practices are variously accused of being too neoliberal, too Western, too reformist (rather

Nehal Bhuta, Florian Hoffmann, Sarah Knuckey, Frédéric Mégret, and Margaret Satterthwaite, *Introduction* In: *The Struggle for Human Rights*. Edited by: Nehal Bhuta, Florian Hoffmann, Sarah Knuckey, Frédéric Mégret, and Margaret Satterthwaite, Oxford University Press. © Nehal Bhuta, Florian Hoffmann, Sarah Knuckey, Frédéric Mégret, and Margaret Satterthwaite 2021. DOI: 10.1093/oso/9780198868064.003.0001

than revolutionary), too complacent, too elitist, too apolitical, too closely aligned with power, and not powerful enough. This book does not purport to resolve the pressing questions of the ultimate utility of human rights or whether or how human rights can be reformed to better support movements for justice. Rather, it is a book of essays that take as their inspiration for reflection the human rights practice of Philip Alston, whose forty-year career as an international human rights advocate, prolific scholar of human rights law, teacher, and active participant in the making of the contemporary international human rights system, yields much grist for the mills of those trying to evaluate the possibilities for change offered by human rights today. Alston has maintained that the challenges facing human rights today require us to 'urgently rethink many of [our] assumptions, re-evaluate [our] strategies, and broaden [our] outreach, while not giving up on the basic principles'. The essays in this volume all engage in this challenge, following the long arc of Alston's career as a prism to evaluate and critically reflect upon some of the themes that have come to define international human rights practice and scholarship in the past decades.

The collection begins by examining a series of foundational debates that have been at the heart of the evolution of the human rights project, a project that has always justified itself by an appeal to more than legal positivism, and that remains haunted by some of its foundational dilemmas (Part I). It then looks at some of the key issues involved in the current effort to, continuously, push the substantive development of human rights: although initially 'proclaimed', it seems that human rights are always 'reinventing themselves' as normative horizons, and tracking this evolution is as challenging as it is a necessary exercise for both human rights practitioners and theorists (Part II). Much of the development of the project over the last half-century, in this context, has been dominated by the seemingly mundane but often politically intractable question of how to best make the rights project concrete: what kind of institutions or mechanisms should be developed so that rights do not remain merely hortatory (Part III)? Despite all this drive towards institutionalization, there remains an intractable dimension to human rights that is not reducible to technocratic or even legal devices: a space for political challenge, more or less spontaneous ordering and bottom-up mobilization (Part IV).

Alston's career is exemplary not only in the sense that it is remarkable, but also because it is emblematic of all these themes. It is illustrative of a certain mode of engagement in international human rights, one that mixes institutional involvement and activism, as well as scholarship and teaching. Alston has been central to the development, use, and critique of human rights, as both a practitioner and critical scholar of human rights. He has worked in and worked to reform the UN and regional human rights systems. He has also taught future generations of activists, government lawyers, and academics. Alston's career as a practitioner has included work as a human rights officer at the UN Centre for Human Rights in Geneva, a legal advisor to UNICEF, member and Chair of the Committee for Economic, Social and Cultural Rights, Special Advisor to the UN High Commissioner for Human Rights, Independent Expert to the UN General Assembly, and as Special Rapporteur (first, for unlawful killings, and then on extreme poverty and human rights). He has also been a commissioner for UN Commissions of Inquiry, including in the Kyrgyz Republic and the Central African Republic. His scholarly contributions are vast, and have pushed forward knowledge in innumerable areas, including labour rights, socioeconomic rights, tax, development, the use of force, children's rights, the European Union, and the UN.

Alston's teaching has also been core to his work as an advocate and as a scholar. He frequently developed entirely new courses to grapple with emerging topics in human rights (such as the critical examination of human rights fact-finding, or the relationship between international criminal law and human rights), creating new syllabi to push his own learning and to debate new questions with young scholars. And through his teaching, generations of students have worked with him on his UN and other work, learning while doing. As Gerard Quinn writes in Chapter 11, 'echoes of [Alston's] heart' can be found in myriad human rights efforts led by Alston's former students. Alston's commitment to the education of new generations, discussed by John Tobin in Chapter 13 on the purposes and methods of teaching human rights, has supported the development of legions of engaged scholars and critical advocates around the world.

At the same time, the critique of human rights has never been far behind its rise in global significance. While the rhetorical question 'Who can be against human rights?' seems to admit of only one answer, as a historical matter, contemporary human rights have faced numerous internal and external challenges to their value, validity, and efficacy. For example, Koskenniemi's contribution to this volume suggests that the attempt by parts of the human rights movement to stand outside—or above—politics, has led to its inefficacy, and even complicity in current crises. Koskenniemi concludes that human rights are at once too broad and too narrow to adequately respond to the current political challenges of populisms. Rodríguez-Garavito's contribution argues for a need to reform and rethink current modes of doing politics through human rights, in order to make them more adequate and apposite to the nature of contemporary crises. He maintains that human rights can develop new methods of mobilizing that connect more explicitly to other political movements, and that gives greater 'attention to narratives, emotions, and frames capable of connecting with larger constituencies and other social justice movements'. The strong association of human rights with political liberalism can render them susceptible to both conservative and leftist critiques, and—as Steiner demonstrates in his chapter—the relationship between human rights and democracy has never been stable, and remains in flux. Human rights charters from a variety of regional systems, as well as the international treaties, do not adopt any singular approach but seem to leave the issue in the realm of political contestation.

Human rights' genealogical connections to Western modernity means that they are sometimes considered with wariness (or their mainstream content is challenged) by indigenous groups, peasant movements, and others seeking to preserve or build space outside the neoliberal order. Their birth during, and historical and contemporary coexistence with, patterns of racial or colonial domination, and dependence for enforcement on states' pursuit of their own interests, can create suspicion not only but especially in the Global South, as well as in the 'South within the North'. This is in addition to often-stated concerns within the international human rights movement about the lack of teeth of international mechanisms, the resistance of states to implement their commitments, and the elite-driven nature of some of the highly visible modes of human rights advocacy. Perhaps most damning is the continuous egregious abuses committed since the Universal Declaration of Human Rights (UDHR) was presented to the world. The mass killings in Myanmar, the current climate change disasters, the targeting of civilians in Syria and Iraq, systemic racism across the globe, and unprecedented global inequality are highly visible remonstrances against our 'normal' or 'mainstream' political, economic, and social institutions. To the extent that human rights have become a component part of those institutions, are they part of the problem or part of the solution? As the essays collected here show, no dogmatic answer can be given about the possibilities of human rights—it is a question that can perhaps be answered through examining different kinds of practice.

Those committed to human rights often see themselves as committed to action. Advocates elaborate human rights standards and policies, develop human rights institutions, educate, investigate abuse, and attempt to hold actors to account. But, perhaps buoyed by the righteousness of all these endeavours, the field has often had an ambivalent relationship with critique. While many within the field voice trenchant internal critiques of human rights, they are often reluctant to do so more openly for fear of undermining advocacy efforts. Among activists, there is often far too little space for reflection and critique. And some of the more critical scholarly writing is not well grounded in actual human rights practice. Could it be that the significance of Alston's career is that he has modelled how to produce movement-relevant critical theory and to practice critical advocacy? In his roles as scholar and 'independent expert', Alston has oscillated between insider and provocateur, building and buttressing the institutions and repertoires of international human rights even as he highlights limits, blind spots, and failures of imagination or political judgment. Alston's call for human rights activists and institutions to re-examine their modes of organizing and working in light of the rise of populist movements is a good example of a refusal to reduce human rights ideals to a moralizing vantage point on a fallen political reality, and rather to constantly try to test its *political impact* on the struggle for justice, against existing realities. Chapter 23 by Obiora Okafor, in that respect, is emblematic of the effort one needs to invest in one's mandate to reinvent it, in his case from the point of view of a third-world sensitivity.

Alston has been forthright in his critiques of the human rights community, including for its failure to attend to the real and crushing human rights violations experienced by those living in poverty. In his report on the civil and political rights of the poor, he excoriates his own kind, shaming human rights professionals for their 'systematic' neglect of far-ranging violations, such as the use of money bail, criminalization of homelessness, and police torture and killings. He argues that human rights organizations and experts have done grave harm to the indivisibility of human rights, long at the centre of theories about human rights. Alston has also repeatedly criticized the extent to which socioeconomic rights have been devalued by many states, and how for decades they were all but ignored by high profile Western NGOs. Alicia Yamin, in Chapter 12, notes Alston's pivotal contributions, while exploring how the legal idea of a right to health benefited from Alston's visionary work to develop a framework for the recognition and institutionalization of socioeconomic rights, and for holding states and others accountable for their realization. Thomas Hammarberg reflects, in Chapter 16, on the meaning of the 'implementation' of human rights treaty obligations, in the practice of the Committee on the Rights of the Child; and highlights the means through which the effectiveness of such obligations can be improved.

While Alston's contributions to socioeconomic rights have been central to his career, they have not occupied his entire field of vision. His work has shifted the terms of debate on issues ranging from human rights and development through to algorithmic governance and climate change. In Chapter 17 on infrastructure finance and investment, Mac Darrow notes the groundbreaking nature of Alston's work on human rights 'mainstreaming' in the late 1990s, and proceeds to analyse contemporary infrastructure development approaches through a human rights lens. He warns of the human rights risks embedded in infrastructure projects, but in particular 'in the regulatory framework for infrastructure investment and PPPs [public–private partnerships] at the national level'. He urges the incorporation of human rights due diligence into the risk assessment processes of investment and development finance institutions from the outset, rather than only reactive assessments after harm has already occurred. Chapter 14 by Malcolm Langford highlights the originality of Alston's work on the digital welfare state and explores further the difficulties and challenges of applying a human rights based public policy frame to new technologies of algorithmic governance. In Chapter 8 Benedict Kingsbury suggests that this work 'herald[ed] a regrouping and reform for the conventional human rights forces, with new strategy and new tactical training in apposite use of the standard-issue weapons' against encroachments of the digitised state. But Kingsbury also inquires into whether the methods and concepts of human rights are adequate to the sociotechnical realities of the 'making' of artificial intelligence and its specific rationalities and methods.

The 'world of human rights' is broad and far reaching, so much so that its exact reach is sometimes hard to define (does it include international criminal law? International humanitarian law? Labour rights? Property rights? Refugee rights? Cyberspace? The environment?). Which issues can and should be examined through a human rights lens, and which human concerns or needs should be expressed through the language of human rights? Since the UDHR, more and more issues are examined with human rights principles and tools, and more needs and individuals have become protected through expression in legal human rights.

In Chapter 11 on autonomy and decision-making in the UN Convention on the Rights of Persons with Disabilities (CRPD), Quinn highlights Alston's early influence in that area. He goes on to argue that the CRPD develops a new paradigm of the personhood of disabled persons, emphasizing supported autonomy over guardianship. He also reflects how this new concept may bring a new set of problems. In light of Alston's work to extend rights analysis into new areas, it may seem ironic that one of his early influential articles argued against 'conjuring up new human rights'.[1] However, a retrospective of Alston's career makes clear that his concern was with the rush to use human rights to justify claims whenever, as Kingsbury suggests in Chapter 8, 'a plausible use case' had been identified. Alston has instead insisted that human rights law must respond to new challenges while remaining true to its original purposes of expanding equality, reducing suffering, and advancing human potential. Alston's work on poverty and human rights is emblematic of this approach. He has aimed the rights spotlight on concerns that escaped such scrutiny for too long, bringing to light the human rights implications inherent in economic policies like taxation, the work of the World Bank, and the International Monetary Fund (IMF), and the existential crisis of climate change.

Another central area of development in human rights has been the growth in the number and type, and dramatic expansion in activity, of formal human rights mechanisms, from national human rights institutions to regional human rights commissions and courts, to UN treaty bodies, committees, special rapporteurs, and commissions of inquiry, and new mechanisms in specific subject areas, such as human rights and business. While these mechanisms and systems have had innumerable positive impacts, they also can be bureaucratic, slow, ineffective, and removed from the realities of the lives of those directly impacted by abuse. And they can be captured by state interests.

Alston's career and his many appointments in the UN reflect tensions in the field about these mechanisms. Alston has worked within many of these systems, seeking to use them to develop human rights norms and to increase their relevance to those directly impacted by abuse. He has a career-long interest in improving the 'machinery' of human rights, his concerns about their operation informed by an intimate understanding of their operations and weaknesses. The UN system, whether the treaty bodies or special rapporteurs, has drawn considerably on what is conventionally described as 'expertise'. Chapter 20 by Hélène Trigoudja (examining Alston's influence on regional human rights bodies) and Chapter 26 by Frédéric Mégret (exploring Alston's UN visit to report on poverty in the United States)

[1] Philip Alston, 'Conjuring up New Human Rights: A Proposal for Quality Control' (1984) 78 American Journal of International Law 607.

seek to situate the place of special rapporteurships, in particular, within a broader theory of the roles that human rights professional types are called upon to take or perform. The politics of expertise have been criticized, and expertise is a somewhat elusive quality when it comes to human rights: it evidently includes deep knowledge about the issue but also conveys a certain quality of neutrality and impartiality. Quite what that neutrality and impartiality are when it comes to issues as normatively and emotionally loaded as human rights is open to question. And in these 'expert' roles, Alston has also been advantaged by his identity: as a well-educated white man from the West, he has been perceived to be 'neutral' in ways that others, including women and people of colour, may find more difficult.

In Chapter 24 Knuckey and Satterthwaite examine the question of praxis from a different angle by asking if human rights advocacy should itself comport with human rights principles. Examining the field of rights advocacy, they find an embrace of the substantive principles undergirding human rights, including indivisibility and interdependence but a less complete integration of the procedural principles of participation, empowerment, and accountability. Here Alston, Knuckey, and Satterthwaite agree: human rights professionals have all too often been content to 'play down' the difference that class and socioeconomic status plays, even inside rights movements.

Alston has often been at the forefront of efforts to critique international institutions, straddling the outsider line, and sometimes offering very significant proposals in strong terms. A committed supporter of international human rights institutions, as expert and as an official, he has defended the necessity of their effective functioning against attacks aimed at undermining or marginalizing them. Critical of the pathologies of political bodies such as the UN Human Rights Commission and Human Rights Council (HRC), he also cast a cold eye over proposals for reform that threatened to turn universal bodies into entities that might be dismissed as merely Northern or Western. Inclusiveness and representativeness of the world's states of course brought with it countless threats to the integrity of human rights monitoring within these bodies, but the ethos of continuous struggle to build the right kinds of international institutions, warts and all, pervades his steadfast engagement with them.

Vitit Muntarbhorn shares this interest in the *practical* universality of human rights institutions in Chapter 15, examining the positive steps taken by, but also the significant work that remains for, the Association of South-East Asian Nations (ASEAN) to protect and promote human rights in the region. Bruno Simma and Giorgia Sangiulo note, in Chapter 9 examining the mechanisms and possibilities for the justiciability of corporate human rights abuse, that Alston's role in human rights institutions has often been to use the 'margin of manoeuvre' of a given post to address the most crucial issues of the time—from the institutional and conceptual to the theoretical and practical. Simma and Sangiulo go on to argue that the current legal frameworks for dispute resolution, including investment disputes, have perhaps an underexplored 'margin of manoeuvre' to hold corporate actors accountable for human rights violations.

Alston has been able to use his 'expert' appointments for real human rights impact. He seems to have come to illustrate the qualities that make up expertise: knowing the system inside out, being somewhat above the fray yet deeply committed to human rights in ways that denote passion rather than the cold determination of the technocrat. His adroit use of his expert appointments to spotlight the most difficult human rights dilemmas is one of his enduring legacies. Alston's work on targeted killings—referenced in Chapter 21 by Bhuta and Mignot-Mahdavi—exemplifies Alston's ability to bring governmental violations into sharp focus through UN mechanisms while delving into the deeper implications in his scholarship. He pushed what had been a marginal issue onto the international agenda, and through his role as UN Special Rapporteur on Extrajudicial Executions, sought accountability for individual cases of civilian deaths. Bhuta and Mignot-Mahdavi note, however, that Alston's call for greater transparency about targeted killings has generated the paradoxical outcome that certain states have moved their legal rationales for targeted killings from the opaque contexts of diplomatic persuasion to more forthright claims of having successfully reshaped the law. They point to some of the disturbing consequences of this claim of reshaping, in propounding a set of rules that seem to authorize endless war against non-state actors and hostile individuals. In a different vein, Joseph Weiler, in Chapter 3, gestures towards the very moral judgments inherent in the application of legal and political concepts, by asking whether the trial and execution of Jesus Christ could be understood as an 'extrajudicial killing'.

As Georges Abi-Saab writes in Chapter 1, Alston shares something with Antonio Gramsci's ideal type of the 'organic intellectual': refusing to opine from abstraction and instead infusing his theories into a praxis of rights, mechanisms, and advocacy. This praxis has many times made effective use of what Hilary Charlesworth, in Chapter 2, calls 'human rights rituals', moments that transcend the performative to engage the system's capacity to advance real change. Alston's special rapporteur activities exemplify this strategy, drawing on the institutional authority of the mandates to provide a focal point and platform for a domestic human rights actors and social movements to identify and articulate a wide range of lived injustices in human rights terms. The power of the international institution was, in Alston's performance of it, always as a propaedeutic to the democratic and discursive empowerment and visibility of domestic agents for change.

Precisely because of this sensibility of how international human rights institutions might help support the creation of spaces for political and economic justice, Alston was also always a trenchant critic of international organizations and even human rights bodies, on their own terms. This striking ability to embody the promise of human rights mechanisms while nevertheless revealing their limits and failures is discussed by Andrew Clapham in his chapter concerning Commissions of Inquiry, which addresses common dilemmas facing such fact-finding bodies. Alston's distinctive style of critique achieved great visibility in his report concerning the UN's role in Haiti's devastating cholera outbreak, and his long-term critical dialogue with the World Bank and its approach to human rights, which Alston has called, in his typical dry but incisive manner, 'a human rights free zone'. His strident critiques of international financial institutions, and his wider efforts to ensure accountability of international organizations for human rights failings, are explored in José Alvarez's chapter. Alvarez argues that Alston's critiques of the accountability failures of the World Bank, the IMF, and the UN, point to the wider problems of legitimacy and legality that dog international institutions exercising governance functions that impact the lives of millions. Chapter 6 by Euan MacDonald picks up this theoretical problem, and argues that human rights respect or promotion can be *a* reason for granting legitimacy to these institutions, but need not be the only foundations for their legitimacy.

The peculiar 'idealistic realism' of Alston's approach is reflected in his knack for concrete institution-building, not only at the UN Committee for Economic, Social and Cultural Rights, but also through his academic roles as scholar and founding member of Harvard Law School's pioneering Human Rights Clinic in the 1980s, through to his founding and co-leadership of NYU's Center for Human Rights and Global Justice over the past two decades. Alston's visionary institution-building has been undertaken with the goal of making advances in human rights more concrete.

One of the central lessons to be drawn from Alston's long career could be summarized as follows: International human rights institutions can be effective means through which to advance and promote a myriad of struggles against injustice, but only if they constantly negotiate and maintain a space between states' ineluctable political interests, and an overweening utopian legalism that simply promulgates high-minded standards and principles with no real concern for their political conditions of possibility. Alston's scholarly output—prolific and heavily documented—revolves around these preoccupations, often deftly deflating grand but ungrounded normative agendas while excoriating the disingenuous manoeuvres of states and international organizations. In his work as a human rights scholar and practitioner, he never loses track of what human rights really mean, beyond the jargon and the technical specialization that increasingly dominates the field. At ease in the minute reform of treaty bodies, he has also showed that after forty years of working at the heart of the international human rights machinery, his capacity of indignation at what are, at bottom, forms of raw injustice, remains intact. Channelling indignation has long been one of the central motifs in the life of international human rights. At the same time, indignation cannot be its own end. It only succeeds in changing the narrative to the extent it is willing to rewrite it.

PART I

ARGUING ABOUT THE HISTORY, THEORY, AND POLITICS OF HUMAN RIGHTS

1
The Organic Intellectual

Georges Abi-Saab[*]

It was in the fall of 1978, a little more than forty years ago, that I met the young Philip Alston. At that time, I was highly interested in the drive for the establishment of a 'New International Economic Order' (NIEO) and organized a series of round tables at the Graduate Institute in Geneva on the origins of the NIEO, the Charter of Economic Rights and Duties of States, Basic Needs, and so on. And here turns up Philip—who had just been recruited by the Human Rights Division of the UN Secretariat, via Berkeley, to work on the first report on the Right to Development—attending and vigorously intervening in the round tables.

I was immediately struck by his vivid intelligence, quick perception, and very dry sense of humour. We soon discovered that we have what the French call *des atomes crochus*, that is, great affinities, and became very good friends, seizing on every opportunity to be and work together. As time wore on, our bond became tighter and happily survived his departure from Geneva. We managed to get together at least once a year, Philip having continuously kept a foothold in Geneva in one capacity or another. My only regret is that I didn't manage to lure him to come and teach at the Graduate Institute, as every time a window of opportunity opened, he was attracted by brighter prospects elsewhere.

Now, I must tell you a private story ('private' in the same sense as in 'private joke') between the two of us. At the time we met and forged our relationship, there was in Geneva an American Ambassador in charge of human rights who was running around, giving lectures everywhere, claiming that economic, social, and cultural (ESC) rights are not real legal rights but mere aspirations or standards of achievement. Since then, I kept nagging at Philip, telling him that he should write the definitive book on ESC rights that would prove once and for all the genuine legal character of those rights. But of course Philip, being so dynamic, was very busy running all over the world, doing so many things at the same time in defence and promotion of human rights, that he never managed to marshal enough time to sit down and write such a *magnum opus*.

However, pondering retrospectively over the vast spectrum of Philip's efforts and achievements in the service of human rights, I have to admit that what he did has gone much beyond what he would have achieved by devoting a large part of his time to writing the definitive book on ESC rights; a book that might be read or kept on the shelf, however superb it may be. Instead, what Philip did has contributed significantly to insinuating and inculcating these rights into daily social practice. Let me illustrate and expound on this further in what follows. This is of course without forgetting or belittling Philip's other achievements as a charismatic teacher with a vast following and admirers all over the world; having written the best teaching tool of human rights I know of, *International Human Rights in Context* (first with Henry Steiner, then with Ryan Goodman, and now by himself); or his work as legal advisor

[*] I thank Dr Jason Rudall, Assistant Professor of International Law at the Grotius Center, Leiden University, for valuable research assistance.

Georges Abi-Saab, *The Organic Intellectual* In: *The Struggle for Human Rights*. Edited by: Nehal Bhuta, Florian Hoffmann, Sarah Knuckey, Frédéric Mégret, and Margaret Satterthwaite, Oxford University Press. © Georges Abi-Saab 2021. DOI: 10.1093/oso/9780198868064.003.0002

to several international organizations (UNICEF, HCR, etc); not to mention his vast bibliography of edited books, articles, reports, and so on; or his acting as Special Rapporteur for the UN Council of Human Rights or 'Extra-judicial, summary, or arbitrary executions', which had a great resonance on the international scene. Thus, while not forgetting or belittling all these achievements, I shall concentrate on his great contribution to ESC rights and their transformation into palpable social reality.

In so doing, Philip reminds me of something I read in *The Prison Notebooks*[1] of Antonio Gramsci, the great Marxist thinker during the interwar period, about the role of the intellectual in society. Gramsci writes: 'As reasoning beings, all men are intellectuals, but not all have in society the function of intellectuals.'[2] Those who do can be divided, according to Gramsci, in two categories: the 'traditional intellectuals' by the nature of the functions they occupy—involving an intellectual activity rather than a manual or physical one—such as teachers, priests, and administrators, who continue to do the same thing as their predecessors, transmit or apply knowledge as they received it from generation to generation. But according to Gramsci, there is a second category, that of the 'organic Intellectual', a kind of Schumpeterian entrepreneur,[3] who introduces new ideas in society and transforms them into current social practice, or 'praxis' in Gramsci's Marxist lingo, which is defined in the *Shorter Oxford English Dictionary* as: 'being in Marxism the willed action by which a theory or philosophy becomes practical social activity'.[4] I think that this description fits perfectly what Philip has been doing for the ESC rights throughout these forty years.

How did he go about it? It is useful to recall that what is at issue here is not the formal legal status of ESC rights as legal rights. These rights are the subject matter of the first UN Covenant of Human Rights, and they figure in numerous other multilateral, regional, or bilateral conventions to which the overwhelming majority (if not all) of the states of the world have subscribed; and which are legally binding on their parties. But a distinction must be made here, as when we speak, for example, of 'soft-law', between the *instrumentum*—the legal instrument—and the *negotium*—the normative substance embodied in the instrument. Those who deny the legal character of ESC rights do not contest the legally binding character of the instruments. But they contend that these instruments do not yield hard and fast legal rights and obligations. This is because, in their contention, the normative material of these rights, by its very nature, is not, nor is it capable of becoming, sufficiently concrete to be translatable into legal entitlements with corresponding legal obligations.

Countering such a radical negationist representation, the admirable and patient work undertaken by Philip throughout the last four decades, consisted of seizing on any opportunity that was offered him to disprove minutely, bit by bit, this negationist representation; by shedding light on the intrinsic legal characteristics of those rights and the legal means to effectuate and protect them, as well as by exposing egregious cases of their violation and their causes.

Looking back at Philip's efforts during those decades, they seem to have followed, at least with the benefit of hindsight, a pre-planned strategy. For, to borrow the title of a famous book by another Australian, 'Man Makes Himself' not only across the geological ages, but even within the span of a lifetime, through his day-to-day choices and decisions. Clarity and

[1] Antonio Gramsci, Quintin Hoare, and Geoffrey Nowell-Smith, *Selections from the Prison Notebooks of Antonio Gramsci* (1st edn, International Publishers 1971).
[2] ibid 9.
[3] ibid 4.
[4] *Shorter Oxford English Dictionary* (6th edn, OUP 2007).

steadfastness of purpose make for consistency of action that may look retrospectively like premeditated design.

Be that as it may, the emerging pattern from these relentless efforts is akin to a long-term strategy in the form of three concentric circles, ranging from the general and hardly controversial, to the highly pointed and pugnacious type of action.

1.1 Sharpening the Institutional Tools and Framework

This is the largest and least controversial circle. The UN being, from its inception, the breeding ground of international human rights, this led with time to the proliferation of organs dealing with those rights, often working on connected, if not similar, subjects without each knowing what was going on in the others. Philip, since his early work in the Secretariat, became keenly aware of this overlap and lack of communication with the attendant waste of efforts and loss of efficiency. He consistently strove, in whatever position he occupied, for better communication, coordination and rationalization of efforts, and consistency of approaches, if not their unification, between those organs, as well as with the other organization members of the UN family that dealt with the same issues. Moreover, he wrote three important reports, in 1989, 1993, and 1997, as Independent Expert appointed by the UN Secretary General at the request of the General Assembly, on 'Measures to ensure the long-term effectiveness of the UN human rights treaty bodies'.

He also dealt with the issue in his academic writings and in his reports as Special Rapporteur of the Human Rights Council. Thus, for example, in his famous article 'Ships Passing in the Night',[5] Philip criticizes the way the Human Right Community and the Development Community within the UN family, while dealing with the same subject and aiming at the same objective—that is, the Millennium Development Goals (MDGs)—each went their own way, without communicating with each other or taking into consideration each other's work. Of similar inspiration is his description of the World Bank as 'a human rights free zone'; and his criticism of the IMF for glossing over the dire repercussions of its advocated policies on human rights.

1.2 Sharpening the Normative Analytical Tools and Contents of the Rights

As useful as Philip's work on the institutional tools is, its impact remains latent, not easily perceptible at first sight. More significant and directly visible is his work on sharpening the normative analytical tools and contents of the rights, particularly during his tenure as a member of the UN Committee on ESC Rights, which lasted for some fifteen years, from the establishment of the Committee in the mid-1980s to the end of the 1990s; a period throughout which he served either as its Rapporteur or its Chairman. This contribution is clearly reflected in the General Comments that the Committee adopts from time to time, which—though formally issued in the name of the Committee—clearly bore Philip's imprint during his tenure (covering the first ten General Comments). For, on almost all the subjects treated by those

[5] Philip Alston, 'Ships Passing in the Night: The Current State of the Human Rights and Development Debate Seen through the Lens of the Millennium Development Goals' (2005) 27 Human Rights Quarterly 755.

Comments, Philip had previously published long articles, of which the General Comments were the quintessence.

Thus, for example, General Comment No 3 of 1 January 1991, brings important clarifications, as its title indicates, on 'The Nature of States Parties Obligations'.[6] It analyses inter alia the traditional distinction between 'obligations of conduct' and 'obligations of result', which is much used and abused by the negationists. They contend that—unlike civil and political rights, which entail corresponding hard and fast obligations of result, with concrete and well-defined content, whose violations are easily identifiable—ESC rights generate only vague obligations of best efforts or conduct, with blurred, hardly definable contents, of which the performance is impossible to evaluate and the violation to pin down. However, the Comment's analysis of this dichotomy or distinction shows that it is less radical or absolute than it might appear at first sight. Thus, the subject matter of both types of obligation can be vague or well defined; and 'best efforts' are not totally averse to measurement or evaluation. Moreover, the implementation of obligations of 'best efforts' envisaged here involve many other related obligations, some of which are 'obligations of result', such as the obligation of non-discrimination that applies to all conduct related to human rights. The same General Comment No 3 also interprets and fleshes out the obligation of solidarity and cooperation of states parties with the less developed among them, especially through economic and technical assistance, in the progressive realization of said rights.

Other General Comments also expound on and further specify the content of certain rights and corresponding obligations, as well as the concrete requirements for their realization, such as General Comments Nos 4 and 7 on the right to adequate housing; or set out in the same way the rights of certain vulnerable categories, such as persons with disabilities (No 5) and older persons (No 6). Similarly, the General Comments dealing with the institutional and procedural requirements and obligations of states parties to the Covenant highlight these requirements and describe step by step how to fulfil them, eg reporting (No 1), and reception and integration in municipal law (No 9).

All these General Comments render the protected rights as well the corresponding obligations more concrete and visible, hence operable and justiciable, particularly for their final beneficiaries.

1.3 Sharpening the Analysis of Egregious Violations of ESC Rights and of their Underlying Causes

This third and most combative circle of action corresponds to Philip's later activities as Special Rapporteur of the Human Rights Council on Extreme Poverty. The glaring exposure of these violations was effected through a substantial number of thematic and country reports as well as consistent efforts at dissemination and outreach to public opinion at large.

The thematic reports reveal and explain, by vigorous analysis, demonstration, and proof, the tight chain of causality between certain macroeconomic policies—that is, the Washington consensus, structural adjustment programmes, privatizations (with attendant economic insecurity and widening inequality gap)—and flagrant violations and deprivations of ESC rights, particularly those of the poorest, weakest, and most vulnerable segments of society. These reports also show the inextricable relation between egregious violations of

[6] cf Philip Alston and Gerard Quinn, 'The Nature and Scope of States Parties' Obligations under the International Covenant on Economic, Social and Cultural Rights' (1987) 9 Human Rights Quarterly 156.

ESC rights and those of civil and political rights, while imposing unpopular policies detrimental to large segments of society. By contrast, the thematic reports also explore other socio-economic policies more supportive and protective of ESC rights, particularly those of the poorest members of society, even in times of economic adversity, such as the adoption of social protection floors or of a universal basic income.

Country reports concretely illustrate the analysis and conclusions of the thematic reports. They also demonstrate that egregious violations and deprivations of ESC rights are not the preserve of developing countries and that highly developed ones such as the United States and the United Kingdom, by practising the macroeconomic policies alluded to earlier—whose heavy price is invariably borne by the lowest and most vulnerable strata of society—create the conditions of extreme poverty within their own communities.

The dissemination and outreach activities of Philip have been intense. They extend much beyond the international law, human rights, and UN circles to the wider public, through his constant lecturing and participation in conferences and events all over the world, as well as his press statements and interviews, leading to large media coverage, particularly by influential organs like the *New York Times* and the *Guardian*, of some of his most telling reports, such as those on extreme poverty in the United States and the United Kingdom.

In sum, Philip's tireless activities over the past four decades—besides confounding the negationists and demonstrating the irrefutable legal qualities of ESC rights from every angle—have mightily contributed to heightening the general public's awareness of the existence, tenor, and import of ESC rights and of their direct impact on the conditions of daily life of common people all over the world. They have also sharpened the perception of world public opinion as to the flagrancy of violations and deprivations of ESC rights as well as of their underlying causes; thus spurring lawyers to invoke them in courts and judges to apply them, in spite of possible gaps and deficiencies in national legal systems. They have also incited civil society all over the world to bring sustained pressure to bear on legislators and governments to 'take [ESC] rights seriously', through the diligent pursuit of their progressive realization and protection. Whether one calls the total effect of this impressive array of activities *conscientisation* (consciousness raising), mainstreaming, or by any other name, it perfectly illustrates the role of Gramsci's organic intellectual.

I would be remiss to conclude without reverting to my old refrain concerning the definitive book on ESC rights. In fact, by undertaking the abovementioned activities wholeheartedly, Philip has, perhaps unwittingly, written that book; but it is alas too voluminous. For, if we put together all his reports and articles—not to mention the more than a dozen books he co-authored or edited and in each of which he contributed at least one long essay—we will end up with a score of volumes. It would be an exciting challenge for the former students and disciples of Philip, if he cannot do it himself, to distil and synthesize the quintessence of this impressive sum of knowledge and insights into a manageable volume. But perhaps it is too early for that, as Philip's contribution continues to flow abundantly, for a long time I hope, for the benefit and well-being of humanity.

2
Rituals and Ritualism in the International Human Rights System

Hilary Charlesworth[*]

2.1 Introduction

I first encountered Philip Alston in 1975, when he was a tutor in contract law at Ormond College at the University of Melbourne. His keen intelligence and his dry wit immediately engaged us motley group of undergraduates, rendering exposure to the tedious legal doctrines almost enjoyable. Since that time, Philip Alston has devoted his professional life to the field of human rights. He has worked in a wide range of roles in the area, including as a UN official, a member of the UN human rights treaty bodies, an academic, and a Special Rapporteur appointed by the UN Human Rights Council (HRC). Philip is also a generous colleague and mentor who has influenced generations of students and scholars all over the world. Philip's fine intellect, laconic humour, fearless disposition, and acute sense of justice are evident in all these endeavours.

The title of this *festschrift* conceives the realization of human rights as a struggle. The concept may suggest a long-running battle between promoters of human rights principles on the one hand and entities, typically states, that resist them on the other. International lawyers have intervened in the perceived struggle to shore up human rights norms by emphasizing compliance, often in the form of coerced compliance with rules. One example is the sporadic campaign for a global human rights court to implement international human rights treaties, when national systems fail to do so. In 2011 a Swiss government-sponsored panel of eminent jurists called for a World Court of Human Rights that would adjudicate complaints of human rights violations by both states and non-state actors and provide reparations to victims.[1]

Another remedy proposed by international lawyers to strengthen the international human rights system is the erection of greater barriers to participation in the system for states that fail to demonstrate genuine commitment to rights. For example, Oona Hathaway suggests making ratification of human rights treaties probationary for states, in order to discourage 'insincere ratifiers'.[2] The design or reform of monitoring institutions to improve compliance with human rights obligations is also a staple of the human rights literature. The work of the UN human rights treaty-monitoring bodies is a popular focus as it is cumbersome and inefficient in many ways.[3]

[*] Many thanks to Michael McArdle for research assistance and to Darren Dick of the Australian Human Rights Commission for information about the UPR process in Australia.

[1] See Panel on Human Dignity, 'Protecting Dignity: An Agenda for Human Rights' (Report, 2011) 41–92.

[2] Oona Hathaway, 'Do Human Rights Treaties Make a Difference?' (2002) 111(8) Yale Law Journal 1935.

[3] For example, UNGA, 'Effective Implementation of International Instruments on Human Rights, Including Reporting Obligations under International Instruments on Human Rights' (8 November 1989) UN Doc A/44/668; UNGA, 'Status of Preparation of Publications, Studies and Documents for the World Conference: Note by the Secretariat—Addendum: Interim Report on Updated Study by Mr. Philip Alston' (2 April 1993) UN Doc A/CONF.157/PC/62/Add.11/Rev.1; UNCHR, 'Effective Functioning of Bodies Established Pursuant to United

Hilary Charlesworth, *Rituals and Ritualism in the International Human Rights System* In: *The Struggle for Human Rights.* Edited by: Nehal Bhuta, Florian Hoffmann, Sarah Knuckey, Frédéric Mégret, and Margaret Satterthwaite, Oxford University Press. © Hilary Charlesworth 2021. DOI: 10.1093/oso/9780198868064.003.0003

This concentration on institutional reform as the route to transforming the dismal empirical reality of human rights protection underplays the political context of the human rights system. Attempts to streamline institutions and processes are often thwarted by regional coalitions, determined to ensure that state sovereignty trumps human rights scrutiny. As Philip Alston has pointed out in the case of the Swiss-sponsored proposal for a World Court, the capacity of the five permanent members of the UN Security Council to veto enforcement of Court rulings would undermine the Court's work.[4] More generally, giving priority to judicial mechanisms as a response to human rights violations overlooks the limited capacity of international courts to create local cultures of respect for human rights.[5]

International lawyers overall tend to focus on the normative standards and institutional context of the human rights system. By understanding human rights as a site of struggle, lawyers rarely tarry to consider the social practices that surround it. In this chapter, I will investigate the life of international human rights law through two distinct but related practices—rituals and ritualism. I start by introducing these concepts and then consider them in relation to a central mechanism of the UN human rights system, the UPR. I suggest that a human rights ritual such as the UPR may have some power in countering the practice of human rights ritualism.

2.2 Rituals and Ritualism

The international human rights system is replete with ritual.[6] The concept of ritual has generated a vast literature, with anthropologists and sociologists as its chief custodians. Marie-Bénédicte Dembour defines ritual as 'a public, orchestrated event that is intentional and rule-bound'.[7] Repetitive, rhythmic, and patterned forms are critical in this process. The primary function of rituals is that of communication of a particular social order through repeated social encounters,[8] but rituals also shape and transform our experience. Mary Douglas has observed:

> Ritual focuses attention by framing; it enlivens memory and links the present with the relevant past.... So it is not enough to say that ritual helps us to experience more vividly what we would have experienced anyway. It can come first in formulating experience.[9]

Nations Human Rights Instruments: Final Report on Enhancing the Long-Term Effectiveness of the United Nations Human Rights Treaty System' (27 March 1997) UN Doc E/CN.4/1997/74; Philip Alston, 'Against a World Court for Human Rights' (2014) 28(2) Ethics & International Affairs 197, 211.

[4] Alston, 'Against a World Court for Human Rights' (n 3) 204.

[5] ibid 210.

[6] Benjamin Authers and others, 'Introduction: Dossier on Human Righs Rituals' (2018) 9(1) Humanity: An International Journal of Human Rights, Humanitarianism, and Development 63.

[7] The Rituals of Human Rights Workshop, Centre for International Governance and Justice, RegNet, Australian National University, 25–27 June 2014.

[8] Meredith Rossner and Mythily Meher, 'Emotions in Ritual Theories' in Jan E Stets and Jonathan H Turner (eds), *Handbook of the Sociology of Emotions*, vol 2 (Springer 2014) 218.

[9] Mary Douglas, *Purity and Danger: An Analysis of Concept of Pollution and Taboo* (Routledge 2005) 79 quoted in Shadd Maruna, 'Reentry as a Rite of Passage' (2011) 13(1) Punishment & Society 3, 9. Graeme Orr quotes Murray Edelman's definition of ritual: an 'activity that involves its participants symbolically in a common enterprise, calling their attention to their relatedness and joint interests in a compelling way'. Graeme Orr, *Ritual and Rhythm in Electoral Systems: A Comparative Legal Account* (Ashgate 2015) quoting Murray J Edelman, *The Symbolic Uses of Politics* (5th edn, University of Illinois Press 1985) 16.

Emile Durkheim's influential account of rituals emphasized the way that rituals generate solidarity: they bring people together, creating a 'collective effervescence' and encourage common understandings of social, moral, or political questions.[10] Rituals can thus manifest the dominance of a way of thinking or of being: enshrining a practice as ritual reduces contestation.[11] In this sense, rituals can obscure alternative cultural or political orders by imposing a particular logic on a situation.[12]

Another strand in ritualology emphasizes rituals as a more prosaic form of human engagement, helping make sense of the fractured and ambivalent nature of the world.[13] One way that they do this, according to Adam Seligman and co-authors, is by producing 'as if' or 'could be' worlds, creating what they call 'the rhythmic structure of the shared subjunctive'.[14]

Human rights rituals include those of transitional justice and of apology, which mark a break between the old and the new, and signal a society's recognition of certain wrongs, as well as its determination to move on.[15] Such rituals can both establish and entrench a consensus about how a society relates to its past. This can happen in the aftermath of war or in recognition of deep social divides.[16] In a study of rituals of reconciliation in Sierra Leone, Tim Kelsall claims that 'at its most effective, [ritual] has the power to transform perceptions and emotions and therefore situations'.[17] He notes that the reconciliation process in Sierra Leone 'mask[ed] or obscure[d] certain truths in favour of others'.[18] Kelsall suggests, however, that this enabled the reconstruction of community, albeit a community within which 'the unbearable truth of atrocities was partially eclipsed by the more palatable truth of remorse and desire for peace'.[19] Rituals also have the capacity to construct ways of being and relating to the world, such as through particular ideas of manhood and womanhood.[20]

We can also observe rituals at play in state appearances before the UN human rights treaty bodies. Toby Kelly has, for example, studied the behaviour of states before the UN Committee against Torture, highlighting the formal and orchestrated nature of these interactions.[21] In this way, rituals offer a bridge between human rights norms and their implementation.

[10] Maruna (n 9) 9; 'The very fact of assembling is an exceptionally powerful stimulant': Émile Durkheim, *The Elementary Forms of Religious Life* (Carol Cosman tr, Oxford University Press 2001) 162 quoted in Tim Kelsall, 'Truth, Lies, Ritual: Preliminary Reflections on the Truth and Reconciliation Commission in Sierra Leone' (2005) 27 Human Rights Quarterly 361, 388. Durkheim also stated that 'within a crowd moved by a common passion, we become susceptible to feelings and actions of which we are incapable of on our own': ibid 157.

[11] Hilary Charlesworth and Emma Larking (eds), *Human Rights and the Universal Periodic Review: Rituals and Ritualism* (Cambridge University Press 2014) 9.

[12] Sally Merry makes this point more generally about the operation of law; how it produces cultural meanings and identities as an aspect of power: Sally Engle Merry, 'Resistance and the Cultural Power of Law' (1995) 29 Law & Society Review 11, 14.

[13] On this account, rituals are concerned with 'the endless work of building, refining, and rebuilding webs of relationships in an otherwise fragmented world': Adam B Seligman and others, *Ritual and Its Consequences: An Essay on the Limits of Sincerity* (OUP 2008) 180.

[14] ibid 10.

[15] Danielle Celermajer, 'Mere Ritual? Displacing the Myth of Sincerity in Transitional Rituals' (2013) 7 International Journal of Transitional Justice 286.

[16] ibid; Charlesworth and Larking (n 11) 9.

[17] Kelsall, *Culture under Cross-Examination: International Justice and the Special Court for Sierra Leone* (CUP 2009) 390.

[18] ibid.

[19] ibid.

[20] Maruna (n 9) 8–9, citing Catherine M Bell and Reza Aslan, *Ritual Perspectives and Dimensions* (OUP 1997) 101.

[21] Tobias Kelly, 'Two Cheers for Ritual: The UN Committee Against Torture' (2018) 9 Humanity: An International Journal of Human Rights, Humanitarianism, and Development 93; Tobias Kelly, *This Side of Silence: Human Rights, Torture, and the Recognition of Cruelty* (2013) ch 6.

Ritualism, by contrast with ritual, is a term drawn from regulatory theory, found in Robert Merton's classic sociological study of modes of adaptation to a normative order, published in 1968. Merton identified five modes of individual and collective adaptation to cultural values: conformity, innovation, ritualism, retreatism, and rebellion.[22] Ritualism can be defined as 'acceptance of institutionalised means for securing regulatory goals while losing all focus on achieving the goals or outcomes themselves'.[23] It involves the formulaic or perfunctory acceptance of norms or values in the absence of a more substantial commitment.[24]

Scholars have identified regulatory ritualism in various contexts, including aged care and taxation. For example, in a three-country study, Braithwaite, Makkai, and Braithwaite found that nursing home operators rarely actively resisted regulation.[25] It was much more common for operators to avoid confrontation with regulators and to agree to the language and techniques of regulation, for example by changing a policy. This strategy usually favoured the preservation of the status quo both because the new plans or policies were observed in a perfunctory way and because regulators did not have sophisticated follow-up mechanisms.[26]

All five of Merton's modes of adaptation are evident in responses to international human rights regulation, but ritualism is particularly pervasive. The concept of regulatory ritualism captures an important feature of the international human rights system. The high ratification rates of human rights treaties illustrate the preparedness of UN member states to accept the institutionalized normative order. This may be a response to pressures from the international community—for example, ratification of human rights treaties may be a conduit for development assistance; or newly independent countries may accept human rights treaties to signal their membership of the international community. Ratification is a relatively straightforward step, involving a formal bureaucratic process, but implementation is much more costly and complex.

Rights ritualism is a more common response than outright rejection of human rights standards and institutions (rebellion, in Merton's terminology). Ritualism entails embracing the language of human rights precisely to deflect human rights scrutiny and to avoid accountability for human rights abuses, while at the same time gaining the positive reputational benefits or legitimacy associated with human rights commitments. This is well illustrated in Fleur Adcock's study of the ritualism of state responses to the work of the UN Special Rapporteur on Indigenous Peoples.[27] Practices of ritualism can also include ratifying human rights treaties without implementing their provisions domestically, perfunctory reporting to international human rights bodies, failing to provide remedies for human rights breaches or to develop policy to prevent violations, and, in some circumstances, invoking claims of culture to undermine international standards.

The ideas of rituals and ritualism, then, draw attention to different facets of the international human rights system. Rituals are forms of communication that rely on symbols and transmit social meanings. While rituals can be productive, ritualism indicates hollow

[22] Robert King Merton, *Social Theory and Social Structure* (Free Press 1968) 194.

[23] John Braithwaite, Toni Makkai, and VA Braithwaite, *Regulating Aged Care: Ritualism and the New Pyramid* (Edward Elgar 2007) 7 <http://site.ebrary.com/id/10328563> accessed 12 September 2020.

[24] Hilary Charlesworth, 'Swimming to Cambodia: Justice and Ritual in Human Rights after Conflict' (2010) 29 Australia Yearbook of International Law 1, 12; Charlesworth and Larking (n 11) 14.

[25] Braithwaite, Makkai, and Braithwaite (n 23).

[26] The forms of ritualism described by Braithwaite, Makkai, and Braithwaite (n 23) have also been described as 'rituals of verification'; Michael Power, *The Audit Society: Rituals of Verification* (OUP 1997).

[27] Fleur Adcock, 'The UN Special Rapporteur on the Rights of Indigenous Peoples and New Zealand: A Study in Compliance Ritualism' (2012) 10 New Zealand Yearbook of International Law 97.

practices that mask inaction. We can see both human rights rituals and human rights ritualism at play in the central mechanism of the UN HRC, the Universal Periodic Review (UPR).

2.3 The UPR

The UPR involves all 193 UN members being subjected to human rights scrutiny every four and a half years. This is a marked departure from the work of the UN Commission on Human Rights, the HRC's predecessor, which was criticized for its selective focus on a small group of states.[28] The HRC's slogan is cooperation rather than confrontation.[29] The founding resolution of the HRC established the UPR.[30] That resolution declares the basis of the review to be the UN Charter and the Universal Declaration, along with any human rights treaties to which the state is a party and any voluntary commitments undertaken by the state in international fora.

The UPR's purpose is an assessment of the human rights situation in each state in an 'objective, transparent, non-selective, constructive, non-confrontational and non-politicized manner'.[31] Three documents are central to the UPR: a national report by the state (states are encouraged to consult with members of civil society before finalizing their state report); a compilation of existing treaty body reports and any relevant reports from Special Rapporteurs prepared by the Office of the High Commissioner for Human Rights (OHCHR); and a summary of 'credible and reliable' information received by the OHCHR from 'other stakeholders', such as non-government organizations (NGOs). The documents have strict word limits—the state report is just twenty pages; the OHCHR compilation ten pages; and the stakeholder summary ten pages—and there are time frames for preparation.[32]

Three states that are members of the HRC are chosen by lottery to form a 'troika'—a group to manage the UPR for a particular state and to review the documents.[33] The most dramatic public aspect of the UPR is the 'interactive dialogue' of the state under review, conducted in Salle XX in the Palais des Nations in Geneva, in which the state presents its report and other states comment on it and make recommendations.[34] This process is precisely choreographed: from the second cycle onwards, the dialogue has run no longer than three and a half hours. The state has seventy minutes in total for its report and responses to questions. States with questions or recommendations may be allocated tiny amounts of time—such as one and a half minutes—depending on the number of states that wish to intervene.[35]

[28] For example, Kofi Annan spoke of the Commission's 'declining credibility and professionalism' in his 2005 manifesto, Report of the Secretary General, 'In Larger Freedom: Towards Development, Security and Human Rights for All' (2005) UN Doc A/59/2005; Philip Alston, 'Reconceiving the UN Human Rights Regime: Challenges Confronting the New UN Human Rights Council' (2006) 7 Melbourne Journal of International Law 185, 187–88.

[29] UNGA Res 60/251 (15 March 2006) UN Doc A/RES/60/261 para 5(b); UNHRC 'Institution-building of the United Nations Human Rights Council' (18 June 2007) UN Doc A/RES/60/521, annex, para 3(g), cited in Vincent Chetail, 'The Human Rights Council and the Challenges of the United Nations System on Human Rights: Towards a Cultural Revolution?' in Laurence Boisson de Chazournes and Marcelo G Kohen (eds), *International Law and the Quest for Its Implementation: Le Droit International et La Quête de Sa Mise En Oeuvre* (Brill 2010) 22.

[30] UNHRC, 'Institution-building of the United Nations Human Rights Council' (7 August 2007) UN Doc A/HRC/RES/5/1.

[31] ibid, annex, para 3(g).

[32] ibid, annex, paras 15–17.

[33] UN Doc A/HRC/RES/5/1 (n 30) allows states to request that a member from their own regional group be a member of the troika; ibid, annex, para 19.

[34] This is conducted in 'working group' sessions.

[35] The modalities of the UPR are contained in an appendix to UNHRC, 'Review of the work and functioning of the Human Rights Council' (12 April 2011) UN Doc A/HRC/Res/16/21.

Microphones are simply cut off if a speaker exceeds the time limit.[36] All UPR proceedings are webcast. After the dialogue, the troika prepares a draft report, essentially a transcription of the recommendations made, and any immediate responses by the state. The state then has a short period to consider the recommendations and to respond to them.[37]

The final act in this drama is several months later when a compilation of these documents is forwarded to the whole HRC as its report, and this is formally accepted. At this session, which lasts no more than one hour, the state under review can again make a presentation and other states can make observations. It is only at this stage that civil society is allowed to intervene in the proceedings: national human rights institutions and accredited NGOs can make oral statements, within a twenty-minute period. Halfway between one cycle and the next, there is a 'follow-up' process, in which a state can volunteer to provide a 'mid-term' report on progress.

In 2019, at the time of writing, the UPR was halfway through its third cycle. It has generated a remarkable level of coordination and communication on human rights not only between states themselves but also between states, other human rights mechanisms, and civil society. The UPR process illustrates the operation of both human rights rituals and human rights ritualism, as we can see in the case of Australia.

After some clashes with the UN human rights treaty bodies in 2000,[38] Australia appeared to embrace the UPR process. The fact that the UPR involves review by states, rather than by independent experts, seemed to give it a higher status for the Australian government. As of October 2019, Australia has gone through two UPR cycles, in January 2011 and November 2015.[39] Its third UPR appearance was timetabled for November 2020 but was postponed until January 2021.

In both UPR sessions conducted at the time of writing, the Commonwealth government prepared a draft report and conducted a consultation process with civil society groups, and the Australian states and territories. The first report gave a glowing self-assessment of Australia's human rights performance, but also acknowledged some problems, for example, the lower life expectancy rates of Indigenous Australians and the fact that women's earnings are on average lower than those of men.[40] The second report focussed on recommendations from the first UPR. It gave bland assurances of Australia's diligent protection of human rights in all contexts, suggesting that any consultations with civil society had had little impact on its content.[41]

[36] ibid, appendix, para 3. States can later send written comments.

[37] UN Doc A/HRC/RES/5/1 (n 30) paras 28–32. The revised terms that apply to the second and subsequent cycles of the UPR, which began in 2012, require focus on the implementation of the recommendations of the first review cycle; UN Doc A/HRC/Res/16/21 (n 35) annex, para 6. There was much debate about limiting the second cycle to reporting only on *accepted* recommendations—because it would allow states to limit the scope of the review by rejecting recommendations in areas that they do not want to discuss. This emerged as a major area of contention between some Western countries on the one hand and the Non-Aligned Movement, the Organization of the Islamic Conference and the African group on the other, in the context of the 2011 five-year review of the HRC.

[38] Sarah Louise Joseph, 'The Howard Government's Record of Engagement with the International Human Rights System' (2008) 27 Australia Yearbook of International Law 45, 53–55.

[39] Australia's UPR documents are accessible through the Australian Attorney General's website: Government of Australia, 'Australia's Universal Periodic Review' (Attorney General's Department) <https://www.ag.gov.au/rights-and-protections/human-rights-and-anti-discrimination/united-nations-human-rights-reporting/australias-universal-periodic-review> accessed 12 September 2020.

[40] Government of Australia, 'Australia's Universal Periodic Review' (Attorney General's Department 2010) <https://www.ag.gov.au/sites/default/files/2020-03/UniversalPeriodicReview.PDF>.

[41] UNHRC, 'National Report Submitted in Accordance with Paragraph 5 of the Annex to Human Rights Council Resolution 16/21: Australia' (7 August 2015) UN Doc A/HRC/WG.6/23/AUS/1.

The process of preparation of the reports prompted detailed analysis by the Australian Human Rights Commission. In the case of both UPRs, the Commission pointed to a number of pressing human rights issues in Australia, including the treatment of refugees, indigenous people, and prisoners.[42] Australian and international NGOs also produced extensive background information and proposed questions for countries to ask of Australia.[43]

At its first UPR session in 2011, Australia announced several new commitments, for example, establishing a fulltime Race Discrimination Commissioner, tabling concluding observations from the UN human rights treaty bodies and UPR recommendations in parliament; and creating a systematic process for review of Australia's reservations to human rights treaties. Fifty-three countries participated in the 2011 interactive dialogue and themes included congratulations to Australia on Prime Minister Rudd's 2008 Apology to Indigenous Australians; expressions of concern over Australia's treatment of its indigenous people, the rights of refugees and asylum seekers, and protection of children's rights; and encouraging withdrawal of Australia's reservations to human rights treaties.[44]

The HRC's draft report listed 145 recommendations and Australia presented its response in June 2011, after consultation with the states, territories, and Commonwealth government departments. The response seemed positive in the sense that Australia stated that it accepted 90 per cent of recommendations in full or part.[45] However it also rejected some of the major recommendations with little explanation. These included a call to enact a Human Rights Act, to compensate the Stolen Generations of Indigenous Peoples and to end mandatory detention of asylum seekers. The response did not appear to draw on consultations with civil society, although these had taken place.

Following the first cycle of the UPR, Australia developed a Baseline Study on Human Rights and began a consultation to develop a National Human Rights Action Plan (NAP), a voluntary commitment made by Australia during the UPR session. The final version of the NAP was released on 10 December 2012 and served as the interim report on implementation of the UPR to the HRC. After a change of government in September 2013, the new Attorney General indicated that the NAP was no longer government policy.[46] Australia has not since adopted an alternative policy approach to national human rights protection. By Australia's second UPR session in 2015, around 10 per cent of recommendations that Australia had accepted had been fully implemented, and some others had been partially implemented.[47] It is hard to be precise when calculating the extent to which Australia complied with the

[42] Australian Human Rights Commission, 'Taking Stock of Australia's Human Rights Record' (2010); Australian Human Rights Commission, 'Australia's Second Universal Periodic Review: Submission by the Australian Human Rights Commission under the Universal Periodic Review Process' (2015).

[43] See submissions at: Universal Periodic Review, 'Australia: Session 23—Civil Society and Other Submissions—English' (*UPR Info*, 2019) <www.upr-info.org/en/review/Australia/Session-23---November-2015/Civil-society-and-other-submissions> accessed 14 September 2020.

[44] UNHRC, 'Report of the Working Group on the Universal Periodic Review: Australia' (24 March 2011) UN Doc A/HRC/17/10.

[45] Department of the Attorney General, 'Australia's Universal Periodic Review' (n 40).

[46] Senator Penny Wright, 'Estimates: Questioning AG Brandis in L&CA Committee' (29 May 2014) <http://penny-wright.greensmps.org.au/content/estimates/estimates-questioning-ag-brandis-lca-committee> accessed 14 September 2020.

[47] There was some debate on what proportion had been partially implemented. The Australian Human Rights Commission estimated that 65 per cent of the accepted recommendations had been partially implemented, while a joint NGO Submission reported partial implementation of just 19.7 per cent: 2015. Australian Human Rights Commission, 'Australia's Universal Periodic Review' (Australian Council of Hujan Rights Authorities (2014) Progress Report; Human Rights Law Centre, Kingsford Legal Centre and National Association of Community Legal Centres, 'Australia's 2nd Universal Periodic Review: Joint NGO Submission' (2015) Australian NGO Coalition, 2 <https://www.klc.unsw.edu.au/sites/default/files/documents/15%20Final-UPR-Submission-for-website.pdf> accessed 17 March 2021.

recommendations it had accepted in 2011, as the UPR recommendations were often vaguely worded.

Australia's second UPR displayed a more diffident attitude than its first. It is possible that the apparent decline in enthusiasm for the UPR was exacerbated by the 2013 change of government in Australia.[48] One sign was the composition of the delegations: while a government Minister led the delegation for the first UPR, Australia's Geneva-based Ambassador to the United Nations headed the delegation to its second UPR in 2015. The delegation included the Chair of the Australian parliament's Joint Committee on Human Rights, Philip Ruddock.

The issues of Australia's treatment of asylum seekers and attention to the rights of its indigenous people remained prominent in the interactive dialogue.[49] Australia accepted 150 of the 290 recommendations (made by 104 states) and noted fifty to consider further.[50] This figure is of limited value in assessing Australia's engagement with the UPR as many of the recommendations were identical, for example, twenty-seven of them were concerned with ratification of the Optional Protocol to the Convention against Torture (OPCAT). Going against HRC policy,[51] Australia deployed six different rubrics to respond to the recommendations from the second UPR, two more than it did in 2011.[52] These were: 'Accepts'; 'Accepts on the basis of existing law, policy and action'; 'Notes'; 'Notes and will further consider'; 'Notes but will not further consider at this time'; 'Notes pending [various other events]'. In this way, accountability becomes attenuated: Australia could avoid outright rejection of recommendations and obscure its obligations to implement accepted recommendations.

Again, Australia made some important voluntary commitments at its second UPR, such as to hold a referendum on constitutional recognition of indigenous peoples and to increase funding for family violence and the Syrian humanitarian crisis. The government also undertook to work cooperatively with the Australian Human Rights Commission to monitor Australia's progress in implementing the UPR recommendations. This has resulted in page on the Commonwealth Attorney General's Department website that contains Australia's UPR reports, its UN statements, the reports of the UPR Working Group and Australia's responses to them.[53] Australia's mid-term UPR report in 2018 promised the updating of its 'monitoring website' as its centrepiece. While the 'monitoring' site reports Australia's attitude

[48] A Liberal–National Party Coalition government was elected to replace a Labor government in 2013. In general, the Australian Labor Party has been more prepared to engage with the international human rights system than conservative governments. Hilary Charlesworth, 'International Law' in Brian Galligan and Winsome Roberts (eds), *Oxford Companion to Australian Politics* (OUP 2007); Joseph (n 38) 54.

[49] UNHRC, 'Report of the Working Group on the Universal Period Review: Australia' (13 January 2016) UN Doc A/HRC/31/14.

[50] Government of Australia, 'UN Human Rights Council 39th Session: Oral statement—Submission of Australia's Universal Periodic Review (UPR) Monitoring Website as Australia's UPR Mid-Term Report' (Attorney General's Department 2020) <www.ag.gov.au/sites/default/files/2020-03/upr-mid-term-review-statement.pdf> accessed 14 September 2020; There was a general leap in the number of recommendations in the second UPR cycle, compared to the first: Subhas Gujadhur and Marc Limon, 'Towards the Third Cycle of the UPR: Stick or Twist?—Lessons Learned from the First Ten Years of the Universal Periodic Review' (Universal Rights Group 2016) Policy Report 14.

[51] ibid 46. In 2006, the Human Rights Council proposed two categories of response to UPR recommendations: 'supported' and 'noted'.

[52] Fiona McGaughey, 'The Role and Influence of Non-Governmental Organisations in the Universal Periodic Review—International Context and Australian Case Study' (2017) 17 Human Rights Law Review 421, 447.

[53] Government of Australia, 'Australia's Universal Periodic Review' (n 39). According to the government's 'monitoring tool', Australia seems to have reduced its responses to recommendations from six to four categories: 'Accepts', 'Notes', 'Notes (will consider further)' and 'Notes (will not consider further at this time'); Government of Australia, 'Universal Periodic Review Monitoring' (Attorney General's Department) <www.ag.gov.au/rights-and-protections/human-rights-and-anti-discrimination/united-nations-human-rights-reporting/universal-periodic-review-monitoring> accessed 14 September 2020.

to recommendations, and is meant to be updated annually, it does not offer a transparent monitoring mechanism.[54] It is difficult to identify areas of progress, or new problems that have emerged, and there is no sign of the promised collaboration with the Australian Human Rights Commission. In turn, as at October 2019, the Commission's own UPR page had not been updated since 2015.

Australia was elected to the HRC in 2017 for the 2018–20 term and the impact of this on its engagement with the UPR is unclear. Preparations for Australia's third UPR in November 2020 were underway at the time of writing, although there was little public sign of this.[55]

2.4 Rituals and Ritualism in the UPR

The UPR process qualifies as a human rights ritual, meeting Dembour's definition as 'a public, orchestrated event that is intentional and rule-bound'.[56] We can observe ritual practices in the cyclical nature of the process, and its elaborate calendar of events. The procedure itself is intricately managed and formalized, manifested, for example, in the formulaic structure and style of UPR documents.[57] The concept of 'interactive dialogue' is reduced into the sometimes deadening reality of extended formal introductions and rigorously observed time constraints.[58] We can observe an elaborate etiquette of supportive statements as well as rituals of condemnation.

One rationale of the UPR ritual is the performance of universal application of human rights norms. The HRC proudly notes that all 193 UN members have participated in the first two cycles. The appearance of universal participation has sometimes justified stretching the rules of the ritual: for example, in 2008 to accommodate South Africa's failure to observe the relevant timelines for documentation.[59]

When universality is under threat, for example, when Israel announced that it would not participate in its second UPR in January 2013 because of anti-Israel bias in the Council, considerable diplomatic energy was devoted to bringing Israel back into the fold. Israel's review was postponed and there were months of 'dialogue' with Israel, including intervention by the UN Secretary General. Some states pushed for a formal statement of condemnation of Israel for refusing to cooperate. While this was not successful, the Council took the strong step of adopting a resolution critical of Israel by consensus.[60] In the end, Israel's UPR session took

54 Attorney General's Department, 'Universal Periodic Review Monitoring' (n 53). In October 2019, the webpage noted Australia accepts 171 of the recommendations, up from 150 accepted at the time of the second cycle. The increase is due to Australia's ratification of the Optional Protocol to the Convention against Torture in 2018.

55 The government provided a first draft of a UPR national report at an annual NGO forum on 12 December 2019, but this document was not yet public.

56 Walter Kälin, 'Ritual and Ritualism at the Universal Periodic Review: A Preliminary Appraisal' in Charlesworth and Larking (n 11) 52.

57 For example, the HRC's detailed guidelines on the subject matter to be covered in national reports:

> UNHRC, 'Follow-up to the Human Rights Council Resolution 16/21 with Regard to the Universal Periodic Review' (19 July 2011) UN Doc A/HRC/DEC/17/119 para 2; The Council has also introduced strict word limits for working group reports, written views presented by the state under review after the interactive dialogue, and outcome reports: UNHRC, 'Follow-up to President's Statement 8/1' (24 September 2008) UN Doc A/HRC/PRST/9/2.

58 UN Doc A/HRC/DEC/17/119 (n 57) para 8(c).

59 On South Africa's backlog of overdue reports in 2008, see Damian Etone, 'The Effectiveness of South Africa's Engagement with the Universal Periodic Review (UPR): Potential for Ritualism?' (2017) 33(2) South African Journal on Human Rights 258, 265.

60 UNHRC, 'Report of the Human Rights Council on Its Seventh Organizational Meeting' (4 April 2013) UN Doc A/HRC/OM/7/1, 2 Part I, 'Decision OM/7/101: Non-cooperation of a State under Review with the Universal Periodic Review Mechanism'.

place in October 2013. A total of 237 recommendations were made, with Israel rejecting 132 of them. Israel failed to attend the formal adoption of the report, citing a labour strike in its Foreign Ministry.

The ritual of the UPR also reinforces the fiction of the equality of states: it reproduces an image of a body of sovereign, equal nations deliberating together, despite obvious inequalities. For example, the strict time limits for each review, whether it be of China or of Nauru, create a sense of equality between states in terms of human rights scrutiny.

The rituals of human rights can be limiting: all parties must conform to the requirements of the process to secure their participation. As Gerd Oberleitner notes, the concerns of human rights, such as promotion of human dignity and protection of the vulnerable, are translated into processes and procedures. Procedures also limit access to the global system. For example, NGOs that have not been granted 'consultative status' with intergovernmental bodies are excluded from international fora.[61]

The obsession with process can seem to prioritize means over ends and obscure the realities of human rights abuse. There is no possibility of discussion of the root causes of human rights violations, a point Susan Marks has made with respect to the human rights system generally.[62] Moreover, the state-run 'peer review' process is much less comprehensive than the expert review system of the human rights treaty bodies. Indeed, some countries invoke the UPR process precisely to resist the often sharper criticisms of the expert treaty bodies.

Some scholars have focussed on the rituals of the human rights system and interpreted these as evidence of emptiness and ossification.[63] While there is some truth in this, the UPR ritual carries some weight for the country under scrutiny. The fact that the UPR involves states reviewing other states gives it greater diplomatic consequence than review by the UN treaty bodies, which are made up of independent experts. One sign of the bite of the UPR is the strong resistance by some countries to its web casting. Indeed, during the first UPR cycle the internet failed in both China and Iran at the times of these countries' reviews.[64]

While the UPR can be understood as a ritual, it has also been a fertile site for human rights ritualism—the technique of embracing the language of human rights while deflecting human rights scrutiny and avoiding accountability for human rights abuses. UPR ritualism means participation in the process of reports and meetings, but an indifference to or even reluctance to increase the protection of human rights.

As a state-run system of scrutiny, the UPR is affected by regional and global alliances that may support ritualism. One example is the way that, in the first cycle, the interactive dialogue with a country being reviewed could be manipulated by stacking the speakers' list with friendly countries, preventing any tough questions being asked. The effect of the stacking is evident in the gentle scrutiny some countries, such as China, received, a technique described as a 'filibuster of praise'.[65] This technique to evade scrutiny was remedied in the second cycle by a decision to allow all interested states to participate in the dialogue.[66] While this avoids

[61] Gerd Oberleitner, *Global Human Rights Institutions: Between Remedy and Ritual* (Polity 2007) 14.

[62] Susan Marks, 'Human Rights and Root Causes: Human Rights and Root Causes' (2011) 74 The Modern Law Review 57.

[63] For example, Costas Douzinas, *The End of Human Rights: Critical Legal Thought at the Turn of the Century* (Hart Pub 2000); Stephen Hopgood, *The Endtimes of Human Rights* (Cornell University Press 2013).

[64] Interview with officers from the OHCHR, 28 September 2011; on resistance by Arab states, in particular Egypt, see Laura K Landolt, 'Externalizing Human Rights: From Commission to Council, the Universal Periodic Review and Egypt' (2013) 14 Human Rights Review 107.

[65] Landolt (n 64) 118. This contrasts with the much tougher reviews of the other P5 members: Rhona Smith, 'To See Themselves as Others See Them: The Five Permanent Members of the Security Council and the Human Rights Council's Universal Periodic Review' (2013) 35(1) Human Rights Quarterly 1, 13.

[66] UN Doc A/HRC/DEC/17/119 (n 57) paras 5–8.

the problem of filibuster, the change means that the time available for the 'interactive dialogue' (approximately two hours and twenty minutes) is simply divided by the number of states that wish to speak, sometimes leaving less than two minutes per state. It has been observed that the time constraints 'turn[] what should be a dynamic space for peer-to-peer debate and exchange into a stale forum of rushed and often unconnected monologues'.[67]

Other forms of ritualism include the fact that, overall, there is little self-criticism in country reports. This is well illustrated in Australia's national reports, which present a glowing picture of human rights protection. On the contentious issue of offshore detention of asylum seekers in Papua New Guinea and Nauru, for example, Australia's report in its second UPR brushes off responsibility for well-documented human rights abuses.[68] It states that these countries have 'agree[d] to treat transferees with dignity and respect in accordance with relevant human rights standards'.[69] Other countries simply ignore well-documented issues; an example is South Africa's reluctance to refer to HIV-AIDS as a human rights problem.[70] There are many cases where the plea of 'special circumstances' has been made to justify departures from human rights principles. For example, the United Kingdom has relied on the threat of terrorism to explain restrictions on the right to a fair trial;[71] and Australia refers to the 'flow of illegal maritime arrivals' to justify its treatment of asylum seekers.[72]

The broad nature of many UPR recommendations encourages ritualism. Recommendations often contain verbs such as 'consider', 'continue', 'reinforce', 'engage', or 'make every effort', which do not place a clear obligation on the state under review and which are difficult to measure. Australia, for example, was able to accept a recommendation from Trinidad and Tobago at its second UPR to 'engage closely with civil society in the follow-up on the [UPR]' and yet performed this in a token manner.[73] Australia also accepted recommendations with more specific language such as to 'take legislative measures to continue to guarantee rights and equal treatment for the indigenous people in order to ensure national cohesion and social harmony' (made by Angola). It seems that Australia interpreted this as requiring no action, and adequately fulfilled by existing laws.

A further technique of ritualism is to accept a recommendation formally, even if the intention is to reject it. One example is the United Kingdom's 'acceptance' of Russia's recommendation in the first UPR cycle that it consider removing the UK reservation to the Optional Protocol to the Convention on the Rights of the Child on the Involvement of Children in

[67] Gujadhur and Limon (n 50) 4.

[68] Government of Australia, 'National Report of Australia: Universal Periodic Review Second Cycle 2015' (2015) paras 122–39; UNHRC, 'Report of the Special Rapporteur on Torture and Other Cruel, Inhuman or Degrading Treatment or Punishment, Juan E Mendez—Addendum: Observations on Communications Transmitted to Governments and Replies Received' (5 March 2015) UN Doc A/HRC/28/68/Add.1, 7–10.

[69] UN Doc A/HRC/WG.6/23/AUS/1 (n 41) para 127 (footnotes omitted).

[70] In the national report of its second UPR cycle, for instance, South Africa referred to HIV-AIDS through the lens of the Millennium Development Goals, rather than as a human rights issue. UNHRC, 'National Report Submitted in Accordance with Paragraph 5 of the Annex to Human Rights Council resolution 16/2: South Africa' (7 March 2012) UN Doc A/HRC/WG.6/13/ZAF/1 para 38; UNHRC, 'National Report Submitted in Accordance with Paragraph 5 of the Annex to Human Rights Council Resolution 16/21: South Africa' (11 April 2017) UN Doc A/HRC/WG.6/27/ZAF/1.

[71] For example, UNHRC, 'National Report Submitted in Accordance with Paragraph 5 of the Annex to Human Rights Council Resolution 16/21: United Kingdom of Great Britain and Northern Ireland' (8 March 2012) UN Doc A/HRC/WG.6/13/GBR/1, paras 50–52, 63–69.

[72] Government of Australia, 'National Report of Australia: Universal Periodic Review Second Cycle (n 68) para 126.

[73] Government of Australia, 'Recommendation 66' (Attorney General's Department) <https://www.ag.gov.au/recommendations/recommendation-66> accessed 14 September 2020. Australia's 'monitoring tool' suggests that the 'close engagement' occurs annually at the Attorney General's forum on human rights, a one-day meeting at which a great range of human rights issues and mechanisms are discussed.

Armed Conflict.[74] The effect of the reservation is to allow 16- and 17-year-olds in the armed forces to take part in direct hostilities. In a highly legalistic response, the United Kingdom stated that it did not have a reservation, but rather a declaration.[75]

Another popular method of deflecting scrutiny is the deployment of government-organized NGOs, or GONGOs, which then monopolize the NGO speaking slots at the time that a UPR report on a state is formally adopted. This happened, for example, in the first UPRs of China and Cuba. Although the HRC has an NGO coordinator who reviews the credentials of NGOs, there are claims that some states intimidate this office to allow GONGOs to speak and to exclude independent NGOs.[76]

We can observe different regional approaches to ritualism in the UPR. African states and OIC members typically focus on changing procedures to reduce human rights scrutiny, for example, by arguing for longer UPR cycles.[77] Members of the 'Western Europe and Others' group, including Australia, tend to deflect recommendations by claiming 'we do this already', invoking their self-acclaimed image as longstanding human rights protectors.[78]

If the UPR is a site for both rituals and ritualism, can rituals have a role in countering ritualism? As noted already, Seligman and others see rituals as creating 'as if' or 'could be' worlds, generating 'the rhythmic structure of the shared subjunctive'.[79] Sincerity is not critical to this enterprise. On this analysis, we can understand the rituals of the UPR as requiring states to act 'as if' they take their human rights commitments seriously and 'as if' they are political peers.[80] In other words, states care about the process and how they will emerge from it. So, the performative moment itself is powerful. This may not be enough to induce comprehensive compliance, but it encourages states at least to present a positive performance. Jane Cowan has observed that:

> repeated participation in the ritual of the UPR serves to make habitual, customary and normal a specific discourse regarding the nature of sovereignty in relation to human rights. The focus on issues of sincere versus insincere commitment can be a distraction when 'going through the motions' itself has such powerful effects.[81]

[74] UNHRC, 'Universal Periodic Review: Report of the Working Group on the Universal Periodic Review: United Kingdom of Great Britain and Northern island—Addendum: Views on Conclusions and/or Recommendations, Voluntary Commitments and Replies Presented by the State under Review' (25 August 2008) UN Doc A/HRC/8/25/Add.1, para 4.

[75] Leanne Cochrane and Kathryn McNeilly, 'The United Kingdom, the United Nations Human Rights Council and the First Cycle of the Universal Periodic Review' (2013) 17(1) International Journal of Human Rights 152, 158.

[76] Landolt (n 64) 118–19, citing Essam El-Din Mohamed Hassan and others, 'Bastion of Impunity, Mirage of Reform: Human Rights in the Arab Region' (Cairo Institute for Human Rights Studies 2009) Annual Report, 223.

[77] Cochrane and Mcneilly (n 75) 168–69; Jane K Cowan and Julie Billaud, 'Between Learning and Schooling: The Politics of Human Rights Monitoring at the Universal Periodic Review' (2015) 36 Third World Quarterly 1175, 1183–85; Takele Soboka Bulto, 'Africa's Engagement with the Universal Periodic Review: Commitment or Capitulation?' in Charlesworth and Larking (n 11) ch 11; Damian Etone, 'African States: Themes Emerging from the Human Rights Council's Universal Periodic Review' (2018) 62 Journal of African Law 201–23.

[78] One such example is the practice of the United States with respect to the UPR: Constance de la Vega and Cassandra Yamasaki, 'The Effects of the Universal Periodic Review on Human Rights Practices in the United States' in Charlesworth and Larking (n 11) ch 10.

[79] Seligman and others (n 13) 10.

[80] Roy A Rappaport, *Ritual and Religion in the Making of Humanity* (CUP 1999) cited in Kelly, 'Two Cheers for Ritual' (n 21) 101.

[81] Jane K Cowan, 'The Universal Periodic Review as a Public Ritual: An Anthropological Perspective on Emerging Practices in the Global Governance of Human Rights' in Charlesworth and Larking (n 11) 52.

Some scholars have dismissed cooperative peer review in the context of human rights as a weak regulatory measure.[82] However, although states may initially participate in cooperative regulatory regimes in a perfunctory manner, or even for reasons at odds with the stated purposes of the regime, they are sometimes drawn into more effective commitments simply through their representatives' direct experience of participation and a desire to claim virtue in implementation.[83] Thus, Australia's campaign to be elected as a member of the HRC may be a sign that it takes the Council seriously. There is some evidence of such a process at the UPR. For example, Australia has announced human rights initiatives prior to both its reviews, and mission staff in Geneva display a marked willingness to engage with civil society throughout the review process.[84] Although Australia did not formally accept the many recommendations in its second UPR to ratify the OPCAT, the fact that Australia ratified the protocol two years later suggests that the UPR process had some effect. Scrutiny mechanisms such as the UPR can also discourage states from undermining the legitimacy gained initially by signing on to international human rights instruments.[85] It is possible that involvement over time in a cooperative regime leads to an internalization, or socialization, by participants of the regime's goals.[86]

While the UPR rituals sometimes constrain debate on human rights, they also prompt occasions of debate and critique. This creates some space, even if fleeting, for moral reflection and pressure.[87] Toby Kelly has pointed out that the civility of the ritual allows conversation on topics of human brutality that would otherwise be impossible to discuss.[88] Similarly, Jane Cowan has suggested that the ritual, repetitive character of the UPR provides a less confrontational space for difficult human rights issues to be raised.[89]

The UPR rituals also generate the belief that struggles for human rights are more than a series of localized conflicts.[90] Because of its nature, and the participation of state officials, the UPR cannot be dismissed by governments as somehow an illegitimate pressure.[91]

Civil society in the form of national human rights institutions and NGOs plays an important role in the UPR. It can help construct and maintain the 'as if' world of commitments to human rights standards. Thus, civil society can be empowered by a country's treaty ratification, even if the state itself fails to implement it.[92] One example is Egyptian NGOs' use of the UPR, which has fostered sustained human rights activity inside Egypt and at the regional level.[93] At the international level, many of the UPR recommendations were based on information provided by Egyptian civil society.[94]

[82] For example, Eric Neumayer, 'Do International Human Rights Treaties Improve Respect for Human Rights?' (2005) 49(6) Journal of Conflict Resolution 925, 926.

[83] John Braithwaite and Peter Drahos, *Global Business Regulation* (CUP 2000) 555–56..

[84] Ben Schokman and Phil Lynch, 'Effective NGO Engagement with the Universal Periodic Review' in Charlesworth and Larking (n 11) 142.

[85] Wade M Cole, 'Human Rights as Myth and Ceremony? Reevaluating the Effectiveness of Human Rights Treaties, 1981–2007' (2012) 117(4) American Journal of Sociology 1131, 1133.

[86] See generally Ryan Goodman and Derek Jinks, 'How to Influence States: Socialization and International Human Rights Law' (2004) 54 Duke Law Journal 621.

[87] Kelly, 'Two Cheers for Ritual' (n 21) 101.

[88] ibid.

[89] Cowan (n 81) 52.

[90] Kelly, 'Two Cheers for Ritual' (n 21) 103.

[91] Landolt (n 64) 125.

[92] Beth A Simmons, *Mobilizing for Human Rights: International Law in Domestic Politics* (CUP 2009) 125; Grainne de Búrca, 'Human Rights Experimentalism' (2017) 111 American Journal of International Law 277, 284 who suggests that the UPR could be understood as a system of experimentalist governance.

[93] Landolt (n 64) 126.

[94] ibid 122; Karolina M Milewicz and Robert E Goodin, 'Deliberative Capacity Building through International Organizations: The Case of the Universal Periodic Review of Human Rights' (2018) 48 British Journal of Political Science 513.

The staff of the OHCHR can also provide an important counterweight to ritualism. Although bureaucrats, they understand their role as 'keepers of the truth' and have some capacity to shape procedures.[95] One example is in the context of NGO registration. OHCHR staff have resisted pressure on the HRC NGO coordinator from some authoritarian states to register GONGOs, or to not register certain NGOs.[96] In the context of the UPR, members of the OHCHR have worked to preserve 'the voice from the field'.[97]

2.5 Conclusion

The title of this book uses the notion of a struggle in charting the life of human rights: it highlights the sense that human rights will always meet resistance, and perhaps implies that those in the field must gird their loins for a perpetual battle. Paying attention to human rights rituals and the phenomenon of ritualism, by contrast, shifts the focus to the performances surrounding the international system. It allows us to develop a finer-grained analysis of how the international human rights system works.

The concepts of ritual and ritualism emerge from different scholarly traditions, but there are links between them. Drawing on Seligman and others' description of rituals as creating 'as if' or 'could be' worlds, we can understand human rights rituals as requiring states to act as if they take their human rights commitments seriously.[98] Accepting a human rights treaty requires a performance of implementation. While this may often be a ritualized performance, there is some power inherent in the performative moment itself. In the processes of the UPR, despite political posturing by representatives of states presenting accounts of their country's human rights performance, and by delegates from other states who assess and respond to these accounts, there are possibilities for reflection and pressure.

International lawyers' emphasis on compliance with human rights norms overlooks the social life of the law. The international human rights system is highly politicized, but that is not the full story. In fits and starts, it is capable of being mobilized to improve the protection of human rights. The constant challenge is, then, to harness the transformative potential of human rights rituals to undermine human rights ritualism. Philip Alston's many contributions to the international human rights system are inspiring examples of meeting this challenge.

[95] Julie Billaud, 'Keepers of the Truth: Producing "Transparent" Documents for the Universal Periodic Review' in Charlesworth and Larking (n 11) 70–72, 77, 80–82.

[96] Landolt (n 64) 119.

[97] Jane K Cowan and Julie Billaud, 'The "Public" Character of the Universal Periodic Review: Contested Concept and Methodological Challenge' in Ronald Niezen and Maria Sapignoli (eds), *Palaces of Hope: The Anthropology of Global Organizations* (CUP 2017) 116–18.

[98] Rappaport (n 80) cited in Kelly, 'Two Cheers for Ritual' (n 21) 101.

3
The Targeted Killing of Jesus Christ

JHH Weiler

3.1 Targeted Killing?

On its face the very essence of a 'targeted killing' is the execution of a person—guilty or suspect as he or she might be—without the benefit and authority and legitimately of a trial. Jesus stood not one but two trials, before the Sanhedrin and before Pontius Pilate. How could this, then, be a targeted killing? Easily enough. If the trial is a sham with the outcome predetermined in advance, the arrow stuck and the circles then drawn around it, it is no other than a targeted killing executed not by those who nailed him to the cross but by those who ordered such.

Was this the case in this instance? At face value there are two primary suspects: the Sanhedrin and Pontius Pilate. I am going to take Pilate off the suspect list since on the reading of the Gospel accounts (the so-called Synoptics—Mark, Mathew, and Luke) Pilate was just doing the bidding of the Sanhedrin. And according to John (in the Johannine account there was no trial, just an interrogation before the Sanhedrin), he was sent to Pilate because the Jews had no authority in capital cases. So, at this point, our suspect list is reduced to one, the Sanhedrin, speaking unanimously on behalf of 'the Jews'.

3.2 A Brief Methodological Excursion

There are two principal types of literature on the trial of Jesus. The first is pietistic and devotional—the Christ of Faith. Its typical epistemic foundation is what we may call Gospel truth, the belief that the biblical narratives are inspired by the Almighty—for some the inerrant Word of God—and are thus a fully reliable historical source on the life of Jesus, including his trials before the Jewish Sanhedrin and Pontius Pilate. The accounts of the four Gospels do not always agree in the detail. But this, in the eyes of this literature, comes as no surprise as would be the case regarding any historical happening recounted by different witnesses. Sometimes they appear to contradict each other—in John, as I just mentioned, there is no Sanhedrin trial but a mere interrogation, whereas the so-called Synoptics, Marc, Matthew, and (in a truncated manner) Luke, describe such a trial. But these types of contradictions can, in a tradition of centuries, usually be 'harmonized': 'First there was an interrogation and then a trial', to give but one classical example.

The tone of the devotional books on the trial is one of outrage and indignation at what we would call a targeted killing. Typical titles would be Murder at Golgotha; The Illegal Trial of Jesus; The Day Justice was Judged!; The Mistrials of Jesus; Crucify Him; The Most Outrageous Trial in History.

JHH Weiler, *The Targeted Killing of Jesus Christ* In: *The Struggle for Human Rights*. Edited by: Nehal Bhuta, Florian Hoffmann, Sarah Knuckey, Frédéric Mégret, and Margaret Satterthwaite, Oxford University Press.
DOI: 10.1093/oso/9780198868064.003.0004

These books are not ancient history but continue to be published to this day as a quick Amazon search will readily display. One can and should be empathetic to these emotions and not condescend to them. The Gospel narrative invites such emotions. The Jewish authorities are determined, and consequently conspire, to bring about the death of Jesus. The ensuing description of the trial, false witnesses and all, presents a caricature of due process. And the defendant is not 'merely' the Messiah, and the Son of the Blessed (to adopt the Marcan terminology) in relation to which a conviction for blasphemy appears an outrage in and of itself, but a person who throughout his life exuded goodness, preached justice, and harmed no one.

Inevitably these emotions turn into anger and at times even include explicit calls for vengeance against the perpetrators, the Jews. After all, even after the trial, when 'they' had a chance to save Jesus at the offer of Pilate, the brayed for his death in the famous phrase from Matthew: Let his blood be on us and on our children. This turn to the perpetrators is understandable too. It is the human condition when faced with cruelty and injustice to seek the perpetrators and find an outlet for one's outrage and rage.

But I want to point out two features of this literature that will become important later in this short essay. The first is that in addressing the injustice with understandable emotion it is the procedural defects of the trial that are overwhelmingly highlighted: it was an unjust procedure. Nobody should have been convicted following such an aberrational process. Strange as it may seem, the issue of the substantive guilt or otherwise of Jesus, whether he was or was not a blasphemer is almost invariably elided, or dealt with very perfunctorily.

One reason is obvious. Jesus was the Messiah and was divine. How could he be found guilty of anything—let alone blasphemy—if he was telling the truth? His innocence is assumed. But there is another reason why the focus is so overwhelmingly not on the substantive issue of his alleged blasphemy but on the unfairness of the trial and the lack of due process. Lurking below the surface and sometimes not very deeply is the discomforting feeling that if, say, someone today was to come and announce that he is the Messiah and Son of Jesus—among believers the word blasphemy would instantly come to mind, would it not?

The second strand in the vast literature on the trial of Jesus is scientific—the historical Jesus. It has been going on in successive 'quests' for three centuries. It is driven by the realization that the Gospel narratives pose problems for the historian who wants to explore what Jesus 'really' said; what Jesus 'really' did. The problems are readily apparent. What did Jesus 'really' say? Our New Testament accounts are in Greek, but Jesus most certainly taught and conversed in Aramaic and Hebrew, so that there is an immediate problem, with which we would all be familiar in other contexts, as regards the accuracy of the translation. Further, the Gospels were written between one to two generations after his death and relied on disparate oral (and perhaps some written) traditions at times at variance with each other; given the huge impact of Jesus on his immediate followers, the possibility—in good faith to be sure—of some embellishment, of faulty memory, and the like cannot be excluded. Further still, the Gospel writers did not think of themselves as historians—their factual narrative was embedded in the understanding of each of them of the religious significance of Jesus, shaped by the ministry of Paul that preceded them, which again adds to the difficulties. It is, for example, a commonplace, accepted by most but not all, that Luke and Matthew had access to the Marcan narrative. When comparing what each took from Marc and what each left out or modified, one can see how these cohere with the theological outlook of these two Gospels.

And then, in addition, the earliest (incomplete) manuscripts of the four Gospels, which we have dated at best to the second century CE and full manuscripts even later, allowing for the possibility of copyist and scribal error or 'correction'.

On top of all this—and this is no original insight—though all scholars belonging to the historical Jesus school as distinct from the Gospel Truth approach agree on all the above-mentioned, there are fierce debates as to the appropriate scientific tools with which to address these problems and, even more so, their application in practice. It is not uncommon, and this is no condemnation but rather a normal feature of social science, that scholars purporting to use more or less the same toolkit will come to very different and at times opposing conclusions.

Moreover, though in principle the scientific approach of the historical Jesus should be 'disinterested', driven, unlike the devotional literature, neither by religious nor other ideological agendas, this ideal of disinterested science is hard to achieve in any of the social sciences least so here. The scientist himself or herself is inevitably situated with some normative and even epistemic—conscious or subconscious—presuppositions that will then impact the framing of their research questions, the methodology they employ, and ultimately their conclusions. This is evident in sociology and anthropology and other social sciences and perhaps even more so in the historical approach to theological questions in general and to the historical research of Jesus in particular. Numerous scholars have deeply held religious convictions, which many do not hide, and there are almost as many historical Jesuses as there are scholars trying to reconstruct such. This by no means condemns the field—it is inevitable.

Thus, notwithstanding vigorous protests over the centuries, the historical Jesus endeavour is not antithetical to religious faith but rather indispensable since both traditional Judaism and Christianity (and the trial involves both) are historical religions in the sense that they reject any 'founding myth' basis for faith as condescending and reductionist. Christians (and Jews) understand themselves as rooted in historical reality. If Jesus did not live, was not crucified and resurrected, the foundations or traditional Christianity evaporate. And thus, the big debates—and they are fierce—concern only the degree to which one can reconstruct the historical Jesus and the relevance of such to theological understanding. The Catholic Church, for example, has long accepted the validity and importance of the historical endeavour. And it should not surprise one that distinguished traditional Christian theologians, like Ratzinger in German, Pagola in Spanish, or Wright, Dunn, or Brown in English to mention but a few of many, attempt, each in their own way, to integrate their understanding of the uses and misuses of the historical method into their reconstructions of a holistic historical Jesus/Christ of faith.

In what follows I will focus mostly on the Gospel Truth account for a simple reason: It is this account that for centuries and close to two millennia shaped our collective consciousness—and historical or otherwise—has become the living asset of Western civilization.

3.3 Reconsidering the Procedural Issues of the Trial

As mentioned, an overwhelming portion of the popular and theological literature of the trial is directed to show that a miscarriage of justice occurred in Jerusalem. Interestingly, the critics, many of them anguished and angry, and often both, do not protest the fact that a trial took place; they protest the injustice of that trial. And when dealing with the injustice, equally interesting is the tendency to focus on the procedural aspects of the trial rather than issues of the substantive guilt of Jesus.

But why seek to find the trial unjust at all? There is of course the visceral anger at the killing of the Christ. But that, as we shall see when we discuss the theology of the trial, is a motive not without complications, for the whole purpose of the Passion was the divine plan for the sacrifice of the Son as redemption for a sinful humanity. At least one additional factor comes into play. It was not just the killing of Jesus that enrages but the impugning of Jesus, as a criminal and blasphemer.

There is a theological imperative that as the Paschal lamb Jesus must have died blameless, innocent, pure, and without blemish. It is only thus that the redemptive purpose and function of his death could be realized. The problem of the trial is therefore not simply in its result, his death, but in the eyes of many, not least the Evangelists, that the conviction threatens that purity. And thus, independently of the result, the trial itself has to be impugned and Jesus's alleged guilt expunged.

It is not surprising therefore that a huge literature emerges that tries to do just that: impugn the trial as grossly unjust. The procedural approach takes its cue from the Gospel account itself, where it is, indeed, the procedural aspects of the trial and the good faith of the Sanhedrin that are called into question:

> But the Chief Priests and the whole Sanhedrin were seeking testimony against Jesus in order to put him to death, and they were not finding any. For many were giving false testimony against him, and the testimonies were not consistent. And some, having stood up, were giving false testimony against him, saying that 'we have heard him saying that "I will destroy the sanctuary made by hand, and within three days another not made by hand I will build." ' And even so their testimony was not consistent. (Mark 14:55–59)

Or even more egregiously:

> But the Chief Priests and the whole Sanhedrin were *seeking false testimony* against Jesus so that they might put him to death. And they did not find any, although many false testifiers came forward. But at last two, having come forward, said 'This person stated "I am able to destroy the sanctuary of God, and within three days I will build (it)." '[1]

The Mishnah component of the Talmud is far more accessible than the Gemara, so generations of 'trial blazers' have gone to the Sanhedrin Tractate of the Mishnah and have studied the elaborate procedures outlined for criminal trials in general and capital punishment trials more specifically. Taking their cue from the Gospel narrative itself, which, as we have just seen, expresses doubts about the procedural propriety of the trial, and supplementing this with the gleanings of the Mishnah, the road clears to demonstrate with different levels of indignation, outrage, and/or sadness the myriad ways in which the fragmented accounts of the trial in the Gospel violate those procedures. Indeed, they do. On some counts there are said to be no less than twenty-seven conflicts between the Gospel narrative of the trial and Jewish sources on proper criminal procedure. Many of them were not trivial. To contemporize, these were not instances of 'harmless error' but a colossal denial of 'due process' resulting inevitably in a massive miscarriage of Justice. I will illustrate with just a few examples:

- In the Synoptic accounts, the trial took place on the eve of the Passover. The Mishnah forbids the holding of a Capital case on the eve of the Sabbath or a feast day, probably because of the fear that the court would rush the procedure to the detriment of the accused.

[1] Matthew 26:59–60; emphasis added.

- By most Gospel accounts the trial takes place during the night. This again is forbidden by the Mishnah, probably for a similar reason.
- The Mishnah stipulates that witnesses should be given stern warning to speak the truth, that a Capital trial should begin with reasons for acquittal and witnesses heard for the accused. None of this is reported in the Gospel accounts.
- In the Gospel account Caiaphas, the Chief Priest speaks first, in calling for the conviction of Jesus. The Mishnah, worried perhaps that more junior members of the Sanhedrin would be swayed or fear to speak their own mind after hearing the view of senior judges, stipulates that the order of voting commence with the most junior and conclude with the Head of the Sanhedrin.
- The verdict as reported in the Sanhedrin is unanimous. The Mishnah invalidates a unanimous conviction on capital offenses—suspicious that such unanimity may indicate a rigged or railroaded court.

On this analysis, the trial was indeed procedurally a miscarriage of justice. This turn to the Mishnah even by traditionalists represents (inadvertently perhaps) a mélange of the Gospel Truth and historical approaches. But applying that methodology, the conclusions are not without their problems.

First is what one might call the historiography conundrum: How is one to interpret the trial's egregious and widespread disregard of the Mishnah tenets of criminal procedure? To some, these discrepancies are triumphant proof that Jesus was unjustly convicted, even by 'their own' law—see the Mishnah! For others it is proof that the Synoptic trial narrative is at worst a fabrication (extrapolating backwards from the trial before Pilate so as to shift blame from Rome to Jerusalem is one of the favourite theses) and at best that the account in John where there is no trial but a mere interrogation, is to be preferred. For, so the argument goes, the Synoptic narrative cannot be credible since the description of the trial is so at odds with how a veritable trial would have taken place—see the Mishnah! Historiographically speaking, the same premise—the trial's massive deviation from fundamental procedural requirements in the Mishnah—can pretty much sustain either hypothesis.

Be that as it may, still arguing historically, we simply have no way of knowing with any measure of accuracy at all what were the prevailing procedural norms at the time of the trial. As has been pointed out endlessly, the Mishnaic code was redacted 200 years after the Trial. There is very little certainty as to which of its components reflected prevailing norms two centuries earlier and which were the result of subsequent accretion.

It is in fact likely that most of the norms found to conflict were not in place at the time of the trial. Most of the Mishnaic criminal procedure provisions reflect such a revulsion at the thought of convicting the innocent that it must be the most 'pro-defendant' code in legal history. Indeed, these provisions give the distinct impression of an idealized, post-sovereignty code conceived when its authors had no responsibility of administering a functioning criminal legal system. The saying of that period was that a Sanhedrin who executed more than one defendant in seventy years was to be thought of as murderous. Indeed, if any Sanhedrin actually had to operate under those rules of criminal procedure, they would have had trouble securing even that single conviction. It is unlikely that many of its rules were operational when the Jews actually exercised sovereignty over criminal matters.

The result of this brief historical foray is not to argue that the trial was procedurally just. It is simply to say that historically a judgment on this point is difficult to establish from the usual Mishnaic sources cited.

It is instead worth returning to the Gospel account itself and reading it with care. First, though we do not know and have no way of knowing the precise content of the rules of procedure controlling at the time of the trial, the scriptural account itself suggests strongly that procedure mattered. It is clear, for example, that witnesses were needed and that the testimony of witnesses, as prescribed in the Bible itself, had to be consistent.

Second, startlingly, even after two witnesses whose testimony did agree were finally found, it was apparently not sufficient for a conviction and Caiaphas turned to interrogate Jesus himself, who was eventually convicted based on his answers. Procedure, whatever its content, seemed thus to matter a great deal.

It does not come as a surprise that in his recent study Benedict XVI concludes from these very facts that it seems as if they were in search of a procedurally just trial.

Let me suggest for consideration the following propositions based on the Gospel narrative:

Plausible: By Scriptural account, in the eyes of Caiaphas Jesus was no trivial criminal, someone who blasphemed in the marketplace or made idle threats against the Temple, but someone who for some reasons was not only defying and undermining the authority of the Jewish leadership but also risking the entire nation. Jesus appeared sufficiently dangerous and threatening that Caiaphas not only sought his death but was willing to take considerable risks to achieve that result. He risked public humiliation if Pilate refused to carry out the execution.

He risked, perhaps, some popular opposition against such an outcome—especially since it would be him who would be held responsible.

Implausible: If Caiaphas wished to suborn witnesses it is implausible that he could not have arranged for two witnesses to tell whatever incriminating tale would be necessary to secure a conviction. Judas sold his great master for thirty coins of Silver—was there only one Judas in the whole land?

Implausible: That members of the Sanhedrin (whether twenty-three or seventy or whatever number) to the very last would be part of the pretrial conspiracy to kill Jesus. Likewise, it stretches credulity to imagine that at the trial a unanimous verdict would be reached in the face of major procedural defects, especially in a Sanhedrin that was as ideologically and theologically heterogeneous as the one at the time of the trial. It is worth recalling the trial in Acts in which the famous R Gamiliel dissents.

And yet, recall Caiaphas, 'it is expedient for us that one man should die for the people, and not that the whole nation should perish'.[2] The Bible is full of stories of getting rid of enemies by extra judicial means. Think of King David himself at the hour of his death commanding those around him:

> Moreover thou knowest also what Joab the son of Zeruiah did to me, *and* what he did to the two captains of the hosts of Israel, unto Abner the son of Ner, and unto Amasa the son of Jether, whom he slew, and shed the blood of war in peace, and put the blood of war upon his girdle that *was* about his loins, and in his shoes that *were* on his feet. Do therefore according to thy wisdom, and let not his hoar head go down to the grave in peace.[3]

The execution was swift:

[2] John 11:48.
[3] 1 Kings 2:5–7.

> Then tidings came to Joab: for Joab had turned after Adonijah, though he turned not after Absalom. And Joab fled unto the tabernacle of the LORD, and caught hold on the horns of the altar ... So Benaiah the son of Jehoiada went up, and fell upon him, and slew him: and he was buried in his own house in the wilderness.[4]

A clandestine assassination, based on utilitarian notions of justice, would have served Caiaphas well. In fact, that is almost what one could expect. And yet, even though Jesus is conceived—in the Synoptic accounts too—as a serious threat, a veritable target, and even though it would probably be much tidier simply to send a Benaiah son of Jehoiada to cut his throat, that is apparently not on the cards.

I think the best judgment on the procedure must be that we don't know, we can't know.

3.4 Reconsidering the Substantive Issues of the Trial—Theology and the Paths to God

Let us turn from procedure to the substantive part of the trial. With what was Jesus charged? Of what was Jesus actually convicted? True, his alleged statements about the destruction of the Temple seem to have been abandoned. But his responses to the questions of Caiaphas, specifically to the question 'Are you the Messiah the Son of the Blessed?' to which at least in one account he gives an unequivocal Yes, and the claims about sitting to the right of the Power—are these not all self-evident blasphemy?

It may come as a surprise to some that in the trial literature there is huge controversy about these issues. The problems are legion, and none are trivial or specious. The Temple charges are powerful in explaining the enmity against Jesus by, for example, the Priestly cast. They provide motive for moving against him. But it is far less clear how this motive translates into a legal charge, and how it is connected to the conviction for blasphemy. For one, is it not reminiscent of the unsuccessful attempt to convict Jeremiah with similar charges? How and why would Jesus be different? Second, the Gospel itself recounts Jesus' statements and conduct against the Temple. Surely it could not have been too difficult to find (truthful) witnesses who would attest to what Jesus said and did against the Temple and, thus, be done with it. So, what exactly was the charge in the trial? What was Caiaphas trying to ascertain in his examination of the witnesses? And on what issue precisely was it so difficult for them to agree, given the public nature of the sayings and deeds of Jesus? And why, even when, in one account, agreement was found, this apparently was not sufficient for conviction?

In his interrogation of the witnesses and subsequent questioning of Jesus, one has the distinct feeling that Caiaphas was really trying to find out something, the absence of which would not permit the conviction of Jesus. On this reading, Jesus' replies to Caiaphas, did not in and of themselves constitute blasphemy, as is sometime argued as an alternative basis for conviction, but instead provided the missing element of a charge—generically called blasphemy—which the interrogation of the witnesses failed to establish.

I veer to that reading because the notion of blasphemy itself raises more questions than it gives answers. There is the noted lexical issue: There is no certainty as to the Hebrew equivalent of the Greek blasphemy used in the New Testament (NT) and the responses of Jesus in and of themselves correspond neither to the biblical definitions that might constitute such

[4] ibid 2:28, 34.

equivalence nor to the Mishnaic. Is it Kll? Is it Nkv? Is it Gdf? If we examine the circumstances of these three biblical offenses, all translated as 'blasphemy' and all linked to forms of grave and intentional disrespect to God, they do not seem to correspond to the actual answers of Jesus at the trial nor to any action before. The entire testimony of the Gospel is of a Jesus who loves and seeks to follow what he understands is his duty to God. There is not, at first blush, the kind of arrogance we notice in other contexts in the Bible where blasphemy is invoked.

Nor, contrary to present day sensibilities is the Messiahship claim or the Sonship claim, or the sitting next to the power of God claim, self-evidently or even plausibly blasphemous by either biblical or Mishnaic concept of blasphemy. The Mishnaic definition of blasphemy consists in pronouncing the explicit name of God (the Tetragrammaton). It is farfetched to suggest that Jesus did that. When the Talmud recounts (400 years later) the story of the trial—in which there are no Romans and Jesus is convicted and put to death by the Jewish authorities—he is not accused of blasphemy but of incitement. The Talmud sages are not of course a reliable historical source, and they get various historical facts about Jesus, including the time of his life, wrong. But they certainly sought to impugn him in their account and they definitely knew something about Jewish law. The facts and legends as known to them evidently pointed away from the classical biblical and Talmudic rendition of blasphemy.

And so does the Gospel. For in the story of the healing of the paralytic in which Jesus himself forgives his sins, he is considered by the Pharisees to have committed blasphemy by doing something that only God may—again, pointing away from the more specific and technical definitions and more towards a generic offence against God.

Of all the theories put forward to explain both the charge and conviction for blasphemy, I find the most plausible that which regards the use of the Greek word 'blasphemy' not as a legal *terminus technicus* but as a generic and general allusion of some offence against God, the concrete manifestation of which is not spelled out by the non-legal narrators of the NT. The question remains then: Of what was Jesus charged? And what was the specific offence against God that he was perceived by the Sanhedrin to have committed?

The substantive enigma of the trial is not limited to the factual-legal question but also presents some theological challenges; I will raise three. In teaching the trial, every year, in different ways, a delicate moment, pregnant with meaning, presents itself. There will always be a group of students for whom, despite the academic setting, the seminar is an exploration of faith. What I have found, again and again so moving, is their true love for Jesus. It is not a simple fealty to a faith, or commitment to a truth, but an emotional state. Their sense of unfolding injustice is palpable, painful, and understandable in terms of the pathos of the Passion. The Passion evokes passion. The theological imperative of a blemishless and blameless Jesus is complemented with a passion that justice be done and that he be exonerated.

This is so with all martyrdoms. Though we may be inspired by the martyrdom, when we contemplate the events, we truly wish that they would not have taken place—that, for example, the Christian men or women were not thrown to the Lions for professing their belief in Jesus, or that the Jewish men or women were not burnt on the stake for refusing to profess such.

But in this case there always comes the moment where someone raises, one way or another, the question—'Suppose Jesus were exonerated … and then what?' The martyrdom of the Trial, not surprisingly, is unlike any other; for Jesus in the eyes of his believers is unlike any other martyr. In one way because, for his followers and believers the statement, 'I wish it never happened'—is far more complicated. In some profound sense that would negate the entire sense of the Passion, the direction of his short life, his destiny, and the design of God for a sacrifice of the Son, intended to redeem the world. To be sure, in the long history of Christian theology, this 'what if' question has been discussed. All I will permit myself to say is that the answers given may not convince all, (especially if the Original Sin remains intact) and in any event, deprived of Passion, of crucifixion, and resurrection it would be such a different Christianity that discussing this option is rendered overly artificial. At a minimum, the uniqueness of this martyrdom renders reaction to it emotionally and normatively complex.

If we hold on to the Christian traditional view that considers Jesus' fate to have been predestined as a means for God to redeem a humanity tainted by Original Sin, and regards the Passion as leading inevitably to crucifixion and resurrection, a second theological issue emerges. If it is the design of God that Jesus must die, and he must die innocent, for this to happen, some human agent must defy the will of God—for we are surely commanded not to condemn and kill the innocent.

At first blush this seems to be no problem at all. It is not at all uncommon, not least in biblical narrative, that God's design be fulfilled by the wrongful or even evil deeds of people, sometimes even those close to God. Let us briefly consider the story of Joseph and his brothers. It was through a particularly dastardly act, first the plot to kill him and then eventually to sell him into slavery, that Joseph arrived in Egypt. When Joseph finally revealed himself to his brothers with a display of love and forgiveness, their unease was palpable and enduring. And that unease did not dissipate with time. Years later when Joseph's brothers saw that their father was dead, they said, 'Perhaps Joseph will [now] hate us, and may actually repay us for all the evil which we did to him.'

It falls to Joseph to explain the mysterious ways of God:

> But as for you, you meant evil against me; but God meant it for good, in order to bring it about as it is this day, to save many people alive.[5]

Here, then, is an instance of someone (the brothers) doing evil, electing to do evil, though at the end it serves the purposes of God.

But at the trial of Jesus the theological situation is far more delicate and complex. In the case of Joseph, the design of God could have been achieved in many ways not requiring the bad deeds of the brothers. There are myriad ways in which Joseph could have found himself in Egypt, none of them necessitating an egregious defiance of God's will. What is special and complex in the trial situation is that to fulfil the postulate of the divine plan an innocent must be put to death. In the context of the trial an innocent must be found guilty. That of course runs directly contrary to God's law. Evil must occur, God must be defied, his servants must disregard his laws and his wish that humans act justly—in order for the Passion on which salvation hangs to take place. It would be as if the Golden Calf were required for the giving of the Torah. That is quite different from the Joseph situation where it just transpires that an evil deed is then found to have served a divine purpose. I do not want to belabour the point, but it is surely theologically unsatisfying on more than one level, that the design of God and the salvation of mankind be *dependent* on someone defying God.

Finally, a question that is rarely raised concerns the very instrumentality that is used to play the Passion to its climax. Why a trial at all? What is special about a trial rather than, say, some more run-of-the-mill assassination plot? What, if any, is the theological significance that Jesus faced his enemies through a trial?

[5] Genesis 50:20.

At the core of the substantive dimension of the trial, we have observed, then, something of a double enigma. Legally, we are left searching for the specific charge brought against Jesus for which he was convicted. Theologically, among other problems, it is most perplexing that on its own terms, the divine design would require human agents to defy God so that his will be fulfilled.

Let us turn first to the legal question. I think the key is to search for the charge, the indictment, the legal accusation before exploring the conviction. The most explicit Scriptural answer to the question of the Charge is, in fact, to be found in the Gospel, in Acts in the context of the trial of Stephen, which for obvious reasons is almost universally accepted as completing the truncated Jesus trial narrative in Luke:

> For we have heard him say, that this Jesus of Nazareth shall destroy this place, and shall change the customs which Moses delivered us.[6]

There are several reasons why following this Luke/Acts lead is attractive: First, I think one should prefer an explanation to the substantive enigma of the trial that derives as directly as possible from Scripture. Second, of all Gospel narratives this is the only one that explicitly addresses the question of the charge against Jesus. In all other accounts we are required speculatively to reverse-engineer from the interrogation of the witnesses or Jesus by Caiaphas. Third, it harmonizes well with the narrative in the other Gospel accounts (even including John) since the Temple accounts in those narratives would easily fall within the first leg of the Luke/Acts accusation. Fourth, it is consistent with the thesis that renders blasphemy as a generic description of an offence against God, which requires concretization.

In this case I shall argue that there is a ready-made biblical offence that may serve that purpose. And finally, as I shall presently show, it coheres well with the use of 'blasphemy' in the paralytic healing episode and indeed with all other instances where blasphemy is invoked against Jesus in his pretrial days.

I find Deuteronomy XIII 1–6 the most germane biblical passage giving legal form to the account in Acts/Luke and concretizing the generic 'blasphemy' in all accounts. When used in the trial literature it is often referred to as the 'False Prophet' charge following, perhaps, the characterization of that passage in Deuteronomy in some rabbinic literature (a characterization that may, indirectly, have been influenced by the Church–Synagogue conflict). But that is not the characterization used in the Deuteronomy itself. The False Prophet is dealt with in Deuteronomy XVIII and pertains to a different phenomenon. For reasons that will transpire, I think one should avoid that characterization.

As early as the thirteenth century, the Cologne Jewish sage Jacob ben Ahser, the famous Baal HaTurim, suggested the Deuteronomy XIII passage alludes to Jesus; but it was censored out of many editions as offensive to Christianity. Ironically, the possible allusion to Jesus could be thought of as offensive to Judaism since Jesus would be given the dignity of a prophet and messenger of God as stipulated in the Deuteronomy passage. As I shall argue, it need not be thought of as such by Christians or Jews alike.

The chapter opens with the following canonical phrase integral to the re-elaboration of the Mosaic Code.

[6] Acts 6:14.

> What thing so ever I command you, observe to do it: thou shalt not add thereto, nor diminish from it. Deut. XIII:1 (in some Biblical traditions these are the closing words of Ch. XII)

This would seem in many ways to be part of the *Grundnorm* of Mosaic law. We are instructed with that same divine authority that set out the material content of the long list of commandments, that the list is finite and immutable. It may not be touched by us—we can neither add nor delete. It is a common phrase repeated many times in the Pentateuch. The law is not only finite but also eternal, Chukat Olam, a law for ever. And lest someone wonder how long forever is, the Bible is explicit on that too: a thousand generations.

Now, even a novice in public law will know that both 'constitutional precepts'—immutable and eternal—are as stable as their author wishes. The mouth that forbids, is the mouth that permits. Should the Almighty God change his mind, there would be nothing to stop him from not only revising the material content of His law, but also the precepts of immutability and eternity.

So here, in Deuteronomy XIII Scripture tries to do something more radical—it tries to ensure that it would become irreversibly a law 'forever'. Let us return to the legally stunning text of Deuteronomy XIII:

> 1 If there arise among you a prophet, or a dreamer of dreams, and giveth thee a sign or a wonder, 2 And the sign or the wonder come to pass, whereof he spake unto thee, saying, Let us go after other gods, which thou hast not known, and let us serve them; 3 Thou shalt not hearken unto the words of that prophet, or that dreamer of dreams: for the LORD your God proveth [tests] you, to know whether ye love the LORD your God with all your heart and with all your soul. 4 Ye shall walk after the LORD your God, and fear him, and keep his commandments, and obey his voice, and ye shall serve him, and cleave unto him. 5 And that prophet, or that dreamer of dreams, shall be put to death; because he hath spoken to turn you away from the LORD your God, which brought you out of the land of Egypt, and redeemed you out of the house of bondage, to thrust thee out of the way which the LORD thy God commanded thee to walk in. So shalt thou put the evil away from the midst of thee.[7]
>
> *Nota bene*: The prophet who giveth a Sign (Ot) or a wonder (Mofet) is not a magician, a sorcerer or any one of the operators of supernaturalism which the Biblical world and word acknowledges and in certain cases forbids. When God sends Moses and Aaron to Pharaoh they give Signs and Wonders (Otot u Moftim) to verify their provenance and authenticity.[8]

When some of these are precisely replicated by Pharaoh's underlings, that does not make these prophets, and their demonstrations are not divinely authenticating: They are called magicians and sorcerers. And the very same acts or signs or wonders—the terminology for a divine signal—are named 'enchantments' (Lahatutim). An Ot or a Mofet—a sign or a wonder—is the common terminology in the Hebrew Bible to indicate authentic divine authority. It is always used in this manner.

The person in Deuteronomy XIII 1–6 is neither a false prophet in the normal sense. Deuteronomy XVIII:18–22 lays down the general provisions concerning prophets with the

[7] Deuteronomy 13:1–5.
[8] Exodus 4:1–9.

instruction that they must be obeyed and followed, whereas a false prophet must die. The test of the prophet is the veracity of his prophecy over time. The issue of such a prophet advocating straying from the law is not even discussed. As already Maimonides noted, the prophet, whose authority is explicitly derived from the law, would lose all his authority if he himself undermined that very law. You cannot ask to be followed in the name of the law and at the same time claim to be above that law. The authority of the 'normal' prophet is found within the legal system itself. It is subject to the Grundnorm of neither adding nor diminishing.

But what if we step outside the legal system, an appeal to the authority on which that very legal system is predicated?

The people were told that *they* were not to add or diminish from the commandments of God re-elaborated in the Duteronomic Code. But surely if a prophet, adding or diminishing, with the authenticating authority of signs and wonders from God, these can be followed? He who maketh, taketh? Apparently not. For even if the messenger were to exhibit an unmistakable sign and wonder that in all respects replicated the signs that authenticated Moses[9]—in other words, even if it were clear and uncontestable that the prophet was an authentic messenger from God and speaking with the imprimatur of God, at the moment the prophet so authenticated were to inveigh a breach of the Mosaic law, that message was to be taken as sign of a divine test, the real meaning of which is that it should not be followed since we are instructed that the messenger in question, with the authenticating signs and wonders is sent by God, to 'proveth' (menaseh ani otchem)—to test the love, loyalty, and fidelity of the people to God's revealed word to Moses at Sinai, and to no one else.

This is legally ingenious: Should a mere human come along, a brother, a son, a mother, as explicated immediately afterwards in Deuteronomy XIII:7–12[10] and entice one (mesit) to stray from God's commandments, that very fact of enticement would condemn them as violating the law of God, since clearly humans with their own agency may neither add nor diminish. But even if a prophet comes, with signs and wonders authenticating his divinely sanctioned authority, you may not follow him, because the real purpose of exercising that divinely sanctioned authority is in testing you, of proving your loyalty to the Sinaitic event. Heads I win, tails you lose.

It is not only legally ingenious but of unique theological import. It is through the seemingly legalistic device of entrenchment that we come to understand the profundity of the revolution of Covenantal Monotheism.

First is the fact that God reveals himself to the nation as a whole and covenants with a nation, a people, and not with, or through, an individual. This covenant is like a treaty with a nation in international law. It is not extinguished when the specific humans living at the time of conclusion die, for the nation endures beyond the life of any single individual.

Second, what is special about the entrenchment in Deuteronomy XIII is the realization that in binding the community for ever to his eternal law, God has at one and the same time tied his own hands. Only if God were to replicate the conditions that, as in Exodus XIX:9 'And the LORD said unto Moses, Lo, I come unto thee in a thick cloud, that the people may hear when I speak with thee, and believe thee for ever'[11] authenticated Moses as the giver of the law, in front of the entire nation, could he undo the immutability and eternity of the law. A practical impossibility. Any other messenger challenging the eternity and immutability

[9] Exodus 19:9.
[10] Deuteronomy 13:1–2.
[11] Exodus 19:9.

of the law, no matter how authenticated, could, would, and should be construed as coming under the Deuteronomic provision and regarded as a means of God to test the people, put them on trial and through a trial. God binds the community, but at the same time he binds himself.

Does this not contradict God's omnipotence? If God is omnipotent, surely in his omnipotence he should be able to change his mind? The opposite is actually true. When He covenants Chukat Olam, a law for ever, it is covenantal, like a marriage. In human affairs, Till Death Do Us Part, means just that; and in this divine scheme, forever, ad olam, means just that. That is why God can describe the relationship with his elected people as an indissoluble marriage. In the words of Hosea:

> And I will betroth thee unto me for ever; yea, I will betroth thee unto me in righteousness, and in judgment, and in lovingkindness, and in mercies.

If God were unable to tie His own hands, so to speak, he would be prevented from credibly making or creating an eternal covenant—be it the one with all humanity after the Deluge, be it the Mosaic one with Israel, the central content of which is the eternity of His law. If God could not so tie his hands, his covenant would not be eternal, but 'at his pleasure', until he changed his mind.

In the end result, the Mosaic Code ex Deuteronomy XIII is thus not only immutable but eternal.

This raises a second inextricable issue of equal intricacy. Veritable immutability of this kind is inconsistent with a living and functional legal system, especially one with the capacious reach of the Mosaic Code—a law for life. Two classical problems present themselves: First, what if you have, say, in the Code laws regarding divorce, but not laws regarding marriage? Divorce, implies marriage, but the Code is silent. Does the prohibition on 'adding' mean that you are prohibited from enacting and regulating marriage? If so, you would effectively be diminishing divorce, since if no one can marry, no one can divorce. So, there must be a mechanism of deducing from that which is given, *expressis verbis*, that which is implied.

Second, the express provisions of the Code cannot envision all situations, especially as time goes by. Interpretation can give an answer. Interpretation is part of the ontology of any legal code, more so when the code itself is a higher law and even more so if it is designed to be immutable and eternal—where one cannot say: 'Lets leave that to the legislator'; or 'That will require a constitutional amendment'.

One cannot overstate the importance of this point, but one can restate it in slightly different terms. If an immutable Code is to remain also a timeless Code—an eternal covenant, or at least one till the end of days—and not become dead letters written on stone, interpretation becomes its living breath, an essential component.

To say that interpretation is part of the ontology of a Code—be it the Deuteronomic Code or the Constitution of the United States—is not to minimize the delicacy of that proposition and certainly not to suggest what would be the appropriate norms of interpretation. The boundary between legitimate judicial interpretation and illegitimate judicial legislative or constitutional usurpation masquerading as interpretation, is notorious and I am thankful that I do not have to address that issue. But most of us will agree that there is a category difference between an act of interpretation and, by contrast, a decision explicitly amending the law. In the first case, we give huge respect to the code's provisions. We consider them normative and binding. We seek, through interpretation, to determine scope and boundaries. In the second we either disrespect the norm and its author or regard ourselves as enjoying an authority of at least equal value to the lawgiver or constitution maker, an authority that grants us the freedom to mutate the norm, namely to add or to diminish from it.

The practical effect might be exactly the same. The line may sometimes be so difficult to draw that the distinction might seem academic. But let us consider the emotions that overreaching decisions, of, say, the Supreme Court of the United States in interpreting the American Constitution evoke, decisions in which the line between interpretation and judicial legislation is transgressed by whatever standard the observer considers appropriate. For some, the concern is mostly the material content of the decision: If the substantive result serves my interest, I do not care much how they reached it. But to others, many, perhaps most, the process is as important. It is of course in part an issue of institutional power—power that should, say, vest in the legislature or the presidency and is seen to be arrogated by the judicial branch. But the matter goes deeper. The rage is not based on just a calculus of interests. The vocabulary one finds in the heat of these debates is telling: presumption, arrogance, usurpation, and disrespect of the Constitution, disrespect of the people. And the rage is shared by left and right; when, in the eyes of its beholders the Court transgresses the line and strays from its interpretative role it seems to be tampering, subverting, yes, a sacred document. How much more so if one were dealing with a truly sacred document. It is one thing to interpret the laws of God. We cannot do otherwise. It is quite another to arrogate to ourselves the authority to make, amend, or break them. That is one deep reason for the prohibition in Deuteronomy XIII.

Let us now turn from the legal to some moral and theological concerns raised by Deuteronomy XIII. The first is to underline a point made previously in passing. The messenger here is termed a prophet. He is not an 'observer of times, or an enchanter, or a witch. Or a charmer, or a consulter with familiar spirits, or a wizard, or a necromancer'.[12]

It is not at all self-evident, and thus also the subject of considerable speculation, why God would want to test or 'prove' the people in the manner suggested by these verses: If they are transgressing, as they seemed regularly to do throughout the biblical narrative, from Joshua through Chronicles, there is nothing to test or prove. And, if they are actually following the ways of the Almighty and observing his commandments, why seek to entrap them? And yet, Deuteronomy clearly envisages that God contemplates such a test. The 'test' here, as in other biblical contexts, is a complicated term. It is also Nisayon, an experience, a trial—as in trial and error, a test of fire and water. It is a trial from which one may emerge transformed and serve as a beacon for others. We may be inclined to construe the phrase uttered by the Angel to Abraham after his 'test': 'For now I know that you fear God' not in the simple meaning of knowledge acquired as a result of the test, which would jar with an omniscient God, but as a different type of knowledge. You are different after the trial, after the Nisayon, and I know that you are different in that way. These 'tests', of Abraham, of the People in Israel in the Desert, come at unique moments and are formative and transformative in the relationship between God and his subjects.

The giving of the Torah and, indeed, the entire travails of the desert are also described, with the same vocabulary, as a trial, a test, an experience.

A trial and test at this moment also make sense. They come at a moment of a major theological event coupled with a major sociological and anthropological happening, a collective equivalent to the Abrahamic individual moment. It is also clear that the significance of the 'test' or 'trial' is not in their result, but in their experiential impact; in the transformation they

[12] Deuteronomy 18:10–11.

have on their subject, in the lesson they give for the future who are invited, as in the case of Abraham, to contemplate his action and experience as pregnant with significance, rather than the fact that he withstood the test, or acquitted himself well in his 'trial'.

It is not, however, clear in the Deuteronomic XIII text when and how circumstances might be that would justify yet another 'test'. It is hard to imagine another Abrahamic or Sinaiatic moment. It is understandable why God would put Abraham, the father of the nation, the father of all nations, through such a trial, and why he would put the newly covenantal nation through such, but why and when would he want to do that again to His people, especially if they are following his law? The issue remains unsolved.

There is more that is challenging in our passage. I insisted on the agency of the prophet. I argued that the choice of appellation and authentication militate against the possibility of coincidental reliance of the choice of the wrongdoer, one of the classical ways of trying to make sense of the passage. The prophet in this case is the agent of God, an instrument in his design to put Israel to the test. But if this is so, a grave moral dilemma, arises: Why would this agent be put to death? After all, in fulfilling his agency he was following that which God intended for him. Unlike Joseph's brothers, if he is acting in accordance with God's scheme and empowered by God to give signs and wonders, he is innocent. Why then should he die? (The sages were troubled by this and many attempts at resolution have been offered.)

We already saw one theological dilemma—why would God seek to try, to test, to 'entrap' his people in a situation where they are actually following in his ways. Be the answer to that question whatever it may be, why should that test of Israel, their trial, implicate the killing of the innocent messenger of God?

What, finally, from the perspective of his listeners, is evil in the acts of this prophet? He cannot be evil, since he is following the instructions of God; he is sent by God. The evil is in the message in as much as the listeners are concerned. It is in the invitation (which God put in his mouth in order to test His people) not to 'walk after the Lord your God and fear Him, and keep His commandments and obey His voice'.[13] Keeping the commandments and obeying the voice that spoke at Sinai is the way in which the people will manifest that they withstood the test and will 'proveth' that 'ye love the Lord your God with all your heart and with all your soul'.[14] It makes sense: These are the very commandments to which the very same text has instructed us one may neither add nor diminish—with all the attendant problems we have identified in drawing the line between the ontological necessity of interpretation and the theological imperative of not tampering.

How are we to understand 'Elohim Acherim'. The King James and most translators construe this as 'other gods'. This is plausible. But note that elsewhere, for example, just a few phrases later in relation to incitement, the text explicitly refers to 'the gods of the people around you'. Elohim Acherim here can equally mean, in correct Hebrew, a different god, different to the God of Sinai who gave you the commandments. This, too, requires some theological explication. The Monotheistic God is transcendent. In principle, his transcendence means that he can neither be grasped nor depicted except in our limited, reductionist human faculties. But the transcendence is not complete, because the God of Abraham, Isaac and Jacob may, and does, elect to breach his transcendence and reveal himself from time to time. We can only know him through those moments of willed breach of His transcendence, in the form and manner in which He chose to appear. For the Jews as a collectivity, the subjects of the covenant, God elected to reveal himself through his law. They know him as

[13] Deuternomy 13:4.
[14] Deuteronomy 13:3.

the God of the Law, of Torah, of Nomos. It is of course, theologically speaking, not impossible for God to elect to breach his transcendence to others in a different form. Who are we to put such limitations on Him? But the burden of Deuteronomy XIII, and another reason for its fundamental importance is that should anyone claim to be speaking in the name of the God of Abraham, Isaac and Jacob, and present him as disowning his immutable, eternal law, for Israel that would have to be considered Elohim Acherim, a different God. For Israel only knows, and is instructed to know, only one God, that of the Torah, Nomos.

I now return to the life of Jesus and his Passion, as it unfolds in the Gospel narrative and examine such in the light of the Acts/Luke formulation and our juridical, moral, and theological reflections on Deuteronomy XIII.

By inveighing against corruption and hypocrisy by those who follow the ritual but forget the commandments of the heart to do justice and show mercy, Jesus is annoying, threatening, and destabilizing but fully within the prophetic tradition of, say, an Amos or an Isaiah.

But what of the law, the 'customs that Moses gave' in the formulation of Luke? At first it would seem that the Acts/Luke allusion is the least probable. Did not Jesus explicitly claim in the Sermon on the Mount: 'I have not come to change one iota of the law?'

A close reading of all passages where Jesus engages with the law reveals a constant and tantalizing duality, which in turn can lead to an explosive ambivalence in perception—ambivalence exactly at that juncture of change and immutability, interpretation and legislation, submission and original authority.

Let me briefly illustrate this duality starting with a most celebrated instance taken from Mark 2:

> And it came to pass, that he went through the corn fields on the sabbath day; and his disciples began, as they went, to pluck the ears of corn. And the Pharisees said unto him, Behold, why do they on the sabbath day that which is not lawful? And he said unto them, Have ye never read what David did, when he had need, and was an hungred, he, and they that were with him? How he went into the house of God in the days of Abiathar the high priest, and did eat the shewbread, which is not lawful to eat but for the priests, and gave also to them which were with him? And he said unto them, The sabbath was made for man, and not man for the sabbath: Therefore the Son of man is Lord also of the sabbath.[15]

It is of course not the transgression of the Sabbath per se that taxes the Pharisees but the teaching, the casting of the behaviour as normative and, above all, the authority of the new proposed rule. The matter is simple enough. As an exegetical move in the interpretation of the scope of the prohibition on plucking the corn on the Sabbath, the move by Jesus is unexceptional. It is almost trivial; we find debates, even about Sabbath observance, among various Houses of Learning with far greater differences. Not only in result, but in his reasoning, too, Jesus is within the cannon of legalistic rabbinic disputation, not forgetting that that cannon was at that time in its formative years.

It is the very final phrase that gives pause. The extant law is that plucking is forbidden. Jesus teaches that, at least in the circumstances of the incident, it was not forbidden. Is that teaching just a hermeneutic conclusion, based on a kind of analogical reasoning from the incident of David? In which case the final reference to Son of Man being the Lord of the Sabbath would simply be a conclusion applying to all men? Or is the Lord of the Sabbath statement a

[15] Mark 2:23–28.

reference to Jesus himself, exercising an autonomous, non-hermeneutic, original authority, with the power to add or, as in this case, to diminish? Is Jesus acting as a 'mere' rabbi, or is he claiming a much more exalted status? The question is not how I or you would explain the text today—but to understand that the duality reflected in the text reflected a duality in the way Jesus was perceived both by his followers and the authorities.

The Sermon on the Mount is no less tantalizing. The duality is equally present. He says that he does not want to change one iota of the law, but then adds: 'Until the Law is fulfilled'. What is the status of that statement? And how does one explain then the long list of norms in the Sermon in which he actually talks about change, most famously in relation to divorce? Is that interpretation, or is Jesus adding or detracting something? It is possible to show similar duality in practically all passages of legal engagement.

Imagine now, as a mental exercise, the reports coming from the Galilee about his signs, wonders, and teaching, for example, the reports of the Pharisees who were tracking him throughout his wandering and teaching in the Galilee. Imagine further the questioning of those bringing the reports in which the interrogator asks: His legal rulings were clear enough. What was not clear was the authority that he was claiming as a basis for his rulings on the laws, on the 'customs' of Moses. Was he merely interpreting the law? Or was he claiming an original authority to change or even abolish those laws and customs? The fact that even today scholars argue about the burden of the evidence illustrates the ambivalence and the concern that the authorities might have had.

Consider, now, the following passage from Mark:

> {11:27} And they come again to Jerusalem: and as he was walking in the temple, there come to him the chief priests, and the scribes, and the elders, {11:28} And say unto him, By what authority doest thou these things? and who gave thee this authority to do these things? {11:29} And Jesus answered and said unto them, I will also ask of you one question, and answer me, and I will tell you by what authority I do these things. {11:30} The baptism of John, was [it] from heaven, or of men? answer me. {11:31} And they reasoned with themselves, saying, If we shall say, From heaven; he will say, Why then did ye not believe him? {11:32} But if we shall say, Of men; they feared the people: for all [men] counted John, that he was a prophet indeed. {11:33} And they answered and said unto Jesus, We cannot tell. And Jesus answering saith unto them, Neither do I tell you by what authority I do these things.[16]

What is pertinent to the line of analysis being presented here is the fact that the chief priests, the scribes, the elders—indeed all those who subsequently will be involved in the trial of Jesus are not concerned directly with the content of Jesus' teachings, but with the authority that he claims, the authority under which he issues his teachings and rulings. We already noted the paradox that it is precisely the eternal and immutable nature of the law shielding it from a human law maker, that delivers it into the hands of the human interpreter. This is precisely the period that sees the emergence of Rabbinic Judaism, in which the interpreter, rather than the priest comes to the fore.

In and of themselves there is nothing startling in the content of Jesus' legal rulings even when they deviate from reigning custom. The Mishnah is replete with such.

It is not, as regards the content, in a 'ballpark' different from the various teachings of Jesus.

[16] Mark 11:27–33.

His ethical teachings, even those concerning sacrifices in the Temple, resonate with the prophetic messages of, say, an Isaiah or an Amos and likeminded prophets:

> {1:10} Hear the word of the LORD, ye rulers of Sodom; give ear unto the law of our God, ye people of Gomorrah. {1:11} To what purpose [is] the multitude of your sacrifices unto me? saith the LORD: I am full of the burnt offerings of rams, and the fat of fed beasts; and I delight not in the blood of bullocks, or of lambs, or of he goats. {1:12} When ye come to appear before me, who hath required this at your hand, to tread my courts? {1:13} Bring no more vainoblations; incense is an abomination unto me; the new moons and sabbaths, the calling of assemblies, I cannot away with; [it is] iniquity, even the solemn meeting. {1:14} Your new moons and your appointed feasts my soul hateth: they are a trouble unto me; I am weary to bear [them.]{1:15} And when ye spread forth your hands, I will hide mine eyes from you: yea, when ye make many prayers, I will not hear: your hands are full of blood.[17]

These, too, are not in their content in a category different from some of the teachings of Jesus in the Temple, indeed the very teachings that prompted the aforementioned confrontation.

What concerns them is the question of authority. By what authority is he teaching and ruling? Is he claiming the derivative authority of the interpreter, which might render him remarkable and/or exceedingly annoying, but in a category not different from other remarkable and annoying prophets, or is he claiming the original authority of the lawgiver, which would put him in a class all to himself, both in the eyes of his followers, but also in the eyes of the public authorities?

In this vein I would claim that this perspective, the perspective of Mark 11:27 (and the similar passages elsewhere in the Gospels) is the one that will make most sense of the all too cryptic description of the interrogation of Jesus during his trial and the other aspects of his trial.

We may now pull all substantive threads together. I would like to advance two possible hypotheses. The first is modest—I simply want to argue that whilst not perfect, in considering the various legal conundrums of the trial, much is explained by hypothesizing that the central issue was prompted by the perception developed about his teaching, or the implication of his teaching, on the law. Since the material content of his teaching was known, some pretty fundamental rulings on the Sabbath, on the purity of food, on divorce, and so on, the specific concern was to ascertain the authority Jesus claimed when expounding the law in these rulings, a concern accentuated by his popularity and persuasiveness, enhanced by the signs and wonders that accompanied his teachings. Was he simply a Rabbi making classical hermeneutic moves? Or was he actually adding (divorce) or detracting (Sabbath, purity of food) to and from the law, on the basis of some divine authority and thus possibly appearing to the authorities to be the very personage referred to in Deuteronomy XIII:1–6?

The trial on this reading was to establish not the content of his teaching, but the authority he was claiming for himself—and once this becomes clear, the necessary outcome also became clear.

I believe this explanation is comfortably within the parameters of the historical Jesus literature of the trial and coheres well with much in Scripture. It is, for example, in line with the various encounters Jesus had with those trying to 'trick' him—in all but one or two places that is what they were trying to ascertain. It coheres with the reference to blasphemy in the

[17] Isaiah 1:10–15.

paralytic episode—as a healer, Jesus was legitimate; as a 'forgiver' he transgressed the line. It is, too, in line with questioning about the Temple—the 'ability' to destroy and build it—that Jesus would do it, with some form of divine power, rather than God in the prophecies of other prophets such as Jeremiah and Micah.

It is, also, in line with the final impatient questions of Caiaphas: If you claim to be the Messiah or the Son of the Blessed you really are doing something different from mere exegesis. It explains why all factions of the Sanhedrin, which on many other issues would have been at each other's throat, could agree—because on the Deuteronomy XIII 1–6 Pharisees and Saducees would both, from their own perspective, agree that change of biblical law (Saducees) going beyond interpretation and exegesis (Pharisees) was hugely violative. The unanimity becomes plausible.

Interestingly, it may explain why, as told in the Gospel—Jesus seemed so important to his detractors. Why would he be considered as a threat to the very existence of the whole nation?

The usual hypothesis is that somehow his destabilizing activity would threaten the Romans, who in turn would act against the Jews. Some even have suggested, given that this episode comes shortly after the Lazarus incident, that the Romans would fear that his ability to raise from the dead could tilt the military balance in favour of the Jews. I find none of these explanations particularly plausible.

The present hypothesis offers an alternative. The self-understanding of the nation by its leaders, the prosecutors of Jesus, was that of the nation of God, defined by the covenant. The understanding of the nation, the subject of the covenant, is of a holy people constituted as such, by that very covenant, and defined by their observance. It is the covenant and the duty to observe the law that set the Jews apart from others.

This religious specificity had political implications. It was on this basis that the Jews claimed their particular status and privileges from the Romans, such as, for example, total sovereignty and autonomy over the Temple—not even Romans were allowed in. If the law that constitutes the nation was undermined, its subject would disappear too.

Caiaphas may have understood what became so evident later to Paul. In the message of Jesus, through his teaching and actions, religion becomes at one and the same time individual and universal, but not particularistic and national. Thus, the famous Pauline message is but the logical and inevitable implication of the Christian message delivered by Jesus:

> There is neither Jew nor Greek, there is neither bond nor free, there is neither male nor female: for ye are all one in Christ Jesus.[18]

On this hypothesis, the Jewish authorities understood this implication of the teachings of Jesus long before Saul/Paul articulated it so clearly. The significance of Deuteronomy XIII is not simply in obedience. Undermining the law is to undermine not only the content of the covenant, but the very subject with whom God covenants. With no law, on this reading, not only can the covenant as conceived between God and a nation, not endure, but the very subject of the covenant, the nation as such, cannot endure. If the law is completed and has lost its character as immutable and eternal, and if the Jew and Gentile become one in Christ, on what basis do the Jews continue to ask the Romans for their privileges as a distinct community? The people may endure as individual, but the nation would have perished.

[18] Galatians 3:28.

When turning over Jesus to Pilate for execution, this would not be something that they could openly state for obvious reasons. The Romans would hardly be sympathetic to *this* concern; indeed, they might even have an interest in Jesus if that were the effect of his teaching. Obviously, some other explanation had to be given.

I present this as a 'modest' claim simply because it merely hypothesizes that it was possible for the Jewish authorities to suspect Jesus as being the very person referred to in Deuteronomy XIII 1–6, and that this may in fact be the most plausible explanation to the charge, to the interrogation, and to the conviction—regardless of whether Jesus was in fact the Deuteronomic Prophet of XIII 1–6. It is a claim about a subjective truth not an objective truth.

But perhaps it is possible to go beyond this modest and ultimately conventional hypothesis and at least contemplate something theologically more audacious namely that, vis-à-vis the Jews, Jesus was in fact the Deuteronomy XIII personage. Is it, after all, theologically impossible that in the hands of the divine, Jesus could have served more than one purpose?

The theological implications are interesting, and in some respects radical, though they do not affect, and are not intended to affect, Christian and Jewish different ontological understandings of Jesus.

It would, first, solve some of the theological and moral dilemmas indicated earlier. It actually manages to square the circle. On the one hand, under this hypothesis Jesus is indeed entirely blemishless and blameless—he is doing the bidding of God exactly as stipulated in Deuteronomy XIII. He is subjectively innocent and pure—faithfully following, from his perspective, the Father. He is objectively so—God gives or allows him the signs and wonders to prove such.

At the same time this is the one instance whereby convicting him and bringing about his death, his objective and subjective innocence notwithstanding, the Sanhedrin would have been doing God's will, following in this respect too, the Deuteronomic XIII imperative. God instructed them that even a messenger speaking for Him, with all authenticating signs and wonders, but tampering with the eternal law (at God's behest as a means of testing their fealty), must be put to death. On this reading, not only was Jesus on trial but so were those who tried him. They were being put to the test:

> [required to prove] whether ye love the LORD your God with all your heart and with all your soul ... [to] walk after the LORD your God, and fear him, and keep his commandments, and obey his voice, and ye shall serve him, and cleave unto him.[19]

That critical passage in Deuteronomy displayed a weighty moral conundrum: The prophet authenticated by God, and hence blameless and blemishless, was to be put to death. How could one square this with notions of justice?

It is not for me to pronounce on Christian theology in such a delicate matter, but I wonder how unacceptable, if at all, would it be from a Christian perspective to imagine that unknown to the Sanhedrin its fulfilment of God's will in convicting Jesus is what in fact put in motion God's plan and design for everyone else—the crucifixion of Jesus as a redemption? And since the death of Jesus has, in the eyes of his believers, a deeply meaningful and desired-by-God significance, it provides, in this one instance, a different perspective on the moral dilemma about the seemingly unjust fate of the personage in Deuteronomy XIII. One might go even

[19] Deuteronomy 13:4.

further in addressing the moral dilemma of the innocent Deuteronomic prophet being ordered to be put to death. For, from a Christian perspective, this seeming injustice would be cured within three days with the resurrection of Jesus. How could God, to test the Jews, order that His messenger be put to death? He could while knowing that he would be resurrected within three days. This would seem, at least from a Christian perspective, not a specious or trivial solution to the first moral dilemma to which Deuteronomy XIII gives rise.

What of the second dilemma? Why would God want to put 'the Jews' to this test? As already indicated, if they were in a state of disobedience, as seems to have been their sort quite regularly since coming to the Promised Land, there would be no reason to put them to the test since they would be failing it before the test were to begin. If they were in a state of obedience, the test would seem to be a cruel entrapment.

There are certain things we can never know. But we could perhaps speculate that such tests, such trials made sense and were desirable precisely at those moments when major theological changes were taking place in the world, when there was a shift of theological paradigm, as was the case with Abraham and the Covenant at Sinai.

The coming of Jesus, with such an attractive and tantalizing message destined to sweep so much of the world they knew, would be just the right moment to put the Children of Israel, tempted perhaps to abandon their particularistic, eternal, and immutable covenant, to a new test and trial—one that would be able to renew the eternal betrothal as well as give an example for future generations if similarly tempted. As might be expected, the insistence on the endurance of the Sinaiatic Covenant does not rest simply on the formalism of *Pacta Sund Servanda* (Agreements are to be Observed). It is said that God does not make covenants in vain. Though a small people, though a very particularistic code of law and justice surely not intended for all, the insistence of the lawgiver that it endure eternal and immutable till the end of time may be rooted in the importance of a certain type of witness and a particular expression of holiness, hard and difficult, often consecrated in its breach, but at the same time giving reassurance to all, even in moments of great despair regarding not only the faith of man to God but of God to man.

On this reading, in this double trial, that of Jesus and that of the Jews, everyone was following in the path of God. This is not a relativist perspective—everyone has their own truth. Nor is it a syncretic message—it is all one religion and so on. It is a perspective according to which Jews and Christians retain their sharp distinctions, distinctions that, however, are, it is claimed, the expression of God's will as expressed in Scripture.

Is this so shocking?

Do we not find in the very same Scripture, and this too finds its way prominently into Christian dogma, that not only did Jesus predict his death but it was all part of a divine design, willed by the Father whereby the death of his pure and innocent Son, was meant to be a sacrifice offering salvation to humanity? There has been over the centuries some, if scant, speculation concerning this counterfactual. Whatever your own speculation, it would not be Christianity as we know it today. No crucifixion, no resurrection. No salvation.

Yes, the crucifixion of Jesus was a targeted killing. At the hands of God, the Almighty, the Holy One Blessed be He.

4

Rocking the Human Rights Boat

Reflections by a Fellow Passenger

Martti Koskenniemi

4.1 Introduction

Towards the end of a recent text on human rights and populism,[1] Philip Alston asked the question about the role of scholars in responding to the far-right attack on many aspects of post-1968 politics in the West, including human rights. In addition to cautioning against the 'backlash'[2] he also suggested, perhaps surprisingly, that 'it has become fashionable, especially at elite universities in the West, to disparage human rights by accentuating in dramatic and sometimes destructive ways the undoubted shortcomings of international human rights norms and institutions'.[3] It was not that 'elite universities' would have suddenly started to espouse extremist causes but that they had offered a platform for another type of human rights criticism that, Alston suggested, has unwittingly contributed—and is still contributing—to such causes. The work by 'critical scholars' had created the 'unintended consequence' of weakening human rights precisely at the moment when they had been targeted by a massive right-wing onslaught. He illustrated the point by a talk given at New York University 'by one of the world's leading international legal scholars' on the essentially illusionary character of human rights and the speaker's response to a student who had hoped to make a career in human rights practice. What should a distressed student do if human rights have, according to the speaker, no reality about them? But the latter refused to offer another blueprint. It was not the speaker's task, the response had gone, to 'suggest alternative strategies', merely to point to the political 'abyss' offered by human rights.

It is a fair point to remind participants in a political debate not to overlook the unforeseen consequences of how they speak or what they propose. I think Alston believes—at least I believe—that human rights activists and 'critical scholars' share many political objectives. What he suggests is that the latter are now undermining those objectives by eroding the basis on which effective resistance against the right-wing surge can be mounted. 'Do not rock the boat, please', he wants to say. If the boat collapses, we will both drown. I am dubious about this. Taking a break from criticisms of human rights—especially criticisms targeted by Alston—is not likely to strengthen them. I want to make two points. The first has to do with the assumptions on which the invitation not to rock the human rights boat is based. Are the present difficulties of the human rights project *really* caused, in some significant sense, by human rights criticism? I doubt that. Instead, I suggest that they are caused by aspects of intellectual autism in human rights culture. Another point seeks to clarify what the critic is

[1] Philip Alston, 'The Populist Challenge to Human Rights' (2017) 9 Journal of Human Rights Practice 1.
[2] ibid 3.
[3] ibid 13.

Martti Koskenniemi, *Rocking the Human Rights Boat* In: *The Struggle for Human Rights.* Edited by: Nehal Bhuta, Florian Hoffmann, Sarah Knuckey, Frédéric Mégret, and Margaret Satterthwaite, Oxford University Press.
DOI: 10.1093/oso/9780198868064.003.0005

trying to do when rocking the human rights boat. Alston concedes that at least some types of human rights critique have had their usefulness. The point about unintended consequences is not so much about principle as it is about strategy. But a key point of (left) criticism is that human rights are failing precisely as strategy.

In examining Alston's reaction, it is useful to bear in mind the leading role that he has played in international human rights law. He is not only a distinguished academic but an effective operator in international human rights institutions, especially influential within the UN human rights treaty system and as an outspoken expert on arbitrary executions and massive poverty. As captain of the human rights boat Alston is understandably worried about how it is being rocked by the waves of history and politics. This is not meant as an *ad hominem* point, but to signal that how to view his attack depends on whether or not the boat is steadily sailing its course. But as Alston points out, a massive attack has been carried out on the values represented by human rights all over the world, and more is to be expected in the coming years.[4] Authoritarian government appears increasingly attractive to many people. Violent right-wing activism has become an everyday phenomenon and neo-nationalism, xenophobia and targeting of minorities and refugees has entered official party politics. Many governments are cutting measures for development assistance and are attacking human rights organizations and activists. As Alston summarized his concern: 'human rights proponents need to rethink many of their assumptions [and] re-evaluate their strategies, . . . there has not been enough reflection by human rights advocates on the innovative thinking and creative strategizing that are urgently needed'.[5]

According to Alston, human rights criticism will unwittingly support far-right politics that human rights experts and critics *both* reject. The call to look out for the unforeseen consequences of rocking the boat, after all, presumes that the protagonists are in the same boat. I agree. Certainly, human rights people and (left) critics are much closer to each other than either is to the 'backlashers'. We need to cooperate in 'innovative' and strategic thinking. The point about thinking twice is an important reminder in a debate between allies. Critics should be no less self-aware than other people. However, I insist that critics have learned something that human rights experts still, after all these years, continue to ignore. This little response aims to rephrase one set of concerns as a friendly (though not purely internal) rejoinder, hoping to demonstrate that dismissing them as overly sophisticated academism will only perpetuate the strategic problems faced by human rights today. I think more awareness is needed about what the 'backlash' stands for and what might be needed in response to it.

4.2 Rights Genuine and False

One well-known feature of human rights as a set of norms and an ideology is that it can be made to stand for almost whatever claims or policies. In the absence of a litmus test allowing the separation of 'real' rights from merely spurious or pretended rights, the most varied preferences are able to be translated into the rights of their holders. Repeated reference to this point (the so-called indeterminacy thesis) by critics has often been viewed in the human rights camp—and perhaps also by Alston—as an over-theoretical argument with little bite on the real world: 'We know what we stand for. Irrespective of your fancy demonstrations, the human rights world can be shown to have historically supported an easily demonstrable,

[4] ibid 4–8.
[5] ibid 2.

limited set of progressive causes.' Quite so. And this is precisely the problem. Although human rights can in principle be stretched to defend whatever preference—including the right of free speech for racists and the rights of foreign investors against domestic political constituencies—in practice, attempts to do so have remained unsuccessful. Hidden or unarticulated criteria have made it possible for human rights experts to distinguish 'genuine' human rights-protected preferences from other preferences, values that activists regard illegitimate or 'fake'. It is this set of criteria, and especially its clandestine operation, that has outraged the 'backlashers' and particularly right-wing critics to no end. To understand the importance of this problem for the predicament—both strategic and principled—of human rights today, it is useful to recount once more how the human rights culture has proceeded from abstract claims about universality and inalienability to specific and today increasingly controversial policies.

Human rights arose in the late 1960s and 1970s to oppose the deformalization of modern law and administration—the flexibility of open-ended standards and the managerial practice of balancing opposite considerations in view of some utilitarian calculation.[6] The search for responsiveness in modern law allocated (law-applying) authority to powerful actors to determine the way in which people should live. 'Taking rights seriously' meant seeking to empower individuals and formerly excluded groups vis-à-vis those authorities. 'It is my life! Who are you to tell me how I should live!' Conservatives who objected that such individualism would end up eroding the basis of society were dismissed on the liberal side by the retort that society had no legitimate claim to enforce 'morals'. It was only entitled to prevent concrete, demonstrable harm to others.[7] In the extreme from, the individual's claim to protection (against the state usually) took the form of the theory of the trumping power of rights—that a right was a normative claim that could not be overridden by a social value, however historically embedded or however defensible by a calculation of an overall benefit for society at large.[8]

The power of this (liberal) argument led to its expansion in the 1980s and 1990s as an increasing number of preferences had pushed themselves to be redescribed as 'rights' of their holders, worthy of protection against countervailing considerations. By the century's end rights had become ubiquitous in Western administrations and in many international institutions. They had even come to be addressed as a new secular religion of sorts. But already in the 1990s many activists—Alston among them—began to worry about the apparent limitlessness of these translations and the proliferation of institutions purporting to protect them. But where would criteria come from that would enable distinguishing between 'genuine' and 'fake' rights? To do this work, they should not only be independent of rights but also at a *normatively higher level* so as to be able to carry out those discriminations acceptably.

Initially, this did not seem too worrying. If expanding areas of policy came to be perceived in terms of rights advancement, this meant that human rights language and human rights expertise were becoming increasingly powerful. However, as more and more groups—including groups that did not share the original agendas of human rights experts—began to dress their claims in rights terms, increasing amounts of social conflict began to take the form of rights conflict. When property owners—for example, the owners of fur trading

[6] I have made this argument in many places, eg in 'The Effect of Rights on Political Culture' in Philip Alston (ed), *The European Union and Human Rights* (OUP 1999) 99–116

[7] On the famous Hart-Devlin debate in the 1960s, see Patrick Devlin, *The Enforcement of Morals* (OUP 1959). See also HLA Hart, *Law, Liberty and Morality* (Stanford University Press 1963))

[8] Ronald Dworkin, *Taking Rights Seriously* (Harvard University Press 1978).

businesses faced with protests by animal rights activists—began to invoke their right to exclude protestors from their premises, activists cried foul—as if property was no right at all. As long as conflicts between, say, property rights and rights of freedom of speech were 'balanced' in institutions with a human rights ethos (such as the European Court of Human Rights—ECtHR), the problem did not seem too acute. The outcomes would reflect the priorities of human rights experts. But then human rights moved in the adversary's camp.[9]

Take security, for example. Activists have often regarded security concerns as profoundly inimical to rights. The theme 'security versus human rights' appeared to capture an important struggle: which side should win? However, that simple binary ('either you are on our side or theirs') has been completely messed up by the realization that security is also a human rights concern. Already the 1990s notion of 'human security' suggested that, rightly understood, security work was also a work for human rights. This was fine as the language of 'human security' was employed by people in or close to the human rights camp. But then the languages of humanity and human rights entered military service in the 1990s—in debates about intervention and 'responsibility to protect'.[10] In the *al-Jedda* case (2005) the British High Court went as far as to describe the incommunicado detention of a person in Iraq as a human rights measure (the action was taken '[f]or the purposes of restoring and maintaining that peace and security without which there can be no human rights within Iraq').[11] Nor was this necessarily in bad faith: had you interviewed Iraqi inhabitants after 2003, or people in any of the innumerable crisis zones today about what they regard as their most important rights concern, many would undoubtedly say 'security'. Western military and security apparatus was now delighted to think of itself at the service of human rights. They were soon joined by anti-immigrant groups worried over the 'crimes' committed by refugees or migrants. Is not 'security' at home one of the most important rights that public authorities should protect? Would not increasing policing resources and the ubiquitous presence of CCTV cameras in public localities be important as human rights measures?

Now of course, this is not at all what human rights activists think. They would immediately retort that such policies are not part of 'genuine' human rights work. And this is precisely what outrages the 'backlash'—*So you say that everyone's rights are of equal concern—but in your practice, you always override priorities that WE think of as important! Hypocrites!* In the absence of a clear set of criteria to distinguish 'real' human rights from other kinds of claims, the human rights camp seems merely to be making contested political claims behind a facade of humanitarian neutrality. *Why would their political priorities somehow automatically override ours?* Think about economic, social, and cultural (ESC) rights, brought into the canon as a cold war manoeuvre and to finish up the implementation of the Universal Declaration of Human Rights (1948/1966). This seemed especially important to show that human rights have a heart, to avoid the accusation that it was blind to larger social problems and to respond to those who believed that the freedom to sleep under the bridges was no real freedom at all. But how could the ESC rights then be distinguished from social-democratic policies? If they only had a 'programmatic' character (as it was usual to assume), did they not operate as a kind of party programme designed to bind the hands of legislators and finance ministries outside electoral policies? Was human rights in truth a social-democratic policy

[9] See further, Frédéric Mégret, 'Human Rights Populism. What Happens to Human Rights when Populists Invoke its Language?', at https://www.openglobalrights.org/human-rights-populism/.

[10] See eg Anne Orford, *International Authority and the Responsibility to Protect* (Cambridge University Press 2011).

[11] *R (on the application of Al-Jedda) v Secretary of State for Defence* [2005] EWHC 1809 (Admin) [104].

of the welfare state, cleverly disguising itself as a 'non-political' project of realizing pre-existing 'rights'? Of course, as Alston would be the first to admit, intelligent ESC advocacy makes distinctions and compromises: let's at least eradicate the *most significant* ESC problems, the most 'egregious' human rights violations. It is hard to disagree with this. Alston's recent work as rapporteur on extreme poverty is an excellent example of sophisticated human rights policy. But it is also economic policy, and the question is whether it has *any* distance to sophisticated and compromise-ready socialist attention to capitalism's dark side. And if there is no difference—well, then what about the claims about 'universal and inalienable' as well as the view of rights as a non-political *limit* to politics? For those not already committed to these ideas, human rights could only appear as a *leftist policy in unpolitical disguise*.

But there is more. Nobody denies that extreme poverty ought to be eradicated as soon as possible. Many who think this are surely economic liberals who believe that the best way to accomplish this is by lifting the artificial regulations that states have set up for free trade, free movement of investment, and commercial establishment. Trade unions, they might suggest, have distorted the labour market, undermining incentives for companies to hire workers and thus contributed to massive unemployment. In an astonishing feat of historical forgetting, people in the human rights camp have failed to remember that most important rights struggles from the Magna Carta to the American and French revolutions and beyond have been about the recognition of rights to own property. If John Locke is part of the international human rights canon—as Hersch Lauterpacht, for example, firmly believed[12]—then a very strong protection of property is part of the canon, too. Surely it is not insignificant that Lauterpacht and his collaborator Sir Hartley Shawcross played key roles in the *Anglo-Iranian Oil Company* case about the protection of the property rights of the company's British owners against the Iranian government.[13] Surely it is equally relevant that the most important blueprint for today's international investment regime (the Abs-Shawcross plan) came from the same quarters. The protection of investment can easily be (and has been) argued in human rights terms: the investor has the *right* to repatriate the profits gathered from the uses of the property. If present investment lawyers avoid arguing this, it is not because they would not believe in investors' property rights but owing to their (correct) assessment that the human rights establishment would not view the matter in such a way.

Nor is it irrelevant that some of the twentieth century's most visible advocates of liberal economy—Hayek, Röpke, Friedman—were quite comfortable with speaking in rights terms. Opposing Fascism and Communism, the 'neoliberals' wanted to liberate the creative emerges of individuals from oppressive economic planning.[14] When human rights advocates today speak of 'corporate social responsibility' they are over again challenged by business executives arguing that the best way commercial companies can contribute to welfare rights is by filling the expectations of their customers and the pockets of their owners. Nor is this necessarily cynical. It may seem such to human rights activists but only to the extent that they have inherited a *different* economic doctrine—namely a social-democratic or a Keynesian one—that they believe will compel intervention by public authorities. If the rights activist feels that the corporate executive is not 'taking rights seriously'—the latter will see the rights advocate as a closet communist.

Or, finally, think about the conflict between collective and individual rights. Deference to ethnic, religious, or other traditions is surely an important part of rights culture. But what if

[12] Hersch Lauterpacht, *International Law and Human Rights* (Steven & Sons Ltd 1950).
[13] See now, Doreen Lustig, *Veiled Power. International Law and the Private Corporation* (OUP 2020) 144–78.
[14] See Jessica Whyte, *The Morals of the Market. Human Rights and the Rise of Neoliberalism* (Verso 2019).

a group member feels those traditions as unjust obstacles on his or her self-expression? As increasingly more traditionalists learn to speak the rights language, more and more rights practice turns out as balancing between claims of individual and collective rights of equal a priori validity, raising again the question about the institution that should be competent to set the required 'balance'. If this is a 'human rights institution', then the balancing act might raise interesting technical issues worthy of a case comment in a human rights law journal. For those not versed in the intricacies of human rights law, however, balancing will amount to a wholly mystical drawing of a rabbit out of a hat—once again providing demonstration of the human rights cult's refusal to engage with social conflict in open and democratic political forums.

4.3 A Clandestine Politics

Wars, property rights of investors, subordination to and freedom from communal traditions, and many, many other things have been identified in human rights terms. Of course, human rights experts do not think that anything goes. No doubt, they hold many such claims as un-serious or made in bad faith. They have specific, firmly held views on what rights claims are legitimate; and these do not include the priorities of a security specialist, a religious zealot, or a neoliberal economist. They would not, for example, normally include principles of free trade that WTO lawyers would identify as absolutely crucial in human rights terms.[15] Although the rhetoric of human rights may be indeterminate, *the practice is not, and never has been*. As a social group, the human rights camp can without difficulty be identified as standing for certain definite practices, values, and priorities. The camp joins a generation grown up in the secular West between the late 1960s and the 1980s. Many things converged in the period: the break-up of homogenous 'national' cultures and loosening of social and religious norms, the demise of real socialism, and the increased attraction of a commercially incentivized non-conformism. Samuel Moyn has recently summarized this as a 'North Atlantic revolution in moral sensibility, political rhetoric, and non-Governmental advocacy in the 1970s'.[16] Realizing one's identity and supporting the right of everyone else to realize theirs became important—much more important than national greatness or growth of the domestic GNP. They often coincided with calls for cosmopolitan democracy and global justice. As the phenomenon reached the 1980s it converged with a twofold critique of old-style politics. One aimed to set limits to the extent to which public authorities would be entitled to limit individual life choices. In fact, it often seemed that constraining the state was the very point of human rights. Another, related, effort was to formulate one's political objectives in rights terms with little or no necessary connection to domestic histories or practices. Rights claims after all were universal and taking them seriously required greater ambition than seeking to satisfy local constituencies. Both developments were underlain by the supposition that conventional policies were hampered by party politicking and state interests. New types of 'civil society' engagement were needed.

Among institutions undermined were political parties. The change that the human rights generation wanted seemed beyond the capacity of old institutions to attain. Going the way of rights offered an attractively apolitical alternative. Universality and inalienability connoted

[15] Philip Alston, 'Resisting the Merger and Acquisition of Human Rights by Trade Law' (2002) 13 European Journal of International Law 815.
[16] Samuel Moyn, *Not Enough: Human Rights in an Unequal World* (Harvard University Press 2018).

a level of ambition conventional parties had long ago given up. A particularly important moment was when in the 1980s and 1990s when social democrats, panicking over declining electoral support, co-opted human rights as part of the 'Third Way'. Tony Blair and Bill Clinton rose to power by addressing electorates in a human rights idiom, supporting the rights of women, minorities, and disadvantaged groups as well as internationalist agendas of humanitarian intervention and the environment. The door was opened for political activity for groups and themes previously suppressed by dominant political culture. But the neoliberal co-optation of the Third Way in the 1990s fatally undermined its credibility, eventually bringing social democracy down and now threatening to take human rights with it. By the time the financial crisis of 2008 had set in, rights had become infected by their association with a centrist elite that spoke of free trade and privatization and presided over a politics of unending austerity and a massive growth of domestic and international inequality. The political left had lost its bearings and found in its wake an increasingly cynical electorate looking for revenge in populist attacks on political correctness and attachment to nationalist nostalgia.

The 1990s had sealed the collapse of human rights from a language of revolution to that of routine governance in domestic and international institutions. Human rights combined the cultural aspirations of the 1960s with a debilitating blindness about how its anti-state alliance with global trade and finance was seen and felt outside its magic circle. Increasingly large parts of Western electorates were beginning to feel that they had been allocated life in an underclass struggling for 'bullshit jobs' while a global elite spoke human rights and thrived. Those people suddenly found their values and life preferences shut out of doors; they were not represented by anybody any longer—until right-wing manipulators found their way to the stage by breaching the rules of political correctness and directing their scorn at the hypocrisy of human rights as a wholly cynical effort to move elite values outside political contestation. The new politicians were reactionaries, a species not seen in Western democracies in decades: the moral-cultural high ground set up in the 1960s had to be abolished.

4.4 Thinking about the Backlash

So far, human rights people have been unwilling to concede that ideas that animate them—ideas about the position of refugees and minorities, about gender relations, but also about the operation of the economy, ways of treating criminality, the significance of climate change and so on—are not universally shared but specific and controversial. This has made human rights activists appear to their adversaries as a kind of social-democratic splinter group, a role they find hard to inhabit because of the belief that instead of being 'political' they speak about the moral and legal *limits* to politics. This is why they, and many other liberal analysts, have interpreted the 'backlash' less as a political challenge than a social pathology, to be healed by economic reforms. What needs to be done is to support equality and to pick up those 'left behind'. Reference is often made—I, too, have made it—to the 'Elephant Curb' in Branko Milanovic's *Global Inequality*[17] showing that in the period 1988–2008 the economic position of the white lower middle class in Europe and the United States has stagnated while the middle classes in the non-Western world have won, sometimes considerably, as have the richest of the rich, the 1 per cent of the 1 per cent. This has been taken to suggest that the

[17] Branko Milanović, *Global Inequality: A New Approach for the Age of Globalization* (The Belknap Press of Harvard University Press 2016).

right-wing surge expresses an economic grievance that needs to be addressed by policies that better target those constituencies. Alston, too, suggests that what needs to be done now is to address the inequality problem by increased emphasis on economic rights.[18] With more public attention to social welfare and equality legislation, the backlash would dissipate.

I remain sceptical about this proposal. It shares something of the paternalism that often characterizes human rights advocacy. The backlash is not concerned over equality. It is not moved by the annual data produced by Oxfam and others, pointing to the ever-widening gap between the richest of the rich and everyone else. No concern has been expressed by the backlashers about money laundering or tax havens. On the contrary, a backlasher may even admire a billionaire who has been able to trick the system in such a spectacular way. Instead, the backlasher finds it scandalous how the system directs social welfare benefits to all kinds of alien groups, 'illegal immigrants,' mock-refugees, and lazy foreigners flooding Europe and the United States. In reward for the honest labour of the white man they are planning to turn everywhere into a global Mogadishu. Whatever the deep causes, the politics of the backlash have not been about economic deprivation. Nor are the nationalists in Hungary or Poland, or Trump supporters in middle America, 'poor' in any meaningful statistical sense. Measured by almost any global standard they are reasonably well off. The outrage expressed by the backlash is not about hunger, illness, or even the appearance of gated communities for the rich in the holiday resorts they used to visit.[19] Until recently, almost everyone in Europe and the United States, whatever their economic standing, could look at the third world and think, 'well, at least we are not like that'. For most of the post-war period, white privilege used to include justified confidence that one's standard of living would gradually improve and that one's children would be better off than their parents. That is no longer the case in the West—while it may well be so elsewhere. At the same time, that very confidence and the aspirations and values it was related to—the values of white privilege—have been subjected to ridicule and scorn by liberal culture and its human rights avant-garde.

The attack on 'global elites', refugees, and non-governmental and human rights institutions is not about being 'left behind' and the wish to catch up. It is not about economic deprivation and carries no meaningful programme for institutional or policy reform. It is instead about the massive cultural transformation that peaked in the 1960s: civil rights, women's rights, gay rights, minority rights, the environment, the third world ... *café latte*, and so on. It is about the rise of a new cultural and political hierarchy in a West that no longer 'respected' the old values but treated them with more or less open contempt. Women, people of colour, foreigners, and members of innumerable identity groups at home and abroad began to claim and often attain a visibility and status earlier reserved for the white middle classes. The backlashers do not care a whiff for reform but want revenge against those who have supported this new sensibility. Instead of a social pathology, the backlash ought to be seen as a reactionary political movement that hopes to recreate the world before the 1960s—a world before civil rights, before environmentalism, multiculturalism, gender equality, before the time when patriarchy began to seem like a bad word.

The backlashers have no clear reform project beyond returning to a mythical past. They are not interested in institutional niceties. People who possess the kind of expert knowledge that it takes to debate reform of the European Union, WTO, or the climate regime are already in the adversary's camp. Whatever adjustments might be made would only further consolidate the authority of *these* institutions, and *those* people. Already to participate in reform

[18] Alston, 'Populist Challenge' (n 1) 6–9.

[19] See further Malcolm Bull, 'Am I Right to be Angry?' (2018) 40(15) London Review of Books 23–24.

would be to capitulate to an alien system of cultural and political values. Instead, what the backlashers want is revenge against a political and cultural elite that uses the grandiloquent rhetoric about human rights to distribute material values to its friends—aliens, minorities, and 'unaccountable international bureaucrats'. Studies showing that 'Brexit' will hurt its staunchest supporters economically have no effect because the grievance is not about economics but about status. 'Taking back control' addresses that status loss directly. It is neither about justice nor inequality, but about restoring an old system of control—control by white men over their families and their societies. Restoration of a time when feminists, cosmopolitan elitists, Jewish philanthropists, gay journalists, and African refugees did not tell white men how to think or what to do.

4.5 How to Engage?

In his 2016 article, Philip Alston appealed to action: 'each one of us is in a position to make a difference if we want to do so'.[20] But it is not obvious *what* human rights activists should want to do. The left criticism of human rights points to a strategic paralysis engendered by the assumption that the 'backlash' is a social pathology to be cured by economic reform and more efficient human rights work. Even though rising inequality is an enormous problem that needs to be treated, it is insufficient without a strategy to deal with the status concern and the political objectives of the reactionaries in a situation where—to borrow an expression from the American right—human rights increasingly appear as an *opposition party*. Human rights people have often been reluctant to think of themselves as men and women of power in this way.[21] Too often they have been satisfied by having human rights language appear in one or another policy document. But *power cannot be attained or exercised by human rights language because everyone can use it*. Instead, like a true 'opposition party', the human rights camp must learn to identify tangible goals in different policy areas and devise strategies for how they may be reached. Alston appeals for creativity in his essay; and I agree. Creativity requires taking stock of the new situation that has arisen both with respect to liberal-democratic politics and the world of expert governance in the West in the recent decades. The difficulty is that this might necessitate leaving or at least significantly downplaying attachment to rights language and beginning to engage in what today increasingly appears as expert politics.

The first step is making a clear split to neoliberalism and austerity. I agree with Sam Moyn that attention should not only be directed to the floor in terms of distribution but also the ceiling: equality must also be seen to happen. But this is not sufficient. Creativity is needed to imagine politics neither as old-time electoral activism nor as retreat into some pre-technocratic authenticity where values and interests could be implemented independently of what experts say about the ways they can be realized. One of the dramatic post-1960s developments in Western polities has been the collapse of the boundary between politics and knowledge, *what we want to do* and *what experts say we should do*. The backlashers have correctly identified this fact and have been scandalized by it. It has become impossible to attain

[20] Alston, 'Populist Challenge' (n 1) 14.

[21] Or maybe it is not incomprehensible but follows from a conviction that power will corrupt. But fear of corruption reflects insecurity or lack of determination. Human rights activists have sometimes had difficulty imagining themselves as political adversaries of somebody. Aiming at power will inevitably create adversaries—in fact, already speaking clearly about one's objectives will do that.

influence in the regular political process without relying on expert knowledge. And because 'expertise' often appears to be about maintaining the present system by tinkering with its details, the backlashers have understood it as a duplicitous way for the elites to blunt criticism.

Meaningful political engagement today must begin by taking seriously the interpenetration of knowledge and value. Political activism moves *within* the sphere of expertise, of knowledge production itself, and not in some esoteric world of universal value. Although particular forms of expertise—when examined from the outside—seem like homogenous structures of consolidated knowledge, insiders are invariably conscious of disciplinary struggles between orthodoxies and a heterodoxies, leading theories with their accepted commonplaces and a counter-theories with deviating axioms and policy proposals. The internal life of expertise is a constant exchange between these two—a fact that outsiders occasionally glimpse in the ability of political opponents to support themselves by opposing types of expert knowledge.[22] They do this either by enlisting different kinds of expertise (economy versus environment, for example, or security versus constitutional principle) or by drawing from the internal strands of particular expert regimes (free trade versus development economics, military versus human security). Because, as experts themselves are often the first to admit, not only the world of expertise as a whole but also individual fields of expert knowledge are divided against themselves, their best representatives in disagreement about the very premises of those fields (*especially* about the premises). This is why much can be done *within expertise* itself to support the agendas of rights activists. As long as activists limit their imagination to 'human rights', they tend to push themselves unwittingly beyond the margin of political influence.

This is so because, as a form of political engagement, 'human rights' is both too broad and too narrow as a counterpoint to the right-wing surge in Europe and the United States. 'Human rights' is too broad in that it has no specificity but can be translated to support whatever projects—including the 'grievances' of the supporters of cultural reaction (narrowing the definition of hate speech and reinterpreting affirmative action a discrimination, for example). Retorting that it does *not* allow such translations makes its universalist pretensions appear hypocritical. 'Human rights' is too narrow to the extent that it continues to resist being translated into the technical vocabularies that enable ruling over political communities. The latter point calls for a little extension.

Efficient engagement in politics today requires entering debates with experts in areas from security to education, health to housing, environment to agriculture, all areas where governance takes place. For by itself, 'human rights' does not involve expertise in anything specific; it is just a set of very generally expressed preferences. To create social effects, those preferences must be translated to authoritative expert language. In that translation process the human rights activists might find themselves losing voice. Many types of expert knowledge are available and many alternative directions within single fields of knowledge. How is one to choose? I have elsewhere discussed the costs and benefits of integrating in a field of expertise—the way making an effort to understand the problems that experts deal with so as to become a persuasive interlocutor with experts almost automatically makes one sympathize with the complex ways in which the best experts see the world.[23] Taking the time and energy to become a persuasive user of expert speech is likely to dilute or at least complicate

[22] This matter is studied in detail in David Kennedy, *A World of Struggle: How Power, Law, and Expertise Shape Global Political Economy* (Princeton University Press 2016).

[23] Martti Koskenniemi, 'Human Rights Mainstreaming as a Strategy for Institutional Power' (2010) 1 Humanity: An International Journal of Human Rights, Humanitarianism, and Development 47.

one's original intuitions: *Well, apparently there are many ways in which a problem may be dealt with, each involving different, and usually uncertain costs.* One is left swinging between what it requires to act as an efficient bureaucrat, skilfully laying out expert translations for one's preferences, and the need to constantly adjust those preferences by reference to experiences that have accumulated in expert routines in the past. To be in control of that oscillation requires a critical mindset aware of the manner in which expert policies allocate values between human groups.

So, I want to end by suggesting that the leftist critique of human rights points to the apparent paradox that the best human rights policies might not be human rights policies at all. Instead, they would be the best economic policies, best development policies, best agricultural policies, best labour policies, best security policies, and so on, determined in debates with and between experts. When the human critic at NYU appeared to fail the student by refusing to offer a blueprint for the student to follow, that person might have been suggesting something else, and perhaps more valuable, namely that 'human rights' is not the platform on which political battles are won but that this requires engagement in more specific fields of knowledge and expertise, career paths that more directly and with more authority influence the distribution of material and spiritual values. The right-wing backlashers have—correctly—identified expert knowledge, academy, and the principled, scientific search for true answers to questions posed by science as the adversary. On the one side, prejudice, resentment, racism, and descent into obscurity and violence—on the other, truthfulness, the search for knowledge, respect, and peace. Over half of the republican electorate in the United States believes that universities are rather more harmful than useful for American society. If the process and outcomes of engaging in the production of knowledge is associated with being politically on the left, then surely that is an encouraging feature of the world we live in. In the Marxist tradition it was once taken for granted that the criterion of truth of a proposition lay in the way it contributed to emancipation. The contemporary experience that universities and expert knowledge are among the first targets of the extreme right constitutes a practical confirmation of that old adage.

5
The State of Human Rights Consciousness: Not Yet Endtimes

Sally Engle Merry

5.1 Introduction

Human rights are increasingly described as being in crisis. Some scholars argue that the system of human rights has become too formalized and professionalized and is therefore too remote from those who need its protection. Others insist that it is a Western ideology that has failed to escape its colonial past. Observers of the contemporary political situation note that some authoritarian governments have threatened or closed human rights organizations in their countries. The enthusiasm for globalization and a universal order of justice of the 1990s was transformed by the 2010s, in part by the growing inequality generated by economic globalization, including the increasing wealth and cosmopolitanism of the few and the poverty and isolation of the many. In place of a celebrated globalism there is now a rising populist tide that puts nation, religion, and race first, and that poses new kinds of threats to human rights.

But are human rights really on the verge of disappearing? It is certainly the case that many human rights institutions have become more bureaucratic and stodgier; and that human rights organizations in many parts of the world are under threat. Yet the appeal of human rights has always resided in the ideal of justice, fairness, and equality that they represent. These remain appealing ideas globally, even if the institutions designed to promote and enforce human rights are in themselves increasingly unable to do so. Indeed, it is notable that one of the scholars arguing that we are at the end of human rights, Stephen Hopgood, distinguishes between Human Rights and human rights, capital letters and small letters. The former refers to national and international institutions of human rights such as the International Criminal Court (ICC), Responsibility to Protect (R2P) doctrines, major human rights organizations, and laws, while the latter refers to human rights language where global laws and precedents play some role in promoting local causes. Advocates of this latter use of human rights do not, he says, aspire to hegemony but see rights as malleable and often integrated into other belief systems as one political language among others.[1] In other words, human rights refer to everyday uses of the concept. It is only the Human Rights side that he thinks is in trouble and has failed to deliver. Indeed, he sees possibilities in human rights as 'a globally unowned and unknowable claim of human moral equality as the anchor of fair treatment and nothing more'.[2] Ideally, human rights can be a place where 'diversity of motivations and outlook is prized in the furtherance of concrete improvements in everyday lives on all measures: nutrition and health, disease, security, education'.[3] It is the idea of an

[1] Stephen Hopgood, *The Endtimes of Human Rights* (Cornell University Press 2013) 14–15.
[2] ibid 22.
[3] ibid 22.

Sally Engle Merry, *The State of Human Rights Consciousness: Not Yet Endtimes* In: *The Struggle for Human Rights*. Edited by: Nehal Bhuta, Florian Hoffmann, Sarah Knuckey, Frédéric Mégret, and Margaret Satterthwaite, Oxford University Press. © Sally Engle Merry 2021. DOI: 10.1093/oso/9780198868064.003.0006

impartial moral authority with democratic legitimation under the influence of American pragmatism that he expects to be swamped by the new importance of religion and nationalism along with American insistence on its exceptionalism.[4]

In Mark Goodale's recent review of two major books on human rights, Kathryn Sikkink's (2017) enthusiastic view of its successes in improving life conditions for many (although she acknowledges that there is much more to be done), is juxtaposed to Samuel Moyn's (2018) far more doomsday analysis of human rights that has accepted a goal of sufficiency—a floor to an adequate life—rather than equality, thus ignoring the material inequalities of wealth in the world.[5] Goodale concludes with the case of Bolivia, arguing that in countries like it, especially at the margins where global capital has not yet reached, there may be hope for greater justice.[6] In a recent article, Kathryn Sikkink and Geoff Dancy present empirical evidence of the accomplishments of the human rights approach.[7]

Human rights, in this sense, refer to a set of ideals about how governments should treat their citizens and about how all humans should be treated. These ideals, moreover, have the imprimatur of a global consensus. Although there has been a great deal of sophisticated and valuable scholarship about whether human rights are 'effective', measured 'effectiveness' is not the only way to evaluate the importance of human rights. After all, we do not judge the value of national laws because they are effective, but because they articulate goals that we would like to make effective. Most—national and international—laws in fact have an impact in the absence of sanctions, operating instead on the basis of voluntary compliance with a set of rules and ideas that people (or collectives) come to accept. But they are also routinely violated. Thus, even nation-state law is fundamentally a cultural project, an articulation of a vision of society that many, but not all, aspire to have. Lack of compliance with these laws is not viewed as an indication that the cultural project has failed. The same understanding should apply to human rights law and norms.

Considerable ethnographic research in local communities shows that human rights are widely appropriated, adopted, and redefined to fit particular social issues and struggles. I have called the cultural dimension of this process vernacularization. This term refers to the way an idea or norm is redefined and represented in a way that is more or less compatible with the existing social world. This does not mean its meaning is changed entirely (although it may be reframed), but rather that it has an altered mode of presentation. New ideas of gender equality coming from other parts of the world might, for example, be presented through conventional figures in a familiar genre of a street play or painted on kites that are sold for kite-flying contests so that the kites land in random back yards when the strings break, carrying their message with them. The new idea is dressed in the clothes of the old to render it more understandable, acceptable, and relevant. In time, the human rights idea may lose its grounding in the normative system in which it arose and become part of a different cultural formation.

Recognizing the continuing importance and strength of human rights requires looking for them in different places. These places are not simply the HRC or the regular meetings of

[4] ibid 22–23.

[5] Mark Goodale, 'What Are Human Rights Good For?' (2018) Boston Review <http://bostonreview.net/global-justice/mark-goodale-what-are-human-rights-good> accessed 28 July 2020.

[6] Kathryn Sikkink, *Evidence for Hope: Making Human Rights Work in the 21st Century* (Princeton University Press 2017).

[7] Geoff Dancy and Kathryn Sikkink, 'Human Rights Data, Processes, and Outcomes: How Recent Research Points to a Better Future' in Stephen Hopgood, Jack Snyder, and Leslie Vinjamuri (eds), *Human Rights Futures* (CUP 2017) 24–59.

the committees seeking to monitor compliance with human rights treaties but also the offices of small NGOs and the streets of poor neighbourhoods. Understanding human rights *in practice* requires looking at the way the ideas they promote have become part of everyday life for many people around the world. César Rodriguez-Garavito advocates this kind of locally defined and relevant approach to human rights as a human rights practice developing in the global South.[8] He cites the need for spaces for new actors, themes, and strategies and the importance of recognizing its diversity. He suggests seeing the field as an ecosystem, rather than as a unified movement or institutional architecture with an emphasis on symbiotic relationships and connections between the discrete contributions of members of the ecosystem.

The resilience of some broad conception of human rights in communities around the world rests in part on the universal concern with justice, although it is defined in many ways. Every society has conceptions of justice, although the specific norms and procedures used to produce it are quite variable. Many of these conceptions are grounded in religion while others are based on community standards or state enactments. Human rights differ, however, in that they offer a relatively secular conception of justice rooted not in a particular state but in the consensus of a large majority of states. Thus, they are legitimated by a transnational consensus that gives them a kind of power beyond that of state law. It is far from the only transnational conception of justice, of course. Many religions are transnational and carry these ideas, such as liberation theology, while political ideologies such as Marxism and democracy and the rule of law provide alternative ideas of justice.

This does not mean that there are not problems with human rights as a global model for justice. It offers an over-individualized idea of justice that does not always address the structural causes of inequality. It establishes a platform below which no person or society should fall, but it does not explicitly tackle inequality. Although it covers social and economic rights as well as civil and political ones, the former are often not as well supported and implemented. Human rights as a global justice ideology have not resolved the difficult question of the incompatibility of universal applicability and respect for local cultural practices. States that feel threatened by human rights activism are increasingly shutting down human rights organizations. Yet, human rights ideas remain a major force in global consciousness.

Framing ideas of justice in human rights terms offers at least three important benefits to social justice activists engaged in local struggles. First, the global consensus about human rights adds legitimacy to a moral claim made by local actors. Using the human rights language suggests that these are not just ideas from a local community or even country, but ideas that have been created and agreed upon by virtually all the countries of the world. Whether or not these human rights are implemented, the process of their creation through global debate and agreement provides an important level of legitimacy. Second, calling a social justice claim a human rights claim produces allies. Groups concerned with housing rights, poverty alleviation, educational inequality, racial discrimination in health benefits,

[8] César A Rodríguez Garavito, 'The Future of Human Rights: From Gatekeeping to Symbiosis' (2014) 11 Sur Journal <https://papers.ssrn.com/abstract=2553200> accessed 9 September 2020; Malcolm Langford, César A Rodríguez Garavito, and Julieta Rossi, *Social Rights Judgments and the Politics of Compliance Making It Stick* (CUP 2017); Rochelle Cooper Dreyfuss and César A Rodríguez Garavito (eds), *Balancing Wealth and Health: The Battle over Intellectual Property and Access to Medicines in Latin America* (1st edn, OUP 2014); César A Rodríguez Garavito (ed), *Business and Human Rights: Beyond the End of the Beginning* (CUP 2017); César A Rodríguez Garavito, 'A Human Right to a Healthy Environment? Moral, Legal and Empirical Considerations' in John H Knox and Ramin Pejan (eds), *The Human Right to a Healthy Environment* (CUP 2018).

and so on, can all join together as advocates of human rights, a process I observed among activists in New York City.[9]

Third, describing a particular issue as a human rights one renders it legible to a wider audience. For example, in 2008 a group seeking to promote the rights of battered women in New York City family courts turned to a human rights framework to show how the everyday struggle abused women faced in being heard and not losing custody of their children in court was an instance of a larger justice issue. By translating the difficulties these women faced in court into violations of their human rights, they presented these issues in ways that other justice activists could understand even if they might not have encountered this particular problem themselves.[10]

Focusing on how human rights travel and how they are transformed offers an invaluable corrective to those perspectives locating human rights only in formal institutions and laws. It shows how human rights are embedded in everyday social practice and activism. It challenges the idea that human rights are an entirely Western construct resisted by the postcolonial world by showing how these ideas are appropriated in countries around the world and how the international human rights norms and architecture are shaped by these countries' experiences. And it makes clear that although measuring compliance is important, this is not the only way to assess what human rights do. By examining the human rights system as a social justice ideology with universal aspirations, flexible enough to be reinterpreted and redefined in a variety of contexts and for a broad range of problems, it is possible to develop a more comprehensive and useful understanding of the way human rights work in our contemporary world.

In my work on human rights and gender violence, I found that even in relatively remote local communities, many activists and even some victims had an awareness that there was an international system of human rights according to which women could 'stand up for themselves'.[11] The existence of a transcendent system of human rights, even vaguely defined, gave strength to local demands for justice. That the human rights system is a legal one was clearly important to its legitimacy and power. In a subsequent collaborative study with Peggy Levitt focused on local activists in the United States, China, India, and Peru, we saw how they reinterpreted and vernacularized global standards about women's rights, making them understandable within local systems of meaning and practice.[12] At the same time, these ideas of justice remain tethered to the conception of a global, universal system of law, although the ties are sometimes long and tenuous.

To assess whether we are really in the 'end times' of human rights, it is important to expand what we think human rights do in the world. While they are sometimes imagined as a form of law that must be asserted and enforced, they have two other important functions as well. The legal enforcement of human rights laws through the treaty body process, individual complaints, and the decisions of regional human rights courts is clearly an important dimension of what human rights do and is fundamental to understanding human rights in practice. However, there are two other important functions for human rights. One is providing an ideology of social justice for social movements and the other is documentation

[9] Sally Engle Merry and others, 'Law From Below: Women's Human Rights and Social Movements in New York City: Women's Human Rights and Social Movements' (2010) 44 Law & Society Review 101.

[10] ibid.

[11] Sally Engle Merry, *Human Rights and Gender Violence: Translating International Law into Local Justice* (University of Chicago Press 2006); Merry and others (2010) (n 9).

[12] Vernacularization on the ground: local uses of global women's rights in Peru, China, India, and the United States; see Peggy Levitt and Sally Engle Merry (2009) 9(4) *Global Networks* 441–46.

of injustice: making violations of the most vulnerable known to the world. Both are critically important dimensions of what human rights do, equally if not more important than the narrower legal processes. However, the existence of the laws and the formal legal process gives added legitimacy to the social justice ideology and to the processes of fact-finding and documentation.

In fact, the imposition of human rights law is probably the least successful of these three. But as I have already argued, we do not abandon law because it is unsuccessful in producing consistently law-abiding behaviour, but view legal regulation as an ongoing process. Indeed, legal regulation is often a game between regulators and regulated as the regulated seek to get around regulation.

5.2 Human Rights as a Social Justice Ideology

There is a great deal of ethnographic evidence that human rights as an ideology of justice is actively used around the world in a variety of ways, many of which are vernacularized or reinterpreted in forms of analysis and presentation that make sense within local context but are still loosely tethered to the global system of law. Sometimes vernacular uses of human rights pay close attention to the text of the rights, but at other times they are understood broadly, and the important fact is that they exist as an international system of justice.

For example, a recent edited collection exploring the travel and transformation of human rights investigates their mobilization in Nepal and the Dominican Republic,[13] Vietnam,[14] and China.[15] In Vietnam, local activists use digital strategies to protest widespread use of torture by the state while international human rights activists turn to formal institutions such as the Uniform Periodic Review process of the HRC. State resistance to human rights inhibits the effectiveness of these strategies, but McLean argues that these two strands of activism are beginning to come together.[16] In China, despite a crackdown on human rights and international human rights organizations since 2013, training in the right to health by US-based NGO Asia Catalyst, in conjunction with Chinese health rights activists, taught local activists to see themselves within a global movement, to embed human rights governance principles in their practice, and to improve the effectiveness of their advocacy skills. Davis and Mohamed find that these skills were used by programme participants in their interactions with government actors.[17] Some of the participants initiated successful programmes, although they tended to be micro-level interventions that did not directly challenge state power. Those that continued their health advocacy work focused on issues that were very local and had pragmatic aims while avoiding international human rights mechanisms that might trigger government crackdowns.[18]

However, the process of translating human rights into local understandings and basis for action is hardly simple and straightforward. As Harri Englund shows in his study of human

[13] Samuel Martinez, 'Upstreaming or Streamlining? Translating Social Movement Agendas into Legal Claims in Nepal and the Dominican Republic' in Tine Destrooper and Sally Engle Merry (eds), *Human Rights Transformation in Practice* (1st edn, University of Pennsylvania Press 2018).

[14] Ken MacLean 'New Visibilities: Challenging Torture and Impunity in Vietnam' in Destrooper and Merry (n 13).

[15] Sara LM Davis and Charmain Mohamed, 'Global Rights, Local Risk: Community Advocacy on Right to Health in China' in Destrooper and Merry (n 13).

[16] MacLean (n 14) 175.

[17] Davis and Mohamed (n 15) 231.

[18] ibid 245.

rights in Malawi, the translation of the terms themselves may be so poorly done that the central concepts disappear.[19] Moreover, training programmes designed to tell communities about human rights may fail to address real issues of inequality and injustice.[20] Translating the abstract global norms into local conditions typically requires intermediaries who are conversant with both the human rights world and local conditions, as occurred in the example from China. In the absence of such translation, the impact of human rights ideas is far less. For example, in a study of a UNICEF project on clean water and sanitation in the Democratic Republic of the Congo, Tine Destrooper finds that the local community is interested in some human rights dimensions of the project, such as holding duty bearers accountable, but because of the imbalance of power between UNICEF staff and villagers and the failure of the staff to consult villagers, this human rights awareness is undeveloped.[21] This example underscores the important role that intermediaries play in the vernacularization of human rights. People who are conversant both with the human rights system and the local community and can translate between them are critical actors in the process of human rights vernacularization. Such individuals were not present in the Congo case. Intermediaries sensitive to local issues as well as the global human rights system seem critical to the effective mobilization of human rights ideas. For example, Martinez argues that the top-down actions of international human rights activists in converting the local demands of Haitian descendants in the Dominican Republic not to be deported and those of debt-bondage farmers in Nepal for release from bondage into legal claims narrowed the focus so that, when both cases lost in the legal arena, those seeking to assert rights were less well off.[22]

5.3 Human Rights Documentation and Knowledge Production

While the vernacularization of human rights and their mobilization in local social movements is clearly an important dimension of how human rights act in the world, a third, also very important dimension is the role of human rights activists in making forms of injustice known, publicizing the disadvantages of the most vulnerable. In fact, this may be the most important contribution human rights make to promoting social justice globally. This is a core part of the work of Human Rights Watch, for example, which issued seventy-eight reports of violations around the world in 2018. The centrality of fact-finding to human rights work is exemplified by recent publications on fact-finding and research in human rights, such as the 2017 publication from the Danish Institute of Human Rights, *Research Methods in Human Rights: A Handbook*.[23] An important contribution to this dimension of human rights activism is the publication of a book on fact-finding in human rights based on a major international conference convened by the Center for Human Rights and Global Justice at NYU School of Law, edited by Philip Alston and Sarah Knuckey.[24] As the book argues, fact-finding is becoming increasingly important in human rights work and calls for greater attention to assumptions, methods of research, and modes of analysis and interpretation.

[19] Harri Englund, *Prisoners of Freedom: Human Rights and the African Poor* (University of California Press 2006).
[20] ibid.
[21] Tine Destrooper, 'Localization "Light": The Travel and Transformation of Non-Empowering Human Rights Norms' in Destrooper and Merry (n 13) 208–28.
[22] Martinez (n 13).
[23] Bård-Anders Andreassen, Hans-Otto Sano, and Siobhán Mclnerney-Lankford (eds), *Research Methods in Human Rights: A Handbook* (Edward Elgar Publishing 2017).
[24] Philip Alston and Sarah Knuckey (eds), *The Transformation of Human Rights Fact-Finding* (Oxford University Press 2016).

One of the most impressive exemplars of human rights work in this dimension is that of the special rapporteurs appointed by the HRC. As of December 2018, there were eighty mandate holders, carrying out investigations on a wide range of human rights topics. Often their reports receive considerable media coverage and may serve to frame the way emerging issues are understood. For example, Radhika Coomaraswarmy's 1996 and 2002 reports on violence against women, written during her tenure as the first Special Rapporteur on Violence against Women, contributed significantly to defining the developing field of violence against women.[25]

Philip Alston has of course made many major contributions to the field of human rights, not only from his work on children's rights to social and economic rights through the treaty body system but also through his extensive, thoughtful publications about the nature of human rights and the process of implementing them. One of his most important recent contributions, however, has been his work in fact-finding and reporting, both as Special Rapporteur on Extrajudicial Killings and more recently as Special Rapporteur on Extreme Poverty and Human Rights. While human rights work tends to be done by countries of the global North exploring issues in the global South, he made a widely publicized visit and report on poverty in the United Kingdom in 2017 and the United States in 2018. These reports received significant press coverage and alerted Americans and Britons to the extent of poverty in these countries.

Choosing to visit the United States and the United Kingdom as well as some European countries is an important innovation since human rights are typically viewed by affluent countries as something for others. As Barbara Oomen argues, this is characteristic of the Netherlands and Europe more generally.[26] Despite many efforts to establish strong human rights groups in the United States focused on US issues, the existing groups are radical and creative but remain marginal.[27] Studies of human rights activism in the United States show that despite the long US history of rights activism, the human rights framework itself is not as widely adopted as might be expected, either in fields such as gender-based violence or more generally.[28] Thus, to bring human rights ideas to bear on issues in the affluent global North serves to expand the reach of these ideas and expose the forgotten marginalized populations of these countries.

Another important dimension of human rights knowledge production is the work of the treaty bodies, charged with monitoring compliance with particular human rights treaties. Here also, Philip Alston has made major contributions. As chair of the Committee on Economic, Social and Cultural Rights from 1991 to 1998, he helped to examine countries' efforts to promote these rights as they testified to their actions in complying with the treaties. This is a delicate process in which a country submits a periodic report and committee members ask the country delegates questions over a period of several hours. It is an information gathering process, both

[25] UNCHR, Fifty-second Session 5 February 1996 'Report of the Special Rapporteur on Violence Against Women, Its Causes and Consequences, Ms. Radhika Coomaraswamy, Submitted in Accordance with Commission on Human Rights Resolution 1995/85' UN DOC E/CN.4/1996/54; UNCHR, Fifty-eigth Session, 'Report of the Special Rapporteur on Violence against Women, its Causes and Consequences, Ms Radhika Coomaraswamy, submitted in accordance with Commission on Human Rights Resolution 2001/49: Cultural Practices in the Family that are Violent towards Women' UN Doc E/CN.4/2002/83.

[26] Barbara Oomen, *Rights for Others: The Slow Home-Coming of Human Rights in the Netherlands* (CUP 2014).

[27] Cynthia Soohoo, Catherine Albisa, and Martha F Davis (eds), *Bringing Human Rights Home: A History of Human Rights in the United States* (abridged edn, University of Pennsylvania Press 2009).

[28] Sally Engle Merry and Jessica Shimmin, 'The Curious Resistance to seeing Domestic Violence as a Human Rights Violation in the USA' in Shareen Hertel and Kathryn Libal (eds), *Human Rights in the United States: Beyond Exceptionalism* (CUP 2011) 113–31.

through the written report and the questions about it. Committees draft their responses to the report and discussion, which are labelled as concluding comments. Reports and concluding comments for each country are available online, allowing local NGOs to understand what the committee thought about the report and the discussion. Thus, this mechanism provides another source of information about how well countries are complying with human rights treaties.

Yet it is a slow and time-consuming process for a committee to hear periodic reports from about 150 countries, with each obligated to report usually every four years to each of the committees of the treaties they have ratified. By the 1980s it was clear that the system was becoming overwhelmed. In 1988 the Secretary General asked Philip Alston to suggest reforms to the treaty body system to streamline it and reduce costs, which he did in a series of trenchant reports in 1989, 1993, and 1997.[29]

As this brief overview indicates, Philip Alston has contributed in very significant ways to the information gathering and knowledge production dimension of human rights. Those that are currently engaged in predicting the death of human rights or their failure tend to ignore the contribution of the role of human rights in documenting abuses and expanding the knowledge of human rights violations. By focusing largely on enforcement of rules, they miss the critically important process of human rights vernacularization and the contributions to social justice of the efforts to expose and make known abuses of human rights globally, in affluent countries as well as in poor ones.

5.4 Conclusions

Perhaps Kathryn Sikkink's position is a more accurate assessment of the place of human rights in the contemporary world than that of Hopgood or Moyn. While Hopgood despairs that Human Rights have not served to cement a liberal democratic order and Moyn regrets the inability of the human rights system to grapple with inequality, human rights as a social justice ideology is being appropriated in myriad ways by local and national activists seeking to deal with a range of particular problems. The established global institutions, such as the ICC or the HRC seem unable to produce a human rights compliant world, yet ideas of rights have spread, not as the only ideology of social justice, but as one important alternative. They merge with other justice ideas in various locations, inspire activists either directly or indirectly, and constitute a secular set of ideas rooted in the sphere of the international world rather than in that of religion or state. This is not a system closely controlled by international human rights institutions. It is a fragmented, varied, and shifting set of ideas and practices, often merging with the cultural logics of those who have appropriated and used them. Nevertheless, as one of several justice systems, it occupies an important place among global social movements and has consequences for local people and their experiences with injustice around the world.

[29] Note by the Secretary General, 'Effective Implementation of International Instruments on Human Rights, Including Reporting Obligations Under International Instruments on Human Rights' (1989) UN Doc A/44/668; UNGA; Note by the Secretary General, 'Interim Report on Updated Study by Mr. Philip Alston' (1993) UN A/CONF.157/PC/62/Add.11/Rev.1; UNCHR, 'Final Report on enhancing the Long-Term Effectiveness of the United Nations Human Rights Treaty System' (1997) UN Doc E/CN.4/1997/74.

6
Human Rights, Legitimacy, and Global Governance

Euan MacDonald[*]

6.1 Introduction

Can human rights play a role in addressing the 'legitimacy crisis'[1] in global governance—and in particular its 'democratic deficit'?[2] If so, what? These are my questions in this contribution. They are questions that have formed an important element of Philip Alston's theoretical work over the years; often in relation to the international human rights regimes,[3] but also with regard to global governance institutions more generally.[4] One such occasion was in 2002, in response to Ernst-Ulrich Petersmann's startling claim that the *only* way for governance bodies such as the WTO to gain the democratic legitimacy that they lacked was to 'integrate' international human rights law into their own jurisprudence.[5] Alston demurred, arguing that empowering the WTO to adjudicate on human rights matters would fatally undermine the very legitimizing force that it sought to co-opt.[6] Of course, these claims could both be true. If so, too bad for the WTO. Or, perhaps, for human rights.

Since the Petersmann–Alston exchange, the literature on the legitimacy of global governance institutions has grown considerably. Much has been from a political science perspective, with a focus on 'sociological' understandings of legitimacy.[7] But there has also been an increase in interest from the perspective of normative legal and political philosophy, and an attempt to set out, in general terms, an appropriate 'standard of legitimacy' for global governance.[8] Within this literature, there is an emerging 'cosmopolitan functionalist'

* I would like to thank Luís Duarte d'Almeida, Chloë Kennedy, Ismael Martinez Torres, and Lea Raible for their detailed comments on an earlier draft of this chapter; and audiences at workshops at NYU and Edinburgh University for helpful comments and criticisms.

1 For example, Johan Karlsson Schaffer, 'Legitimacy, Global Governance and Human Rights Institutions: Inverting the Puzzle' in Andreas Føllesdal, Johan Karlsson Schaffer, and Geir Ulfstein (eds), *The Legitimacy of International Human Rights Regimes: Legal, Political and Philosophical Perspectives* (CUP 2013) 213.

2 For example, Steven Wheatley, 'A Democratic Account of the Right to Rule in Global Governance: Democracy and Global Governance' (2012) 18 Swiss Political Science Review 158, 160–62.

3 For example, Philip Alston, 'Reconceiving the UN Human Rights Regime: Challenges Confronting the New UN Human Rights Council' (2006) 7 Melbourne Journal of International Law 185; Philip Alston, 'Hobbling the Monitors: Should UN Human Rights Monitors Be Accountable?' 52 Harvard Human Rights Journal 561.

4 For example,Philip Alston, 'The Myopia of the Handmaidens: International Lawyers and Globalization' (1997) 8 European Journal of International Law 435.

5 Ernst-Ulrich Petersmann, 'Time for a United Nations "Global Compact" for Integrating Human Rights into the Law of Worldwide Organizations: Lessons from European Integration' (2002) 13 European Journal of International Law 621.

6 Philip Alston, 'Resisting the Merger and Acquisition of Human Rights by Trade Law: A Reply to Petersmann' (2002) 13(4) European Journal of International Law 815.

7 For a recent set of examples, see Jonas Tallberg and Michael Zürn, 'The Legitimacy and Legitimation of International Organizations: Introduction and Framework' (2019) 14(4) The Review of International Organizations 581.

8 For example, the contributions in Føllesdal, Schaffer, and Ulfstein (n 1).

Euan MacDonald, *Human Rights, Legitimacy, and Global Governance* In: *The Struggle for Human Rights*. Edited by: Nehal Bhuta, Florian Hoffmann, Sarah Knuckey, Frédéric Mégret, and Margaret Satterthwaite, Oxford University Press. © Euan MacDonald 2021. DOI: 10.1093/oso/9780198868064.003.0007

mainstream,[9] characterized by the rejection both of more robust 'global democracy-based' or 'global justice-based' approaches, and of minimalist accounts that equate legitimacy with state consent. Instead, these authors stress the provision of global public goods, with an important but limited role for the protection of core human rights and certain procedural guarantees, which are held to vindicate 'democratic values' sufficiently to secure legitimacy. In what follows, I want to offer a broadly sympathetic yet significantly different account of the legitimacy of global governance institutions—one that is I think better suited to address democratic concerns in particular—and of the role that human rights can play in this.

To keep things manageable, I will limit my focus to one key cosmopolitan functionalist account: that offered by Allen Buchanan and Robert Keohane in 2006.[10] I focus on this, first, because it remains one of the most sophisticated and influential contributions to date; and second, because it gets most of the important things wrong in highly instructive—and widely shared—ways. In particular I will argue that they (1) 'weaken' the dominant conception of 'legitimate authority' in an ad hoc and incoherent manner; and that this leads them to (2) mistake the normative role that human rights play in legitimizing global governance; and (3) ignore entirely the important role that *consent* plays in underpinning demands for democratic legitimacy in particular.

One final note before I proceed. This argument has a lot of moving parts. A full defence of any of them would require a paper (at least) of its own. My goal here is to do enough to get the account I offer on the table as a potentially plausible one; nothing more.

6.2 Conceptual Criteria, Normative Standards

'In order to remain democratically acceptable, global integration law (e.g. in the WTO) must pursue not only "economic efficiency" but also "democratic legitimacy" and "social justice" as defined by human rights'.[11] This claim of Petersmann's is striking for a number of reasons. First, it puts democratic concerns at the heart of the legitimacy crisis in global governance institutions. It thus moves beyond the traditional model that viewed the consent of participating states—regardless of their own internal political structure—as both necessary and sufficient for legitimacy. At the same time, it proposes that we address legitimacy issues *within* the functionally differentiated institutional framework through which global governance is currently conducted, eschewing any grand democratic institution-building project at the global level. Petersmann can thus be read as an example of the 'cosmopolitan functionalism' that now forms the mainstream thinking regarding the legitimacy of global governance institutions. His account is cosmopolitan in its view that what matters morally are individuals and their universal rights; it is functionalist in its understanding of both why we have and why we ought to keep broadly the current set of institutions. The solution to the legitimacy crisis will come not from building anew but from 'constitutionalising' what we have.[12] Human rights have perhaps *the* key role to play in this process. Legitimacy demands nothing less than the full 'integration' of international human rights law into the law of 'worldwide institutions'. The promotion of human rights is thus cast not merely as a sufficient

[9] Schaffer (n 1) 213–14.
[10] Allen Buchanan and Robert O Keohane, 'The Legitimacy of Global Governance Institutions' (2006) 20(4) Ethics & International Affairs 405.
[11] Petersmann (n 5) 624.
[12] ibid 623.

but also a necessary condition for the legitimacy of global governance institutions, regardless of its particular area of competence.

The strength of Petersmann's claims makes them controversial. It is one thing to assert that global governance institutions like the WTO should respect human rights in the conduct of their governance activities;[13] quite another to claim that '[t]here is no reason why ... the WTO Appellate Body should be less capable than politicized UN bodies, or than the ECJ [European Court of Justice], to protect human rights in the trade policy area'.[14] Similarly, it is one thing to claim that any organization that effectively promotes human rights would be presumptively legitimate;[15] quite another to claim that no institution that *fails* to do so can be legitimate.[16] Within the 'cosmopolitan functionalist' mainstream there is widespread agreement on some version of the former proposition within each pair. However, among those that have set out more developed philosophical accounts of legitimacy beyond the state, there is much less appetite for endorsing the latter. Among the most important of these is that offered by Allen Buchanan and Robert Keohane in 2006. It is in dialogue with this contribution that I will, in what follows, set out my own views on the role that human rights play in securing the legitimacy of global governance.

Buchanan and Keohane start with the concept of 'legitimate governance'. To call a governance institution 'legitimate' is to assert that it has the moral 'right to rule'. Legitimacy assessments are a way of providing support for valuable institutions that strike a middle ground between rational self-interest on one hand, and evaluation as morally optimal on the other. Legitimacy makes moral, and not merely prudential, demands of governance institutions; but its standard is that of moral acceptability rather than full justice. Legitimacy assessments thus make possible coordinated support—and support for the right reasons—for valuable institutions operating under nonideal conditions, including uncertainty and disagreement over the correct standards of global justice.

This much seems widely agreed. Buchanan and Keohane insist that the dominant view of what makes governance legitimate, developed in the context of the state, are too strong for the global level.[17] There are, they claim, two main facets to this view.[18] From the institutional perspective, 'ruling' (or governing) involves promulgating rules, and using coercive force both to secure compliance and to exclude all other governance institutions from operating within a given domain. *Legitimate* governance institutions are morally justified in acting in this manner. From the individual perspective, dominant accounts insist that those subject to legitimate governance have a content-independent moral *obligation* to comply with its rules (ie an obligation that they have regardless of their view on the merits of the rules in question).

Both elements here seem too strong to capture what might be meant by 'legitimate governance' (or the 'right to rule') at the global level.[19] Few global governance institutions even use force to ensure compliance with their rules; even fewer claim a justified monopoly on governance (let alone force) within their domain of competence. And nor do they, generally, even claim to impose a content-independent moral obligation even on those directly

[13] Alston, 'Resisting the Merger and Acquisition' (n 6) 829. As Alston himself notes, this is 'a proposition with which almost any proponent of human rights would be sympathetic'.

[14] Petersmann (n 5) 642.

[15] Recall that Alston's objection was precisely that giving eg the WTO Appellate body competence over human rights questions in the domain of trade policy would result in a failure to genuinely promote human rights.

[16] I will return to the distinction between 'respecting' and 'promoting' human rights in much more detail later.

[17] They suspect—and I agree—that it may also be too strong for the domestic level, but that is beyond the scope of the current essay.

[18] A point further developed by Buchanan in slightly later work.

[19] Buchanan and Keohane (n 10) 411.

subject to their rules (still usually states)—let alone on the individuals who are ultimately affected by them. They thus propose a 'weakening' of the state-based accounts to render them appropriate to global governance. First, 'ruling' is to mean simply 'promulgating rules, and attempting to secure compliance with them by attaching costs to non-compliance and/or benefits to compliance'.[20] Their having the 'right' to rule means, from the institutional perspective, that they are morally justified in so acting. Individuals have strong reasons *not to interfere*, and must change their 'practical attitudes' to legitimate institutions:

> Generally speaking, if an institution is legitimate, then this legitimacy should shape the character of both our responses to the claims it makes on us and the form that our criticisms of it take. We should support or at least refrain from interfering with legitimate institutions ... Judging an institution to be legitimate, if flawed, focuses critical discourse by signaling that the appropriate objective is to reform it, rather than to reject it outright.[21]

Buchanan and Keohane then move on to the standard that global governance institutions must meet to justifiably claim this weakened 'right to rule'. General state consent is rejected as too little;[22] full-blown global democracy as too much.[23] Their proposed 'complex standard' has two parts. The first is a set of substantive criteria, the second a set of epistemic-deliberative virtues, designed to accommodate the facts of moral uncertainty and disagreement about global justice.

The first of the substantive criteria is 'minimal moral acceptability': 'Global governance institutions, like institutions generally, must not persist in committing serious injustices. If they do so, they are not entitled to our support'. Human rights violations are the 'primary instance' of serious injustices. Not just any human rights, however: the facts of moral uncertainty and disagreement mean that we must not require too much in this regard, lest our 'presumptive necessary condition', and hence our standard of legitimacy, become too demanding to be met under current conditions:

> There is disagreement amongst ... theorists of human rights as to exactly what the list of human rights includes and how the content of particular rights is to be filled out. There is agreement, however, that the list includes the rights to physical security, to liberty (understood as at least encompassing freedom from slavery, servitude, and forced occupations), and the right to subsistence. Assuming this is so, we can say at least this much: global governance institutions (like institutions generally) are legitimate only if they do not persist in violations of the least controversial human rights.[24]

The authors acknowledge that this is 'a rather minimal moral requirement for legitimacy' and that we might expect institutions to do better 'as we gain greater clarity about the scope of human rights';[25] but they claim this is the most we can currently demand. They then draw an important distinction between *respecting* human rights on one hand and *promoting* them

[20] ibid 405.
[21] ibid 407.
[22] ibid 413. The consent of non-democratic states 'cannot transfer legitimacy for the simple reason that there is no legitimacy to transfer'. The consent of *democratic* states is, however, presumptively necessary.
[23] ibid 416. '[T]he social and political conditions for democracy are not met at the global level, and there is no reason to think that they will be in the foreseeable future'.
[24] ibid 420.
[25] ibid.

on the other. All legitimate global governance institutions must respect at least these most basic of human rights—a point on which we would find both Petersmann and Alston in agreement.[26] *Pace* Petersmann, however, they deny that legitimacy requires all institutions to promote human rights *even if they have the capacity to do so*. This would only hold if, as well as the capacity to promote human rights, the institution in question has a duty of justice to do so—something that must be established independently.

The other two substantive criteria, 'comparative benefit' and 'institutional integrity', can be dealt with more quickly. The main reason we have global governance institutions is instrumental: they can provide us with certain benefits that we could not otherwise obtain. If a governance institution cannot effectively provide the benefits that justify its existence, then this 'undermines its claim to the right to rule'. Effectiveness here is not *optimal*, but *comparative*: there must not be 'an institutional alternative, providing significantly greater benefits, that is feasible, accessible without excessive transaction costs, and meets the minimal moral acceptability criterion'.[27] The third criterion of 'institutional integrity' requires merely that there not be an 'egregious disparity' between actual institutional performance on one hand, and its own procedures or goals on the other.

These three requirements are not to be viewed as 'necessary conditions *simpliciter*', but merely as 'presumptive' ones. There may be circumstances in which an institution fails to meet one or two but remains legitimate nonetheless. For example, an institution may lack integrity but still do important work in promoting human rights that no alternative institution could achieve. Instead, we are to view the three conditions as 'counting principles', that have their own dimension of weight in legitimacy assessments, with success in one capable of offsetting deficiencies in the others: 'the more of [the substantive conditions] an institution satisfies, and the higher degree to which it satisfies them, the stronger its claim to legitimacy'.[28]

These three presumptively necessary conditions are not yet cumulatively sufficient for institutional legitimacy. They must, in order to meet the problems of 'factual knowledge' and 'moral disagreement and uncertainty',[29] be supplemented by certain 'epistemic-deliberative' virtues. These include 'broad transparency' (making information accessible to external actors) and 'broad accountability' (in which the terms of accountability themselves are up for grabs).[30]

Any global governance institution that enjoys the ongoing consent of democratic states, meets the three substantive criteria, and possesses these 'epistemic virtues' will also sufficiently vindicate—in the absence of even a possible global democracy—the values that underpin the demand for democratic legitimacy at the global level. These values are: 'equal regard for the fundamental interests of all persons'; 'decision-making about the public order through principled, collective deliberation'; and 'mutual respect for persons as beings who are guided by reasons'. As a result, it will be justified in making rules and seeking to ensure compliance with them; and we will all have content-independent moral reasons to support, or at least not interfere with, it as it does so. It will, in short, be legitimate.

[26] Alston, 'Resisting the Merger and Acquisition' (n 6).
[27] Buchanan and Keohane (n 10) 422.
[28] ibid 424.
[29] ibid 425.
[30] ibid 425–29.

6.3 Conceptualizing 'Legitimate Governance'

Let's look again at the multifaceted 'weakening' to the dominant view that Buchanan and Keohane propose:

> Legitimacy in the case of global governance institutions, then, is the right to rule, understood to mean both that institutional agents are morally justified in making rules and attempting to secure compliance with them and that people subject to those rules have moral, content-independent reasons to follow them and/or to not interfere with others' compliance with them.[31]

This looks, at first glance, like a plausible set of moves, producing a conception more appropriate to governance at the global level. 'Governing' is weakened by removing both coercion and exclusivity, referring only to rule-making and attempting to secure compliance. The entitlement claimed by institutions is weakened from a moral duty-creating power to a 'justification' (or permission) to 'govern' in the aforementioned sense; and the normative upshot of governance for the governed is weakened both in kind (it is no longer duties or obligations that are created, but mere reasons) and in content (the reason is now 'to comply, or at least to not interfere'). Upon closer inspection, however, each move begins to appear problematically ad hoc. Being clear about why will be crucial to the arguments that follow.

6.3.1. What is 'Governance'?

Buchanan and Keohane are clearly right that the correct concept of 'governance' at the global level cannot require either coercion or a demand for exclusivity. We cannot, however, simply remove these requirements and call what remains 'governance'. One role they are playing in the dominant view is to distinguish the kind of *public* governance of interest to us from the activities of clubs, corporations, and other private associations. Many if not most of these will make rules, and 'attach costs to non-compliance and/or benefits to compliance'. Yet this does not entitle us to view them as 'ruling', or as claiming the 'right' to do so.

Nor can the weakened 'normative upshot' rescue this situation—such that only legitimate *governance* would generate the requisite content-independent reasons 'to comply, or at least not interfere'. Indeed, a similar criticism applies here. The distinction between 'obligations' and 'reasons' in this context, when it is drawn at all,[32] is drawn on the basis of the distinctive nature of authoritative directives.[33] The creation of mere 'content-independent reasons' to

[31] ibid 411.

[32] Many discussions of the 'obligation to obey' the law seem to gloss over the distinction between content-independent reasons and duties. For example, MBE Smith, 'Is There a Prima Facie Obligation to Obey the Law?' (1973) 82(5) Yale Law Journal 950.

[33] Joseph Raz, 'The Obligation to Obey the Law' in Joseph Raz (ed), *The Authority of Law: Essays on Law and Morality* (2nd edn, OUP 2009) 234–35. Raz claims that 'an action is obligatory (p.235) only if it is required by a protected reason which does not derive merely from the fact that adherence to it facilitates realization of the agent's goals ... [F]or most people an obligation to obey the law ... means something far more demanding than a prima facie reason. It means a peremptory reason best explained in keeping with my general analysis of obligation, as a categorical protected reason'.

The extent to which Buchanan endorses this is not fully clear. Elsewhere, he assumes that the content-independent reasons to comply/not interfere are 'substantial' *because* they are 'peremptory', where the latter term means 'ruling out certain reasons for not complying *ab initio*' (such as compliance being to our personal disadvantage). This seems less strong than the Razian version, but it is hard to be sure; and it is also difficult to see what, in Buchanan's account, is the particular feature of legitimate governance that grounds reasons with this feature; Allen

comply is insufficiently determinative, because an individual or institution can have the power to create *these* without having, or claiming, any entitlement to govern.[34] Likewise, we will often have content-independent reasons not to interfere with things that cannot plausibly be understood as 'governance' of any sort. So the *authority-individuating* aspect of the normative upshot for the governed—that moral reasons of a particular *kind* are created—is lost.

To the extent that we can extract a definition of 'governance' from the Buchanan and Keohane account, then, it seems over inclusive. With its exclusive focus on rule-making (and compliance securing), however, it is also under inclusive. It takes no account of the fact that, increasingly, things like standard setting and even mere data collection and publication are important modalities of global governance.[35] Not all rule-makers govern; and not all governors make rules. Our definition of 'governance' must reflect this.

To say this is not to criticize Buchanan and Keohane; it was never their goal to define 'governance' beyond the state. Yet the task remains an important one, even if I can do no more than gesture at a way forward here. In other work, Buchanan has suggested limiting the focus to 'international law-making institutions'.[36] This would certainly help refocus on the *public* element of governance that is lost in reference to mere 'rule-making'. But it would again be under inclusive: as Raz pointed out some forty years ago, even state governments increasingly govern in ways that do not involve the exercise of legal authority, for example, through use of their economic muscle to change or entrench certain behaviours.[37] Unlike lawmaking (or interpreting, or applying), such activities become public governance due to the nature of the *actor*, rather than the *action*.

This suggests a possible way forward. First, we should stop talking about 'authority' and 'governance' beyond the state as if these were the same thing. 'Governance' should instead be recognized as the more extensive category, incorporating exercises of authority and much else besides. Were we to abandon completely talk of 'ruling' in the context of legitimate global governance, we would rid ourselves of much unhelpful baggage at no cost. We should then conceive of 'governance' as action aimed at influencing the actions of others that is either public in nature (such as making or applying the law, or perhaps the provision of certain basic services) or carried out by a public institution. When we see that the latter can delegate aspects of their governance activities to other actors, public or private, and formally or informally, we can make progress towards a conception that captures the varied modalities of contemporary global governance.[38]

Buchanan, 'The Legitimacy of International Law' in Samantha Besson and John Tasioulas (eds), *The Philosophy of International Law* (OUP 2010) 83–84.

[34] For example, a friend's request for a favour arguably creates content-independent moral reasons to do as requested.

[35] For example, Kevin E Davis, Benedict Kingsbury, and Sally Engle Merry, 'Indicators as a Technology of Global Governance: Indicators' (2012) 46 Law & Society Review 71.

[36] See generally Buchanan (n 33). We would presumably need to expand this to include law-applying and (authoritative) law-interpreting institutions.

[37] Joseph Raz, 'The Obligation to Obey: Tradition and Renewal' in Joseph Raz, *Ethics in the Public Domain: Essays in the Morality of Law and Politics* (Rev edn, repr, Clarendon Press 1995) 346.

[38] Thus, for example, a private certification scheme might come to be used as a standard in government procurement decisions, and in doing so become a 'public' form of governance that ought to be subject to corresponding standards of legitimacy, for example, Errol Meidinger, 'The Administrative Law of Global Private-Public Regulation: The Case of Forestry' (2006) 17 European Journal of International Law 47.

6.3.2. What is 'Legitimate' Governance?

Our conception of 'governance' has important implications for the nature of the 'right' to govern that legitimate institutions have. As Raz noted, when governors govern without authority, they 'can do so justly as well as unjustly'.[39] They can also, we might add, do so legitimately as well as illegitimately. But then we cannot understand 'legitimate' governance as consisting in the existence of a moral duty-creating power, as we might 'legitimate' authority. It makes no sense to understand the legitimacy of governance generally by reference to the existence of a power that need not even be claimed.

We should, then, as Buchanan and Keohane propose, understand this 'entitlement' in terms of a moral justification or permission. Doing so gives us a conception of legitimacy that can be fully general across types of governance (and has the additional benefit of being generalizable to almost all our uses of the term 'legitimacy' in other contexts).[40] Nor does this commit us to any controversial view on the nature of authority. It is usually—wrongly—thought that the 'permissibility-based' and 'power-based' accounts are mutually exclusive. In fact, they can be complementary. Exercising a power—moral or otherwise—is an *action*; and we can ask of any action whether or not it is morally permitted. We can have moral powers without being permitted to exercise them.[41] So we can affirm a permission-based account of legitimacy while remaining agnostic on whether the correct conception of legitimate *authority* requires the permissible exercise of a moral duty-creating power. If there are global governance institutions that exercise moral authority of this sort—I leave this open—they do so legitimately when they do so permissibly.

The proposed weakening of the normative upshot of this entitlement for the governed is more puzzling. On the dominant view, the creation of content-independent, peremptory reasons for action is conceptually tied to the entitlement justifiably claimed by legitimate authorities. It is *because* authorities claim the power to create moral duties for their subjects, and legitimate authorities do so truthfully, that legitimacy has the normative upshot of creating moral reasons for the governed.[42] It is not enough to simply 'weaken' both sides of this equation, as Buchanan and Keohane do; we must ensure that the relations between them continue to obtain. But when we 'weaken' the power-based account to a permissibility-based one, we lose the most familiar reason for conceiving of legitimate governance in terms of the new moral reasons it creates for the governed. That an action is permissible does not entail that anybody else has reasons not to interfere.

Buchanan and Keohane do offer an independent argument in support of this criterion. Legitimate institutions satisfy the 'comparative benefit' criterion; they thus produce goods that could not be otherwise produced. This requires coordination, which gives those to whom its rules are addressed a content-independent reason to comply, and everybody else a content-independent reason not to interfere.[43] As a result, that an institution is

[39] Raz, 'The Obligation to Obey: Tradition and Renewal' (n 37) 346.

[40] See Euan MacDonald, 'Legitimacy as Liberty' (unpublished, 2020) for an argument to this effect.

[41] We might, for example, make a valid promise that we ought, morally, not to have made. In such cases, we have exercised our power, but impermissibly. Tasioulas misses this possibility in his response to Buchanan when he says 'it is not obvious what justified *governing* could be other than the issuing of directives that are genuinely content-independent reasons for action'. John Tasioulas, 'The Legitimacy of International Law' in Besson and Tasioulas (n 33) 97, 99.

[42] A John Simmons, 'Justification and Legitimacy' (1999) 109 Ethics 739, 749. Simmons is typical: 'State legitimacy... includes an exclusive power over subjects to impose duties and enforce them coercively, which correlates with obligations on others to refrain from these tasks. It also includes a right, held against subjects, to be obeyed.'

[43] It is not clear that the latter reason is 'content independent', at least in the same sense as the former.

legitimate if flawed means that the 'appropriate objective is to reform it, rather than to reject it outright'.[44]

Even assuming that we are dealing with 'objective' public goods—goods that any reasonable person would value—there are two problems here. First, from the fact that a governance body produces such goods, it does not follow that *every* governance action it takes plays a role in doing so. It is difficult to see—without further argument—why a moral reason not to interfere with the production of a public good would extend to governance actions that are not plausibly playing that role. Second, where the action in question *is* contributing to the production of the good in question, it is difficult to see why the existence of my reason not to interfere should be dependent upon institutional legitimacy in any way. Imagine, for example, a governance body that effectively guarantees international peace; but commits serious violations of human rights in the process. Imagine further that these rights violations are sufficiently serious to render the institution illegitimate overall. Intuitively, although interference may even be morally required, I still have *some* reason not to; the fact that I will thereby be undermining world peace makes some kind of regret—often a marker of defeated reasons—seem appropriate. But if *this* is right, then the generation of reasons not to interfere is conceptually independent of legitimacy judgments.

Of course, it is plausible that there will often—perhaps even usually—be moral reasons not to interfere with legitimate governance. I do not think that Buchanan and Keohane's argument can show more than this. But this shows, at best, that the presence of reasons not to interfere is a typical feature of legitimate governance; not that it is a conceptually necessary one. There is no way to infer the latter from the former. Other accounts that try to tie political legitimacy into duties of non-interference, which proceed by way of examples in which such a duty plausibly arises and conclude that its presence is thus necessary for legitimacy, seem to make this mistake; a sort of conceptual variant of the *post hoc ergo propter hoc* fallacy.[45]

There are thus good reasons to reject Buchanan and Keohane's 'weakened' version of the normative upshot of legitimate governance in favour of an even weaker one: that the legitimacy of governance is exhausted by the question of its permissibility, and thus does not *entail* the creation of any new reasons for action for the governed. As we will see, from this perspective accounting for the fact that reasons of non-interference will nonetheless typically accompany legitimate governance is a relatively straightforward matter.

6.3.3. Legitimacy, Permissions, and Reasons

The terms 'permission', 'justification' (or 'justification-right'), and 'liberty' are, in the literature on legitimacy, often used interchangeably. This is an artefact of conceiving of legitimate governance in terms of an 'entitlement' to govern. It is not without risks. For while there is a sense in which 'justified' and 'permissible' action is synonymous, and a sense in which a 'permission' can be equated to a 'liberty-right', they are not the same sense. The following from Buchanan is instructive:

[44] Buchanan and Keohane (n 10) 407.

[45] For example, William A Edmundson, 'Legitimate Authority without Political Obligation' (1998) 17 Law and Philosophy 43.

> 'Justified' in the phrase 'being justified in governing' is itself ambiguous between (a) having a liberty-right to govern, that is, it being morally permissible to govern; and (b) there being good moral reasons in favour of (the institution's) governing.[46]

Buchanan here understates the ambiguity between 'liberty-right' and 'permissibility'; and overstates it between 'permissibility' and 'there being good moral reasons in favour'. Note, first, that a 'liberty-right' is something that an individual *agent* possesses; while 'permissibility' is a feature of *action*. Second, after Hohfeld it is natural for us to think of liberty rights as *directional* (the absence of a directed duty not to take the action in question). But we often use 'permissibility' to refer to an *overall* judgment: that *it is not the case that the action in question ought not to be taken*. On the assumption that directed duties create only *pro tanto* reasons (reasons that *support*, but do not determine, overall ought claims), the difference between 'liberty rights' and 'permissibility' is clear: we might easily have a liberty-right to do something relative to some individual, but it may remain impermissible overall. On the assumption that directed duties do not exhaust the field of moral reasons, an action might be impermissible even though we have a liberty-right to take it relative to *everybody*. Likewise, the fact that we owe someone—even many people—a duty not to take an action (ie we have, relative to them, no liberty-right to take it) does not determine its impermissibility overall.

My proposal is that we understand legitimacy in terms of permissibility, and permissibility in terms of overall 'not-the-case-that-ought-not'. An action, therefore, is legitimate if and only if it is permissible; and it is permissible if and only if it is not the case that it ought not to be taken. By extension, an action is *il*legitimate if and only if it ought not to be taken (ie if we are required not to take it). On the grounds that an action's being morally required entails that it is permissible (ie if we ought to take it then it is not the case we ought *not* to take it), the illegitimacy of an action entails the legitimacy of not taking it.

Clarifying this has several advantages, even in Buchanan and Keohane's own terms. First, it gives us a straightforward account of the relation between moral reasons and legitimacy judgments. A moral reason is a fact that supports—that is, that has some independent weight in determining the truth of—some 'ought' claim. A reason for action supports some ought claim—positive or negative—about whether an action ought to be taken. Any reason *for* an action supports the claim that it is required (ie that it ought to be taken); and, by entailment, that it is permissible. Any reason for an action thus supports the claim that it is legitimate. Any reason against the action supports the claim that it is *im*permissible, hence illegitimate. We can thus call the reasons in favour of any action 'legitimacy reasons' with regard to that action; and those against it 'illegitimacy reasons'.[47] An action is permissible (hence legitimate) if and only if the overall valence of the set of applicable reasons is either neutral[48] or positive (in the former case, it is optional, meaning that either doing it or not doing it is permissible; in the latter case, it is required). An action is impermissible (hence illegitimate) if and only if the overall valence of the set of applicable reasons is negative.

[46] Buchanan 'The Legitimacy of International Law' (n 33) 83.

[47] The class of 'legitimacy reasons' is, I think, broader than 'reasons for an action'. In particular there exist reasons that support 'not-the-case-that-ought' claims directly and only, and not by entailment by also supporting 'ought not' claims. This idea has proved surprisingly hard to articulate, and impossible by means of our standard 'balancing' metaphor for reasons. Luís Duarte d'Almeida and I have tried to account for this new class of reason in Euan MacDonald and Luís Duarte d'Almeida '*Contra Tantum* Reasons' (unpublished, 2020).

[48] For example, if the reasons for and against are equally balanced; or if there are no applicable reasons in play at all.

This helps us with the puzzle of the relationship between legitimacy and justice highlighted by Buchanan and Keohane: that 'legitimacy' is a distinct and less demanding standard than 'full justice', but that some things are illegitimate precisely because they are seriously unjust. That an action would be unjust is a reason against taking it—an illegitimacy reason. If the injustice is serious enough, it will be near impossible for there to be competing reasons that could offset this sufficiently to return the overall valence of the set of applicable reasons to neutral or positive. But on the assumption that not all reasons against an action are reasons of injustice, we readily see how an action might be just but illegitimate; likewise, on the assumption that not all positively valenced reasons are reasons of justice, we can see how an action might be (somewhat) unjust, but remain legitimate.

This is why Buchanan overstates the ambiguity between 'permissibility' and 'good moral reasons in favour': the latter is not a distinct sense of 'justification', but merely one way in which an action can come to be permissible overall. This helps us account for the fact that individuals will often, but not always, have a reason not to interfere with legitimate governance. Governance actions will often be actions that the institution *ought*, morally, to take. In such cases their permissibility (hence legitimacy) is entailed by this requirement. It seems plausible that we always have a *pro tanto* moral reason not to interfere with an institution (indeed, with anybody) doing something that they are morally required to do. Thus, any legitimate governance action that is morally required will give rise to such reasons; any that is merely morally optional, however, will not. And these will be ordinary reasons. They will not be 'content-independent' in any obvious way. And I can see no reason why they would have 'a privileged status vis-à-vis our reasons for acting'.[49]

Actions can be permissible or impermissible. Institutions cannot. Adopting the approach half-endorsed by Buchanan and Keohane, and fully here, means taking the notion of 'legitimate action', and not that of the 'legitimate institution', as primary.[50] A 'legitimate institution' is an institution that is, in general, permitted to take the actions that it takes (or claims to be permitted to take). This gives us a straightforward way of making sense of the uncontroversial idea that 'legitimate institutions can sometimes act illegitimately', deploying the *same sense* of 'legitimacy' in each use. If this is right, then it is unhelpful to think of legitimacy in terms of an 'entitlement' at all; to do so shifts focus away from the action and back to certain features of the actor, and risks confusing overall permissibility with directed liberties. Talking of legitimate governance in terms of a 'right to rule' thus reveals itself to be misleading pretty much in its entirety.

6.4 The Normative Role of Human Rights

These clarifications help us see that Buchanan and Keohane's heavy circumscription of the list of human rights currently relevant to legitimacy judgments is unwarranted; and that their claim that respect for human rights can function as a 'counting principle' in such judgments is mistaken.

[49] Buchanan (n 33) 83.

[50] Buchanan seems to oscillate on this point. In one article, he claims that 'political legitimacy is an agent-justification notion, having to do only with the normative sufficiency of the justification for the act of imposing rules'; Allen Buchanan, 'Political Legitimacy and Democracy' (2002) 112 Ethics 689, 695; but elsewhere he insists on 'the primacy of institutional legitimacy', such that 'international laws are legitimate only if the institutions that make them are legitimate'; Buchanan (n 33) 79–80.

The distinction they draw between 'respecting' and 'promoting' human rights is an important one. To fix ideas, I will say that an institution *respects* human rights when it is not responsible for an increase in the number of human rights violations in the world. I will say it *promotes* human rights when it is responsible for a decrease in the number of human rights violations in the world. And I will assume that promoting human rights is good, and failing to respect them is bad.

6.4.1. Reasons or Conditions?

Buchanan and Keohane, like most authors in the field, conceive of legitimacy as an entitlement: something that certain kinds of institutions possess. Their focus is thus on the *status* of the institution *qua* right holder. The inquiry then naturally becomes one into the conditions, necessary and sufficient, for acquiring that status.

Merely respecting human rights—even fully respecting all human rights—cannot be a sufficient condition of institutional legitimacy. A governance institution must be instrumentally justified (ie it must actually produce the benefits for which it was established) if it is to be legitimate. And clearly not all violations of just any human right are sufficient to render a governance institution illegitimate, even presumptively so. Violations of human rights sufficiently serious to rise to this level are in; those that aren't are out. As the latter are neither necessary nor sufficient conditions of legitimacy, there is no normative role for them to play—or so the thought seems to be.

Buchanan and Keohane are correct that some, but not all, human rights violations are so serious as to render a governance institution presumptively illegitimate. But necessary and sufficient conditions—even 'presumptive' ones—are somewhat blunt instruments. And while it may be normal to think in these terms when inquiring into the acquisition of an individual or institutional status (such as 'right holder'), it is not at all our natural way of thinking about justified—permissible—*action*. In the latter case, we usually think instead of the balance of applicable reasons. A reason can be normatively significant—even determinative, in context—without ever rising to the level of a presumptively necessary or sufficient condition of permissibility in the abstract.

Fully endorsing a permissibility-based approach helps us both retain what is plausible in Buchanan and Keohane's proposal and to see where they go wrong. That a governance action would violate human rights is a reason against it, an illegitimacy reason. That it would do so seriously is a weighty illegitimacy reason, unlikely to be outweighed by positively valenced legitimacy reasons. Because a claim of 'institutional legitimacy' is shorthand for judgments of the permissibility of institutional action, even a single very serious violation of human rights could undermine that claim. (It seems plausible, for instance, that a very serious violation of a duty in some institutional role could render it morally impermissible for an individual to continue in that role, or to perform it again in the future.) The absence of very serious violations of human rights can thus be viewed as a presumptively necessary condition of legitimacy, because it is hard to imagine a scenario in which such violations could be offset by sufficiently strong legitimacy reasons.

We can even grant that Buchanan and Keohane's truncated list of the most important rights are the only ones that rise to this level. None of this means that those human rights violations that we *can* imagine being offset are therefore irrelevant. Note first that Buchanan and Keohane overstate the degree of disagreement on the broader set of human rights. Certainly, there is much disagreement about the full extent of what each of these covers, and how they ought to be balanced with competing considerations. But this fact does not preclude there being widespread agreement both that a broader set of rights exist, and that certain actions would be clear violations of them. All violations of human rights are illegitimacy reasons; and any single violation, however trivial, will be sufficient to render an action illegitimate if the set of applicable legitimacy reasons is not sufficiently strong to offset it. And were most a governance institution's actions to be of this type—rendered illegitimate by relatively trivial but undefeated illegitimacy reasons—we would have no reason to think the institution itself legitimate.

Fully endorsing the permissibility-based account shifts our focus from agent to action, and from necessary and sufficient conditions to applicable reasons. When we do so, we see that we ought not to limit the set of 'legitimacy-relevant' human rights in the manner proposed.

6.4.2. Reasons and Deniers

A shift in focus from 'conditions' to 'reasons' is already incipient in the Buchanan and Keohane approach. The suggestion that their substantive criteria are also 'counting principles' speaks to a dimension of *weight* that seems to belong to the realm of reasons, and not that of necessary conditions.

That some of their criteria have this feature does seem right. Take 'comparative benefit'. It is plausible to think that the more of a public good is secured by the actions of a global governance body or the more important the good in question, the greater the legitimacy of the institution. But can human rights, with their relevance limited in the manner that Buchanan and Keohane propose, play this role? Recall that we are here dealing with 'minimal moral acceptability', understood as respecting (ie not violating) the most basic of human rights. It is difficult to see how the mere fact that a global governance institution doesn't violate very basic human rights could be thought to count in its favour. Certainly, if it violated human rights, this would count against it. And arguably, if it promoted human rights (rather than merely respecting them), then this would count in its favour. But the mere absence of a bad-making feature is not a good-making feature.

Again, thinking in terms of reasons makes the point clearer. Reasons have this offsetting, balancing feature—we can weigh a reason for a particular action against a whole set of reasons against it and find the action justified overall, if the initial reason is strong enough. But it is a truth about reasons in general that the absence of a reason against something is not itself a reason for it. So were an ice cream to taste of engine oil,[51] that would be a reason against my eating it. But the fact that it doesn't taste of engine oil is not a reason *for* me to eat it. It should not have positive weight in my deliberations; it merely indicates the absence of something that would—if present—have had negative weight. It would be absurd for me to think of balancing my reasons not to eat ice cream (such as the fact that it will cause me to gain weight) against the fact that it doesn't taste of engine oil if trying to decide whether I am justified in eating it.

In much the same way, the fact that a global governance body achieves some minimum standard of moral acceptability cannot be used to offset legitimacy deficiencies elsewhere. Indeed, the same is true even of maximal respect for all human rights. The absence of an

[51] On this, see generally Jonathan Dancy, *Ethics without Principles* (OUP 2004) 44–45.

illegitimacy reason is not a legitimacy reason. We need a further term to refer to those facts about a governance body's actions that pick out the absence of features that would otherwise contribute to its illegitimacy. I propose that we call these *illegitimacy deniers*, to keep them distinct from legitimacy reasons. Both are important in the overall legitimacy calculus, but play different normative roles: the former, such as respecting human rights, operate to remove considerations that would otherwise have negative weight; the latter, including promoting human rights, contribute positive weight of their own.

This gives us a further reason to concur with Buchanan and Keohane, *contra* Petersmann, that the *promotion* of human rights is not in general necessary for institutional legitimacy. Failure to promote human rights—an absence of a legitimacy reason—is not an illegitimacy reason. That a governance institution fully respects human rights is enough to keep its legitimacy slate clean in this regard; and this alone will suffice for its legitimacy *in the absence of further illegitimacy reasons*. Of course, in the current climate, further illegitimacy reasons are not hard to come by. But there is one, I think, that everyone has missed.

6.5 The Consent of the Governed

According to Buchanan and Keohane, that a governance institution meets their 'complex standard' suffices for its legitimacy; in part because, although 'global democracy' is unfeasible, the standard also serves key democratic values. I think it fails to serve perhaps the most important democratic value of all; and that, as a result, their claim that the '[s]atisfaction of the minimal moral acceptability condition rules out the more serious moral objections'[52] that might undermine institutional legitimacy is false. The value I have in mind speaks to the importance of individual consent—actual consent—to legitimate governance.

There are two main objections to treating the actual consent of individuals as relevant to the legitimacy of global governance institutions in general. The first is specific to the global setting: states, not individuals, are the subjects of global governance. The second generalizes to all governance and is the reason why few scholars today take actual consent to be important to its legitimacy: almost nobody actually consents.[53] I will consider each in turn.

6.5.1. Who are 'the Governed'?

Individual attitudes feature in two ways in Buchanan and Keohane's account. First, they are an important consequence of legitimacy judgments. A main reason for an institution to secure legitimacy is to change individuals' 'practical attitudes' towards it. Second, they have a role—albeit a highly limited one—in enabling an institution to be legitimate:

> It is important not only that global governance institutions be legitimate, but that they be perceived to be legitimate. The perception of legitimacy matters, because, in a democratic era, multilateral institutions will only thrive if they are viewed as legitimate by democratic publics. If one is unclear about the appropriate standards of legitimacy or if unrealistically

[52] Buchanan and Keohane (n 10) 436.

[53] Those that *do* still take it to be important tend to conclude on this basis that there is little or no legitimate governance. For example, A John Simmons, 'The Anarchist Position: A Reply to Klosko and Senor' (1987) 16 Philosophy and Public Affairs 269:'There are no morally legitimate states.'

> demanding standards are assumed, then public support for global governance institutions may be undermined and their effectiveness in providing valuable goods may be impaired.[54]

This is a common view. But there is something weird about it. On one hand, the legitimacy crisis in global governance is understood, in part, in democratic terms: the 'distance' between global decision-making and democratic publics is identified as problematic, the consent of democratic states is viewed as necessary, and it is held to be important that our legitimacy standard vindicate key democratic values. It is, moreover, acknowledged that global governance impacts hugely on individual interests. And yet the normative significance of the actual attitudes of actual individuals is reduced to a whisper. Negative attitudes register only as the possibility that obstructive individuals might make it difficult for a governance body to effectively pursue its goals, and thus meet the efficacy threshold of legitimacy. It is hard to square this commitment to 'democratic values' on one hand with the reduction of individual attitudes to 'barrier to effective operation' on the other. Surely one important thought underpinning democratic legitimacy is that actual individual attitudes *matter*, in some direct and robust way, to the legitimacy of governance.

The common view is justified on the basis that states, not individuals, are the subjects of global governance. But there are two reasons to reject this. The first follows from our definition of governance. While it may be true that states are (usually) the subjects of international *law*, we have no reason to limit our conception of governance to exercises of legal authority—or of 'the governed' to the formal subjects of legal authority. The second follows from the nature of the governance relation itself. It is *transitive*, such that, if A governs B, and in doing so requires B to govern C, we can say that A has governed C. So, when a global governance institution requires states to govern their citizens in a particular way, the individual citizens have been governed by the institution.

To see this, take the most commonly cited example—usually held to be exceptional—of a global body governing individuals: the listing mechanism of the UN '1267' Sanctions Committee. This Committee lists actors, including individuals, who are held to be involved in terrorism, and states are required to ensure that certain restrictions (on travel, on access to funds) apply to such individuals. The legitimacy of this governance has been widely held to require the establishment of *individual* redress mechanisms at the global level; something that has, to an extent, occurred.[55] But look at what happens formally here: the UN Security Council places certain obligations on states, who can respond then by placing further obligations (including obligations not to exercise contractual powers) on other actors (airlines, banks). The impact on the interests of the listed individuals takes place across a range of formal governance relations between different legal orders; and, crucially, the legal entitlements of the listed individuals, even under the state legal order, *need not change at all* for the dramatic impact on their interests to take effect.[56]

To view such individuals as globally governed is to concede both that governance need not require an exercise of legal authority over the governed, and that the governance relation is transitive in nature. And if these points are conceded, we lose our justification for thinking

[54] Buchanan and Keohane (n 10) 407.

[55] For a recent discussion, see Nadeshda Jayakody, 'Refining United Nations Security Council Targeted Sanctions: "Proportionality" as a Way Forward for Human Rights Protection' (2018) 29 Security and Human Rights 90.

[56] Generally speaking, placing actors under a duty not to do business with a particular individual need not result in a change in that individual's formal entitlements—at least so far as these can be captured in Hohfeldian positions. But it would be hard to argue that such individuals have not been 'governed'.

of things like the listing mechanism as exceptional, given the widely acknowledged impact that global governance more generally has on individual interests. Global governance bodies *typically* govern individuals. This explains our democratic concerns for their legitimacy in the first place.

6.5.2. The 'Nobody Consents' Objection

If individuals are globally governed, and the consent of the governed matters to the legitimacy of governance, then individual consent matters to the legitimacy of global governance. If so—the objection may run—then all global governance is illegitimate, because pretty much nobody actually consents to it. This objection has been around (at least) since Hume; and—anarchists aside—is widely taken to be fatal to consent-based approaches to legitimacy. 'Actual consent' is viewed as too strong a standard for democratic legitimacy *within the state*; and state-based standards as too strong for the global realm. Tying the legitimacy of global governance in any way to the actual consent of individuals is thus a non-starter.

But not so fast. There are certain elements to the rejection of consent in the state context that—if what I have argued is correct—do not apply here. First, the debate normally centres on whether consent is a necessary condition of legitimacy. I agree that it is not; to do so would give every individual a legitimacy veto. But I have argued that we must move beyond the 'necessary/sufficient condition or bust' model of normative significance. The fact that an individual does not consent to his or her governance can be viewed as an illegitimacy reason even if it is not sufficiently strong to amount to a necessary condition, 'presumptive' or otherwise. An institution can legitimately govern without the consent of many—perhaps even all—if the other applicable legitimacy reasons are strong enough to offset this.

Second, we must look at the question to which 'consent' has been offered as an answer. The question of legitimate governance within the state has been thought by most to be closely linked to the question of political obligation. 'Consent' is the suggested answer to the question of how we, as autonomous agents, can become *bound* to do as another says. Consent of this sort is understood as a form of promising or contracting. It is held to require some kind of *performative element*, some explicit act of self-binding. This is plausible; I cannot create moral duties for myself just by adopting some mental state. Since few people make this kind of performance in relation to the institutions that govern them, few people actually consent to their governance.

But we are no longer interested in governance as the creation of moral duties. We are interested in governance as permissible action. And there is another model of consent; a model concerned not with the role of consent in the creation of duties, but with the part it plays in making permissible actions that would otherwise be impermissible. Its paradigm is not consent as contract, but rather consent to sex.

The literature on the latter is divided on whether consent to sex requires a performative element, or whether a mental state alone can be 'morally transformative'.[57] Elsewhere, I have defended in detail a version of the latter view.[58] There, I argue that consent should be

[57] Amongst those who propose a 'performative' view, see, for example, Alan Wertheimer, *Consent to Sexual Relations* (CUP 2003); for an opposing view see, for example, Heidi M Hurd, 'The Moral Magic of Consent' (1996) 2 Legal Theory 121.

[58] Euan MacDonald, 'Sex and the City' (unpublished, 2020). My claim is not that a mere mental state suffices for 'permissibility' in the case of sex; only that it is enough to change the applicable reasons for action.

understood as an overall desire: a desire that the individual in question not owe us a duty not to take the action in question (in circumstances in which *not* wanting this would be sufficient to trigger the duty not to act). I further argue that 'consent' of this sort should not be understood as the exercise of a moral power of authorization, which also plausibly requires a performative element.[59] So 'consent to sex' is importantly different from 'consent to waive a duty to pay monies owed', even though both have a part to play in making permissible the otherwise impermissible.[60] Authorization is an *action*, and mental states are not actions. In the former case, on the other hand, the mental state is merely one of the background conditions necessary to trigger the reason in question. There is nothing untoward or mysterious about mental states like desires playing *this* normative role. I cannot rehearse the arguments for these claims here. But note that all that is needed to turn the 'no actual consenters' objection is that *some version* of the claim that morally transformative consent consists in a mental state of the consenter succeeds.

Consent to sex is the paradigm, but it does not exhaust the field. In fact, consent of this sort is far more common, and more important to our everyday lives, than is consent-as-contract.[61] It does not create reasons for the consenter to perform the action in question; rather, it removes reasons for others *not* to. The strength of these reasons can vary from effectively necessary conditions of permissibility (in the case of sex) to the largely trivial, depending on the act in question. In the terms I have proposed here, consent of this sort is thus an *illegitimacy denier*. This makes the *absence of consent* an illegitimacy reason.

This is how consent thus comes into the permissibility-based theory of legitimate governance: there is *a moral reason not to govern someone without their consent*.[62] This reason is triggered by the actual attitude that individuals have to their governance. No performance is needed, as the consenter is neither creating duties for themselves, nor waiving them for others. Individually, this reason is perhaps not very strong, and can be readily outweighed by countervailing legitimacy reasons. The greater the set of non-consenting individuals, and the higher the intensity of their non-consent, the harder it will be to outweigh.

When they claim that we should seek to secure institutional legitimacy in order to change individual attitudes, Buchanan and Keohane get the relationship between individual attitudes and institutional legitimacy precisely backwards. Rather, we should seek to change individual attitudes in order to secure institutional legitimacy.

6.5.3. Consent and Human Rights

If this is right, Buchanan and Keohane are wrong that meeting their complex standard suffices for institutional legitimacy. There may be global governance institutions that meet this standard but remain illegitimate because they do not command the consent of the

[59] Tom Dougherty, 'Yes Means Yes: Consent as Communication:' (2015) 43 Philosophy & Public Affairs 224.

[60] A might have a duty to pay B £50. B can consent to waive this right, releasing A from their duty and authorizing non-payment. But A's duty does not seem to be well-described as a 'duty-to-pay-B-£50-unless-B-authorizes-nonpayment' (ie the power to waive is not part of the content of the duty itself). Contrast the case of sex: it does not seem plausible that A has a general duty-not-to-have-sex-with-B, which B can then waive in an analogous manner. Rather, A has a duty-not-to-have-sex-with-B-without-B's-consent. Here, consent *is* plausibly part of the content of the duty itself. And while the former right can—usually—be waived, the latter cannot be.

[61] In Hurd's well-known formulation, consent of this sort 'turns a trespass into a dinner party; a battery into a handshake; a theft into a gift; an invasion of privacy into an intimate moment'; Hurd (n 57) 123.

[62] This is just to say that non-consensual governance bears a higher burden of justification than does consensual governance.

individuals that they ultimately govern. Indeed, the view that there is a 'legitimacy crisis' in global governance *in general* might be mistaken. The degree of legitimacy of each global governance institution will depend, in significant degree, on the general level of individual consent towards it. It seems plausible that different global governance institutions currently enjoy varying levels of individual consent, in the sense outlined earlier. This is an empirical question with normative implications. Maybe some aren't in crisis at all.

A strong showing in the 'comparative benefit' criterion could be used to offset an absence of individual non-consent. Respect for human rights, however, cannot. The inverse also holds: as consent and respect for human rights are both illegitimacy deniers, neither can be used to offset deficiencies in the other. Of course, if a failure—even a perceived failure—to respect human rights was *causing* a lack of individual consent, then rectifying the former ought to help with the latter.

The *promotion* of human rights could be used to offset a lack of individual consent. Indeed, under certain circumstances it might be unreasonable for individuals *not* to consent to an institution that did so successfully. Arguably, this would have the effect of weakening the strength of the illegitimacy reason created by their non-consent.[63] But as a legitimacy-improving strategy, this path seems fraught with danger. First, there is the risk, emphasized by Alston, that any institution that states were willing to empower in this way would promote 'human rights' in name only. This would not only undermine the legitimizing force of human rights; it also carries the further risk that, with the right publicity, *it might work*: that individuals might be persuaded to consent on the false belief that genuine human rights were being effectively promoted. This would have the perverse effect of genuinely improving moral legitimacy (by removing an illegitimacy reason) *but for bad moral reasons* (a false belief of moral progress, and the undermining of human rights).

Even if such an institution *did* successfully promote at least a permissible interpretation of human rights, there is still significant risk. For empowering global institutions that lack consent to rule on highly disputed questions of morality is likely only to increase both the number of non-consenters and the intensity of their non-consent; and thus increase the strength of the set of applicable illegitimacy reasons. Nor is promoting a permissible interpretation of human rights sufficient to attenuate the non-consent in the manner suggested earlier. Only an interpretation that it was unreasonable *not* to endorse—a much higher bar—would have that effect. In such cases, the treatment could end up as bad, if not worse, than the cure. Promoting human rights is not a straightforward solution to the problem of individual non-consent to global governance. Merely respecting them is no solution at all.

[63] Dancy (n 51) 42. Unreasonableness would thus function as what Dancy has called an 'attenuator': a fact that is not itself a reason, but operates to weaken other reasons in play.

7
Democracy and Democracies

*Henry J Steiner**

7.1 Introduction

'How would you briefly describe the kind of constitution and government that we in the United States have?', I might ask my compatriots. Most would answer: 'A democracy of course.' I might persist: 'But why a democracy? What makes us one? Do we possess certain distinctive characteristics or engage in certain behaviours that qualify us for that description? Do we have none that would disqualify us?' Our conversation could proceed and deepen.

Such are the questions that this essay poses from a particular vantage point. It starts with the common observation that people who are partisan to the post-war human rights movement also tend to believe in democratic government. Most of these people would have much the same ideas about what rights purport to 'do', and what they require, protect, and forbid. But their ideas can be remarkably diverse about what democracy means, what it requires and forbids. Exploring the relationships between human rights, particularly civil-political rights, and democracy becomes a principal theme in this chapter. (In recent decades, economic and social rights have assumed more significance for an understanding of democracy, particularly in the hands of academic scholars and in the world of theory but also in an increase in the number of state constitutions and judicial opinions that refer to democracy. This chapter, however, examines only civil-political rights.)

One could explore this topic by concentrating on several states that are broadly viewed as democratic, each with its own set of constitutionally based rights (often influenced or even determined by international human rights), each perhaps with its distinctive notions about and institutional structure of democracy. But this essay unfolds within an international context. It looks to universal and regional treaties on human rights and on democracy, as well as to opinions of international (including regional) courts and views of international commissions addressing both rights and conceptions of democracy.

Particularly since World War II, the use of the term 'democracy' to describe state governments has proliferated around the world. The signal characteristic of a state so terming itself over this period—or as important, so termed by other states—involved competitive political participation of its people through genuine periodic elections under universal suffrage. In most cases, it included to some degree a government's observance of civil-political human rights. The number of states viewed as democratic rose significantly in the period

* My research for this chapter involved substantial foreign legal and political materials. I wish to express my appreciation for the highly valued assistance in this research that I received from (1) Raymond Atuguba, associate professor at the University of Ghana Law School and Henry J Steiner Visiting Professor in Human Rights at Harvard Law School; and (2) Angel Gabriel Cabrera Silva, now a candidate from Mexico for the SJD degree at Harvard Law School. I also wish to acknowledge the invaluable help in obtaining domestic and foreign materials that I received from Michelle Pearse, Senior Research and Data Librarian at Harvard Law School.

Henry J Steiner, *Democracy and Democracies* In: *The Struggle for Human Rights*. Edited by: Nehal Bhuta, Florian Hoffmann, Sarah Knuckey, Frédéric Mégret, and Margaret Satterthwaite, Oxford University Press. © Henry J Steiner 2021.
DOI: 10.1093/oso/9780198868064.003.0008

following the disintegration of the Soviet Union. Scholars came to refer to the ebb and flow of the number of democratic states as distinct 'waves' of democracies' expansion. In several countries, events in recent years suggest that we may be entering or are now within a period of strong and persistent challenges to and even decline of democratic governments, while different versions of populist governments and authoritarian regimes struggle to take their place.

Being widely viewed as democratic can also benefit a state in a practical sense on the world stage. It can gain respect, improve international relations with the democratic world that may help it to achieve a speedier entrance into the 'developed' world, attract more foreign investment, or perhaps be invited to become a member state of powerful international organizations like the European Union. On the other hand, the allure of that term can lead to almost farcical results when it becomes part of certain states' names such as the German Democratic Republic, Democratic Kampuchea, and the Democratic People's Republic of North Korea. Recall Mao's 1949 reference to creation of the People's Democratic Dictatorship.

Putting aside for the moment the question of similarities in their structures of government, do democratic states display among themselves similar relationships between government and citizens, and similar social and economic systems? Do they express and advance similar values? Or does it seem to be an easier task to identify government structures and practices that mark authoritarian states like autocracies, hereditary monarchies, military juntas, theocratic regimes, or states with ideologically defined controlling groups?

Surely political leanings, socio-economic policies, and cultural formations vary greatly among democratic states: from policies of neoliberalism to pervasive regulatory intervention, from market fundamentalism to goals of social justice, from extreme to narrow gaps in wealth and income, from individualism to more communitarian ideals, from polarization among different factions to cooperative deliberative relationships, from religious to secular orientations, from passive acceptance of racism to its criminalization, from a strong nationalist ideology inviting isolationism to a cooperative internationalism.

In its first part, this chapter reviews some basic differences within today's democratic world in understandings of democracy, and gives particular attention to relationships between human rights and democracy. The later parts illustrate that discussion by drawing on international institutions and on international documents like treaties, decisions of intergovernmental commissions, and opinions of international courts.

7.2 Part One

Article 25 of the International Covenant on Civil and Political Rights of 1976 (ICCPR), probably the most prominent and consulted treaty of the universal human rights system, offers a useful point of departure. In one respect, it is an odd vehicle for exploring what human rights and democracy have to do with each other, for the article offers no general observations or definitions of 'democracy' as such. (The term appears three times in the Covenant, but to modest effect.) The article does, however, declare a citizen's 'right' to political participation, which places it in the worlds of both human rights and political democracy.

Over the decades following World War II, contemporary 'rights' rhetoric became instituted worldwide in legal, political, and moral discourse as the universal and regional human rights movements rose to prominence. State constitutions—independently or by internalizing the international human rights treaties to which they were subject—declared rights that were to be assured by states to their citizens. One could imagine the two traditions of individual rights and democracy as allied and interdependent, indeed as two sides of the same coin. Or one could imagine them as significantly different, each with its distinct character, role, and functions in the government of states. After all, human rights mostly address individual rights against the state, while the notion of democracy embraces the political structure and character of an entire polity.

Article 25 (which incorporates the anti-discrimination and equal protection requirements of Covenant Article 2) declares that citizens have the right to 'take part' in the conduct of public affairs directly or through freely chosen representatives, and to 'vote' at 'genuine periodic elections' that are by 'universal and equal suffrage' and 'held by secret ballot, guaranteeing the free expression of the will of the electors'. (Article 21 of the UDHR of 1948 is to much the same effect.) The article is now widely understood to require plural, competitive political parties. It stresses the theme of equality. One of the article's distinctive aspects lies in its not only setting forth the essence of the right (to vote), but also including a political and moral justification for that right, namely the guarantee that through elections, a government serves as 'the free expression of the will of the electors'. The voters consent to the government that they have elected.

Article 25 describes two intimately related political rights. The first, the less noted and invoked of the two, declares without elucidation that citizens can 'take part' in public affairs. The second is more specific in its assurance of the vote at elections. Is voting the only way in which citizens can 'take part' and participate politically? Or does the article cover a wealth of familiar modes of taking part, such as joining or financially supporting associations like interest groups or political parties; canvassing and marshalling potential voters; lobbying in favour of a cause; or advocating and criticizing through speeches, publications, debates, social media, mass meetings, and marches?

A substantial number of such activities are enshrined in specific human rights. Consider four illustrative categories of rights in the ICCPR and other human rights treaties:

(1) Traditional protections for physical security such as forbidding torture serve to protect against abuse by the police or military forces that may be intended to intimidate citizens from overtly supporting an opposition candidate. 'Torture as the price of dissent' imposes too high a price on many potential dissenters.

(2) Norms of due process and observance of the rule of law in relationships between courts or other governmental institutions and citizens go a long way toward curbing government's ability to silence its opponents by denying defendants due process and forcing courts to serve as platforms for 'show trials'.

(3) Equal protection clauses, one of the most powerful and effective provisions for advancing the human rights movement, prohibit invidious discrimination by the state in its regulation of myriad activities. One striking example could be the state's exclusion of members of designated political, religious, sexual, gender, or racial groups from running for a political office.

(4) The expressive rights of speech, press, assembly, and association must supplement Article 25 for a democracy to prosper, indeed for genuine political participation even to exist. One common understanding of democracy emphasizes its role as a framework for active public debate of pressing issues and for collective deliberation in small groups and statewide organizations as a path toward decision-making about policy issues.

The preceding illustrations stress the instrumental role of rights in creating an environment conducive to broad political participation and democracy. One might then describe these rights as bound up in and fully part of contemporary notions of a democratic polity. They serve not simply as helpful companions to Article 25, but as essential ingredients of a larger conception of public engagement in government. Such a role surely does not exhaust the social and individual value of these rights, which may also be understood from other perspectives including their inherent value in attracting citizens and voters to develop their social and moral views as active members of the community.

General Comment No 25 of the ICCPR's Human Rights Committee explicates Article 25 in numerous significant ways. It notes that the article 'lies at the core of democratic government based on the consent of the people'; gives several illustrations of what 'take part' might include in the way of political participation; declares that states must take 'effective measures' to make the right to vote realizable, as well as 'positive measures' to overcome obstacles to voting like illiteracy or poverty; emphasizes several rights that are particularly relevant to political participation like those to speech and association; and refers to 'reasonable limitations' on financing campaigns to avoid 'disproportionate expenditures' on behalf of a candidate or party.

The General Comment notes that the ICCPR 'does not impose any particular electoral system'. This remark may go no further than to point out that no form or realization of democracy is obligatory. In fact, neither the ICCPR nor any other universal treaty requires states parties to institute a particular form of government such as democracy. (The regional African and inter-American treaty systems, and several aspects of the European system, here differ.)

It is not that these early markers of the human rights movement lacked boldness in the obligations that they imposed on states parties. To the contrary, in its foundational documents following the UDHR, that movement showed imagination, creativity, and extraordinary reach in requiring states to respect, promote, protect, and provide support for individual rights. Despite states' long-standing claims under international law of territorial sovereignty and domestic jurisdiction, these requirements set strict new international principles on how states behaved within their own territory toward their own citizens. These treaties reached far higher than had familiar treaties over the centuries in diverse fields of commerce, state boundaries, taxation, trade, or diplomatic immunities. They restated as treaty commitments new norms based on legal, political, and moral ideals so demanding and far-reaching that no state party could fully honour them.

To be sure, the substantive provisions spelling out the content, reach, and limits of rights developed more rapidly than did effective provisions for enforcement and sanctions following violations of those rights. However defined, and whatever their formal legal effects under international law, rights could be understood by treaty parties as aspirations, as goals to be achieved at a more measured pace and pursuant to more modest enforcement provisions than the uncompromising treaty commands and prohibitions might first suggest. Nothing rubs against states' views about their traditional right to self-management and their inherent sovereignty as strongly as do pressures for compliance and actual sanctions issuing from other states and international organizations.

To have gone further at an early stage of the human rights movement by explicitly requiring states parties to institute a designated form of government would have been even more astonishing. Nonetheless, the ICCPR seems to lead its parties in that direction, at least with respect to a democracy's fundamental features. Could indeed a state party to the ICCPR be viewed by other states and international organizations as complying satisfactorily with the major rights-based provisions of that Covenant, and *not* be viewed as a democratic state? Would some degree of compliance with the International Covenant on Economic, Social and Cultural Rights (ICESCR) also be viewed as essential?

If we assume that compliance with the major provisions of the ICCPR is tantamount to being a democratic state, what discretion is left to each state about how it will understand and implement that democracy? Examples abound of the many choices that must be made about matters of high significance and great consequence. Is a universal treaty a plausible path toward answering the important questions that are certain to arise, both at the time of a state's creation and recurrently thereafter? Such a path would be unlikely to attract a substantial number of states parties in view of its unyielding and dysfunctional insistence on imposing near-total conformity on its members. States need some breathing space and room to manoeuvre, some minimum degree of self-determination in their basic political arrangements, some room to learn from their experiences and adapt to new circumstances. The critical choices could be matters for the people to decide within the ordinary processes of a representative democracy through elections and popular pressures, through forms of direct democracy such as referenda, initiatives, and ratifications, or through constitutional amendments—in other words, through a familiar and broad political process of change within a democratic framework.

International human rights institutions frequently recognize the legitimacy of these choices by states and the breadth of the discretion left with them. One could point to the role of the elastic margin of appreciation within the European human rights framework. Through its application, the European Court of Human Rights (ECtHR) can defer to decisions reached by member states, preferably through traditional democratic processes.

Consider the different ways in which the framework of a democracy can be constructed and changed: selection of a parliamentary, presidential, or mixed system of government; elections based on proportional voting, first-past-the-post electoral districts, some mixture of the two, or other schemes; separation of powers among branches of government and situations of overlap of such powers (such as an executive veto over bills approved by the legislature, a legislative power to remove a chief executive from office, a measured or extensive power of judicial review by courts); the degree to which the legislature delegates power, including law-making and adjudicative powers, to the administrative agencies it creates; federal or unitary government and if federal, with one or another division of powers between national and local governments; unlimited or limited terms of office for members of a legislature, top executive officials, or appointed judges; and public funding of electoral campaigns or private funding through limited or unlimited contributions. Can it be doubted that such choices could strongly influence which interests or political parties governed, and thus the course of the country?

There doesn't seem to be an agreed-upon 'red line' that, if crossed by a state making substantial changes in vital arrangements, would lead many to question whether the suspect state remained a democracy. Of course situations can arise where dramatic changes approaching a transformation, brought about perhaps by a military coup or economic collapse, can lead many to believe that democracy itself is in jeopardy, even fatally injured. In general, the situation will be far less clear. Barring a government's opponents from expressing criticism of political leaders poses a far different threat to free speech than do prohibitions of pornography or blasphemy. Expansion of executive power to rule by decree may affect a few selected areas of the economy or cripple a legislature's power over major fields like taxation or criminal procedure. A state may continue to comply with many democracy-related rights while emasculating others. Such actions may lead to different judgments among national or international institutions about their consistency not only with international human rights but also with democracy. How far downhill, at what pace, and with what consequences may all be relevant to a decision.

For such reasons, self-styled democracies may often be better evaluated not by assigning them to simple 'yes-no' categories, but rather by assigning them to places within a ranking system that takes account of multiple factors. Several influential governmental and non-governmental organizations prefer this approach. The Polity IV Project, for example, ranks many countries over periods of years on a scale of −10 to +10 ranging from extreme autocracies or exercises of governmental authority to strong and stable democracies. Freedom House engages in research and advocacy on democracy, political freedom, and human rights. Its annual reports feature scales of 'Freedom in the World' covering political rights and civil liberties in a large number of states. Evaluations may determine the place of states within such polar categories as genuine or sham democracies, liberal or illiberal democracies, strong or weak democracies, and stable or threatened democracies. As noted earlier, the advances of economic and social rights within the human rights movement have influenced the meaning of democracy in numbers of states and contributed to relatively new categories like social democracy or welfare-state democracy.

In contrast with democracy, rights are the subject of legal obligations for states to comply as required by a multitude of treaties and constitutions. They stand at the core of claims for judgment and relief brought before national and international courts and commissions. Rights have rapidly become an indelible part of world law and politics, a widespread and powerful language of justice. Their invocation by masses of people in protest meetings, people shouting 'give us our rights', cannot be simply ignored by rights-denying governments. To be sure, the demand for democracy in similar circumstances may have similar effects. That demand at the core of angry demonstrations aimed at authoritarian regimes may also have momentous evocative power, expressed by chants and slogans familiar to the history of democracy like 'here the people rule', 'government by consent', 'government by and for the people', or more simply 'give us the vote'.

Differences and similarities between rights and democracy affect what matters are brought before courts for decision-making. They also affect the work of organizations that monitor states and publicize the results of their inquiries. National and international organizations, both governmental and nongovernmental, engage in such work. Consider the vital role in the global human rights system that human rights NGOs play. For the most part, they deal with rights, a word often included in their formal names like Human Rights Watch. A fact-finding mission of a human rights NGO may deal with press censorship, torture, assassinations, and incarceration. The more confined range and greater specificity of individual rights allow for a more focused investigation and better reasoned decision about a violation. If exploring whether the targeted state is a 'democracy', an NGO would have a harder task in framing its definition and in setting boundaries to its inquiry. What sanctions could be imposed on that state, by what actor and on what authority? It is doubtful at the outset that NGOs would dispatch missions instructed to examine the question of democracy. These tasks of monitoring, investigating, and reporting would likely be undertaken by other kinds of authors and institutions, from journalists and academic scholars to advocacy groups and governmental agencies.

7.3 Part Two

This section illustrates the different kinds of understandings of democracy that the international human rights movement's treaties and other documents, institutions, officials, and bureaucrats express in today's world.

The following nine illustrations describe (1) the provisions of two treaties and an international body concerned with democracy; and (2) the views and arguments about democracy in six opinions of three international human rights courts functioning within three regional human rights systems: Africa, the Americas, and Europe. These illustrations involve treaties, human rights institutions and their members, officials and bureaucrats within human rights regimes, and courts with an official status within the three regional human rights systems. They do not draw directly on writings of legal or political theorists, social scientists, philosophers, or historians. Nor are they of an academic character.

The small number of illustrations makes clear that this essay stops far shy of offering a systematic study that might have permitted larger generalizations about today's understandings of democracy. By the same token, the article makes no effort based on these illustrations to distinguish among the three regional systems, perhaps by suggesting distinctive approaches of one or the other to the question of democracy. Differences among them might stem from such phenomena as Chapter II on 'Duties' in the African Charter on Human Rights (African Charter on Rights). That Chapter suggests a more communitarian and less individualistic spirit in defining duties of individuals towards their families, national communities, and African cultural values.

7.3.1 The European System

7.3.1.1 *Refah (The Welfare Party) v Turkey*

The Turkish Welfare Party (Refah) came to power in 1996 by forming a coalition government after an electoral victory. It tried to institute its religious agenda. The Turkish Constitutional Court ordered its dissolution, partly on the ground that its activities were contrary to principles of secularism.[1] Refah claimed that dissolution violated its rights under the European Convention for the Protection of Human Rights and Fundamental Freedoms (ECHR), particularly its Article 11 (right to freedom of association). That article cautions that no restriction shall be placed on the right to associate unless it is 'necessary in a democratic society' for reasons stated in Article 11, including national security. The case came to the Grand Chamber of the European Court of Human Rights (ECtHR).

The Court affirmed that democracy was a 'fundamental feature of the European public order',[2] and that the Convention was designed to promote ideals of a democratic society. There was indeed a 'very clear link between the Convention and democracy'.[3] No one can rely on the Convention's provisions in order to 'weaken or destroy the ideals and values of a democratic society'.[4] Within that society's public order, the Convention protected religion's

[1] *Refah Partisi (The Welfare Party) and Others v Turkey* App nos 41340/98, 41342/98, 41343/98 and 41344/98 (ECHR, 13 February 2003).
[2] ibid [86].
[3] ibid [99].
[4] ibid.

role through its provisions on freedom of thought, conscience, and religion. In some circumstances, the state could limit the freedom to manifest a religion publicly, as by wearing an Islamic headscarf, if allowing that freedom 'clashes with the aim of protecting rights and freedoms of others, public order and public safety'.[5] Thus a political party that incites to violence, or advances a policy that fails to respect democracy, or flouts rights and freedoms recognized in a democracy (as evidenced by the ECHR), can't rely on the Convention's protection.

The Court concurred in the Chamber's view about Sharia, 'which clearly diverges from Convention values'[6] in several sectors of Turkish life such as criminal law, legal status of women, and ways in which the state intervenes in spheres of private and public life in accord with religious precepts. For such reasons, the Turkish courts were justified in concluding that Refah's policy of establishing Sharia 'was incompatible with democracy'.[7] Indeed, Refah 'did not exclude recourse to force in order to implement its policy'.[8] All such considerations 'made the danger to democracy more tangible and more immediate'.[9] The dissolution ordered by the Turkish Constitutional Court 'may reasonably be considered to have met a "pressing social need"'.[10] It follows that Refah's dissolution may be regarded as 'necessary in a democratic society' within the meaning of Article 11. There was no violation of that article.

Earlier in its opinion, the Court referred with approval to its statement in a previous decision that, in light of the clause 'necessary in a democratic society', democracy appeared to be the only political model contemplated by the Convention as well as the only one compatible with it.

7.3.1.2 *Hirst v United Kingdom (No 2)*

A national of the United Kingdom who had been convicted of the crime of manslaughter and therefore imprisoned was denied under UK law the right to vote in an election while serving his prison sentence. He claimed that the United Kingdom had thereby violated Article 3 of the First Protocol to the European Convention on Human Rights, which obligated it to hold 'free elections' under conditions ensuring 'the free expression of the opinion of the people'. His case against the United Kingdom came to the ECtHR.[11]

The Grand Chamber of the Court stressed that the right to vote in Article 3 was 'crucial' to maintaining the foundations of a 'meaningful democracy governed by the rule of law'.[12] Through the gradual extension of the franchise over the centuries, 'universal suffrage has become the basic principle'.[13] The Court, however, noted that the right was not absolute but left space for certain limitations. The state was to be allowed some margin of appreciation. There were 'numerous ways of organising and running electoral systems and a wealth of differences, *inter alia*, in historical development, cultural diversity and political thought within Europe which it is for each Contracting State to mould into their own democratic vision'.[14] One cannot expect a democratic society to allow harm to itself by not imposing any conditions on activities that may injure the society and its rights by undermining the rule of law or the foundations of democracy.

[5] ibid [92].
[6] ibid [125].
[7] ibid.
[8] ibid [132].
[9] ibid.
[10] ibid.
[11] *Hirst No 2 v the United Kingdom* App no 74025/01 (ECHR, 6 October 2005).
[12] ibid [58].
[13] ibid [59].
[14] ibid [61].

However, this particular legislative prohibition on voting imposes a 'blanket restriction' on a significant category of persons, without taking account of factors like the seriousness of the crime or length of sentence. The prohibition is imposed in an 'indiscriminate' way. There is no place under the Convention system, within which tolerance and broadmindedness are the acknowledged hallmarks of democratic society, for automatic disenfranchisement based purely 'on what might offend public opinion'.[15] Hence this prohibition must be seen as falling outside any acceptable margin of appreciation, however wide that margin might be, and as being incompatible with this Convention right. The United Kingdom had violated the Convention.

7.3.1.3 Admission of States to the European Union

The European Council agreed in 1993 on criteria for admission of additional states to the European Union, following the dissolution of the Soviet Union and the new independence of East and Central European countries that sought or would likely seek admission. Those criteria, a few of which appear here, extend to a range of economic, social, legal, and political matters. They include a requirement that a candidate country had achieved stability of institutions guaranteeing 'democracy', the rule of law, human rights, and respect for and protection of minorities.

In 1997, the Commission of the European Communities issued a document noting that '[t]he effective functioning of democracy is a primordial question in assessing the application of a country for membership of the Union'.[16] To determine to what extent an applicant state met this condition, the Commission looked beyond a description of a state's formal legal-political provisions. It sought to assess under 'detailed criteria' how democracy 'actually works in practice'.[17] That assessment included how 'various rights and freedoms, such as the freedom of expression, are exercised through, for example, political parties, NGOs, and the media'.[18]

Referring to a number of applicant countries that it had investigated, the Commission observed that, on the whole, their 'constitutions ... guarantee democratic freedoms, including political pluralism, the freedom of expression, and the freedom of religion'.[19] It also found that these countries had held 'free and fair elections' permitting alternation in power of different political parties.

The Commission several times referred to the need for a 'stable' democracy. A democratic state could not be considered stable if rights and obligations of major institutions like the presidency or the constitutional court 'can be put into question by the government itself and if the legitimate role of the opposition in parliamentary committees is not accepted'.[20] An applicant state must have achieved stability of institutions guaranteeing democracy, the rule of law, human rights, and respect for the protection of minorities. Many applicant countries 'have minority populations, whose satisfactory integration into society is a condition for democratic stability'.[21]

[15] ibid [70].
[16] Commission, Agenda 2000—For a Strong and Wider Union' COM (1997) 2000 final, 42.
[17] ibid.
[18] ibid 42–43.
[19] ibid 43.
[20] ibid 42–43.
[21] ibid 44.

7.3.2 The Inter-American System

7.3.2.1 American Democratic Charter of 2001

Ideas about democracy figure importantly in the several institutions and official documents that form the backbone of the Inter-American Human Rights System (IAHRS). This has been so from the start. The Preamble of the Charter of the Organization of American States (OAS) of 1948 refers to 'representative democracy' as an 'indispensable condition for the stability, peace and development of the region'.

One among these documents stands out: the Inter-American Democratic Charter of 2001 approved by state members of the OAS. Article 1 sets the tone for the document's ambitious agenda by declaring that the peoples of the Americas 'have a right to democracy and their governments have an obligation to promote and defend it'. The Charter strengthens its message through its interactions with major instruments and institutions including the principal treaty in the IAHRS, the American Convention on Human Rights (American Convention). The excerpts that follow from the opinions of the Inter-American Court of Human Rights draw principally on the provisions of that Convention, which, although containing some distinctive provisions, declares civil and political rights similar to those in the ECHR. The Democratic Charter itself declares in its Preamble that the Convention contains 'the values and principles of liberty, equality, and social justice that are intrinsic to democracy'. The judicial opinions below also draw on this Charter.

The Charter's Article 3 describes the 'essential elements' of democracy as (1) access to the exercise of power in accord with the rule of law; (2) elections that the Charter describes similarly to Article 25 of the ICCPR; (3) a pluralistic political party system; and (4) separation of powers as well as independence of the branches of government. To this list of essential characteristics, Article 4 adds transparency, respect for social rights, and freedoms of speech and the press. It underscores that respect for the rule of law is 'equally essential to democracy'. The Charter notes a few specific requirements, including elimination of all forms of discrimination and respect for ethnic, cultural, and religious diversity that will contribute to strengthening democracy and citizen participation. Article 12 observes that poverty, illiteracy, and low levels of human development adversely affect the growth of democracy, and that OAS member states are committed to generate more productive conditions.

At first read, the breadth and depth of the Democratic Charter truly astonish. The ground that it covers starts from a minimalist notion that democracy requires political participation principally through elections evidencing the consent of the people. It embraces some familiar structural elements, like separation of powers, and reaches further into underlying characteristics of a political-legal system like transparency, rule of law, and social justice. It notes only a few rights. Moreover it enters the domain of economic and social rights by incorporating issues like a state's responsibility for providing popular education and giving attention to environmental problems. The Charter is no mere catalogue of random thoughts about democracy, but rather a studied aspiration for what today can be achieved.

7.3.2.2 *Gelman v Uruguay*

Multiple episodes of violent crimes committed by the state arose during a period of military dictatorship in Uruguay. The *Gelman v Uruguay* case involved a state-enforced disappearance of a pregnant woman, who then gave birth to a daughter.[22] The daughter was then

[22] Inter-American Court of Human Rights, *Gelman v Uruguay* (2011) Ser C No 221.

removed from her mother (hence the charge of kidnapping) and given to the care of a family anxious to adopt and raise a child. The state later failed to investigate these events and punish the guilty persons.

After Uruguay had resumed democratic government, the state enacted the so-called Expiry Law of 1986, an amnesty law shielding those who had committed crimes during the military dictatorship from prosecution. The procedures for enactment of the Expiry Law followed the state's normal democratic process. After enactment, the law was approved on two separate occasions by popular referenda.

The claim against Uruguay, based on the enforced disappearance and kidnapping, had to overcome the amnesty provisions of the Expiry Law. The case eventually reached the Inter-American Court of Human Rights. The Court found that the disappearance and kidnapping were serious violations of the American Convention. The Expiry Law could not block punishment because it was incompatible with the spirit of the American Convention. The Court's arguments follow.

A basic purpose of human rights is to protect the minority against the majority. Consequently, the Court cannot automatically grant the majority the power to defeat a minority, even if the statute being challenged was properly enacted under democratic process. It is not sufficient to argue that not only was the statute enacted under valid process, but also the two referenda on the amnesty that were approved by popular majorities were instances of direct democracy and must prevail.

As the Democratic Charter makes clear, respect for human rights is a requirement of democracy. The amnesty law's validity doesn't turn on formal process, but rather depends on its substance. As recognized by treaties like the American Convention, protection of human rights sets an impassable limit on the power of the majority. Other courts too have spoken of the limits of what can be achieved through a democratic political process when the protection of fundamental rights is at issue.

7.3.2.3 *Yatama v Nicaragua*

Yatama participated in elections in Nicaragua as a 'popular association' before it became a regional political party formed out of ethnic and indigenous communities. It sought to promote regional self-government partly by engaging in political participation as a way of preserving its autonomy and the ethnic survival of the community. Its aim was to foster a democratic community within the larger framework of democracy for the Nicaraguan state.

The question posed in *Yatama v Nicaragua* was whether Nicaragua had violated several articles of the American Convention, including its Article 23 declaring the right of citizens to 'take part' in the conduct of public affairs, and specifically to vote and be elected in genuine periodic elections. Nicaragua's Electoral Act compelled Yatama to register as a political party.[23] However, because of legal technicalities, the candidates proposed by Yatama were excluded from the options available to voters, thereby imposing a 'direct limitation to the exercise of the vote and [affecting] negatively the broadest and freest expression of the will of the electorate, which implies grave consequences for democracy'.[24] The Court concluded that Nicaragua had violated the Convention.

Combining observations in earlier cases decided by the Court with fresh observations, the opinion restated that representative democracy was a determining factor in the IAHRS, and a 'principle' reaffirmed by American states in the OAS Charter, the system's basic instrument.

[23] Inter-American Court of Human Rights, *YATAMA v Nicaragua* (2005) Ser C No 127.
[24] ibid [226].

The opinion also noted that instituting requirements for exercising political rights was not per se an undue restriction of those rights, which were not intended to be absolute. Nonetheless, any state regulation limiting those rights must observe 'the principles of legality, necessity and proportionality in a democratic society'. The regulation must be necessary to satisfy 'an urgent public interest'.[25]

The following observations appeared in one of several concurring opinions (Judge Diego Garcia-Sayan):

> The OAS Charter declared that respect for human rights was a fundamental obligation of states. Such respect for the essential human rights and the principle of democracy were conceived as interdependent. Other official documents within the American human rights system have referred to the 'conceptual unity of human rights and democracy.'[26] In such respects the Democratic Charter has exercised a large influence. Human rights themselves are not a static list but are evolving, even as political rights are also developing. This movement has led to references by some to 'the human right for democracy.'[27]

7.3.3 African System

7.3.3.1 African Charter on Democracy, Elections, and Governance

Member states of the African Union agreed to the African Charter on Democracy, Elections, and Governance in 2007 (African Charter on Democracy) and committed themselves in Article 4 to 'promote democracy, the principle of the rule of law and human rights'. (Most of the human rights referred to were set forth in the African Charter on Human Rights). Compared with the Inter-American Democratic Charter, this Charter gives more attention to the central concern of the structure and processes of government and to closely related concepts like the rule of law, transparency, and separation of powers. Note, for example, the three words in the Charter's title.

The states parties had far less experience than Latin American countries as independent states. The process of decolonization after World War II continued for a good number of years. The decades following independence saw periods of massive violence, destruction, and high death tolls among the civilians as well as warriors, all the way to genocide. Concern about this background likely had its effect on this Charter, for the notion of steady achievement of a continent of democratic and peaceful states within the requirements of human rights must have seemed almost chimerical. Although showing high aspirations, the Charter also demonstrates caution in the breadth and extent of the demands that it puts on states.

Parties undertake in Article 11 to 'establish and strengthen a culture of democracy'. The states commit themselves to ensuring that citizens enjoy fundamental freedoms and human rights. Much attention is given to democratic elections that meet criteria similar to those stated in Article 25 of the ICCPR, as well as to possible sanctions against states in the event of their unconstitutional changes of government. The Charter gives special attention to a few rights, such as freedom of expression and of the press, that are closely related to the

[25] ibid [206].
[26] ibid [4].
[27] ibid [7].

characteristic processes and practices of a democratic state. It gives some attention to social rights, including basic education and literacy.

7.3.3.2 *Actions pour la Protection des Droits de L'Homme v Republic of Cote d'Ivoire (Ivory Coast)*

An Ivorian NGO involved in the defence of human rights brought this case against Ivory Coast before the African Court on Human and Peoples' Rights.[28] It asked the Court to rule that Law 2014-335 recently enacted by Ivory Coast's National Assembly, providing for the organization and functioning of an Independent Electoral Commission, was not in conformity with international instruments ratified by Ivory Coast, particularly the African Charter on Democracy, Elections and Governance, and the African Charter on Human Rights.

One function of this Commission was to manage elections. The problem in this case stemmed from the provisions of Law 2014-335 on membership in the Commission, which included a personal representative of the president of Ivory Coast and a personal representative of the president of the National Assembly. The state's Constitutional Council had decided that the challenged provisions were in conformity with the Constitution.

The African Court held that the Commission should be constituted according to law in a way that guaranteed its independence and impartiality; and that it should be perceived by the public as such. In this situation, it was necessary to assure the public that the composition of the Commission was balanced. The Court found, however, that under the actual arrangements, the government was represented by eight members as against four members for the opposition. The composition of the Commission thus failed the test of impartiality. In view of Article 17(1) of the African Charter on Democracy, providing that member states should '[e]stablish and strengthen independent and impartial national electoral bodies responsible for the management of elections', it was necessary to cure this imbalance.

The Court found that Ivory Coast had also violated other treaties by denying rights to equality, equal protection, and political participation. It cited provisions in the African Charter on Human Rights, and the International Covenant on Civil and Political Rights.

Though the subject matter of this litigation involved issues bearing directly on elections, and the Court based its judgment partly on provisions in the African Charter on Democracy, the opinion does not mention the term 'democracy'.

7.3.3.3 *Tanganyika Law Society v Tanzania*

Tanganyika Law Society, an NGO, brought claims against Tanzania to the effect that the state, through certain amendments to its laws and Constitution, had violated its citizens' right of freedom of association, the right to participate in public/governmental affairs, and the right against discrimination.[29] The amendments prohibited an independent candidate from contesting presidential, parliamentary, and local government elections. A candidate running in such elections was required to be a member of, and be sponsored by, a political party. The provisions said to bar such a limitation involved Articles 2, 10, and 13(1) of the African Charter on Human Rights, which assured individuals of equality and equal protection of the law, the right to free association, and the right to participate freely in government directly or through freely chosen representatives. Since requirements for forming a political

[28] African Court on Human and Peoples' Rights, Actions pour la Protection des Droits de l'Homme v The Republic of Côte d'Ivoire (2016) 001/2014.

[29] African Court on Human and Peoples' Rights, Tanganyika Law Society and Legal and Human Rights Centre v United Republic of Tanzania (2013) 009/2011.

party were onerous, and since one could not run for office without belonging to a party, the Tanganyika Law Society argued that effectively there was no freedom of association. The state argued that this limitation was the best way to avoid uncontrolled liberty leading to anarchy, and that the prohibition was necessary for good governance, national security, public peace, and morality.

The case came before the African Court on Human and Peoples' Rights. That Court observed that any restrictions on participation in elections as a candidate must be justified as 'necessary in a democratic society', and as 'reasonably proportionate to the legitimate aim pursued'.[30] The argument drew upon the provisions of Article 27(2) of the African Charter on Human Rights, to the effect that rights of an individual 'shall be exercised with due regard to the rights of others, collective security, morality and common interest'. The Court concluded that the state had failed to show that its restrictions on the right to participate freely in government fell within the provisions of Article 27, and that the restrictions were not proportionate to the alleged aim of fostering national unity and solidarity. Any law requiring a citizen to join a political party before becoming a candidate for high office 'is an unnecessary fetter' that denies to the citizen the right of direct participation and amounts to a violation.[31]

7.4 Part Three

The decades following World War II witnessed the spread of democracy among states (with periods of recession that describe in significant respects our contemporary situation), and a related expansion in the ways that many 'official actors' understood its content. By 'official actors', I refer to persons and institutions making decisions or drafting international instruments or otherwise acting within their defined authority in international contexts and systems—for example, the illustrations in section 7.3. This section draws on those illustrations to offer observations about them as a group.

The preceding judicial decisions in the African and inter-American regional systems refer to the charter on 'democracy' in each system. The American Democratic Charter of 2001 is the more striking, stating in its first article that peoples in the Americas 'have a right to democracy' and that their governments have an 'obligation to promote and defend it'. That Charter declares that democracy's 'essential elements' include requirements similar to ICCPR Article 25's requirements for elections. It also embraces broader and more diffuse characteristics of a democracy like separation of powers and transparency. The Charter notes that a few specific rights such as those to speech and press are also 'essential'. The rule of law is 'equally essential to democracy'. The Charter refers to the American Convention on Human Rights as containing 'the values and principles of liberty, equality and social justice that are intrinsic to democracy'. Moreover, it draws upon the rise in importance of economic and social rights to declare that social justice is 'intrinsic to democracy'.

On their face, several judicial opinions described in section 7.3fortify these observations. For example, *Refah* (section 7.3.1.1) affirms democracy as a 'fundamental feature of the European public order' and asserts that the ECHR was designed to 'promote ideals of a democratic society'. It declares a 'very clear link between the Convention and democracy' and speaks critically of a political party that fails to respect democracy or flouts rights and freedoms 'recognized in a democracy'. *Gelman* (section 7.3.2.2) asserts that respect for

[30] ibid [106, 1].
[31] ibid [109].

human rights is a requirement of democracy. In cases of 'serious violations of nonrevocable norms of International Law', the protection of human rights constitutes 'an impassable limit to the rule of the majority' in a democratic context. A concurring opinion in the *Yatama* decision (section 7.3.2.3) states that respect for the essential human rights and for the principle of democracy 'were conceived as interdependent'. Other official documents within the American human rights system have referred to the conceptual unity of human rights and democracy.

On several occasions, official actors have offered small lists of essential ingredients of democracy. Those lists are far from identical. Indeed they have a somewhat random character. It is difficult to imagine a satisfactory explanation as to why specific human rights appear on one list but not another. The rights that most frequently appear in the illustrations generally include those related to association, expression, press, religion, freedom from discrimination, and protection of minorities. It is plausible to conclude that these fundamental rights are selected because of their close association with democracy's cardinal insistence on political participation and elections.

The democracy charters for Africa and the Americas, as well as several of the discussed judicial opinions, include as essential features of a democratic state more abstract characteristics of a legal system. The descriptions reach beyond the core notions of political participation and elections, and beyond the inclusion of several related human rights. Examples from the illustrations include broad values like liberty and equality, as well as the rule of law, transparency, and social justice. Judges gave no indications about their understanding of these inclusions, or of how the inclusions were germane to resolving the concrete issues before the court.

Perhaps 'rule of law' is the most often invoked of these basic conceptions that are frequently associated with democracy. This momentous phrase appears in foundational documents such as the UDHR, whose preamble declares that 'human rights should be protected by the rule of law'. Often the term is employed to mean a political and moral ideal captured in widely known phrases such as (in its modern secular version) 'not under man but under law'. It follows that the phrase rule of law itself is subject to a multitude of interpretations. At a minimum, it requires a government to follow some regular and well-understood processes in making law, and to establish legal regulation that is knowable by the public subject to it, all in contrast to laws imposed by the dictates of autocratic leaders to achieve whatever purposes animate them. Courts, for example, would be protected against mandates from or outright coercion by other parts of government. They would be understood to decide cases pursuant to rules and principles 'within the law' or consistent with general perceptions of how the judicial system functions, rather than by following a partisan ideology or deciding by whim (or bribery). Since the global spread of international human rights as a source of or inspiration for law, the rule of law has come to embrace a requirement that a government provide for and protect specified human rights that are of particular salience for a democracy. Those rights concern matters like voting, free speech, and equality before the law. The boundaries of the rule of law are then fluid and expanding, now embracing principles as broad and fundamental as respect for human dignity.

The illustrations throughout section 7.3 suggest ways in which the rule of law enters the discussion. The document 'Admission of States to the European Union' (section 7.3.1.3) includes a requirement that a candidate country achieve stability of institutions guaranteeing democracy, the rule of law, human rights, and respect for protection of minorities. The *Hirst* decision (section 7.3.1.2) describes the right to vote as 'crucial' to 'a meaningful democracy governed by the rule of law'. It declares that a democratic state could take action to protect itself from activities that might injure the society by undermining the rule of law or the foundations of democracy. The court, however, does not discuss why or how the concept is relevant to its judgment in the case, in the sense of finding that certain governmental conduct violated the court's understanding of the rule of law.

The two dominant notions figuring in this chapter, political democracy and human rights, have each been in flux for a long time. Had the discussion reached back to the eighteenth and nineteenth centuries, the contrast between 'democracy' as understood not only in the opening decades of the United States but for decades thereafter and today's understanding would have been strong and clear. One could describe the change in meaning over this period as a transformation if not quite a revolution. 'International' human rights as a legal, political, and moral phenomenon achieved global significance only after World War II. It too experienced significant growth, in its case to permeate many national legal and political systems as well as to become a vital component of international law and discourse. This essay, however, has addressed a briefer period. It has explored only over recent decades and from an international perspective the developing understandings of 'official actors' about democracy and its relation to international human rights. The flux will doubtless continue. Given the myriad expanding and novel dangers to which our world is subject, democracy and international human rights will struggle to preserve their deep contributions to humanity while adapting to our challenging if not ominous circumstances.

PART II

SETTING THE RIGHTS AGENDA

8
Human Rights in a Use Case World

Benedict Kingsbury

> The new institutions currently being set up by the UK government in the area of big data and AI focus heavily on ethics. While their establishment is certainly a positive development, we should not lose sight of the limits of an ethics frame. Ethical concepts such as fairness are without agreed upon definitions, unlike human rights which are law. Government use of automation, with its potential to severely restrict the rights of individuals, needs to be bound by the rule of law and not just an ethical code.[1]

8.1 Introduction

The languages and practices of international human rights law and those of digital engineering/data science, having evolved largely in isolation from one another in earlier decades, are now spoken in overlapping settings and sporadically interwoven. These co-locutions notwithstanding, a wide gulf can be expected to subsist in core concepts and in ways of thinking and doing. Nonetheless, for the future they will share a common space, at least in places where human rights persist as some sort of lingua franca and deep commitment. This chapter reflects on that cohabitation. Whereas terms such as 'ethics', 'fairness', and 'community guidelines' have been offered from the tech sector as a traveller's Esperanto, these do not reach the fundamental differences in modes of thought. This chapter struggles with the near-ubiquitous digital tech-design notion of the 'use case' as an illuminating representative of the myriad puzzles in this enterprise for the public lawyer, and in particular for the international human rights lawyer. The chapter takes the digital-algorithmic welfare state—for which the software and systems have been designed and built with innumerable use cases—as a setting where human rights and the use case meet, albeit often with limited real convergence. Toward the end of the chapter it will be suggested that framing this meeting ground as infrastructure might be one unexpectedly promising means of bringing them into deeper commonality.

[1] OHCHR, 'Statement on Visit to the United Kingdom, by Professor Philip Alston, United Nations Special Rapporteur on Extreme Poverty and Human Rights' UN News (London, 16 November 2018) <https://perma.cc/7CKJ-92FB> accessed 15 September 2020.

Benedict Kingsbury, *Human Rights in a Use Case World* In: *The Struggle for Human Rights*. Edited by: Nehal Bhuta, Florian Hoffmann, Sarah Knuckey, Frédéric Mégret, and Margaret Satterthwaite, Oxford University Press. © Benedict Kingsbury 2021.
DOI: 10.1093/oso/9780198868064.003.0009

8.2 Human Rights Law

The UN Special Rapporteur on Human Rights and Extreme Poverty marching out into the field to do battle with the algorithmic administration of the UK welfare state's universal credit system has become a symbolic moment for the international human rights law establishment in its grappling with digital government services. This is not because the important deeds that were done that day were unusually heroic—Philip Alston, who earlier in his career had been UN Special Rapporteur on Summary and Arbitrary Executions, had worked on (and in) more horrific and dangerous settings than this official visit to the United Kingdom entailed. Nor was it quite the shot that was heard around the world—a rippling upheaval with momentous consequences reverberating for decades. But it did herald a regrouping and reform for the conventional human rights forces, with new strategy and new tactical training in apposite use of the standard-issue weapons, in the face of the digitalization and automation of massively important public-facing government services.[2]

Philip Alston himself pointed to some of the reasons this engagement had been slow in coming:

> Despite the enormous stakes involved not just for millions of individuals but for societies as a whole, these issues have, with a few notable exceptions, garnered remarkably little attention. The mainstream tech community has been guided by governmental pre-occupations with efficiency, budget-savings, and fraud detection. The welfare community has tended to see the technological dimensions as separate from the policy developments, rather than as being integrally linked. And those in the human rights community concerned with technology have understandably been focused on concerns such as the surveillance state, the potentially fatal undermining of privacy, the highly discriminatory impact of many algorithms, and the consequences of the emerging regime of surveillance capitalism.[3]

Now, it was hoped, the arrival of the international human rights lawyers would cast upon the rushing gov-tech machine an enmeshing filigree of formal law, reaching beyond that of the specialized 'digital rights' movement, that might produce enough accountability and constraint to make a difference. These legal rules, techniques, institutions, and values did not have to be newly concocted—for the most part, the need was just to articulate and deploy them at speed and in the right ways.

One component is the lawyer's fundamental commitment to legality as an essential requirement for exercises of state power toward persons.[4] The possibilities and legal value of this were attested to by human rights-related litigation in national courts on use of automated or predictive-targeting digital technologies in governmental administration of welfare legislation. Illustrations of such legality-assertion include notable cases involving, respectively, human rights and data protection law, administrative law, and the private law of unjust enrichment and tort.

[2] The landmark report on this early phase was UNCHR 'Report of the Special Rapporteur on Extreme Poverty and Human Rights' (11 October 2019) UN Doc A/74/48037.

[3] Philip Alston, 'What the "Digital Welfare State" Really Means for Human Rights' (OpenGlobalRights, 8 January 2020) <https://perma.cc/3TSP-3NRK> accessed 15 September 2020.

[4] Jeremy Waldron, 'The Concept and the Rule of Law' (2008) 43 Georgia Law Review 1; Jeremy Waldron, 'The Rule of International Law' (2006) 30 Harvard Journal of Law & Public Policy 15; cf Fleur Johns, *Non-Legality in International Law: Unruly Law* (CUP 2013).

In the Netherlands, the Hague District Court ruled that the Syri big-data aggregation and analysis system (Systeem Risico Indicatie), used by the Dutch government to try to detect welfare benefits and taxes fraud, was unlawful because it breached Article 8 of the European Convention on Human Rights (right to private life).[5] The risk model and risk indicators were not disclosed, nor did the targets know the process was occurring, hence review and scrutiny were lacking. Moreover, when triggered the Syri system took in a huge range of personal data (usually for a whole neighbourhood), raising concerns about the European law obligation of data minimization, and no single body conducted a unified overview to test whether all the data was in fact truly necessary in the specific instance. Instead, individual government units made this determination for portions of data for which they were responsible. Thus, the extra scale achieved by big data was not accompanied by a comparably comprehensive assessment.

The English Court of Appeal ruled unlawful an idiosyncratic artefact of the digital system design that resulted in certain people being denied some of their universal credit payment if their employer happened to pay their monthly salary slightly earlier than scheduled due to bank closed days.[6] The government's lawyer admitted this was arbitrary and that there was no policy reason for it.[7] The government emphasized 'the importance to the system as a whole of having a simple way of identifying inputs required for the automated calculation of the monthly award for many millions of claimants',[8] which the court accepted could be a legitimate aim. However, the situation suffered by the affected persons in this case was so needlessly adverse that no reasonable Secretary of State could have decided not to fix the problem. A government official responsible for the digital build testified that it was not possible for there to be an automated change to address this particular issue; the changes needed to solve this problem would 'require a new version of the calculator to be essentially rebuilt from scratch'.[9] But the court was not prepared to accept this techno-determinism: with such a vast and complex computerized system as was deployed for universal credit, the court simply asserted that it must be capable of adjustment to deal with this egregious problem.

In Australia, the Federal government's 'Robodebt' system which automatically alleged and demanded return of overpayment to certain recipients of welfare monies by using big data to impute to them an averaged extra income they had not necessarily received, was challenged in various courts. The allegation that the government was unjustly enriched when it received back funds to which the beneficiaries should have been entitled was so clearly well-founded in law that the government conceded and refunded 373,000 people.[10] The further questions of whether the government owed a duty of care and had been negligent in the design and operation of the computerized scheme—which might have brought legal evaluation directly to bear on data science and digital infrastructure building practices—were postponed to a later day.

Collectively, these and many other court cases—including several in which claimants did not succeed or were victorious only due to procedural defects that governments quickly fixed—bring formality and the rule of law to appraise the algorithmic practices of welfare

[5] *Federation of the Dutch Trade Movement v State of the Netherlands*, Rechtbank Den Haag [District Court of the Hague], C/09/550982 HA ZA 18-388 (5 February 2020) <https://perma.cc/RB9J-N6TJ>.
[6] *Secretary of State for Work and Pensions v Johnson & Ors* [2020] EWCA Civ 778 [2020] WLR(D) 360.
[7] ibid [47] (Lady Justice Rose).
[8] ibid [34].
[9] ibid [78].
[10] Luke Henriques-Gomes, 'Robodebt: Government to Refund 470,000 Unlawful Centrelink Debts Worth $721m' The Guardian (29 May 2020) <https://perma.cc/7GCQ-6FWY> accessed 15 September 2020.

state reform.[11] This surge of litigation and judicial action, including important arguments about discrimination and about economic rights to housing or social security, was intensified by the public health epidemic that from 2020 increased pressure on welfare states and heightened governmental use of digital technologies (and redoubled the imperative of universal internet access and proficiency). Many welfare state reforms, and some COVID-19 digital responses, had been launched without full attention to legality, or compliance was waved off as being too hard. In most legal systems, however, claims challenging algorithmic government only become ripe to be lodged late in the process, or ex post; and only very rarely would courts reverse a completed algorithmic roll-out. In complex cases courts may not find it easy to determine legal responsibility for digitally constructed injustices. The international law-textbook emphasis on establishing legal responsibility for human rights violations is challenged in relation to digital government, with many hands (perhaps located in many countries) involved in each digital design making attribution difficult, inadvertent co-production of unforeseen risks through multiple systems operating at once, and new-era problems of attributing responsibility to 'intelligent' machines or machine–human combinations.[12]

A second component thus must be ex ante regulation. What techniques, however, would human rights-inspired regulation of gov-tech be able to use effectively? Statutory provisions experimented with requiring algorithmic and/or data protection impact assessment,[13] a human in the loop in some governmental decision-making,[14] design rules such as privacy-by-design, testing, and debiasing, and other controls on data inputs including artificial intelligence (AI) training data.[15] To address demands for accountability for the use of algorithms and some curbs on automation, global administrative law-type accountability devices were often proposed and occasionally implemented: transparency, explainability/reason-giving, monitoring, and auditing of use of algorithms by governmental bodies.[16] It might be doubted whether this was enough to exert real leverage from the standpoint of fundamental human rights in the basic conflicts about resources, welfare, and poverty that underlie these struggles about welfare state 'reform'. It was moreover unsurprising, if mildly ironic, that this

[11] For US cases, see Rashida Richardson, Jason Schultz, and Vincent Southerland, 'Litigating Algorithms 2019 US Report: New Challenges to Government Use of Algorithmic Decision Systems' (AI Now 2019) <https://ainowinstitute.org/litigatingalgorithms-2019-us.pdf>.

[12] Karen Yeung, 'A Study of the Implications of Advanced Digital Technologies (Including AI Systems) for the Concept of Responsibility within a Human Rights Framework' (Council of Europe 2019) MSI-AUT(2018)05 rev <https://rm.coe.int/a-study-of-the-implications-of-advanced-digital-technologies-including/168094ad40>.

[13] Dillon Reisman and others, 'Algorithmic Impact Assessments: A Practical Framework for Public Agency Accountability' (AI Now 2018) <https://ainowinstitute.org/aiareport2018.pdf>.

[14] Katherine J Strandburg, 'Adjudicating with Inscrutable Decision Rules' in Marcello Pelillo and Teresa Scantamburlo (eds), *Machines We Trust: Getting Along with Artificial Intelligence* (MIT Press 2020); David Spiegelhalter, 'Should We Trust Algorithms?' (2020) 2 Harvard Data Science Review 1.

[15] Some European examples are listed in Matthias Spielkamp, 'Automating Society: Taking Stock of Automated Decision-Making in the EU' (AlgorithmWatch and Bertelsmann Stiftung 2019) <https://perma.cc/5PG5-LTH2>. On the history of some European approaches from 1970: Meg Leta Jones, 'The Right to a Human in the Loop: Political Constructions of Computer Automation and Personhood' (2017) 47 Social Studies of Science 216; an influential but not implemented proposal for legislation in the United States was Arthur R Miller, *The Assault on Privacy: Computers, Data Banks, and Dossiers* (1st edn, University of Michigan Press 1971); a menu of proposals for India is in Amber Sinha, Elonnai Hickok, and Arindrajit Basu, 'AI in India: A Policy Agenda—The Centre for Internet and Society' (The Centre for Internet & Society, 5 September 2018) <https://perma.cc/FA73-KH9J> accessed 16 September 2020.

[16] Council of Europe Committee of Ministers, 'Recommendation CM/Rec(2020)1 of the Committee of Ministers to Member States on the Human Rights Impacts of Algorithmic Systems' (Adopted by the Committee of Ministers on 8 April 2020 at the 1373rd meeting of the Ministers' Deputies); Lorna McGregor, Daragh Murray, and Vivian Ng, 'International Human Rights Law as a Framework for Algorithmic Accountability' (2019) 68 International and Comparative Law Quarterly 309.

panoply of measures for determining or nudging choices made by coders through regulation *of* algorithms, bears no little family resemblance to the various means through which regulation *by* algorithms is intended to shape behaviour.[17] The conventional human rights agenda thus remained unfulfilled by the designs in this important but choppy regulatory grab-bag.

The staging ground for the judicial and statute-making encounters just described—the ancient venues of law courts and legislative chambers, backed by drafters still more sure about quill pens or ink brushes than Github code repositories—gives law the upper hand. The public-lawyerly preoccupation was with the failure of the state to adopt adequate and enforceable public-regarding law, and concomitant apprehensiveness about government deferral to the widespread tendency of the tech sector (and government partners) to create its own extra-legal analogues—AI ethics commissions, vague principles of fairness, and community guidelines. These analogues were thought to be wholly insufficient, a risky deformalization that the formality and legal character of human rights law could and should overtake, and in government instances largely supplant. 'Move fast and break things', 'blitzscale', 'fail fast', and other Silicon Valley business mantras cannot defensibly be migrated into traditional governmental responsibility for life and livelihood or the corresponding public law culture. All of this is well known. The intention of this chapter is to focus attention on a different fissure that the language and concepts of human rights law need to bridge and perhaps can bridge. In the engine rooms of digital tech construction, in coding sprints, in data warehouses, and indeed in the high levels of national civil services embracing digital techniques for government,[18] an almost unrecognizably different language and way of thinking predominates. One term in frequent use there, which may be enough at least to open some basic discussion here, is the 'use case'.

8.3 Use Cases

The 'use case' has its origins as a means of specifying requirements in software development, using text and often flow diagrams. In its software development reference, a use case is prepared to aid in the designing, testing, documenting, and modifying of software, and in particular to ensure all the specific requirements are known so they can be written into the code. It begins with identification of the primary actor and all other actors. It is usually prepared from the standpoint of the primary actor to specify all the ways in which the primary actor interacts with a computer system to achieve a specified and observable goal. The primary actor may be a human, or a non-human such as another computer system. A standard example is of a human using a bankcard to withdraw cash at a bank machine. The primary actor initiates the process, the system responds and may send a prompt or request information, and a back and forth continues until the result is reached. Other actors may also feature in the process flow. The result (the termination outcome) may be success (the customer

[17] A typology of ways in which regulation by algorithm operates is in Karen Yeung, 'Algorithmic Regulation: A Critical Interrogation' (2018) 12 Regulation & Governance 505, 507–12. When deployed predictively to regulate or pre-empt behaviour that has not (yet) occurred, based on patterns in historic data, algorithms may be designed to: focus limited intervention resources at areas of highest risk of harm; to manage risk pools in actuarial fashion and bring harm down to tolerable levels; and to use profiling, surveillance, and other risk-classifiers to target different resources to different cohorts to maximize alignment with policymakers' preferences. See further Karen Yeung and Martin Lodge (eds), *Algorithmic Regulation* (1st edn, OUP 2019).

[18] Patrick Dunleavy and Mark Evans, 'Australian Administrative Elites and the Challenges of Digital-Era Change' (2019) 4 Journal of Chinese Governance 181; Michael Veale and Irina Brass 'Administration by Algorithm? Public Management Meets Public Sector Machine Learning' in Yeung and Lodge (n 17).

receiving their cash) or failure with regard to the initial goal. The basic path to success, and any alternative flows to success, are depicted. Preconditions, exceptions (which may occur during the process, such as the cash not being issued due to insufficient funds in the account), and post-conditions (the things that will be true at the end) are all specified.[19] Any single use case may well have associations with (and differentiations from) numerous other use cases. However, the aim of the single use case is to provide a complete description so that all aspects of the use are exhaustively stated and can then be built by software engineers writing code.

The 'use case' phrase has come to be employed by people in digital industries to refer more broadly to ways in which a user can (or might want to) use a digital system. A use case is neatly bounded, and fully separable from another use case even if they may share some of the same software library or hardware. This is an artefact of daily software design, but when abstracted, this method of separation blends with larger business methods and ultimately with public and political justifications. It is common for tech companies, and politicians, when announcing a new digital initiative to offer up a particular 'use case' as the reason. If artfully chosen, that use case will seem to the audience to respond to a pressing need and perhaps a demand from people who wanted (even if they did not yet know it) exactly this, and who will be glad to have this facility once offered. Ideally the use case slogan will connote the socially desirable and even compelling: 'banking the unbanked',[20] 'income smoothing', '24/7 access', 'prevent fraud'. That the same tech platform or data collection system, once built out for this use case, will also support and make viable many other uses that would at the outset be controversial or shocking, goes strategically unmentioned, and indeed may not have been thought about by the use case developers. In cynical form, the method of justification through separating use cases resembles the political-military strategy of making gains by salami slicing, taking a little bit at a time so that the next step does not seem major or is finally normalized or inevitable.[21] In practice, though, ordinary tech professionals in welfarist democracies don't usually understand their own purposes and beliefs in cynical terms, but if anything tend more to the genuinely hopeful and high-minded. Critiques of such liberal-tech high-mindedness postures may be cultural, but more fundamentally they are structural,[22] some pointing in the United States to the decline of both blue-collar and middle-class life possibilities, the intensification of wealth concentration in tech sector business, and the production by the 'progressive clerisy' of welfare-related ideas such as universal basic income as a means to smooth over opposition to these massive displacements and gradients.[23]

Many are suspicious of 'solutionist' tech mindsets, or that the aesthetic novelty and mass embrace of tech gadgets and culture have led to attention being diverted from fundamental issues of poverty, dignity, voice, and freedom. Some of these concerns are neatly articulated

[19] Examples of the general approach are set out at <IBM Knowledge Center available at https://perma.cc/ER4B-U9DB> and <Usabilility Gov available at https://perma.cc/GY3T-X99K>; SmartDraw's website says: 'A use case diagram is a dynamic or behavior diagram in UML. Use case diagrams model the functionality of a system using actors and use cases. Use cases are a set of actions, services, and functions that the system needs to perform. In this context, a "system" is something being developed or operated, such as a web site. The "actors" are people or entities operating under defined roles within the system', available at https://perma.cc/SFD4-EDUD.

[20] Rob Aitken, '"All Data Is Credit Data": Constituting the Unbanked' (2017) 21 Competition & Change 274.

[21] Thomas Schelling, *Arms and Influence* (Yale University Press 1966) 66.

[22] Julie E Cohen, *Between Truth and Power: The Legal Constructions of Informational Capitalism* (OUP 2019); Nick Couldry and Ulises Ali Mejias, *The Costs of Connection: How Data Is Colonizing Human Life and Appropriating It for Capitalism* (Stanford University Press 2019); Catherine D'Ignazio and Lauren F Klein, *Data Feminism* (The MIT Press 2020); Colin Koopman, *How We Became Our Data: A Genealogy of the Informational Person* (University of Chicago Press 2019); Shoshana Zuboff, *The Age of Surveillance Capitalism: The Fight for a Human Future at the New Frontier of Power* (1st edn, PublicAffairs 2019).

[23] Joel Kotkin, *The Coming of Neo-Feudalism: A Warning to the Global Middle Class* (Encounter Books 2020).

in Shannon Mattern's critique of 'methodolatry' in relation to digitization of 'smart cities', which parallels Alston's critique of digitization of government welfare administration:

> Imagine … researchers merging massive streams of data to map all real-time traffic, weather, energy use, mobile device use, financial transactions, criminal activity, etc.—producing on their multiple flat-screens a map so rich that it becomes a territory itself. Then imagine that processed data, filtered through algorithms, feeding back into and transforming urban space or affecting human behavior in real-time (or pretty darn fast): re-syncing the streetlights or rerouting cabs to areas of high cell-phone activity. Morozov has identified the impulse behind such approaches as 'solutionism', which recasts 'complex social situations either as neatly defined problems with definite, computable solutions or as transparent and self-evident processes that can be easily optimized—if only the right algorithms are in place!' … Morozov says, 'In promising almost immediate and much cheaper results', solutionist techniques 'undermine support for more ambitious, more intellectually stimulating, but also more demanding reform projects'. If we can simply automate the depersonalized dispensation of social welfare, there may not be sufficient motivation to get our hands dirty digging for root problems like poverty, unequal access to healthcare and information services, and socioeconomic disparity in school performance.[24]

But with all the warnings and apprehensions, the embrace of digital tech can be expected to profoundly change government, more so in the future than has happened thus far. How might the actual operationalization of digital welfare systems, and the refashioning of the sociocultural and political basis on which they depend, be accomplished in ways that mesh the universal justice articulated by human rights, and the engineering of use case practicality?

One pathway is to situate the specialized languages and techniques of digital engineering and of law—the digital 'technology' and the legal-administrative technology—in a wider framing in which their combined connections with the social, economic, and organizational can be foregrounded. 'Gov-tech', 'tech', 'digital welfare state', and 'automated digital system' all put the focus too much on the technology. 'Law' or 'human rights law' as framings place the focus too much on law. Potentially suggestive in-between framings include 'platform' and 'ecosystem'. Especially promising, however, is 'infrastructure'. The remainder of the chapter will explore 'thinking infrastructurally' as a way for human rights and use cases thinking to come together.

8.4 Infrastructure

'Infrastructure' is a concept that has physical referents—nearly all accept that the global system of fibre optic cables, internet exchange points, and data centres is an infrastructure

[24] Shannon Mattern, 'Methodolatry and the Art of Measure' (2013) Places Journal <https://placesjournal.org/article/methodolatry-and-the-art-of-measure/> accessed 26 September 2020. Her reference is to Evgeny Morozov, *To Save Everything, Click Here: The Folly of Technological Solutionism* (1st edn, Public Affairs 2013).The characterization 'solutionism' was originally used dismissively, sometimes to evoke dreadful dystopias, but its dialogical role can be reconstructed as being a rhetorical device to try to make space for contestation; cf UNCHR 'Report of the Special Rapporteur on Extreme Poverty and Human Rights' (11 October 2019) UN Doc A/74/48037 para 56: 'digital services risk eliminating, almost entirely, much of the human interaction and compassion that are likely to be indispensable components in providing at least some welfare recipients with the care and assistance they need. The assumption that there is always a technological fix for any problem is highly likely to be misplaced in various aspects of a humane and effective system of social protection.'

(frequently called, with some irony, the cloud), and the same with interconnected systems of electric generation stations, log-distance transmission cables, substations, and local wiring (labelled the electricity grid), or an immense structure of waterways, locks, and supply lakes (encompassed in most references to the Panama Canal). New infrastructure, and new forms of information-management and logistics, are routinely announced as creating the possibilities for better realization of all kinds of human rights. In many developing countries, modernization projects such as supermarket-based food provision with new long-distance supply logistics are presented as vindications of such rights as food and food security.[25] The algorithmic welfare states, like these more tangible infrastructures, are large sociotechnical systems that enact complexity by connecting to and intertwining with assemblages of humans and non-humans.[26] For present purposes, ways of thinking that have developed in relation to traditional infrastructure, 'thinking infrastructurally', are of particular value.[27] To think infrastructurally about the digital innovations of the welfare state entails study not only of the 'technical': user interfaces, software packages, data accumulations, and machine-automated communications. It is also organizational: the siloed java-script code-writers imagining (or failing accurately to imagine) the users, the frontline case workers, the claimants, and the job centres where improbable employment applications are made and boxes duly checked. And it is social: the new social meanings of the digital ID or the thumbprint scanner matching against the financial access card; the workarounds by caseworkers to maintain some of the old flexibility;[28] the new expertise of people helping claimants grapple with the internet platform in public libraries or community centres; the self-conscious visibility of the welfare-entitled when required to use an emblazoned stigmatizing card or to stand in a food bank line due to an unjust delay in payment of a benefit.[29] As Paul Edwards put it, 'we now live in a world governed not by algorithmic systems per se, but rather by interacting ecologies of algorithmic systems, human individuals, social groups, cultures, and organizations'.[30]

Human rights law and modern welfare states each have many origins and local specificities, but one orthodox view from 1940s–1950s United Kingdom and Europe (and some other places) saw their development as part of an overall project that was broadly liberal, in the sense of a 'political rationality that emphasizes individual freedom, mainly the protection of individuals from arbitrary interference, the rule of law, and market governance ... also, in practice, deeply reliant on illiberalisms of all sorts; on the imposition of order, authority and coercion'.[31] Their development and internationalization were understood as linked to

[25] Amy Cohen and Jason Jackson 'Rights as Logistics: Notes on the Right to Food and Food Retail Liberalization in India' in Katharine G Young (ed), *The Future of Economic and Social Rights* (CUP 2019) 407.

[26] Mike Ananny and Kate Crawford, 'Seeing without Knowing: Limitations of the Transparency Ideal and Its Application to Algorithmic Accountability' (2018) 20 New Media & Society 973, 974.

[27] Benedict Kingsbury, 'Infrastructure and InfraReg: On Rousing the International Law "Wizards of Is"' (2019) 8 Institute for International Law and Justice 171.

[28] Jennifer Raso, 'Displacement as Regulation: New Regulatory Technologies and Front-Line Decision-Making in Ontario Works' (2017) 32 Canadian Journal of Law and Society 75. This work extends the literature on experiences of beneficiaries by focusing on frontline agency caseworkers, who in Ontario over many decades have been the object of efforts to regulate them by legalization, judicial review, and de-skilling by discretion reduction. Discretion, however, persists, implemented in some cases by workarounds of the confines of exhaustive drop-down menus and computer system-defined decision paths.

[29] UNCHR 'Report of the Special Rapporteur on Extreme Poverty and Human Rights' (11 October 2019) UN Doc A/74/48037.

[30] Paul N Edwards, 'We Have Been Assimilated: Some Principles for Thinking About Algorithmic Systems' in Ulrike Schultze and others (eds), *Living with Monsters? Social Implications of Algorithmic Phenomena, Hybrid Agency, and the Performativity of Technology* (1st edn, Springer 2018) 19, 23.

[31] Suzan Ilcan and Rob Aitken, 'Postwar World Order, Displaced Persons, and Biopolitical Management' (2012) 9 Globalizations 623, 625–26.

transnational market-opening and post-1945 reconstructive ordering, but also to an engagement with health, population, food, agriculture, and other dimensions of human life with a postcolonial (or end-of-empire) sensibility, and among some an explicitly global view of the field of social action. The rise of neoliberalism in both right wing and Labour/social democrat versions involved demands for repurposing or at least for new narratives of both the welfare state and human rights. The (supposedly) freely choosing individual was no longer to be a docile subject constituted by state action and disciplinary power, but instead to be influenced through state-market action, which framed (and priced) the allowable choices, later extended to a cognitive-science of nudging.[32] The language of human rights became implicated in this project.[33] In this framing the welfare state became not primarily a set-off for jobs lost or health impaired, but a means for individuals to learn to plan themselves like an enterprise, become economically agile, avoid dependency, and find their own place in the economy. Where the project was motivated in that way, digitization was the next technology for pursuing a social and organizational process that was fully under way.[34]

The digital operations of the welfare state are infrastructural in nature. Diverse computerized systems are meshed together; frequently the mesh-builders are confronted with misalignments or missing links. Conversion of data from system to system—employers to tax office, tax office to welfare office—is beset by discordant legacy formats, and software designed for another purpose cobbled onto new welfare project-specific software. Some parts of the digitizing project move forward, others fall behind constituting a 'reverse salient' of cost and vulnerability. That there can be huge advantages for many users of digital systems is attested in their rapid voluntary uptake by individuals all over the world, and by high levels of user satisfaction with some online government services. Almost nowhere, however, has digital uptake become 'universal'. No convincing solution has been found for the digitally unable, and those who do not have the internet access and devices necessary for 'user interfaces'. The automatic digital systems for government services thus tend to be layered on top of existing bureaucracies and service offices,[35] and can spur the growth of new cadres of suppliers of assistance, often in the voluntary sector, but sometimes as costly intermediaries (including data extractors and loan sharks) paid for, knowingly or unknowingly, by hard-pressed welfare beneficiaries. These symbioses are unspoken forms of public–private partnerships (PPPs), in which the infrastructure of digital government opens business opportunities. This has been an explicit aim in government outsourcing of digital provision including through use of 'open source' software, and in efforts to stimulate private markets in digital service supply for these government–society transformations. The latter have had highly uneven results, as when the British effort to spur a competitive private market for

[32] An account of this kind is offered by Mitchell Dean, *Governmentality: Power and Rule in Modern Society* (2nd edn, Sage 2010).

[33] Jessica Whyte, *The Morals of the Market: Human Rights and the Rise of Neoliberalism* (Verso Books 2019); cf Wendy Brown, *In the Ruins of Neoliberalism: The Rise of Antidemocratic Politics in the West* (CUP 2019).

[34] In Alston's terms: 'the embrace of the digital welfare state is presented as an altruistic and noble enterprise designed to ensure that citizens benefit from new technologies, experience more efficient government, and enjoy higher levels of well-being. Often, however, the digitization of welfare systems has been accompanied by deep reductions in the overall welfare budget, a narrowing of the beneficiary pool, the elimination of some services, the introduction of demanding and intrusive forms of conditionality, the pursuit of behavioural modification goals, the imposition of stronger sanctions regimes, and a complete reversal of the traditional notion that the state should be accountable to the individual' UN Doc A/74/48037 (n 29) para 5.

[35] ibid para 49: 'there should always be a genuine non-digital option available'.

supply of log-on identity authentication for different government agencies saw the suppliers dwindle to two, with one of the competitors using the other's system.[36]

Arguments made in relation to traditional infrastructure have been closely paralleled by those made in human rights-oriented critiques of digital welfare states. Among these have been the following:

- Demands for public oversight and transparency in the government's own welfare infrastructure processes, and contestation of governmental practices of opacity intended to prevent both gaming and criticism.
- Efforts to set bounds on government outsourcing of tech development to private companies,[37] and to challenge excessive deference to their claims for business confidentiality and trade secrets.
- Robust public-interest based regulation of PPPs, a neoliberal era staple of physical infrastructure projects,[38] and increasingly significant in digital infrastructure provision, including for healthcare and epidemic disease control.
- Extending the bite of hard-to-adjudicate substantive rights (such as rights to social security, to an adequate standard of living, to food, to mental health) by attaching to them both more readily adjudicable requirements such as non-discrimination, and statements of core values such as human dignity and subsistence.
- Co-design (more ambitious than the—sometimes-sham—mantra of stakeholder engagement): 'in order to reduce the harm caused by incorrect assumptions and mistaken design choices, digital welfare systems should be co-designed by their intended users and evaluated in a participatory manner'.[39]
- Realistic cost and benefits estimates; as opposed to the established pattern of achieving political buy-in via wilful underestimation of capital and maintenance costs and frequent overestimation of project benefits, in deciding to build large physical infrastructure projects.[40]
- Sophisticated cost–benefit analysis, including not only financial balance sheets but also 'the fiscally invisible intangibles that underpin human rights. Values such as dignity, choice, self-respect, autonomy, self-determination, privacy'.[41]
- Taking sober account of the likely reality of digital projects: 'every government technology project seems doomed to arrive late, underperform and come in over budget'.[42]

Whereas the articulation of human rights objectives in relation to digital welfare state projects only slowly took on this infrastructural orientation, the deployment of 'use case'

[36] Victoria Adelmant, 'The Gatekeepers of Government Services: Authentication in the Age of Digital Identity' (unpublished 2020).

[37] Cf UNHCR 'Report of the Special Rapporteur on Extreme Poverty and Human Rights' (26 September 2018) UN Doc A/73/396.

[38] Mariana Valverde, Fleur Johns, and Jennifer Raso, 'Governing Infrastructure in the Age of the "Art of the Deal": Logics of Governance and Scales of Visibility' (2018) 41(118) Political and Legal Anthropology Review.

[39] UN Doc A/74/48037 (n 34) para 49.

[40] Bent Flyvbjerg, 'The Fallacy of Beneficial Ignorance: A Test of Hirschman's Hiding Hand' (2016) 84 World Development 176; Bent Flyvbjerg, Nils Bruzelius, and Werner Rothengatter, *Megaprojects and Risk: An Anatomy of Ambition* (CUP 2003).

[41] UN Doc A/74/48037 (n 34) para 63.

[42] ibid para 66, quoting Helen Margetts, 'Back to the Bad Old Days, as Civil Service Infighting Threatens UK's Only Hope for Digital Government' The Conversation (9 April 2016) <http://theconversation.com/back-to-the-bad-old-days-as-civil-service-infighting-threatens-uks-only-hope-for-digital-government-47683> accessed 26 September 2020.

methodologies in relation to digital infrastructure is well established.[43] How then might human rights law and the use case both be located within an infrastructural framing, blending the technical, the organizational, and the social?

At first this might seem an improbable pursuit. Surely 'human rights' are to 'use cases' what gazelles are to gazebos?[44] One vibrant, creational, its future somewhat precarious, carrying the hopes and possibilities of the living; the other engineered, repetitive, deeply engrained in practice, functional but generally of little moral value. The scale of justification offered for a human rights claim is normally much more expansive than the justification offered for a use case. All else being the same, a human right is, or should be, held equally by everyone. A human right, and the duty the government is placed under by that right, is a justified one if (to take the Kantian approach) the underlying maxim is one that would be morally right if it applied universally.[45] By contrast, an engineer presenting a use case needs only to articulate a justification apposite to the specific ambit of this case—another use would need to be justified separately. Extending this contrast, a rough analogy might be made to:

> an interesting distinction between top-down planning (where a bunch of people begin with an overall goal or the specification of complex action that they want to achieve, and deliberately and methodically carve it up into its component parts, assigning each part to some person or agency), which is what legislation is like, and bottom-up planning (where the overall plan is constructed on the wing as it were, **by** people who begin with some of the subplans and as they go along develop a sense of how they might mesh together in a larger project), which is what the emergence of common law doctrine is like.[46]

The observation that in style of thought and argument human rights work universal-down, whereas use cases work micro-up, does not, however, imply that they remain so far apart. For human rights to be operational, and balanced off with other human rights and with the constraints of limited resources or support in contemporary societal norms, a whole array of use cases are necessarily produced. Insofar as this is done through iterative legal adjudication, the edifice is constituted by thousands of small decisions. The whole gets meaning through technical doctrine and argumentation, organization forms that are parts of the whole operation, and the social structures and agents that produce, reproduce, and change the meanings, the practices, and their influence. Conversely, the digital use case starts from small structures and is tweaked with numerous slight modifications. It may, however, be integrated with adjacent use cases, embedded in the 'minimum viable product', and prove to have extraordinary scalability. Mantras of revisability and software engineer expectations of upgrading to meet technical debt notwithstanding, digital design decisions may come to be features (or bugs) embedded in vast systems that become prohibitively costly to change, just

[43] For example: in 'infrastructure as a service' cloud provision (storage, hardware, networking); in 'internet of things' networking; and in cybersecurity, such as the sector-by-sector infrastructural cybersecurity protections promoted by the US National Institute of Standards and Technology (NIST) <https://perma.cc/L5GC-23JV>.

[44] The imagery of gazebos and gazelles is from a trope, popularized around 2007 in the work of digital engineer Alistair Cockburn, in an internecine debate about relations of use cases to user stories. It might at first seem that a human right and a use case are categories with nothing in common. The number of 'human rights' is small, and barriers for new entrants into this category are high, whereas design teams proliferate use cases freely and with abandon. But this chapter posits that illuminating insights may from evaluating together the concept of 'human rights' and the concept of 'use cases'.

[45] Immanuel Kant, *Groundwork for a Metaphysics of Morals* (1785).

[46] Jeremy Waldron, 'Planning for Legality' (2011) 109 Michigan Law Review 883, 888–89 commenting on Scott Shapiro, *Legality* (Harvard University Press 2010).

as happens in other infrastructures. This is exactly the argument the UK government made in *Johnson*—that the early design decisions not to build in a solution for the 'non-banking day salary shift' use case were by now too deeply embedded in the code to be changed. As in other decisions on Universal Credit, the Court of Appeal did not insist on a perfect solution but declared that legality required some kind of patch or workaround for the standard situations that constituted at least the bulk of the persons detrimentally affected.[47]

In form a use case is complete in itself once the user has been identified and the alternate paths and exceptions have been specified and embodied in the computer code. By contrast, a human rights claim tends to be open in its signification, reflecting the idea of universalizability.[48] In practice, though, this contrast is not so sharp. Because use cases are also socially and organizationally embedded, the justifications implicit in one established use case rapidly diffuse to justify others, and in reverse a normatively problematic use case may blow back to unsettle hitherto uncontroversial ones. A human rights claim, once refined as a legal argument and trimmed to meet the various tests for assessing the justifiability of state restrictions and implications for the due rights and needs of others, often becomes precise, narrow, and closed-ended.

This flickering spark of convergence between the use case and the human rights legal claim could become a flare as interest grows in rendering legal rules in digital code and (somewhat) capable of automatic application.[49] Could human rights be expressed within digital code, rather than being a cassation positioned outside of digital government? Already core ideas of anti-discrimination, transposed into the idiom of fairness and anti-bias, have had considerable traction among machine learning and big data professionals[50] and in courts.[51] Might legal adjudication, drawing on big data patterns processed through deep machine learning and with encoded inputs of numerous case-specific 'facts', become so granular that the address to universalizability becomes just a ritual acknowledgement?[52] These questions are too reductionist to be quite the right ones to debate. But the sense that techniques accepted and embedded now will shape a long future has given the human rights mobilization

[47] *Johnson* (n 6). See also *R (oao TP, AR and SXC) v Secretary of State for Work and Pensions* [2020] EWCA Civ 37, declaring unlawful a 'cliff edge' when beneficiaries with severe disabilities became arbitrarily worse off when they move from one local authority area to another.

[48] Philip Alston's well-known critique of sprawling proliferations of promulgations of new human rights—the human right to tourism, etc.—could be restated as an objection to a methodology in which it is sufficient justification for announcing a new human right that a plausible use case has been diagrammed. Philip Alston, 'Conjuring Up New Human Rights: A Proposal For Quality Control' (1984) 78 American Journal of International Law 607.

[49] Some simple algorithmic methods have long been used in decision-making on legal matters, for example, in adjudicating mass claims, as in the UN Compensation Commission after the 1990–1991 Gulf War. However, to adapt this to simple forms of intelligible rule-based automated digital decision-making calls for precise rules capable of being rendered in computer code—so to embrace this means in effect to dissolve general standards and then resolidify the fragments as rules. In some situations, such detailed rules might themselves be made algorithmically. Katherine J Strandburg, 'Rulemaking and Inscrutable Automated Decision Tools' (2019) 119 Columbia Law Review 1851. Deep-learning systems such as neural networks can produce their new outputs by derivation from past data and decision patterns, and/or from goal specifications, rather than needing a host of pre-specified prospective rules.

[50] Solon Barocas, Moritz Hardt, and Arvind Narayanan, *Fairness and Machine Learning: Limitations and Opportunities* (work in progress 2020) <https://fairmlbook.org/>.

[51] Cf *Ewert v Canada (Correctional Service)* 2018 SCC 30 [2018] 2 SCR 165, in which the Supreme Court of Canada upheld a challenge made to the use of five psychological and actuarial risk assessment tools by the Correctional Service of Canada (CSC) to assess an offender's psychopathy and risk of recidivism, on the basis that they were developed and tested on predominantly non-indigenous populations and that no research confirmed that they were valid when applied to indigenous persons.

[52] Christoph Busch and Alberto De Franceschi, 'Granular Legal Norms: Big Data and the Personalization of Private Law' in Vanessa Mak and others (eds), *Research Handbook in Data Science and Law* (Edward Elgar Publishing 2018) 408; Christopher Busch and Alberto de Franceschi (eds), *Data Economy and Algorithmic Regulation* (Hart 2020).

toward the automated welfare state and the digitally empowered pandemic government a more portentous shading.[53]

Promising efforts have been made to develop the concept of 'affordances' as an organizing idea that is apposite to infrastructure and seems potentially operable in both use case and human rights modes.[54] Laurence Diver argues for imposing thin 'constitutional' design requirements on user-facing code, to provide some degree of contestability, choice, transparency, oversight, and delay.[55] These might be complemented by sociotechnical initiatives, such as some professional training and certification on relevant human rights infrastructure matters for a cadre of software designers and programmers working on governmental algorithmic systems,[56] as well as for those drawn by the inevitable commercially driven demand for lawyers-who-code.[57]

Infrastructure studies open at least three additional lines of inquiry on the meeting of human rights and use case constructs in the digital welfare state. First are issues of time and maintenance. Internet-based mass-participation systems preserve an aura of the new and the future, although they antedate the childhoods of an ever-growing proportion of users. Their embrace overlapped neoliberal enthusiasm for innovation and legacy-industry disruption. These in turn coincided with a devalorization of knowledge of existing systems and their repair, and a chronic under-funding of maintenance. The belittling or outright loss of (low-valued) previous learning and experience (often marked by lack of new training on old systems, and redundancies or retirement of seasoned personnel) has imperilled maintenance of many older infrastructural systems that lumber on unnoticed until they suddenly fail.[58] Digital systems also get old. Many from earlier computer eras are still propped up with

[53] The debate has been slower than that regarding autonomous weapons and predictive, tactical, and strategic AI in military and policing structures. Cf Nehal Bhuta and others (eds), *Autonomous Weapons Systems: Law, Ethics, Policy* (CUP 2016).

[54] Julie E Cohen, 'Affording Fundamental Rights: A Provocation Inspired by Mireille Hildebrandt' (2017) 4 Critical Analysis of Law <https://cal.library.utoronto.ca/index.php/cal/article/view/28151> accessed 26 September 2020; Mark Nunes, 'The Affordances of Place: Digital Agency and the Lived Spaces of Information' (2019) 3 Media Theory 215.

[55] Laurence Diver, 'Digisprudence: The Affordance of Legitimacy in Code-as-Law' (PhD thesis, University of Edinburgh 2019) <https://perma.cc/JFF8-7BBZ>.

[56] Martin Lodge and Andrea Mennicken, 'Reflecting on Public Service Regulation by Algorithm' in Yeung and Lodge (n 17) 179, referring to Science and Technology Select Committee, *Algorithms in Decision-Making* (2017–2019, HC 351).

[57] The transposition of the agenda and techniques of 'corporate social responsibility' (CSR) into private, private–public, and governmental digital power formations (with slogans such as digital social responsibility) is unsurprising but problematic. As noted in Cohen (n 22) 245–46: 'CSR advocates and initiatives occupy a uniquely equivocal position within corporate decision-making processes and network-and-standard-based governance arrangements ... From one perspective, initiatives such as the UN Global Compact represent pragmatic and flexible solutions to pressing global governance problems; from another, they are powerful expressions of neoliberal governmentality ... they project an image of consensus around virtuous privatization of rights enforcement.' Comparable questions arise about the value of transposing other slogans and techniques such as 'human rights mainstreaming' and 'human rights impact assessments'. More effective might be decision paths requiring that well-equipped lawyers review all key design decisions, policy documents, and rules before adoption; but these also draw substantial opposition if lawyers introduce high legalisms or repeatedly reject proposals. The history of partly-analogous debates on roles of lawyers in the World Bank is appraised in Dmitri van den Meersche, 'The World Bank's Lawyers—An Inquiry into the Life of Law as Institutional Practice' (PhD Thesis, European University Institute 2019).

[58] Electricity grid failures in cities unaccustomed to outages bring this home to many people. The 2003 North-East USA grid failure is a much-studied case. 'During this time, the city was "re-materialized". The visiting Brazilian architect Fernando Lara later wrote: "Forget Virilio and Baudrillard and the virtual realities, there is no compression of time and space anymore. You are left alone with the disvirtual reality of space". Suddenly it was not possible to mediate one's relation to the built environment, which had to be measured by the body and its ability to climb, to walk, and to adjust.' Quoted from online adaptation at David Nye, 'When the Lights Went Out: On Blackouts and Terrorism' (MIT Press Reader, 14 August 2019) <https://thereader.mitpress.mit.edu/blackouts-terrorism-history/> accessed 26 September 2020.

recycled parts and ancient disk drives. Some users do not dare seek replacement of digital systems because of the risk of incompatibility with other infrastructural components. Others are stuck with relatively new but poorly selected systems, and cannot internalize the enormous waste (and new cost) of stripping out or abandoning digital infrastructure that was a misguided choice when made. Digital welfare state systems of the recent era may well pose these problems for the next generation, raising combined human rights and use case challenges, some of which are already anticipatable and should be addressed at the outset.

Second are issues of use and purpose. Infrastructure is continuously being constructed and extended, degraded and neglected, ruined and refashioned. Its use cases in life are often far from anything the original designers imagined, and the imagined use cases may barely ever have been fully actuated. After rounds of patching and user modification, governmental and private repurposing, semantic shifts, and organizational reform, the infrastructure may have an almost entirely different valence, and the human rights dimensions must be reframed accordingly.

Third are effects infrastructure can have that reconfigure scale and space. Infrastructures can bring significant returns to scale, including through network effects and interoperability managed by gateways. Low marginal costs after large start-up costs have made scalability (and connectability) integral to many digital business models. Welfare state digitization is pursued with similar aspirations to extendability.[59] Whereas the normalization of scalability has been met by counter-power movements in relation to large physical infrastructural and agro-business projects,[60] traction vis-a-vis large private social media or search platforms has been limited, and the pursuit of massive scalability of government digital surveillance or e-government infrastructure has remained orthodox. Scaling may be tempered, however, by constraints in the configuration of space. Whereas free data flow and the undivided global internet of 1990s digital lore is still vigorously promoted in US-led and Japan-led international trade agreements,[61] assertions of digital sovereignty (in China, the European Union, India, the United States, and many other countries) have buttressed a pro-local or pro-regional motif in digital government, intensified by concern about global extraction of health data in epidemic management. 'Data jurisdictions' *could* become more like the 'national jurisdictions' of classic international human rights and rule-of-law models. But the human rights-based legal control of private, hybrid, and even purely governmental automated data-building and decision-making systems remains relatively elusive. Characterizations of the challenges of real application of human rights law to extraterritorial state conduct do not seem entirely inapt as assessments of challenges posed by digital systems:

> in practice ... the bearers of such rights are citizens without effective sovereigns, or with effective governors who are not *their* sovereigns; and the rights themselves may be 'bare' rights, indeterminate entitlements of uncertain content: values and principles interpreted in myriad ways by a range of actors, and subject to a variety of exigencies in any given context. The beneficiaries of these bare rights have the consolation of having the status of

59 Alston expressed concern, for example, about the UK government plans to develop in relation to welfare benefits a 'fully automated risk analysis and intelligence system for fraud and error', mentioned in Department for Work and Pensions, *Rolling Out Universal Credit* (2017–2019, HC 1123) 61.

60 Anna Lowenhaupt Tsing, 'On Nonscalability: The Living World Is Not Amenable to Precision-Nested Scales' (2012) 18 Common Knowledge 505.

61 Benedict Kingsbury and others (eds), *Megaregulation Contested: Global Economic Ordering after TPP* (1st edn, OUP 2019).

> 'rights-holders', but can have recourse only to the judges of Strasbourg or the expert committees of Geneva to appreciate, in the end, whether this amounts to anything at all.[62]

It might be thought that the issues being confronted in relation to digitization and digital infrastructure of the welfare state in long-prosperous societies such as the United Kingdom are not so much problems of algorithmic government as of basic and longstanding political disagreement about the desirability and sustainability of the 1940s-era UK welfare state.[63] That earlier ideal of universal human rights embodied in the welfare state has come under pressure linked both to political forces and to large changes in the nature of the capitalism in which the welfare states of the early to mid-twentieth century had emerged, and the opportunity structures in fast-growing economies are vastly different from those facing relative decline. Philip Alston indeed took a strong substantive position advocating for that fundamental conception of the welfare state and its purposes, and urging core measures to reverse or mitigate the huge rise in social inequality and radically uneven life chances.[64] This political antinomy, while heated and in some places visceral, should not obscure the profound issues posed by digital infrastructure, machine learning, and algorithmic government, which are more tectonic and prospectively irreversible. The meeting of human rights law and use case engineering may not be in the right register for an effective response, let alone a register in which to generate grand and viable solutions. But pursuing the agenda sketched here might prove empowering in the daunting but indispensable task of thinking into being a better common future than the one techno-power, AI, sporadic dangerous confrontation, and resigned apathy produce on their own.

[62] Nehal Bhuta, 'The Frontiers of Extraterritoriality: Human Rights Law as Global Law' in Nehal Bhuta (ed), *The Frontiers of Human Rights: Extraterritoriality and Its Challenges* (1st edn, OUP 2016) 1, 19.

[63] David Garland, *The Welfare State: A Very Short Introduction* (1st edn, OUP 2016).

[64] Alston very bluntly concluded that the UK government had pursued 'a parallel agenda to reduce benefits by every means available, including constant reductions in benefit levels, ever-more-demanding conditions, harsher penalties, depersonalization, stigmatization, and virtually eliminating the option of using the legal system to vindicate rights. The basic message, delivered in the language of managerial efficiency and automation, is that almost any alternative will be more tolerable than seeking to obtain government benefits. This is a very far cry from any notion of a social contract, Beveridge model or otherwise, let alone of social human rights.' UNCHR 'Report of the Special Rapporteur on Extreme Poverty and Human Rights' (17 July 2019) UN Doc A/HRC/41/39/Add.1, Annex I para 95.

9

Advocating an Ad Hoc Forum for Business and Human Rights Disputes

Bruno Simma and Giorgia Sangiuolo

Preface by Bruno Simma

Before I met Philip more than thirty years ago, my approach to human rights had been as far away from the practical necessities of the subject as you can imagine. It was my work with Philip in a newly established UN Committee on Economic, Social and Cultural Rights that fundamentally changed the way I regarded human rights: as a moral challenge, heavy on my conscience, instead of a mere philosophical construct, a black box. Under Philip's leadership, the Committee became much more than yet another institutional fig leaf, as most observers were expecting (if not hoping), and it turned into a driver and a mover among the UN human rights treaty-monitoring bodies. The broad margin of manoeuvre that the Committee enjoyed, subject only to the UN regime of cooperation with NGOs, gave us the freedom to gradually develop the reporting procedure foreseen in the Covenant into something meaningful. Let me just mention, among other achievements, the development of guidelines for reporting, the handling of overdue reports, the elaboration of a follow-up procedure with 'a bite', and the first steps towards an optional protocol to the Covenant allowing individual applications. All these achievements that make me proud still today were triggered by Philip and I supported them as well as I could. I fondly remember the countless Sunday nights preceding Committee sessions that Philip and I spent together (if possible, over pleasant dinners) developing and discussing ideas on the next challenge to put before our fellow Committee members and states parties.

Since I left the Committee twenty-four years ago, Philip's and my professional ways have parted. Contrary to Philip's career, my dedication to human rights became again very much part time, essentially academic and theoretical. At least until very recently. I am now happy to report that the feeling of being an institution builder, of actually moving something in the field, which I experienced in Philip's company, is back: about two years ago I became involved in a project that I hope will make a meaningful contribution to human rights in the world of business. It is the legal-political points of departure of that project that I will describe in the following, in co-authorship with Giorgia Sangiuolo, to whose devotion and energy the project owes more than could possibly be expressed here.

9.1 Introduction

Our contribution to Philip's *Festschrift* is devoted to a recently completed project in which both of us were participating. The project is designed to solve disputes on compliance by

Bruno Simma and Giorgia Sangiuolo, *Advocating an Ad Hoc Forum for Business and Human Rights Disputes* In: *The Struggle for Human Rights*. Edited by: Nehal Bhuta, Florian Hoffmann, Sarah Knuckey, Frédéric Mégret, and Margaret Satterthwaite, Oxford University Press.
 DOI: 10.1093/oso/9780198868064.003.0010

businesses with human rights obligations by means of arbitration. The initiative to elaborate an ad hoc set of arbitral rules to adjudicate disputes on this matter was taken a few years back by a group of international lawyers, practitioners as well as academics, seeking to contribute to the implementation of the UN Guiding Principles on Business and Human Rights (UNGPs), the so-called 'Ruggie Principles'.[1] In a 2017 manifesto, the group set out the broad guidelines and a working plan to draft the arbitration rules.[2] A year later, with the support of the City of The Hague, the group passed the task to draft these rules on to a Drafting Team.[3] Involving two public consultations regarding the most controversial issues on the scope and functioning of the rules, the Team spent several hundred hours on this task, which essentially consisted in the adaptation of the 2010 UNCITRAL Rules[4] to the business and human rights (BHR) project's specific purpose. On 12 December 2019, at a launch symposium held at the Hague Peace Palace, the final product of the work of the Team—the Hague Rules on Business and Human Rights Arbitration (Hague Rules)[5]—was presented to the public. During the symposium, the first author symbolically handed the first hard copies of the Hague Rules to the Netherlands Human Rights Ambassador, Dr Bahia Tahzib-Lie, and the Deputy Mayor of The Hague, Ms Saskia Bruines.[6]

Within the limited space available to us here, we cannot discuss the Hague Rules in detail. Equally, an adequate analysis of the most problematic knots being debated in the drafting of the Rules would require much more space. Instead, we intend to assess how existing international judicial and arbitral institutions have dealt with BHR disputes in their case law, if at all, and whether an ad hoc mechanism would be better placed to protect and offer redress to victims of human rights abuses by businesses. Our conclusion is that, while existing instruments have attempted to cope with the challenge of delivering some sort of 'justice' in BHR matters, an international consensual ad hoc mechanism like the Hague Rules remains necessary, in the sense of filling a gap, for the effective prevention and redress of violations of corporate social responsibility (CSR) obligations committed by businesses. In fact, the principal limit to the involvement of existing international courts and tribunals in BHR disputes lies in their mandate: beyond structural issues in terms of standing or scope of jurisdiction; all the analysed institutions filter their approach to human rights through the lenses of the specific aim for which they were set up. Thus, the ICJ remains a 'generalist' court wary of opening up to issues that are less related to situations typically encountered by and between states;

[1] UNHRC 'Promotion and Protection of All Human Rights, Civil, Political, Economic, Social and Cultural Rights, Including the Right to Development—Protect, Respect, and Remedy: A Framework for Business and Human Rights' (7 April 2008) UN Doc A/HRC/8/5 (UNGPs).

[2] Claes Cronstedt, Jan Eijsbouts, and Robert C Thompson, 'International Business and Human Rights Arbitration' <www.cilc.nl/cms/wp-content/uploads/2018/03/INTERNATIONAL-ARBITRATION-TO-RESOLVE-HUMAN-RIGHTS-DISPUTES-INVOLVING-BUSINESS-PROPOSAL-MAY-2017.pdf> accessed 16 May 2021; UNHRC 'Promotion and Protection' (n 1).

[3] The Drafting Team is chaired by the first author. Giorgia Sangiuolo is a member of the team. All the documents relating to the Hague Rules are accessible on the webpage of CILC (the Dutch Center for International Legal Cooperation), which functions as the project leader of the Hague Rules 'The Hague Rules on Business and Human Rights Arbitration' (Center for International Legal Cooperation, 2019) <https://www.cilc.nl/project/the-hague-rules-on-business-and-human-rights-arbitration/> accessed 29 September 2020.

[4] UNGA Res 31/98 (1977) UN Doc A/RES/31/98.

[5] The authentic text of the Hague Rules is available on the website of the Permanent Court of Arbitration 'Other Conventions and Rules' (Permanent Court of Arbitration) <https://pca-cpa.org/en/documents/other-conventions-and-rules/the-hague-rules-for-business-and-human-rights-arbitration/> accessed 29 September 2020.

[6] The report of the launch is available on the webpage of CILC at 'The Hague Rules on Business and Human Rights Arbitration' (n 3); a video of the launch is available at CILC, 'Watch the Launch of the Hague Rules on Business and Human Rights Arbitration' (23 December 2019) <www.youtube.com/watch?v=ASYoEgdO_vU> accessed 30 September 2020.

the ECtHR is hesitant to outgrow its function of 'watchdog' of states and to fully take up the task of delivering justice to individuals; investment tribunals only look at human rights in the context of the economic disputes before them, if at all; and the EU judicial system uses human rights principally as a tool to pursue integration. In contrast, bespoke settlement by arbitration of BHR disputes as now provided by the Hague Rules appears to us to be capable of injecting into the 'DNA' of the resolution process BHR-specific values and principles that will orientate its outcome. In a 'lesson learnt' exercise we will attempt to define the desiderata of effective BHR dispute settlement under the UNGPs based upon an analysis of the mechanisms currently in existence. Our conclusion is that effective protection of human rights in the business world would be best served by a network of different remedies flexible enough to adapt to the fluid relationships among all parties involved. The Hague Rules develop around these principles.

Our contribution is structured in three sections. In section 9.2, we will provide some background on the development of CSR or BHR obligations and introduce the Ruggie Principles. In section 9.3 we will then move to the core of our discussion, that is, an overview on the approach taken by some of the most relevant international judicial and arbitral mechanisms regarding disputes possessing a BHR element. Building on this analysis, in section 9.4, we turn to our 'lesson learnt' exercise and present some concluding thoughts.

9.2 The Background of BHR Arbitration

The discussion on the responsibility of business to ensure that its cross-border activities do not perpetrate, or contribute to perpetrating, human rights violations—also known as BHR obligations, CSR, or, earlier, 'social responsibility'—has not developed in a vacuum. Rather, it arose in the context of a structural shift in international law that, departing from a state-centred paradigm, has moved towards the realization of the idea that individuals can, and should, turn into decisive players in the development of the law.[7]

Since the end of World War II, individuals and their rights have become the subject of an increasing number of international treaties and conventions in a variety of fields, far beyond the scope of international human rights law in the narrow, technical, sense. In the course of this process, the position of individuals has grown beyond that of passive addressees of international law to that of active participants in the lawmaking process. Viewed from an angle characterized more by attention to reality than by doctrinal limits, the impact of individuals or groups on the law has grown immensely.

Yet, such enhanced power of private actors, including business, to influence public life was not accompanied by an increase in corresponding responsibilities. Adapting the national and international legal and regulatory frameworks to the new balances of rights and obligations has proved to be very challenging. Principal among these challenges has of course been the establishment of a 'grip' for international human rights law on international business in the absence of agreement about an international legal personality of the corporate entities involved. The lack of agreement on the question of which 'human rights' businesses should respect also factors in the difficulty of regulating their activity. Suffice it here to mention that even the Charter of Fundamental Rights of the European Union—adopted by 'like-minded'

[7] The history of CSR has been traced to the work of Howard R Bowen, *Social Responsibilities of the Businessman* (Harper 1953) (as cited in Archie B Carroll, 'Corporate Social Responsibility: Evolution of a Definitional Construct' (1999) 38(3) Business & Society 268).

states—suffers from various opt-outs[8] and state resistance to the direct application of its provisions. The cross-border dimension of the duty of corporations to respect and protect fundamental rights adds a further layer of complexity to the definition of a BHR framework. The aforementioned legal 'grip' on businesses, the way around the absence of a straightforward recognition of an international legal personality of corporations, rests on their control by certain states. But state borders limit the jurisdiction of national administrative and judicial institutions tasked with the control of business activity and require a degree of coordination among states that is often difficult to achieve in practice.

The discussion on how to overcome these difficulties is taking place in a variety of international fora. To date, the stepping stone in the development of BHR obligations is to be seen in the UNGPs.[9] The UNGPs define the framework of duties of states and businesses in relation to the protection, promotion, and respect of the human rights involved in the latter's activities in thirty-one principles. These principles are divided into three 'pillars': the first pillar, concerned with states, identifies and defines states' existing obligations to respect, protect, and fulfil human rights and fundamental freedoms. The second pillar frames a duty of international businesses to comply with human rights obligations, to prevent violations, and to redress them when they occur, in their cross-border activities. The third pillar, most relevant for the purposes of our discussion, is addressed to both states and businesses and calls for the creation of appropriate and effective judicial and non-judicial remedies to deal with BHR violations. Under the third pillar, such 'effective' remedies should be legitimate, accessible, predictable in their outcomes, equitable, transparent, rights-compatible, a source of continuous learning, and ensure dialogue and engagement.

The 'Ruggie Principles' thus summarized have undoubtedly had an enormous impact on the conception and delineation of BHR obligations. They have led to a remarkable level of alignment of key standards across jurisdictions and the emergence of global, regional, and national initiatives cutting across regions and business sectors.[10] However, the UNGPs constitute 'soft law', and this stands in the way of their effective implementation, especially on the remedies side. In an attempt to fill this gap, the Hague Rules propose to further the realization of the 'effectiveness' requirement under Pillar III of the UNGPs by means of setting up a private, flexible, and specialized international arbitral forum built ad hoc for BHR disputes—a baseline of international protection in addition to the network of existing national and international remedies.

9.3 Existing International Dispute Settlement Mechanisms and Their Limits

While national courts are to remain the preferred forum to deal with BHR disputes, their role is often limited in actual practice. National courts of the country in which a breach of BHR obligations occurs may be perceived by claimants as unable to deliver justice due to a lack of independence or impartiality. Equally, the doctrine of separate legal personality

[8] By Ireland and the United Kingdom.

[9] UNHRC 'Promotion and Protection' (n 1).

[10] Including OECD, *OECD Guidelines for Multinational Enterprises, 2011 Edition* (OECD 2011) <https://www.oecd-ilibrary.org/governance/oecd-guidelines-for-multinational-enterprises_9789264115415-en> accessed 30 September 2020; National Action Plans, the European Union, the Council of Europe, the Organization of American states, the ASEAN Intergovernmental Commission on Human Rights, the Inter-American Commission on Human Rights, and the Inter-American Court of Human Rights.

may obstruct the possibility for victims of bringing a claim against the parent companies of the subsidiary to which an alleged violation is attributed before the courts of their home jurisdictions. Bringing claims before courts in the home jurisdictions of parent companies may be all the more desirable where such jurisdictions recognize higher standards of protection of fundamental rights compared to the standards upheld by courts operating in the jurisdiction where the alleged violation of such rights occurs. An exemplary instance of the accountability gap created by the limited jurisdictional reach of national courts is the recent case of *Okpabi v RDS and SPDC*. In this case, the Nigerian Ogale community brought a claim against Royal Dutch Shell Plc (RDS), a company incorporated and with registered office in the United Kingdom, for the environmental damage caused by oil spills originating from its oil pipelines and associated infrastructure managed by Shell Petroleum Development Company of Nigeria Plc. Fearing a lack of due process before the Nigerian courts, the Ogale community filed the damage claim in the courts of the United Kingdom. However, both on first instance and on appeal, the UK courts declined jurisdiction on the damages claim, considering that RDS did not have a 'duty of care' over its Nigerian subsidiary.[11]

Admittedly, as the recent decision of the UK Supreme Court in the *Vedanta Resources* case shows,[12] national courts do at times take a more liberal approach to claims brought against parent companies in BHR disputes. Similarly, legislators have begun to develop normative tools to fill the accountability gap we just described.[13] However, uncertainties arising from the existing fragmented network of case law and national legislations will continue to exist for a long time—demonstrating that international fora may often still be the only available avenue for claimants to obtain redress for non-compliance with CSR obligations. But what fora? In the absence of a specific/specialized settlement mechanism for BHR disputes, various international courts and tribunals have become, directly or indirectly, involved in such cases, in some instances considerably stretching their jurisdiction to fill gaps in the protection of basic human rights vis-à-vis corporate activity. Yet, despite commendable efforts, these courts all suffer from deficiencies that stand in the way of their delivering a genuinely 'effective' adjudication of BHR disputes under the UNGPs.

The following paragraphs will describe these deficiencies by taking as examples the practice of the ICJ, the ECtHR, investment tribunals, and the Court of Justice of the European Union (CJEU), in relation to human rights and CSR. Beyond structural issues in terms of standing and jurisdiction, the main obstacle that these courts and tribunals encounter in their attempts to deliver justice in BHR disputes appears to lie in what they understand to be their 'mandate'. What we will thus find is that these courts and tribunals are locked in the roles foreseen for them in their constitutive instruments, which ultimately limit their ability and willingness to effectively remedy violations of human rights on the part of businesses.

[11] *His Royal Highness Emere Godwin Bebe Okpabi and Others and Lucky Alame and Others v Royal Dutch Shell Plc and Shell Petroleum Development Company of Nigeria Plc* [2017] EWHC 89 (TCC); *Okpabi v Royal Dutch Shell Plc* [2018] EWCA 89 Civ 191.

[12] *Vedanta Resources PLC v Lungowe* [2019] UKSC 20.

[13] *Loi* n° 2017-399 du 27 mars 2017 relative au devoir de vigilance des sociétés mères et des entreprises donneuses d'ordre, 1.

9.3.1 International Courts

9.3.1.1 The International Court of Justice

In a discussion of possible judicial avenues for the protection of human rights at the international level, the one institution that might come to mind to a non-specialized audience is the ICJ. As the principal judicial organ of the United Nations, provided with general jurisdiction, as the 'World Court', the ICJ enjoys a special status, not only in the law but also in the social imaginary.

And indeed, one of us has been able to witness *sur place* that the Court has more recently warmed up to issues going beyond the traditional areas of inter-state relations and conflicts, among them human rights.[14] Yet, this slow shift of perspective of the Court remains far from allowing it to make meaningful 'direct' contributions to BHR disputes: despite a certain move towards the 'humanization' of the law,[15] the ICJ remains 'genetically' a generalist court operating at the level of states and international organizations. Hence, the role of the Court in the juridical enforcement of human rights—even in general, not to mention the BHR context—will remain modest for what could be called 'structural' reasons. In the Peace Palace, human rights and their enforcement will unavoidably be approached from a 'wrong angle', as it were: viewing human rights problems, above all the issue of violations, from an *inter*-state perspective can only bring to the fore certain limited aspects of these problems. What this means is that the ICJ will deal with violations of human rights as a matter of state responsibility, and the rules on state responsibility are typically 'law by States for States'.[16] Before the International Court, individuals lack standing; thus, in interstate proceedings the individual victims of human rights violations will not have a voice, they remain mute and invisible (as parties before the Court, that is). If a state decides to espouse the claims of individual victims by exercising diplomatic protection in the form of suing the perpetrator in the Hague Court, the almost century-old spirit (or should we say, ghost?) of *Mavrommatis* will remain present, a rigid straitjacket will thus be in place for the admissibility of claims,[17] even though the affected individual might become at least a little more visible in our picture if the Court followed the precedent it set in the *Diallo* case.[18] The task of the ICJ, however, is precisely the settlement of inter-state disputes; only states can sue each other before the Court, while affected individuals have to watch from the gallery in the Great Hall of Justice.

It should thus be clear by now that the Hague Court is miles away from presenting a forum for BHR disputes, structurally as well as regarding legal policy. The only human rights-related activity of the Court that we consider relevant for our topic is what could be called the juridical 'mainstreaming' of these rights, in the sense of integrating human rights into the fabric of international law. Thus, the Court can, and does, render human rights arguments more acceptable to international law generalists by interpreting and applying human rights norms in what could be called 'orthodox' ways, compared, for instance, to the not-infrequent handling

[14] cf, eg Bruno Simma, 'Human Rights before the International Court of Justice: Community Interest Coming to Life?' in Christian J Tams and James Sloan (eds), *The Development of International Law by the International Court of Justice* (OUP 2013) 302.

[15] Theodor Meron, *The Humanization of International Law* (Martinus Nijhoff Publishers, 2006).

[16] Robert McCorquodale, 'Impact on State Responsibility' in Menno T Kamminga and Martin Scheinin, *The Impact of Human Rights Law on General International Law* (OUP, 2009) 235.

[17] *Mavrommatis Palestine Concessions (Greece v UK)* (Judgment, Objection to the Jurisdiction of the Court) [1924] PCIJ Rep Series A No 2, 12.

[18] *Ahmadou Sadio Diallo (Guinea v Democratic Republic of the Congo)* (Judgment, Preliminary Objections) [2007] ICJ Rep 07, 96.

of such norms by UN human rights treaty bodies in a spirit of wishful thinking rather than by proper legal analysis. Further, the Court can devise solutions for more 'technical' legal problems arising at the interface of human rights and more traditional international law, and it can thus play a major role in determining the international legal framework within which international human rights operate. In this direction, the Court has already made quite substantial contributions, albeit with differing degrees of success (depending on the viewpoint of either human rights-minded or more 'statist' observers).[19] None of this will be BHR specific, of course, but it will still be part of the development of international human rights within which BHR arbitration will move.

9.3.1.2 The European Court of Human Rights

The history of the ECtHR mirrors the post-war 'humanization' of international law. Created by the ECHR and Fundamental Freedoms under the auspices of the Council of Europe in 1950, the ECtHR was not originally open to applications by individuals. Access to the Court was 'filtered' through state action and a European Commission of Human Rights. Indeed, the Strasbourg Court was conceived as a tool supporting national institutions as an 'early warning system to sound the alarm in case Europe's fledgling democracies began to backslide toward totalitarianism', rather than integrating them.[20] In 1998, various amendments radically changed its functioning and opened it to direct recourse from individuals. Yet, the ECtHR remains 'supervisory' and 'supporting' in nature, and this bars it from becoming a one-stop forum for the enforcement of CSR obligations.

The evolution of the Court's case law

Unlike the ICJ, the ECtHR now affords direct access to private actors, including individuals, groups, and NGOs, within the jurisdiction of the parties to the European Convention for the protection of a vast array of fundamental rights.[21] Significantly, the nationality of individual applicants is irrelevant in terms of standing.[22] The Convention commits its contracting parties to uphold a number of rights falling within the potential scope of BHR litigation.[23] If the Court finds a violation of the Convention or one of its Protocols, it can award 'just satisfaction' to the complaining party.[24] The judgments of the ECtHR are final and legally binding in international law[25] and their execution is monitored by the Committee of Ministers of the Council of Europe.

Admittedly, the Strasbourg Court's jurisdiction only covers disputes between private parties and a state; it thus excludes litigation among private parties, including on BHR issues. However, the Court has devised certain mechanisms to overcome this limitation and ensure compliance by private entities with the Convention rights by developing the concepts of negative and positive obligations on contracting states.

To begin with, the Court has understood its jurisdiction as extending to acts of corporations acting as state agents or under the control of the state. The Court has adopted a rather practical approach to this question: disregarding formal qualifications, it focuses

[19] Simma (n 14).

[20] Laurence R Helfer, 'Redesigning the European Court of Human Rights: Embeddedness as a Deep Structural Principle of the European Human Rights Regime' (2008) 19(1) European Journal of International Law 125, 125.

[21] Convention for the Protection of Human Rights and Fundamental Freedoms (ECHR, as amended) art 34.

[22] ibid arts 40, 44(3).

[23] Ranging from the right to life (ibid art 2) to the right to property (ibid art 1).

[24] ibid art 41.

[25] ibid art 44.

on the 'institutional and operational characteristics' of the corporation at issue, such as its legal status and the nature of its activity.[26] The end result of this interpretative approach is a broadening of state accountability for the acts of corporations. On this basis, in the *Ališić* case, the Court found Serbia and Slovenia responsible for the debts of the Sarajevo branch of Ljubljanska Banka Ljubljana and the Tuzla branch of Investbanka towards two individuals who, following the dissolution of the Republic of Yugoslavia, were not able to withdraw 'old' foreign currency savings from their accounts.[27]

Further, the Court has developed the concept of positive obligations on states to take all 'reasonable' and 'appropriate' steps to protect human rights; specifically in relation to corporations acting as third parties. In the *Fadeyeva* case, the Court found that the state's (Russia) failure to regulate emissions of a steel plant owned and operated by a private corporation that had caused the applicant severe health problems violated the latter's right to private life under Article 8(1) of the Convention.[28] For the Court, the fact that Russia 'was in the position to evaluate the pollution hazards and to take adequate measures to prevent or reduce them' was sufficient to ascertain a 'nexus between the pollutant emissions and the State to raise an issue of the State's positive obligations under Article 8 of the Convention'.[29]

The ECtHR also recognizes negative obligations on states. In the *Wilson* case, reasoning on grounds of effectiveness of the rights guaranteed in the Convention, it found the United Kingdom responsible for the acts of an employer who had offered financial incentives to his employees to renounce to their rights to collective bargaining. Specifically, the Court found that UK law allowing employers to seek to limit collective bargaining on a voluntary basis by offering substantial pay rises to employees who acquiesced in the termination of collective bargaining, had the effect of frustrating the ability of trade unions to strive for the protection of its members' interests and made the protection under Article 11 of the Convention, on the freedom of assembly and association, illusory.[30]

From still another standpoint, the Court also upholds BHR obligations by means of the right to fair trial (Article 6 of the Convention) and the right to an effective remedy (Article 13 of the Convention). Illustrative in this sense is the *Steel and Morris* case in which the Court found that the non-availability of legal aid to the applicants, two environmental activists, in a lengthy case for defamation against a powerful multinational, McDonalds, resulted in an unacceptable inequality of arms that the state should have addressed.[31]

Limits to the Court's case law

Yet, the commendable interpretative efforts of the Strasbourg Court to afford relief to those affected by alleged BHR violations do not make up for several standing recurrent issues, which ultimately all boil down to the fact that the Court remains an organ of supervision of non-compliance by states, rather than an upfront protector of individual rights.

To begin with, the ECtHR lacks jurisdiction over disputes between private parties, so that the protection that the Court can offer in BHR cases appears merely indirect and insufficient to qualify as an 'effective remedy' under the third pillar of the UNGPs. The possibility for the Court to find a violation also encounters the limit of the margin of appreciation, that is, the

[26] *Ališić v Bosnia and Herzegovina* App no 60642/08 (ECtHR, 16 July 2014) para 114; *Liseytseva v Russia* App nos 39483/05 and 40527/10 (ECtHR, 9 January 2015) paras 187–90.
[27] *Ališić* (n 26).
[28] *Fadeyeva v Russia* App no 55723/00 (ECtHR, 9 June 2005).
[29] ibid paras 89–92.
[30] *Wilson v UK* App nos 30668/96, 30671/96 and 30678/96 (ECtHR, 2 October 2002) para 41.
[31] *Steel v UK* App no 68416/01 (ECtHr, 15 May 2005).

wide space of discretion it normally allows states as to how to regulate and control corporate activities endangering human rights.[32]

A second factor limiting the effectiveness of the ECtHR as a forum for addressing BHR disputes lies in its territorial jurisdiction: Article 1 of the Convention limits the Court's jurisdiction to the territory of those states (currently forty-seven) that have accepted its jurisdiction. Such acceptance can also be partial, limited by opt-outs. It is true that the Court appears to adopt a broad understanding of 'jurisdiction', linked to the 'exercise of public powers' by a state on a certain territory, wherever that exercise may take place, rather than defined by the formal concept of state borders.[33] Yet, the interpretative efforts of the Court on extraterritorial obligations remain limited to cases of gross violations perpetrated by state agents (eg troops in war zones), premised on the assumption that the state exercises a certain control over a territory, to non-refoulement cases, or direct state actions linked to the violation.[34]

The concerns expressed so far are made more acute by the fact that the jurisdiction of the ECtHR is subsidiary to that of national courts: Article 35 of the Convention provides that access to the Court is subordinate to the applicants having exhausted all available remedies before national courts (or showing a good reason not to have done so). This procedural requirement, aimed at giving states a chance to remedy illegalities before their actions are scrutinized by an international body, appears as a serious shortcoming for BHR disputes: most of these cases will deal with threats that are better remedied within a short time. Also, applicants will often lack the economic resources to go through multiple layers of national jurisdictions before being able to resort to Strasbourg. This is especially true if we consider that the member states of the Council of Europe are not required to give direct effect to the European Convention in their domestic law and that the status and rank of the Convention is thus determined by the domestic legal systems of the state parties. Thus, in national litigation, individuals might not be able to rely directly on the rights afforded to them by the Convention, but only on their—possibly more restrictive—national law equivalents.

9.3.2 Investment Tribunals

In times characterized by a 'backlash' of states and civil society against 'secret private tribunals' allegedly serving the interest of multinationals and threatening states' rights to regulate in the public interest, the mere establishment of a link between the international protection of human rights and investment arbitration might appear to some almost heretic. Yet, investment treaties do share one specific feature with human rights treaties: both protect rights of beneficiaries other than states parties to the treaties concerned. Indeed, both human rights treaties and investment treaties confer direct protection—in the form of direct access—to individuals of analogous rights, such as the right to property (protection against expropriation); non-discrimination on grounds of nationality (national treatment, most favoured nation clauses); and fair trial (dispute settlement clauses). Further, both investment and human rights treaties operate to shield these rights against the ephemeral will of the governments of their contracting parties. Thus, the 'third party rights' element of human rights treaties has been considered determinative for arguments on automatic succession of states to such

[32] *Hardy v UK* App no 31965/07 (ECtHr, 14 February 2012) para 218.
[33] *Al-Skeini v UK* App no 55721/07 (ECtHr, 7 July 2011) paras 134–38.
[34] *Treska v Albania and Italy* App no 26937/04 (ECtHr, 29 June 2006) p 12.

treaties, while survival or sunset clauses in investment treaties 'immunize' investors against changes in the actual will of states.

It is perhaps significant that both debates, on protection of foreign investors and on protection of fundamental rights of individuals, developed in the aftermath of World War II—characterized by large-scale violations of both basic civil rights (life, association, family life, etc.) and economic rights (in particular property rights, in the form of uncompensated expropriations, first of Jewish and then of German properties, after the war).[35]

Probably because of such a common rationale, investment tribunals have grown increasingly interested in human rights—even in the BHR context. Yet, the focus of activity of investment tribunals remains limited to a narrow set of rights—economic rights—and this circumstance affects not only the overall design of the investor-state system, but often also the mandate that investment tribunals perceive to have to pursue.

9.3.2.1 The evolving jurisdiction of investment tribunals

Investment arbitration is an extraordinary remedy for two reasons. Not only do investment agreements normally give direct standing to a certain category of individuals, investors, to bring claims against states that have violated their rights under the treaties in question. These agreements also widely abolish the condition of exhaustion of domestic remedies, which is still the rule under the ECHR.

Arbitral tribunals have shown increasing receptiveness to human rights considerations. First, investment tribunals have referred to human rights in the analysis of property rights of both the investor and third parties involved. In *Tecmed v Mexico*, the arbitral tribunal relied on the case law of both the European and the Inter-American Court of Human Rights to ascertain whether the non-renewal to the claimants of a permit to operate a landfill and the closure of the site by Mexico amounted to illegal expropriation under the Spain–Mexico BIT.[36] Further, in line with Article 31(3)(c) of the Vienna Convention on the Law of the Treaties, the Tribunals in *Spyridon Roussalis*[37] and *Vivendi*,[38] to name two early decisions, explicitly recognized that states' international obligations under the BITs could be expanded to include human rights obligations deriving from other treaties to which they were parties, the *Spyridon Roussalis* tribunal explicitly referring to the ECHR.[39]

Tribunals have also engaged in the discussion of whether respect for human rights by foreign investors should be assessed when deciding on the violation of treaty standards. *Urbaser v Argentina*, a case arising out of the insolvency of a concessionaire for the supply of water and sewage services as a consequence of Argentina's emergency measures adopted in the aftermath of the 2001 financial crisis, is relevant in this sense.[40] The tribunal not only

[35] The leading figures in the development of a system of protection that would later give international investors standing to protect their rights, Hermann Josef Abs, the proposer of a 'Magna Carta for Investment Protection', and Aaron Broches, the father of the ICSID Convention, had themselves first-hand experience with states' wrongdoing, albeit from opposite sides, as it were. Taylor St John, *The Rise of Investor-State Arbitration: Politics, Law, and Unintended Consequences* (OUP 2018) ch 3, 68–109.

[36] *Técnicas Medioambientales Tecmed SA v The United Mexican states*, ICSID Case No ARB (AF)/00/2 (29 May 2003).

[37] *Spyridon Roussalis v Romania*, ICSID Case No ARB/06/1 (2 December 2011).

[38] *Suez, Sociedad General de Aguas de Barcelona SA v The Argentine Republic*, ICSID Case No ARB/03/17, Decision on Liability (30 July 2010).

[39] *Spyridon Roussalis* (n 37) [312]. The Tribunal clarified, however, that in that case the application of the BIT was to prevail, given the higher and more specific level of protection offered by this latter instrument compared to the ECHR.

[40] *Urbaser SA and Consorcio de Aguas Bilbao Bizkaia, Bilbao Biskaia Ur Partzuergoa v Argentina*, ICSID Case No ARB/07/26 (8 December 2016).

affirmed jurisdiction on Argentina's counterclaim that Urbaser's failure to provide the necessary level of investment in the supply services led to violations of the human right to water, but also stated that the BIT was construed in a way to allow reference to sources of law external to the BIT, including treaties and general international law, which imposed obligations binding on the claimant, including human rights obligations such as that correlative to the right to water. While the counterclaim in *Urbaser* was eventually dismissed on the merits, the decision seems to have awakened the 'human rights' awareness of successive tribunals.

In *Aven v Costa Rica*, relating to the legality of injunctions adopted on environmental grounds by the Costa Rican authorities against the investors' project of developing a large tourist area, the tribunal, in order to assert its jurisdiction, adopted a wide interpretation of the possibility of an investor to be an addressee of obligations under the Dominican Republic–Central America Free Trade Agreement.[41] While acknowledging that the treaty in principle foresees as parties—and addressees of obligations—only the contracting states, the tribunal admitted that its provisions nevertheless recognize 'at least implicitly' some obligations on investors, 'especially with respect to the environmental laws of the host State'.[42] Reasoning on the basis of *Urbaser*, the tribunal observed that environmental obligations constitute obligations *erga omnes* and that, for that reason, 'it can no longer be admitted that investors operating internationally are immune from becoming subjects of international law'.[43]

The tribunal in *Bear Creek v Peru*, a case revolving around the issue of whether a host state's reaction (or lack thereof) to social unrest by the local population, which barred the investor from exploiting a gold mine, amounted to a violation of several provisions of the Canada–Peru BIT, did not go as far as imposing on the investor a duty to engage in public consultation and outreach with the local population.[44] However, the dissenting opinion of one of the arbitrators puts forward the suggestion that respect by investors of legal obligations—in that case relating to the fundamental rights of the local population under the ILO Convention on Indigenous and Tribal Peoples—should be taken into account at the stage of awarding damages.[45]

9.3.2.2 Amending investment treaties to accommodate human rights obligations

Decisions of investment tribunals dealing with human rights, either of the investor or of other private parties involved in the investment, remain heavily influenced by the normative framework set up by the investment treaty, which circumscribes their jurisdiction and powers. Greater attention to human rights obligations is today made possible through a variety of reforms in treaty making, which include the explicit incorporation of human rights and sustainable development considerations into the treaty text, enhanced transparency, the explicit protection of states' rights to regulate, the possibility of counterclaims, and, in some cases, even the explicit imposition of obligations on investors.[46]

41 *David R Aven and Others v Republic of Costa Rica*, ICSID Case No UNCT/15/3 (18 September 2018).

42 ibid [732].

43 ibid [738].

44 *Bear Creek Mining Corporation v Republic of Peru*, ICSID Case No ARB/14/21(30 November 2017).

45 ibid (dissenting opinion of Philippe Sands). Sands points out that it is ultimately for the investor to obtain a 'social license' to carry out its investment and that the contributory fault of the investor in that case should have led to the halving of the damages awarded.

46 2018 Dutch Model BIT, art 7, at: <https://globalarbitrationreview.com/digital_assets/820bcdd9-08b5-4bb5-a81e-d69e6c6735ce/Draft-Model-BIT-NL-2018.pdf >; Reciprocal Investment Promotion and Protection Agreement between the Government of the Kingdom of Morocco and the Government of the Federal Republic of Nigeria (signed 3 December 2016), art 24.

Yet, such more favourable interpretation by investment tribunals, and even the more substantive systemic changes at the treaty level over the last few years, appear insufficient to regard investment arbitration as an effective path to adjudicate BHR disputes. Investment arbitration remains a legal regime essentially built around the idea of protecting not human rights in general but certain rights of a distinctive group of individuals—the investors. For the same reason, investment arbitration is naturally a shield for investors, and will hardly be turned into the 'sword' to oversee the effective implementation of CSR obligations. The scope of investment arbitration is the relationship between individuals and states. Wrongdoings by businesses that do not fall, at least indirectly, within the scope of investment treaties remain outside the scrutiny of investment tribunals. Equally, investment arbitration is only accessible to investors and states, so that private parties that do not qualify as investors cannot start proceedings over the respect by businesses of their CSR and see their participation in pending proceedings limited by the wording of the treaties in question, which, at best, give them a right to submit *amicus curiae* petitions for consideration by the tribunal. They thus are not 'parties', entitled to bring claims and obtain compensation. The fragmented case law of investment tribunals regarding the role of human rights in investment disputes also continues to show a certain reluctance, arguably justified to an extent, to engage in human rights discourse in the absence of an express mandate in the treaties that confer them jurisdiction.

9.3.3 The EU System of Judicial Protection

Defining the judicial system of the European Union as 'international' will raise more than a few eyebrows among EU lawyers. Yet, just like the other mechanisms discussed until now, the EU judicial system arises out of international treaties and responds to a mandate by states, in this case to oversee integration among the member states. The EU judicial system is, however, unique in the sense that it functionally combines the courts at the Union level, namely a General Court and the Court of Justice (together labelled the CJEU), with the national courts of the member states,[47] with these, despite of course formally remaining state organs, becoming part of the judicial system of the European Union when adjudicating EU law matters; as their role is to offer the effective judicial protection provided in the treaties, if necessary by disapplying competing national law.

9.3.3.1 Jurisdiction of the EU courts over BHR disputes

The CJEU has been the motor of the development of protection of fundamental rights in the European Union ever since its inception. Admittedly, fundamental rights were not originally intended to be part of EU law: while the Court of Justice was supposed to have jurisdiction on certain economic rights of the 'peoples' of Europe—namely the four freedoms—the protection of fundamental rights understood in the traditional sense was left to its 'sister' court, the ECtHR, created under the auspices of the Council of Europe.

Yet, this division of labour did not quite develop as foreseen. The CJEU soon planted the seeds for a systemic change in the EU approach to fundamental rights by qualifying individuals as direct addressees of EU law in its seminal decision in *Van Gend en Loos*.[48] Starting

[47] Consolidated Version of the Treaty on European Union [2012] OJ 326/12 art 19; Dutch Model BIT (n 46) arts 267, 344.

[48] Case 26-62 *NV Algemene Transport-en Expeditie Onderneming van Gend & Loos v Netherlands Inland Revenue Administration* [1963] EU:C:1963:1.

with *Internationale Handelsgesellschaft*, the Court of Justice embraced a broad understanding of its jurisdiction and developed a full doctrine of protection of 'EU fundamental rights'.[49] That doctrine has greatly evolved over time and has arguably changed the face of the European Union: today, fundamental rights can in certain instances even trump the four freedoms that had characterized the Union of the origins.[50] The fundamental rights of the Union have been codified in the Charter of Fundamental Rights of the EU, which, after the modifications brought about by the Treaty of Lisbon, since 2009 enjoys the 'same legal status' as the founding treaties.[51]

While the principles of conferral, proportionality, and subsidiarity limit the scope of EU law and the jurisdiction of its courts, the CJEU has become progressively more interested in complaints by individuals of violations of their fundamental rights on the part of businesses. Indeed, the 'horizontal' nature of human rights their *'Drittwirkung'*, which cuts across several areas of law, can trigger scrutiny by the EU judicial system in multiple ways.[52] The most relevant text for our purposes is probably the aforementioned Charter, which safeguards a vast array of individual rights relevant in BHR disputes and sets up a baseline of protection throughout the European Union for all private entities—whether incorporated in the European Union or not. Although the primary addressees of the Charter are the EU institutions (and the member states, when implementing EU law), the CJEU has progressively enlarged the applicability of the Charter by means of interpretation. Thus, a series of judgments of the Court of Justice allows private entities and individuals to rely upon the Charter not only as against EU institutions and member states but also, on some occasions, horizontally in their relationship with other individuals. This development bears a promising potential for the effective adjudication of BHR disputes, as illustrated particularly well by the joined cases of *Wuppertal v Bauer* and *Willmeroth v Martina Broßonn*.

This decision of the Grand Chamber originated from a preliminary reference by the *Bundesarbeitsgericht* (German Federal Labour Court).[53] The question at issue was whether Article 31(2) of the Charter—ensuring a right to paid annual leave—could be invoked by the widows of two workers whose employers had refused, after the latter's decease, to liquidate the amount of annual leave payment overdue to them. The claimants had based themselves on Article 31(2) of the Charter and Article 7 of EU Directive 2003/88 on certain aspects of the organization of working time.[54] After having highlighted the 'particularly important' nature of the right to paid leave, the Court of Justice was faced with the dilemma that Directive 2003/88 was not directly applicable to one of the claimants, given the private nature of the

[49] Case 11-70 *Internationale Handelsgesellschaft mbH v Einfuhr- und Vorratsstelle für Getreide und Futtermittel* [1971] EU:C:1970:114, para 4. The court held that 'respect for fundamental rights forms an integral part of the general principles of law protected by the Court of Justice. The protection of such rights, whilst inspired by the constitutional traditions common to the Member States, must be ensured within the framework of the structure and objectives of the Community'.

[50] For example, Case C-36/02 *Omega Spielhallen- und Automatenaufstellungs-GmbH v Oberbürgermeisterin der Bundesstadt Bonn* [2004] ECR I-09609.

[51] Treaty on European Union (Maastricht Treaty) art 6.

[52] Including disputes on environmental law, migration law, anti-discrimination law, international investment and trade law, public procurement, consumer protection law, jurisdiction, recognition and enforcement of judicial decisions in civil and commercial matters, applicable law and judicial assistance in cross-border situations, and corporate law.

[53] Joined Cases C-569/16 and C-570/16 *Stadt Wuppertal v Maria Elisabeth Bauer* and *Volker Willmeroth v Martina Broßonn* [2018] EU:C:2018:871.

[54] Directive 2003/88/EC of the European Parliament and of the Council of 4 November 2003 concerning certain aspects of the organization of working time, OJ L 299/2003, p 9.

employer of her late husband.[55] The Court overcame this impasse by affirming that, where appropriate, private entities such as the employers sued in the underlying national litigation, bear direct obligations to comply with the Charter of Fundamental Rights of the European Union.[56] That was the case, the Court held, in relation to the right to paid annual leave, whose 'mandatory and unconditional nature' does not need any implementing provisions in national law to be given concrete expression by employers. The decision is as significant in its content as it is in its effects in the EU legal system: the general and binding nature of preliminary rulings of the Court of Justice makes the decision in *Wuppertal* binding both for all private employers operating under EU law,[57] and for all national courts of the EU when adjudicating comparable issues.

Claimants in BHR disputes falling within the scope of the EU's action in the fields of international trade and investment can, in some instances, also directly activate the jurisdiction of the CJEU. The key provision for this remedy is Article 263(4) of the Treaty on the Functioning of the European Union, which gives standing to individuals and groups of individuals to bring direct actions against EU institutions for the annulment of an EU legal act when that act is either addressed to them, or 'is of direct and individual concern' to them, or when they take action 'against a regulatory act which is of direct concern to them and does not entail implementing measures'. As far-fetched as it might appear, the remedy provided for in Article 263(4) is not to be underestimated in BHR disputes, as it can lead to the annulment of EU legislation on the basis of which businesses operate.

The case of *Frente Polisario v Council*[58] is exemplary in this sense. The National Liberation Movement for Western Sahara—Frente Polisario—sought the annulment of the EU Council Decision adopting the 2010 EU–Morocco Agreement on agricultural, processed agricultural, and fisheries products before the General Court on the grounds that, by means of that agreement, the European Union was benefitting from the exploitation by Morocco and Moroccan firms of the disputed territory of Western Sahara. After accepting jurisdiction,[59] the General Court granted Frente Polisario's application and annulled the challenged Council Decision insofar as it approved the application to Western Sahara of the agreement. Importantly, the General Court found that the EU's obligation to respect the fundamental rights of the population of the partner country's territories extends to a duty to avoid 'indirect violations', which, in turn, translates into a duty of care on the EU institutions to ascertain the absence of any such direct or indirect violations before proceeding to the signature of trade agreements. The General Court's decision in *Frente Polisario* was later set aside by the Court of Justice, but nevertheless remains an important precedent for BHR litigation. To begin with, it clarifies that the Court may offer a forum to adjudicate BHR disputes arising out of indirect consequences of international agreements to which the EU is a party. Secondly, the appeal decision of the Court of Justice did not dismiss the argumentation of the General Court relating to indirect violations and the duty of care, rather it quashed the General Court's decision on grounds of jurisdiction. Thus, the relevance of *Frente Polisario* for our topic remains unchallenged. Finally, the reasoning of the Court of Justice on the issue

[55] EU law provides for the direct effect of directives between private parties only under limited circumstances, on the grounds that private parties cannot be afforded direct obligations under EU law for as long as member states do not implement them.

[56] *Wuppertal v Bauer* (n 53) para 87.

[57] ibid para 90.

[58] *Front populaire pour la libération de la saguia-el-hamra et du rio de oro (Front Polisario) v Council of the European Union* [2015] EU:T:2015:953 (hereafter '*Frente Polisario*').

[59] ibid paras 50–53.

of standing of the National Liberation Movement for Western Sahara is to be read in the context of the scope of the trade agreement in question: for the Court of Justice, Frente Polisario did not have a 'direct and individual concern' in the dispute because the application of the agreement to Western Sahara—a disputed territory—could not be 'implied'. A BHR dispute brought in the context of an EU trade agreement of unquestioned territorial application could thus overcome such exclusion.

9.3.3.2 A matter of integration

Despite of what we just described, the activity of the CJEU in terms of protection of fundamental rights among private individuals still falls short of rendering the EU judicial system an 'effective' forum under Pillar III of the UNGPs. To begin with, the EU judicial system suffers the important limitation of being available only in situations falling within the scope of EU law, and, in principle, only for actions against the institutions and member states. Equally, the EU 'duty of care' in the context of external relations is less prominent than a direct obligation to uphold human rights vis-à-vis companies: arguably, a well-reasoned impact assessment on the part of the EU institutions might be sufficient to 'tick the box' of compliance with the EU duty of care. *Frente Polisario* also confirms that the Charter adopts a narrow understanding of the requirement of 'individual concern' to start an action under Article 263(4) TFEU, only covering situations in which individuals are affected 'by reason of certain attributes which are peculiar to them or by reason of circumstances in which they are differentiated from all other persons and by virtue of these factors [are distinguished] individually just as in the case of the person addressed'.[60] The outcome of various cases brought by NGOs in environmental matters[61] shows that this condition is almost impossible to fulfil with regard to measures that affect the public interest, such as the environment or fundamental rights, which by definition are not peculiar to a certain individual or group of individuals.

The rationale of these exceptions arguably points, once again, to the mandate—or at least the perception of the mandate—entrusted to the CJEU. The case law of the Court on human rights was originally triggered by integrationist aims—that is, the desire to overcome the resistance of national courts to the full primacy and effectiveness of EU law in the member states.[62] Its evolution is marked by similar considerations. Thus, as it became apparent in *Melloni*, the creation of a EU set of fundamental rights was to be regarded as a device to standardize the protection of these rights throughout the member states.[63] Equally, the Court is wary of allowing interferences with the 'keystone' of the EU judicial system, that is, its own relationship with the national courts, by means of accepting a privileged recourse to other courts, be they international (see the opinion on the accession of the to the ECtHR)[64] or national, by means of direct actions.[65]

[60] *Plaumann & Co v Commission of the European Economic Community* [1963] EU:C:1963:17.

[61] For example, *Stichting Greenpeace Council and Others v the Commission* [1998] EU:C:1998:153; *Marie-Thérèse Danielsson and Others v Commission* [1995] EU:T:1995:219.

[62] In the face of the Court of Justice's initial stance of not getting involved in the adjudication of fundamental rights, certain constitutional courts of member states, and particularly the Italian and German constitutional courts, claimed jurisdiction on EU law affecting fundamental rights, affirming that they would have refused to give EU law primacy if it had been shown that it negatively affected these rights.

[63] Case C-399/11 *Stefano Melloni v Ministerio Fiscal* [2013] EU:C:2013:107.

[64] Case Opinion 2/13 *Pursuant to Article 218(11) TFEU* [2014] EU:C:2014:2454.

[65] Case C-263/02 P *Commission of the European Communities v Jégo-Quéré & Cie SA*. [2004] ECR I-03425.

9.4 Lessons Learnt

The impression we get from our analysis of how existing international courts and tribunals have dealt with BHR disputes so far is that, in line with the humanization of international law,[66] all of them, to varying degrees, have warmed up to the idea that individuals can be holders of rights as much as obligations under international law. In the instances pertinent to our topic, namely those of 'individuals' of particular robustness, namely transnational corporations, not yet being recognized as directly subjected to international obligations, a consensus has arisen that legal ways must be developed to bring them within the grip of such obligations at least indirectly. In this direction, the ECtHR has found ways around the limitation of its jurisdiction to individual-to-state disputes by means of a broad interpretation of state-owned or state-controlled enterprises, as well as by setting up a doctrine of indirect state responsibility for the actions of private actors. Investment tribunals increasingly have made efforts to accommodate rights and obligations of individuals and companies in proceedings before them. The decisions of the CJEU that confer direct effect to the EU Charter and address the duty of care of EU institutions in external relations contribute to reinforcing the central position that human rights have in the EU legal system. At the most traditional tip of the scale, even the ICJ, the states' court par excellence, appears to be becoming more receptive to the new perspectives and tools required in the evolving landscape of international law. Yet, in all these instances, various limitations—including standing and scope of protection—create barriers to considering the tools of protection 'effective' under Pillar III of the UNGPs and render them somehow unfit for use in relation to human rights violations perpetrated by businesses.

At this state of affairs, is the creation of an ad hoc general mechanism to uphold business human rights obligations preferable? Our analysis would appear to suggest that procedural amendments will not be sufficient to turn the courts and tribunals just discussed into mechanisms that are effectively capable of delivering justice in BHR disputes, considering that the main obstacle to their capacity to deal with BHR obligations in a satisfactory manner lies in their own understanding of their role, as inscribed in their founding instruments.[67] Along this line, EU courts look at BHR disputes through the 'integrationist' lenses characterizing the EU project. The ECtHR still bears the legacy of its origins of being a 'supervisor' of states' action, rather than an upfront defender of individual rights. This appears even more true for the ICJ, which remains a 'generalist court' hesitant, arguably with good reason, to get directly involved in issues of human rights protection. Investment tribunals, among the few existing mechanisms able to offer effective protection to individuals under international law, remain a shield for the economic rights of investors, rather than a sword for protecting human rights more generally. Hence, an ad hoc forum to solve BHR disputes does appear desirable, or even necessary, to ensure full protection. Such a forum, like the arbitral tribunals foreseen by the Hague Rules, would be able not only to respond to the particular nature of BHR disputes in terms of its design but, most importantly, it would also present an opportunity to set up a mechanism whose DNA is injected with human rights—and BHR-specific values and principles, orientating decision-making in a perspective of 'system-building'.

[66] Meron (n 15).

[67] Karen J Alter, 'Tipping the Balance: International Courts and the Construction of International and Domestic Politics' (2011) 13 Cambridge Yearbook of European Legal Studies 1, 1.

This is not to downplay the role of national courts in the context of BHR.[68] In our view, national systems of protection remain in principle the most effective avenue of redress, given their proximity to the victims and their extensive powers. Yet, from a transnational perspective human rights are arguably best safeguarded by means of a multilayered system of protection formed of alternative, parallel routes, all equally accessible. An ad hoc international mechanism for the settlement of BHR disputes can thus fill gaps left not only by the limited territorial jurisdiction of national courts, but also by the possible unavailability or incapacity of such courts to safeguard individual rights, in developing countries as much as in developed countries.

That said, is arbitration the way forward for BHR disputes? While an in-depth analysis of this question is beyond the scope of our contribution, our answer in the light of what we have learnt in the process of drafting the Hague Rules is a firm 'yes'; the reason being that the flexibility and transnational nature of arbitration allow it to adapt to the complexities of BHR disputes and deliver justice cross-border.[69]

It is perhaps significant to note that, at present, the only instrument already activated to date to uphold BHR obligations is a transnational agreement concluded between private parties, namely the 'Accord on Fire and Building Safety in Bangladesh',[70] as updated,[71] which includes an arbitration clause. This Accord sets out legally binding obligations on brands and trade unions in the ready garment industry in Bangladesh in the wake of the Rana Plaza collapse in 2011 to ensure safer labour conditions. It is estimated to have led to the inspection of over 1,500 factories and to have identified numerous hazards to the safety of workers. Arguably, the effectiveness of the Accord is due in large measure to its provision for arbitration, which differentiates it from most other CSR mechanisms. In 2016 the clause allowed two trade unions to bring two recalcitrant multinational companies before an international tribunal administered by the Permanent Court of Arbitration in The Hague.[72] The proceedings led to a settlement that can arguably be regarded as a victory for the claimants; and demonstrated that the dispute settlement mechanism of the Accord did have 'bite' as a tool in the hands of smaller claimants to enforce workers' rights against 'Goliath' respondents. The case also brought much needed public attention on certain human rights violations by multinationals that, regrettably, we are often too used to notice.[73] Yet, the Accord appears to have become the victim of its own success: the developments we have just described raised the discontent of factory owners lamenting the difficulty to keep up with the standards embodied in the agreement, as well as that of the Bangladeshi government, which apparently does not want to harm its exporting industry.[74] Thus, after the expiry of the Accord's original

[68] The Hague Rules do not aim at replacing existing or future means of redress, including national litigation. Rather, they want to add an effective complementary, cooperative, and constructive component to the toolbox of existing and future remedies.

[69] Cronstedt and Thompson (n 2) 66.

[70] '2018 Accord on Fire and Building Safety in Bangladesh: May 2018' (The Accord 2017) <https://bangladesh.wpengine.com/wp-content/uploads/2020/11/2018-Accord.pdf> accessed 16 May 2021.

[71] ibid.

[72] *IndustriALL Global Union and UNI Global Union v Private Respondent* (Permanent Court of Arbitration) (2018) Joined Cases 2016-36 and 2016-37.

[73] See comments of Valter Sanches, IndustriALL General Secretary 'Global Unions Reach US$2.3 Million Bangladesh Accord Settlement with Multinational Brand' (IndustriALL, 22 January 2018) <http://www.industriall-union.org/global-unions-reach-us23-million-bangladesh-accord-settlement-with-multinational-brand> accessed 11 October 2020; Graham Dunning QC, 'The Bangladesh Accord—A Model for Environmental Dispute Resolution' <https://s3-eu-west-2.amazonaws.com/sqe-essexcourt/wp-content/uploads/2018/09/08152804/Bangladesh-Accord-lecture.pdf>.

[74] 'Bangladesh Government Must Intervene to Secure Garment Factory Safety' (IndustriALL, 5 March 2019) <http://www.industriall-union.org/call-for-high-level-intervention-by-bangladesh-government-to-secure-factory-safety-in-bangladesh> accessed 29 September 2020.

five-year term, its continued operation until 2021 was challenged in court by the government, which declared its readiness to assume responsibility for the safety controls of the over 1,500 factories covered by the Accord. According to recent news, an agreement was found between the government and the trade unions: the Accord will remain in force for about a year, following which its safety programme will continue to operate under the oversight of the Bangladeshi government, importantly, maintaining a role for local and global trade unions.[75] It remains to be seen whether this arrangement will actually safeguard the improvement of working conditions for Bangladeshi garment industry workers. In a sense, the 'nationalization' of an originally 'state-free' system we currently face in Bangladesh also throws light on the obstacles that many domestic courts are likely to encounter in the pursuit of justice in the BHR context.

In conclusion, many challenges still lie ahead to ensure full justiciability of human rights violations by businesses, but so do many opportunities. At the time of writing, an Open-ended Intergovernmental Working Group, on a mandate conferred by the UN Human Rights Council, is attempting to elaborate an international treaty on the matter, more specifically 'an international legally binding instrument to regulate, in international human rights law, the activities of transnational corporations and other business enterprises'.[76] For the supporters of this project, the main advantage of the envisaged treaty will be that of turning CSR obligations into hard law. While, at least at the present stage, the draft treaty does not include an ad hoc remedy for the violation of such obligations, the amendments published in July 2019 make an interesting addition in terms of justiciability of human rights violations on the part of businesses: Article 4.14 mandates states to 'provide effective mechanisms for the enforcement of remedies for violations of human rights, including through prompt execution of national or foreign judgements or awards'.[77] If this text were maintained, the draft could be understood as opening the door to coordination with arbitral mechanisms like the BHR project.

Whatever the future may hold for BHR disputes and BHR arbitration, one thing is certain: the creation of a system of protection through effective remedies under Pillar III of the UNGPs will require cooperation from all parties involved, including states, national courts, and businesses, as well as courage and responsibility by the adjudicators, be they judges or arbitrators.

[75] 'Questions Raised after Agreement Reached on Bangladesh Accord' (Clean Clothes Campaign, 21 May 2019) <https://cleanclothes.org/news/2019/questions-raised-after-agreement-reached-on-bangladesh-accord> accessed 11 October 2020.

[76] UNHRC Res 26/9 (14 July 2014) UN Doc A/HRC/RES/26/9.

[77] Open-ended Intergovernmental Working Group, Legally Binding Instrument to Regulate, in International Human Rights Law, the Activities of Transnational Corporations and other Business Enterprises, Article 4.14, Revised draft of 19 July 2019, < https://www.ohchr.org/Documents/HRBodies/HRCouncil/WGTransCorp/OEIGWG_RevisedDraft_LBI.pdf> accessed 16 May 2021.

10

A Duty to Negotiate in Good Faith as Part of the Duty to Cooperate to Establish 'An International Legal Order in which Human Rights can be Fully Realized'

The New Frontier of the Right to Development

Olivier De Schutter

10.1 Introduction

'Lasting progress towards the implementation of the right to development requires effective development policies at the national level, *as well as equitable economic relations and a favourable economic environment at the international level*.'[1] When the diplomats participating in the World Conference on Human Rights convened in Vienna in June 1993 decided to include that statement in the Declaration and Programme of Action closing the conference, they were not entering new territory. Already in 1986, the Declaration on the Right to Development[2] defined corresponding states' obligations both at the national and international levels: in adopting the Declaration, states had accepted 'the primary responsibility for the creation of *national and international* conditions favourable to the realization of the right to development';[3] and they had acknowledged that 'Steps should be taken to ensure the full exercise and progressive enhancement of the right to development, including the formulation, adoption and implementation of policy, legislative and other measures *at the national and international levels*.'[4] In 2010 the High-Level Task Force established to make proposals on the implementation of the right to development concluded therefore that the right to development implied three levels of states' responsibility, including not only (1) states acting individually as they formulate national development policies and programmes affecting persons within their jurisdiction and (2) states acting individually as they adopt and implement policies that affect persons not strictly within their jurisdiction but also (3) states *acting collectively* in global and regional partnerships.[5]

In the terminology of international human rights law,[6] such duties to 'act collectively' correspond to *global* obligations: as actors in international relations, states should contribute to

[1] UNGA 'Vienna Declaration and Programme of Action' (12 July 1993) UN Doc A/CONF.157/23 para 10.

[2] UNGA Res 41/128 (4 December 1986) UN Doc A/RES/41/128 (Declaration on the Right to Development).

[3] ibid art 3(1).

[4] ibid art 10.

[5] UNHRC 'Report of the high-level task force on the implementation of the right to development on its sixth session' (8 March 2010) UN Doc A/HRC/15/WG.2/TF/2/Add.2 Annex.

[6] Maastricht Principles on Extraterritorial Obligations of States in the Area of Economic, Social and Cultural Rights, Principle 8 (defining 'extraterritorial obligations' as encompassing '(a) obligations relating to the acts and omissions of a State, within or beyond its territory, that have effects on the enjoyment of human rights outside of

Olivier De Schutter, *A Duty to Negotiate in Good Faith as Part of the Duty to Cooperate to Establish 'An International Legal Order in which Human Rights can be Fully Realized'* In: *The Struggle for Human Rights*. Edited by: Nehal Bhuta, Florian Hoffmann, Sarah Knuckey, Frédéric Mégret, and Margaret Satterthwaite, Oxford University Press.
DOI: 10.1093/oso/9780198868064.003.0011

the establishment of bilateral, regional, and global cooperation agreements, including for the setting up of international agencies, and they should exercise their rights within intergovernmental organizations, in accordance with the requirements of the right to development. This requires that states overcome the collective action problems that impede the establishment and maintenance of global public goods, by cooperating with each other. Article 3(3) of the Declaration on the Right to Development provides in this regard that 'States have the *duty to co-operate with each other* in ensuring development and eliminating obstacles to development. States should realize their rights and fulfil their duties in such a manner as to promote a new international economic order based on sovereign equality, interdependence, mutual interest and co-operation among all States, as well as to encourage the observance and realization of human rights.' This is further clarified in Article 4, which stipulates a duty of all states 'to take steps, individually *and collectively*, to formulate international development policies with a view to facilitating the full realization of the right to development', with 'sustained action [being] required to promote more rapid development of developing countries'. The Vienna Declaration and Programme of Action further confirms that 'States should *cooperate with each other* in ensuring development and eliminating obstacles to development. The international community should promote effective international cooperation for the realization of the right to development and the elimination of obstacles to development.'[7]

Thus, the fulfilment of human rights, and of the right to development in particular, requires collective action by states: a joint, coordinated effort to reshape the international environment in order to support the implementation of human rights at domestic level. The Charter of the United Nations itself provided in Article 56 that 'All Members pledge themselves to take *joint and separate action* in cooperation with the Organization' to achieve the purposes of the organization as set out in Article 55 of the Charter, including: 'universal respect for, and observance of, human rights and fundamental freedoms for all without distinction as to race, sex, language, or religion'.[8] And the UDHR refers in Article 28 to the right of everyone to the establishment of a social and international order in which all the rights of the UDHR can be realized.[9] The repeated pledges made by states to work together in order to realize the goals of the international community[10] is thus particularly relevant to the fulfilment of human rights.

that State's territory; and (b) obligations of a global character that are set out in the Charter of the United Nations and human rights instruments to take action, separately, and jointly through international cooperation, to realize human rights universally'). The Maastricht Principles were adopted on 28 September 2011 by a range of human rights research institutes, independent academics, and mandate-holders of the HRC. They aim to contribute to the progressive development of international human rights law; Olivier de Schutter and others, 'Commentary to the Maastricht Principles on Extraterritorial Obligations of States in the Area of Economic, Social and Cultural Rights' (2012) 34 Human Rights Quarterly 1084.

[7] UN Doc A/CONF.157/23 (n 1) para 10.

[8] Charter of the United Nations (adopted 26 June 1945, entered into force 24 October 1945) 1 UNTS XVI.

[9] Universal Declaration of Human Rights (adopted 10 December 1948 UNGA Res 217 A(III) art 28; the UDHR is generally considered today to have acquired the status of customary international law (see UNGA 'Final Act of the International Conference on Human Rights – Proclamation of Teheran' (22 April–13 May 1968) UN Doc A/CONF 32/41 para 2 (in which it was agreed unanimously that the Declaration 'states a common understanding of the peoples of the world concerning the inalienable and inviolable rights of all members of the human family and constitutes an obligation for all members of the international community')).

[10] For example, UNGA Res 55/2 (18 September 2000) UN Doc A/RES/55/2 para 2 (in which the heads of states and governments recognized unanimously that: 'in addition to our separate responsibilities to our individual societies, we have a collective responsibility to uphold the principles of human dignity, equality and equity at the global level').

This chapter is an attempt to clarify the scope of the duty to conclude new international agreements in order to contribute to full realization of human rights. Section 10.2 asks whether such a duty exists. It identifies the sources of the duty in human rights instruments and in the Declaration on the Right to Development, and it replaces the duty in the broader framework of general international law. But isn't the very idea suspicious? If indeed global obligations in the field of human rights include duties to seek to conclude *new* agreements, or to establish new international organizations tasked with the management of certain global public goods,[11] is this not a contradiction in terms? After all, if, as emphasized by the Permanent Court of International Justice in its very first case, 'the right of entering into international engagements is an attribute of State sovereignty',[12] what could it possibly mean that there exists a *duty* to cooperate internationally, including by the conclusion of treaties? Section 10.3 seeks to provide an answer, by clarifying the distinction between the duty to negotiate in good faith for the attainment of certain objectives, and a duty to reach agreement. Section 10.4 offers a brief conclusion.

10.2 Is There a Duty to Cooperate by the Conclusion of Conventions?

10.2.1 The Duty to Cooperate in Human Rights Law

It is common for human rights treaties to refer to a duty of international cooperation, and to include in the definition of such a duty the duty to seek to conclude agreements with other states. A duty to cooperate for the full realization of human rights is included, for instance, in the Convention against Torture and Other Cruel, Inhuman or Degrading Treatment or Punishment,[13] which requires states parties to provide each other 'the greatest measure of assistance in connection with criminal proceedings' relating to torture including 'the supply of all evidence at their disposal necessary for the proceedings'.[14] A comparable commitment is contained in the International Convention for the Protection of all Persons from Enforced Disappearance.[15] Similarly, the Convention on the Rights of Persons with Disabilities,[16]

[11] The notion of 'international organizations' is understood here, as under Vienna Convention on the Law of Treaties (adopted 23 May 1969, entered into force 27 January 1960) 1155 UNTS 331 (Vienna Convention) art 2(1)(i) or under Vienna Convention on the Law of Treaties between States and International Organizations or between International Organizations (18 February–21 March 1986) UN Doc A/CONF.129/15 art 2(1)(i) as organizations set up by states in order to favour intergovernmental cooperation. In principle, the members of such international organizations are states, who conclude among themselves a treaty in order to establish the organization.

[12] *SS 'Wimbledon'* PCIJ Rep Series A No 01, 25 (the Court in that case 'decline[d] to see in the conclusion of any Treaty by which a State undertakes to perform or refrain from performing a particular act an abandonment of its sovereignty. No doubt any convention creating an obligation of this kind places a restriction upon the exercise of the sovereign rights of the State, [...] But the right of entering into international engagements is an attribute of State sovereignty').

[13] Convention against Torture and Other Cruel, Inhuman or Degrading Treatment or Punishment (adopted 10 December 1984, entered into force 26 June 1987) 1465 UNTS 85, as modified by 24 ILM 535 (1985) (Torture Convention).

[14] ibid art 9(1).

[15] International Convention for the Protection of all Persons from Enforced Disappearance (adopted 20 December 2006, entered into force 23 December 2010) 2716 UNTS 3 art 15, which provides that 'States Parties shall cooperate with each other and shall afford one another the greatest measure of mutual assistance with a view to assisting victims of enforced disappearance, and in searching for, locating and releasing disappeared persons and, in the event of death, in exhuming and identifying them and returning their remains.'

[16] Convention on the Rights of Persons with Disabilities (adopted 13 December 2006, entered into force on 3 May 2008) 2515 UNTS 3.

'recogniz[ing] the importance of international cooperation and its promotion, in support of national efforts for the realization of the purpose and objectives of the present Convention', commits states parties to 'undertake appropriate and effective measures in this regard, between and among States and, as appropriate, in partnership with relevant international and regional organizations and civil society, in particular organizations of persons with disabilities'.[17] The Convention on the Rights of the Child[18] also provides that states parties shall take measures for the implementation of the economic, social, and cultural rights of the child, 'where needed, within the framework of international co-operation',[19] leading the Committee on the Rights of the Child to note that 'When States ratify the Convention, they take upon themselves obligations not only to implement it within their jurisdiction, but also to contribute, through international cooperation, to global implementation.'[20]

While some instruments refer simply to a duty of international assistance and cooperation without referring explicitly to the conclusion of new international agreements, others do provide such an explicit reference, where the conclusion of such agreements is seen as essential for the fulfilment of the aims of the convention. Thus for instance, the Optional Protocol to the Convention on the Rights of the Child on the Sale of Children, Child Prostitution and Child Pornography,[21] provides that 'States Parties shall take all necessary steps to strengthen international cooperation by multilateral, regional and bilateral arrangements for the prevention, detection, investigation, prosecution and punishment of those responsible for acts involving the sale of children, child prostitution, child pornography and child sex tourism.'[22]

The duty of international assistance and cooperation is given particular emphasis in the International Covenant on Economic, Social and Cultural Rights. Article 2(1) of the Covenant provides that the states parties to the Covenant undertake to 'take steps, individually *and through international assistance and co-operation*, especially economic and technical', to the maximum of their available resources, 'with a view to achieving progressively the full realization of the rights' recognized in the Covenant. The notion of international cooperation is also mentioned in relation to the right to an adequate standard of living in Article 11(1) of the Covenant, according to which 'States Parties will take appropriate steps to ensure the realization of this right, recognizing to this effect the essential importance of international co-operation based on free consent'. Under Part IV of the Covenant, which relates to the measures of implementation, two provisions relate to international assistance and cooperation. Article 22 states that the Economic and Social Council may bring to the attention of other UN bodies and agencies concerned with furnishing technical assistance any information arising out of the reports submitted by states under the Covenant that 'may assist such bodies in deciding, each within its field of competence, on the advisability of

[17] ibid art 32(1).

[18] Convention on the Rights of the Child (adopted 20 November 1989, entered into force on 2 September 1990) 1577 UNTS 3.

[19] ibid art 4.

[20] Committee on the Rights of the Child, 'General Comment No. 5: General Measures of Implementation for the Convention on the Rights of the Child' CRC/GC/2003/5 para 5.

[21] Optional Protocol to the Convention on the Rights of the Child on the Sale of Children, Child Prostitution and Child Pornography (adopted 25 May 2000 UNGA Res 54/263).

[22] ibid art 10(1); Optional Protocol to the Convention on the Rights of the Child on the involvement of children in armed conflict (adopted 25 May 2000 UNGA Res 54/263, entered into force on 12 February 2002) art 7(1) provides for a duty of States parties to 'cooperate in the implementation of the ... Protocol, including in the prevention of any activity contrary thereto and in the rehabilitation and social reintegration of persons who are victims of acts contrary thereto, including through technical cooperation and financial assistance. Such assistance and cooperation will be undertaken in consultation with the States Parties concerned and the relevant international organizations.' It is less explicit, however, on the conclusion of new agreements to that effect.

international measures likely to contribute to the effective progressive implementation of the present Covenant'. Article 23 specifies the different forms international action for the achievement of the rights recognized in the Covenant may take; including:

> such methods as the conclusion of conventions, the adoption of recommendations, the furnishing of technical assistance and the holding of regional meetings and technical meetings for the purpose of consultation and study organized in conjunction with the Governments concerned.[23]

It has thus become relatively routine for human rights instruments to impose on states parties that they conclude new international agreements (beyond the treaty itself they are parties to), to ensure that domestic efforts are supported by an enabling international framework. The Maastricht Principles on the Extraterritorial Obligations of States in the Area of Economic, Social and Cultural Rights[24] sought to codify this duty. Under the heading 'Obligation to create an international enabling environment', they specify that 'States must take deliberate, concrete and targeted steps, separately and jointly through international co-operation, to create an international enabling environment conducive to the universal fulfilment of economic, social and cultural rights, including in matters relating to bilateral and multilateral trade, investment, taxation, finance, environmental protection, and development cooperation'; the duty, the authors of the Maastricht Principles noted, includes 'elaboration, interpretation, application and regular review of multilateral and bilateral agreements as well as international standards'.[25]

Beyond human rights instruments

While the aforementioned examples related to human rights instruments, similar illustrations of treaties imposing duties to negotiate new international agreements can be found in other areas.[26] Indeed, a duty to negotiate may even do so in the absence of a conventional basis to that effect. In general international law, an obligation to negotiate emerges in particular in situations where states are recognized to have conflicting rights, which can only be reconciled through a process of negotiation clarifying the respective rights and duties.[27] A duty to cooperate (whether this requires to enter into negotiations or not) may also emerge in situations where the effective protection of the rights of the individual require that states combine their efforts, as may occur in particular in situations of a transnational nature. The jurisprudence of the ECtHR provides some illustrations in this regard,[28] and

[23] CESCR 'General Comment No 12: The Right to Adequate Food (Art 11 of the Covenant) (12 May 1999)) UN Doc E/C.121999/5 para 36, the implication is that, for instance, in order to comply with the right to food, 'States parties should, in international agreements whenever relevant, ensure that the right to adequate food is given due attention *and consider the development of further international legal instruments to that end*' (emphasis added).

[24] Maastricht Principles (n 6).

[25] ibid Principle 29(a).

[26] Treaty on the Non-Proliferation of Nuclear Weapons (signed 1 July 1968, entered into force on 5 March 1970) 729 UNTS 161 (Non-Proliferation Treaty) art VI provides that: 'Each of the Parties to the Treaty undertakes to pursue negotiations in good faith on effective measures relating to cessation of the nuclear arms race at an early date and to nuclear disarmament, and on a treaty on general and complete disarmament under strict and effective international control.'

[27] *Fisheries Jurisdiction Case (UK v Iceland)* (Merits) [1974] ICJ Rep 3 [73] (negotiations are required between Iceland and Great Britain who both have legitimate fishing rights in certain maritime areas).

[28] In *Güzelyurtlu and Others v Cyprus and Turkey* App no 36925/07 (ECtHR, 29 January 2019) a Chamber of the ECtHR noted, in the context of a murder that occurred in Cyprus and could only be effectively investigated

it is on that same logic that the Committee on Economic, Social and Cultural Rights relies when it encourages states to cooperate in order to ensure that victims of human rights abuses involving transnational corporations operating in different jurisdictions have access to effective remedies: 'Improved international cooperation', the Committee noted in its General Comment No 24 on State obligations under the International Covenant on Economic, Social and Cultural Rights in the context of business activities, 'should reduce the risks of positive and negative conflicts of jurisdiction, which may result in legal uncertainty and in forum-shopping by litigants, or in an inability for victims to obtain redress. The Committee welcomes, in this regard, any efforts at the adoption of international instruments that could strengthen the duty of States to cooperate in order to improve accountability and access to remedies for victims of violations of Covenant rights in transnational cases.'[29]

It is submitted that, in addition, a state may be duty-bound to negotiate with a view to reaching an international agreement in situations where, in the absence of a negotiation, that state would have to resort to unilateral measures in order to achieve certain results that the international community has defined as desirable. This is particularly relevant to understanding the potential implications of Article 28 of the UDHR, or of the duty of states to '*co-operate with each other* in ensuring development and eliminating obstacles to development', stipulated in Article 3(3) of the Declaration on the Right to Development. Indeed, the establishment of an international environment enabling the full realization of the rights of the UDHR or implementing the right to development requires that states cooperate towards these goals. Yet, while assigning such objectives to the international community, the UDHR and the Declaration on the Right to Development did not authorize states to act unilaterally in order to enforce the duty of another state to adopt measures at domestic level that shall contribute to these objectives, for instance by the adoption of discriminatory trade measures or of other forms of economic sanctions. Indeed, the Declaration on the Right to Development states explicitly that the realization of the right to development 'requires full

(and the perpetrators prosecuted) with the cooperation of the Turkish authorities, that 'Where there are cross-border elements to an incident of unlawful violence leading to loss of life, the fundamental importance of Article 2 requires that the authorities of the State to which the suspected perpetrators have fled and in which evidence of the offence could be located, of their own motion, take effective measures in that regard [. . .]. Otherwise, those indulging in cross-border attacks will be able to operate with impunity and the authorities of the Contracting State where the unlawful attacks have taken place will be foiled in their own efforts to protect the fundamental rights of their citizens and, indeed, of any individuals within their jurisdiction'; in an inadmissibility decision of adopted in the case of *Kevin O'Loughlin and Others v the United Kingdom* App no 23274/04 (ECtHR, 10 August 2004) concerning the explosion of car bombs in the Republic of Ireland (in Dublin and Monaghan) on 17 May 1974 and the alleged failure of the authorities in Northern Ireland to effectively cooperate in the investigation, the Court had already remarked that 'where suspected perpetrators of a bombing attack carried out elsewhere are known to be present within the jurisdiction of a Contracting State, and evidence of a criminal offence may be secured, the fundamental importance of Article 2 [of the ECHR, guaranteeing the right to life] requires that the authorities of that State of their own motion take effective measures in that regard. Otherwise, those indulging in cross-border attacks will be able to operate with impunity and the authorities of Contracting State where the unlawful attacks have taken place will be foiled in their own efforts to protect the fundamental rights of their citizens.' The application was found inadmissible, however, due to the time limit of six months having been exceeded.

[29] CESCR, 'General Comment No 24 (2017) on State obligations under the International Covenant on Economic, Social and Cultural Rights in the context of business activities' (10 August 2017) UN Doc E/C.12/GC/24 para 35; UNHRC 'Improving accountability and access to remedy for victims of business-related human rights abuse—Report of the UN High Commission for Human Rights' (10 May 2016) UN Doc A/HRC/32/19 para 31(c). The Committee refers in this regard to the recommendation included in the report on accountability and access to remedy for victims of business-related human rights abuse, prepared by the Office of the UN High Commissioner for Human Rights at the request of the HRC. According to that report, states should 'take steps, . . . to improve the effectiveness of cross-border cooperation between State agencies and judicial bodies, with respect to both public and private law enforcement of domestic legal regimes'.

respect for the principles of international law concerning friendly relations and co-operation among States in accordance with the Charter of the United Nations'.[30] These principles in turn commit each state to 'refrain in its international relations from the threat or use of force against the territorial integrity or political independence of any State, or in any other manner inconsistent with the purposes of the United Nations', and not to 'use or encourage the use of economic, political or any other type of measures to coerce another State in order to obtain from it the subordination of the exercise of its sovereign rights and to secure from it advantages of any kind', consistent with the 'inalienable right' of each state 'to choose its political, economic, social and cultural systems, without interference in any form by another State'.[31] The right to development therefore does not justify the adoption of unilateral measures as a means to obtain from a state that it changes its course of conduct; quite to the contrary, the Declaration of Principles of International Law Concerning Friendly Relations and Co-operation among States in accordance with the Charter of the United Nations recalls that 'States have the *duty to co-operate with one another*, irrespective of the differences in their political, economic and social systems, in the various spheres of international relations, in order to maintain international peace and security and to promote international economic stability and progress, the general welfare of nations and international co-operation free from discrimination based on such differences' (emphasis added).[32] In the Declaration on the Right to Development, this is further echoed in Article 6(1), which provides that 'All States *should co-operate* with a view to promoting, encouraging and strengthening universal respect for and observance of all human rights and fundamental freedoms for all without any distinction as to race, sex, language or religion' (emphasis added).

By referring in Article 3(2) to the Principles of International Law Concerning Friendly Relations and Co-operation among States in accordance with the Charter of the United Nations, the Declaration on the Right to Development therefore expresses a preference for multilateralism; and cautions against the adoption of unilateral measures by states to impose compliance with the right to development. In its various resolutions on unilateral coercive measures, the HRC has also emphasized the threat to human rights, including the right to development, that could result from the adoption of such measures, as well as the risk that multilateralism be circumvented by the most powerful states, who are best placed to impose their views by resorting to unilateral measures.[33] But there is a positive obligation implied

[30] UN Doc A/RES/41/128 (n 2) art 3(2).

[31] Declaration of Principles of International Law Concerning Friendly Relations and Cooperation among States in accordance with the Charter of the United Nations (adopted 24 October 1970) UNGA Res 265(XXV); UNHRC 'Report of the Independent Expert on the effects of foreign debt and other related international financial obligations of States on the full enjoyment of all human rights, particularly economic, social and cultural rights, Cephas Lumina—Guiding principles on foreign debt and human rights' (10 April 2011) UN Doc A/HRC/20/23 paras 25–26 (referring in the context of states borrowing from foreign lenders, to 'the sovereign and inalienable right [of states] to implement a process of national development independently and free from pressure, influence or interference from external actors, including other States and international financial institutions').

[32] Indeed, threatening a state with the denial of certain advantages in order to force the state to conclude an international agreement would constitute coercion in the meaning of the Vienna Convention on the Law of Treaties (n 11) art 52; Declaration on the Prohibition of Military, Political or Economic Coercion in the Conclusion of Treaties (26 March–24 May 1968 and 9 April–22 May 1969) UN Doc A/CONF.39/26) para 1 (which 'condemns the threat or use of pressure in any form, whether military, political, or economic, by any State in order to coerce another State to perform any act relating to the conclusion of a treaty in violation of the principles of the sovereign equality of States and freedom of consent').

[33] For example, UNHRC 'Human rights and unilateral coercive measures' (7 April 2017) UN Doc A/HRC/RES/34/13; UNHRC 'Human rights and unilateral coercive measures' (3 October 2014) UN Doc A/HRC/RES/27/21 (establishing the mandate of the Special Rapporteur on the negative impact of unilateral coercive measures on human rights).

in this condemnation of unilateral coercive measures: it is to cooperate in good faith in the search of solutions through multilateral approaches.

Such a duty to enter negotiations in order to find solutions through multilateralism has been regularly affirmed in the new area of sustainable development. Principle 12 of the 1992 Rio Declaration on Environment and Development[34] expresses a strong encouragement for the search for solutions at the multilateral level:

> Unilateral actions to deal with environmental challenges outside the jurisdiction of the importing country should be avoided. Environmental measures addressing transboundary or global environmental problems should, as far as possible, be based on international consensus.

Similarly, paragraph 2.22(i) of Agenda 21, also adopted at the 1992 Earth Summit, provides:

> Governments should encourage GATT, UNCTAD and other relevant international and regional economic institutions to examine, in accordance with their respective mandates and competences, the following propositions and principles: ...
> (i) Avoid unilateral action to deal with environmental challenges outside the jurisdiction of the importing country. Environmental measures addressing transborder problems should, as far as possible, be based on an international consensus.

If, on the one hand, the international community defines certain objectives as desirable, yet disapproves of states seeking to achieve such objectives by unilateral action, should it not follow that all states have a duty to at least *seek to arrive at a negotiated agreement*? The question is relevant for all situations where a particular objective can only be attained by states acting collectively, rather than by the adoption of measures at domestic level only. It is relevant, in other terms, for the creation and maintenance of global public goods—goods that must be produced because of the interdependence of states, which requires them to act together to address a particular problem. The establishment of a social and international order in which all the rights of the UDHR can be realized (to paraphrase Article 28 of the UDHR) is, par excellence, such a global public good.

10.3 Is the Duty to Cooperate by the Conclusion of Conventions Purely Rhetorical?

Whether the duty to cooperate is made explicit (as it is in several human rights instruments, as noted earlier), or whether it is derived from the condemnation of unilateral measures to achieve ends that the international community has set for itself that require collective action by states, the next question that emerges is whether such commitments have any legal significance at all. What, exactly, can be expected from states imposed such obligations? Imposing an obligation on a state to enter into any form of international agreement or to negotiate such an agreement may seem both odd and impractical, since it can hardly be reconciled with the principle of state sovereignty—one of the implications of which is that states cannot be forced to enter into agreements against their will.

[34] UNGA 'Report of the United Nations Conference on Environment and Development' (12 August 1992) UN Doc A/CONF.151/26.

A most authoritative voice has dismissed as purely hortatory, rather than binding, provisions in international treaties that call on parties to negotiate further agreements. Such provisions, it has been written:

> are *pacta de contrahendo*, which cannot be enforced if the parties do not reach agreement. There is no way in which an agreement can be forced upon them and there is likewise no way in which they can be compelled to negotiate. The assertion that the duty to negotiate or to conclude an agreement implies a duty to negotiate in good faith is an empty one. Unless appropriate machinery has been set up, no court or other agency can determine whether a State has or has not negotiated in good faith and what the duty to negotiate in good faith requires. In the relations of States, a complaint that negotiations have not been carried on in good faith is mere rhetoric.[35]

This, however, conflates a duty to *negotiate in good faith*, with the duty to *reach an agreement*; yet the former may be imposed without the latter necessarily following. The Permanent Court of International Justice established this distinction long ago.[36] It is again a distinction relied on by Judge Charles de Visscher in his dissenting opinion to the Advisory Opinion delivered by the International Court of Justice on the *International status of South-West Africa*, where the question arose of the duty of the Union of South Africa, having received a mandate under the mandates system established under the League of Nations, to enter into an agreement to join the trusteeship system under the newly created organization of the United Nations: 'the mandatory Power', Judge de Visccher wrote, 'while remaining free to reject the particular terms of a proposed agreement, has the legal obligation to be ready to take part in negotiations and to conduct them in good faith with a view to concluding an agreement'.[37]

The duty to negotiate in good faith, as opposed to the duty to reach an agreement, should be treated as an obligation of means: the state should deploy its best efforts to cooperate internationally with a view to finding such agreement. The responsibility of the state cannot be engaged merely due to its failure to arrive at an agreement. A state may, however, be accountable for its failure to seek, in good faith, to conclude new partnerships. Indeed, the precedents cited earlier in the field of sustainable development[38] were referred to by the Appellate Body of the WTO when, in the *Shrimp/Turtle* dispute, it took the view that the requirement of non-discrimination under Article XI:1 of the 1994 General Agreement on Tariffs and Trade prohibited the adoption of unilateral measures, unless such measures have been preceded by good faith attempts to reach an agreement with the trading partners on the adoption of common standards achieving the desired objective. The Appellate Body condemned in that case 'the failure of the United States to engage the appellees, as well as other Members exporting shrimp to the United States, in *serious, across-the-board negotiations with the objective of concluding bilateral or multilateral agreements for the protection and conservation*

[35] RR Baxter, 'International Law in Her Infinite Variety' (1980) 29(4) International and Comparative Law Quarterly 549, 552.

[36] *Railway Traffic Between Lithuania and Poland* (Advisory Opinion) PCIJ Rep Series A/B No 42 p 115 (about the duties following from a resolution of the Council of the League of Nations recommending that 'the two governments [Polish and Lithuanian] . . . enter into direct negotiations as soon as possible' concerning the railway connections between the two countries); Martin A Rogoff, 'The Obligation to Negotiate in International Law: Rules and Realities' (1994) 16 Michigan Journal of International Law 141–85, 148 (emphasizing the importance of distinguishing the obligation to negotiate from the obligation to conclude an agreement).

[37] *International status of South-West Africa* (Advisory Opinion) ICJ Rep 1950, 188.

[38] UN Doc A/CONF.151/26 (n 34).

of sea turtles, before enforcing the import prohibition against the shrimp exports of those other Members'.[39] The Appellate Body could of course not require that such agreement be reached: unilateral measures remain available to the WTO members, as a last resort, should multilateralism fail. In its view, however, it would not be acceptable for a member to impose on other members compliance with certain standards, without giving at least a fair chance for a joint approach to succeed.

The case illustrates that it is possible, in such a quasi-judicial context, to assess the 'seriousness' of the efforts of a country to search for a negotiated solution to the issue at hand, by examining, for instance, the time and energy that went into searching for such a solution, the reasonableness of the offers made to the other parties, and so forth.[40] For the understanding of global obligations corresponding to the realization of the right to development, this can be essential, since the right to development is inter alia about the duty to contribute to design solutions through bilateral or multilateral partnerships, including partnerships at regional level, that can lead towards shaping an international environment enabling development efforts deployed at domestic level.

Widely diverging views coexist, however, as to the extent of this obligation of means. At one end of the spectrum, the duty to negotiate could be given the narrowest of meanings, and constitute little else than a requirement that, before resorting to unilateral measures or to litigation, a state provide a clear indication of its intention to address an issue, thus providing other states an opportunity to come up with proposals that might lead to a negotiated settlement. The interpretation by the ICJ of the compromissory clause of Article 22 of the International Convention on the Elimination of All Forms of Racial Discrimination (ICERD) provides an example. That clause suggests that the ICJ should only play a subsidiary role in the settlement of disputes related to the interpretation or application of the ICERD, where such a dispute 'is not settled by negotiation or by the procedures expressly provided for in this Convention [which includes a provision on interstate communications filed with the Committee on the Elimination of Racial Discrimination]'.[41] In the case

[39] United States—Import Prohibition of Certain Shrimp and Shrimp Products (12 October 1998) WT/DS58/AB/R para 166 <http://docsonline.wto.org> accessed 21 July 2021. At issue in this case was s 609 of Public Law 101–162, adopted by the United States in 1989. This provision required the imposition of an import ban on imports from countries where shrimp were harvested with technology that could adversely affect certain sea turtles, unless the countries concerned were certified by the president, on an annual basis, as having a regulatory programme governing the incidental taking of sea turtles in the course of harvesting comparable to that of the United States, or having an average rate of incidental taking of sea turtles comparable to that by US vessels using turtle-excluding devices, or having a fishing environment such that there exists no threat of incidental taking of sea turtles in the course of such harvesting. Faced with this unilateral measure adopted by the United States, the Appellate Body regretted the failure of the United States to seek a negotiated solution. The resort to unilateral trade measures is condemned in the following terms: 'an alternative course of action was reasonably open to the United States for securing the legitimate policy goal of its measure, a course of action other than the unilateral and non-consensual procedures of the import prohibition under Section 609. It is relevant to observe that an import prohibition is, ordinarily, the heaviest "weapon" in a Member's armoury of trade measures. The record does not, however, show that serious efforts were made by the United States to negotiate similar agreements with any other country or group of countries before (and, as far as the record shows, after) Section 609 was enforced on a world-wide basis on 1 May 1996. Finally, the record also does not show that the appellant, the United States, *attempted to have recourse to such international mechanisms as exist to achieve cooperative efforts to protect and conserve sea turtles* before imposing the import ban' (emphasis added) (para 171).

[40] Michel Virally, 'Panorama du Droit International Contemporain: Cours Général de Droit International Public' in Collected Courses of the Hague Academy of International Law (1983) 240. Virally writes that 'in assuming an obligation to negotiate, a State reserves the right to disagree—and therefore the right to prevent a settlement—on the sole condition that it acts in good faith', a condition, he adds, 'which may be difficult to verify'. It is argued here that this may be too pessimistic a view. Certain criteria can be identified, allowing to assess the seriousness with which a state enters into a process of negotiation.

[41] International Convention on the Elimination of All Forms of Racial Discrimination (adopted 21 December 1965, entered into force on 4 January 1969) UNGA Res 2106 (XX) art 22, which reads: 'Any dispute between two or more States Parties with respect to the interpretation or application of this Convention, which is not settled

concerning the *Application of the International Convention on the Elimination of all Forms of Racial Discrimination (Georgia v Russian Federation)*, Russia questioned the jurisdiction of the ICJ because, it asserted, 'there has never been the slightest negotiation between the Parties on the interpretation or application of the Convention on the elimination of racial discrimination'.[42] The Court rejected the argument. While acknowledging that 'Article 22 does suggest that some attempt should have been made by the claimant party to initiate, with the Respondent Party, discussions on issues that would fall under CERD',[43] it noted that:

> such issues have been raised in bilateral contacts between the Parties, and, [...] these issues have manifestly not been resolved by negotiation prior to the filing of the Application; [...] in several representations to the United Nations Security Council in the days before the filing of the Application, those same issues were raised by Georgia and commented upon by the Russian Federation; [...] therefore the Russian Federation was made aware of Georgia's position in that regard; and [...] the fact that CERD has not been specifically mentioned in a bilateral or multilateral context is not an obstacle to the seisin of the Court on the basis of Article 22 of the Convention.[44]

At the other end of the spectrum, attempts have been made to define the specific duties that are implied by a general obligation to negotiate 'in good faith'. In the recent case concerning the *Obligation to Negotiate Access to the Pacific Ocean (Bolivia v Chile)* presented to the ICJ, Bolivia claimed that Chile had in fact committed to negotiate 'in order to reach an agreement granting Bolivia a fully sovereign access' to the Pacific Ocean—an access essential to Bolivia, which suffers important negative consequences from its situation as a landlocked country. Intervening on behalf of Bolivia, Mr Vaughan Lowe submitted during the hearings that:

> the duty to negotiate under international law entails, at a minimum, the following specific obligations:
>
> *(a)* First, the duty to receive communications and proposals put forward by another State concerning the adjustment of any matters of serious concern to that State.
> *(b)* Second, the duty to consider any such communications or proposals, taking into account the interests of the other State.
> *(c)* Third, the duty to participate, in a considered and reasoned manner, in official meetings to discuss such communications and proposals, if invited to do so.
> *(d)* Fourth, the duty to look for ways of overcoming any problems that stand in the way of resolution of the matter.

by negotiation or by the procedures expressly provided for in this Convention, shall, at the request of any of the parties to the dispute, be referred to the International Court of Justice for decision, unless the disputants agree to another mode of settlement.'

[42] *Application of the International Convention on the Elimination of all Forms of Racial Discrimination (Georgia v Russian Federation)* (Provisional Measures) [2008] ICJ Rep 140 [102].
[43] ibid [114].
[44] ibid [115].

All this in good faith and in a timely manner.[45]

Chile, Mr Lowe continued, 'must engage with the issue, and actively consider what steps it might take to resolve the problem, even if that requires contemplating a shift from its previously declared position. It must give serious, informed and timely consideration to the substance of any proposal or communication put forward in good faith by Bolivia and give a response that engages in a reasoned manner with the substance of the proposal or communication.'[46]

Although this does go much further than the vague duty to make the other party aware of one's position in order to give a chance for negotiations to commence (as in the case concerning the *Application of the International Convention on the Elimination of all Forms of Racial Discrimination (Georgia v Russian Federation)*, referred to earlier), it still is distinct from any duty to reach an agreement, let alone to achieve a particular outcome. In its judgment of 1 October 2018, the Court carefully distinguishes in this regard the duty to *negotiate in good faith* from a duty to *agree*:

> 86. While States are free to resort to negotiations or put an end to them, they may agree to be bound by an obligation to negotiate. In that case, States are required under international law to enter into negotiations and to pursue them in good faith. As the Court recalled in the *North Sea Continental Shelf* cases, States 'are under an obligation so to conduct themselves that the negotiations are meaningful, which will not be the case when either of them insists upon its own position without contemplating any modification' (*I.C.J. Reports 1969*, p. 47, para. 85). Each of them 'should pay reasonable regard to the interests of the other' (*Application of the Interim Accord of 13 September 1995 (the former Yugoslav Republic of Macedonia* v. *Greece), Judgment, I.C.J. Reports 2011 (II)*, p. 685, para. 132).
>
> 87. Negotiations between States may lead to an agreement that settles their dispute, but, generally, as the Court observed quoting the Advisory Opinion on *Railway Traffic between Lithuania and Poland (P.C.I.J., Series A/B No. 42*, p. 116), 'an obligation to negotiate does not imply an obligation to reach an agreement' (*Pulp Mills on the River Uruguay (Argentina* v. *Uruguay), Judgment, I.C.J. Reports 2010 (I)*, p. 68, para. 150). When setting forth an obligation to negotiate, the parties may, as they did for instance in Article VI of the Treaty on the Non-Proliferation of Nuclear Weapons, establish an 'obligation to achieve a precise result' (*Legality of the Threat or Use of Nuclear Weapons, Advisory Opinion, I.C.J. Reports 1996 (I)*, p. 264, para. 99). Bolivia's submissions could be understood as referring to an obligation with a similar character.
>
> 88. As the Court observed in its Judgment on the preliminary objection, 'Bolivia does not ask the Court to declare that it has a right to sovereign access to the sea' (*I.C.J. Reports 2015 (II)*, p. 605, para. 33). What Bolivia claims in its submissions is that Chile is under an obligation to negotiate 'in order to reach an agreement granting Bolivia a fully sovereign access' (*ibid.*, para. 35).
>
> 89. In its Judgment on Chile's preliminary objection, the Court determined 'that the subject-matter of the dispute is whether Chile is obligated to negotiate in good faith Bolivia's sovereign access to the Pacific Ocean' (*ibid.*, para. 34). As the Court observed, this alleged

[45] *Obligation to Negotiate Access to the Pacific Ocean (Bolivia v Chile)* (Oral Proceedings—Translation) [2018] ICJ Rep 153 [9].
[46] ibid [12].

obligation does not include a commitment to reach an agreement on the subject-matter of the dispute.

It is worth emphasizing that the duty to negotiate in good faith remains an obligation of means, distinct from a duty to reach an agreement (which would be an obligation of result), even where the objective of the negotiation is clearly defined—in the case of the Bolivia–Chile dispute, to ensure sovereign access of Bolivia to the Pacific Ocean. Where such an objective is agreed on by the parties, the negotiation shall serve to identify the means through which it shall be attained, including the allocation of the burden between the parties, the timelines, and so forth. It may well be that, in the end, no agreement shall be reached. This does not imply that it shall not be possible for a court or a quasi-judicial body to assess whether a state has negotiated 'in good faith', in other terms: that is not refused to reconsider its initial positions in the light of proposals made by other parties; that, in formulating its proposals, it has paid 'reasonable regard' to the interests of the other parties; and that, where the objectives of the negotiation are agreed, it has worked constructively towards the attainment of such objectives by putting forward proposals (or answering to proposals from the other parties) that contribute to this end.

10.4 What Implications Follow from a Duty to Cooperate in the Negotiation of Conventions Supporting the Right to Development?

If there exists a duty to negotiate in good faith with a view to the conclusion of agreements (or to the revision of existing agreements) in support of the implementation of the right to development, which criteria should be taken into account to assess compliance with such a duty? It is submitted that, in order to make such an assessment, it shall be required to consider: first, whether they have put forward proposals, with a view to strengthening international cooperation, that are sufficiently concrete, or have responded to proposals made by others; and second, whether such proposals or counterproposals have a reasonable chance of attracting support.

10.4.1 The Procedural Requirement to Negotiate

The first requirement is of a procedural kind. It is that states do not remain passive but make concrete steps towards reaching an international agreement—minimally, by responding in a timely fashion to the proposals made by other parties. Under the ICESCR, states are expected to take steps towards the progressive realization of the rights recognized in the Covenant that are 'deliberate, concrete and targeted as clearly as possible towards meeting the obligations recognized in the Covenant'.[47] A similar requirement could be imposed, at the level of global obligations, as regards the duty to put forward proposals that could move towards an international environment supporting domestic-level efforts at achieving the right to development. Thus, though this obligation is procedural in nature, it is not simply a pro forma obligation to be open to discussions or to acknowledge receipt of proposals filed

[47] CESCR 'General Comment No 3: The Nature of States Parties' Obligations (Art. 2, Para 1, of the Covenant)' (14 December 1990) UN Doc E/1991/23 para 2.

by other parties: rather, to borrow from the language of the *Graeco-German* Arbitration, the engagement should be 'meaningful'.[48]

10.4.2 The Substantive Requirement to Put Forward Reasonable Proposals

The second requirement concerns the substance of the negotiation position taken. The proposals states put forward in negotiation fora should be reasonably tailored to attain the objectives pursued. Though there exists no clear consensus on precise benchmarks in this regard, it may be suggested that this requires assessing the potential impacts of the proposals put forward in order to examine:

a) whether such proposals shall enable the states to whom such proposals are addressed to respect, protect and fulfil human rights, consistent with their international obligations;
b) whether they shall benefit, as a matter of priority, the most marginalized groups within the states concerned; and
c) whether, in the distribution of the burdens and benefits, such proposals take into account the principle of common but differentiated responsibilities and respective capabilities.

Thus, the reasonableness of a proposal for a new international agreement may be assessed on three criteria. The first criterion is that the agreement should not make it more difficult, or impossible, for the states concerned to comply with their duties to respect, protect, and fulfil human rights. This follows from the principle of *pacta sunt servanda*,[49] as well as from the axiomatic rule according to which states may not escape pre-existing treaty-based commitments by the conclusion, with other parties, of another treaty covering the same subject, whose provisions would in some way conflict with the earlier treaty: the posterior treaty could not be invoked against the parties to the earlier treaty, for whom it is a *res inter alios acta*.[50] Indeed, even if it were suggested that all states parties to a human rights treaty be involved in negotiations on a new agreement reducing these pre-existing obligations, the

[48] In this case, in which Greece argued that Germany was under an obligation under Agreement on German External Debts (adopted 16 September 1953) 333 UNTS 3 (London Debt Agreement) art 19, to enter into negotiations to settle certain outstanding claims, the Arbitral Tribunal explained that: 'To be meaningful, negotiations have to be entered into with a view to arriving at an agreement. Though … an agreement to negotiate does not necessarily imply an obligation to reach an agreement, it does imply that serious efforts towards that end will be made' (Graeco–German Arbitration (1972) 91 RIAA p 57). The duty, the Tribunal stated, is to 'negotiate, bargain, and in good faith attempt to reach a result acceptable to both parties' (ibid p 56).

[49] Vienna Convention on the Law of Treaties (n 11) art 26.

[50] ibid art 30 (specifically, art 30 § 4, b); GG Fitzmaurice, 'Third Report' (1958) ILC 20. As explained by Special Rapporteur Fitzmaurice: 'Since anything that some of the parties to a treaty do *inter se* under another treaty is clearly *res inter alios acta*, it cannot in law result in any formal diminution of the obligation of these parties under the earlier treaty, or affect juridically the rights or position of the other parties, which remain legally intact and subsisting'; for further discussions of the rule, see in particular Charles Rousseau, 'De la compatibilité des normes juridiques contradictoires dans l'ordre international' in A Pedone (ed), *Revue générale de droit international public, vol 39* (1932) 133–92; EW Vierdag, 'The Time of the "Conclusion" of a Multilateral Treaty: Article 30 of the Vienna Convention on the Law of Treaties and Related Provisions' (1989) 59 British Yearbook of International Law 92; W Czaplinski and GM Danilenko, 'Conflict of Norms in International Law' (1990) 21 Netherlands International Law Review 12; Jan B Mus, 'Conflicts between Treaties in International Law' (1998) 45 Netherlands International Law Review 208.

status of human rights norms as norms that cannot be derogated from by mutual agreement because of their peremptory character would prohibit such an agreement from entering into force;[51] if it were to be signed and ratified by the states concerned, it would have to be considered as null and void.[52] Such an agreement, in any event, would have to be treated as incompatible with Article 103 of the UN Charter, and thus inapplicable.[53]

The second criterion on the basis of which the reasonableness of a proposal may be assessed is by asking whether, if accepted, the proposal would contribute to the reduction of inequalities. The prohibition of discrimination is a core obligation of states both under the UN Charter and international human rights law. Discrimination constitutes any distinction, exclusion, restriction or preference or other differential treatment that is based on any ground such as race, colour, sex, language, religion, political, or other opinion, national or social origin, property, birth, or other status, and which has the purpose or effect of nullifying or impairing the recognition, enjoyment, or exercise by all persons, on an equal footing, of all rights and freedoms. Any proposal for an international agreement that would entail discrimination thus defined would not pass the reasonableness test. But human rights law goes further. It also prohibits any action or omission that disproportionately affects members of a particular group, in the absence of a reasonable and objective justification, thus constituting de facto discrimination.[54] Thus, proposed international agreements should be assessed to ensure that they shall not have such impacts. Such agreements may, however, provide for differential treatment benefiting certain categories of the population facing systemic disadvantage. Indeed, in order to eliminate de facto discrimination, states may be under an obligation to adopt special measures to attenuate or suppress conditions that perpetuate discrimination. Such measures are legitimate to the extent that they represent reasonable, objective,

[51] Vienna Convention on the Law of Treaties (n 11) art 53 (defining a peremptory norm of international law as 'a norm accepted and recognized by the international community of States as a whole as a norm from which no derogation is permitted and which can be modified only by a subsequent norm of general international law having the same character'); disagreements persist as to whether the full list of human rights recognized in the International Bill of Rights have the status of *jus cogens*, however. For example, Erika De Wet and Jure Vidmar (eds), *Hierarchy in International Law: The Place of Human Rights* (OUP 2012). The debate is not new: fifty years ago, Judge Tanaka was already suggesting in his dissenting opinion in the *South West Africa* case that human rights law belonged to the *jus cogens*, which is imperative, as opposed to the *jus dispositivum*, that states could freely dispose of: 'If we can introduce in the international field a category of law, namely jus cogens, recently examined by the International Law Commission, a kind of imperative law which constitutes the contrast to jus dispositivum, capable of being changed by way of agreement between States, surely the law concerning the protection of human rights may be considered to belong to the jus cogens' *South West Africa (Ethiopia v South Africa)* (Judgment) [1966] ICJ Rep 46 (Judge Tanaka, dissenting opinion); *South West Africa* (*Liberia v South Africa*) (Judgment) [1966] ICJ Rep 47 (Judge Tanaka, dissenting opinion). The issue of peremptory norms of general international law (*jus cogens*) is currently under examination within the ILC, with a view to contributing to the codification and progressive development of the topic.

[52] Vienna Convention on the Law of Treaties (n 11) art 64.

[53] Whereas a treaty found to be in violation of a *jus cogens* norm is void and must be considered to have never existed, a treaty incompatible with obligations flowing from membership in the United Nations does not disappear; however, as a result of art 103 of the UN Charter, it shall not be applied to the extent of such an incompatibility. Pierre-Marie Dupuy, *L'unité de l'ordre juridique international: cours général de droit international public, vol* 297 (Martinus Nijhoff 2003) 305; ILC, 'Fragmentation of International Law: Difficulties Arising from the Diversification and Expansion of International Law' (18 July 2006) UN Doc A/CN.4/L.702 para 41 '(a) A rule conflicting with a norm of *jus cogens* becomes thereby *ipso facto* void; (*b*) A rule conflicting with Article 103 of the United Nations Charter becomes inapplicable as a result of such conflict and to the extent of such conflict'; Jean Combacau, 'Logique de la validité contre logique d'opposabilité dans la Convention de Vienne sur le droit des traités' in Michel Virally (ed), *Le Droit international au service de la paix, de la justice et du développement: Mélanges Michel Virally* (A Pedone 1991) pp 195–203.

[54] UNHRC, 'CCPR General Comment No 18: Non-discrimination' (10 November 1989) UN; CESCR 'General Comment No 20: Non-discrimination in economic, social and cultural rights (art 2, para 2 of the International Covenant on Economic, Social and Cultural Rights)' (2 July 2009) UN Doc E/C.12/GC/20.

and proportionate means to redress de facto discrimination and are discontinued when substantive equality has been sustainably achieved.

The third criterion is that the agreement put forward takes into account the principle of common but differentiated responsibilities and respective capabilities. This principle originally emerged in international economic law to justify positive discrimination in favour of developing countries: as an illustration, the Second UNCTAD conference expressed itself in favour of 'the early establishment of a mutually acceptable system of generalized, non-reciprocal and non-discriminatory preferences beneficial to the developing countries in order to increase the export earnings, to promote the industrialization, and to accelerate the rates of economic growth of these countries'.[55] It then penetrated international environmental law, inspiring the 1987 Montréal Protocol on Substances that Deplete the Ozone Layer to the 1985 Vienna Convention for the Protection of the Ozone Layer.[56] Principle 7 of the Rio Declaration describes it as follows:

> States should co-operate in a spirit of global partnership to conserve, protect and restore the health and integrity of the Earth's ecosystem. In view of the different contributions to global environmental degradation, States have common but differentiated responsibilities. The developed countries acknowledge the responsibility that they bear in the international pursuit of sustainable development in view of the pressures their societies place on the global environment and of the technologies and financial resources they command.

As illustrated by the UN Framework Convention on Climate Change and the Convention on Biological Diversity, the first examples of the implementation of the principle of common but differentiated responsibilities agreed on in Rio,[57] this principle requires that the allocation of responsibilities between states should take into account both each state's contribution

[55] United Nations, 'Report of the United Nations Conference on Trade and Development on its Second Session' (1968) Resolution 21(ii). This commitment resulted, in particular, in the adoption of decisions granting waivers from the most-favoured nation principle under the General Agreement on Tariffs and Trade, allowing for General Systems of Preferences to be set up in order to accelerate the integration of developing countries in international trade, see Decision relating to the establishment of generalized, non-reciprocal and non-discriminatory preferences beneficial to the developing countries (25 June 1971) BISD 18S/24; Decision on Differential and More Favourable Treatment, Reciprocity and Fuller Participation of Developing Countries (28 November 1979) BISD 26S/191, 203 (providing that 'contracting parties may accord differential and more favourable treatment to developing countries, without according such treatment to other contracting parties').

[56] Vienna Convention for the Protection of the Ozone Layer (adopted 22 March 1985, entered into force on 1 January 1989) 1513 UNTS 293. In the Preamble of the Montréal Protocol, the parties acknowledge that 'special provision is required to meet the needs of developing countries, including the provision of additional financial resources and access to relevant technologies, bearing in mind that the magnitude of funds necessary is predictable, and the funds can be expected to make a substantial difference in the world's ability to address the scientifically established problem of ozone depletion and its harmful effects'; ibid art 5 (providing for specific treatment of developing countries).

[57] UN Framework Convention on Climate Change (adopted 9 May 1992, entered into force on 21 March 1994) 1771 UNTS art 3(1) (States parties should act 'on the basis of equity and in accordance with their common but differentiated responsibilities and respective capabilities'); Convention on Biological Diversity (adopted 5 June 1992, entered in force on 29 December 1993) 1760 UNTS 79 art 20(4) ('The extent to which developing country Parties will effectively implement their commitments under this Convention will depend on the effective implementation by developed country Parties of their commitments under this Convention related to financial resources and transfer of technology and will take fully into account the fact that economic and social development and eradication of poverty are the first and overriding priorities of the developing country Parties'); the principle of common but differentiated responsibilities has now grown into a general principle of international environmental law, see Philippe Cullet, *Differential Treatment in International Environmental Law* (Ashgate 2003); Lavanya Rajamani, *Differential Treatment in International Environmental Law* (OUP 2006); Tuula Honkonen, *The Common but Differentiated Responsibility Principle in Multilateral Environmental Agreements: Regulatory and Policy Aspects* (Kluwer Law International 2009).

to the issue to be addressed through international cooperation,[58] and each state's ability to contribute to addressing that issue (capabilities, as measures by financial resources and technologies).[59] In its New Delhi Declaration of Principles of International Law relating to Sustainable Development, adopted at the Seventieth Conference of the ILA held in New Delhi on 2–6 April 2002, the ILA described the principle thus:

> 3.1. States and other relevant actors have common but differentiated responsibilities. All States are under a duty to co-operate in the achievement of global sustainable development and the protection of the environment. International organizations, corporations (including in particular transnational corporations), non-governmental organizations and civil society should co-operate in and contribute to this global partnership. Corporations have also responsibilities pursuant to the polluter-pays principle.
>
> 3.2. Differentiation of responsibilities, whilst principally based on the contribution that a State has made to the emergence of environmental problems, must also take into account the economic and developmental situation of the State, in accordance with paragraph 3.3.
>
> 3.3. The special needs and interests of developing countries and of countries with economies in transition, with particular regard to least developed countries and those affected adversely by environmental, social and developmental considerations, should be recognized.
>
> 3.4. Developed countries bear a special burden of responsibility in reducing and eliminating unsustainable patterns of production and consumption and in contributing to capacity-building in developing countries, inter alia by providing financial assistance and access to environmentally sound technology. In particular, developed countries should play a leading role and assume primary responsibility in matters of relevance to sustainable development.

At the World Summit on Sustainable Development held in Johannesburg in August–September 2002, at which the implementation of the Agenda 21 and the Rio Declaration on Environment and Development was discussed, heads of state and governments pledged to take 'concrete actions and measures at all levels and to enhancing international co-operation, taking into account the Rio principles, including, inter alia, the principle of common but differentiated responsibilities as set out in principle 7 of the Rio Declaration on Environment and Development'.[60] The principle of common but differentiated responsibilities also appears in the 2030 Development Agenda, particularly in targets 10.a and 12.1 of the Sustainable Development Goals (SDGs), and in the Addis Ababa Action Agenda of the Third International Conference on Finance for Development.[61]

Perhaps the chief obstacle to the operationalization of the principle of common but differentiated responsibilities—allowing the principle to guide international negotiations and to assess the reasonableness of proposals and counterproposals presented in negotiation

[58] In international environmental law, this may be seen as a manifestation of the polluter-pays principle, see ILA, 'New Delhi Declaration on Principles of International Law relating to Sustainable Development' (6 April 2002) published in UN Doc A/57/329, Principle 3.

[59] These two dimensions, which are respectively looking backward and looking forward, shall often converge: an inequitable trading system, for instance, shall often be the result of past unfair trading practices, and the partner having benefited most shall have greater capacities to remedy the resulting imbalances.

[60] United Nations, Johannesburg Summit, 'Plan of Implementation of the World Summit on Sustainable Development' (2002) paras 2, 81 <http://www.un.org/jsummit/> accessed 21 July 2021.

[61] UNGA Res 69/313 (17 August 2015) UN Doc A/RES/69/313 para 59.

fora—is that there exists no unanimous agreement on how countries should be classified in order to implement the principle. The category of 'developing countries'—leaving aside even its implicit but highly contestable suggestion that there would exist a single pathway to development, one 'script' that all countries should follow—is hardly helpful to identify the countries' differentiated responsibilities. Today, the group of 159 'developing countries', categorized as such by the United Nations, is widely heterogenous: they include countries whose situations, trajectories, and prospects differ widely, leading the World Bank to reject the use of this category since the 2016 edition of its *World Development Report*.

Other classifications are barely more helpful, however. The World Bank classifies countries as 'low income', 'lower middle income', 'upper middle income' and 'high income', on the basis of their GNI per capita, using a three-year average exchange rate to avoid the classification being influenced by short-term changes in currency values.[62] However, though for most countries there is a strong correlation between GNI per capita and social indicators,[63] GNI per capita remains a crude proxy to assess the level of development of a country. It does not, for instance, take into account adequately the activity in the informal sector or the non-monetary segments of the economy. Nor does it reflect fully the nature of the challenges certain countries may be facing: small island developing states and landlocked developing countries, for instance, face specific constraints due to their geography, which may have to be taken into account, although such constraints may not be reflected in their position on a GNI per capita ranking; similarly, poor countries with a high level of debt face challenges of their own, which were recognized when a separate category of 'heavily indebted poor countries' eligible for special assistance from the IMF and the World Bank was defined when the HIPC initiative was launched in 1996. Finally, a separate classification is based on the list of least-developed countries (LDCs). This list is decided upon by the UN Economic and Social Council and, ultimately, by the General Assembly, on the basis of recommendations made by the Committee for Development Policy, using a set of criteria including per capita GNI, a human assets index and an economic vulnerability index.[64]

These various approaches were each designed for specific purposes and in specific institutional settings, and they are more or less well-suited to those ends. But they appear insufficient to capture the full spectrum of conditions that countries face. Classifying countries in 'groups', separated by more or less arbitrarily defined boundaries, may not be the most justifiable approach. Instead, taking into account the principle of common but differentiated responsibilities and respective capabilities for the implementation of the right to development may require to identify for each country (1) the contribution that it has made in the past to the emergence of environmental problems and, more generally, of unsustainable forms of growth; (2) the capacity of each country to contribute to the right to development, based on the resources (natural, financial, technological, and human) that it could

[62] The classification is published on http://data.worldbank.org and is revised once a year on 1 July, at the start of the World Bank fiscal year. For instance, for the current 2018 fiscal year, low-income economies are those with a GNI per capita of US$1,005 or less in 2016; lower-middle-income economies are those with a GNI per capita between US$1,006 and US$3,955; upper-middle-income economies are those with a GNI per capita between US$3,956 and US$12,235; high-income economies are those with a GNI per capita of US$12,236 or more. World Bank 'World Bank Country and Lending Groups—World Bank Data Help Desk' (World Bank) <https://datahelpdesk.worldbank.org/knowledgebase/articles/906519> accessed 5 November 2020.

[63] Neil Fantom and Umar Serajuddin, 'The World Bank's Classification of Countries by Income' (2016) World Bank Group Policy Research Working Paper <http://documents.worldbank.org/curated/en/408581467988942234/pdf/WPS7528.pdf> accessed 5 November 2020.

[64] United Nations (ed), *Handbook on the Least Developed Country Category: Inclusion, Graduation, and Special Support Measures* (United Nations 2008).

mobilize to that effect; and (3) the constraints (including geographical constraints, the debt burden, and the lack of diversification of the economy) the country faces. The classification of countries based on these criteria could be regularly updated, ideally on an annual basis, in order to arrive at a shared understanding of which efforts can be expected from each state, where the burden of realizing the right to development should be shared between countries. Proposals to improve the international social and economic order should be assessed on the basis of whether they take account the respective responsibilities of countries, based on this set of criteria.

10.5 Conclusion

Human rights instruments include numerous references to the duty of international cooperation, inter alia by the conclusion of new international agreements; and the duty is key to the implementation of the right to development proclaimed by the UN General Assembly. Yet, it continues to be an 'imperfect' obligation: it remains formulated at a highly general level, and its content is still vague and contested, making the obligation unenforceable unless and until it is further clarified.[65] This chapter has sought to propose a way forward. It emphasized the distinction between the duty to negotiate in good faith with a view to reaching an agreement, and the duty to agree. The former is an obligation of means; that is not to say that it is empty, or that it cannot be objectively assessed. Three criteria, it has been suggested, could be relied upon to guide the evaluation of the reasonableness of the positions adopted by a state in negotiation fora in which new instruments are proposed to implement the right to development. First, a proposal should only be deemed reasonable if it supports, rather than impedes, the realization of human rights at domestic level. Second, it should contribute to the reduction of inequalities and focus on the most vulnerable and marginalized groups of the population. Third, finally, the distribution of the burden between countries should take into account the principle of common but differentiated responsibilities and respective capabilities. Any proposal that cannot be justified in the light of these three conditions should be considered with caution, since it gives rise to the suspicion that the proposal is put forward merely to preserve the state's reputation, rather than to contribute, constructively, to the progress of human rights in general, and of the right to development in particular.

In 2020, when we celebrate the seventieth birthday of Philip Alston, whose international career started with the preparation, on the UN Secretary General's behalf, of a study on the right to development,[66] we shall also celebrate the seventieth birthday of the Advisory Opinion delivered by the International Court of Justice on the International status of South-West Africa. In his dissenting opinion, Judge Charles de Visscher remarked that:

> The obligation to be ready to negotiate with a view to concluding an agreement represented the minimum of international co-operation without which the entire régime contemplated and regulated by the Charter would have been frustrated. In this connexion one must bear

[65] The notion of 'imperfect obligations', though originally derived from Kant, is inspired here by Amartya K Sen, 'Rights and Capabilities' in Amartya Sen (ed), *Resources, Values, and Development* (Oxford: Blackwell 1984) pp 310–15; Amartya Sen, *The Idea of Justice* (Harvard University Press 2011) 360.

[66] Report of Secretary General, 'The International Dimensions of the Right to Development As a Human Right in Relation with Other Human Rights Based on International Co-Operation, including the Right to Peace, Taking into Account the Requirements of the New International Economic Order and the Fundamental Human Needs' (2 January 1979) UN Doc E/CN.4/1334.

> in mind that in the interpretation of a great international constitutional instrument, like the United Nations Charter, the individualistic concepts which are generally adequate in the interpretation of ordinary treaties, do not suffice.

The closing sentences of his dissenting opinion could be ours now, simply by replacing the reference to Article 76 of the UN Charter (outlining the basic objectives of the trusteeship system) by a reference to Article 55 (referring to the objectives of international economic and social cooperation). It would read:

> Under Article 55 of the Charter, the United Nations shall promote 'universal respect for, and observance of, human rights and fundamental freedoms for all without distinction as to race, sex, language, or religion', as a means to create 'conditions of stability and well-being that are necessary for peaceful and friendly relations among nations based on respect for the principle of equal rights and self-determination of peoples'. In recognizing their obligations to be ready to negotiate with a view to concluding new agreements for the realization of human rights and for the implementation of the right to development, all states, without thereby jeopardizing their freedom to accept or refuse the terms of such an agreement, cooperate in a particularly important field in the attainment of the highest objectives of the United Nations.[67]

[67] The actual quote is the following: 'Under Article 76 of the Charter, "the basic objectives of the Trusteeship System" conform to "the purposes of the United Nations laid down in Article 1 of the present Charter". In recognizing its obligation to be ready to negotiate with a view to concluding a Trusteeship Agreement, a mandatory Power, without thereby jeopardizing its freedom to accept or refuse the terms of such an Agreement, co-operates in a particularly important field in the attainment of the highest objectives of the United Nations'.

11

Reconsidering Personhood—From 'Civil Death' to 'Civil Life' for Persons with Disabilities

Reflections on Article 12 of the UN Convention on the Rights of Persons with Disabilities

Gerard Quinn

11.1 Introduction

The adoption of the United Nations Convention on the Rights of Persons with disabilities (UNCRPD or 'the Convention') in 2006 was a landmark event.[1] It extends the reach of general human rights norms taken for granted by many to persons with disabilities who were hitherto effectively excluded. About 177 states have ratified.[2]

Although much has been written about the drafting of the Convention, less is known about Philip Alston's pivotal role in paving the way for it.[3] As chair of the UN CESCR he oversaw the adoption of the very first General Comment in the UN treaty system on disability and human rights in 1994.[4] It was far ahead of its day by rejecting paternalistic approaches and it also laid the groundwork for the normative content of the Convention that would be concluded nearly twenty years later.

Furthermore, several of his graduates and interns went on to lead, or be part of, delegations during the drafting of the Convention. Two of them wrote the pivotal 2002 UN Study that helped start the process of drafting the Convention.[5] Another drafted the Chair's Draft of the Convention in 2004 that formed the basis for negotiations. One led the delegation of global national human rights institutions at the drafting sessions. Yet another went on to become the chair of the new treaty monitoring body—the UN Committee on the Rights of Persons with Disabilities (the Committee). And one served ably on the delegation of the Office of the High Commissioner throughout. All took personal inspiration from Professor Alston's teaching and research and especially his commitment to lesser-heard voices. It is probably fair to say that he has had an outsized influence on a global instrument that touches 800 million persons with disabilities around the world.

[1] For a general treatment of the evolution of the convention see Arlene S Kanter, *The Development of Disability Rights under International Law: From Charity to Human Rights* (Routledge 2015).

[2] The main website of the convention and its mechanisms including ratification data: United Nations Human Rights Office of the High Commissioner, <www.ohchr.org/EN/HRBodies/CRPD/Pages/CRPDIndex.aspx> accessed 10 August 2021.

[3] For commentary on the drafting of each article see Ilias Bantekas, Michael Ashley Stein, and Dēmētrēs Anastasiou (eds), *The UN Convention on the Rights of Persons with Disabilities, a Commentary* (1st edn, OUP 2018).

[4] General Comment No 5: Persons with Disabilities (adopted 9 December 1994) E/1995/22 (UN Committee on ESC Rights).

[5] Gerard Quinn and Theresia Degener, 'Human Rights and Disability: The Current Use and Future Potential of Human Rights Instruments in the Context of Disability' (UN OHCHR 2002) HR/PUB/02/1.

Gerard Quinn, *Reconsidering Personhood—From 'Civil Death' to 'Civil Life' for Persons with Disabilities* In: *The Struggle for Human Rights*. Edited by: Nehal Bhuta, Florian Hoffmann, Sarah Knuckey, Frédéric Mégret, and Margaret Satterthwaite, Oxford University Press.
 DOI: 10.1093/oso/9780198868064.003.0012

The drafters expected that the Convention would be a simple tract setting out the equal opportunities/non-discrimination approach to disability—something that had been perfected in the Anglo-American world throughout the 1990s. Indeed, at the very outset of negotiations, Finland tabled a 'non-paper' to that effect. That non-paper proposed a draft with only one or two operative paragraphs that would simply proscribe discrimination on the ground of disability. It did not particularize the barriers faced by persons with disabilities in the enjoyment of their various rights. Nor did it formulate general as well as targeted or specific obligations to overcome them. In the event, the drafters went far beyond the Finnish non-paper and adopted what Professor Arnardottir calls an equality treaty based on 'multi-dimensional disadvantage equality'.[6]

The drafters also added something else. Conscious of the abuses of social welfare and social security systems to effectively entrap people with disabilities at the margins of society (or 'purchase their absence'), the drafters recast ESC rights to ensure that they genuinely provided the material means by which persons with disabilities could take full advantage of new pathways into the mainstream of society. That is why there is such an interesting blending of civil and political rights alongside social and cultural rights in the Convention. All of this was of course anticipated by the 1994 General Comment adopted under Professor Alston's chairmanship of the CESCR (the monitoring body for the ICESCR).

Last but not least, the drafters tackled what was/is the underlying cause of so much exclusion—the literal invisibility of persons with disabilities in mainstream society and—just as important—the normative invisibility of persons with disabilities within general human rights instruments. They reckoned that there was little point opening up new opportunities and providing the material means to take advantage of them if new barriers are likely to appear. And that was bound to happen if—as in the past—the very personhood of persons with disabilities continued to be doubted or discounted. That is to say, the root cause of much exclusion had to do with the fact that persons with disabilities were either heavily discounted as persons or not viewed as persons all. They just didn't count. Or (to use the dyspeptic language of ethics) they were deemed to be 'persons of lessor moral considerability'.[7] That had to be tackled head-on and reversed. And it was. Hence, the centrality of personhood issues in the Convention (and especially in Article 12 on autonomy and legal capacity).

A longstanding flashpoint in the more specific context of disability has always been autonomy and a recognition (or non-recognition) of persons with disabilities as persons capable of directing their own lives. Comparative law reflected this and had tended to view persons with intellectual and psycho-social disabilities in particular as suffering 'civil death'.[8] One result was that their legal capacity to exercise their own autonomy was either fully or partially withdrawn. Decision-making was typically placed in the hands of third parties under various types of guardianship regimes. In retrospect this seems like a strange reaction to the weakness of voice—to take it away altogether instead of seeking ways to spark it or to

[6] Oddný Mjöll Arnardóttir, 'A Future of Multidimensional Disadvantage Equality' in Oddný Mjöll Arnardóttir and Gerard Quinn (eds), *The UN Convention on the Rights of Persons with Disabilities: European and Scandinavian Perspectives* (Brill 2009) 41–66. Her chapter presaged the content of UNCRPD, 'Convention on the Rights of Persons with Disabilities (General comment No 6 on equality on non-discrimination)' (26 April 2018) UN Doc CRPD/C/GC/6.

[7] On moral considerability theory see Mark H Bernstein, *On Moral Considerability: An Essay on Who Morally Matters* (OUP 1998).

[8] The suggestive phrase 'civil death' is originally used in Sir William Blackstone, *Commentaries on the Laws of England in Four Books, vol 1* (1753), 442–45, 1765 when describing the effect of marriage on married women. The idea of civil death', which explains the merger or effective disappearance of her separate legal personhood upon marriage is also a metaphor used to describe slavery and guardianship.

augment it. Until the UNCRPD, the focus in law and public policy (if there was one) was on the process of regularizing guardianship and not on challenging its foundational premises.

All this changed under Article 12 of the UNCRPD, which was drafted to restore visibility, full personhood, and legal capacity to all persons with disabilities regardless of the nature of their disability or its severity. Article 12 is probably the most famous—and certainly the most contentious—Article in the UNCRPD. It seeks to reverse centuries of law and policy by effectively outlawing all forms of guardianship. In its place, it recommends a new 'support paradigm' to assist persons with disabilities to exercise their legal capacity where needed. Mostly this means support with respect to decision-making. But decision-making assumes a developed sense of self, which may itself be the question especially after years of institutionalization. The support paradigm can also extend to supports that are designed to spark a sense of self in precarious situations.[9]

Curiously enough, this new paradigm has had little traction in law reform around the world. True, many governments are innovating by introducing new support regimes. But, at the same time, most of these governments retain the option of imposing guardianship regimes. They hedge their bets with part of a new paradigm sitting alongside parts of the old paradigm. Maybe this is no surprise given that the move to the new paradigm profoundly disrupts traditional power relationships by taking power away from those used to exercising it (formally or informally). Third parties (like service providers and even families) who have been comfortable making decisions for persons with disabilities need to move to completely new business models, which is seldom easy.

But one senses there is also a deeper reason for the limited impact of Article 12 so far. Persons with disabilities were not the only ones to suffer 'civil death' or a lack of legal personhood throughout legal history. Most famously, this embraced persons of colour as well as women. This was reversed in most of the world on an understanding that the alleged material difference of race and gender (*vis* the alleged lack of rational or cognitive ability) was not in fact real. However, one senses a lingering doubt about persons with disabilities. That is to say, one suspects that the persistence of 'civil death' in the form of traditional guardianship for persons with intellectual disabilities has something to do with a belief that, due to the specific impairment of mental or cognitive capacity, enough of a material difference exists to justify the continued existence of guardianship regimes. If this—the existence of a certain minimal level of cognitive ability—continues to be one of the unspoken and yet essentialist criteria of personhood and legal capacity, then it is no surprise that the new paradigm has not made much headway.

The unspoken nature of this essentialist criterion is even woven into the background assumptions of international human rights law. It is not for nothing that the very first article of the UDHR (1948) asserts that 'all human beings are endowed with reason'. This is not quite the same as saying that a human being with less reason counts for less as a person—but it probably leaves enough space for traditional assumptions that persons with limited cognitive ability count as 'less morally considerable', thus leaving space for guardianship and other regimes that effectively silence their voices. All of this shows just how embedded these cultural assumptions about the centrality of cognition to personhood are.

This chapter is structured as follows.

In section 11.2, I will place the UNCRPD in a broader context. Article 12 with its support paradigm does not in fact announce a radical new departure. It makes sense when viewed

[9] See generally Piers Gooding, *A New Era for Mental Health Law and Policy: Supported Decision-Making and the Un Convention on the Rights of Persons with Disabilities* (CUP 2017).

against the backdrop of developments across a range of disciplines that have been silently evolving over the past two decades or more. These new theories are about the nature, function, and outer boundaries of personhood. Interestingly, many of them come from within the hard sciences. They all, in their own way, debunk the idea that cognitive capacity is a central or 'essentialist' criterion of personhood. It is suggested that it is these changes that convert the seemingly utopian ideal of Article 12 into a valid legislative and policy goal for states into the future.

Second, I want to reflect on the UNCRPD, its centre of gravity and the moral and legal steer it gives to law reform. It is probably fair to say that the Convention expresses or encapsulates a new approach. But again, what makes that new approach cogent is not so much what is said in the Convention but how received understandings of personhood have in fact changed in a variety of disciplines in recent times. One might even say that Article 1 of the UDHR itself needs to be revised or at least contextualized.

Third, I want to address how we give life and real meaning to the issue of 'civil life' as against 'civil death' for persons with disabilities. That is to say, we need to move away from a traditional human rights default that aims to police how we limit rights (as in guardianship) to a human rights perch that explores how to give life to rights (through appropriate supports).[10] This entails a completely different policy imagination. In saying so, I do not want to portray the new framework as Nirvana or problem free. New paradigms always bring their own boundary issues and problematics as well as dilemmas for legislators. What are they? And how can they be handled in a way that doesn't repeat the mistakes of the past?

11.2 Reconsidering Personhood—Is Cognitive Ability Really an Essentialist Criterion?

But first, how and why did cognitive ability assume centre stage as the main essentialist criterion of personhood? How have our underlying understandings of personhood shifted? And why is cognitive ability no longer seen as central to personhood?

11.2.1 Why was Cognitive Ability Traditionally Considered an Essentialist Criterion of Personhood?

This is important if we are to get beyond a formalistic understanding of the Convention and develop a less legalistic case for change. Dean Roscoe Pound used to insist that 'all law decays inevitably'.[11] What he meant was that, either the social realities of what the law was intended to address have materially altered or that the values that originally animated the law have themselves changed. Law reform to him meant a readjustment of the law to meet current exigencies with new animating values.

The facts here have not altered. Persons with intellectual disabilities continue to be persons with intellectual disabilities and often with severe cognitive impairments. What has altered—and altered very significantly—is how we see, frame, and value persons with

[10] On the bridge between the first wave of human rights (tidying up guardianship) and the latest wave (eliminating guardianship) see Oliver Lewis, 'Advancing Legal Capacity Jurisprudence' (2011) 6 European Human Rights Law Review 700.

[11] Roscoe Pound, 'Mechanical Jurisprudence' (1908) 8 Columbia Law Review 605, 607.

intellectual disabilities. In this regard the Convention reflects, confirms, and reinforces rather than establishes profound shifts that have been happening for other reasons and in many domains beyond the law.

To grasp this let me try to describe where we are coming from. There is a debate about what/who a human is in biology. Many criteria are purely internal to the person (like having a body, having a mind, having consciousness, having a certain degree of cognitive capacity) and many are outward facing (like sociability, emotional connectedness, empathy, being able to project oneself into the future, etc.). None are unproblematic. Cognitive ability is one factor among many. The empirical biological question about 'who is a human' is separate from, but informs, the more normative question in ethics as to whether the human is 'morally considerable' or has full moral status as a person. Recall that one doesn't have to be a human to be a person. After all, corporations also enjoy at least some recognition as persons before the law.[12]

In the field of ethics, it is interesting to note that not all individuals with intellectual disabilities are embraced as persons. Ethicists have long disputed whether persons with intellectual disabilities, because of their relative lack of cognitive ability, are 'morally considerable' or possess 'full moral status' to be considered the fitting subjects of a theory or practice of justice. Why? This is so for one very simple reason. Rather unlike the biologists, the ethicists tend to consider cognitive capacity to be the key to 'full moral status'. That is to say, they use the indicator of cognitive ability to distinguish between (1) those entities with full moral status ('normal' humans or even corporations up to a point); (2) those with lesser moral status (persons with intellectual disabilities); and (3) those with no moral status at all (like a rock). This view within ethics is not without challenge. It is challenged especially by a prominent ethicist, Professor Eva Feder-Kittay, who happens to have a daughter with a disability.[13] But it is striking that the field of ethics still tends to assign a lesser moral status for persons with intellectual disabilities contrasted to those without such disabilities.

This reveals a lot. If our underlying understanding of ethics is one that effectively excludes persons with intellectual disabilities from the 'moral community' then can it be any surprise that the law has followed suit? This serves to make the point that our cultural default—which is to view cognitive disability negatively—has very deep roots.

Quite why cognitive ability was fixed on as the core essentialist criterion for full moral status within the field of ethics is open to speculation. Presumably, a being that is (and could be seen by others to be) self-aware, self-conscious, and capable of navigating the lifeworld through rational appraisal of the facts, though a rational shifting of one's options for action or inaction, through a rational processing of risks and benefits, could thereby qualify for 'full moral status'. Those that did not, did not. Of course, there are a myriad of other characteristics that could have been chosen as the essentialist criterion of personhood like a capacity for empathy, a capacity for social interaction (sociability), a capacity for an interior emotional life, a capacity to engage in human relations, or just sentience itself. But the point is they were not.[14]

[12] For interesting analysis see Daniel Greenwood, 'Person, State or Not: The Place of Business Corporations in Our Constitutional Order' (2015) 2(87) University of Colorado Law Review 351–436.

[13] See especially Eva Feder Kittay and Licia Carlson (eds), *Cognitive Disability and Its Challenge to Moral Philosophy* (Wiley-Blackwell 2010); Kittay, *Learning from My Daughter: The Value and Care of Disabled Minds* (OUP 2019).

[14] History is of course inconsistent. If cognitive ability is the main essentialist criterion of personhood then many humans who possessed it in abundance were still denied equal personhood in the past, including slaves and women. And, indeed, if cognitive ability plays such a central role, then why confine personhood to humans? Many animals also have high levels of cognitive ability. In fact, most arguments for animal rights are predicated on

11.2.2 The Steady Erosion of the Centrality of Cognition

What we have witnessed over the past two or three decades is the unravelling of that image of the atomized rational man or woman—the unravelling of the 'standard account' of personhood. It is this unravelling that gives us fresh space to think anew about autonomy and disability—which neatly coincides with the UN Convention—but is separately driven.

First, there is a long strain of thought in the humanities leaning toward the notion of the social self. Much of the literature is expertly brought together by Laura Kathryn Davy in a recent edition of *Hypatia*.[15] In it she captures brilliantly the notion of intersubjectivity or shared personhood especially in feminist legal and political thinking and applies it to the sphere of intellectual disability.

But the emphasis on the social self is not confined to the traditional humanities any longer. Modern science is itself displaying the true extent to which the 'self' is a social construct. At one pessimistic extreme is the field of sociobiology or evolutionary psychology. It can lead to the view that the 'self', like the 'mind', is an illusion.[16] Certainly, if taken to such extremes it places not just an asterisk but also a huge question mark over all decision-making by 'normal' people or persons with intellectual disabilities alike.

Additionally, much modern neuroscience is yielding new theories of the mind that have been conspicuously absent from orthodox debates about the 'self' including decision-making. Antonio Damasio, for example, is famous for his thesis that the brain is 'wired to connect'.[17] He does not say that the brain of those with higher cognitive functioning is 'wired to connect'. He says that all brains are wired to connect. In essence the 'self' emerges from these connections. Our 'selves' are intersubjective from the outset and our autonomy is fundamentally 'relational'. Similarly, in the field of clinical psychology, Bruce Hood develops the idea of the 'social brain'.[18] The point is that modern neuroscience debunks the 'standard account' of a hermetically sealed and disconnected mind. What it points to instead is the quality of the social connectors in our lives and especially in the life of the mind.

One pithy way of putting this is that our personhood is primarily shared—although it is necessarily experienced individually. Bernadette McSherry's perceptive article in the 2015 issue of *Laws* shows how the new 'discovery' techniques being opened up by neuroscience have positive potential in the future to reveal formerly unknown and unknowable persons as the science evolves.

Added to recent literature in clinical psychology is the burgeoning field of behavioural economics. The standard account of mind, consciousness, and rational decision-making underpins much classical economics and animates many econometric models. Yet the explanatory power of these models has been found wanting. Contemporary economists have been reassessing the role of rationality in economic decision-making. Indeed, the 2015 World Bank World Development Report focuses on exactly this: 'Mind, Society and Behavior'.[19] The 2015 Report characterizes decision-making (for all of us) along three axes: (1) automatic

cognitive ability: see Steven M Wise and Jane Goodall, *Rattling the Cage: Toward Legal Rights for Animals* (Basic Books 2000).

15 Laura Davy, 'Philosophical Inclusive Design: Intellectual Disability and the Limits of Individual Autonomy in Moral and Political Theory' (2015) 30 Hypatia 132.

16 See generally John Alcock, *The Triumph of Sociobiology* (OUP 2003).

17 Antonio Damasio, *Self Comes to Mind: Constructing the Conscious Brain* (Vintage Books 2012).

18 Bruce M Hood, *The Self Illusion: How the Social Brain Creates Identity* (OUP 2013).

19 World Bank, 'World Development Report 2015: Mind, Society, and Behavior' (The World Bank 2014) <http://elibrary.worldbank.org/doi/book/10.1596/978-1-4648-0342-0> accessed 10 August 2020.

decision-making; (2) social decision-making; and (3) mental decision-making models. It insists that the vast majority of decisions are made automatically with little or no in-depth deliberation. By social thinking is meant the reflex in all of us to fit in with and be valorized by our group affiliation (if we are lucky enough to have one). Indeed, the report insists we 'imitate the behavior of others almost automatically'.[20] Lastly, the report insists that we come to decision-making with baggage—narrow windows through which we make sense of the world (bypassing our cognitive functioning).

These disciplines are telling us loud and clear that cognitive ability is just one part of a menu of capacities that most humans possess. They are telling us that personhood is primarily shared and that it is wholly natural to focus on the dialectic between supports and threats that are integral in all our decision-making. And they are telling us that new discovery techniques are available and are evolving to enable us to divine the will and preference of the person even in circumstances where we thought they were unknowable to us.

That should be enough to force change. Why persist with laws and policies that rest on assumptions that are plainly at odds with new insights from the hard sciences? If there ever was 'evidence-based policy-making' then clearly our old policies stand in clear need of reform. How does the UNCRPD reflect and advance these insights?

11.3 The UN Convention—Advancing the New Paradigm of Universal Personhood and Moral Agency

Probably the best way to understand the Convention is in light of these underlying movements away from the 'standard account' of what it means to be human and a person—even away from Article 1 of the UDHR. If one takes the shift seriously—admittedly a big 'if'—then the task of the Convention is simple: restore full 'moral agency' to those who previously failed the test of a certain minimal level of cognitive ability and who can, with the right kind of support, plot their own way in their own lives.

11.3.1 Article 12—Restoring Personhood and Moral Agency

So how does Article 12 seek to restore 'moral agency'?[21] The text of Article 12 is as follows:

Article 12 Equal recognition before the law

1. States Parties reaffirm that persons with disabilities have the right to recognition everywhere as persons before the law.
2. States Parties shall recognize that persons with disabilities enjoy legal capacity on an equal basis with others in all aspects of life.
3. States Parties shall take appropriate measures to provide access by persons with disabilities to the support they may require in exercising their legal capacity.

[20] ibid 26–39.

[21] See generally Anna Arstein-Kerslake, *Restoring Voice to People with Cognitive Disabilities: Realizing the Right to Equal Recognition before the Law* (CUP 2017).

4. States Parties shall ensure that all measures that relate to the exercise of legal capacity provide for appropriate and effective safeguards to prevent abuse in accordance with international human rights law. Such safeguards shall ensure that measures relating to the exercise of legal capacity respect the rights, will and preferences of the person, are free of conflict of interest and undue influence, are proportional and tailored to the person's circumstances, apply for the shortest time possible and are subject to regular review by a competent, independent and impartial authority or judicial body. The safeguards shall be proportional to the degree to which such measures affect the person's rights and interests.
5. Subject to the provisions of this article, States Parties shall take all appropriate and effective measures to ensure the equal right of persons with disabilities to own or inherit property, to control their own financial affairs and to have equal access to bank loans, mortgages and other forms of financial credit, and shall ensure that persons with disabilities are not arbitrarily deprived of their property.

The first subparagraph effectively announces a theory of universal legal capacity even in the face of severe decision-making frailties. Article 12 therefore does not rest on a view that persons with disabilities are only contingently persons if they pass a certain cognitive test. It asserts that they are persons *simplicitor*. This is a rather large step forward relative to contemporary state practice.

The second subparagraph (12.2) assures persons with disabilities a right to enjoy legal capacity '*on an equal basis with others*' and in all spheres of life. The reference to '*on an equal basis with others*' could go two ways. Of course, it is open to states parties to assert (and many of them strenuously do so) that there are significant material differences (ie in levels of cognitive ability) between persons with severe intellectual disabilities and others to fully justify the withdrawal or limitation of legal capacity. Indeed, not to do so might even be framed as a failure to take adequately into account the material difference of cognitive disability. This is so because most states still see the presence of a certain minimal level of cognitive ability as the essence of personhood.

However, the third subparagraph (perhaps one of the most discussed provisions in any international human rights treaty) points to a wholly new departure point in the context of personhood and decision-making frailty. It speaks of a right of 'access' to 'supports' to enable a person 'exercise' their legal capacity. True, it does not, at least on its face, proscribe guardianship. However, its overall thrust is unmistakable—at the first sign of decision-making frailty states should not resort to guardianship. Instead, the states parties should endeavour to promote access to a web of supports to enable a person to exercise their inherent legal capacity. The obligation does not fall directly on the state. In other words, such supports most often occur naturally in social settings (a sort of untapped and natural deposit of social capital) and it is the task of the state to open up access to these naturally occurring supports in the community. This is a tall order where no such community exists for the individual in question. A more muscular state obligation going beyond facilitating access may arise when the individual lacks any other person or acquaintance in their lives and the experience of extreme isolation (eg as a result of institutionalization) requires the direct provision of support by the state.

If Article 12.3 points in a new direction, Article 12.4 reintroduces an equivocal note. It specifies a slew of safeguards that are usually associated with guardianship (that the interventions be time-limited, that conflicts of interest should be regulated, etc.). There is therefore a tension between subparagraphs 3 and 4. That is to say, the various safeguards envisaged in subparagraph 4 do seem to contemplate the continuance of some form of substitute decision-making (guardianship) thus presenting an interesting interpretive conundrum for the treaty monitoring body.

In effect, the Committee has taken the view that the safeguards—whilst hinting at guardianship—should in fact be engrafted onto a new support paradigm. This interpretive turn on the part of the Committee makes sense mainly because of how the 'standard account' of personhood has in fact shifted over time. However, if you are inclined to the anachronistic view that cognitive ability is still the essence of what it means to be a person then the interpretive turn taken by the Committee probably makes little sense. But if you have already grasped how the ground has shifted—especially in the hard sciences—then it makes perfect sense.

Subparagraph 4 famously interjects the language of 'will and preferences' of the person. This is a curious formula that also seems to point in two different directions. The mention of 'preferences' seems to assume a traditional approach whereby it is assumed (until proved to the contrary) that the person can rationally process his or her options and rationally pronounce a preference. In other words, they possess sufficient cognitive ability to do the same. However, the mention of 'will' seems to point in exactly the opposite direction—toward naked preferences formed more by instinct and impulse than by rationality. This tension aside, most people rightly use the term 'will and preferences' as a term of art that refers essentially to the choice of the person (howsoever formed) as distinct from choices imposed upon the person by a third party.

Subparagraph 5 deals with the right to legal capacity on the context of decision-making over property and financial affairs. Strictly speaking, this was not necessary since the reference to 'all aspects of life' in subparagraph 2 should have been sufficient to cover it. What probably moved the drafters to include a specific provision on it was the widespread prevalence of financial abuses.

What Article 12 is really insisting on is that persons with intellectual disabilities are to be treated as 'moral agents' in their own right—with the right to construct their own legal universe (no matter how minimal) in a web of voluntarily chosen reciprocal arrangements. This is, to be sure, complicated and perhaps at times distorted. But what a remarkable turnaround Article 12 represents—from an assumption of 'civil death' to a search for ways to make 'civil life' a reality.

11.3.2 General Comment 1—An Assertion of Universal Legal Capacity Regardless of Disability

As if to underscore Article 12 as the fulcrum of the whole Convention, the UNCRPD Committee chose to issue its very first General Comment on it in 2014. Though not, in a strict legal sense, legally binding, the General Comment put forward a treaty monitoring body's understanding of a provision and the correlative obligations incumbent on states parties. The General Comment opens by asserting that there has been a:

> general failure to understand that the human-rights based model of disability implies a shift from the substitute decision-making paradigm to one that is based on supported decision-making. (para 3)

This can't be strictly true since early attempts to regulate guardianship in the 1990s also emanated from a human rights perspective.[22] What it is essentially saying is that the old human rights-based agenda of regularizing guardianship of the 1990s has been superseded by a newer human rights-based approach to replace guardianship altogether.

The General Comment continues by asserting that the right to equal recognition before the law:

> implies that legal capacity is a universal attribute inherent in all persons by virtue of their humanity and must be upheld for persons with disabilities on an equal basis with others. (para 8)

So, the General Comment posits a theory of 'universal' legal capacity regardless of cognitive ability. The reasoning is somewhat conclusory since being a human does not necessarily mean that one was a person in law in the past. And as already noted, some entities are persons in law despite not being human (eg corporations).

What follows from this is the separation out of tests of 'mental capacity'—which varies—from the question of 'legal capacity'—which it assumes is universal (para 13). In other words, the presence of even a severe cognitive incapacity does not equate to (and can indeed never equate to) a legal incapacity.

If guardianship is not the appropriate response to mental incapacity, then the General Comment asserts that 'will and preferences' should replace the old theory of 'best interests' (para 21). In other words, the process of exploring (excavating) the 'self' and identifying his or her own choices is primary. The endeavour of controlling the actions of substitute decision-makers through the application of controlling notions like 'best interests' is not only secondary—it doesn't exist at all under the new paradigm.

Interestingly, the General Comment asserts that the obligation to provide 'access' to supports partakes of the nature of a civil and political right and therefore must be implemented immediately (para 30). This is certainly debatable since 'access' is not in itself a robust state obligation and it has the look and feel of an obligation that is to be 'progressively realized'.

To be sure, all the aforementioned jurisprudence of the UN Committee seems starkly ahead of state practice. If you bring the assumptions of the 'standard account' of personhood based on cognitive ability to it, then it probably doesn't make much sense. However, if you have already begun to move away from the 'standard account' then it begins to make sense. So, in a way it bubbles to the surface a very profound debate that actually goes far beyond disability: Who or what are we as persons and are there essentialist criteria against which we measure them?

11.3.3 A New Departure—Our Personhood is Shared and Support is Natural

The concept of 'support' in Article 12.3 is key to any new paradigm of 'civil life' as against 'civil death'. Can it work—are we asking too much of it? It must be first noted that Article 12.3

[22] The first wave stems from some early judgments of the ECtHR to regularize guardianship and is best exemplified in Committee of Ministers of the Council of Europe, 'Recommendation No R 99(4) on Principles Concerning the Legal Protection of Incapable Adults' (1999) (adopted on 23 February 1999) <www.coe.int/t/dg3/healthbioethic/texts_and_documents/Rec(99)4E.pdf> accessed 10 August 2020.

refers to 'support' to enable a person '*exercise their legal capacity*'. This goes far beyond support for just decision-making. Indeed, decision-making can be seen as something at the very end of a spectrum that begins first of all with the very stuff of personhood.

Implicitly at least, the support concept assumes that our personhood is primarily shared—that the essence of our personhood emerges from and through an ongoing and iterative process with 'others'. Our sense of self—our sense of our 'selves' in the world, our sense of our relationship to the world, our very identity—is a function of these iterative interactions and attachments. This depends on a minimum level of social interaction, and on the existence of and our immersion in dense social networks that occur naturally for most people.[23]

The point is that many people with intellectual disabilities lack this social space or capital. Because their personhood is assumed to be unknown or unknowable, they are separated from normal social intercourse into institutions and segregated schools and workplaces. Many (most) live at home—which is not really their own 'home' but that of their ageing parents. And mostly it is the small decisions that matter in building both confidence and competence. Just having the chance to make a decision and to experience regret would be a huge step forward.

Although persons with intellectual disabilities are generally well 'known' to close family members who can divine their intentions, the soft techniques of discovery that emerge naturally and over time in closed circles of love are seldom replicated beyond and especially in services that disproportionately affect their lives. The resulting isolation, segregation, and institutionalization has the wholly predictable effect of further degrading their latent capacities—making their 'civil death' appear almost like a self-fulfilling prophesy.

It is no surprise therefore that 'supports' to enable individuals to exercise their legal capacity primarily means putting in place social networks to spark the individual's personhood, which, though flickering and faint, still exists. This is a form of support to enable a person to exercise legal capacity no less than a support to enable a person to make a decision. Indeed, the reference in subparagraph 3 to 'access' itself infers that these supports occur naturally and primarily in dense social networks—so much so that we are hardly conscious of them in our own lives.

It follows that the main role of government is to open up that zone of rich social interaction to persons with intellectual disabilities. Success in embedding these kinds of supports will (it is hoped) enable the person to emerge and manifest his or her 'self' to others. This does not necessarily mean that the person manifests as strongly or as coherently as 'others' do in our lives. And it certainly does not mean that we 'find' the person primarily through their rational expression or in formal communication. But it does mean that there is a spark of their humanity hidden somewhere that stands a better chance of emerging when the social context we take for granted for everyone is layered back in.

If our personhood is shared, if 'we' are to be found echoed and echoing in our close relationships and are 'held' by those close to us, and if those close to us have privileged access to who we are as persons (not necessarily through rational dialogue) then it is only natural to try to find us or gain access to us (reveal our sense of self, our identity, and our broad preferences in the world) in those others. It is in these intimate circles of love and support that the person—otherwise unknown to the broader world—can emerge and count as a person.

[23] On the role of social capital in augmenting legal capacity see Gerard Quinn, Jo Watson, and A Gur, 'Ageism, Moral Agency and Autonomy: Getting Beyond Guardianship in the 21st Century' in Israel Doron and Nena Georgantzi (eds), *Ageing, Ageism and the Law: European Perspectives on the Rights of Older Persons* (Edward Elgar Publishing 2018) 50–71.

11.4 Darkness at the Edge of the New Paradigm—Boundary Issues and a New Set of Problems

So much for ideas and philosophy! How can we take things forward? Where are the new lines drawn and how can they be mediated especially in law?

Thomas Kuhn's theory of paradigm shift does not suggest that there is an end point.[24] He uses the idea of a paradigm as a heuristic—something that shines a light on an old set of problems—but that will inevitably pose problems of its own. No matter how much one might applaud the new paradigm of Article 12, it does bring with it a new set of problems and boundary issues and it is important to be honest about them.

There are at least four distinct sets of risks with respect to supported decision-making. Some will need to be dealt with in legislation. Others will have to be dealt with as part of a new regulatory environment or codes of practice that have yet to evolve.

The unknown or unknowable self: First of all, take the case of a person who is, as yet, unknown and, to all intents and purposes, unknowable to the world. Support, here, means much more than supported decision-making. It entails, through broad-ranging social inclusion strategies, a process of building up the 'moral agency' of the person—revealing the 'self' first to itself and then to the outside world.

This is a highly sensitive endeavour but also a highly necessary one, especially for those who are coming out of institutions.

One danger is that we (those involved in providing the support) will manufacture the 'self' or contrive it into a false existence. Maybe a variant on this, stems from the fact that it is the state or emanations of the state that will likely perform this task in circumstances where there is no one in the life of the person. A more subtle danger here is not so much that the 'self' will be manufactured along implicit social or ideological lines but that it will instead be moulded to fit the level of currently available social resources. Instead of becoming the total of what you consume you might become just the sum of what 'we' can afford.

How do we counter these risks? First, every arrangement, every regime will be open to the charge that the person is being sculpted and not revealed. There is a sense in which this is inevitable. There will nearly always be a nudge element whichever way we look at social services.[25] The first variant of the risk might be mitigated by trying to embed the person in social contexts that offer alternatives in the hope that the self that emerges will be true to itself or truer to itself than might otherwise be the case.

It is the second variant of the risk that is seemingly intractable—sculpting the person according to what 'we' can afford. It is probably part of the human condition that those deeply embedded in a social system who provide a support like this will to some extent reflect the exigencies of that system. Some intentional strategy will be needed to counteract it. Some dreams are nevertheless part of who we are even though they will never be realized. I dream of a Lamborghini but own a Citroen. Even though the dream is unrealistic it is part of who I am.

The CRPD Committee seems to believe that in such extreme cases where the person is unknown or currently unknowable that 'the 'best interpretation' of the person's will and preference will do.[26] I remain to be fully convinced. 'Best' according to what meta-theory

[24] Thomas S Kuhn, *The Structure of Scientific Revolutions* (2nd edn, enl University of Chicago Press 1970).

[25] On nudge theory see Richard H Thaler and Cass R Sunstein, *Nudge: Improving Decisions about Health, Wealth and Happiness* (Penguin Books 2009).

[26] UN Doc CRPD/C/GC/6 (n 6) para 21.

of the person? Best relative to what has been disclosed in the past of the person's personal biography? But aren't we all free to diverge from our own biographies? New techniques of discovery are being validated almost weekly.[27] Yet it is probably best to be frank about the problem and then focus intentionally on avoiding any semblance of a sculpted sense of self.

Interpretive leeway: The second risk has to do with the means of interpretation used to reveal the 'self' and his or her preferences. Carl Llewellyn, the great legal realist, used to say that the problem of canons of interpretation is that they run in pairs of opposites.[28] To put it bluntly, if you use one interpretive tool you get one result and if you use another you get another. That's what 'result oriented jurisprudence' is all about. This places a premium on having the right interpretive tools and using them correctly.

This problem will probably only occur in a minority of cases where resort to informal methods of communication is necessary. I think it is fair to say that this is not only an evolving but also a maturing field. I can do no better than to point to the sterling work of Dr Jo Watson at Deakin University in this regard.[29] But the point is that any new regulatory apparatus that emerges to operationalize the new paradigm should take this in hand and develop broad guidelines and protocols on tools of interpretation.

Supports (and supporters) that undermine and not underpin the self: The third risk is how do we guard against the supporters undermining rather than underpinning the person? This can take two forms. In the first instance a supporter might unself-consciously nudge the person in a certain direction—towards a certain set of preferences. This risk is ever-present—after all, we have all nudged our children in certain directions and (perhaps even our spouses—or they us)! The only answer has to do with self-awareness training and especially self-awareness about unconscious biases (we all have them).[30] This is no sure-fire guarantee against unconscious bias, but it can hopefully be corrected enough to give the 'moral agency' of the person a chance of being effectuated.

The second form is more straightforward and has to do with conscious or intentional manipulation perhaps with the material interests of the supporter being uppermost in mind. One would hope that the kind of person attracted to becoming a supporter would narrow the field down to those with a genuine interest. Yet human ingenuity constantly surprises. The only answer to this is vigorous monitoring by an outside agency. Will it catch every instance of violation? Probably not. It is hard to legislate for human nature. But can we probably keep it to the absolute minimum? Probably yes. And certainly, the overall gains are worth it. This sounds like a utilitarian calculus. Yet I do think that the near inevitability of some intentional wrongdoing is not a reason for not moving forward. If we can get our regulatory apparatus right, then the benefits of legislating far outweigh the risks of the outlier supported.

Conflicts between the supporters: A fourth risk has to do with conflicts between supporters—assuming there are more than one. At a certain level this is entirely natural and not unexpected. What we are not talking about here are conflicts with regards to the person's best interests or a choice that is best for the person. That is gone if the prime directive of support is to give effect to the 'moral agency' of the person. What we are talking about here are

[27] The substantial work of Dr Jo Watson at Deakin University (Melbourne) stands out in this regard.

[28] John M Breen, 'Statutory Interpretation and the Lessons of Llewellyn' (2000) 33(2) Loyola of Los Angeles Law Review 263.

[29] Jo Watson, 'The Role of Speech-Language Pathology in Supporting Legal Capacity' (2019) 21(1) Journal of Clinical Practice in Speech Language Pathology 25, 1.

[30] For example, Mahzarin R Banaji and Anthony G Greenwald, *Blindspot: Hidden Biases of Good People* (Bantham Book 2016).

differences in understanding the person—or interpreting their will. Perhaps this will happen most when the bigger decisions are at stake.

My first reaction to this is that it should be welcomed. What we don't want is a formalistic or purely logical unpacking of the person. It is an art as well as a science. And we don't want groupthink among the supporters. We have to understand this potential tension between the supporters as natural—something that works itself pure over time. In most cases this will be enough. In a minority of cases, and probably because of a breakdown in trust, it will not. What then are the options?

All things being equal, the person should be able to remove one or more supporters. Regular reviews of the support arrangements should provide an occasion to do this—assuming it is possible. The supporters might themselves apply to have the arrangement reviewed. Or perhaps a third party with a *bone fide* interest might apply (not just family). I don't think that the possibility of dissension among the supporters is a cause for moral panic. There should be ways contrived to break out of impasses and the task of doing so should not derail the move toward legislation.

11.5 Conclusions

What then are my conclusions?

First, we are all at the very beginning—not the middle or the end—of a larger discussion about what it means to be person and the role of cognitive ability—if any—in defining what it means to be human. The debate implicates disability—but actually sweeps much broader. It is likely to become a core focus in bioethics as we try to come to terms with new entities that merge AI with human biology in the future—creating so called transhumans.[31]

Second, our focus in the past was on mitigating the effects of 'civil death'. But our focus now is on enabling 'civil life' to those who previously suffered 'civil death'.

Third, the animating philosophy of Article 12 isn't about Tea Party libertarianism—it has to do with social inclusion and tending to the 'scaffolding of the self'. Apparently, Mohammad Ali wrote a poem with only two words: 'Me. We.' This sums it all up. The support we talk about isn't just about decision-making—it is also about the very stuff of the self. To some extent the decision comes at the end of a chain—a chain that implies self-identity, a personal story, and a sense of place and belonging in the world—exactly the things that were denied in the past to many persons with disabilities.

Finally, the human liberation agenda of the Convention sustained many of its drafters during the labyrinthine process of negotiations. Some of them had the benefit of Philip Alston's teaching and research. Echoes of his heart can be found throughout.

[31] A good introduction to the field is Michael Bess, *Make Way for the Superhumans: How the Science of Bio-Enhancement is Transforming Our World, and How We Need to Deal with It* (ICON 2016).

12

On Principle and Persuasion: Examining Philip Alston's Contribution to Economic and Social Rights through the Lens of Health

Alicia Ely Yamin

12.1 Introduction

There is arguably no single scholar-practitioner who has done more to build the field of economic and social rights (ESR) than Philip Alston. At a time when human rights, and ESR in particular, are increasingly under critique by progressives for being a 'powerless companion' on the steady march of Croessus;[1] irrelevant to social justice as too associated with liberal elitism;[2] or even complicit in the deepening degradation of neoliberalism;[3] Alston has been among the few leading figures from within the field of human rights, and ESR in particular, who has steadfastly insisted on critical introspection and constant reinvigoration of both our theorization and advocacy. In typically blunt remarks in a speech at the London School of Economics, shortly after Donald Trump's election in 2016, Alston noted, 'dejection and despair are pointless and self-defeating. It's assuredly not a lost cause, but we should not be fooled into thinking that it's ever going to be a wining cause; it's an ongoing struggle.'[4]

Although relatively little of Alston's scholarly or other work has been directly related to health, his enormous contribution to the clarification and development of ESR norms, as well as the linkages to development paradigms and practice have greatly contributed to the field. Moreover, patterns of health are a keen reflection of social (in)justice within and between countries; health has been at the centre of recent development paradigms; and health access and outcomes are profoundly subject to influence by non-state actors in the global economic order, both directly and indirectly. Thus, the area of health rights provides a particularly relevant lens through which to examine some of Alston's contributions to the larger field of ESR. This chapter takes up the framework Alston proposed as UN Special Rapporteur on Extreme Poverty and Human Rights for advancing ESR: '(a) the need to accord legal recognition to the rights; (b) the need for appropriate institutional arrangements to promote and facilitate realization of the rights; and (c) the need for measures that promote governmental accountability'.[5] I explore each component of his 'Recognition, Institutionalization,

[1] Samuel Moyn, 'A Powerless Companion: Human Rights in the Age of Neoliberalism' (2014) 77 Law and Contemporary Problems 147; Samuel Moyn, *Not Enough: Human Rights in an Unequal World* (Belknap Press of Harvard University Press 2019).

[2] Stephen Hopgood, *The Endtimes of Human Rights* (Cornell University Press 2013).

[3] Naomi Klein, *The Shock Doctrine: The Rise of Disaster Capitalism* (Knopf Canada 2007).

[4] Philip Alston, 'The Populist Challenge to Human Rights' (2017) 9 Journal of Human Rights Practice 1, 4.

[5] UNHRC, 'Report of the Special Rapporteur on Extreme Poverty and Human Rights' (28 April 2016) UN Doc A/HRC/32/31 para 21.

Alicia Ely Yamin, *On Principle and Persuasion: Examining Philip Alston's Contribution to Economic and Social Rights through the Lens of Health* In: *The Struggle for Human Rights.* Edited by: Nehal Bhuta, Florian Hoffmann, Sarah Knuckey, Frédéric Mégret, and Margaret Satterthwaite, Oxford University Press. © Alicia Ely Yamin 2021. DOI: 10.1093/oso/9780198868064.003.0013

and Accountability' (RIA) framework, in the context of evolving struggles for the health-related rights over the last three decades.

In the chapter I examine both the significance of Alston's approach to building ESR in the context of the right to health and human rights-based approaches to health (HRBAs). In section 12.2 I consider the imperative of recognizing health, and other ESR, as real legal rights, focusing on the significance of the UN CESCR General Comment 3, as well as debates about the 'sufficientarianism' of ESR.[6] I contrast the approach in General Comment 3 with respect to a minimum essential level of ESR with that of the CESCR in General Comment 14, arguing that the latter undermines critical understandings of the usefulness of the minimum core concept, and misconceives the appropriate role of treaty monitoring bodies (TMBs) in oversight. In section 12.3 I examine Alston's argument for the need to meaningfully institutionalize ESR, through national institutional arrangements. Here, I focus on understanding health systems as social institutions, which require democratization of decision-making, including bottom-up diagnosis of problems and proposals for solutions. I go on to contrast Alston's nuanced call for synergies between human rights and development—without denying challenges—with tendencies toward instrumentalizing and 'operationalizing' human rights in health through global health governance. Finally, in section 12.4 I explore Alston's call for accountability, and the challenging role of courts vis-à-vis other democratic institutions, with respect to a right for which the entitlements and obligations are far from obvious. I conclude by arguing that Alston's twin commitments to building a coherent architecture of international human rights law, and to critical praxis in the field, have been key to the enormous contributions he has made, and continues to make, to the ongoing struggle to deploy human rights for social justice.

12.2 Recognition

In his 2016 report to the UN HRC as Special Rapporteur on Extreme Poverty and Human Rights, Alston noted that the legal recognition of ESR, such as health, 'matters a great deal', for philosophical, doctrinal, and political reasons, among others. First, 'the two sets of rights are indispensable elements in enabling individuals to live dignified and fulfilling lives'.[7] Second, 'The equal status of the rights recognized in the Universal Declaration of Human Rights' was 'the glue that has held the package together and the understanding that enables the reconciliation of otherwise starkly competing visions'.[8] Alston further notes that the failure to pay sufficient heed to ESR, and economic inequality, undermines both democracy and the credibility of international human rights law in general.[9]

Despite the title of an NYU Law School working paper containing his report—'Re-thinking ESR'—this is hardly a recent insight for Alston himself. In 1987, together with Gerard Quinn, Alston published their 'Working Paper on The Nature and Scope of States' Obligations under the International Covenant on Economic, Social and Cultural Rights' in the *Human Rights Quarterly*.[10] That paper emphasized the importance of legal recognition,

[6] Axel Gosseries and Lukas H Meyer (eds), *Intergenerational Justice* (OUP 2009).
[7] UN Doc A/HRC/32/31 (n 5) para 12.
[8] ibid para 12.
[9] ibid para 16.
[10] Philip Alston and Gerard Quinn, 'The Nature and Scope of States Parties' Obligations under the International Covenant on Economic, Social and Cultural Rights' (1987) 9 Human Rights Quarterly 156.

as part of a good faith interpretation of the treaty consistent with international law. They concluded:

> The challenge of giving substance to those obligations in practice is one that, after too many years of neglect, must now urgently be taken up by the peoples of the world who are the Covenant's chief beneficiaries, by the nongovernmental groups who profess a concern for *all* human rights, by all governments that have recognized the validity of the concept of economic, social, and cultural rights, and by the newly created United Nations Committee on Economic, Social, and Cultural Rights.[11]

A few years later—just as the global political order was definitively shifting, in 1990—that newly created UN CESCR adopted General Comment 3: 'The Nature of State Parties Obligations', which built on the previous working paper of Quinn and Alston, who was the Rapporteur for the General Comment. It also built on Alston's previous reflections on the CESCR's reporting procedure and the imperative that governments be asked to 'identify benchmarks or standards which they consider to be the essential minimum requirement in their country for the realization of each of the rights recognized in the Covenant'.[12] This approach, Alston and his co-author argued at the time:

> would enable the Committee to focus much more decisively on the single issue that is its proper *primary* concern: i.e., the extent to which the most disadvantaged individuals in any given society are enjoying a basic minimum level of subsistence rights. In addition, it would place the principal burden of establishing appropriate national standards, against which compliance with the obligations in the Covenant could be measured, on the government.[13]

Given Alston's involvement in drafting it, it is unsurprising that General Comment 3 asserts the notion of an essential or existential minimum, which had been linked (and since the proliferation of social constitutions has been far more so) to the purposes of the modern welfare state or 'democratic state of law', as opposed to the traditional liberal state where freedom was believed to require only restraint from government interference.[14] CESCR asserted that without such an essential minimum the treaty 'would be largely deprived of its *raison d'être*'—which is protecting human dignity.[15] Thus, CESCR found: 'a State party in which any significant number of individuals is deprived of essential foodstuffs, of essential primary health care, of basic shelter and housing, or of the most basic forms of education is, *prima facie*, failing to discharge its obligations under the Covenant'.[16] In sum: (1) protecting human beings from the degradation of extreme poverty is not merely a programmatic aspiration, but a *legal obligation* of parties to the ICESCR; (2) mere declarations of lack of resources

[11] ibid 222.

[12] Philip Alston and Bruno Simma, 'First Session of the UN Committee on Economic, Social and Cultural Rights' (1987) 81 American Journal of International Law 747, 750.

[13] ibid.

[14] For an example from Mexico's Supreme Court, which sets out this reasoning carefully, see Amparo en revisión 1780/2006. Lempira Omar Sánchez Vizuet. 31 de enero de 2007. Cinco votos. Ponente: José Ramón Cossîo Dîaz. 172545. 1a. XCVII/2007. Primera Sala. Novena Época. Semanario Judicial de la Federación y su Gaceta. Tomo XXV, Mayo de 2007, 793.

[15] CESCR, 'General Comment No 3: The Nature of States Parties' Obligations (Art. 2, Para. 1, of the Covenant)' (14 December 1990) UN Doc E/1991/23 para 10.

[16] ibid para 10.

are insufficient to escape the obligations—states parties bear the burden of proof that they have made every effort consistent with maximum available resources; and (3) the CESCR's oversight mandate entails requiring justification from states through the state reporting process, while allowing that there may be reasons or trade-offs that a TMB is not as well-placed as those from a specific context to determine. Further, in light of current arguments about whether ESR only require subsistence, it is critical to underscore that this minimum level—including 'essential primary health care'—was never intended to substitute for, or to be read in isolation from, obligations relating to the progressive realization of the right to health and other ESR.[17]

By contrast, ten years later, CESCR issued General Comment 14 on the 'Right to the Highest Attainable Standard of Health', the third in a series of general comments focused on specific rights in the Covenant, which takes a very different approach. General Comment 14 sets out an extensive list of 'basic obligations' (para 43(a-f)),[18] and a second set of obligations 'of comparable priority', (para 44(a-e)).[19] This enumeration of theoretically minimum obligations undermines substantially the premises in General Comment 3, as these lists are neither supported by any coherent rationale nor close to being met in practice, even by wealthy states. Thus, it does not put the focus sharply on states' priorities and muddies the threshold legal obligation.[20] Further, these obligations are theoretically *non-derogable* as opposed to the presumption established in General Comment 3, which acknowledged the importance of the process for states to justify their actions. The non-derogable nature of these many core obligations was quickly remedied in CESCR's General Comment 15 but given that, as some have noted, General Comment 14 has taken on virtually Biblical stature among the communities working on health rights, it continues to have unfortunate effects on health rights scholarship and advocacy. In my view, it would have been far preferable to place a heavy burden of proof on the governments, and to develop further the criteria and processes through which shortfalls could be justified. The Siracusa Principles,[21] already reflected elsewhere in international law, provide elements of such guidance as does drawing on the language on 'limitations' in Article 4 'only insofar as this may be compatible with the nature of these rights and solely for the purpose of promoting the general welfare in a democratic society'[22]—which arguably entails a democratic decision-making process for 'law', as opposed to decrees issued for countless health reforms and austerity policies in relation to health that affect both progressive realization and the minimum core.

Some scholars have attempted to update or substitute their proposals for 'essential primary health care'. For example, John Tobin has advocated as a starting point a 'selective primary health care model' suggested by UNICEF.[23] John Tasioulas suggests a slightly different starting point, which includes some basic public health preconditions. Although the specifics differ, an emphasis on *primary health care* (PHC) has been repeatedly reiterated in global health forums and was abundantly justified as an empirical matter during the

[17] ibid para 9.

[18] CESCR, 'General Comment No. 14: The Right to the Highest Attainable Standard of Health (Article 12 of the International Covenant on Economic, Social and Cultural Rights)' (11 August 2000) UN E/C.12/2000/4 para 43(a–f).

[19] ibid para 44 (a–e).

[20] John Tobin, *The Right to Health in International Law* (OUP 2012) 240.

[21] UNCHR, 'The Siracusa Principles on the Limitation and Derogation Provisions in the International Covenant on Civil and Political Rights' (28 September 1985) UN Doc E/CN.4/1985/4.

[22] International Covenant on Economic, Social and Cultural Rights (adopted 16 December 1966, entered into force 3 January 1976) 993 UNTS 3 (ICESCR) art 4.

[23] Tobin (n 20) 250–51.

COVID-19 pandemic.[24] Adding 'emergency care, which should not be conflated with all life-saving care, is now widely recognized as one of the core functions of a health system as recognized in much domestic law, and is particularly essential from a gender perspective as obstetric emergencies are largely unpredictable and unpreventable. As a normative matter, maintaining a focus on PHC and emergency care, which invariably entails a system for referrals and prioritization, would allow governments to enter into dialogue on their compliance with the CESCR, recognizing that there are various ways of making fair choices on the path to progressive realization of the right to health, within and beyond health systems, but some trade-offs are simply unjust and run counter to fundamental human rights as well as ethical principles.[25] It should be noted that CESCR's General Comment 22 on the 'Right to Sexual and Reproductive Health', which takes General Comment 14 as its starting point, reduces the number of core obligations and goes considerable distance in correcting other flaws, in a topic area that is particularly resistant to democratic debates in many societies.[26]

In her informative review of the distinct approaches to 'minimum core'—which discusses both a minimum threshold for all ESR and the nature of a minimum set of obligations for specific rights—Katherine Young notes the significance of that 'Essence Approach'—as she calls the one adopted in General Comment 3. Young argues that the 'Essence Approach':

> is helpful in ensuring that advocates are able to articulate the minimum core of rights through vocabularies that draw attention to the important ethical justifications for economic and social rights (as for all human rights). This approach is consistent with the insight that rights belong to a category of legal entitlement that is, for special reasons, immune to the vagaries of short-term politics or cost-benefit decision-making.[27]

Young, however, goes on to characterize the debates between expansive lists of minimum core and existential minimums as involving normative disputes between proponents of human flourishing and of basic survival, with which I do not agree.[28] Rather, I see these disputes relating to the nature of minimum core obligations as also, or even principally, implicating important questions regarding normative as well as the sociological legitimacy of TMBs.

Nonetheless, it is certainly true that the paths to go *beyond* a minimum threshold level are deeply contested. Indeed, the right to health may be the most ill-suited to positivistic interpretations of specific items in a minimum core, as well as other specific priorities, due in part to its inherent instability, given technological, epidemiological, and demographic shifts as well as social structures and development levels. Further, as opposed to other rights perhaps, there is not anything like a normative consensus on what constitutes health justice; there will always be reasonable disagreements on the criteria and ranking of different factors, from population characteristics to effectiveness of interventions to severity of condition. As the Rawlsian philosopher and ethicist, Norman Daniels, has written of health specifically,

[24] The World Health Organization's Declaration of Alma-Alta was signed by 134 countries at the International Conference on Primary Health Care, Alma-Ata, USSR, 6–12 September 1978. The commitment to Alma-Alta principles was reaffirmed at the Global Conference on Primary Health Care, Astana, Kazakhstan, 25–26 October 2018.

[25] WHO, *Making Fair Choices on the Path to Universal Health Coverage: Final Report of the WHO Consultative Group on Equity and Universal Health Coverage* (WHO, 2014).

[26] CESCR, 'General Comment No 22: The Right to Sexual and Reproductive Health (Article 12 of the Covenant)' (2 May 2016) UN Doc E/C.2/GC/22.

[27] Katherine Young, 'The Minimum Core of Economic and Social Rights: A Concept in Search of Content' (2008) 33 Yale Journal of International Law 113, 138.

[28] ibid.

'[r]ights are not moral fruits that spring up from bare earth, fully ripened, without cultivation'.[29] In sum, the task of justice is precisely to justify the conditions under which health entitlements can be legitimately specified, not to specify them from on high by a TMB whose authoritative interpretation is defeasible.

Further, as Alston appeared to envision, the state reporting process need not *and should not* be a formality, obfuscated by meaningless information provided to independent 'experts' with varying degrees of familiarity with the topic and free time to read through the reams of material they receive. It can—and should—be a way for states to clarify their own minimum—and progressive—obligations through reasoned arguments. It also should permit the states' arguments for legislation and measures they have adopted—and the outcomes they have achieved—to be assessed by a genuinely independent body outside of the political currents within a given state, in light of the requirements of fundamental principles such as formal and substantive non-discrimination, attention to the most vulnerable/marginalized, and the like.

In short, the legal recognition of health in international and domestic law is essential for conceiving of *health* not as a development objective, a matter of charity or merely a technical issue to be determined purely in accordance with specialized expertise. Part of that legal recognition has entailed historically, and continues to entail, setting minimum thresholds without which the right would be meaningless. General Comment 3 was issued by CESCR just as the Cold War was coming to a close and new possibilities were emerging for understanding human rights. In that context, it contributed greatly to fostering the understanding, already sown in human development,[30] that the foundations of extreme poverty are predictable, and therefore subject to change through political choices, including enactment and implementation of certain ESR; and that extreme poverty is not an amorphous state that exists in a vacuum (ie to be measured by a decontextualized GDP/capita metric) but rather is fundamentally relational and is (re)produced through unjust power relations along class, race, gender, and other axes of identity. General Comment 3 did *not* produce the understanding of ESR as rights to 'subsistence'. The implacable incursions of neoliberal economic governance, based on principles and norms that contradicted a democratic state of law, and eliminated policy space for ESR, including health, have accomplished that. It is the approach taken in General Comment 14, not that of General Comment 3, which undermines the development of stronger argumentation in advancing the progressive realization of health rights, including in relation to global inequalities.[31]

12.3 Institutionalization

12.3.1 The Domestic Level

In health, we too often neglect the fact that rights realization requires more than norms and standards. Using legal norms that recognize health as a right requires fostering a (re)arrangement of social institutions that are fit for purpose in a democratic society, as John Rawls

[29] Norman Daniels, *Just Health: Meeting Health Needs Fairly* (CUP 2008) 15.

[30] Amartya Sen, *Poverty and Famines: An Essay on Entitlement and Deprivation* (Clarendon Press 1981); UN Development Programme, *Human Development Report 1990* (OUP 1990) <http://books.google.com/books?id=j_UuAAAAMAAJ> accessed 11 September 2020.

[31] For more detailed discussion regarding these issues, see Alicia Ely Yamin, *When Misfortune Becomes Injustice: Evolving Human Rights Struggles for Health and Social Equality* (Stanford University Press 2020).

elaborated at length. Alston means *institutionalization* in a reasonably narrow but important sense, largely as shorthand for domestication through policies and programmes and the promotion of wider understanding of ESR. In his 2016 report as Special Rapporteur on Extreme Poverty and Human Rights, he notes regarding ESR generally (but the same is applicable to health in particular): 'In terms of institutions for the promotion of economic and social rights, scholars and others have focused almost all of their attention in recent years on courts' but 'judicial enforcement is not the same, however, as institutional promotion.'[32] Alston goes on to argue that, at the domestic level, two types of actors are most relevant: government ministries, such as health in the case of the right to health; and national human rights institutions (NHRIs).

Alston is circumspect in his appraisals of the scope of HRBAs in institutionalization, just as in the scope of the remit of the CESCR in defining normative contours: 'This is not to argue, as is sometimes suggested in the literature on rights-based approaches to development, that everything these ministries do should be guided by and seen through the lens of human rights.'[33]

Alston notes with respect to NHRIs that: 'The most detailed scholarly study of those institutions yet undertaken concludes that, if they "can be faulted as a group for one thing, it is an insufficient challenge to the material conditions that perpetuate human rights violations".'[34] He concludes: 'A key factor in explaining this fundamentally unbalanced approach may be the relative absence in the work of many national human rights institutions of genuinely consultative approaches that would enable the affected communities to influence priorities and approaches and participate in developing policy responses and recommendations.'[35] It is arguable that mandates in the majority of NHRIs also need to be changed, as well as human and financial resource levels.

Nonetheless, what might such a more consultative, bottom-up practice look like, as compared to what is too often done? After the first UN Technical Guidance on A Human Rights-based Approach to Health (in the Context of Preventable Maternal Mortality and Morbidity) was adopted by an inter-governmental resolution of the HRC in 2012,[36] UN agencies considered ways of further institutionalizing it, together with the UN Technical Guidance on Under 5 Mortality.[37] Different UN agencies and consultants had created manuals on HRBAs.[38] Checklists and manuals assume that global-level bureaucrats and their consultants have the 'technical expertise' to know exactly what should be done, and how it should be done; how rights should be regulated and interpreted in far-flung contexts, and that doing so is a matter of following their specialized knowledge. Not surprisingly, such manuals produce bureaucratic and insular approaches to human rights work in health and beyond. By contrast, as lead consultant to the OHCHR, I suggested a different methodology—'Summary Reflection Guides'—which were intended to spur bottom-up processes to identify problems and suggest proposals in four constituencies: (1) health policymakers; (2) health

[32] UN Doc A/HRC/32/31 (n 5) para 36.
[33] ibid para 36.
[34] ibid para 38.
[35] ibid para 39.
[36] UNHRC, 'Technical Guidance on the Application of a Human Rights-based Approach to the Implementation of Policies and Programmes to Reduce Preventable Maternal Morbidity and Mortality' (2 July 2012) UN Doc A/HRC/21/22.
[37] UNHRC 'Technical Guidance on the Application of a Human Rights-based Approach to the Implementation of Policies and Programmes to Reduce and Eliminate Preventable Mortality and Morbidity of Children Under 5 Years of Age' (30 June 2014) UN Doc A/HRC/27/31.
[38] For example, see UNFPA and Harvard School of Public Health, 'A Human Rights-Based Approach to Programming: Practical Information and Training Materials' (UNFPA 2010).

workers; (3) NHRIs; and (4) judiciaries. This methodology was initially met with significant resistance—as insufficiently technical and prescriptive; however, with support from the OHCHR, eventually these Summary Reflection Guides were published jointly by OHCHR, PMNCH, UNFPA, WHO, and the Harvard FXB Center for Health and Human Rights, where I was the policy director at the time.

The NHRI Guide, and each Summary Reflection Guide, opens with similar language: 'It is essential that group reflection [within the NHRI itself as well as with communities] includes frank and open discussion of what problems are happening to whom and where; why they are happening; and who and what institution is responsible for taking action'.[39] After noting that contexts vary dramatically, and that technical knowledge and capacity is of course essential, it goes on to note that 'overcoming political and organizational obstacles to change also requires collective deliberation' on the part of people and actors affected by policies and those charged with responding, including NHRIs. Thus, rather than start with preformulated directives, the idea was to provide points of departure for conversations among people who actually live with the impact of laws and conditions regarding their understanding of the problems and the 'necessary changes in policy and practice that will lead to effective implementation' of human rights in health.[40] The Summary Reflection Guides were a small effort—among many—to take seriously the need to multiply the potential arenas for democratic practices of discussion, and to surface ways in which power operates within institutional contexts in health systems, as well as at the interface of communities and health systems. The Summary Reflection Guides have been used from Malawi to Mexico, India to Uganda, and have been adapted organically by different NGOs, as is entirely appropriate.

To be clear: corrupt and indifferent health ministries are regularly making decisions that ignore the human rights of the people they ostensibly serve. Nevertheless, as Alston notes in his RIA framework and has given due deference to throughout his career, 'vernacularization' of rights in relation to health inherently necessitates discussion by people who are actually affected and understand their realities to collectively think through problems and solutions in a specific context.[41] The more we promote HRBAs that call for little more than bureaucrats to check boxes, the more human rights falls victim to being a modular project removed from social structures and relations, and indifferent to the process of empowerment that is so critical in any human rights endeavour.

12.3.2 The International Level

Alston's work has shown consistent recognition of the limitations of exclusively focusing on domestic institutionalization in the context of an egregiously unequal world order. Many cite his 2005 article on the MDGs and human rights, 'Ships Passing in the Night',[42] for reflections on the missed opportunities between the human rights community and the development community during the MDGs, as well as his candid denunciations of the impunity of multilateral institutions—for example, the 'World Bank as a human rights-free zone'[43]—in more

[39] OHCHR and others, 'Summary Reflection Guide on a Human Rights-Based Approach to Health: Application to Sexual and Reproductive Health, Maternal Health and under-5 Child Health' (HRBA Portal 2016) 5.
[40] ibid.
[41] UN Doc A/HRC/32/31 (n 5) para 71.
[42] Philip Alston, 'Ships Passing in the Night: The Current State of the Human Rights and Development Debate Seen through the Lens of the Millennium Development Goals' (2005) 27 Human Rights Quarterly 755.
[43] Philip Alston, 'The World Bank as a Human Rights-Free Zone' (2017) NYU School of Law <www.ssrn.com/abstract=3079899> accessed 10 September 2020.

recent work. But just as with the struggle for legal recognition, as Alston himself wrote in 2005, 'endeavors to promote meaningful and productive linkages between the agendas of [the development and human rights] communities are hardly new'.[44] And such endeavours have certainly been critical elements of Alston's own career. In the 1970s Alston was involved in the drafting of the UN Declaration of the Right to Development and frequently addressed proposals for an NIEO.[45] In the 1980s Alston was engaged in the drafting of the Convention on the Rights of the Child, in which children's rights were seen by James Grant, the director of UNICEF at the time, as integral to the child survival revolution and human development.[46] In the late 1990s Alston was special advisor to then-UN High Commissioner for Human Rights Mary Robinson on the MDGs, which laid the groundwork for the adoption of the 'UN Common Understanding on Human Rights-based Approaches to Development Assistance' in 2003.[47]

Among other things, I take Alston's original intent as aiming to raise awareness of synergies and challenges with respect to: (1) promoting mutual reinforcement of development and human rights; and in turn (2) the need for international institutions beyond the inner circle of traditional human rights bodies to play constructive roles in the advancement of human rights, and especially ESR. For example, early in the 1990s as the UN regime began expanding tremendously, Alston pointed to the need to go beyond TMBs to 'the *authentically human-rights conscious* UN agencies, such as the International Labor Organization (ILO and the UN Educational Scientific and Cultural Organization UNESCO)'.[48] Notably, although the list is not exhaustive, Alston does not mention the WHO, which despite having the right to health in its preamble has historically been widely perceived by scholars to be 'mired in powerful states' political interests and its own ineffectiveness [which make it] largely unable to effectuate these ideals [of health for all]'.[49]

In an era where these global health institutions are increasingly mainstreaming and operationalizing HRBAs to health, some scholars have pointed to the need to carefully evaluate the meaning of 'mainstreaming' in institutions of global health governance.[50] However, others cite Alston's 'authentically human rights conscious' language from over twenty years ago and appear to argue that after having developed a normative framework, operationalization through these institutions can achieve 'human rights through global health governance'.[51] This latter approach arguably hollows out the intent of Alston's arguments, which have consistently focused on the need to identify and address the gaps between ideals and practice through pragmatic, yet principled argument.[52] Bureaucratic mainstreaming and top-down 'operationalization' through global governance forecloses rather than opens spaces for dialogue and argument.

44 Philip Alston, Mary Robinson, and New York University (eds), *Human Rights and Development: Towards Mutual Reinforcement* (OUP 2005), 1.
45 UNGA, 'Declaration on the Right to Development' (4 December 1986) UN Doc A/RES/41/128.
46 UNGA Convention on the Rights of the Child (adopted 20 November 1989, entered into force 2 September 1990) (1990) A/RES/44/25.
47 For example, see Philip Alston, 'The Rights Framework and Development Assistance' (1995) 34 Development Bulletin 9.
48 Philip Alston, 'Critical Appraisal of the UN Human Rights Regime' in Philip Alston (ed), *The United Nations and Human Rights: A Critical Appraisal* (OUP 1995) (emphasis added).
49 Jennifer Prah Ruger, *Global Health Justice and Governance* (1st edn, OUP 2018), 18.
50 Paul Hunt, 'Configuring the UN Human Rights System in the "Era of Implementation": Mainland and Archipelago' (2017) 39(3) Human Rights Quarterly 489.
51 Benjamin Mason Meier and Lawrence O Gostin (eds), *Human Rights in Global Health: Rights-Based Governance for a Globalizing World* (OUP 2018).
52 Alston, 'The Populist Challenge to Human Rights' (n 4).

Further, no human rights scholar-practitioner has more vigorously argued for reconstruction of UN and multilateral institutions when they have fallen short of their promise. Although Alston has not focused on health per se, it is worth pointing out that despite the rhetoric of 'human rights in health' or 'the right to health', global health institutions are increasingly controlled, not just by powerful states, but by philanthro-capitalist and corporate interests, and over-ridden by 'value for money' imperatives.

For example, although the Gates Foundation sets agendas for global health, including approaches taken to address the COVID-19 pandemic, there is no meaningful accountability for the actions implemented, the means deployed, and metrics selected to measure progress. Nor are the priorities set (and not set) subjected to public scrutiny in the countries in which they operate or in the institutions they fund, ranging from the GAVI, The Vaccine Alliance to the Global Fund for AIDS, TB, and Malaria, to the many different entities in the WHO orbit including the WHO itself.[53] The disastrous impact of the Gates Foundation's influence on public health agenda setting became painfully apparent in 2020 in light of the Foundation's staunch support for intellectual property rights over the sharing of technologies and know-how for a life-saving vaccine in the midst of a global pandemic.[54] More broadly, as Linsey McGoey has pointed out, philanthro-capitalists from the Gates to even the progressive founder of the Open Society Initiatives, George Soros, earned their billions through business tactics (eg currency trading) that have 'compounded financial instability, eroded labor protections and entrenched economic inequalities' across the world.[55] In short, relying on bureaucratic operationalization through these institutions under current circumstances appears not just distant from Alston's vision of authentically promoting human rights in lived realities. Arguably, it reduces human rights rhetoric to whitewashing larger trends in neoliberalism that undermine both health and other ESR across the globe, and for which the human rights movement is so deeply criticized today.

12.4 Accountability

The third prong of Alston's RIA framework is accountability. Alston does not merely focus on courts but adopts a broader approach, including: '(a) sharing information with the media; (b) using community or peer pressure; (c) collecting and publishing data; (d) complaining to an authoritative body or person; and (e) evaluating and reporting'.[56]

As Alston argues, the legislature plays a critical oversight role, which can get played out in power struggles of constitutional dimensions—as of late in the United States.[57] Nonetheless, as Alston notes, 'most of these [accountability] methods assume that, at the end of the day,

[53] Chelsea Clinton and Devi Lalita Sridhar, *Governing Global Health: Who Runs the World and Why?* (OUP 2017) 203.

[54] Rohit Malpani, Brook Baker, and Mohga Kamal-Yanni, 'Corporate Charity – Is the Gates Foundation Addressing or Reinforcing Systemic Problems Raised by COVID-19?' *Health Policy Watch*, 31 October 2020 <https://healthpolicy-watch.news/gates-foundation-address-systemic-covid-19/> accessed 4 November 2020.

[55] Linsey McGoey, *No Such Thing as a Free Gift: The Gates Foundation and the Price of Philanthropy* (Verso 2016) 9.

[56] UN Doc A/HRC/32/31 (n 5) 40.

[57] For example, Kim Wehle, 'How Alabama's Abortion Ban Could Wind up Reversing Roe' *The Hill* (16 May 2019) <https://thehill.com/opinion/judiciary/444039-would-roe-reversal-make-abortion-illegal-what-the-right-to-abortion-really> accessed 21 September 2020; Abigail Weinberg, 'House Dems Vote to Block Trump Attack on Obamacare' (*Mother Jones*, 17 May 2019) <www.motherjones.com/politics/2019/05/house-dems-vote-to-block-trump-attack-on-obamacare/> accessed 11 September 2020.

there will be a mechanism in place to which the claim can ultimately be brought for vindication in the absence of self-correction by the duty holder',[58] which has generally been interpreted to be judicial accountability, in health and ESR broadly. Here, taking Alston's report as a starting point, I detail some of the advances and limitations of relying on judicial accountability in health specifically, focusing on sexual and reproductive health and rights (SRHR); the right to health beyond one specific treatment/intervention; implementation; and remedies.

The first challenge in accountability is using the norms in creative and principled ways to expand legal interpretations that did not recognize ESR as fundamental enforceable rights. Indeed, the history of ESR and health rights litigation has been developing trenchant arguments against *obvious*, and formalistic, interpretations of rights. This has enabled advocates and judiciaries to break down fallacious distinctions between 'fundamental' civil and political rights and ESR as unenforceable 'directive principles', for example, as Alston points to in his 2016 report and has worked at throughout his career.

Similarly, SRHR and other ESR rights advocates have transformed understandings of the boundaries between the so-called 'public' and 'private' spheres in the liberal state, the interpretation of formal and substantive equality, the conditions necessary to promote equal participation of diverse members of society, and the demands of the social contract in a welfare state or democratic state of law. In health specifically, anti-formalist constructions of international and constitutional law have enabled us to perceive, for example, the way gender stereotypes operate to prevent women from enjoying SRHR,[59] gender-based violence in health facilities and private homes as cruel and inhuman treatment,[60] and the 'family' as an ever-evolving institution not dependent upon hetero-normative and patriarchal assumptions, with implications for an array of issues from benefits to access to services in health.

However, the history of litigation relating to health rights specifically reveals the significance of institutions and procedures to defining how rights function in practice, which is what Alston calls upon us to focus on. After the groundbreaking litigation in different countries enforcing access to antiretroviral treatment as a right, the right to health has proliferated to include a great number of issues and has become a deeply polarized issue in many countries in Latin America.[61] There is not reliable empirical evidence that, *but for judicial enforcement*, governments would be making more rational decisions, which would benefit others more greatly. Nonetheless, ad hoc judicial concessions of individual entitlements often entail substantial transactional costs and do not promote systemic equity across health systems

[58] UN Doc A/HRC/32/31 (n 5) 40.

[59] Rebecca J Cook and Simone Cusack, *Gender Stereotyping: Transnational Legal Perspectives* (University of Pennsylvania Press 2011) <http://VH7QX3XE2P.search.serialssolutions.com/?V=1.0&L=VH7QX3XE2P&S=JCs&C=TC0000606387&T=marc&tab=BOOKS> accessed 11 September 2020.

[60] For example, 'IV v Bolivia' (Inter-American Commission on Human Rights 2008) 40/08, Petition 270-07 http://cidh.org/annualrep/2008eng/Bolivia270.07eng.htm accessed 11 September 2020; 'María Mamerita Mestanza Chávez v Peru' (Inter-American Commission on Human Rights 2003) 71/03-Petition 270-07 <www.cidh.oas.org/annualrep/2003eng/Peru.12191.htm> accessed 11 September 2020; 'Mariana Selvas Gomez and Others v Mexico' (Inter-American Commission on Human Rights 2011) 158/11-Petition 512-08; OAS, 'Inter-American Convention on the Prevention, Punishment and Eradication of Violence against Women ("Convention of Belem do Para")' (9 June 1994).

[61] Octavio Luiz Motta Ferraz, 'Moving the Debate Forward in Right to Health Litigation' (2016) 18 Health and Human Rights Journal 265; Daniel Wei L Wang, 'From Wednesbury Unreasonableness to Accountability for Reasonableness' (2017) 76(3) The Cambridge Law Journal 642.

with chronic regulatory and compliance gaps.[62] Thus, as Alston argues, 'it might be argued that the focus on justiciability has become the tail that is wagging the analytical dog'.[63]

If health is understood as a right, in my view, health systems must be understood as democratic social institutions that embed normative values such as solidarity, autonomy, and dignity; they are not just mechanisms for delivering goods and services. As guardians of our constitutional commitments, courts have an inherent role to play in interpreting those values.[64] Thus, for example, high courts have often been able to establish principles and criteria relating to the functioning of a democratic health system, including: obligations of comprehensive and continuous care; regulation of private providers and insurers; fair processes relating to determination of benefits; and rights to information (related to care as well as social determinants of health).[65]

But Alston poses a challenge other than the competence of courts, which is that 'the implementation of positive judicial outcomes and the search for more creative remedies have been "an analytical and practical blind spot"'.[66] Here I take Alston to be raising two related, but distinct, issues: (1) low levels of implementation, which undermine inter alia the sociological legitimacy of the tribunal, as well as reducing effective enjoyment of the ESR; and (2) a lack of creative thinking with respect to structural remedies.

First, implementation is no doubt an enormous problem, driven by lack of social legitimacy as well as normative legitimacy. Yet, after much criticism there is increasing institutional attention to the implementation of decisions at regional, international, and national levels—from the Inter-American System to the 'follow-up procedure' adopted recently by the CESCR.[67] Of note here, the ECtHR has begun to utilize what Cali and Koch term as a 'deliberative compliance model' that also affects the kinds of creative remedies that the Court might adopt.[68] That is, the ECtHR does not provide specific details about what actions a state should take to comply with decisions requesting structural remedies, but rather enters into discussions with the state and maintains continuing supervision.

Second, and relatedly, creative approaches to designing structural remedies—such as the 'deliberative compliance model' of the European Court, have been adopted by national courts in the last decade that also acknowledge to greater and lesser degrees that courts and tribunals need to catalyse political action to effectively implement decisions relating to ESR, including health. Indeed, it has been through adopting 'dialogical' as opposed to formalistic 'command and control' remedies for violations of health and related social rights that various high courts—from South Africa to India, and Argentina to Colombia, have been

[62] Paola Bergallo, 'Argentina: Courts and the Right to Health: Achieving Fairness Despite 'Routinization' in Individual Coverage Cases?' in Alicia Ely Yamin and Siri Gloppen (eds), *Litigating Health Rights: Can Courts Bring More Justice to Health?* (Human Rights Program, Harvard Law School: Harvard University Press 2011) 43–75.

[63] UN Doc A/HRC/32/31 (n 5) para 40.

[64] Alicia Ely Yamin, 'Democracy, Health Systems and the Right to Health: Narratives of Charity, Markets and Citizenship' in Silja Voenecky and Gerald Neuman (eds), *Human Rights, Democracy and Legitimacy in a World of Disorder* (Cambridge University Press 2018) 185–208; Keith Syrett, *Law, Legitimacy and the Rationing of Healthcare: A Contextual and Comparative Perspective* (Cambridge University Press 2007) <www.cambridge.org/core/product/identifier/9780511495380/type/book> accessed 11 September 2020.

[65] Yamin (n 31) ch 6.

[66] UN Doc A/HRC/32/31 para 48.

[67] Víctor Abramovich, 'From Massive Violations to Structural Patterns: New Approaches And Classic Tensions in the Inter-American Human Rights System' (2009) 6(11) SUR International Journal of Human Rights <https://papers.ssrn.com/abstract=1706715> accessed 11 September 2020; Basak Cali and Anne Koch, 'Enforcing Civil and Political Rights: Lessons from European Court of Human Rights' (International Symposium, Bogota, 7 May 2010); Malcolm Langford, César A Rodríguez Garavito and Julieta Rossi, *Social Rights Judgments and the Politics of Compliance Making It Stick* (CUP 2017).

[68] Cali and Koch (n 67).

able to catalyse greater political action. These forms of 'soft' or 'weak' judicial review have enabled us to understand the variety of ways that law exercises power beyond black-letter rulings that dictate or prohibit behaviour. Rather, we see direct and indirect material effects, as well as political, institutional, and discursive effects, and the appropriation of a sense of having rights, as in the case of people living with HIV in South Africa.[69] Indeed, 2018 marks ten years since two large structural judgments regarding health-related rights were decided in Colombia and Argentina,[70] both of which established 'dialogical remedies' meant to catalyse democratic deliberation and action by multiple actors, including critically civil society.

What is clear from these judgments, together with the Indian Right to Food case and Campaign,[71] and the famous TAC-PMTCT litigation in South Africa,[72] is that strategic litigation in health and other social rights, has always faced the paradox of being most useful to achieve social and policy reform when there are blockages in the political realm; and these thwart converting progressive legal standards into effective enjoyment of health and other social rights in practice. Judicialization is most successful when it intensifies political action, connecting litigation with social demands and participation, and in turn incentivizing democratic debates and actions by the executive and legislative branches of government.

In sum, accountability in health and other ESR should not be conceptualized solely in terms of combatting impunity. The goal should be more than returning a situation to the status quo ante, or merely securing guarantees of non-repetition, as important as these are in specific cases. Accountability in health and other ESR fundamentally entails transforming systems and institutions, which, as Alston underscores, requires far more than court-centred strategies from the ESR community.

12.5 Conclusions

I have had the great good fortune of having Philip Alston as a professor in law school, as well as a mentor and colleague for the last thirty years. Further, as this volume attests, I am among a large cadre of people in the human rights field whose professional lives and thinking have been indelibly shaped by Alston and his work. The RIA framework, which in 2016 set out many of the same challenges Alston was addressing as early as the 1980s, indicates how Sisyphean the struggle for ESR has been over his career, and will always be.[73]

At the same time, at a time when critics of human rights abound, Alston is unflinching in his defence of using the law. Citing Karl Klare, he notes: 'There are no "law-free" zones in modern societies to which activists can repair so as to avoid entanglement with law and system.... Legal entitlements (including those formulated as "rights") strongly influence the distribution of wealth and power and partially construct identities. Social change movements cannot avoid engagement on this terrain'.[74] In other words, it is an illusion to believe we can

[69] Roberto Gargarella, 'Dialogic Justice in the Enforcement of Social Rights: Some Initial Arguments' in Yamin and Gloppen (n 62) 232–45; César Rodríguez-Garavito, 'Beyond the Courtroom: The Impact of Judicial Activism on Socioeconomic Rights in Latin America' (2011) 89 Texas Law Review 1669; Bergallo (n 62).

[70] Sala Segunda de Revisión julio 31, 2008, MP: Manuel José Cepeda Espinoza, Sentencia T-760/08 (Colom) (Corte Constitucional); Mendoza Beatriz Silva et al v. State of Argentina et al, File M 1569 XL (Corte Suprema de Justicia de la Nación).

[71] *People's Union for Civil Liberties v Union of India & Others (PUCL)* SCC (Civil) No 196/2001 (India).

[72] *Minister of Health v Treatment Action Campaign (TAC)* 2002 5 SA (CC) [721].

[73] UN Doc A/HRC/32/31 para 2.

[74] ibid para 3.

create social change—*including in relation to the neoliberal economy*—without law, and legal recognition of rights remains extraordinarily important, even if a perpetual struggle.

In unpacking the three elements of the RIA Framework in relation to struggles for health-related rights in this chapter, it becomes clear that although not directly working on health, Alston has made extraordinary contributions to the coherent normative construction of ESR as real legal rights; the need for and challenges to linking human rights and development; and in analysing mechanisms and meanings of accountability in ESR beyond standard formulas. Further, part of the contribution Alston has made to an otherwise overly self-congratulatory field is to have remained ever critical and clear-eyed about both external challenges and internal limitations to deploying human rights in social justice struggles.

As other contributors to this volume no doubt will note, Alston's effectiveness as both critical and constructive scholar in the field, would not have been the same without his commitment to praxis, that is, using theory to inform practice and vice versa. For example, as Special Rapporteur on Extrajudicial, Summary, or Arbitrary Executions in Guatemala, Alston saw close up the painful effects of the tired stereotypes of civil and political rights as negative 'cost-free' rights (versus ESR as programmatic aspirations). He then argued in a report to the HRC in 2007:

> The reason the executive branch of the Guatemalan state has so little money to spend on the criminal justice system is that the Congress resist the imposition of all but the most perfunctory taxes. To put this in perspective, as a percentage of GDP, Guatemala's total tax revenue in 2005 was 9.6 per cent of GDP [well below the 15 per cent recommended as a minimum even by the IMF][75]

The same lack of tax justice led Guatemala to have some of the worst health (and other ESR) indicators in the region, but by noting this in a report on extrajudicial, summary, or arbitrary executions Alston made the principle that much more persuasive.

Alston's persuasion is far from pacification of those in power. Indeed, despite—or perhaps in part because of—what he himself readily acknowledges as his own position of privilege as a white man, Alston continually goes out of his way to draw the wrath of governments to garner public attention to the issues he highlights,[76] and in turn to empower diverse social movements and marginalized communities that require an interlocutor to amplify their voices in desperately needed public conversations. In one recent interview, Alston noted about the United Kingdom that, 'What is most striking about the UK case is how deliberate it has been'. He said, 'What [the government is] trying to engineer is the simple message that you wouldn't want to be on welfare. It is going to be very unpleasant, and you will find yourself wanting to do almost anything else rather than going through it.'[77]

[75] UNHRC, 'Civil and Political Rights, Including the Questions of Disappearances and Summary Executions—Report of the Special Rapporteur on Extrajudicial, Summary or Arbitrary Executions, Philip Alston' (29 January 2007) UN Doc A/HRC/4/20.

[76] For example, OHCHR, 'Statement on Visit to the USA, by Professor Philip Alston, United Nations Special Rapporteur on Extreme Poverty and Human Rights' *UN News* (Washington, 15 December 2017) <www.ohchr.org/EN/NewsEvents/Pages/DisplayNews.aspx?NewsID=22533> accessed 11 September 2020; OHCHR, 'Statement on Visit to the United Kingdom, by Professor Philip Alston, United Nations Special Rapporteur on Extreme Poverty and Human Rights' *UN News* (London, 16 November 2018) <www.ohchr.org/en/NewsEvents/Pages/DisplayNews.aspx?NewsID=23881> accessed 11 September 2020.

[77] Robert Booth, 'UK's Brexit Obsession Will "diminish" Country, Says UN Poverty Expert' *The Guardian* (30 April 2019) <www.theguardian.com/politics/2019/apr/30/philip-alston-uks-brexit-obsession-will-diminish-country-says-un-poverty-expert> accessed 11 September 2020.

Perhaps what has struck me most over the last thirty years of observing Alston's indefatigable scholarly and practical work in the ESR field, is that he genuinely cares about the vast swathes of diverse people around the world in rich and poor countries alike whose lives are darkened by deprivation and degradation. His critical appraisals, his evident indignation, and his continually urging more to be done, comes from understanding that real human beings are suffering the consequences of corrupt and callous governments, indifferent bureaucracies, unfettered private greed, ineffectual advocacy, and flaccid scholarship. We should all be driven so implacably by the urgency of that imperative.

13
Teaching Human Rights
Four Key Capabilities

John Tobin

13.1 A Reflection

In 1998 I was undertaking a Master of Laws at the University of London. For my minor thesis I decided to embark on an analysis of the East Asian financial crisis through the prism of human rights. It was an ambitious project and I quickly found myself floundering. In need of assistance I cast my net into the relatively shallow pool of academics who were working on the intersection between the international financial institutions and human rights at the time. One of my emails was directed into the inbox of an Australian who like myself had grown up in Melbourne, now attending Melbourne Law School and who was a Professor at the European University Institute. I decided I would at least try to make a connection based on our shared background but didn't hold huge hope. Why would a law professor take the time to respond to a student from another university? To my surprise, an email came back within twenty-four hours with an offer to read my draft paper. As luck would have it, my partner and I had booked a weekend to Florence and I found myself traipsing up the hill to Fiesole with a backpack in 35-degree heat. I finally found respite in the beautiful grounds of the Villa Salviati and was directed to the office of one Professor Philip Alston. We have remained colleagues and friends ever since.

Three things struck me about our first meeting. First, how on earth did an Australian who grew up not 5 km from where I grew up find himself working and living in such an extraordinary location? For those who have not visited, the European University Institute is like nirvana for academics. My conclusion was that he must have been bloody good at what he does. Second, why is it that someone with such an acclaimed status would bother to make the time to meet with me, a mere Master's student? My second conclusion was that he must be an exceptionally generous person (a quality from which I have been the repeated beneficiary over many years). Third, why did he have pieces of paper all over the floor of his office with extracts from cases, UN documents, and articles attached with sticky tape? The answer, when I inquired, was that he was preparing an updated copy of his coursebook on human rights. And my reflection at the time, was wow, this bloke really takes his teaching seriously.

13.2 The Prompt

It is this last observation that has provided the prompt for this chapter. Teaching human rights is something many of us do. Its place in a university curriculum may have once been contentious,[1] but one would be hard pressed to find a law school that does not offer at least

[1] J Paul Martin, 'Human Rights—Education for What?' (1987) 9 Human Rights Quarterly 414 <www.jstor.org/stable/761882> accessed 25 July 2020 (examining the merits of the arguments for teaching human rights).

John Tobin, *Teaching Human Rights* In: *The Struggle for Human Rights*. Edited by: Nehal Bhuta, Florian Hoffmann, Sarah Knuckey, Frédéric Mégret, and Margaret Satterthwaite, Oxford University Press. © John Tobin 2021. DOI: 10.1093/oso/9780198868064.003.0014

one subject on human rights with specialist centres and programmes continuing to flourish alongside the appointment of dedicated human rights academics.[2] Increasingly the teaching of human rights is also extending beyond the cloisters of law schools and can be found in the syllabi of other disciplines such as health, politics, history, sociology, social work, and education. However, while there is an expanding business of teaching human rights and an expanding market of materials from which to draw when preparing our classes,[3] there is scant guidance and/or reflection on what we are teaching, how we should teach it, and why. To date the pedagogy of human rights has been largely ignored. There have been some thoughtful and provocative contributions, Peter Rosenblum's paper from 2002 on Teaching Human Rights: Ambivalent Activism, Multiple Discourses and Lingering Dilemmas[4] is a must read for anyone in this sector as is Gerry Simpson's 'On the Magic Mountain: Teaching Public International Law'.[5] But beyond these pieces the recent pickings are slim[6] and tend to focus on clinical programmes.[7]

This chapter is an attempt to ignite a conversation about this issue. It consists of two parts. First, section 13.3 offers a discussion about the role of an academic when teaching human rights. Drawing on the work of John Hattie and his model of Visible Learning,[8] it suggests that human rights teachers need not be activists, advocates, sceptics, or agnostics but should focus on being activators who engage in deliberate interventions to promote cognitive change in their students. Critical to the success of this model is the importance of clear

[2] Elizabeth Griffin, 'The Dilemmas of the Postgraduate International Human Rights Law Educator' (2015) 7 Journal of Human Rights Practice 18 <https://doi.org/10.1093/jhuman/huu017> accessed 25 July 2020, 22; Henry Steiner, 'The University's Critical Role in the Human Rights Movement' (2002) 15 Harvard Human Rights Journal 317 < https://harvardhrj.com/wp-content/uploads/sites/14/2020/06/15HHRJ317-Steiner.pdf> accessed 25 July 2020; Alperhan Babacan and Hurriyet Babacan, 'The Transformative Potential of an Internationalised Human Rights Law Curriculum' (2012) 10(4) Journal of Transformative Education 199 <http://journals.sagepub.com/doi/10.1177/1541344613478470 > accessed 25 July 2020.

[3] Christina Binder and Jane A Hofbauer, 'Teaching International Human Rights Law: A Textbook Review' (2017) 28(4) European Journal of International Law 1397 <https://academic.oup.com/ejil/article/28/4/1397/4866321> accessed 25 July 2020.

[4] Peter Rosenblum, 'Teaching Human Rights: Ambivalent Activism, Multiple Discourses, and Lingering Dilemmas' (2002) 15 Harvard Human Rights Journal 301<https://heinonline.org/HOL/P?h=hein.journals/hhrj15&i=306> accessed 25 July 2020.

[5] Gerry Simpson, 'On the Magic Mountain: Teaching Public International Law' (1999) 10 European Journal of International Law 70 <https://doi.org/10.1093/ejil/10.1.70> accessed 25 July 2020.

[6] For example, Griffin, 'The Dilemmas of the Postgraduate International Human Rights Educator' (n 2) 18;Safia Swimelar, 'Visual Culture and Pedagogy: Teaching Human Rights with Film and Images' (2009) 3(10) 21st Century Global Dynamics <www.21global.ucsb.edu/global-e/november-2009/visual-culture-and-pedagogy-teaching-human-rights-film-and%C2%A0images> accessed 25 July 2020; Gillian MacNaughton and Diane Frey, 'Teaching the Transformative Agenda of the Universal Declaration of Human Rights' (2015) 103 Radical Teacher 17 <https://doi.org/10.5195/rt.2015.232> accessed 25 July 2020; Santiago Legarre, 'The Art of Human Rights: Enriching the Life of the Law School through Drawings' 80 Prudentia Iuris 251; Caroline Bettinger-Lopez and others, 'Redefining Human Rights Lawyering through the Lens of Critical Theory: Lessons for Pedagogy and Practice' (2011) 18(3) Georgetown Journal on Poverty Law and Policy 337. This is to be contrasted with the general teaching of international law, which has been subject to significant discussion. See the bibliography compiled by Thomas Jefferson School of Law at <www.tjsl.edu/slomansonb/6th_Teach_Bib.pdf>; Florian Hoffmann, 'Teaching General Public International Law' in Jorg Kammerhofer and Jean D'Aspremont (eds), *International Legal Positivism in a Post-Modern World* (CUP 2014).

[7] For example, Ben Saul and Irene Baghoomians, 'An Experiential International Law Field School in the Sky: Learning Human Rights and Development in the Himalayas The Teaching-Research Nexus in Law: Opportunities and Challenges' (2012) 22(2) Legal Education Review 273; Jocelyn Getgen Kestenbaum, Esteban Hoyos-Ceballos, and Melissa C Del Aguila Talvadka, 'Catalysts for Change: A Proposed Framework for Human Rights Clinical Teaching and Advocacy' (2012) 18(2) Clinical Law Review 459; Hurwitz, 'Lawyering for Justice and the Inevitability of International Human Rights Clinics' (2003) 28(2) Yale Journal of International Law 505 <https://digitalcommons.law.yale.edu/yjil/vol28/iss2/12> accessed 25 July 2020; Arturo Carillo and Nicolás Yaksic, 'Re-Imagining The Human Rights Law Clinic' (2011) 26(1) Maryland Journal of International Law 80.

[8] Ivo Arnold, 'John Hattie: Visible Learning: A Synthesis of over 800 Meta-Analyses Relating to Achievement' (2011) 57(1–2) International Review of Education 219.

learning intentions and success criterion that enable teachers to evaluate the impact of their teaching on their students' learning. Section 13.4 engages with a discussion about the potential learning intentions for a human rights class and offers a model that is focussed on the development of the capabilities of students across four broad domains—technical, critical, strategic, and reflective. A student's *technical capability* refers to their doctrinal knowledge and understanding of international human rights law; their *critical capability* refers to their ability to identify and critique the underlying values and limitations of this body of law; their *strategic capability* refers to their understanding of how to use a range of techniques to advance and implement international human rights law; and their *reflective capability* refers to their ability to assess the role and place of their own personal values in their understanding and engagement with this normative framework.

13.3 An Activator not an Activist

What then is the role of the academic who teaches international human rights law? Simpson talks about the fear that we may see ourselves as apologists or imposters sitting among colleagues teaching the 'real' law subjects like property law, contracts, and constitutional law.[9] Our disciplinary gown is much like the Emperor's clothing—spectacular and bold with high-minded aspirations but nothing more than an illusion when pitted against the traditional law subjects that are championed and enforced in the highest courts of a nation. In our quest for legitimacy we may elect to adopt a focus on doctrine and legalism in our teaching to demonstrate that international human rights law is indeed real law. We may see our role as that of the dispassionate expert disseminating information about human rights to the student body in a measured and bipartisan way. We may turn to a reliance on cases and treaties to mimic the positivist case law method so common in law schools that was originally used to elevate the status and teaching of law from trade schools to the civility of universities.[10] In many respects, this possibly remains the traditional conception of an academic in a tertiary setting. It imagines a capacity for passive and objective delivery of information with no agenda beyond the transfer of information and knowledge to students.

Of course, for many of our colleagues this model is illusory at best and deceptive at worst. If international human rights law is accepted as being a deeply political and contested discourse, the very notion that it can be taught in a neutral and objective manner becomes if not intolerable then at least very tenuous. The meaning of the right to life, a discussion about the universality of rights or the legitimacy and effectiveness of the HRC cannot be reduced to an incontestable mathematical equation like Newton's law of universal gravitation. Political and moral forces are always at play in these discussions as is the reality of state sovereignty. For the philosophers among us, they may make the counter argument that it is possible to reduce human rights to a grand foundational theory of justice. But even they too would have to concede that not everyone would share their theory or theories. Thus, what we teach and how we teach international human rights law necessarily involves a complex set of decisions that are informed by values and judgments that are both overt and invisible to us.

[9] Simpson (n 5) 72–73.

[10] Albert James Harno, 'The Case Method' in Albert James Harno, *Legal Education in the United States* (Bancroft-Whitney Company 1953); A Benjamin Spencer, 'The Law School Critique in Historical Perspective' (2012) 69 Washington and Lee Law Review 1949, 1960–64, 1973–75 <http://www.ssrn.com/abstract=2017114> accessed 25 July 2020; Susannah Furnish, 'The Progression of Legal Education Models: Everything Old Is New Again' (2013) 6(1) Northeastern University Law Journal 7.

This politicized reality of teaching human rights continues to spawn debates about whether we are or should be activists in our classrooms. Griffin's survey of human rights academics tends to suggest a preference for the activist model or 'at least some ideological attachment to human rights as a project for social change'.[11] This begets a broader question as to the conception of human rights that our colleagues believe we are, or should be, advocating for in our classrooms. Griffin's research suggests that teachers of human rights are likely to have a broad and shared commitment to this discourse and thus be more likely to be an advocate for the idea of international human rights and the systems that have been developed to support its implementation. Yet she still pauses to take heed of the words of Henry Steiner, the founder of the Harvard Human Rights Program, that 'academic freedom permits many choices about the terms of professors' engagement with the movement and about their ideological orientation in teaching a class'.[12] Thus, an activist may just as easily be someone who *actively* seeks to undermine and/or destabilize this concept as someone who is its greatest champion.

Moreover, there is no reason to resist the idea that an academic can assume one persona in the classroom and be an activist or advocate *outside* the classroom—what Cesar Rodriquez-Garavito refers to as the 'amphibious' academic.[13] Indeed Philip Alston, is best perhaps the greatest illustration of this ability to traverse these different worlds such that a student of mine in a reflective piece posed the question, 'Is Philip Alston the "Real" Aquaman?' (the movie, *Aquaman* was being released at the time!). But for those who have read Philip's coursebook or sat in one of his classes, it would be difficult to label him as an activist in his capacity as a classroom teacher. His Socratic mind constantly leaps into action and pushes students and readers to contemplate a range of competing possibilities. In the textbook and classroom, at least, he does not overtly insist on a fixed position. Of course, when lobbying the United Nations to provide compensation to the Haitian people who were victims of the cholera outbreak spread by UN peacekeepers[14] or the UK government to arrest the impact of poverty on its people,[15] he is clearly a passionate and determined advocate.

These debates about whether human rights academics are or should be activists, atheists, sceptics, or agnostics are to be encouraged. This is not because we need to determine *the* right answer to this question or to align ourselves with a particular position. No, these debates are important because they should force us to reflect on our role as a teacher in a university classroom and the extent to which our teaching is *effective*. These broader inquiries take us away from our human rights bubble and the level of our commitment or otherwise to the 'cause' and demand that we think more deeply about what it means to provide *effective teaching* for our students. Such inquiries also mean that we have to leave the common terrain of human rights and venture into pedagogical waters that many of us may have never explored. So where might this journey take us?

Much has been written about the characteristics of an effective teacher and effective teaching in the tertiary sector.[16] However, John Hattie's work, *Visible Learning: A Synthesis of*

[11] Griffin (n 6) 24.

[12] ibid 25 citing Henry Steiner 'The University's Critical Role in the Human Rights Movement' (2002)15 Harvard Human Rights Journal 317, 321.

[13] César Rodríguez-Garavito, 'The Future of Human Rights' (*OpenGlobalRights*) <www.openglobalrights.org/the-future-of-human-rights/> accessed 25 July 2020.

[14] UNGA 'Report of the Special Rapporteur on Extreme Poverty and Human Rights' (2016) UN Doc A/71/367.

[15] UNHRC 'Report of the Special Rapporteur on Extreme Poverty and Human Rights Visit to the United Kingdom of Great Britain and Northern Ireland' (2019) UN Doc A/HRC/41/39/Add.1.

[16] For example Paul Ramsden, *Learning to Teach in Higher Education* (2nd edn, Routledge Falmer 2003); John B Biggs and Catherine Tang, *Teaching for Quality Learning at University: What the Student Does* (4th edn, McGraw-Hill, Society for Research into Higher Education & Open University Press 2011); Michael Prosser and

over 800 Meta-Analyses Relating to Achievement, offers the most comprehensive analysis of the evidence regarding effective teaching to date.[17] His conclusions therefore warrant consideration. For Hattie 'the act of teaching requires deliberate interventions to ensure that there is cognitive change in the student'.[18] Under this model a teacher is not merely a facilitator but an *activator* and deliberate change agent in a student's learning.[19] Note here that under this model a teacher is not an activist for a particular position with respect to human rights but an expert who plays an active role in enabling a student to construct his or her understanding and knowledge of human rights. To be sure, they must be passionate. As Hattie explains, 'we rarely talk about passion in education as if doing so makes the work of teachers seem less serious, more emotional than cognitive, somewhat biased or of lesser import'.[20] But the research indicates that teachers who are passionate about the process of learning and relish the opportunity to play an active role in their students' learning are actually more effective teachers.[21]

For Hattie, student learning must also be *visible* to both the student and teacher. For this to occur the 'key ingredients are awareness of the learning intentions [and] knowing when a student is successful in attaining those intentions'.[22] Learning intentions are what 'we want the students to learn in terms of the skills, knowledge, attitudes and values' within a particular course or unit of study.[23] An effective teacher is therefore one who has clearly defined learning intentions (and success criteria), a range of teaching strategies to realize these intentions, and a process to evaluate the impact of these strategies on student learning. What then are the consequences of this model for human rights academics in the classroom? The first is that we need to develop clear learning intentions but what should they be?

13.4 Learning Intentions for the Human Rights Classroom

As tertiary educators, human rights academics teaching human rights generally have the luxury of being unburdened by the demands of a set curriculum. This contrasts with teachers in primary and secondary schools who will invariably have to teach a curriculum determined by an external authority. Even our academic colleagues who are teaching compulsory law subjects are likely to have certain topics that must be covered as part of the established canon of knowledge in their area of expertise whether it be constitutional law or contract law. But human rights is almost always offered as an elective subject that can be shaped and fashioned to align with the interests of the teacher. As such the learning intentions of human rights subjects are likely to be multifarious. In the world of university learning where freedom of expression is cherished, it is therefore as legitimate for a teacher

Keith Trigwell, 'Student Learning and the Experience of Teaching' (2017) 4 HERSDA Review of Higher Education <https://www.herdsa.org.au/herdsa-review-higher-education-vol-4/5-27> accessed 25 July 2020; Ken Bain, 'Popular Teachers and Great Ones' (2012) 10 Revista de Docencia Universitaria 11; Susan Ambrose and others, *How Learning Works: Seven Research-Based Principles for Smart Teaching* (1st edn, Jossey-Bass 2010).

[17] John Hattie, *Visible Learning: A Synthesis of over 800 Meta-Analyses Relating to Achievement* (Routledge 2009); John Hattie, 'The Applicability of Visible Learning to Higher Education' (2015) 1 Scholarship of Teaching and Learning in Psychology 79.
[18] Hattie *Visible Learning* (n 17) 23.
[19] ibid 25.
[20] ibid 23.
[21] ibid 24.
[22] ibid 23.
[23] ibid 163.

to have the learning intention that *students recognize the 'abyss in front of anyone seeking to take human rights seriously'*[24] as it is to have the intention that *students recognize and develop the skills necessary to traverse the abyss*. Where a teacher sits on this spectrum of learning intentions ranging from futility to hope will be influenced by their own personal views about the merit and legitimacy of the human rights project (and the extent to which they are able to draw sufficient enrolments in the class!).

The traditional model of legal education involves the teacher, as the expert, delivering content knowledge in the form of rules to students who demonstrate their knowledge by applying these rules to a hypothetical set of facts in an exam or an assignment.[25] My own experience of studying human rights at both the undergraduate and graduate level certainly mirrored this 'signature pedagogy'.[26] Moreover, a review of the leading human rights textbooks still displays an overwhelming preference for a *content based approach* to teaching human rights. Few of these texts explicitly state their learning intentions. However, they are relatively easy to infer from even a cursory review of the table of contents, which tends to indicate that the dominant learning intention is invariably focussed on enabling students to develop their knowledge and understanding about several core features of the human rights project. These features typically include:

- the history of human rights;
- the nature of the international human rights system;
- the tension between the categories of human rights;
- the meaning of specific human rights;
- the human rights enjoyed by specific cohorts such as women, children, refugees, and persons with a disability; and
- the relevance of human rights in certain contexts such as business, climate change, armed conflict, and development.

Interestingly the content of most textbooks does not extend to a significant discussion of the contentious nature of international human rights. As Binder and Hofbauer observed in their review of several leading human rights textbooks, most 'tend to assume the existing human rights framework (often uncritically) as given. They validate it by pointing to its origins in natural justice and, thereby, presenting human rights as a legalized form of universally applicable morality'.[27] As Binder and Hofbauer warn, however, this approach creates the danger of students taking 'human rights for granted and disregarding the political context in which they apply'.[28] This in turn creates a further a risk that 'students will fail when trying to effect change if they are left oblivious to the legal intricacies arising in human rights practice'.[29]

Significantly the original coursebook prepared first by Philip and Henry Steiner and then with Ryan Goodman adopts a broader lens to the teaching of human rights by injecting

[24] Philip Alston, 'The Populist Challenge to Human Rights' (2017) 9 Journal of Human Rights Practice 1, 13 (referring to a response given by one of the world's leading international legal scholars to a student who was hoping to make a career defending and promoting human rights).
[25] Mary Keyes and Richard Johnstone, 'Changing Legal Education: Rhetoric, Reality, and Prospects for the Future' (2004) 26 Sydney Law Review 537.
[26] Sally Kift, '21st Century Climate for Change: Curriculum Design for Quality Learning Engagement in Law' (2008) 18 Legal Education Review 1, 15.
[27] Christina Binder and Jane Hofbaeur, 'Teaching International Human Rights: A Textbook Review' (2018) 28(4) European Journal of International Law 1397, 1399.
[28] ibid 1397, 1399.
[29] ibid 1400–01.

critical commentary into the discussion of each topic. Under this model, as Binder and Hofbauer observe, 'the variety of opinions reflected in the materials provides a good basis to give students a balanced view on the scope and content of the international human rights framework'.[30] Philip's approach to teaching therefore represents an advance on a narrow content-based approach to the teaching of human rights because it offers critical commentary on the weaknesses, deficiencies, and challenges associated with international human rights. He may not be prepared to jump ship, but he is clearly prepared to rock the human rights boat and challenge its structural integrity. That said, the learning intentions of his textbook do not extend to enabling students to acquire and develop the skills necessary to traverse the 'abyss' that, for some scholars, confronts the implementation of international human rights law. This is not to say that in his work, and no doubt in his classroom where anecdotes from the field are routinely shared, students are shown and told how to advance the protection of human rights in practice. However, the focus of his coursebook remains on content, albeit subject to critical assessment and commentary, and not the practice of human rights.

13.5 Looking Beyond Content to Capabilities

When I first taught human rights twenty years ago, there were no discussions about 'learning intentions'. It was all about 'course aims'; and my aim, which was largely influenced by Philip's textbook and which I used in my teaching, was to enable students to develop a deep and critical understanding of the international system for the protection of human rights. However, as each course commenced, I would ask my students about their expectations for the subject and a recurring theme was the hope that I could demonstrate to them how human rights could be applied in practice—not an easy task in a country like Australia. That said, as I engaged in various advocacy projects myself and followed the work of Philip and other leading human rights practitioners, I began to build up a repertoire of insights and understandings about how to translate the aspirations of the international human rights project into practice. This process also transformed my understanding of how to approach my own teaching of human rights. For too long I had presented human rights to my students as an object to observe and critique—a bit like a museum exhibit. But what if it were treated as a dynamic design project that was constantly evolving and that rather than being bystanders or observers of this project, students could actually become active participants in the ongoing construction of international human rights law? What if they could become the normative entrepreneurs that Rosenblum speaks about when they mined the texts of human rights treaties? What if rather than showing them the abyss confronting human rights, I could equip my students with the skills to build the bridge or bridges that could span that abyss?

If I were to have such ambitions, learning intentions that focussed on content and critical commentary of the human rights project would be insufficient. Thus, what I outline in this section is a model for teaching human rights that has the learning intention of stretching students' capabilities across four discrete domains—technical proficiency, critical engagement, strategic implementation, and reflective practice in relation to the international human rights project. Underling this model is an attempt to convince students to see international human rights law not simply as a static canon of law that is to be revered and conquered or

[30] ibid 1408.

condemned and criticized but as an evolving system of norms and processes in which students can become actively and critically involved should they choose to do so.

13.5.1 Capability 1: Technical Proficiency

Several years ago I invited the President of the Victorian Court of Appeal into my human rights class. He spoke to the students about the skills required to be an effective human rights lawyer. The first among those skills he listed was the need to be a technically proficient lawyer. Passion and empathy will only take you so far, he told the students. If you want to help your client, you need to know the law. So positivism, despite all its limitations, still has a central place in the teaching of human rights under a capabilities approach. But why is this the case when there is so much talk about the demise of human rights and its lack of enforceability? In the mind of the Victorian judge it was quite clear as he had announced in one of his decisions that:

> The Court will encourage practitioners to develop human rights-based arguments where relevant to a question in the proceeding; Practitioners should be alert to the availability of such arguments, and should not be hesitant to advance them where relevant; [and] Since the development of an Australian jurisprudence drawing on international human rights law is in its early stages, further progress will necessarily involve judges and practitioners working together to develop a common expertise.[31]

The students in my classes were literally being invited to become the future lawyers who would be called upon to make these submissions and I had to teach them how to do so. They were also being called upon to prepare what is known as statements of compatibility, which involve an assessment of proposed domestic legislation against international human rights standards; to prepare submissions outlining the human rights implications for inquiries on all manner of policy issues; to prepare complaints to be lodged before the various human rights treaty monitoring bodies; to prepare alternative reports for submission to these bodies as part of the reporting process; and to advise NGOs and multinational corporations on the human rights implications of their work. As lawyers, policymakers, and advocates working within government, the private sector, and civil society my students need to know (a) what processes and systems are in existence to monitor and guard the protection of international human rights at the international and domestic level and (b) the relevant law to be applied in these circumstances.

The detail and manner in which human rights academics might teach their students to become technically proficient in international human rights law is a matter on which views will naturally differ. In my view, however, it requires students to gain an understanding of:

(a) the international human rights system, its institutions, processes, and normative frameworks (including any regional systems that may be relevant to the jurisdiction in which the course is being delivered);

[31] *Royal Women's Hospital v Medical Practitioners Board of Victoria* 15 VR 22 (2006) VSCA 85 [71].

(b) the status and relevance of international human rights within the domestic law of the jurisdiction in which the course is being delivered (including any intersection with domestic systems for the protection of rights);
(c) the meaning of substantive human rights (or at least a methodology for generating a meaning for each right);
(d) the nature of the obligations imposed on states under civil and political rights and ESC rights; and
(e) how to determine when an interference with a human right is justified.

When I undertook my own review of several leading human rights textbooks[32] I discovered that explicit attention to (a) was common; (b) was relatively rare, which is unsurprising given these textbooks are targeted at audiences beyond one jurisdiction; (c) was common but not standard; (d) was common; and (e) was rarely if ever given any detailed treatment.[33]

This last observation is a concern. Most debates and complaints about human rights arise from allegations that this discourse is too idealistic and unable to resolve complex and competing rights claims. However, far too little attention and recognition, is given to the fact that international human rights law offers a methodology to resolve these claims. It is a methodology that is rooted in the principles of legality, legitimacy, and proportionality[34]—principles that are also found in various guises within domestic systems of constitutional law. Under human rights law, a state can kill someone, treat them differently, restrict their speech, and deprive them of their liberty provided it has a legal basis, which is clear and accessible; a legitimate aim (such as the rights of others, national security, or public health) *and* the measures taken to achieve that aim are necessary and proportionate.

Most debates about human rights fixate on the legitimacy of the aim—states are quite happy with this because it means that the populist causes invoked by states like 'national security' invariably win the political battle. However, a substantive rights analysis actually demands that states must justify their actions as being necessary and proportionate to achieve their aim as opposed to simply being popular. Moreover, a proportionality assessment involves two broad inquiries—was there a nexus between the measure being taken and the aim ought (the rational connection test); and if so, were there alternative measures reasonably available that would have minimized interference with the right (the minimal impairment principle)? When this test is employed it not only demands an evidence-based approach to the resolution of rights claims it also demands a level of rigour that human rights is so often accused of lacking.

Students need to be familiar with this methodology and practice its application in all manner of contexts if they are to develop the technical skills necessary for human rights practice—whether it be the legitimacy of exemptions for religious schools from

[32] The textbooks reviewed were: Philip Alston, Ryan Goodman, and Henry J Steiner, *International Human Rights: Text and Materials* (OUP 2013); Rhona KM Smith (ed), *International Human Rights Law* (8th edn, OUP 2018); Adam McBeth, Justine Nolan, and Simon Rice, *The International Law of Human Rights* (2nd edn, OUP 2017); Walter Kälin and Jörg Künzli, *The Law of International Human Rights Protection* (2nd edn, OUP 2019); Daniel Moeckli, Sangeeta Shah, and Sandesh Sivakumaran (eds), *International Human Rights Law* (2nd edn, OUP 2014); Olivier de Schutter, *International Human Rights Law: Cases, Materials, Commentary* (CUP 2010).

[33] The only text that addresses this issue in any detail is de Schutter (n 32) 288–325; Kalin and Kunzli (n 32) 99–103 and Moeckli and others (n 32) 99–102 offer a brief discussion of the limitations on human rights.

[34] See generally UN ECOSOC, 'Status of the International Covenants on Human Rights' (28 September 1984) UN Doc E/CN.4/1985/4, Annex—Siracusa Principles on the Limitation and Derogation Provisions in the International Covenant on Civil and Political Rights.

discrimination laws,[35] the legality of corporal punishment of children,[36] or the grounds on which a patent can be granted to restrict distribution of a medicine.[37] Philip's coursebook in fact gives little attention to this issue. However, his work as the Special Rapporteur on Extrajudicial and Arbitrary Executions is replete with examples of high quality technical human rights analysis. In his report on targeted killings, in which he examined the regulation of this practice under international law, he noted that under human rights law:

> A State killing is legal only if it is required to protect life (making lethal force *proportionate*) and there is no other means, such as capture or non- lethal incapacitation, of preventing that threat to life (making lethal force *necessary*). The proportionality requirement limits the permissible level of force based on the threat posed by the suspect to others. The necessity requirement imposes an obligation to minimize the level of force used, regardless of the amount that would be proportionate, through, for example, the use of warnings, restraint and capture.[38]

He then went on to detail the implications of these broad principles when they are applied to the practice of targeted killings. Indeed, a close reading of this report reveals a meticulous attention to the provision of high quality technical legal analysis that is the foundation stone upon which the skills of a human rights *lawyer* must be erected. But if enabling a student to develop their technical capability in human rights law is a necessary learning intention, it is far from sufficient.

13.5.2 Capability 2: Critical Engagement

For students to engage in deep rather than surface learning effectively they must experience cognitive dissonance[39]—their preconceptions and underlying values and assumptions must be challenged and engaged by the new ideas and thinking introduced by us as teachers. When teaching human rights law, the opportunities to create cognitive dissonance are everywhere. A simple question about the origins of human rights in the first class when underpinned by a reading of Dembour's article on the various schools of thought[40] will no doubt shake things up for many students. A subsequent class on universalism versus relativism may well lead to further destabilization of the idea of international human rights while a further class in which the work of critical scholars such as Kennedy, Hopgood, Moyn, and Posner[41] is

[35] John Tobin, 'Should Discrimination in Victoria's Religious Schools Be Protected? Using the Victorian Charter of Human Rights and Responsibilities Act to Achieve the Right Balance' (2010) 36 Monash University Law Review 16.

[36] *Freedom of Religion South Africa v Minister for Justice and Constitutional Reform, YG et al CCT320/17 [2019] ZACC 34; YG v S* (A263/2016) [2017] ZAGPJHC 290; 2018 (1) SACR 64 (GJ) [2017] (decisions of the South African High and Constitutional Courts ruling that the defence of reasonable chastisement was an unjustified interference with the rights to dignity; bodily integrity and equal treatment before the law).

[37] John Tobin, *The Right to Health in International Law* (OUP 2012).

[38] UNHRC, 'Report of the Special Rapporteur on Extrajudicial, Summary or Arbitrary Executions, Addendum Study on Targeted Killings' (28 May 2014) UN Doc A/HRC/14/24/Add.6 para 32.

[39] Ramsden (n 16) 146 (explaining that 'helping students to become aware of their current conceptions' is critical to encouraging deep approaches to learning).

[40] Marie-Bénédicte Dembour, 'What Are Human Rights? Four Schools of Thought' (2010) 32 Human Rights Quarterly 1.

[41] David Kennedy, 'The International Human Rights Regime: Still Part of the Problem?' in Robert Dickinson and others (eds), *Examining Critical Perspectives on Human Rights* (CUP 2013) 19; Stephen Hopgood, 'The Endtimes of Human Rights' in Doutje Lettinga and Lars van Troost (eds), *Debating the Endtimes of Human Rights* (Amnesty

unleashed on the students might not only leave some students at the edge of the abyss but actually push them over. And if they are still standing, subsequent classes which highlight the fact that none of the processes to monitor human rights at the international level have any coercive power and are riddled with inefficiencies, may well see them jump off the human rights boat entirely.

Developing students' capacity to critically engage with the international human rights project is a therefore tricky exercise. Too little exposure to critical commentary on issues such as the origins of rights, the legitimacy of the rights project and the effectiveness of the international human rights system can leave students without an appreciation of the complex, contested and political nature of this project. On the other hand, too much exposure to all its limitations and deficiencies can destroy whatever faith or interest a student may have had in this project. Moreover, research tells us that our students come into our classes with 'preconceptions about how the world works' and that we as teachers 'need to engage with this initial understanding otherwise the students may fail to grasp the new concepts and information'.[42]

My own response to this dilemma is to, first, identify the expectations of my students and their broad position with respect the human rights project (advocate, agnostic, champion, critic, etc) and then try to adopt a balanced response by providing students with a diverse range of materials with conflicting views on the merit or otherwise of international human rights. Thus, while Moyn's work holds a place on my reading guide, de Deburca's review of his work also earns a spot;[43] Kennedy's *The Dark Sides of Virtue*[44] is also there but so too is Rodriquez's and Sikkink's more hopeful vision;[45] and while Philip's work on poverty and human rights is included[46] it sits beside Posner's challenge to this nexus.[47] I do not insist on any position and seek to create a learning environment in which my students are encouraged to construct their own understanding of international human rights. Moreover, my aim in developing a student's critical capability is not merely about enabling them to identify the deficiencies in international human rights, what might be termed negative critique. It also extends to encouraging them to consider the ways in which the deficiencies of this project could be ameliorated, to create in the words of Richard Falk, the 'the possible histories of the future'.[48] However, if they are to create these possible histories, they need more than a technical and critical capability.

International Netherlands 2014) 11–18; Samuel Moyn, *Not Enough: Human Rights in an Unequal World* (Belknap Press of Harvard University Press 2019).

[42] Hattie *Visible Learning* (n 17) 245.

[43] Grainne de Búrca, 'Shaming Human Rights' (2018) NYU School of Law Public Law Research Paper 2/18 <https://ssrn.com/abstract=3233063> accessed 25 July 2020.

[44] David Kennedy, *The Dark Sides of Virtue: Reassessing International Humanitarianism* (Princeton University Press 2005).

[45] Cesar Rodríguez-Garavito, 'For Human Rights to Have a Future, We Must Consider Time' *OpenGlobalRights* (10 June 2019) <www.openglobalrights.org/for-human-rights-to-have-a-future-we-must-consider-time/> accessed 5 August 2021; Kathryn Sikkink, *Evidence for Hope: Making Human Rights Work in the 21st Century* (Princeton University Press 2017).

[46] UNHRC, 'Report of the Special Rapporteur on Extreme Poverty and Human Rights' (28 April 2016) UN Doc A/HRC/32/31.

[47] Eric A Posner, 'Should Human Rights Law Play a Role in Development?' (2016) 30(1) The World Bank Economic Review 16.

[48] Richard A Falk, 'New Approaches to the Study of International Law' (1967) 61(2) American Journal of International Law 477, 487.

13.5.3 Capability 3: Strategic Engagement

More recently in my teaching and in response to student evaluations, I have included a class in which we discuss the qualities of leadings human rights practitioners. The reading materials include a news article on Philip's work as Special Rapporteur on Extrajudicial Killings in which the journalist reports that:

> those in the field say Alston has been able to significantly re-invent the position—both with respect to his specific mandate and to special rapporteurs generally. He's built on this ability with his innovation, persistence, fierce independence and skill at exploiting the news media. 'Whether it's a case of bucking the system or just doing things people haven't done before,' says James Ross, legal and policy director at Human Rights Watch, 'he's been very effective'.[49]

Indeed, for anyone who follows Philip's work there is a distinct pattern of innovation and creativity—he is constantly trying to develop methods that will traverse the abyss. He has mastered the art of creating a media headline—'Guatemala is a good place to commit a murder because you will almost certainly get away with it';[50] and 'The World Bank treats human rights more like an infectious disease than universal values and obligations';[51]—phrases that have catapulted his work as a rapporteur from the normal obscurity associated with these reports onto the pages of the *New York Times* and social media.[52]

Beyond his use of the media he is also constantly developing innovative strategies to advance and protect human rights in complex situations. Many will remember the harrowing images shown on the Channel 4 News in the United Kingdom of Sri Lankan forces executing members of the Tamil tigers. An 'official' government inquiry claimed that the video was fabricated. Philip, who was Special Rapporteur on Extrajudicial Killings at the time, had deep reservations about the impartiality of the government inquiry, so he commissioned experts in forensic pathology, forensic video analysis, and firearm evidence to examine the video.[53] Their conclusion, which Philip reported to the HRC, was that the video was authentic and, as such, he recommended that there should be an independent inquiry into the possible commission of war crimes.

How to undertake effective *fact finding* and engage with the *media* are not skills that are generally not taught in law school (unless students are undertaking a clinical subject); they are certainly not skills that receive much attention in human rights textbooks. Nor is the art of storytelling,[54] effective messaging,[55] the use of social media; submission writing;

[49] Paul Tullis, 'The UN's Death Squad Watchdog' *Pacific Standard* (3 May 2017).

[50] Cited in James Painter, 'Crime Dominates Guatemala Campaign' *BBC* (10 May 2007) ; David Grann, 'A Murder Foretold' *The New Yorker* (28 March 2011) ;Philip Alston, 'A Good Place to Commit Murder' in Greg Grandin, Deborah T Levenson, and Elizabeth Oglesby (eds), *The Guatemala Reader: History, Culture, Politics* (Duke University Press 2011).

[51] UNGA, 'Report of the Special Rapporteur on Extreme Poverty and Human Rights' (4 August 2015) UN Doc A/70/274.

[52] For example, The Editorial Board, 'The World Bank Should Champion Human Rights' *The New York Times* (27 June 2016); Jess Staufenberg, 'The World Bank Treats Human Rights like 'an Infectious Disease' Says UN Expert' *The Independent*, (24 October 2015).

[53] 'Deeming Sri Lanka Execution Video Authentic, UN Expert Calls for War Crimes Probe' *UN News* (7 January 2010).

[54] For example Rachel Ball, 'When I Tell My Story, I'm in Charge' (Victoria Law Foundation Community Legal Centre 2013) 60; Journal of Human Rights Practice 2010 2(2), which is a special edition on Storytelling and Human Rights Advocacy.

[55] For example, Anat Shenker-Osorio, 'A Brilliant Way of Living Our Lives: How to Talk About Human Rights' (2018) <https://socialcarefuture.files.wordpress.com/2020/10/87e39-a-brilliant-way-of-living-our-lives-how-to-

negotiation skills; human centred design[56] or the sociology of behavioural change[57] even though in practice human rights advocates are increasingly drawing on these skills in their work. In fact, very little attention is given to the range of skills that are necessary to overcome the reality that the implementation of human rights is rarely if ever a matter of simply lodging a complaint with a committee or commencing legal proceedings in a regional or domestic court. It is for this reason, that the development of an understanding of the strategic skills necessary for the implementation of human rights should be a key learning intention of human rights classes.

The challenge, however, is that most of us teaching human rights in law schools do not have expertise in any of these skills. We can of course learn about these skills from extending our own learning, from talking with our clinical and professional colleagues. We can also draw upon specialists in these fields who can present their knowledge to our students. Moreover, we should not feel burdened that in the space of one semester and one subject, we must find sufficient time to enable our students to become experts in all the capabilities required for effective human rights lawyering. Raising an awareness about the fundamental principles that underlie these capabilities and showing our students where and how they can develop them further will often be all we can reasonably achieve. That said, where resources allow for the development of a human rights programme, this can provide students with the opportunity to undertake a range of subjects including experiential learning opportunities and attend additional workshops and seminars that allow students to develop their skills and understanding incrementally. However, whether teaching a single subject or running a human rights programme, a core learning intention must also be enabling students to understand the importance of self-reflection.

13.5.4 Capability 4: Reflective Practice

David Kennedy's book, the *Dark Sides of Virtue*, undoubtedly finds a place in the readings of many of us who teach human rights. Whether we all agree with his suggestion that the human rights movement may have done more harm than good is debatable. What is irrefutable, however, is that his work does force anyone working in the field of human rights to reflect upon the motives for their involvement in this project and their contribution to it aims. Reflective practice has long been recognized as a core attribute of professional life in areas such as a social work, childcare, and primary and secondary education. Less so, however, in legal practice and by extension human rights lawyering. As lawyers we simply administer the law and as human rights lawyers we can make the grander claim that we are administering a

talk-about-human-rights.pdf> accessed 5 August 2021; Michele Leiby and Matthew Krain, 'The Human Rights Lab: Using Experiments to Craft Effective Messaging' (*OpenGlobalRights*, 3 May 2017) <www.openglobalrights.org/human-rights-lab-using-experiments-to-craft-effective-m/> accessed 25 July 2020; Anat Shenker-Osorio, 'Messaging This Moment: A Handbook for Progressive Communicators' <https://communitychange.org/wp-content/uploads/2017/08/C3-Messaging-This-Moment-Handbook.pdf> accessed 25 July 2020; A Guide to Hope-Based Communications' (*OpenGlobalRights*) <www.openglobalrights.org/hope-guide/> accessed 25 July 2020.

[56] For example, the work of Margaret Hagen, the director of the Legal Design Lab at Stanford Law School: Margaret Hagan, 'Pharos: Human Rights Media' (*Margaret Hagan*) <www.margarethagan.com/design-projects/pharos-human-rights-media/> accessed 25 July 2020; César Rodríguez-Garavito, the founder of *Just Labs*, César Rodríguez-Garavito, 'Cesar Rodriguez-Garavito' (*JustLabs*) <www.justlabs.org/cesar-rodriguezgaravito> accessed 26 July 2020.

[57] Ryan Goodman and Derek Jenks, 'Sociological Theory Insights into International Human Rights Law' (IILJ 2008).

law that has as its foundation the inalienable rights of all persons enshrined in international covenants and treaties. The moral high ground is ours for the taking.

Our task then is twofold. First, to ensure that our students realize that the moral ground is not as stable as they might assume. Unlike any other law subject, students need to be encouraged and taught to reflect on how their own values, assumptions, and prejudices can influence their understanding of human rights law. For whom will they be acting, how and why? Second, students must also be taught that as lawyers, they are not the high priests or priestesses of human rights. They are not the gatekeepers. Reflective practice requires a willingness to identify not only one's personal deficiencies and prejudices but also the weaknesses and limitations of the discipline in which law students are trained and the approaches that the human rights movement has adopted. As Philip himself explained in an address at the London School of Economics in 2016:

> the human rights movement needs to develop a spirit of introspection and openness. Historically, it has not responded well to criticism. As long as the critics were mainly governments seeking to defend themselves or despairing deconstructionist scholars, it was not difficult to continue with business as usual. Going forward, it will be highly desirable for the movement to be open to reflecting on its past shortcomings and to involve a broader range of interlocutors in its reflections than has been the case in the past.[58]

For him, self-reflection for the human rights community entails 'expanding its horizons in terms of thinking about which other actors it can work with' including the private sector; devoting 'more time and effort to being persuasive and convincing, rather than simply annunciating our principles as though they were self-evidently correct and applicable'; and adopting a 'much more instrumentalist than we have been in the past' by 'thinking [about] why the other side is not doing what we consider to be the right thing ... [because] a great many human rights issues are quite complex and a concerted effort to understand the other side, to address their formal as well as their real concerns, and to seek to identify constructive ways forward, will bring much greater results'.[59] It will come as no surprise that I agree with these observations. But I also believe that this call for self-reflection must be explicitly embedded as a learning intention in the teaching of human rights.

13.6 Conclusion—An Evolving and Dynamic Project

I remember my huge sense of dissatisfaction when I studied international human rights law as an undergraduate student. If none of the treaties could be enforced, what was the point. I didn't abandon my commitment to social justice, but for me human rights law had little to offer. After graduating from law school I practised as a commercial lawyer, a government lawyer, and a defence lawyer for children in the criminal justice system. I found myself looking for an emancipatory discourse to respond to the injustices and systemic failures I witnessed in practice, which led me to undertake a Master of Law. I remember picking up a copy of Philip's coursebook in a library and flicking through its pages to see if it offered any hope for my own project. I read a section in which he discussed the meaning of 'enforcement' in the context of international human rights. In pedagogical terms it was a moment of

[58] Alston, 'The Populist Challenge' (n 24) 4.
[59] ibid 11.

cognitive dissonance. I suddenly realized that my undergraduate gaze had been constrained by an expectation that 'real law' was enforced in the courts. As a graduate student I suddenly realized that the legitimacy of the human rights project did not necessarily rest on its enforcement in domestic courts.

Looking forward twenty years I now realize that I have been involved in a constant and ongoing process in which I have continued to construct my own understanding of what is a complex and contested area of law. Much like the floor of Philip's office I visited in Florence, I have been constantly cutting and pasting ideas and concepts together to make sense of international human rights law for both myself and my students. This process is evolving and dynamic. Critically for my teaching to be effective it cannot simply involve me preaching my vision of the human rights project whether it be one of pessimism or hope. Instead, I need to ensure the development of clear learning intentions that extend beyond the orthodox approach to ensure that students are empowered to construct their own understanding and level of engagement with the human rights project. Whether the capabilities approach that I outline in this chapter is an effective model is something to be debated. But surely a robust discussion about the pedagogy of human rights is long overdue?

14
Alston and Artificial Intelligence

Malcolm Langford

14.1 Introduction

In launching his 2019 report to the UN General Assembly, Philip Alston announced that the world was 'stumbling zombie-like into a digital welfare dystopia'.[1] Pushing back against the 'cheerleaders' of the digitalization, Alston, as UN Special Rapporteur for Extreme Poverty and Human Rights, brandishes and advances this self-described 'dystopic vision'.[2] In partnership with the private sector, governments are digitalizing the welfare state to 'automate, predict, identify, surveil, detect, target and punish' and create, in the process, a 'human rights free zone'.[3]

Far from going gently into that good night, Alston's report is a quintessential (and elegant) rage against the dying of the light. Seeking to hold the line in the face of new challenges to economic, social, and cultural (ESC) rights realization, he calls on a broad range of actors to think more deeply and critically about the implications of the Fourth Industrial Revolution. Digitalization and artificial intelligence (AI)[4] is neither a panacea or failsafe solution in the quest to make social welfare provision fairer and effective.

With a neat symmetry, this report bookends four decades worth of work by Alston on ESC rights. His first two scholarly publications on these rights both appeared in 1979: 'The United Nations' Specialized Agencies and Implementation of the International Covenant on Economic, Social and Cultural Rights'[5] and 'Human Rights and Basic Needs: A Critical Assessment'.[6] These two articles represent also the two genres that have long marked Alston's human rights scholarship. The first is *visionary*, providing new and often optimistic perspectives on international human rights law and architecture together with opportunities for enforcement and action. The second is *critique*, shredding with a healthy pessimism the latest fad or fashion for its doctrinal weakness, empirical fallibility, or theoretical infirmity.

[1] OHCHR, 'World Stumbling Zombie-like into a Digital Welfare Dystopia, Warns UN Human Rights Expert' (OCHHR, 17 October 2019) <www.ohchr.org/EN/NewsEvents/Pages/DisplayNews.aspx?NewsID=25156&LangID=E> accessed 29 July 2020.

[2] Note by the Secretary General, 'Report of the Special rapporteur on Extreme Poverty and Human Rights' (2019) UN Doc A/74/48037 para 8.

[3] ibid.

[4] AI can be understood in many ways. Functionally, it compromises any device, programmed or data-driven, that *perceives* its environment and *takes actions* that maximize its chance of successfully achieving *its goals*. Most AI is focused on specific rather than multiple tasks (so-called general AI) and in the field of welfare systems takes on the form of automated advice, detection, or decision-making.

[5] Philip Alston, 'The United Nations' Specialized Agencies and Implementation of the International Covenant on Economic, Social, and Cultural Rights' (1979) 18 Columbia Journal of Transnational Law 79, 18.

[6] Philip Alston, 'Human Rights and Basic Needs: A Critical Assessment' (1979) 12 Revue des droits de l'homme 19.

Malcolm Langford, *Alston and Artificial Intelligence* In: *The Struggle for Human Rights*. Edited by: Nehal Bhuta, Florian Hoffmann, Sarah Knuckey, Frédéric Mégret, and Margaret Satterthwaite, Oxford University Press. © Malcolm Langford 2021.
DOI: 10.1093/oso/9780198868064.003.0015

These two genres run like a red thread through Alston's countless academic publications on ESC rights, UN reports as a special rapporteur, and general comments and concluding observations issued as Chair of the UN CESCR. In many respects, these dual strands have allowed Alston to play the two leading archetypal figures in the theory of collection developed by Nobel Prize in Economics winner Elinor Ostrom. He is the far-sighted 'conditional co-operator' that builds group trust and understanding and the 'willing punisher' that is prepared to enforce group consensus.[7]

Four decades later, Alston's visionary role in ESC rights scholarship and jurisprudence has mostly subsided. Other scholars, rapporteurs, and committee members have taken on the task of identifying ever new venues, interpretations, and applications of ESC rights. Indeed, his digital welfare report is notable for its stunning lack of law. The post-structuralist philosopher Michel Foucault is cited more (three times) than the International Covenant on Economic, Social and Cultural Rights (only twice).[8] For early followers of Alston's work, it might come as a great surprise. Has Alston gone all Marti Koskienniemi on us, they might ask? But Alston's critique is distinct, grounded, and multifaceted as always. Whether it is populism,[9] inequality,[10] proposals for a world court,[11] or the effectiveness of the human rights movement,[12] there is a clear focus on the ills and solutions, with legal gymnastics and diplomatic niceties afforded little place.

And, as always, the critique is unsparing—unsurprising for us that shared some of Philip's journey. In 2000 I arrived as a Master of Law student at the European University Institute in Florence, when Philip was seemingly at the height of his critical powers. Ulrich Petersmann was being dressed down for appropriating human rights for trade law,[13] the ILO chastised for diluting international labour standards,[14] the United Nations scolded for charging user fees for treaty information,[15] and the CESCR upbraided for unnecessary activism and poor legal craftsmanship. Ostrom is not wrong when she speaks of the 'considerable level of scorn' used by 'willing punishers' for those that transgress the commons. One day remains etched in memory. The classroom swung open and Philip stormed into class, flinging copies of the CESCR's newly minted General Comment No 14 on the Right to Health across the room. The instructions to us were clear. We were to read it, analyse it, and critique it. And the tactic (or indoctrination) worked, as time would tell.[16]

This brief essay takes up Alston's latest critical foray, the digitalization of the welfare state. Technology and AI first emerge in Alston's extrajudicial killings work on drones and targeted

[7] Elinor Ostrom, 'Collective Action and the Evolution of Social Norms' (2000) 14 Journal of Economic Perspectives 137, 142.

[8] Compare text and references in notes 5, 103, and 112 with notes 98 and 99.

[9] Philip Alston, 'The Populist Challenge to Human Rights' (2017) 9 Journal of Human Rights Practice 1.

[10] Philip Alston and Nikki Reisch (eds), *Tax, Inequality, and Human Rights* (OUP 2019).

[11] Philip Alston, 'Against a World Court for Human Rights' (2014) 28 Ethics & International Affairs 197.

[12] Philip Alston, 'The Challenges of Responding to Extrajudicial Executions: Interview with Philip Alston' (2010) 2 Journal of Human Rights Practice 355.

[13] Philip Alston, 'Resisting the Merger and Acquisition of Human Rights by Trade Law: A Reply to Petersmann' (2002) 13 European Journal of International Law <https://www.ssrn.com/abstract=332440> accessed 1 August 2020.

[14] Philip Alston, '"Core Labour Standards" and the Transformation of the International Labour Rights Regime' (2004) 15 European Journal of International Law 457.

[15] Philip Alston, 'Charging for Access to International Law Treaty Information: Time for the UN to Rethink a Perverse Initiative' (2001) 12(2) European Journal of International Law 351.

[16] The Alstonian stamp can be found in the work I have done in drafting various international standards and general comments on ESC rights. See the discussion of drafting in Malcolm Langford and Jeff King, 'UN Committee on Economic, Social and Cultural Rights: Past, Present and Future', in Malcolm Langford (ed), *Social Rights Jurisprudence: Emerging Trends in International and Comparative Law* (CUP 2008) 477–516.

killings (2011)[17] and lethal robotics (2012)[18] and later in extreme poverty country reports on the United States (2018)[19] and United Kingdom (2019).[20] However, his latest report is notable for its full-scale and comprehensive engagement with the technological present and future for ESC rights. In this respect, the report is welcome, if not ground-breaking, and section 14.2 sets out Alston's findings in a broader scholarly context. This is followed by a closer reading of the report through the lens of *critical empiricism*. While the report is notable for its commitment to empirical insights, questions can be raised about the construction of technological imaginaries and the ease with which emancipation and repression in AI-marked futures can be identified.

14.2 Alston's Dystopia

Alston paints a picture of welfare states in the throes of digital disruption. His report begins with the empirical observation that the 'era of digital governance is upon us' and ends with a normative call for a 'sober reflection on the downsides'.[21] Advances in biometric identification, digitization, and automation of processes, use of beneficiary data for predicting and controlling behaviours, and moves toward automated lawmaking are together transforming social protection and assistance. Yet, its dark sides are occluded by the 'altruistic' and 'noble' claims of improved efficiency, accessibility, and security.[22] Instead, the digital welfare state has, unwittingly or not, provided a useful 'neutral' cover for long-standing neoliberal policies, whether it is reducing welfare budgets, narrowing the beneficiary pool, entrenching conditionalities, or enhancing sanctions.

In typical fashion, Alston castigates the human rights community's neglect of the issue.[23] Their attention span has been limited, focused on privacy concerns in surveillance states and capitalism rather than a broader swathe of impacts on human rights. Most poignantly, Alston points to a fundamental change in welfare state rationality, which should be troubling from a human rights perspective. There is a reversal of the 'traditional notion that the State should be accountable to the individual'.[24] Digitalization makes instead the individual transparent to the state. Drawing on Foucault, Alston concludes that 'citizens become ever more visible to their Governments, but not the other way around'.[25] In this respect, it is part of a broader trend that moves beyond asking 'whether an AI is "fair" and "for good"' to 'how is AI shifting power?'[26]

[17] OHCHR, 'Report of the Special Rapporteur on Extrajudicial, Summary or Arbitrary Executions, Philip Alston, Study on Targeted Killings' (28 May 2010) UN Doc A/HRC/14/24/Add.6.

[18] Philip Alston, 'Lethal Robotic Technologies: The Implications for Human Rights and International Humanitarian Law' (2012) 21(2) Journal of Law, Information and Science 35.

[19] UNHRC, 'Report of the Special Rapporteur on Extreme Poverty and Human Rights on His Mission to the United States of America' (4 May 2018) UN Doc A/HRC/38/33/Add.1.

[20] UNHRC, 'Visit to the Lao People's Democratic Republic, Report of the Special Rapporteur on Extreme Poverty and Human Rights' (23 April 2019) UN Doc A/HRC/41/39/Add.1.

[21] OHCHR (n 1) paras 1, 78.

[22] ibid para 5.

[23] For earlier critiques, see amongst others Philip Alston, 'Ships Passing in the Night: The Current State of the Human Rights and Development Debate Seen through the Lens of the Millennium Development Goals' (2005) 27 Human Rights Quarterly 755.

[24] OHCHR (n 1) para 5.

[25] ibid. Alston refers to Michel Foucault's description of panoptic systems, in which those under surveillance are 'seen, without ever seeing', see Michel Foucault, *Discipline and Punish: The Birth of the Prison* (1st US edn, Pantheon Books 1977) 202.

[26] Pratyusha Kalluri, 'Don't Ask if Artificial Intelligence is Good or Fair, Ask How it Shifts Power' (2020) 583 Nature 169.

To be sure, critical analysis of the underbelly of welfare state digitalization is not new to academic scholarship. While the early adoption of algorithmic governance in policing and security garnered most attention,[27] its arrival in welfare state has not gone unnoticed.[28] For example, in the United Kingdom, Omar, Weerakkody, and Sivarajah describe the bureaucratic race against 'digital Darwinism', the fear of being left behind that generates top-down, paternalistic, and failure-prone digital welfare reforms;[29] Harlow and Rawlings worry that 'the good governance triad of transparency, accountability and participation may be restricted, even reversed', especially through the loss of reason giving and discretion;[30] Larkin argues that the absence of digital literacy can hinder access to social services;[31] Burton demonstrates that face-to-face and telephonic services may be more appropriate for serious and urgent social welfare cases;[32] and Tomlinson indicates how digitalization of appeals tribunals may be transforming traditional administrative processes into more adjudication-like procedures.[33]

What marks Alston's report though is its global reach, succinct identification of common trends across highly diverse countries and welfare states, and clear-eyed human rights perspective. It is also eclectic in its sources, drawing on sixty submissions from twenty-two governments and NGOs; NHRIs, academics, and individuals in thirty-four countries; as well as grey and academic literature.

The first half of the report outlines six key areas of concern. The first is the abusive use of *biometric information* in which the digital registration and identification of social security beneficiaries is used as much to extend services as engage in surveillance, with concrete examples from India and Kenya. The second is automated *eligibility assessments*, which are conducted in various Western states with off-the-shelf IBM software. In the first year of operation of the system in Ontario there were 1,132 cases of errors, affecting US$101 million worth of payments and causing considerable distress.[34] The third is *calculations and payments* of benefits, and Alston rightly references the 'robo-debt' scandal in Australia. The government automatically issued approximately half a million flawed debt notices to the tune of US$0.85 billion.[35] He also describes the rise of electronic debt cards that embed new

[27] Rosamunde Van Brakel and Paul De Hert, 'Policing, Surveillance and Law in a Pre-Crime Society: Understanding the Consequences of Technology-Based Strategies' (2011) 20 ResearchGate 163.

[28] Joanna Redden, 'Democratic Governance in an Age of Datafication: Lessons from Mapping Government Discourses and Practices' (2018) 5(2) Big Data & Society 1; Caroline Sheppard and John Raine, *Administrative Justice in the 21st Century* (Hart Publishing 1999) <https://www.bloomsburycollections.com/book/administrative-justice-in-the-21st-century> accessed 29 July 2020; John W Raine, 'Modernising Courts and Tribunals through ICTs—Lessons from The London Parking Appeals Service' (2001) 9 International Journal of Law and Information Technology 115.

[29] Amizan Omar, Vishanth Weerakkody, and Uthayasankar Sivarajah, 'Digitally Enabled Service Transformation in UK Public Sector: A Case Analysis of Universal Credit' (2017) 37 International Journal of Information Management 350.

[30] Carol Harlow and Richard Rawlings, 'Proceduralism and Automation: Challenges to the Values of Administrative Law' in Elizabeth Fisher, Jeff King, and Alison Young, *The Foundations and Future of Public Law* (OUP 2020).

[31] Philip M Larkin, 'Universal Credit, "Positive Citizenship", and the Working Poor: Squaring the Eternal Circle?' (2018) 81 Modern Law Review 114.

[32] Marie Burton, 'Justice on the Line? A Comparison of Telephone and Face-to-Face Advice in Social Welfare Legal Aid' (2018) 40 Journal of Social Welfare and Family Law 195-215.

[33] Constitutional Law Group, 'Joe Tomlinson: The Policy and Politics of Building Tribunals for a Digital Age: How "Design Thinking" is Shaping the Future of the Public Law System' (*UK Constitutional Law Association*, 21 July 2017) <https://ukconstitutionallaw.org/2017/07/21/joe-tomlinson-the-policy-and-politics-of-building-tribunals-for-a-digital-age-how-design-thinking-is-shaping-the-future-of-the-public-law-system/> accessed 29 July 2020.

[34] CA$140 million, as at November 2015.

[35] AU$1.25 billion. See Terry Carney, 'Robo-Debt Class Action Could Deliver Justice for Tens of Thousands of Australians Instead of Mere Hundreds' (*The Conversation*, 17 September 2019) <http://theconversation.com/robo-debt-class-action-could-deliver-justice-for-tens-of-thousands-of-australians-instead-of-mere-hundreds-123691> accessed 10 August 2020.

forms of control by restricting the purchase of certain goods and services.[36] The fourth is *fraud detection* and he points to efforts by the United Kingdom, amongst others, to develop data matching technologies. The fifth is the use of *risk scoring and assessment* technologies to determine potential abuse and levels of assessment. The sixth is *communication*, and the challenges of digital literacy and access for many social security beneficiaries are comprehensively charted.

This catalogue of risks resonates clearly beyond the states sampled in the report. It can be extended easily to some of the world's most democratic welfare states (eg Norway) and its most authoritarian (eg China). In Norway, fraud detection technologies based on machine learning are used to detect abuse of student benefits.[37] Experiments show that detection is more accurate but what happens when these technologies are rolled out across the welfare state for more complex cases remains to be seen. Indeed, a new Norwegian study shows that issues of discrimination and bias, digital literacy and access, and surveillance and ethics feature poorly in digitalization initiatives within the state.[38] Moreover, the current welfare scandal in Norway reveals a remarkable degree of surveillance in a state ranked as first on the global WJP Rule of Law index. Social security agencies used digital footprints (emails, bank records, etc) to track recipients' travel outside the country, which was met with benefit suspension, debt claims, and prison sentences, all contrary to EU law.[39]

Turning to China, the rise of digital authoritarianism is casting a shadow on the country's rudimentary social welfare system. In different cities and regions, social credit ratings affect, for example, access to subsidies for winter heating, bicycle-sharing services, credit, tickets for high-speed trains, and free health services.[40] The national government has now set itself the goal of developing a nationwide social credit system from 2020.[41]

Some of Alston's points deserve particular attention and their deeper implications could have been expanded upon. For example, Alston briefly notes that risk technologies personalize risk and overlook structural disadvantages based on inequality, poverty, and racism.[42] This is an important recognition that technology possesses constitutive power. Not dissimilar to law itself, Miller argued already in 1978 that technology creates its 'own forms of consciousness', we view it 'truer, or more transparent, or more objective than others'.[43] Technology begins as an instrumental means and becomes an inevitable end,[44] reshaping how we see the world. It privileges 'linear, incremental, causal forms of thought' in understanding social phenomena and legitimates 'efficiency' narratives.[45] This makes technology

[36] Alston engages in an extended dialogue with the Australian government on the agency effects for indigenous communities and others in Alston, 'Mandate of the Special Rapporteur on Extreme Poverty and Human Rights' (30 January 2018), OL AUS 1/2018.

[37] Marius Jørgenrud, 'Lånekassen tar i bruk kunstig intelligens for å avdekke juks' (*Digi.no*, 22 January 2018) <https://www.digi.no/artikler/lanekassen-tar-i-bruk-kunstig-intelligens-for-a-avdekke-juks/426299> accessed 29 July 2020.

[38] Heather Broomfield and Lisa Reutter, 'Towards a Data-Driven Public Administration: An Empirical Analysis of Nascent Phase Implementation' (2021) 25(2) Scandinavian Journal of Public Administration 73.

[39] 'Norwegian Public Prosecutor Expects More Cases in NAV Social Security Scandal' (13 November 2019) <https://www.thelocal.no/20191113/norwegian-public-prosecutor-expects-more-cases-in-nav-social-security-scandal> accessed 29 July 2020.

[40] Sergey Golubev, 'Digital Dystopia as a Model of Panopticon in Society' (*Medium*, 3 February 2019) <https://medium.com/@sergiygolubyev/digital-dystopia-as-a-model-of-panopticon-in-society-27d7dbcdab12> accessed 29 July 2020.

[41] ibid.

[42] See particularly the discussion in OHCHR (n 1), footnote 59.

[43] Carolyn R Miller, 'Technology as a Form of Consciousness: A Study of Contemporary Ethos' (1978) 29 Central States Speech Journal 228, 236.

[44] ibid 230.

[45] ibid 231–32.

a singular and independent rather than contingent cause of historical change. Technology and society engage in a mutually constitutive relationship,[46] generating new political settlements—which, in themselves, constitute a form of institutional power. Thus, further research on the cognitive effects of digital transformation for human rights thought is needed.

Moving beyond concerns, Alston sets out a human rights approach to digital welfare reform in the final part of the report. His emphasis is clearly on risk reduction or elimination, a Pareto-optimization logic in which no individual is made worse off through efficiency improvements. In his eight-point list, Alston demands that states (1) view the field as ripe for regulation; (2) ensure that there is a legal basis for the reforms; (3) engage with the 'vast digital underclass' by promoting equality in digital literacy and access and permitting non-digital options;[47] (4) respect the right to social security by maintaining access levels together with eligibility fairness and human dignity in procedures; (5) protect civil and political rights through privacy constraints and limits on use of data to harass and surveil; (6) democratize decision-making on digital policy choices; (7) regulate private actors; and (8) hold both public and private actors accountable.

The report ends with six accompanying recommendations, although the last strikes a different tone. Alston concedes briefly the potential positive use of technology to advance ESC rights. However, the possibility is reframed a critique given its absence in practice:

> [A]stonishingly little attention has been paid to the ways in which new technologies might transform the welfare state for the better. Instead of obsessing about fraud, cost savings, sanctions and market-driven definitions of efficiency, the starting point should be how existing or even expanded welfare budgets could be transformed through technology to ensure a higher standard of living for the vulnerable and disadvantaged and to devise new ways of caring for those who have been left behind and more effective techniques for addressing the needs of those who are struggling to enter or re-enter the labour market. That would be the real digital welfare state revolution.[48]

This critique of the absence of empowering legal technology is salient. Despite the promise of a legal assistance revolution through technology,[49] legal technology is rarely directed towards public interest, rights-enhancing projects.[50] Almost all of the global US$18 billion private legal technology market is devoted to commercial uses—for example, tools for lawyers or basic legal services for small businesses—and only a fraction for public interest or services for everyday citizens.[51] Likewise, governments have engaged in digital transformation with primarily costs savings and efficiency foremost in mind rather than improved public services or accountability.[52]

[46] Donald A MacKenzie and Judy Wajcman (eds), *The Social Shaping of Technology* (2nd edn, Open University Press 1999).

[47] OHCHR (n 1) para 44.

[48] ibid para 84.

[49] Richard E Susskind, *Tomorrow's Lawyers: An Introduction to Your Future* (2nd edn, OUP 2017).

[50] Malcolm Langford, 'Who Benefits? Legal Technology and Distributive Justice' (Annual Meeting on Law and Society, Toronto, June 2018); Brian Sheppard, 'Incomplete Innovation and the Premature Disruption of Legal Services' (2016) 2015 Michigan State Law Review 1797.

[51] Jonathan Marciano, 'LegalTech Hits $1 Billion Investment as Lawyers Belatedly Embrace Automation | by Jonathan Marciano | Becoming Human: Artificial Intelligence Magazine' (*Medium*, 3 December 2018) <https://becominghuman.ai/legaltech-hits-record-1-billion-investment-in-2018-71d4e60d6bf2> accessed 29 July 2020.

[52] Jannick Schou and Morten Hjelholt, *Digitalization and Public Sector Transformations* (1st edn. 2018, Springer International Publishing 2018).

14.3 Grounded Technological Critique

Alston's engagement with the digital welfare state is as much classical critique as standard human rights analysis. There is a distinct Gramscian flavour with his focus on new digital hegemonies and alienation of a new and old sub-altern.[53] However, in the spirit of critical empiricism, it is worth probing the framing and evidence in the report.[54] Critique itself should be subject to 'relentless reviewing of processes and methods and continual reinvention of vocabulary'.[55]

The first question to pose concerns Alston's underlying *definition of technology*. It appears to be 'artefact'-centric, focused on digital techniques and method. In science and technological studies, technology is instead commonly understood as the complex assemblages of components and know-how that make up 'technological systems'.[56] This systemic perspective raises questions as to whether Alston's frame of 'digital' welfare states enlightens as much as it obscures. This is because social welfare states are based also on 'systems' that have been in development from at least the late nineteenth century—and can be easily described as a form of technology. Indeed, one of the distinctive aspects of the General Comment No 19 on the Right to Social Security is that the first element of the right is the existence of a 'system'. A system must be established to provide coverage if pre-determined risks materialize.[57] At the same time, we know that social welfare systems, in a Weberian fashion, have long been tools for control, exclusion, and surveillance. As Duncan Kennedy observed, this dark side helped spur the turn to rights across the political spectrum in the 1970s:

> The dominant rhetoric of critique was civil libertarian, and permitted a de facto alliance of left and right, quite similar to that which had linked the social democratic and fascist versions of the social now under attack. The critique targeted the procedural dimension of the social welfare program, that is, its antiformalism. In family law, criminal law, labor law, public housing, the law of civil commitment, and in the law of prisons, mental hospitals, and juvenile homes, the social program involved the creation of new institutions … The civil libertarians attacked the institutions as denying individual rights and their administration as arbitrary and implicitly authoritarian.[58]

Moreover, features such as automation are not necessarily novel in social welfare systems. As Schartum observes, 'the first example of a fully automated legal decision-making process in government administration [in Norway]—with no elements of human assessment—dates back to the Housing Benefit System of 1972.'[59] Other examples could be named.

[53] Esteve Morera, 'Gramsci's Critical Modernity' (2000) 12 Rethinking Marxism: A Journal of Economics, Culture & Society 16.

[54] This critique is first rehearsed in Malcolm Langford, 'Taming the Digital Leviathan: Automated Decision-Making and International Human Rights' (2020) 114 AJIL Unbound 141.

[55] Steve Redhead, 'Toward a Theory of Critical Modernity: The Post-Architecture of Claude Parent and Paul Virilio' (2005) 14 TOPIA: Canadian Journal of Cultural Studies 37.

[56] James E McClellan and Harold Dorn, *Science and Technology in World History: An Introduction* (3rd edn, Johns Hopkins University Press 2015).

[57] CESCR 'General Comment No. 19 on the Right to Social Security' (4 February 2008) UN Doc E/C.12/GC/19 para 11.

[58] Duncan Kennedy, 'Three Globalizations of Law and Legal Thought,' in David M Trubek and Alvaro Santos, *The New Law and Economic Development: A Critical Appraisal* (CUP 2006) 61; For a similar description of an alliance at the international level, see Samuel Moyn, *The Last Utopia: Human Rights in History* (Belknap Press of Harvard University Press 2012).

[59] Dag W Schartum, 'Law and Algorithms in the Public Domain' Nordic Journal of Applied Ethics (2016) 15, 19.

The problem therefore with an artefact-centric critique of the 'digital welfare state' is that it leads to a reification and part romanticization of an earlier and imagined 'human/e welfare state'. We may forget that the welfare state has always been a technology, a complex and hierarchical amalgam of rules, algorithms, coercion, institutions, and spaces in which humans in their physical and cognitive dimensions are just one element. It is thus essential that the emerging critique of welfare states do not succumb to an atemporal reflex. Recent digitalization trends must be located in the *longue durée*. Alston partly does this by showing how digitalization can camouflage a neoliberal agenda, but several of the concerns he highlights pre-date neoliberalism. Thus, the key question to ask is how digital technologies strengthen or relieve the long-standing abusive aspects of the social welfare state. In some cases, the solution may be limited or slowed digitalization; in other cases, other aspects of the system may require more attention.

The second question to ask concerns the *evidence* of the ills of the digital welfare state. One perennial challenge in both critical theory and human rights fact-finding is the preference for the anecdotal and qualitative. There is often a reluctance to engage in or with aggregative and condition-based empirical research of a quantitative or medium-N nature. As discussed earlier, various large-N studies support several conclusions of Alston's report. But at other times one wonders whether there is cherry-picking. For example, the eligibility errors in the Ontario software were clear in 2015 but I have struggled to find evidence of the same problem in the Auditor General reports in the period 2016 to 2018. Is this because the Ontario government managed to fix the problems with automation after an experimental phase?

This potential slippage goes to the heart of the debate on the uptake of AI technologies. What metric do we use to evaluate its upsides and downsides? We have known for a long time that there is 'black box' in human decision-making. Our cognition is inflected and shaped by implicit bias, racial animus, arbitrariness and custom, laziness and error. This pre-digital understanding is sometimes lost in discussions of the dangers of the computational 'black box', whether it is the structural bias, determinism, and atheorism of data-driven approaches or the bluntness, inflexibility, and errors of programming-based approaches. Discussions of the weaknesses of the welfare state should be guided by a logic of minimizing danger, regardless of its origins. While Alston is right to place his thumb on the critical end of the scale when it concerns digital solutions, given most lean on the cheerleading end, we also require human rights-inflected public policy tools of a general nature. There are difficult choices over the extent, speed, and sequencing of digitalization in the welfare state, which require a fine-tuned human rights perspective.

Finally, there is the question of how to hold the digital welfare state *accountable*. Surprisingly, the accountability section of the report is short and bereft of content. Alston himself often stated that accountability was the *raison d'être* of human rights. However, it is here that Alston's point on the transformative power of digitalization is most pertinent and profound. Holding the digital Leviathan to account will often require digital tools. Indeed, the robo-rights scandal traversed by Alston was first challenged through digitalized mobilization and a website for automating complaints.[60] Thus, the human rights community must not only ready itself to challenge digital developments it must also develop digital weapons

[60] Shannon Farley, 'Legal Tech is Opening the System to Those Who Need Legal Representation Most' *TechCrunch* <https://techcrunch.com/2018/03/13/legal-tech-is-opening-the-system-to-those-who-need-legal-representation-the-most/?guccounter=1&guce_referrer=aHR0cHM6Ly93d3cuZ29vZ2xlLmNvbS8&guce_referrer_sig=AQAAAKSpnHlquUyNRlOFhdQYFmEuB9e_Kq_8dfBsnDHt70Dk1lYTSHI64AGEg6COe7ZScb8i1WP1382vawcOaRvZ1PexhX5aWufgb-6zgysuZPDK3tHC3dO81ehFDSa9vJ7fJcltfuBMYF58ya2kMdKaZGWUesIQCFdHfwv7GIZAb8oP> accessed 13 March 2018.

that match new forms of bureaucratic and private power in the welfare state. A digital arms race is concededly a more pragmatic response to the digital welfare state. But it is also consistent with a human rights tradition that has sought to both fight immediate injustice and speak truth to power over the long term.

That said, Alston's report on the digital welfare state remains a defining and central moment in the emergent and insurgent field of social rights and technology. With his razor-sharp analysis and street-wise public communication, Alston has fashioned a report that is now a standard reference in public policy and research as a quick Google search demonstrates. Through his long career Alston has not only bequeathed a scholarly legacy and community of practice, he continues to shape how we think about and engage with the future.

15
Towards ASEAN Human Rights Law

Vitit Muntarbhorn[*]

15.1 Introduction

One of the key developments in international law, since the end of World War II, has been the rise of a large range of regional organizations set up by states, including those dealing with human rights.[1] The value added of the latter has been to help establish standards at the regional level to complement and amplify international standards, while providing further guarantees for human rights protection, especially where the remedies for violations at the national level are inadequate or where local remedies have been exhausted. Today, these organizations can be found in Europe, the Americas, and Africa, and they are anchored on a variety of treaties and related instruments.[2] They have also set up various bodies, such as Commission, Committee, and/or Court on human rights to help monitor the implementation process and enforce the standards as part of the evolving system.

Yet, there is no equivalent organization in Asia, partly because of the varied geography and heterogeneity of this vast continent. Instead, there have emerged various subregional organizations of a political-economic nature.[3] This study aims to examine a key subregional organization found in the Southeast Asian region—ASEAN. Even though it is not a human rights organization, in recent years it has expanded the scope of its work, in principle, to cover human rights' promotion and protection. It has concretized various instruments, in the form of binding treaties and or non-binding declarations, which deserve analysis to see whether they help to raise international standards. Moreover, the range of challenges facing human rights implementation in the subregion should not be overlooked.

[*] Vitit Muntarbhorn is a Professor Emeritus at the Faculty of Law, Chulalongkorn University. He has helped the United Nations in a variety of capacities, including as a former UN Special Rapporteur, UN Independent Expert, and member of UN Commissions of Inquiry on human rights. He was the alternate Thai member of the ASEAN High Level Panel that drafted the terms of reference establishing the AICHR. He is currently a member of the UN Secretary General's Civil Society Advisory Board on Prevention of Sexual Exploitation and Sexual Abuse, and a member of the ILO's Committee of Experts on the Application of Conventions and Recommendations. All views in this study are personal. The chapter has been adapted from an earlier paper presented at the Regional Seminar on ASEAN: Legal Perspective and Regionalism, at the Universitas Padjadjaran, Bandung, Indonesia, 2017.

[1] For introduction, see Bob Reynalda (ed), *Routledge Handbook of International Organisation* (Routledge Press 2013); Clive Archer, *International Organizations* (4th edn Routledge Press 2015).

[2] Tanja A Birzel and Thomas Russe (eds), *The Oxford Handbook of Comparative Regionalism* (OUP 2016).

[3] In addition to ASEAN, examples of subregional organizations include the South Asian Association for Regional Cooperation; Pacific Islands Forum; Arab League and Gulf Cooperation Council.

Vitit Muntarbhorn, *Towards ASEAN Human Rights Law* In: *The Struggle for Human Rights.* Edited by: Nehal Bhuta, Florian Hoffmann, Sarah Knuckey, Frédéric Mégret, and Margaret Satterthwaite, Oxford University Press. © Vitit Muntarbhorn 2021.
DOI: 10.1093/oso/9780198868064.003.0016

15.2 Background

ASEAN was established in 1967 and celebrated its fiftieth birthday in 2017.[4] Its ten members are: Brunei Darussalam, Cambodia, Lao People's Democratic Republic, Indonesia, Malaysia, Myanmar, Singapore, Thailand, the Philippines, and Vietnam. It should not be forgotten that when the organization was founded and then during its first decades, the Southeast Asian region was embroiled in a heated regional and international conflict—the Indochina war was raging in the vicinity. Later in the century, on a more propitious note, the various protagonists were brought together under the regional umbrella, thus bringing peace to the region.

In 2019 Thailand was 'chairing' the ASEAN as part of the annual rotation and there was emphasis on advancing sustainability; this is linked with the SDGs adopted by the global community for the 2015–2030 period, bearing in mind that this global commitment has also enjoyed great 'buy-in' from the region.[5] In retrospect, the organization has progressed well in accommodating differences between countries and has contributed much to fostering peace and cooperation in the regional setting.

What is the physiognomy of ASEAN? It is worth remembering that ASEAN is principally a political-economic organization. From the outset it was not and is not a human rights organization. It has always been an intergovernmental, inter-executive organization. Moreover, it is not a supranational organization. It works on the basis of consensus and it does not have organs that can promulgate laws that are directly applicable to the member states and are of direct effect/directly enforceable in the domestic courts.

Parallel to this, there is the fact that most ASEAN countries are not democratic and even in countries that enjoy democracy, there are key human rights challenges. On the human rights front, expectations from this regional organization would thus have to be modest. However, some elements of human rights may burgeon even in such a setting and this is discussed later.

The legal situation of each ASEAN country at the national level also differs in its relationship with international law, including international human rights law; while some ASEAN countries (such as the Philippines[6]) adopt the monistic approach of incorporating international law into the domestic setting automatically without the need for a national law, other countries (such as Thailand[7]) adopt the dualistic approach of integrating such law only where there is a domestic law transforming international law into national law.

[4] For background, see Alison Broinowski (ed), *Understanding ASEAN* (Macmillan 1982); Vitit Muntarbhorn, *The Challenge of Law: Legal Cooperation among ASEAN Countries* (Institute of Security and International Studies (ISIS), 1987) ; Sharon Siddique and Sree Kumar (Compilers), *The 2nd ASEAN Reader* (Institute of Southeast Asian Studies (ISEAS) 2003); Rodolfo C Severino, *Southeast Asia in Search of an ASEAN Community* (ISEAS 2006); ASEAN, *A Resilient and Innovative ASEAN Community: Annual Report 2017–2018* (ASEAN Secretariat 2018); ASEAN Annual Report (annual) at <https://asean.org/> accessed 10 May 2021.

[5] Transforming Our World : The 2030 Agenda for Sustainable Development UN Doc A/RES/70/1 (October 2015).

[6] See, for example, the Constitution of the Republic of the Philippines 1987:

Section 2. The Philippines renounces war as an instrument of national policy, adopts the generally accepted principles of international law as part of the law of the land and adheres to the policy of peace, equality, justice, freedom, cooperation, and amity with all nations.

[7] See, for example, the Constitution of the Kingdom of Thailand 2017:

Section 178

[...]

Any treaty which provides for a change in Thai territories or external territories over which Thailand has sovereign right or jurisdiction under a treaty or international law, or which requires the enactment of an Act for implementation, and other treaties which may have wide scale effects on the security of economy, society, or trade or investment of the country must be approved by the National Assembly. In this regard, the National Assembly shall complete its consideration within sixty days as from the date

15.3 Human Rights Instruments

The relationship between ASEAN countries and international human rights treaties (and related procedures) can first be noted, followed by a survey of key instruments emerging from ASEAN as an organization.

With regard to the international human treaties that are the backbone of international human rights law, currently, there are nine core international human rights conventions and all ASEAN countries are parties to only three of them: the Convention on the Elimination of All Forms of Discrimination against Women, the Convention on the Rights of the Child, and the Convention on the Rights of Persons with Disabilities.[8] About half are parties to the Covenants on Civil and Political Rights and Economic, Social and Cultural Rights, as well as the International Convention on the Elimination of all Forms of Racial Discrimination against Racial Discrimination. The record varies in regard to the other treaties. The least ratifications have been regarding the International Convention for the Protection of All Persons from Enforced Disappearance and the Convention on the Protection of the Rights of All Migrant Workers and of their Families, implying the sensitive nature of the issues in a region much attached to national sovereignty.

With respect to the various procedures and processes connected with the UN Charter interlinked with international human rights law, all ASEAN countries engage with the UN HRC and all have been involved in the peer review process known as the Universal Periodic Review (UPR), with ensuing (non-binding) recommendations for implementation.[9] Increasingly, they are also opening the door to entry by UN Special Procedures (such as the UN special rapporteurs on various themes) to undertake a country assessment of the human rights situation and share it with the world community.

With regard to instruments evolved by ASEAN itself, the primary entry point must be the ASEAN Charter 2007, which is the mini-Constitution of the group.[10] However, the Charter is mostly concerned with the functioning of ASEAN as a regional organization, and it mentions human rights only in brief. It is not, in substance, a human rights instrument. It is also riddled with other challenging concepts such as non-interference in the internal affairs of a state that has an uneasy relationship with human rights. The only substantive article on human rights in the ASEAN Charter is Article 14, which calls for the establishment of an ASEAN human rights body. Subsequently, the ASEAN Intergovernmental Commission on Human Rights (AICHR) was established pursuant to this Article.[11] This was paralleled by the setting up of a sectoral body on women's and children's rights, namely the ASEAN Commission on the Rights of Women and Children (ACWC).[12]

> of receipt of such matter. If the National Assembly does not complete the consideration within such period of time, it shall be deemed that the National Assembly has given approval (The original version is in Thai)

[8] See further <https://bangkok.ohchr.org/> accessed 10 May 2021. For more information on the Southeast Asian region, see <https://bangkok.ohchr.org/> accessed 10 May 2021.

[9] ibid.

[10] ASEAN, The ASEAN Charter, Singapore, 20 November 2007 (entered into force 15 December 2008): <https://asean.org/asean/asean-charter/charter-of-the-association-of-southeast-asian-nations/> accessed 10 May 2021.

[11] *ASEAN Intergovernmental Commission on Human Rights Terms of Reference (TOR)* (ASEAN Secretariat 2009): <https://www.asean.org/storage/images/archive/publications/TOR-of-AICHR.pdf> accessed 10 May 2021. See also Vitit Muntarbhorn, *Unity in Connectivity? Evolving Human Rights Mechanisms in the ASEAN Region* (Brill/Nijhoff 2013).

[12] ASEAN Commission on the Rights of Women and Children Terms of Reference (TOR) (ASEAN Secretariat 2009): <https://www.asean.org/wp-content/uploads/images/2012/Social_cultural/ACW/TOR-ACWC.pdf> accessed 10 May 2021.

The AICHR then drafted the ASEAN Human Rights Declaration (AHRD) which was adopted in 2012. The Declaration starts with basic principles, ringing a universal tone, inter alia:

1. All persons are born free and equal in dignity and rights. They are endowed with reason and conscience and should act towards one another in a spirit of humanity.
2. Every person is entitled to the rights and freedoms set forth herein, without distinction of any kind, such as race, gender, age, language, religion, political or other opinion, national or social origin, economic status, birth, disability or other status.
3. Every person has the right of recognition everywhere as a person before the law. Every person is equal before the law. Every person is entitled without discrimination to equal protection of the law.
4. The rights of women, children, the elderly, persons with disabilities, migrant workers, and vulnerable and groups are an inalienable, integral and indivisible part of human rights and fundamental freedoms.
5. Every person has the right to an effective and enforceable remedy, to be determined by a court or other competent authorities, for acts violating the rights granted to that person by the constitution or by law.[13]

There follow sections on civil and political rights; economic, social, and cultural rights; right to development; right to peace; and cooperation in promotion and protection of human rights. While it has some innovative elements, such as the call to protect persons with HIV/AIDS, and advocacy of the right to development and peace, the AHRD has been heavily criticized by analysts as not being congruent with international human rights standards[14] and this is elaborated upon in section 15.5.

Importantly, as with all declarations, the AHRD is non-binding (even though it might reaffirm customary rules of international law, such as freedom from slavery and torture). Precisely because of the aforementioned fact that the Declaration was critiqued for not complying with international human rights standards, when the Declaration was forwarded to the Summit of the ASEAN Heads of Government for formal adoption, the Summit adopted another declaration in the form of the Phnom Penh Statement to accompany the AHRD as a kind of damage control exercise.[15] The Phnom Penh Statement on the Adoption of the AHRD thus insists that implementation of the AHRD should comply with international human rights law, in particular the 1948 UDHR, the Vienna Declaration and Programme of Action of the 1993 World Conference on Human Rights and international human rights treaties to which ASEAN countries are parties.[16]

On another front, the only convention or treaty emerging from the ASEAN with bearing on human rights, to date, is the ASEAN Convention against Trafficking in Persons, especially

[13] ASEAN, *ASEAN Human Rights Declaration and the Phnom Penh Statement on the Adoption of the ASEAN Human Rights Declaration (AHRD)* (ASEAN Secretariat 2014): <https://www.asean.org/storage/images/ASEAN_RTK_2014/6_AHRD_Booklet.pdf> accessed 10 May 2021..

[14] See, for example, comments from the International Commission of Jurists, which condemns the fatally flawed ASEAN Human Rights Declaration: <https://www.icj.org accessed> 10 May 2021.

[15] ASEAN, *ASEAN Human Rights Declaration and the Phnom Penh Statement on the Adoption of the ASEAN Human Rights Declaration (AHRD)* (n 13).

[16] These instruments were mentioned specifically in the TOR of the AICHR as applicable to ASEAN countries: ASEAN Intergovernmental Commission on Human Rights Terms of Reference (TOR) .(n 11).

Women and Children (ACTIP) 2015[17] (accompanied by its ASEAN Plan of Action (APA)). The ACTIP is the first substantive treaty in the region on a specific issue with human rights implications. While it is an anti-crime instrument, the elements of protection and recovery offered to victims invites a human rights-oriented approach. The provisions of this regional Convention underline a broad definition of human trafficking based on 'exploitation'; the need for criminalization of the trafficking; criminalization of related money laundering, obstruction of justice, and corruption; possible universal jurisdiction; prevention measures; cross-border cooperation; protection of victims such as measures on victim identification, medical, and other assistance, and safety of return; effective law enforcement; confiscation of assets of the culprits; and mutual legal assistance and cooperation.

In addition, ASEAN has evolved other instruments, such as declarations (and plans of action), which have bearing on human rights, even though not directly titled human rights. Most pertinent is the ASEAN Declaration on the Elimination of Violence Against Women and Elimination of Violence Against Children 2013,[18] advocating more cooperation to tackle the violence through responsive laws, policies, and practices, with national focal points. The strategies include investigation, prosecution, and punishment of perpetrators; protection of women/child victims and survivors/witnesses; access to justice; counselling; awareness against revictimization; and family support services. This has been complemented by training sessions and seminars, and practical programming such as improving standards for service delivery.

There is also the ASEAN Declaration on the Protection and Promotion of the Rights of Migrant Workers 2007,[19] which acts as a gentle call for cooperation between source and destination countries. After an impasse of several years concerning the preparation of another instrument on the issue, that Declaration has now been supplemented by the ASEAN Consensus on the Protection and Promotion of the Rights of Migrant Workers 2018.[20]. There is an update on migrant workers' rights, followed by a section on the obligations of sending states and another section on obligations of receiving states. However, many of the provisions are subject to national legislation, which means that the guarantees for the rights of migrant workers are likely to be lower than international standards. For example, in various ASEAN settings, migrant workers do not enjoy fully the right to freedom of association since they are not allowed to sit on the boards of trade unions. Yet, arguably, the main value added of the Consensus is to support the mechanism established pursuant to the 2007 Declaration—the ASEAN Committee on the Implementation of the ASEAN Declaration on the Protection and Promotion of the Rights of Migrant Workers[21] (ACMW, also a sectoral body), to adopt a more concrete action plan to implement the consensus and share best practices on the matter.

[17] ASEAN, ASEAN Convention Against Trafficking in Persons, Especially Women and Children, 21 November 2015 (entered into force 8 March 2016): <https://www.asean.org/wp-content/uploads/images/2015/November/actip/ACTIP.PDF> accessed 10 May 2021.

[18] <Declaration-On-The-Elimination-Of-Violence-Against-Women-And-Children-In-ASEAN-1.pdf. https://asean.org/?static_post=declaration-on-the-elimination-of-violence-against-women-in-the-asean-region-4> accessed 10 May 2021.

[19] ASEAN Declaration on the Protection and Promotion of the Rights of Migrant Workers (13 January 2007): <https://asean.org/?static_post=asean-declaration-on-the-protection-and-promotion-of-the-rights-of-migrant-workers> accessed 10 May 2021.

[20] ASEAN Consensus on the Protection and Promotion of the Rights of Mirant Workers (Jakarta, March 2018): https://asean.org/storage/2019/01/3.-March-2018-ASEAN-Consensus-on-the-Protection-and-Promotion-of-the-Rights-of-Migrant-Workers.pdf accessed 10 May 2021..

[21] On the sectoral bodies, see further *Unity in Diversity? Evolving Human Rights Mechanisms in the ASEAN Region* (n 11).

Most recently, there emerged the ASEAN Enabling Masterplan 2025 Mainstreaming the Rights of Persons with Disabilities;[22] this helps to integrate into the regional context the CRPD. The strength of the Masterplan is that the drafting process of this plan brought together key mechanisms from both the regional and national levels to work together on an issue of common concern. Thus, the AICHR worked hand in hand with one of the sectoral bodies, the ACWC and the Senior Officials of the Ministries on Social Welfare and Development (SOMSWD) to concretize the Masterplan with a shared sense of ownership.

Parallel to the aforementioned, there is the 2016–25 ASEAN Community framework for the ASEAN beyond 2015 under the caption 'Forging Ahead Together'.[23] Human rights appear particularly in the ASEAN Political Security Blueprint and the ASEAN Sociocultural Community Blueprint. The Political Security Blueprint emphasizes a rules-based, people-oriented, and people-centred community,[24] with a list of actions on the promotion and protection of human rights, including strengthening of domestic legislation and human rights education; accession to and implementation of human rights treaties; engagement with the United Nations and its UPR; support for the AICHR; exchange of information and strengthen implementation of the AHRD; mainstreaming of human rights; encouragement of interaction among the AICHR, sectoral bodies, and civil society organizations (CSOs); support for AICHR's research work on various themes; consideration, as appropriate, of review of AICHR's TOR; encouragement of consultations among ASEAN organs and bodies on the AHRD, the Hanoi Declaration on Enhancement of Welfare of Women and Children (2010), and the Bali Declaration on Enhancement of the Role and Participation of Persons with Disabilities in ASEAN (2011); and support to accelerate the work of the ACMW in developing the relevant instrument on migrant workers.

In regard to the ASEAN Sociocultural Community Blueprint,[25] the directions interrelated with human rights include: promotion of regional mechanisms for vulnerable groups; financing for social protection; tackling of traditional practices that affect human rights negatively; action against discrimination, trafficking, harmful practices, violence against women and children, persons with disabilities, youth, migrant workers, the elderly, victims of trafficking, and ethnic minorities; increasing attention to the rights of the elderly such as through the Brunei Declaration on Strengthening Family Institutions in Caring for the Elderly (2010); and strengthening of interest on the ASEAN Declaration on the Rights of Migrant Workers.

In sum, the region is not short of instruments. While the process of adopting these instruments exemplifies the so-called ASEAN way of consensus building, at times the contents of these instruments fall short of international standards, precisely because of the quid pro quo needed to reach such consensus. Added to that, there is the test of implementation, or constrained implementation, particularly when much of the region remains undemocratic and reticent towards the indivisibility of human rights, particularly civil and political rights, which are the backbone of democracy.

[22] ASEAN Enabling Masterplan 2025: Mainstreaming the Rights of Persons with Disabilities (15 November 2018): <https://asean.org/storage/2018/11/ASEAN-Enabling-Masterplan-2025-Mainstreaming-the-Rights-of-Persons-with-Disabilities.pdf> accessed 10 May 2021..

[23] ASEAN, *ASEAN 2025: Forging Ahead Together* (The ASEAN Secretariat 2015) <https://www.asean.org/storage/2015/12/ASEAN-2025-Forging-Ahead-Together-final.pdf> accessed 10 May 2021.

[24] ASEAN, *ASEAN Political-Security Community Blueprint* (The ASEAN Secretariat 2009): <https://asean.org/wp-content/uploads/archive/5187-18.pdf> accessed 10 May 2021.

[25] ASEAN, *ASEAN Socio-Cultural Community Blueprint 2025* (ASEAN Secretariat 2016): <https://asean.org/wp-content/uploads/archive/5187-19.pdf> accessed 10 May 2021..

15.4 Implementation Implications

From the angle of implementation of international human rights law through ASEAN, the relevant institutions would be those at the national level pertaining to all the rights covered by the international human rights treaties. They call into play the three pillars of the state (executive, legislative, judicial). The role of national human rights institutions such as human rights commissions has also come to the fore. Currently, there are national human rights commissions in five countries: Indonesia, Malaysia, Myanmar, Thailand, and the Philippines. Parallel to this, there is the important role of civil society through NGOs. Some CSOs are now able to apply for accreditation and have more access to dialogue with ASEAN mechanisms, such as to the AICHR.

From the angle of the AHRD, the most pertinent institution is the AICHR. However, the role adopted to date by the AICHR has been more targeted to promotion of human rights, for example, organizing seminars and supporting research studies, than protection of human rights, such as to accept communications of alleged violations, investigate complaints, and call for remedies and accountability. There are also ASEAN sectoral bodies, particularly the ACWC, which has a similar promotional role, and the ACMW, which is more of a meeting of bureaucrats working on labour issues, trying to evolve more actions on migrant labour in the ASEAN. The AICHR in particular has declined to consider cases of alleged human rights violations concerning individual countries, and this is exemplified poignantly by the situation concerning the Rohingya people from Myanmar who have had to seek asylum in neighbouring countries due to persecution at home.[26]

Over and above the AICHR, there is a hierarchy of possible pressure points including (upwards) the ASEAN Foreign Ministers, the other ASEAN ministers drawn from a variety of ministries at the national level meeting at the ASEAN level (such as on women, children, and migrant workers), and at the apex, the Summits of Heads of Government. Interestingly, it was the ASEAN Foreign Ministers that took an initiative at the beginning of 2019 to address the Rohingya/Myanmar issue, albeit in an overly soft manner.[27] They agreed to support the ASEAN Humanitarian Action Centre to help the Myanmar Government in its repatriation plans concerning Rohingyas who had left the country, as well as to provide humanitarian assistance to Rakhine State where several Rohingyas and other minorities are currently found in Myanmar. They have avoided supporting UN fact-finding regarding accountability[28] and have remained silent on the International Criminal Court's investigations regarding crimes perpetrated by various individuals related to the Rohingya exodus.[29].

[26] For refugee related reports, see, for example, UN High Commissioner for Refugees (UNHCR), *Up to 15,000 refugees stranded near Bangladesh-Myanmar border* (17 October 2017): <https://www.unhcr.org/news/briefing/2017/10/59e5c73f4/15000-refugees-stranded-near-bangladesh-myanmar-border.html> accessed 10 May 2021.; UNHCR, *Rohingya refugee returns must meet international standards* (24 November 2017): <https://www.unhcr.org/news/briefing/2017/11/5a16fe014/unhcr-rohingya-refugee-returns-must-meet-international-standards.html> accessed 10 May 2021.

[27] See further, Press Statement by the Chairman of the ASEAN Foreign Ministers' Retreat, Chiang Mai, 17–18 January 2019. ASEAN, *Press Statement by the Chairman of the ASEAN Foreign Ministers' Retreat, Chiang Mai* (17–18 January 2019): <https://asean.org/storage/2019/01/Press-Statement-by-the-Chairman-of-the-ASEAN-Foreign-MInisters-Retreat-Chiang-Mai-17-18-January-2019-FINAL-FINAL.pdf> accessed 10 May 2021.

[28] 'Report of the Detailed Findings of the Independent International Fact-Finding Mission on Myanmar' (September 2018) UN Doc A/HRC/39/CRP/2.

[29] Press Release: ICC Pre-Trial Chamber I rules that the Court may exercise jurisdiction over the alleged deportation of the Rohingya people from Myanmar to Bangladesh (6 September 2018) https://www.icc-cpi.int/Pages/item.aspx?name=pr1403accessed 21 May 2019.

In essence, the ASEAN approach is basically pro-cooperation and non-confrontational—the heart of the so-called ASEAN way. If the issue is implementation of international human rights law through the ASEAN, cooperation can be multi-pronged. It might be cooperation at the national level, bilateral/subregional level, and/or at the ASEAN regional level. This would entail cooperation in regard to the variety of rights, with a panoply of possible cooperation and implementation measures, including laws, policies, practices, mechanisms, monitoring and data generation, resources, education and capacity development, remedies, and networking/mobilization for space for reform and related action. However, ASEAN countries are reticent to cooperate on human rights protection, especially regarding reception of and investigation of complaints of human rights violations, precisely because these countries are still steeped in their attachment to national sovereignty and the non-interference principle.

En passant, it is interesting to note that if the issue is cooperation in regard to the AHRD, the AHRD advocates as follows:

> COOPERATION IN THE PROMOTION AND PROTECTION OF HUMAN RIGHTS
>
> 39. ASEAN Member States share a common interest in and commitment to the promotion and protection of human rights and fundamental freedoms which shall be achieved through, *inter alia*, cooperation with one another as well as with relevant national, regional and international institutions/organizations, in accordance with the ASEAN Charter.
>
> 40. Nothing in this Declaration may be interpreted as implying for any State, group or person any right to perform any act aimed at undermining the purposes and principles of ASEAN, or at the destruction of any of the rights and fundamental freedoms set forth in this Declaration and international human rights instruments to which ASEAN Member States are parties.[30]

The trend is thus that the AICHR will address and cooperate on thematic issues and it has, to date, tended to organize conference after conference with little follow-up. The most constructive output has been the variety of youth debates on human rights that open the door to human rights advocacy through young voices from the region—daring to say what the adults dare not. The AICHR has also carried out various studies such as on business sector and human rights, and women in disaster-related situations. Yet, it avoids focus on the situations of individual countries. Moreover, while it will emphasize the rights of particular groups such as children, women, and persons with disabilities, it eschews the broad range of civil and political rights that are sensitive to several ASEAN countries, particularly those with a 'democracy deficit'. Given such limitations, it is important to access other checks and balances that might address a comprehensive range of human rights issues in a more balanced manner, as voiced in the final section of this study.

15.5 Current Challenges

Despite the many outward commitments to human rights from the ASEAN region, a key challenge pervading the landscape is that the space for human rights (and democracy) is shrinking on many fronts. Civil and political rights are particularly constrained

[30] *ASEAN Human Rights Declaration and the Phnom Penh Statement* (n 15).

in non-democracies. Even in some of the democracies, instances of arbitrary killings and violence also take place, coupled with the vulnerability of various groups, such as political dissidents, refugees and asylum seekers, women, children, indigenous peoples, minorities, including those linked with sexual orientation and gender identity, and human rights defenders.

Implementation measures for human rights might also be less than effective in several contexts. They vary from the (poor) quality of laws to policies, practices, mechanisms, monitoring and data, resources, education/capacity building, accountability related remedies, and public participation/mobilization for reform. Lax law and policy enforcement is compounded by lack of political and social will, aggravated by non-transparent systems (corruption!) subjected to political instrumentalization.

The AHRD suffers from the fact that various parts of the document are not congruent with international human rights law.[31] The stumbling blocks include the appearance of regional particularities (alias, 'ASEAN values'?) in the text, which might undermine universally recognized human rights. These include the overt mentioning of 'duties/obligations' (of persons) instead of paramount emphasis on human rights; reference to 'national and regional context', which might override universal standards, with components of cultural relativism; omission of various internationally guaranteed rights, particularly the right to freedom of association; overly broad limitations on human rights in the guise of 'morality'; emphasis on 'non-confrontation', which interplays with the ASEAN governmental attachment to national sovereignty and their claim that human rights-related action should not interfere in the internal affairs of states; and subjection of human rights, particularly the right to seek asylum, to national law (bearing in mind that most ASEAN states are not parties to the international refugee agreements).

Those nuances can be seen in the wording of the AHRD as follows:

6. The enjoyment of human rights and fundamental freedoms must be balanced with the performance of corresponding duties as every person has responsibilities to all other individuals, the community and the society where one lives. It is ultimately the primary responsibility of all ASEAN Member States to promote and protect all human rights and fundamental freedoms.
7. All human rights are universal, indivisible, interdependent and interrelated. All human rights and fundamental freedoms in this Declaration must be treated in a fair and equal manner, on the same footing and with the same emphasis. At the same time, the realisation of human rights must be considered in the regional and national context bearing in mind different political, economic, legal, social, cultural, historical and religious backgrounds.
8. The human rights and fundamental freedoms of every person shall be exercised with due regard to the human rights and fundamental freedoms of others. The exercise of human rights and fundamental freedoms shall be subject only to such limitations as are determined by law solely for the purpose of securing due recognition for the human rights and fundamental freedoms of others, and to meet the just requirements of national security, public order, public health, public safety, public morality, as well as the general welfare of the peoples in a democratic society.

[31] ICJ (n 14).

9. In the realisation of the human rights and freedoms contained in this Declaration, the principles of impartiality, objectivity, non-selectivity, non-discrimination, non-confrontation and avoidance of double standards and politicisation, should always be upheld. The process of such realisation shall take into account peoples' participation, inclusivity and the need for accountability [. . .]
16. Every person has the right to seek and receive asylum in another State in accordance with the laws of such State and applicable international agreements.[32]

The AHRD should never be read by itself but must be read with the Phnom Penh Statement mentioned earlier. Concomitantly, there is the lacuna that ASEAN human rights mechanisms, such as the AICHR, decline to address human rights violations concerning individual countries, thus opening a 'protection gap' in the ASEAN setting.

Nor is the ACTIP without blemish. While more commitment to help victims of human trafficking is welcome, it is important to note that the ACTIP itself omits the issue of refugee protection, which is covered by the international treaty on human trafficking—The Protocol to Prevent, Suppress and Punish Trafficking in Persons, especially Women and Children (Palermo Protocol) attached to the UN Convention against Transnational Organized Crime, to which most ASEAN countries are parties.[33] The following provision from the Palermo Protocol is missing from the ACTIP:

Article 14:
'Saving clause
1. Nothing in this Protocol shall affect the rights, obligations and responsibilities of States and individuals under international law, including international humanitarian law and international human rights law and, in particular, where applicable, the 1951 Convention and the 1967 Protocol relating to the Status of Refugees and the principle of non-refoulement as contained therein.
2. The measures set forth in this Protocol shall be interpreted and applied in a way that is not discriminatory to persons on the ground that they are victims of trafficking in persons. The interpretation and application of those measures shall be consistent with internationally recognized principles of non-discrimination.'[34]

On a more novel front, while the most recent Masterplan on the rights of persons with disabilities exemplifies welcome cooperation between the regional and national mechanisms, the opaque situation of persons with mental disabilities is disquieting. Statal powers to use electric shocks and other coercive means still exist in the region in dealing with this group.[35]

It is thus necessary to be vigilant against any retrogression when new declarations, treaties, or programmes are evolved in and from the ASEAN region. The regional system should provide a value added to enhance the international system and shun the value subtracted, which may be tantamount to backtracking.

[32] *ASEAN Human Rights Declaration and the Phnom Penh Statement* (n 15).
[33] *A Protocol to Prevent, Supress and Punish Trafficking in Persons, Especially Women and Children, supplementing the United Nations Convention against Transnational Organized Crime*, 2237 UNTS 319, New York, 15 November 2000 (entered into force 25 December 2003).
[34] ibid.
[35] For instance, Thai Law on mental disabilities: http://pcmc.swu.ac.th/EC/document/form/dw_form4/21.pdf accessed 21 May 2019.

15.6 Stepping Stones

The march towards respect for human rights thus invites much patience to realize that the approach from the region is step-by-step. Yet, it needs to become more oriented towards protection of human rights rather than the mere promotion of human rights. While cooperation, rather than accountability, is essentially the key to the ASEAN (governmental) way, it needs to advance a holistic agenda for human rights protection that must not be obscured by overemphasis on the promotional aspects—if it is to be credible and meaningful in the long run.

Given that currently the ASEAN system avoids delving into country situations and related violations, *ad interim* the quest for remedies has to look elsewhere for channels of redress, such as via the national mechanisms (eg the local courts and human rights commissions (if they exist and if they are effective)), and or the international human rights system through the United Nations, such as the UN special rapporteurs who will receive complaints from individuals and advocate redress, and the various bodies related to human rights treaties.

There is thus the need to build checks and balances between the national, regional, and international levels. Stepping stones for the future include the call to the ASEAN countries/ASEAN to:

- Accede to all the international human rights treaties as binding law and implement them effectively at the national level and through the ASEAN with comprehensive, measures premised on civil, political, economic, social, and cultural rights in their totality (such as by means of responsive laws, policies, and practices).
- Follow through the recommendations from the UN treaty bodies, UPR and Special Procedures.
- Build national systems for effective human rights protection, while opening the door to regional mechanisms if there are no national remedies, possibly to enable the AICHR and related mechanisms to take complaints and act thereon and, conversely, even if the regional mechanisms do not take complaints, to enable them to cross refer cases to the national or UN mechanisms that can deal with protection issues.
- Ensure that there is no retrogression when ASEAN instruments are drafted and adopted; there should be value added to advance and not undermine international standards.
- Enlarge the space for people's participation in the ASEAN through more people-centred channels and activities based on inclusivity and the international Rule of Law, with more access by ASEAN parliamentarians,[36] strong People's Forum,[37] networking between judges,[38] and ultimately, an independent and transparent regional court in the ASEAN structure.[39]

[36] There is the ASEAN Interparliamentary Assembly that enjoys interface with the ASEAN but it is not yet an official organ of the latter. There is also the ASEAN Parliamentarians for Human Rights organization, which is more akin to a CSO.

[37] Various peoples' forums are organized parallel to ASEAN meetings. However, there is no official peoples' organization as part of the ASEAN formal, official structure and at the most recent ASEAN Summit in Thailand in mid-2019 no people's forum took place: <https://www.nationthailand.com/asean-plus/30371418> accessed 7 May 2021.

[38] There are various periodic meetings of chief justices from the ASEAN region. See further: <https://www.aseanlawassociation.org/> accessed 7 May 2021 .

[39] See, for example, the ongoing work of the civil society Working Group for an ASEAN Human Rights Mechanism, which decades ago put forward ideas for various mechanisms, including a Court: https://aseanhrmech.org/ accessed 7 May 2021.

PART III

HUMAN RIGHTS MECHANISMS: BUILDING, REFORMING, AND CRITIQUING INSTITUTIONS

16
Implementation of Treaty Obligations
Political Measures Expected of State Parties

Thomas Hammarberg

16.1 Introduction

'Further standard setting should no longer be given priority, focus should instead be put on implementation.' That comment has quite often been heard among human rights activists. One reason of course is the fact that there now exist international treaties covering wide areas of human rights problems. However, behind this opinion is also a degree of impatience about slow or totally lacking enforcement of the international human rights agreements.

No doubt, the agreed treaties on human rights, including the UN Conventions, have been of very great importance. The drafting, adoption, and ratification procedures have given attention to the crucial issues behind them. The final texts have given interested governments and civil society groups valuable instruments for national and local human rights initiatives. Standards have been set and spread.

The UN Committees, established to monitor implementation of the respective treaty, have invited governments to public hearings, usually at the UN Headquarters in Geneva. Following such sessions they normally issue 'Concluding Observations', which would include recommendations on further steps towards protecting and promoting the rights. The intention is that the state parties would study these advisory documents carefully and organize transparent discussions about their recommendations with civil society groups, parliamentarians, and other relevant parties. This procedure has been taken seriously by many state parties.

However, it is also true that the agreed standards have not been respected in several cases and situations. There have been political obstacles. Illiberal governments have tended to ignore human rights. In war situations, when respect for the norms would be particularly crucial, they are often massively violated. Security concerns and economic problems have often been allowed to trump protection of justice.

These trends make it even more important to reflect on what ought to be done to enhance a serious implementation of the adopted and ratified human rights treaties. A careful reading of the Conventions themselves is obviously a first step. They are in specific articles setting out some overall obligations on political and other measures to ensure and promote implementation.

The Covenant on Civil and Political Rights underlines the need to adopt legislative or other measures to give effect to the rights in the treaty. Further, state parties should ensure that there is an effective remedy for any person whose rights are violated(Article 2).

The Covenant on Economic, Social and Cultural Rights states that each state party should take steps to the maximum of its available resources to achieving progressively the full

Thomas Hammarberg, *Implementation of Treaty Obligations* In: *The Struggle for Human Rights.* Edited by: Nehal Bhuta, Florian Hoffmann, Sarah Knuckey, Frédéric Mégret, and Margaret Satterthwaite, Oxford University Press.
DOI: 10.1093/oso/9780198868064.003.0017

realization of the rights recognized in the treaty. It also stresses particularly the adoption of legislative measures (Article 2).

The Convention on the Rights of the Child requests the state parties to take 'all appropriate legislative, administrative, and other measures' for the implementation of the rights therein. State parties should also undertake measures to guarantee ESC rights 'to the maximum extent of their available resources' (Article 4). Other obligations specifically mentioned are measures to make the Convention known to both adults and children and to circulate implementation reports widely (Articles 4, 42, and 44 para 6).

Such articles in other UN human rights treaties also emphasize the importance of legislation in line with the agreed norms. The need for necessary resources is also repeated, though with room for a progressive approach when necessary. Another requirement in these agreements is that the rights should be applied without discrimination.

Some of the Committees have produced General Comments on articles in the respective treaty. Their purpose is to offer a more thorough interpretation of the norms and thereby serve implementation efforts. They are based not least on the experience of dialogues with state party representatives. These comments have been understood as a sort of guidelines for decision makers and others involved.

The Committees relating to the three aforementioned treaties have all issued such focused comments. Those by the Committee on the Rights of the Child were produced more recently and are more extensive. I will refer here to the efforts by that Committee to illustrate thinking on ways of making the interpretation in the state parties more solid. Similar discussions have also been held in other Committees.

Within the Committee on the Rights of the Child there was a feeling for several years that implementation of the Convention was far less effective than anticipated. Different factors appeared to have contributed to this situation in different countries, but one fundamental cause appeared to be common: *absence of a systematic, comprehensive approach to children's rights as a political priority.*

Concerns for children were not given top priority in politics. The Committee noticed that ministers responsible for children's affairs tended to be junior and to stand outside the inner circles of power. When political issues were divided into 'soft' and 'hard' ones, those relating to children were dealt with as 'soft-soft'. Often these issues were seen as non-political and sometimes simply trivial. This was not considered within the Committee as consistent with the intentions behind the Convention.

16.2 Basic Obligations

The Committee on the Rights of the Child referred to the three types of basic obligations that should be honoured by a ratifying state: an obligation of result, an obligation of conduct, and an obligation of transparent assessment of progress.

(a) *An obligation of result:* Article 2 of the Convention requires states to 'respect and ensure the rights set forth in the Convention to each child within their jurisdiction'. The authorities therefore have an obligation not only to respect the rights themselves, but also to make sure that others do so as well (eg by preventing and combating abuse and discrimination in society). States should create the necessary conditions for children's rights to be effectively enjoyed. Even when it is foreseen that a right can be implemented gradually (eg the right to health or the right to education), there is an obligation to achieve progressive results. The successful adoption of a law could be one such 'first-step' result.

(b) *An obligation of conduct:* Implementation of the Convention is not only measured by tangible results; a major emphasis is also on the *efforts* governments make. States should be able to show that they have undertaken 'all appropriate legislative, administrative, and other measures for the implementation of the rights recognized in the present Convention'. Indeed, much of the discussion between the Committee on the Rights of the Child and states' representatives has been precisely on whether sufficient action has been taken to realize children's rights. This focus has made the Convention particularly relevant for national political debate.

(c) *An obligation of transparent self-assessment:* The periodic reports to the Committee are therefore essential for the implementation process. They should contain information on the process of implementation of the Convention, including facts about measures taken and on results achieved, as well as on the factors and difficulties hindering further progress. The reports are expected to be self-critical and objective, giving the Committee a comprehensive understanding of the reality in the country and enabling it to make meaningful suggestions and recommendations. In line with this concern for transparency, states are also required to make their periodic reports widely available to the public in their own countries. The reports should therefore play an important catalytic role, contributing to the promotion of a national debate on children and their rights, encouraging the participation of NGOs, and generally fostering a process of public scrutiny of governmental policy on children.

There is of course a clear interrelationship between the three obligations mentioned here. In all of them the purpose is to ensure that children can enjoy their rights. The obligations on 'conduct' and 'self-assessment' aim at results as well but start from a more indirect position. They recognize implicitly that full realization will never be reached. Implementing children's rights is by nature a permanent and endless process; there is always room for improvement. What is expected is a constant cycle of conduct–result–assessment. From the assessment one might learn to improve the conduct in order to achieve better results, and so forth.

Still, the distinction between the different kinds of obligations is important, not least for the identification of relevant *indicators* to measure the level of progress achieved for the rights of the child. Benchmarks are needed both on what is to be achieved (progress and final results) and on measures taken. In this process, statistics are of importance.

16.3 Concrete Measures of Implementation

One the basis of field visits and its discussions with state and civil society representatives, the Committee developed checklists on the standard measures that serious governments ought to take. The list of ten points that follow is one attempt to summarize the issues raised not least during the hearings with government representatives.

16.3.1 Improving the Laws

The law can be critical for the promotion and protection of children's interests. Some countries have adopted the Convention as a national law; others have reviewed and amended existing legislation in the light of the provisions of the Convention. Whatever method is chosen, it is important that the law of the land be harmonized with the Convention. This should be done consciously in order to provide real guidance to government agencies, the judiciary, legal professionals, and the public at large. It is important, for example, to give serving judges and other key personnel in the courts updated information and orientation on how to interpret and apply children's rights legislation. The law could also be used to establish an aspect of public morality; the anti-smacking laws that several countries now have adopted is one example.

16.3.2 Promoting Systems for Independent Monitoring

National commissions or ombudsmen for children may have different mandates, though the main intent is usually to facilitate an independent monitoring and systematic discussion of children's issues. The effective autonomy of these offices is critical, and it is especially important that they are free from day-to-day political and bureaucratic influence. In some settings it may be more rational to ensure a child dimension in a broader ombudsman concept; in other environments a separate ombudsman focusing solely on children would be more effective. Whatever model is adopted, there should be sufficient resources for more than individual casework; studies into structural problems are necessary as well. An independent press and other media, together with an active non-governmental sector, are essential actors for truly independent monitoring. It is also useful to establish procedures to make monitoring easier. The government—at both central and local levels—could, for instance, be required to submit annual reports on the status of children and their rights to the parliament or the local assembly for review and debate.

16.3.3 Adjusting Government Structures

The national agenda should be promoted through an effective administration. Governments tend to reflect their priorities in the way they organize themselves. Matters relating to children should be mainstreamed into the activities of all relevant ministries. At the same time, a coordinating mechanism within the government should be created to ensure that the different ministries march in the same direction in regard to children's rights. For instance, one ministry could have this as a special task and/or an inter-ministerial Committee could be set up. A mechanism is also needed for coordinating national policymaking with local administration. In most countries, key decisions on children are taken at a local level rather than in the capital city.

16.3.4 Adopting a National Strategy

All serious governments should have a national strategy, plan, or agenda on how the rights of the child should be ensured. Whatever plan or policy is adopted, it needs to be based on the whole Convention and address the needs and rights of all children, without discrimination. It should result from widespread consultation, including with NGOs and involving children themselves in the process. Often more important than the actual plans and policies is the process by which progress against the plans and policies is reviewed and results fed back into the planning and implementation processes. Again, this ongoing review of implementation should take place in open and democratic forums, with provisions for hearing the views of relevant constituencies, including children themselves.

16.3.5 Giving Children Room in the Budget Process

The budget reflects priorities. The Convention states that the maximum extent of available resources should be allocated to the implementation of children's rights. The term 'maximum extent' needs to be further clarified. In addition, processes should be developed to facilitate a serious public discussion about children's interests. Environmental impact analyses are now a common element in most major decisions about public works and many private construction projects throughout the world. In some developing countries, the World Bank has led the way in promoting and providing technical assistance for these studies. Such impact analyses need to become a common element in decision-making that affects children, at both national and local levels. The idea of a 'child appendix' to national or local government budgets, reflecting the child-related dimensions of the various allocations, should be developed.

16.3.6 Assessing Child Impact

New procedures clearly need to be introduced to ensure a higher priority for children in political decision-making. 'Child impact analyses' could create a basis for decisions in the best interests of the child. The idea is that decision makers should find out—ideally before making their decisions—what consequences different options would have on children. One element in this methodology is to solicit the views of children themselves. Such procedures should be applied not only for decisions relating directly to an individual child, but also for broader political issues affecting children as a group.

16.3.7 Collecting and Using Relevant Data

Relevant and accurate data are essential as a basis for discussions concerning reforms. Data should be organized and appropriately disaggregated so that possible patterns of disparities, discrimination or neglect can be identified and analysed. Some work has been done on the development of relevant indicators to measure progress in fulfilling the rights of the child, but much more is needed in terms of both the indicators themselves and the mechanisms for monitoring the quality, consistency, and meaning of the data over time.

16.3.8 Creating Awareness

The school is one of the most important environments for the promotion of children's rights. If the school system can bring the spirit of the Convention to coming generations of children, a major change will have been initiated. Few things therefore can be as important as finding the best approach to introducing children's rights in the school—and ensuring an impact on the school itself, including on school governance. Broad awareness campaigns for adults, with an emphasis on parenting education, are also important. In particular people working with children should be offered a genuine possibility to understand both the specific provisions of the Convention and its overall spirit. Professional groups of particular relevance are teachers, health personnel, institutional staff, judges, social workers, police officers, and journalists. Those who are closest to children in their everyday worlds have the greatest opportunity to fulfil the Convention's goal that children's own views be heard and taken seriously. This goal represents a formidable 'training' challenge.

16.3.9 Cooperation with the Civil Society

NGOs have been crucial for the efforts made so far to implement the Convention: their advocacy, support programmes, and monitoring have made a clear difference in many countries. As they increasingly involve NGOs in carrying out public programmes, governments should avoid co-opting these organizations and instead fully respect their independence. They should also make every effort to include NGOs working for—and genuinely involving—children themselves. Few governments have created formal structures for consulting with NGOs on children's issues, a step that is much needed and long overdue. The time has also come to involve the private commercial sector in the fulfilment of children's rights. The co-operation of its more responsible elements can be a critical strategy for addressing the economic exploitation of children, for instance, or for protecting children from the negative influences of mass media.

16.3.10 Priority to Children in International Cooperation

The Convention explicitly calls for international cooperation to help achieve full realization of children's rights. This requirement means that donor countries ought to prioritize children's rights in their aid programmes and that recipient countries ought to do the same in cooperation negotiations. Multilateral resources should be channelled to a larger extent to children's needs, particularly education and health. International cooperation is also needed to develop common 'child-friendly' policies and strategies, and to tackle issues that clearly transcend national borders (eg the need to protect children during armed conflicts, to assist refugee children, to prevent the trafficking of children, and to combat abuses in connection with intercountry adoption).

16.4 Making the Proposed Measures Useful

These recommendations have several characteristics in common. Each relies on public debate and transparent procedures. Each advocates a priority, a 'first call', for children, while recognizing the need to integrate efforts for the realization of their rights into existing administrative structures and procedures. The idea is that children's issues should be moved from the exclusive realm of charity onto the political agenda—and placed high thereon. Each recommendation also includes aspects that in themselves reflect the spirit of the Convention, for instance, by giving children a voice in the procedures.

The recommendations are also mutually reinforcing. A serious national agenda would include all the other points; non-governmental groups would advocate their priorities and the ombudsman or commissioner would scrutinize and report on implementation. Effective coordination of government programmes would be necessary to live up to the expectations. The data collection and child impact analyses serve decision-making, including the budgeting work. In an interrelated world, international cooperation will also be necessary in this field and should draw on the various national experiences covered in the other recommendations. In fact, there is a clear synergy to be gained by combining the various recommendations.

The recommendations can be used as a checklist against which governments can measure the current situation and decide what further measures are needed. Clearly, no government can honestly suggest that their work in this area is complete. In its discussions with government representatives, the Committee on the Rights of the Child has realized that there is no ground for complacency anywhere in the world, even in countries where legislation has been harmonized and an office for children's rights monitoring created.

Although the measures formulated here are focused on the national level, several are also relevant for the *local level*. Indeed, the lives of children are heavily influenced by decisions made in the immediate community. The Agenda 2030 envisages a role for local communities, including children, in the protection of the natural environment. This has been a useful signal and has had an impact in some countries, especially where the local assemblies have been free to take on the challenge and encouraged to do so.

In some communes in Sweden, local ombudsmen for children have been appointed. The idea of adopting a local agenda is also beginning to spread in some other countries, its main objective being to give priority to children in the local budget. Using child impact analyses when preparing decisions that might affect children is of course also relevant at the local level. Such processes should include consultation with children, which is likely to be easier to organize meaningfully at the local level.

16.5 Relevant Measures Relating to Several Conventions

How relevant is the approach of the Committee on the Rights of the Child to the other UN human rights treaties? In fact, most of the ten measures recommended would be of direct relevance to bodies promoting implementation of UN human rights standards:

- A *legislation* covering the treaty norms—through incorporation or transformation—is a must for all state parties.
- The existence of an *ombudsman structure* to which people could complain is also essential.
- The importance of effective *government structures* on different levels is obvious.
- Producing a *national plan* with a strategy for implementation is required. Preferably it should be the result of wide consultations and approved by the parliament.
- The idea of ensuring that national and local *budget*s protect social interests is certainly relevant even beyond concerns for children.
- The method of assessing the child impact on various political and administrative decisions cannot be easily transformed to fit other groups. However, the underlying message is relevant and important: decisions affecting *vulnerable people* require special care.
- A competent *data collection* is necessary for the work on a national plan but also to service a meaningful public debate
- Keeping *people aware* on needs and remedies is another obligation. It should include information on the Convention to the public as well as offer training to relevant professionals.
- No serious work on human rights is possible without a constructive relationship between authorities and *civil society.*

- Aspects of *international cooperation* are specifically mentioned in some of the treaties. One ambition is to promote assistance for the implementation of human rights.

16.6 Responding to Criticism

The application of the measures that have been proposed here is not just a question of good planning, organization, information techniques, budgeting, and other technical skills. The major problems relate to attitudes.

Politicians and key officials are of course influenced by the cultural environment in which they live, with its particular views and prejudices. They are faced with the dilemma of whether they want or are able to spearhead modernization, and to what extent. In the current political climate human rights seem unfortunately not to be considered as an attractive message during election campaigns in numerous countries.

The general goodwill towards children does not automatically translate into support for their rights as formulated in the Convention. The fact that the United States has not yet ratified this treaty appears to be the result of a lobby representing 'family rights', which has opposed the Convention on the grounds that it undermines the status of parents.

Though opposition to this Convention has been low-key in most countries, some issues appear to ignite public debate and delay effective implementation. Opponents to the Convention claim that parental rights are more important than rights for children, that there should be a balance between children's rights and their duties and obligations, and that there are not enough resources to implement the Convention. These claims need to be questioned.

In principle, there is no contradiction between the interests of the parents and those of children. Children need a positive family environment—the Convention clearly emphasizes this point. There are, however, extreme situations when authorities have a duty to intervene to protect the life and well-being of a child under threat from the very person(s) who should be his or her security. To construct an artificial conflict in the public discourse between parental rights and children's rights is therefore a reactionary position that could be, and sometimes is, used as a justification for repressing children.

The argument that children's rights must be balanced with duties is also misused. Of course, children have duties and responsibilities, and so they should. Generally children all over the world are under heavy pressure within the family, in school, and from their peers to fulfil certain responsibilities. In most cases, there is no need to increase that burden. Behind the argument on children's duties lurks the notion that children's rights should be conditioned by their having formal duties, in law or otherwise. Such conditionality is not part of any international human rights Convention. The argument is, in fact, a frontal attack against the whole concept of children's rights and should be answered accordingly.

During the hearings in Geneva, government representatives have sometimes referred to financial restrictions as an explanation for lack of implementation efforts. Clearly, poor countries have genuine problems here. In fact, those who drafted the Covenant on Economic, Social and Cultural Rights as well as the Convention on the Rights of the Child did not ignore the realities of economic problems in some countries. Both treaties foresee a gradual, progressive implementation of some articles, given possible resource constraints. However, this should not be used as an escape clause. There must be serious efforts to move towards full implementation. Also, these efforts should be transparent and accounted for.

Furthermore, the Conventions mention *international cooperation* as a possibility to be considered by all parties. During hearings Committee members have raised this issue with donor governments deemed able of providing assistance. Also, there have been recommendations to relevant UN agencies to include the needs of children in their priority setting. Furthermore, discussions have been held with recipient states on how they have used such assistance from outside.

Though real and genuinely difficult, especially in low-income countries, resource limitations should therefore not be an obstacle to taking the treaty obligations seriously. The greater the difficulties, the more reason to act with a clear political will and address problems in a systematic fashion. Indeed, it is particularly in times of crisis that the state has to affirm its commitment to needy people and their rights.

Economic policies that have been pursued on national and global level in recent years have resulted in growing gaps between the rich and the poor in countries all over the world. Growing inequalities have victimized children and other vulnerable groups.

16.7 Political Priorities

The Convention on the Rights of the Child has been considered a relatively successful treaty, at least compared to some of the others. Universal ratification was obtained quickly (with the exception of the United States), a number of ombudsmen for children have been appointed, child-friendly laws have been enacted in several countries, and serious conferences on child-related issues have been organized.

UNICEF has played an important role in this development as have Save the Children and other NGOs. It is also obvious that the focus by the Committee on concrete implementation measures has had an impact. It has made the dialogue with governments more substantive and given the civil society activists an additional agenda for their lobbying.

Still, civil society groups working in this field report that key politicians appear to have lost interest and that there seems to be a lowering of the priority of children's rights in political life. The vacuum created has tended to be filled by political gestures and charity rather than serious debate.

Reports from groups working on human rights in general have exposed alarming tendencies. Some governments not only violate basic rights directly they also promote an atmosphere of xenophobia and intolerance. These current trends call for further and stronger efforts to make reality of the agreed human rights norms.

The political measures of implementation mentioned in this essay have a purpose: to serve as the basis of programmes that would make real the principles and provisions of the agreed treaties.

The seriousness of governments will be judged by the degree to which they mobilize political, legal, budgetary, administrative, and other resources in support of the measures spelled out in such recommendations.

In the end this is a question of *political will.*

17

Up the Stream without a Paddle

Human Rights Challenges in Mega-infrastructure Finance and Investment

Mac Darrow

17.1 Introduction

One Sunday evening in Canberra, in early 1997, I received a phone call from Philip Alston at the European University Institute, Florence, offering me a temporary position there as his research assistant. I had met Philip through my master's course at the Australian National University and had contacted him a few weeks earlier to seek career advice. But the invitation (which I accepted on the spot) came as a complete surprise. Within a matter of weeks I had resigned from my job-for-life in the Attorney General's Department, packed my life into two large suitcases, and was winging my way—Italian dictionary in hand—to the cradle of the Renaissance.

The main focus of work would be a project examining the 'mainstreaming' of human rights in the work of the UN system, with a particular focus on development. In this, as in many other things, Philip was well and truly ahead of the game. The international human rights movement had taken enormous strides since the 1970s, in terms of doctrinal evolution and strategies for political and social mobilization. However, international human rights law and practice were still heavily compartmentalized, interdisciplinary scholarship and praxis were limited, and—even more than today—human rights advocacy rarely engaged in more than a tokenistic or tangential way with economic injustices.

The mainstreaming project, conceived in the early 1990s, offered an antidote to the rigidity and myopia of conventional human rights praxis. The project was predicated upon the simple (yet underappreciated) premise that the realization of human rights depends at least as much upon finance and trade ministries as justice and foreign ministries; on international development and finance institutions as much as specialized human rights bodies; on private actors as much as states; and on economic and other social science perspectives as much as the law. The project was intended to draw human rights praxis from its comfort zone and, through an interdisciplinary approach, analyse the political economy and root causes of human rights violations, rather than (or in addition to) their manifestations, and highlight those aiding, abetting, or enabling violations, far from the site of suffering, as well as the perpetrators themselves. 'Upstreaming', rather than mainstreaming, may have been a more apt (though even less elegant) metaphor.

The prescience of this premise was quickly proven when, in July 1997, former UN Secretary General Kofi Annan promulgated a major initiative to 'mainstream' human rights across all major areas of the UN system's work. During this period, UN development agencies began to experiment with 'human rights-based approaches' to development. However,

Mac Darrow, *Up the Stream without a Paddle* In: *The Struggle for Human Rights.* Edited by: Nehal Bhuta, Florian Hoffmann, Sarah Knuckey, Frédéric Mégret, and Margaret Satterthwaite, Oxford University Press.
DOI: 10.1093/oso/9780198868064.003.0018

the evaluations mostly fell short of aspirations. The concept of 'mainstreaming' has since wilted somewhat under critical scrutiny, linked to philosophical objections to human rights and suspicions about their proponents.[1] At a more practical level, human rights praxis has struggled to keep pace with the evolution of global financial governance and engage effectively with sites of economic power. 'Mainstreaming', in practice, has succeeded to varying degrees when framed as tinkering or tweaking rather than transplanting or transforming, and where the human rights tributary runs roughly in the same direction as the development Amazon. But where there are strong counter-currents, human rights are often swept into a harmless eddy, or are swamped or assimilated entirely. At the same time, institutional inertia, cynicism, fatigue, ritualism, bureaucratization, conflicting accountabilities, and mismatched incentives have taken a toll on the mainstreaming mission within individual organizations. Recent geopolitical shifts, threats to the post-World War II institutional architecture, the rise of authoritarian populism, nativism, and parochialism, and the COVID-19 pandemic now pose existential threats to international human rights, whether mainstreamed or quarantined.

Yet the essential idea underpinning 'mainstreaming'—that is to say, that human rights embody higher-order values and norms that should be taken into account by all influential actors—has enjoyed remarkable staying power. Newton's third law of motion holds that for every action there is an equal and opposite reaction. So, in recent years, we have seen authoritarian overreach provoking uprisings, progressive political campaigns, social movements, and grassroots demands for human rights. Somewhat against the run of play, the 2030 Agenda for Sustainable Development contains a raft of important human rights commitments, and states explicitly that the Agenda should be implemented in accordance with existing international law.[2] The idea of policy coherence is now commonplace in international development agreements, and the doctrine of 'systemic integration' (or contextual interpretation) has emerged in response to the challenges presented by the fragmentation of international law.[3] Businesses, investors, and development actors are increasingly adopting human rights policies and safeguards, and empirical research increasingly bears out the importance of human rights for development.[4] The pertinence and subversive potential of the human rights enterprise are also evident, paradoxically, in the energy and resources marshalled against it in intergovernmental bodies, international development and financial organizations, and among national elites.

This is by no means a linear progression. Progress is often more rhetorical than real, and can easily be reversed. But nowhere does the human rights challenge appear more pressing than in relation to the 'billions to trillions' mega-infrastructure investment agenda of the G20 and international financial institutions (IFIs), an ambitious plan to re-engineer development finance and increase global investment in transport, energy, water and sanitation,

[1] For example, Martti Koskenniemi, 'Human Rights Mainstreaming as a Strategy for Institutional Power' (2010) 1 Humanity: An International Journal of Human Rights, Humanitarianism, and Development 47; cf Grainne de Búrca, 'Human Rights Experimentalism' (2017) 111(2) American Journal of International Law 277(drawing upon experimentalism governance theory in support an account of the positive impact of international human rights law).

[2] UNGA Res 70/1 (2015) UN Doc A/RES/70/1, paras 10, 18–20.

[3] Campbell McLachlan, 'The Principle of Systemic Integration and Article 31(3)(C) of the Vienna Convention' (2005) 54(2) The International and Comparative Law Quarterly 279.

[4] The World Bank, 'Human Rights, Inclusion and Empowerment' (*World Bank*) <https://www.worldbank.org/en/programs/program-template> accessed 28 May 2021.

and other key infrastructure sectors in order to achieve the SDGs.[5] The human rights implications of any single infrastructure project, such as a major highway or hydroelectric dam, are relatively easy to imagine and anticipate: for example, ensuring adequate information and consultation at the design stage, avoiding forced evictions and labour rights violations, avoiding gender-based violence from labour influx, ensuring that services are available on a non-discriminatory basis and are accessible and affordable, protecting human rights and environmental defenders, and so forth. These kinds of issues are standard fare for human rights practitioners.

However, as we will shortly see, when aggregated to the level of national and regional (and in some cases, cross-regional) plans, and when the political economy of mega-infrastructure projects and investment and financing policy implications are factored in, human rights risks are magnified considerably, and systemic risks emerge. At the same time, paradoxically, ('micro') human rights issues can easily be forgotten in the utilitarian cost–benefit analysis of mega-infrastructure investment and can be obscured by the complexity of the financing and investment structures involved. At the time of writing, COVID-19 appeared to have taken steam out of the mega-infrastructure investment agenda. But the financial interests, neoliberal economic assumptions, and institutional incentives underpinning 'big infrastructure development' run deep. COVID-19 has graphically exposed the conceptual frailties, injustices, and ideological biases in the dominant economic model. A direct interrogation of mega-infrastructure investment paradigm through the prism of human rights may help us to envisage and construct more just and enduring post-COVID economic and financial arrangements.

17.2 Human Rights Implications of the G20's Mega-infrastructure Investment Agenda

In recent years, G20 finance ministers and the multilateral development banks (MDBs) have been working to increase global investment in mega-infrastructure projects, including large dams, oil and gas pipelines, ports, highways, and railways. According to the IMF's Managing Director Christine Lagarde, US$90 trillion of infrastructure investment may be needed globally between the year 2016 and 2030.[6] Ms Lagarde observed, no doubt rightly, that the quality of investment in transport, energy, water, and other major infrastructure sectors 'could radically affect the quality of life on the planet—for all of us'.[7]

Following the eleventh G20 Summit in Hangzhou, China, in September 2016, a Global Infrastructure Connectivity Alliance was created to link regional infrastructure master plans, facilitate trade, increase economic activity, and—it is hoped—stimulate growth.[8] An annual Global Infrastructure Forum was inaugurated in the year 2016 to enhance coordination among the MDBs and facilitate project financing. The World Bank Group and other MDBs have established several infrastructure financing and project facilitation platforms in

[5] African Development Bank and others, 'From Billions to Trillions: Transforming Development Finance' (2015) <http://pubdocs.worldbank.org/en/622841485963735448/DC2015-0002-E-FinancingforDevelopment.pdf> accessed 28 May 2021.

[6] Christine Lagarde, 'The Role of Emerging Markets in a New Global Partnership for Growth by IMF Managing Director Christine Lagarde' (*IMF* 4 February 2016) <https://www.imf.org/en/News/Articles/2015/09/28/04/53/sp020416> accessed 1 September 2020.

[7] ibid.

[8] Report: Global Infrastructure Connectivity Alliance Initiative, <http://www.g20.utoronto.ca/2016/global-infrastructure-connectivity-alliance.pdf> accessed 28 May 2021.

order to attract private investment, standardize investment contracts and regulations, and help meet global demand. Moves are underway to financialize infrastructure as an asset class and create pipelines of 'bankable' projects to attract the trillions of dollars held by institutional investors such as pension funds and sovereign wealth funds that, in a climate of negative interest rates, are desperate for higher yields.

Infrastructure, if well-conceived and implemented, is vital for economic growth and national security.[9] However, the motivations for infrastructure investment are often as much political as economic,[10] and the G20's plans are laden with un-assessed human rights risk. Large dams, pipelines, major highways, and other mega-infrastructure projects have been lightning rods for social conflict, land grabs, and serious human rights violations, in all regions of the world. Recently reported examples include the Brumadinho dam collapse in Brazil,[11] the Ponte Morandi bridge collapse in Italy,[12] the North Dakota pipeline project in the United States,[13] the Kabira slum evictions in Nairobi,[14] and as reported by Philip in 2019, the Attapeu dam disaster in Lao PDR.[15] Even relatively modest infrastructure projects like the Agua Zarca dam in Honduras can have major adverse consequences for both communities and investors, if the appropriate preconditions and due diligence are not in place.[16]

When taken to scale, the risks are compounded. Regional infrastructure master plans include up to 100,000 km of new roads in Africa and 579 new projects in Latin America including highways, hydroelectric dams, and pipelines. China's Belt and Road Initiative (BRI), backed by the US$40 billion Silk Road Fund, AIIB, and China Development Bank, spans over seventy countries and includes transport links through conflict-ridden areas of Pakistan, Myanmar, and Central Asia's Fergana Valley.[17] The Delhi–Mumbai Industrial Corridor, the world's largest infrastructure project, may adversely affect up to 180 million people.[18] Land conflict around agribusiness and extractive projects in Indonesia was recently

[9] Cf 'TSC IntelBrief: U.S. Infrastructure a Serious Threat to National Security' (*The Soufan Center* 19 December 2017) <https://thesoufancenter.org/u-s-infrastructure-a-serious-threat-to-national-security-security/> accessed 1 September 2020.

[10] Bent Flyvbjerg, 'What You Should Know about Megaprojects and Why: An Overview' (2014) 45 Project Management Journal 6; Nicholas Hildyard, *Licensed Larceny: Infrastructure, Financial Extraction and the Global South* (Manchester University Press 2016) 55–84.

[11] For example, Dom Phillips, '"That's Going to Burst": Brazilian Dam Workers Say They Warned of Disaster' *The Guardian* (Brumadinho, 6 February 2019) <https://www.theguardian.com/world/2019/feb/06/brazil-dam-collapse-workers-say-they-warned-owners> accessed 1 September 2020.

[12] For example, Colin Caprani, 'Genoa Bridge Collapse a Sign of Things to Come If Infrastructure Maintenance Ignored' *ABC Australia* (16 August 2018).

[13] OHCHR, 'Native Americans Facing Excessive Force in North Dakota Pipeline Protests—UN Expert' *UN News* (Geneva, 15 November 2016) <https://www.ohchr.org/EN/NewsEvents/Pages/DisplayNews.aspx?NewsID=20868> accessed 1 September 2020.

[14] For example, Malavika Vartak, 'End Brutal Evictions, They Only Confirm Lip Service to Housing' *Nation* (30 September 2018) <https://nation.africahttps://nation.africa/kenya/blogs-opinion/opinion/end-brutal-evictions-they-only-confirm-lip-service-to-housing-93090> accessed 1 September 2020.

[15] OHCHR, 'UN Expert: Lao PDR's Economic Strategy Entrenches Poverty' *UN News* (Vientiane, 28 March 2019) <https://www.ohchr.org/EN/NewsEvents/Pages/DisplayNews.aspx?NewsID=24416&LangID=E> accessed 1 September 2020.

[16] Zeid Ra'ad Al Hussein, 'Human Rights Are Trampled in the Push to Build Infrastructure in Indigenous Regions | Miami Herald' *Miami Herald* (8 March 2017) <https://www.miamiherald.com/opinion/op-ed/article136884218.html> accessed 1 September 2020.

[17] Hildyard (n 10) 55–84; William W Grimes, 'The Belt & Road Initiative as Power Resource: Lessons from Japan | The Asan Forum' (15 April 2016) <http://www.theasanforum.org/the-belt-road-initiative-as-power-resource-lessons-from-japan/> accessed 1 September 2020. Counterintuitively, the world 'belt' refers to planned road and rail networks and 'road' refers to sea routes.

[18] Rina Chandran, 'More than 11 Million Face Eviction, Displacement as India Booms | Reuters' *Reuters* (Bangkok 9 April 2019) <https://www.reuters.com/article/us-india-landrights-eviction/more-than-11-million-face-eviction-displacement-as-india-booms-idUSKCN1RL1ER> accessed 1 September 2020; Raksha Kumar, 'Delhi Mumbai Corridor: How the World's Largest Infrastructure Project Is Uprooting Indian Farmers | Cities | The Guardian' *The Guardian* (15 September 2015) <https://www.theguardian.com/cities/2015/sep/15/

described as a 'brutal class war.'[19] The involvement of MDBs can help improve project quality but cannot compensate for governance gaps and weaknesses across transboundary projects and regional plans. In any case, MDB social and environmental safeguard policies are generally limited to the project footprint. The MDBs' increasing focus on leveraging private investment may curtail their direct involvement in projects and thereby limit the positive impacts of their safeguard policies.[20]

The dominant narrative in mega-infrastructure investment is 'de-risking' for investors, not for the individuals whose lives may be disrupted or ended by projects. The unspoken, or sometimes spoken, narrative seems to be that you need to break a few eggs to make an omelette. With disarming candour, the President of the AIIB has reportedly described people resisting forced resettlement as 'irrational' and that families should be willing to 'sacrifice' in the public interest.[21] In 2016 the former World Bank president, Dr Jim Kim, when questioned about the risks of hydro-dam projects and the killing of indigenous leader Berta Cáceres earlier that year in Honduras, remarked that 'you cannot do the work that we are trying to do and not have some of these "incidents" happen.'[22] Not to be outdone, at a panel event at the October 2016 Annual Meetings of the World Bank and IMF, the Oxford University economist Paul Collier railed against donor countries for continuing to fund social development ('the smiling face of the child') rather than subsidizing private sector infrastructure investment in African countries. Professor Collier's diatribe against moralizing opponents of urbanization and hydropower speaks eloquently to the mega-infrastructure zeitgeist:

> We need to completely reshape aid budgets from paying for the smiling face on the child, which has been the social agenda for the last 15 years, to actually doing the serious stuff of getting proper firms to go to countries that there is not a lot of money in. . . .NGOs are fixated on helping peasants, and it's just a false agenda. . . .[*And on energy policy*] . . . Governments won't let you use coal, and NGOs won't let you use hydropower. I grew up in Sheffield which flooded villages in order to make a dam. Now, there'd be moral outrage, human rights. My

indias-future-dmic-delhi-mumbai-industrial-corridor> accessed 1 September 2020; 'Delhi–Mumbai Industrial Corridor: Development Dilemmas' (*CauseBecause* 7 March 2016) <https://causebecause.com/delhi-mumbai-industrial-corridor-development-dilemmas/4495> accessed 1 September 2020; Hildyard (n 10) 55–57.

[19] ibid 73.

[20] Office of the UN High Commissioner for Human Rights and Heinrich-Böll-Stiftung, *The Other Infrastructure Gap: Sustainability Human Rights and Environmental Perspectives* (OHCHR and Heinrich Böll Foundation 2018), 118–19.

[21] Notes from AIIB seminar, 26 June 2016, Beijing, 'Infrastructure and Global Economic Growth' (on file with author).

[22] Dr Kim's statements are available at Union Theological Seminary, 'The Principle of Mercy: World Bank President Jim Yong Kim' (6 April 2016) 59:32", 1:01:47" <www.youtube.com/watch?v=tJWZ102R4LA>. For criticisms, see 'Open Letter / Unacceptable Statements of World Bank President Jim Kim on Berta Cáceres' Murder (09052016)' (*Initiativo Mesoamericana de Mujeres Defensoras de Derechos Humanos* 8 May 2016) <http://im-defensoras.org/2016/05/carta-publica-inaceptables-declaraciones-del-presidente-del-banco-mundial-sr-jim-kim-sobre-asesinato-de-berta-caceres/carta-banco-mundial-08052016-english/> accessed 1 September 2020; Abogadas y Abogados para la Justicia y los Derechos Humanos, AC, 'Letter to President Kim Ref. to Berta Caceres and Dams' (11 May 2016) <https://aida-americas.org/sites/default/files/featured_pubs/letter_to_dr._kim_ref._berta_caceres_and_dams_more_than_300_org_may_2016.pdf> accessed 1 September 2020; for the World Bank's response see Dr Jim Yong, 'World Bank Group Fact Sheet: Honduras and Indigenous People' (*The World Bank*, Honduras 11 May 2016) <https://www.worldbank.org/en/topic/indigenouspeoples/brief/honduras-and-indigenous-people> accessed 1 September 2020; for a rebuttal of Dr Kim's assertions regarding resettlement and large dams see Peter Bosshard, 'Setting the World Bank President Straight On Large Dams' *Huffpost* (26 April 2016) <https://www.huffpost.com/entry/setting-the-world-bank-pr_b_9782060> accessed 1 September 2020.

> human right to have a drink would be ignored in the interest of the human rights of a few villagers running around.[23]

The message is clear: the business of infrastructure is no place for the faint-hearted, let alone the bleeding-hearted.

But the bleeding hearts have a highly compelling case. Globally, the construction industry, along with fishing, textile, and agriculture, is pervaded by forced labour, both on the construction site and in the building materials supply chain.[24] According to Transparency International, corruption in the construction sector is a bigger problem than in mining, real estate, or even the arms market, resulting in unnecessary, unreliable, dangerous, and overpriced projects, poverty, and loss of life.[25] Moreover concrete was recently described by the *Guardian* newspaper as 'the most destructive material on earth', given health, habitat, carbon emissions, water over-consumption, and other environmental effects, as well as corruption and the increasing control over sand production by armed groups.[26] In order to supply BRI projects, China's largest cement producer has announced plans to construct a hundred cement factories in fifty countries.[27] Unless production and sourcing techniques improve dramatically, absent positive shifts in the political economy of concrete production, the cumulative adverse impacts may be colossal and irreversible.

Human rights problems typically begin with poor transparency and consultation guarantees and practices. Regional infrastructure master plans are rarely if ever consulted or subjected to public debate. National disclosure requirements for major infrastructure projects are often very weak, and information is withheld under overly broad commercial-in-confidence or national security exceptions.[28] In a recent independent survey of eight hundred people affected by infrastructure and extractive industries projects world-wide, 94 per cent stated that they had never been consulted about their development priorities for the country or region, 88 per cent said that they had not been consulted during the planning phase of the project, 85 per cent stated that they didn't think that their ideas or opinions were incorporated into project plans, and 64 per cent said that they did not know where to find project information.[29] Only 10 per cent expressed the view that the project in question would benefit their communities.[30] Failure stakeholder engagement in turn frequently leads to social conflict and failed projects.[31]

[23] Namrata Brar, 'IMF: Toward Better Infrastructure in Developing Countries' (5 October 2016) 12'25", 44'50", 45'25" <www.imf.org/external/POS_Meetings/SeminarDetails_archive.aspx?SeminarId=177> accessed 1 September 2020.

[24] Von Elgg and Jantine Werdmuller, 'Hidden in Plain Sight Modern Slavery in the Construction Industry' White Paper. London: LexisNexis Business Insight Solutions, 2016 <https://bis.lexisnexis.co.uk/pdf/whitepapers/Modern_Slavery_in_Construction_Full.pdf> accessed 10 August 2021

[25] 'Preventing Corruption on Construction Projects' (*Transparency International* 20 February 2005) <https://www.transparency.org/en/news/preventing-corruption-on-construction-projects> accessed 1 September 2020.

[26] Jonathan Watts, 'Concrete: The Most Destructive Material on Earth' *The Guardian* (25 February 2019) <https://www.theguardian.com/cities/2019/feb/25/concrete-the-most-destructive-material-on-earth> accessed 1 September 2020.

[27] Angus McNeice, 'China to Build 100 Cement Plants in Belt and Road Region' *China Daily* (London, 13 December 2017) <//global.chinadaily.com.cn/a/201712/13/WS5a3015c8a3108bc8c672b094.html> accessed 1 September 2020.

[28] OHCHR (n 20) 36, 44.

[29] Ryan Schlief and International Accountability Project, 'What Development Is and What It Could Be' (*Mediun*) <https://medium.com/@accountability/what-development-is-and-what-it-could-be-ddf47eaa0608> accessed 1 September 2020.

[30] ibid.

[31] Graham Watkins and others, 'Lessons from Four Decades of Infrastructure Project-Related Conflicts in Latin America and the Caribbean' (Inter-American Development Bank 2017) <https://publications.iadb.org/handle/11319/8502> accessed 1 September 2020.

There are particularly serious shortcomings in the mega-infrastructure investment from a gender perspective. The problems begin at a deep, structural level, as the mega-infrastructure world is populated by the traditionally male-dominated professions of finance and engineering, and success is measured by size and speed rather than sustainability of outcomes or quality of process or due diligence.[32] In transport projects, the World Bank has noted that project designs often privilege men's commuting patterns rather than women's needs and uses, and fail to include differentiated assessment of personal security needs and affordability constraints.[33] In energy projects, men have typically dominated decision-making, and very little attention has been given to identifying, monitoring, and mitigating adverse project impacts on women.[34] Women frequently suffer discrimination in connection with employment, and compensation payments from energy projects are typically paid to the male heads of households, to the detriment of the human rights of women and girls.[35]

Infrastructure projects and plans may be discriminatory in more subtle and structural ways, mirroring and reinforcing existing patterns of social stratification. For example, in the United States, certain infrastructure programmes have reportedly contributed to 'metropolitan fragmentation that facilitated white flight and class stratification', while minority populations remained in high-density inner-city high rises. Subsequently, as inner-city areas gentrified, the highway systems reportedly had the effect of 'stitching together the affluent, white components of the fragmented metropolis',[36] thereby perpetuating segregation. Water infrastructure projects may be associated with user fees or connection charges that limit or preclude access by low-income populations, contrary to international human rights law.[37] Project designs are also frequently insensitive to the accessibility concerns and human rights of persons with disabilities.[38]

Infrastructure projects and other development initiatives are increasingly being implemented in hostile political conditions and at great risk to human rights defenders. In the year 2016, more than one thousand people in twenty-five countries were reportedly murdered, harassed, imprisoned, or intimidated while defending their community's rights.[39] Women, often first to defend their homes and children, accounted for more than half of those killed.[40] In the vast majority of cases, killings were preceded by warnings, death threats, and intimidation, which were reported to police authorities but ignored.[41] Development projects have been among the greatest causes of displacement of communities, with approximately fifteen

[32] For a light-hearted but thought-provoking reflection along similar lines see Jeff Delmon, 'Mythbusters: Overcoming Macho Tendencies in Funding Toll Roads' (World Bank 1 December 2016) <https://blogs.worldbank.org/ppps/mythbusters-overcoming-macho-tendencies-funding-toll-roads> accessed 1 September 2020; for evidence of gender bias in the EIB *see* Maïa de La Baume, 'Macho Time Warp at the European Investment Bank' *Politico* (25 August 2017) <https://www.politico.eu/article/european-investment-bank-a-mens-club-at-the-top/> accessed 1 September 2020.

[33] Koskenniemi (n 1).

[34] OHCHR (n 20) 61, 72.

[35] ibid 61, 72.

[36] ibid 79; Mason B Williams, 'The Precedent for Donald Trump's Infrastructure Plan—The Atlantic' *The Atlantic* (7 January 2017) <www.theatlantic.com/politics/archive/2017/01/trump-infrastructure-cities/512432/> accessed 1 September 2020.

[37] OHCHR (n 20) 68–69.

[38] ibid 73–73.

[39] Paola Totaro and Matthew Ponsford, 'Politics of Death: Body Count Mounts in Worldwide Wars over Land' *Reuters* (London, 20 June 2017) <https://www.reuters.com/article/us-landrights-violence-activists-idUSKBN19B02H> accessed 1 September 2020; 'Murdered for Their Rivers: A Roster of Fallen Dam Fighters' (*International Rivers*) <www.internationalrivers.org/murdered-for-their-rivers-a-roster-of-fallen-dam-fighters/> accessed 1 September 2020.

[40] ibid.

[41] ibid.

million people having been forced off their land per year since the mid-2000s.[42] Following his recent visit to Lao PDR, for example, Philip remarked: 'High profile instances of reprisals, arrests, and disappearances of people who have pushed ever so gently against the envelope send chilling and highly effective messages to Lao people who want to participate in addressing important and complex public issues.'[43]

This crisis is occurring amidst worsening conditions for civil society organizations generally. The incentives of government authorities and national elites to victimize those opposing infrastructure projects can be powerful and do not depend on a country's level of development. In the United States, for example, following protests over the Dakota Access Pipeline, lawmakers in six states introduced legislation protecting drivers of motor vehicles who kill or injure protestors.[44] Governments worldwide have increasingly been clamping down on NGOs, curtailing the right to freedom of peaceful assembly, attacking independent media organizations, increasing state censorship, promulgating draconian anti-terror laws, encouraging vilification and incitement to violence against opposition groups, and engaging in surveillance, arbitrary detention, torture, and disappearances. In some countries, punitive laws and special law enforcement agencies have been created specifically to protect investors' interests.[45]

Beyond the project footprint, mega-infrastructure projects can also impact negatively on human rights indirectly by creating a drain on public budgets and limiting the resources available for the progressive realization of economic and social rights. Megaprojects have a poor track record of implementation,[46] particularly in low-income countries and non-competitive sectors. It has been reported that nine out of ten mega-infrastructure projects are beset by cost overruns.[47] Megaprojects are often driven by political motives and 'delusional optimism' that occlude proper assessment of the potential benefits and risks,[48]

[42] Alexandra Bilak and others, 'Global Report on Internal Displacement' (Internal Displacement Monitoring Centre 2016), 44 <https://www.internal-displacement.org/globalreport2016/> accessed 1 September 2020.

[43] OHCHR (n 15).

[44] The states are North Dakota, North Carolina, Florida, Tennessee, Texas, and Rhode Island, although as of 2020 none of the bills had yet passed into law. Dakin Andone, 'These States Have Introduced Bills to Protect Drivers Who Run over Protesters' *CNN* (19 August 2017) <https://edition.cnn.com/2017/08/18/us/legislation-protects-drivers-injure-protesters/index.html> accessed 1 September 2020; for further evidence of intimidation and victimization of environmental defenders in the United States see Yulia Genin and others, 'Dangerous Work: Increasing Pressure on Environmental NGOs and Activists in the Countries of the Former Soviet Union and the US' (Crude Accountability 2017) <http://crudeaccountability.org/wp-content/uploads/DangerousWorkReport.pdf>, 57–63.

[45] Examples include Pakistan Khurram Husain, 'Hidden Costs of CPEC' *DAWN* (29 September 2016) <http://www.dawn.com/news/1286698> accessed 1 September 2020 and Mexico 'Gendarmería debe proteger derechos de personas y no intereses empresariales' (*Fundar, Centro de Análisis e Investigación* 21 October 2014) <https://fundar.org.mx/gendarmeria-debe-proteger-derechos-de-personas-y-intereses-empresariales/> accessed 1 September 2020.

[46] Flyvbjerg (n 10) 6–19; World Bank, *World Bank Group Support to Public–Private Partnerships: Lessons from Experience in Client Countries, FY02–12* (World Bank 2015) <http://elibrary.worldbank.org/doi/book/10.1596/978-1-4648-0630-8> accessed 1 September 2020 (noting a range of challenges in connection with the World Bank's support to PPPs including a lack of adequate focus on fiscal implications of PPPs and a lack of data on the impacts on the poor).

[47] Flyvbjerg (n 10) 9.

[48] Bent Flyvbjerg, Massimo Garbuio, and Dan Lovallo, 'Delusion and Deception in Large Infrastructure Projects Two Models for Explaining and Preventing Executive Disaster' (2009) 51(2) California Management Review 170, 5; for an illustration see Nadia Naviwala, 'Pakistan's $100B Deal with China: What Does It Amount To?' *Devex* (Islamabad, 24 August 2017) <https://www.devex.com/news/sponsored/pakistan-s-100b-deal-with-china-what-does-it-amount-to-90872> accessed 1 September 2020, noting that 'Chinese [infrastructure] financing is driven by their own need to deploy excess human, financial and technical resources … What they offer coincides with the interests of politicians who are looking for short-term gains—much like Pakistan's current government, which is in a rush to conclude agreements and get projects off the ground during its term, which started in 2013 and will end with elections in 2018.'

including human rights risks. Promoters of large-scale infrastructure projects often have incentives to deliberately underestimate complexity and inflate the benefit–cost ratio at the early stages of a project, in order to compete successfully for project funding. In what some have called 'debt-trap diplomacy', governments may also be tempted to trade off their own country's longer-term sovereignty and economic well-being for the short-run rush of a big-ticket mega-infrastructure project.[49] The long timeframe of many mega-infrastructure projects usually ensures that those responsible for poor planning are free from any adverse consequences when the project goes (sometimes literally) off the rails.[50] These pathologies are captured in what Bent Flyvbjerg from Oxford University's Said Business School describes as the 'iron law' of megaprojects: 'Over budget, over time, over and over again.'[51]

Another indirect but potentially profound way that human rights can be impacted negatively by mega-infrastructure projects is through the failure to integrate climate resilience and sustainability at the design stage, thereby risking locking in carbon-intensive technology for generations. As a key input to concrete, cement is responsible for approximately 8 per cent of global carbon dioxide emissions each year.[52] The driving rationales of the G20's and MDBs' mega-infrastructure agenda include increased connectivity, competition, trade facilitation, economic stimulus, and a desire to support global and national efforts to meet the SDGs, including Goals 6–9 and 13.[53] However, on the current state of things, regional infrastructure master plans, which are rarely the subject of parliamentary debate or public consultation, risk locking in an environmentally and socially destructive 'extract and export' model of development, potentially exacerbating inequalities between population groups and sowing the seeds for serious human rights violations for generations to come.[54] Even if project designs could be improved, national regulatory and institutional capacities and incentives to manage mega-infrastructure projects are often weak.[55]

[49] For example, 'The Perils of China's "Debt-Trap Diplomacy"' *The Economist* (6 September 2018) <https://www.economist.com/asia/2018/09/06/the-perils-of-chinas-debt-trap-diplomacy> accessed 1 September 2020.

[50] Flyvbjerg and others (n 48) 15–16.

[51] Bent Flyvbjerg, 'Introduction: The Iron Law of Megaproject Management' in Bent Flyvbjerg (ed), *The Oxford Handbook of Megaproject Management* (OUP 2017) ch 1, 1–18, at 11.

[52] Johana Lehne and Felix Preston, 'Making Concrete Change: Innovation in Low-Carbon Cement and Concrete' (Chatham House 2018) p 1 <https://www.chathamhouse.org/sites/default/files/publications/2018-06-13-making-concrete-change-cement-lehne-preston-exec-sum.pdf> accessed 28 May 2021.

[53] Goal 6: Ensure availability and sustainable management of water and sanitation for all; Goal 7: Ensure access to affordable, reliable, sustainable and modern energy for all; Goal 8: Promote sustained, inclusive and sustainable economic growth, full and productive employment and decent work for all; Goal 9: Build resilient infrastructure, promote inclusive and sustainable industrialization and foster innovation; Goal 13: Take urgent action to address climate change and its impacts. The latter goal was something of a placeholder, and has been monitored principally through the more specific subsequent provisions of the 2015 Paris Agreement. United Nations, 'Sustainable Development' <https://sustainabledevelopment.un.org/topics/sustainabledevelopmentgoals> accessed 8 September 2020.

[54] 'Infrastructure: For People or for Profit? The Crucial Role of Responsible and Democratic Governance' (Heinrich Böll Foundation North America, undated); Pétalla Brandão Timo, 'Development at the Cost of Violations' (2017) 10(18) SUR International Journal of Human Rights, 136–57 <https://sur.conectas.org/en/development-cost-violations/> accessed 8 September 2020; Hildyard (n 10). The fact that the master plans connect with one another also implies that global sourcing and the transportation and externalities that this entails may displace local sourcing on a significant scale. Fossil fuel subsidies and use contribute to significant health and air quality problems, and coal mines are disproportionate consumers of energy and water resources. Big hydro projects may generate significant greenhouse gas emissions, and the benefits to local consumers, particularly those in rural areas, are frequently oversold.

[55] For example, 'The 2015 Infrascope: Evaluating the Environment for Publc Private Partnerships in Africa' (The Economist Intelligence Unit 2015), 13–17 noting that only one country (South Africa) out of the fifteen surveyed had 'developed' institutional capacities to manage infrastructure PPPs; ibid 22, where the local capacities of eight of the fifteen sampled countries was assessed only as 'nascent'.

Financing arrangements for infrastructure have very significant (even if indirect) human rights implications. The 'billions to trillions' agenda is predicated upon a radical reconceptualization of official aid as a means of subsidizing infrastructure investment and risk-taking by the private sector in so-called frontier markets. Mega-infrastructure projects have potentially lengthy construction and operation phases, with significant fiscal risks for governments and commercial risks for investors and operators. Depending upon how financing for a given project is structured, and depending upon the kinds of guarantees and other inducements that are offered to investors, infrastructure projects may create unsustainable fiscal burdens for governments and unaffordable services for many population groups. The lure of infrastructure investment, competition among financers, and demands of foreign investors may create incentives for a regulatory race-to-the-bottom on environmental protection, labour rights, social protection, personal security, and other vital issues.[56]

PPPs have become the instrument of choice for mega-infrastructure investment, apparently driven as much by theology as evidence, and often contain lopsided risk guarantees and damaging off-budget liabilities as the price for private sector participation.[57] Investment agreements, PPP laws, and PPP contracts may create a regulatory 'chill', constraining states from exercising their right (and duty) to regulate in the public interest and implement relevant international environmental and human rights agreements.[58] Political risk guarantees (such as 'Material Adverse Government Action' provisions in PPP contracts) may unfairly protect investors for losses relating to war, riots, and other events over which the host government may have little if any control, and—where strike action is included—may create incentives for oppressive labour practices and violations of the rights to freedom of association, freedom of expression, the right to form trade unions, and a potential raft of other human rights.[59] Investor–State Dispute Settlement (ISDS), a standard feature in PPP contracts, has been criticized as being inherently biased towards investors and beyond repair.[60]

For governments already facing fiscal austerity, contingent liabilities from PPPs may displace critical investments in socio-economic rights and environmental protection, and in some cases even lead to unsustainable debt burdens and macro-economic crisis. In Portugal, for example, the government's over-exposure to PPP liabilities allegedly contributed to an economic crisis which, in May 2011, forced it to seek an international bailout.[61] Fiscal risks of this kind may be compounded in the future through the creation of asset-based securities such as collateralized debt obligations and credit default swaps, designed to fully exploit infrastructure as an asset class.[62] The bundling of interests in infrastructure into new

[56] For a more comprehensive analysis of financing risks see OHCHR (n 20) 115–50.

[57] ibid 35–39, 75–79, 139–40.

[58] ibid 95–99.

[59] ibid 107.

[60] ibid 17, and more generally 90–114.

[61] OHCHR (n 20) 139–40. The European Parliament has expressed concerns regarding the EIB's support for infrastructure PPPs, noting that 'flawed PPPs have turned into an expensive system of public financing of the private sector, generating public debt', and that 'such operations often face problems of opacity as well as asymmetric information in the execution clauses between the public and private agents, normally in favour of the private sector'; 'European Investment Bank Annual Report' (2013) P8_TA(2015)0183 para 21.

[62] OHCHR (n 20) 39, 46–47; Kenneth Rapoza, 'China Blowing Major Bubbles In 2017' (*Forbes* 19 December 2016) <https://www.forbes.com/sites/kenrapoza/2016/12/19/china-bubble-economy-2017/#8daeae947452> accessed 8 September 2020; Maha Khan Phillips, 'Are Investors Expecting Too Much from Infrastructure?' (*CFA Institute* 12 January 2016) <https://blogs.cfainstitute.org/investor/2016/01/12/are-investors-expecting-too-much-from-infrastructure/> accessed 8 September 2020; Arleen Jacobius, 'Supply-Demand Issue to Hit Infrastructure' (*Pensions & Investments* 26 January 2015) <https://www.pionline.com/article/20150126/PRINT/301269981/supply-demand-issue-to-hit-infrastructure> accessed 8 September 2020; for a critique of the European Commission and EIB's 'Project Bonds Initiative' (PBI), designed to improve the ratings of infrastructure bonds and attract institutional investors, see 'The Castor Project' (*Counter Balance* 3 January 2014) <http://www.

financial products and putative new asset classes may conceal and inadvertently magnify human rights risks inherent in the underlying infrastructure assets, and may complicate the quest for accountability when things go wrong.[63] The mortgage-backed security bubble in 2007 brings to mind the potential folly of financial engineering of this kind absent full transparency and a strong regulatory framework.

17.3 Genocide as an Infrastructure Risk

One place where these risks converge quite dramatically is Myanmar. Myanmar is a resource-rich country, however, its long period of political and economic isolation, and the armed conflicts that continue to ravage the country, have seriously impeded the country's development prospects and eroded its infrastructure. As of the year 2017, only 20 per cent of Myanmar's roads were sealed, and 65 per cent of the population lacked access to the national electricity grid.[64] The Asian Development Bank (ADB) has estimated that the 'infrastructure gap' in Myanmar—the difference between investment needs and current investment levels—will be US$120 billion between now and the year 2030.

Since the year 2012, international investors and development financing institutions have descended upon Myanmar in droves, hopeful for high-yielding investments in infrastructure and other economic sectors. Interest has been stimulated by Myanmar's abundant natural resources, governance reforms, economic liberalization, and relatively youthful labour force. Also relevant is the fact that Myanmar is situated at the intersection of China and India, two of the world's most important emerging markets. Myanmar's geographic location makes it an important component in the BRI, offering China an important sea route and source of energy through its landlocked Western provinces.[65] Infrastructure projects supported by MDBs have included rural roads, major highways, port construction, telecommunications projects, cement production, energy transmission and distribution facilities, gas-fired power plants, and water and other basic services. The Myanmar government has announced its intention to begin work on projects under the China–Myanmar Economic Corridor agreement, which is part of the BRI.[66] The projects reportedly include the controversial (and stalled) Myitsone Dam and Kyaukphyu-Kunming Railway projects, and economic cooperation projects in the border regions of Shan and Kachin.[67]

Infrastructure investment in Myanmar, while sorely needed, presents particular human rights risks for investors and development financing institutions to consider. Many of the human rights risk factors outlined earlier may be relevant to any given infrastructure project in the Myanmar context, such as forced displacement and livelihood destruction; land seizures; human trafficking and sexual violence; abusive labour practices; and so on. A major

counter-balance.org/the-castor-project/> accessed 8 September 2020; European Parliament (n 61) paras 32–33, directing the EIB to evaluate problematic as well as profitable PBI projects and to undertake remedial actions in relation to the Castor Project in Spain, where the EIB's environmental due diligence was reportedly weak).

[63] OHCHR (n 20) 72, 120–26.

[64] Baker McKenzie, 'Building Myanmar: Bridging the Infrastructure Gap' (The Economist Corporate Network 2017), 5, 12.

[65] ibid 7.

[66] Nan Lwin, 'China's Six Belt and Road Projects in Myanmar to Watch in 2019' *The Irrawaddy* (Yangon, 24 January 2019), <https://www.irrawaddy.com/specials/chinas-six-belt-road-projects-myanmar-watch-2019.html> accessed 8 September 2020.

[67] ibid.

highway project in Kachin state, part of BRI's East–West Economic Corridor, has been associated with armed conflict, forced displacement, poor consultation practices and environmental damage.[68] Poor stakeholder engagement was reportedly among the factors leading to the suspension of the Myitsone Dam joint venture between China and Myanmar.[69] Telecommunications tower construction and fibre cable projects have been associated with child labour, debt bondage, and other labour rights violations.[70] Up to twenty thousand indigenous persons may have lost their livelihoods when their lands were confiscated during the construction of the crude oil pipeline between Kyaukpyu, in Rakhine state, and Kunming, China.[71]

The push for PPP financing and operating arrangements for infrastructure projects in Myanmar,[72] should significant commitments materialize, may raise particularly high fiscal risks arising from contingent liabilities and unfair risk allocation between investors and the public, given Myanmar's relatively weak administrative capacities and poor traditions of transparency and public accountability. Corruption may exacerbate fiscal risks. In Myanmar, or any militarized state or weak governance environment, user fees and other infrastructure project revenue streams may easily find their way into the pockets of the perpetrators of human rights abuses. Moreover, China's investment in a special economic zone in Kyaukpyu, southern Rakhine state, which includes a US$7.3 billion deep seaport and oil and gas pipelines from Rakhine to China's Yunnan province, has generated fears that the government of China may be seeking to exercise leverage over Myanmar through the imposition of unsustainable debt obligations.[73]

The government's recent ethnic cleansing campaign against the Rohingya raises the risks and stakes in infrastructure investment. Conflict-related risks are (or should be) well known to investors and development financing institutions in Myanmar, however, the situation in northern Rakhine state demands heightened vigilance and universal condemnation. In August 2017, in circumstances that are well known, a 'slow genocide'[74] against the minority Rohingya population in northern Rakhine state rapidly escalated into full-blown ethnic cleansing operations, killing thousands of people and eventually expelling nearly 800,000

[68] Su Myat Mon, 'An Army, a Mountain and the Asian Development Bank' *Frontier Myanmar* (2018) <https://www.frontiermyanmar.net/en/an-army-a-mountain-and-the-asian-development-bank/> accessed 8 September 2020; Su Myat Mon and Thomas Kean, 'ADB Puts Brakes on Kayin State Quarry' *Frontier Myanmar* (2018) <https://www.frontiermyanmar.net/en/adb-puts-brakes-on-kayin-state-quarry/> accessed 8 September 2020.

[69] Aung Zaw, 'Myitsone Dam Is Now a Sovereignty Issue' *The Irrawaddy* (1 April 2019) <https://www.irrawaddy.com/opinion/commentary/myitsone-dam-now-sovereignty-issue.html> accessed 8 September 2020.

[70] 'Myanmar ICT Sector-Wide Impact Assessment' (Myanmar Centre for Responsible Business, Institute for Human Rights and Business, Danish Institute for Human Rights 2015) 194–200.

[71] Nava Thakuria, 'With India in Sleep Mode on Myanmar Project, China Begins Pipeline | Tehelka—Investigations, Latest News, Politics, Analysis, Blogs, Culture, Photos, Videos, Podcasts' *Tehelka* (8 November 2017) <http://old.tehelka.com/with-india-in-sleep-mode-on-myanmar-project-china-begins-pipeline/> accessed 18 September 2020; Subir Bhaumik, 'Why Do China, India Back Myanmar over the Rohingya Crisis?' *South China Morning Post* (18 October 2017) <https://www.scmp.com/week-asia/geopolitics/article/2115839/why-do-china-india-back-myanmar-over-rohingya-crisis> accessed 18 September 2020.

[72] For example, Juliet Shwe Guang, 'IFC Pushes for PPP Projects to Spruce up Myanmar Infrastructure' *Deal Street Asia* (17 January 2018) <https://www.dealstreetasia.com/stories/elevated-expressway-yangon-draw-400m-private-investment-90203/> accessed 8 September 2020.

[73] Bhaumik (n 71); Nyshka Chandran, 'Ethnic Cleansing in Myanmar Threatens Chinese Investments. Beijing Is Taking Action' *CNBC* (22 November 2017) <www.cnbc.com/2017/11/22/chinas-peace-plan-for-myanmar-has-a-business-agenda.html> accessed 8 September 2020; China's investment in the Hambantota port in Sri Lanka has been criticized on similar grounds, see Kai Schultz, 'Sri Lanka, Struggling With Debt, Hands a Major Port to China' *The New York Times* (12 December 2017) <https://www.nytimes.com/2017/12/12/world/asia/sri-lanka-china-port.html> accessed 8 September 2020.

[74] Amartya Sen, 'The Slow Genocide of the Rohingya' (21 May 2016), particularly from 1'30" to 2'10" <www.youtube.com/watch?v=ugHhAwARb98 > accessed 8 September 2020.

over the border to Bangladesh. The abuses by the Myanmar authorities attracted widespread condemnation from governments, civil society organizations, major business entitles and investors, and certain MDBs (notably, the World Bank and ADB). In December 2017 the UN High Commissioner for Human Rights remarked that the abuses carried out against the Rohingya may meet the legal threshold for the crime of genocide.[75] The February 2021 military coup has been associated with allegations of possible crimes against humanity.[76]

In September 2018 an 'independent and impartial fact-finding mission' (FFM) established by UN Human Rights Council resolution 34/22 (2017) reported on evidence of gross human rights violations, crimes against humanity, and war crimes in Kachin, Shan, and Rakhine states and evidence of genocidal intent in the crimes committed against the Rohingya.[77] The FFM's report found that there was sufficient information to warrant the investigation and prosecution of senior officials in the military chain of command, so that a competent court could determine their liability for genocide in relation to the situation in Rakhine State. The report listed a number of alleged perpetrators as priority subjects for investigation and prosecution, and documented how the political economy of development had contributed to the causes of conflict.[78] Of direct relevance to Myanmar's future development plans, the report also identified a number of geographic areas where Myanmar authorities had bulldozed razed Rohingya villages or were constructing new roads, housing, or other infrastructure, as part of an apparent effort to conceal evidence of international crimes.[79]

In a noteworthy methodological development for a UN human rights mechanism, the FFM's reporting included a detailed analysis of the economic interests of the Tatmadaw, using financial databases to trace domestic and foreign ownership of commercial enterprises associated with senior military figures.[80] The FFM's reporting has informed subsequent international criminal prosecutions[81] and provides a valuable roadmap to guide the due diligence of would-be investors and financers of infrastructure in Myanmar, particularly in helping to identify and navigate the extreme human rights risks in Shan, Kachin, and northern Rakhine states. Some risks are more obvious than others; for example, the building of new resettlement camps for displaced Rohingya may effectively preclude the latter from returning to their homes,[82] and hence should not be supported. The FFM has documented how the construction of approximately eight hundred houses in the Muangdaw township, an area heavily hit by the ethnic cleansing operations, disproportionately benefits ethnic Rakhine and other population groups (to the detriment of the Rohingya), in an evident attempt to

[75] Nick Cumming-Bruce, 'Myanmar's Rohingya Actions May Be Genocide, U.N. Official Says' *The New York Times* (Geneva, 5 December 2017) <www.nytimes.com/2017/12/05/world/asia/myanmar-rohingya-genocide-un.html> accessed 8 September 2020.

[76] See <https://www.ohchr.org/EN/NewsEvents/Pages/DisplayNews.aspx?NewsID=26989&LangID=E> accessed 14 July 2021.

[77] UNHRC, 'Report of the Detailed Findings of the Independent International Fact-Finding Mission on Myanmar' (17 September 2018) UN Doc A/HRC/39/CRP.2.

[78] ibid paras 382–88 (on military leaders' responsibilities), paras 98, 110–11, 407, 413, 746 (on links between development and conflict).

[79] ibid paras 1182, 1216–244.

[80] UNHRC, 'The Economic Interests of the Myanmar Military' (12 September 2019), UN Doc A/HRC/42/CRP.3.

[81] Most notably, see *Application of the Convention on the Prevention and Punishment of Genocide (The Gambia v Myanmar)* [2020] ICJ 178, [22], [27]–[28], [46], [54]–[55], [71]–[72].

[82] Francesca Morano, '"We Will Lose Any Hope of Going Home": Rohingya Live in Fear of Resettlement' *The Guardian* (Sittwe, 2 May 2019) <https://www.theguardian.com/global-development/2019/may/02/we-will-lose-any-hope-of-going-home-rohingya-live-in-fear-of-resettlement-myanmar-rakhine-state> accessed 8 September 2020.

change the demographic composition of northern Rakhine state.[83] The military coup has imperilled the Rohingya further.[84]

But other risks are more novel and subtle, rooted in the deeply ingrained discrimination, lack of citizenship rights and freedom of movement of the Rohingya and other Muslim minority groups. Even ostensibly benign (and desperately needed) projects like the extension of the electricity grid and connection of basic services may have the effect of excluding the Rohingya, if the systematic denial of their rights prevents them from taking advantage of development opportunities on the same footing as others. The government's acquisition of 'burned lands' under Myanmar's Natural Disaster Management Law creates additional barriers.[85] Should the infrastructure plans for Rakhine state in any way frustrate the safe, sustainable return of displaced Rohingya populations to their homes, those financing or investing in those projects may be complicit in ethnic cleansing. Should international firms or development financing institutions provide raw materials or financial or other support for roads, buildings, or other infrastructure development on or around potential crime scenes, as documented by the FFM or its successor body,[86] they may frustrate international criminal investigations and, effectively, be complicit in genocide.

17.4 Concluding Thoughts

This chapter is not an argument against infrastructure investment in conflict-affected contexts or elsewhere. To the contrary: it is an argument in favour of human rights due diligence, which—from an investor's or development finance institution's perspective—is principally an obligation of conduct. The complexities that have been discussed cannot be boiled down to a binary question of 'to invest or not to invest', or 'do I stay or do I go'. However, human rights policies of firms and development financing institutions (which are a threshold component of human rights due diligence)[87] should certainly include a description of the circumstances in which a responsible exit may be warranted, within a broader discussion of mitigation responsibilities, partnerships, leverage mechanisms, and redress options. A human rights policy of this kind, backed by effective monitoring, public reporting, and an independent accountability mechanism, may contribute greatly to sustainable infrastructure investment and operate as a defence for development finance institutions when—despite best efforts—things go wrong.

Human rights risks have been well documented in the design and implementation phases of energy, transport, water, and other infrastructure projects, but have been addressed by human rights organizations in mostly a reactive way in practice, often after the damage is done. This is not to impugn 'reactive' strategies, which may be the last line of defence for affected populations. Far from it. But as we have seen, human rights risks are also embedded in the design of regional and national infrastructure master plans, in financing and investment policy, and in the regulatory framework for infrastructure investment and PPPs at the

[83] UNHRC, 'Report of the Detailed Findings' (n 77) paras 1224–229.

[84] See <https://www.un.org/sg/en/content/note-correspondents-joint-statement-un-special-adviser-the-prevention-of-genocide-and-un-high-commissioner-for-human-rights-myanmar> accessed 14 July 2021.

[85] ibid paras 1217–219.

[86] UNHRC, 'Situation of Human Rights of Rohingya Muslims and other Minorities in Myanmar' (3 October 2018) UN Doc A/RES/39/2 paras 22–23.

[87] 'Guiding Principles on Business and Human Rights' (Office of the UN High Commissioner for Human Rights 2011) HR/PUB/11/04, Principle 15.

national level. The latter risk factors are comparatively less well known, but a more concerted focus at these levels could serve an important preventive function, as a critical complement to the vital life-saving and restorative work undertaken by human rights and development practitioners on the ground.

In 2018, Philip submitted a report to the UN General Assembly on privatization.[88] The report exposes the mixed evidence on privatization in different domains, critically analyses competing narratives and the track record of human rights organizations, and excoriates the proponents of privatization as an ideology of governance. Infrastructure, social services, and the public goods are discussed, and in his press release accompanying the report Philip warned: 'There is a real risk that the waves of privatisation experienced to date will soon be followed by a veritable tsunami.'[89]

Philip's privatization report has been vindicated *post facto* by the COVID-19 pandemic which, among many other things, has revealed the calamitous human and economic costs of weak regulation and underinvestment in public health, education, and social protection systems. For human rights practitioners, Philip's report provides a welcome reminder of the power of narrative, the need to embrace complexity, and the importance of engaging with the political economy and competing ideological frames through which human rights are achieved or denied. The report is partly an admonishment of human rights practitioners, or at least, those wedded to conventional biases. But it is also a timely invitation to pull our canoes from the reeds and eddies, check our bearings, and paddle hard upstream.

[88] Note by the Secretary General, 'Extreme Poverty and Human Rights' (2018) UN Doc A/73/396.

[89] 'UN Poverty Expert Warns against Tsunami of Unchecked Privatisation' *UN News* (New York, 19 October 2018) <https://www.ohchr.org/EN/NewsEvents/Pages/DisplayNews.aspx?NewsID=23740&LangID=E> accessed 8 September 2020.

18
Dilemmas Facing Commissions of Inquiry

Andrew Clapham

18.1 Introduction

Philip Alston was amongst the first to herald the significance and effectiveness of international Commissions of Inquiry (COIs) as a response to human rights violations.[1] He nevertheless also presented to the UN HRC a critical analysis of the shortcomings of *national* COIs.[2] He served on various Commissions, including the Commission set up by the Security Council on the Central African Republic, and this chapter seeks to build on some of the ideas that he advanced in this context. I know Philip would be disappointed by a chapter that simply recounted his exploits and described the increasing resort to international COIs, so I have sought to offer an 'insider perspective' on some of the dilemmas faced by international Commissions in the contemporary context. It was Philip who, early on in my career, impressed on me the importance of revealing one's perspective, and of setting up counterarguments before demolishing them. His marker of a good academic piece, he once told me, was detection of a liberal deployment of the words 'nevertheless' and 'however'.

I will cover six selected dilemmas as they arise—more or less chronologically—over the life of a Commission. They are related to the legal framework, questioning witnesses and suspected perpetrators, and future access to sensitive material.

18.2 The Beginning and End of Armed Conflict

COIs are often asked to report on situations that involve an armed conflict. Despite a level of resistance from some states, Commissions have inevitably resorted to reporting on violations of the laws of armed conflict, or international humanitarian law. Alston himself was central to the task of explaining the legitimacy of Special Procedures at the UN HRC framing their reports of violations in terms of international humanitarian law (IHL).[3] More recently, it has been noted that 'it has become regular practice that HRC commissions make findings of IHL violations and international crimes that stem from, or occur in connection with, human rights violations'.[4] But any debate over whether the HRC should deal with international

[1] Philip Alston, 'The Darfur Commission as a Model for Future Responses to Crisis Situations' (2005) 3 Journal of International Criminal Justice 600.

[2] UNHRC, 'Report of the Special Rapporteur on Extrajudicial, Summary or Arbitrary Executions, Philip Alston' (2008) UN Doc A/HRC/8/3; Philip Alston, 'Introduction: Commissions of Inquiry as Human Rights Fact-Finding Tools' (2011) 105 Proceedings of the ASIL Annual Meeting 81.

[3] Philip Alston, Jason Morgan-Foster, and William Abresch, 'The Competence of the UN Human Rights Council and Its Special Procedures in Relation to Armed Conflicts: Extrajudicial Executions in the "War on Terror"' (2008) 19 European Journal of International Law 183.

[4] Larissa van der Herik and Catherine Harwood, 'Commissions of Inquiry and the Charm of International Criminal Law: Between Transactional and Authoritative Approaches' in Philip Alston and Sarah Knuckey (eds), *The Transformation of Human Rights Fact-Finding* (OUP 2016) 241.

Andrew Clapham, *Dilemmas Facing Commissions of Inquiry* In: *The Struggle for Human Rights.* Edited by: Nehal Bhuta, Florian Hoffmann, Sarah Knuckey, Frédéric Mégret, and Margaret Satterthwaite, Oxford University Press. © Andrew Clapham 2021.
DOI: 10.1093/oso/9780198868064.003.0019

humanitarian law is a separate question from determining the scope of application of this law. In particular when exactly did the armed conflict start and which parties does it bind? This is especially tricky when the Commission is reporting during an armed conflict, and even harder when a cessation of hostilities or a peace agreement comes in the middle of the reporting period. Determining that there has been a resort to the armed conflict—as opposed to an outbreak of violence involving criminal activity—is to accuse one party of breaching the agreement and potentially triggering a collapse of a fragile peace. One also has the risk of contradicting those officially charged with cease-fire monitoring. In the run up to reporting on violations, and establishing responsibility, a Commission may have to choose very carefully between a determination that potentially incorrectly extends the conflict and the regime that allows for the prosecution of war crimes, and a premature finding that the conflict is over. An international court has the luxury of making these determinations many years after the events without antagonizing the parties from whom the Commission is seeking cooperation. And yet international courts will nevertheless be relying on the reports of such Commissions precisely as evidence of the exact day when the conflict finished.[5]

I found Alston's use of public statements from the International Committee of the Red Cross (ICRC) goes some way of cracking this particular nut. As long as the ICRC is reporting that it is explaining the principles of IHL to the parties, this seems to open the door for a possible application of IHL. Of course the ICRC may be pre-emptively explaining the rules in the light of an upcoming armed conflict, but a judicious use of this public pronouncement can insulate a Commission from accusations that it has come to an unsustainable conclusion over the application of the law of armed conflict with the attendant regime for individual responsibility for war crimes. But while the ICRC may provide public references to the applicability of IHL over the past year, this does not of course help to resolve the dilemma of whether to conclude that, notwithstanding the signing of a cease-fire or peace agreement, an armed conflict exists for the purposes of the application of IHL.

It certainly helps that the ICRC has recently taken an approach suggesting that even a formal agreement to end the fighting does not necessarily end the application of IHL. Their new Commentary states:

> armed confrontations sometimes continue well beyond the conclusion or unilateral pronouncement of a formal act such as a ceasefire, armistice or peace agreement. Relying solely on the existence of such agreements to determine the end of a non-international armed conflict could therefore lead to a premature end of the applicability of humanitarian law in situations when in fact a conflict continues.[6]

At a formal level a Commission can perhaps avoid fixing an exact time and date for the beginning and end fear any armed conflict that occurs during its mandate. But in situations where the Commission has the cooperation of the authorities, and is engaged with them, a choice must be made whether to express oneself in the language of the laws of war or simply

[5] See the discussion by Agnieszka Jachec Neale, 'Human Rights Fact-Finding into Armed Conflict and Breaches of the Laws of War' (2011) 105 Proceedings of the ASIL Annual Meeting 85.

[6] ICRC, *Commentary on the First Geneva Convention* (2nd edn,CUP 2016) para 490; Gabriella Venturini, 'The Temporal Scope of the Conventions' in Andrew Clapham, Paola Geeta and Marco Sassòli (eds), *The 1949 Geneva Conventions: A Commentary* (OUP 2015) 61, 61–62: 'The 1995 *Tadić* Decision held that in the case of internal conflicts, IHL applies until a "peaceful settlement is achieved". In the *Haradinaj* Decision, the ICTY clarified that once the threshold of violence is met, a decrease in the intensity of fighting (or, one might add, degree of organization of an armed group involved) cannot end the applicability of IHL.'

rely on human rights norms. When dealing with military personnel, judges from Courts Martial, and the leaders of opposition groups the Commission may feel that referencing the Geneva Conventions or the laws and customs of war may find more traction than provisions more associated with law enforcement and the police academy. When raising basic rules associated with the Geneva Conventions I have always been told that everyone has been trained to respect this law and that violations are always punished. No one will tell you that the fighting has dipped below the level necessary for the application of humanitarian law, or that the organizational capacity of the group has diminished so that they are no longer bound by the obligations in the Geneva Conventions that protect the victims of war.

If we are honest it is precisely in the chaotic conditions when government forces are seeking to claim control and insurgent groups are fragmenting in a disorderly way that a COI is most likely to have to document atrocity crimes. In short, faced with the dilemma of asking whether the situation fits within the framework of the law of armed conflict, there will usually be good reasons to continue to apply it even when the fighting ceases, as one does not know at that moment when it will resume.

Such an approach, nevertheless, needs to be carefully considered as an international or national criminal court could consider this rather determinative for the question as to whether war crimes could be committed during the period in question.

The Central African Republic COI report that Alston jointly authored addresses the problem head on:

> In reaching its conclusions on the qualification of the conflict, the Commission seeks to balance two competing considerations that it believes should guide its analysis. The first calls for caution in suggesting too many changes over time in the classification of the conflict....
> The second consideration is the need for some precision in the determination of the nature of the conflict in order to avoid the possibility that prosecutions will be undertaken for war crimes, which will subsequently fail because the defence is able to show that there was no armed conflict in existence at the time the alleged offences were committed....
> In balancing these two considerations, the Commission considers that it is best to err on the side of caution and to avoid blunt classifications that may provide a greater degree of legal certainty and facilitate the continuing and uninterrupted application of international humanitarian law but that do not accurately reflect the nature of the events on the ground.[7]

The dilemma is spelled out with exquisite clarity; *however*, there is here a real risk that Commissions get drawn into quasi-judicial findings that make it harder to engage the actors on the ground and protest certain acts relating to weapons or explain duties of command responsibility. This is especially the case in the context of Commissions that are of a longer duration (at the time of writing the Syria COI has been running for nearly ten years) and where lulls in the fighting or reconfigurations of the parties lead to uncertainty over whether or not the law of armed conflict continues to apply, notwithstanding the high levels of violence and atrocities.

A further dimension to this dilemma is that the inclusion or exclusion of IHL may be seen as favouring one or other of the parties. We have come a long way from a simplistic approach

[7] UNSC 'International Commission of Inquiry Report on the Central African Republic—Final Report' (22 December 2014) UN Doc S/2014/928 paras 99–101.

that associates human rights with peace-time and IHL with war.[8] The work in this area often concludes that the legal regimes overlap and that each one has to be interpreted in the light of the other.[9] Nevertheless, the debate may turn on whether a specific act of violence is to be considered part of hostilities or part of a general protest that ought to be met with a response that better reflects law enforcement rather than combat. The situation concerning the demonstrations in Gaza near the fence with Israel was seen by some as a law enforcement problem, and by others as an armed conflict between Israel and an organized armed group. The COI explained its approach to applicable law as follows:

> Both Israel and the State of Palestine are party to the International Covenant on Civil and Political Rights, other core international human rights treaties and the Geneva Conventions of 1949, and are bound by customary international law. Within Gaza, the de facto authorities led by Hamas bear human rights obligations given their exercise of government-like functions.
> Israel and Palestinian organized armed groups (Izz al-Din al-Qassam Brigades and Al Quds Brigades, the military wings of Hamas and Palestinian Islamic Jihad respectively), as parties to the armed conflict, are bound by international humanitarian law. As the occupying Power, Israel is also bound by the rules on occupation under international treaty and customary law.[10]

So we have the application of IHL for at least three separate entities: the State of Palestine, the State of Israel, and Hamas; the application of IHL for Israel as an occupying power; as well as the parallel application of IHL between Israel and two armed groups—Izz al-Din al-Qassam Brigades and Al Quds Brigades. The Commission avoids being caught on the horns of a dilemma between human rights law and IHL, a choice that would inevitably give rise to accusations of bias, but instead explains that 'during the same event, the conduct of hostilities paradigm applies to targetable individuals; while against (rioting/violent) civilians, the law enforcement paradigm applies'.[11] It then proceeds to an examination of the individual incidents rather than broad brush assertions of the more appropriate legal framework.

18.3 Identifying the Applicable Human Rights Law

One might think that determining the applicable human rights law would be less problematic than determining the applicability of the laws of war. However, dilemmas may arise. In the context of South Sudan, some reporting, and indeed some formal petitions, at the international level suggested that South Sudan was bound by the human rights treaties to which Sudan was bound, because South Sudan had become bound as a succeeding state. The

[8] Yuval Shany, 'The End of the War/Peace Limit on the Application of International Human Rights Law: A Response to Andrew Clapham' in Bardo Fassbender and Knut Traisbach (eds), *The Limits of Human Rights* (1st edn, OUP 2019).

[9] Mona Rishmawi, 'Peace and Justice: Human Rights Fact-Finding in Raging Conflicts' in Fannie Lafontaine and Franćois Larocque (eds), *Doing Peace the Rights Way: Essays in International Law and Relations in Honour of Louise Arbour* (Intersentia 2018) especially 190–94.

[10] UNHRC, 'Report of the Independent International Commission of Inquiry on the Protests in the Occupied Palestinian Territory' (6 March 2019) UN Doc A/HRC/40/74 paras 11–12.

[11] UNHRC, 'Report of the Detailed Findings of the Independent International Commission of Inquiry on the Protests in the Occupied Palestinian Territory' (18 March 2019) UN Doc A/HRC/40/CRP.2 para 110, footnotes omitted.

arguments in favour of a seceding state to automatically succeed to the Genocide Convention and human rights treaties have been set out by Judge Weeramantry in a separate opinion in the *Application of the Genocide Convention Case*.[12] Interestingly he includes as part of the argument the report of the meeting of chairpersons of human rights treaty bodies in 1994. The report states: 'The chairpersons are, however, of the view that successor States are automatically bound by obligations under international human rights instruments from their respective date of independence and that the respect of their obligations should not depend on a declaration of confirmation made by the new Government of the successor State'.[13]

This is not the place to examine these arguments. A Commission might, however, face the dilemma of choosing whether to take this path of assumed human rights obligations. In the context of South Sudan, the Commission could rely on the state's clear-cut obligations under the African Union human rights treaties that South Sudan had chosen to join. In time, South Sudan went on to become a party to several UN human rights treaties, including treaties Sudan had chosen not to join. This meant not only did the range of treaties grow but, just as importantly, the government of the Republic of South Sudan was in a position to point to these steps as progress as well as to adapt national law to ensure the international obligations could apply domestically. One could say that under this route there was a greater sense of 'ownership' of the relevant human rights norms.

There is then a choice for a COI on whether to insist on all the possible obligations that could be laid at the foot of a state, or to work with a government and perhaps relevant armed groups to encourage a focus on those norms that have the best chances of traction. The dilemma is whether to insist on a maximalist catalogue of all the human rights applicable—or to concentrate on those norms that seem to illicit the greatest familiarity or legitimacy. Most COIs will have to navigate a complex landscape of human rights norms with competing pressure to gravitate towards the UN standards, the regional norms, or the national law. The risk of a comprehensive approach is that one misses the opportunity to generate a genuine appreciation of the rules concerned. Less can be more.

18.4 Distinguishing Abuses from Violations and the Danger of Applying a Skewed Approach

There is an unspoken assumption that when mandates refer to human rights violations and abuses that this is a green light to report on and determine human rights responsibility with regard to both government actors and non-state actors. Clearly, reporting only on the government's actions and omissions while leaving unexamined atrocities committed by any opposition or terrorist group would leave the Commission open to accusations of bias and would fail the victims of those non-state actors. Furthermore, it would betray one of the rationales for establishing such Commissions: to inform the international community about the facts of a situation and make recommendations to prevent a deterioration of the situation and to promote accountability.

Recent research has revealed that international bodies such as the Security Council, the General Assembly, and the HRC use the expressions 'human rights violations' and 'human

[12] *Application of the Convention on the Prevention and Punishment of the Crime of Genocide (Bosnia and Herzegovina v Serbia and Montenegro)* (Preliminary Objections) [1996] ICJ Rep 1996.

[13] UNGA, 'Report of the Fifth Meeting of Persons Chairing the Human Rights Treaty Bodies' (19 October 1994) UN Doc A/49/537 para 32.

rights abuses' rather arbitrarily even if COIs generally favour the word violations,[14] although some human rights lawyers still prefer to draw a strict distinction, reserving the word abuses to describe the transgressive acts of non-state actors. Some commentators and organizations still consider that only state acts represent violations of breaches of international human rights law, while the same acts committed by armed groups merely signify breaches of the moral expectations of the international community with regard to human rights.[15]

In the practice of special rapporteurs, the Security Council, and COIs, any dichotomy between legal obligations and non-legal moral responsibility is dissolved when reporting on armed groups that are considered to be carrying out governmental type functions and controlling territory.[16] As special rapporteur, Philip Alston sometimes simply used human rights 'abuses' to refer to both the acts of government forces and armed non-state actors.[17] The Security Council monitors six 'grave violations' of children's rights in armed conflict, listing governments and armed groups without distinction. COIs often report on the acts of non-state actors as violating human rights obligations under international law and determine responsibility for both governmental and opposition forces without nuance.

Even those commentators who at one time had opposed at a doctrinal, or theoretical, level the idea that non-state actors had any international human rights obligations, have more recently pointed to a 'modified traditional view'.[18] In the words of the late Sir Nigel Rodley, such a modified traditional view is 'the at least theoretical acceptance that if another entity—a non-state actor (NSA)—exercises "effective power" analogous to that of the state, then such an entity should logically be seen as capable of being obliged to respect the human rights of those subject to that power'.[19]

In fact, Philip Alston himself was confronted in his work as Special Rapporteur on Extrajudicial, Summary, or Arbitrary Executions with the dilemma of how to report on and engage non-state actors,[20] without seemingly lending them legitimacy by treating them 'like a state'. His early statement on Sri Lanka grounds the obligations in the UDHR and the demands of the international community:

> As a non-State actor, the LTTE does not have legal obligations under ICCPR, but it remains subject to the demand of the international community, first expressed in the Universal

[14] Jessica Burniske, Naz K Modirzadeh, and Dustin A Lewis, 'Armed Non-State Actors and International Human Rights Law: An Analysis of the Practice of the U.N. Security Council and the U.N. General Assembly' (2017) Harvard Public Law Working Paper 17–37 <www.ssrn.com/abstract=2994907> accessed 01 August 2020; Annyssa Bellal, 'Human Rights Obligations of Armed Non-State Actors: An Exploration of the Practice of the UN Human Rights Council' (2016) <https://www.geneva-academy.ch/research/our-project/detail/4-armed-non-state-actors-and-the-human-rights-council> accessed 1 August 2020.Ginevra Le Moli, 'From "Is" to "Ought": The Development of Normative Powers of UN Investigative Mechanisms' (2020) 19 Chinese Journal of International Law 625.

[15] For example, Alexander Breitegger, 'The Legal Framework Applicable to Insecurity and Violence Affecting the Delivery of Health Care in Armed Conflicts and Other Emergencies' (2013) 95 International Review of the Red Cross 83, 89, 103.

[16] See the examples given in Andrew Clapham, 'Non-State Actors' in Daniel Moeckli and others (eds), *International Human Rights Law* (3rd edn, OUP 2018) 557–79.

[17] UNHRC, 'Report of the Special Rapporteur on Extrajudicial, Summary or Arbitrary Executions, Philip Alston, Addendum: Mission to the Philippines' (16 April 2008), UN Doc A/HRC/8/3/Add.2.

[18] Sir Nigel Rodley, 'Non-state Actors and Human Rights' in Scott Sheeran and Nigel S Rodley (eds), *Routledge Handbook of International Human Rights Law* (Routledge 2016) 523.

[19] ibid.

[20] See in particular the dilemmas explained in his UNHRC 'Report of the Special Rapporteur on Extrajudicial, Summary or Arbitrary Executions, Philip Alston, Addendum: Mission to Afghanistan' (6 May 2009) UN Doc A/HRC/11/2/Add.4 para 42.

> Declaration of Human Rights, that every organ of society respect and promote human rights.
>
> I have previously noted that it is especially appropriate and feasible to call for an armed group to respect human rights norms when it 'exercises significant control over territory and population and has an identifiable political structure. This visit clarified both the complexity and the necessity of applying human rights norms to armed groups. The LTTE plays a dual role. On the one hand, it is an organization with effective control over a significant stretch of territory, engaged in civil planning and administration, maintaining its own form of police force and judiciary. On the other hand, it is an armed group that has been subject to proscription, travel bans, and financial sanctions in various Member States. The tension between these two roles is at the root of the international community's hesitation to address the LTTE and other armed groups in the terms of human rights law. The international community does have human rights expectations to which it will hold the LTTE, but it has long been reluctant to press these demands directly if doing so would be to 'treat it like a State.
>
> It is increasingly understood, however, that the human rights expectations of the international community operate to protect people, while not thereby affecting the legitimacy of the actors to whom they are addressed. The Security Council has long called upon various groups that Member States do not recognize as having the capacity to formally assume international obligations to respect human rights. The LTTE and other armed groups must accept that insofar as they aspire to represent a people before the world, the international community will evaluate their conduct according to the Universal Declaration's 'common standard of achievement.[21]

The complexity of the current situation facing various COIs is that some of the armed groups are more like criminal enterprises than governments-in-waiting. Some may have minimal control over territory, and yet move around with their child abductees and targeting those they come across. Some victims may find that control over their town changes from week-to-week or even day-to-day. More complicated still for anyone seeking to draw a bright line between the behaviour of the government and the non-state actors, is that these days many of the groups may be oscillating between opposition and government. As research in other social sciences demonstrates, the idea that there is at all times a clear distinction between state and non-state groups is fallacious. In some contexts armed groups can be better described as 'spin offs' from the state rather than non-state actors, and those same groups may at various stages take on functions that the state chooses not to entrust to its own forces.[22] Add to this the ambiguity over whether some groups have joined or left the government, along with the factor that we may often have different governments within the same state recognized as *de lege* authorities by different parts of the international community, and one can see the impossibility of COI drawing watertight distinctions when labelling specific incidents as violations or abuses.

When international lawyers get involved, they often gravitate to refocusing fact-finding around determining attribution to the state under the rules of state responsibility. The state may indeed be responsible for empowering these groups to carry out governmental

[21] ibid; ECOSOC, 'Report of the Special Rapporteur, Philip Alston, on Extrajudicial, Summary or Arbitrary Executions, Philip Alston, Addendum: Mission to Sri Lanka' (27 March 2006), UN Doc. E/CN.4/2006/53/Add.5 paras 25–27 (footnote omitted).

[22] Klaus Schlichte, 'With the State against the State? The Formation of Armed Groups' in Keith Krause (ed), *Armed Groups and Contemporary Conflicts: Challenging the Weberian State* (Routledge 2010) 45–63.

functions, or for directing operations, or for acknowledging and adopting the action as its own after the events,[23] but the mandate of a COI is to determine which people and entities were responsible, and this means looking at the parallel or dual attribution towards the non-state entities. The readers of these reports really want to know primarily which groups are responsible for atrocities; whether the state might also be indirectly responsible through the complexity of the rules on state responsibility is of secondary importance in this context. The reader needs to know which groups are 'spoilers' and who should be addressed or sanctioned in order to prevent further human rights atrocities.

Furthermore, to suggest that what a government through its agents does violates international law but what the armed groups do remains outside the realm of international accountability is misleading and presents a false dichotomy for a Commission. Apart from the identification of those responsible from all sides for war crimes, crimes against humanity, and genocide, COIs can point to those who could be prosecuted for the human rights crime of torture. This can be particularly effective as the prospects of an extraterritorial prosecution in one of the 166 states parties to the UN Convention Against Torture may be better than for the extraterritorial prosecution of a war crime. The traditional doctrine is keen on pointing out that the human rights violation of torture can only be committed by state agents, according to this approach the same act committed by someone from the non-state actor side falls outside the scope of the Convention and the international law of human rights. But when such cases come to court, judges have, however, been quite flexible and have allowed for prosecutions for torture to proceed against individual non-state actors. Faced with a challenge to their jurisdiction to prosecute a member of Charles Taylor's rebel group in Liberia, a the UK Supreme Court interpreted the expression 'official capacity' in the Torture Convention as it is incorporated into UK law, setting out the contours for prosecuting such an individual who is part of the activities of a non-state actor rather than working for the state:

> 'A person acting in an official capacity' in section 134(1) of the Criminal Justice Act 1988 includes a person who acts or purports to act, otherwise than in a private and individual capacity, for or on behalf of an organisation or body which exercises, in the territory controlled by that organisation or body and in which the relevant conduct occurs, functions normally exercised by governments over their civilian populations. Furthermore, it covers any such person whether acting in peace time or in a situation of armed conflict.[24]

18.5 Whether and How to Warn Witnesses That Their Statements May be Used to Build a Case against Them in a Court of Law

The mandate of Commissions, and the new investigative mechanisms, established for Syria, Iraq, and Myanmar, known as Triple-I Ms, increasingly collect and preserve evidence for

[23] ILC, 'Draft Articles on Responsibility of States for Internationally Wrongful Acts, with Commentaries' (2001) UN Doc A/56/10 arts 5, 8, 11. The UN General Assembly took note of the articles, 'commended them to the attention of Governments', and annexed the Articles to its Resolution 56/83, 12 December 2001; see further James Crawford, *The International Law Commission's Articles on State Responsibility: Introduction, Text, and Commentaries* (CUP 2002).

[24] *R v Reeves Taylor* [2019] UKSC 51, [76] for a discussion of the subsequent dismissal of the charges see Andrew Clapham, 'Challenging the Myths which Suggest that Human Rights Bodies Cannot Address Armed Non-state Actors in Situations of Armed Conflict: With Special Emphasis on the *Case of Agnes Taylor*' in Gloria Gaggioli (ed) *The Role of Human Rights Mechanisms in Implementing International Humanitarian Law* (Elgar forthcoming).

future use in a criminal prosecution. In some contexts, a Commission with its researchers may be interviewing those who might face future prosecution. Evidence from within the armed forces or within an armed group can be essential to building a case, especially where it involves questions of command responsibility. But here comes an unresolved issue: what sort of obligation does a Commission have to warn the interlocutor that what they say could be used in a future prosecution against them? Does one warn someone that they are about to incriminate themselves and risk losing the lead that will enable the Commission to fulfil its mandate to identify those responsible for violations and abuses?

Although an international Commission is not operating like a police force bound by national rules of criminal procedure, many of the lawyers I have discussed this with nevertheless felt at least a moral obligation to offer some sort of warning, or to take down the information in a way that made it less evidentiary with regard to the individual concerned and more probative towards the overall inquiry. There is, for some, a dilemma as to whether to leave this sort of interviewing work to the investigative authorities of the state or an international prosecutorial team, rather than compromising the investigation, or even violating the human rights of the individual. How one resolves this dilemma will, of course, have to depend on the context. In some situations the Commission will be investigating simply as a prelude to later investigation by the prosecutor of an international tribunal, but in other cases the prospect of further investigations may be very remote indeed, and this interview could be the only chance to fill in the gaps in a narrative implicating one or more individuals in international crimes.

The literature and manuals on how to conduct investigations have dedicated considerable attention to the rights of victims and witnesses not to be traumatized, to be treated with cultural sensitivity, and to have carefully explained to them how their information will be used, but there is very little thought given to dealing with the rights of the perpetrators and the ethics of fact-finding in this context.[25]

Clearly no one, victim, witness, or perpetrator, should be 'duped into cooperating with investigators with the expectation of benefitting from interviews',[26] but at what point does a Commission feel the need to point out that the narrative is helping to build a case against the interviewee? If the commander is explaining how indeed they have actually punished troops for war crimes in the past, they are making the case that they had the capacity to do this for the case under investigation; this might not seem obviously self-incriminatory to the person being interviewed. The Commission will be keen to interview those who know the most about any one operation, but those people are those who may be the ones who are most responsible by omission for failing to act on what they knew. The problem is inherent in the methodology of any Commission considering reporting on command responsibility. Perhaps the dilemma must be solved alongside the question tackled in following section.

[25] For example, Sara Ferro Ribeiro and Danaé van der Straten Ponthoz, 'International Protocol on the Documentation and Investigation of Sexual Violence in Conflict: Best Practice on the Documentation of Sexual Violence as a Crime or Violation of International Law' (2nd edn, UK Foreign & Commonwealth Office 2017) <https://www.un.org/sexualviolenceinconflict/wp-content/uploads/2019/06/report/international-protocol-on-the-documentation-and-investigation-of-sexual-violence-in-conflict/International_Protocol_2017_2nd_Edition.pdf> accessed 19 May 2021; International Institute of Higher Studies in Criminal Sciences, *Siracusa Guidelines for International, Regional and National Fact-Finding Bodies: International Institute of Higher Studies in Criminal Sciences* (M Cherif Bassiouni and Christina Abraham eds, Intersentia 2013); Rosette Muzigo-Morrison, 'Victims and Witnesses in Fact-Finding Commissions: Pawns or Principal Pieces?' in Alston and Knuckey (n 4) 180 who does reference the need to consider the dignity of perpetrators when interviewing them in detention.

[26] ibid 181.

18.6 Letters of Cooperation

The problem of warning possible defendants leads naturally to a further dilemma: should a Commission respond to a request for a document to say that an individual has been very helpful in an inquiry, and that this should be taken into account in any future proceedings? One could imagine such information being relevant for a plea bargain or as part of a mitigation plea at the time of sentencing. Of course no Commission would ordinarily have any authority over any criminal court process, but the dilemma remains: should one issue a letter of cooperation or simply refuse?

Requests for such letters are certainly made. To put the choice another way: writing such a letter, even without any promise that it will be taken into account by a court, could lead to more truth telling and increase the prospects of justice, but, on the other hand, there is nevertheless some sort of implied inducement being offered up for testimony that could render such testimony unreliable.

Attention is now turning to ensuring that trials are not compromised by 'transactional testimony'.[27] This term encapsulates the need to avoid compromising testimony by following it up with referrals for health treatment and counselling. The point is to ensure that witnesses are medically treated, and all arrangements made for trauma counselling, before being interviewed. In this way one can preclude some testimony being later challenged in court as being influenced by the prospect of health care. Of course there is the larger problem that in these contexts all stories are at risk of being adjusted to please the Commissioners or fact-finders. As Rothenberg explains:

> those interviewed may adjust the stories they tell because they believe this will be beneficial to them, perhaps aiding in a refugee claim or enabling access to benefits of some type. This is often an issue eve where those gathering testimonies clearly indicate, as most research methodologies require, that participation does not come with any benefits. In addition, some presenting testimonies may adjust their stories out of a desire to meet the needs of those engaging in the interviews. They may try to give the interviewers what they appear to want, for a variety of reasons, including fear, or a desire to be polite and helpful.[28]

So what happens when we move beyond the implied benefits to testimony and onto an explicit arrangement? Imagining that a warning has been given that the statement, which is being taken down verbatim, could later come to be used to build a case against the interviewee, can one go on to suggest that information that allows for others to be pursued for criminal will not only be welcome but that providing such information is likely to be looked on favourably by any sentencing judge? What if the cooperation is not to be presented in open court for fear of reprisal? Should a COI be authorized to provide the details of such cooperation to a judge in the future?

The likelihood is that, by the time the case comes to the sentencing stage the Commission and its secretariat will have long been disbanded. Who then should be charged with the residual duties of a Commission? This takes us to our next topic: the protocols for access to the Commission's evidence and information after it has been dissolved.

[27] I first heard the phrase coined by Chris Dolan and Yasmin Sooka at the workshop on Promoting Access to Justice for Victims of Sexual and Gender-Based Crimes in South Sudan in March 2019.

[28] Daniel Rothenberg, 'The Complex Truth of Testimony: A Case Study of Human Rights Fact-Finding in Iraq' in Alston and Knuckey (n 4) 204.

18.7 Accessing Information Gathered by a Commission

Today, many Commissions and other mechanisms will build up an evidence base, with videos, witness statements, medical reports photos, and so on. Together with such evidence and associated information, it is increasingly common to keep a confidential file with the names and details of suspected perpetrators. This list may be handed over to the Secretary General or the High Commissioner for Human Rights at the end of the Commission.[29] Certain practices have developed over the years to determine who can access such confidential names. In some cases they may be exclusively destined for the prosecutor of an international tribunal, in other cases the information may be available to a wider range of authorities.

In the context of a Commission simply set up to establish the facts and responsibility for a specific incident, the details may be managed fairly easily, but the issues become more complex as Commissions have evolved. The Commission or Mechanism may continue for many years and there may be requests for access to not only the names but also to the associated witness statements and background work. Such requests could be from the territorial state itself, from other states seeking to prosecute a crime based on extraterritorial jurisdiction, or even from plaintiff lawyers for a tort case. Consider, for example, the possibilities in the United States under the Victim Torture Protection Act, which covers not only torture but also extrajudicial killings.[30] In other cases the request might come from immigration authorities looking to confirm or deny immigration status including refugee status. There is no doubt that these authorities already rely on the reports of COIs in performing their 'background checks'.[31]

A choice as to whether to release such information may eventually be faced by the entity holding the archive, but the responsibility for setting the parameters for such decision-making must lie with the Commission itself. As Commissions may now be renewed over a period of several years, requests for information will naturally arrive during the period of the Commission. This in turn means that Commissions need to develop specific criteria for access to such information, both during the life of the Commission and after its dissolution. Each Commission operates in a different environment. What follows are a few suggested key principles:

1. The overriding concern is the *safety of the witnesses and survivors* who shared information with the Commission. This requires an assessment of the dangers at the time of the request for access to information.

[29] See, for example, the practice for the UN Commission of Inquiry on Darfur, the UN Commission of Inquiry on Libya, the UN Commission of Inquiry on Syria, the AU Commission of Inquiry on South Sudan, the UN Commission on Human Rights in South Sudan, the Commission of Inquiry on the Protests in the Occupied Palestinian Territory (2019), and the International Team of Experts on the Kasai region (Democratic Republic of the Congo); for further discussion on this aspect of the work of Commissions see OHCHR, 'Commissions of Inquiry and Fact-Finding Missions on International Human Rights and Humanitarian Law' <https://primarysources.brillonline.com/browse/human-rights-documents-online/commissions-of-inquiry-and-factfinding-missions-on-international-human-rights-and-humanitarian-law;hrdhrd98462015002> accessed 01 August 2020, 12–14.

[30] Torture Victim Protection Act 1991, 28 USC 1350 (2006), s 2(a) '(LIABILITY—An individual who, under actual or apparent authority, or color of law, of any foreign nation—(1) subjects an individual to torture shall, in a civil action, be liable for damages to that individual, or (2) subjects an individual to extrajudicial killing shall, in a civil action, be liable for damages to the individual's legal representative, or to any person who may be a claimant in an action for wrongful death.'

[31] Relayed to the author by a relevant agency.

2. In many situations the information will have been provided to the Commission under the *condition* that it should be shared with a *restricted set of recipients*, and the purposes may be similarly restricted (eg individuals may choose to restrict the use of their statements solely for the purposes of a criminal prosecution, or alternatively solely for use by truth and reconciliation commission). These conditions relating to the consent of the sharing of the information have to be respected. Some witnesses are adamant that their statement should only be used in the event that the suspected perpetrator is arrested and securely detained. Others may have specified that their statement is to be used only before an international court.
3. Should the prosecutorial authorities of a state initiating a criminal investigation request any evidence or information the entity in charge of the COI's information should give consideration to: the nature of the allegations and/or charges, respect for the fundamental principles of *fair trial* in the domestic justice system, the prospects of the *death penalty or disproportionate punishment*, the application of adequate *witness protection* measures, and whether the information or evidence may put *anyone at risk*.

18.8 Final Remarks

Philip Alston participated as Commissioner in various COIs and has highlighted how innovative and essential this work is in the world of monitoring compliance with international law. As an academic he challenges us to think more reflectively about these phenomena:

> This proliferation of major inquiries across a wide range of countries and situations calls into question the common wisdom which portrays the emergence of the various international and mixed criminal courts and tribunals over the past two decades as the most significant development in the human rights field. In contrast, it could reasonably be argued that the explosion in the number and variety of international fact-finding bodies has been a development of comparable significance. It is striking, however, that while the criminal courts and tribunals have generated a veritable industry and a vast literature, fact-finding has been largely neglected as an area for sustained exploration, critique, and refinement.[32]

[32] Alston, 'Introduction: Commissions of Inquiry' (n 2) 84.

19

Quis Custodiet Ipsos Custodes?

Philip Alston

José E Alvarez

19.1 Introduction

Philip Alston has long been preoccupied with making power-wielders responsible. His scholarship, like those of others, contends that '[t]he trigger for accountability is power';[1] that those who exercise power over individuals today include international organizations; and that one of the biggest challenges of our time is to adapt rules and processes originally designed to apply to states to make international organizations accountable.[2] This essay considers Alston's efforts to extend his accountability efforts as a UN special rapporteur, famously directed at states in the past,[3] to the United Nations, the World Bank, and the IMF.

Alston's three reports as Special Rapporteur on Extreme Poverty and Human Rights as UN system organizations have expanded their missions and powers, their operations have sometimes injured individuals in ways that, had those actions been undertaken by states, would have been deemed clear human rights violations. With respect to the United Nations itself, the most famous example remains the counter-terrorism sanctions imposed by the UN Security Council that led to the Kadi rulings by the ECJ.[4] Other notorious examples include sexual abuses attributed to UN peacekeepers—from involvement in human trafficking to rape—and numerous proposals to grapple with them.[5]

As Special Rapporteur on Extreme Poverty and Human Rights, Alston has focused on another notorious UN case: the UN's responsibility for spreading cholera in Haiti starting in 2010.[6] The UN's actions and inactions in Haiti—which, through May 2016, had led to at least 9,145 deaths and 779,212 infected persons[7]—have been the subject of numerous studies, lawsuits, and scholarly accounts and do not require thorough review here.[8] The arrival of

[1] Philip Alston, 'Hobbling the Monitors: Should UN Human Rights Monitors be Accountable?' (2011) 52 Harvard Human Rights Journal 563, 615.

[2] ibid 605–15.

[3] For example, UNHRC, 'Report of the Special Rapporteur on Extrajudicial, Summary or Arbitrary Executions Addendum: Study on targeted killings' (28 May 2010) UN Doc A/HRC/14/24/Add.6.

[4] Joined Cases C-402 and C-415/05P *Yassin Abdullah Kadi and al Barakaat International Foundation v Council of the European Union and Commission of the European Communities* [2008] ECR I-6352 [Kadi I]; Joined Cases C-584/10P, C-593/10P and C-595/10P *European Commission and Others v Kadi* [2013] ECR 00000 [Kadi II].

[5] For example, Marie Deschamps, Hassan B Jallow, and Yasmin Sooka, 'Taking Action on Sexual Exploitation and Abuse by Peacekeepers: Report of an Independent Review on Sexual Exploitation and Abuse by International Peacekeeping Forces in the Central African Republic' (UN) <https://reliefweb.int/report/central-african-republic/taking-action-sexual-exploitation-and-abuse-peacekeepers-report> accessed 10 September 2020.

[6] Note by the Seretary General, 'Extreme Poverty and Human Rights' (2016) UN Doc A/71/367.

[7] ibid para 13.

[8] For example, *Georges v United Nations* 84 F Supp 3d 246 (SD NY 2015); UN Doc A/71/367 (n 6); José E Alvarez, 'The United Nations in the Time of Cholera' (2014) 108 AJIL Unbound 22; Ira Kurzban, Beatrice Lindstrom and Shannon Jonsson, 'UN Accountability for Haiti's Cholera Epidemic' (2014) 108 AJIL Unbound 17; Bruce Rashkow, 'Remedies for Harm Caused by UN Peacekeepers' (2014) 108 AJIL Unbound 10; Mara Pillinger, Ian Hurd, and

José E Alvarez, *Quis Custodiet Ipsos Custodes?* In: *The Struggle for Human Rights.* Edited by: Nehal Bhuta, Florian Hoffmann, Sarah Knuckey, Frédéric Mégret, and Margaret Satterthwaite, Oxford University Press.
DOI: 10.1093/oso/9780198868064.003.0020

a 1,000 person peacekeeping force from Nepal in Haiti coincided with a sudden, unprecedented cholera epidemic in a country that had not seen recorded cases of the disease.[9] After considerable study, it was credibly shown that the strain of cholera found in Haiti was a genetic match to a cholera outbreak that had occurred in Nepal prior to the peacekeepers' departure to Haiti. It was also found that the disease—which ultimately infected at least 7 per cent of the entire population of Haiti—was likely caused by the discharge of raw untreated sewage by the peacekeepers' base camp into a tributary that flows into the Artibonite River, a major source of drinking water in central Haiti.[10] Alston's report contrasts these facts with the UN's efforts to sidestep responsibility by suggesting, first, that there was no conclusive evidence that its peacekeepers were to blame and, later, by taking refuge in the preliminary conclusion reached by a UN panel report that suggested that the epidemic emerged from a 'confluence of circumstances' that included Haiti's post-earthquake vulnerabilities.[11] Alston's report castigates the sixteen-month delay between the filing of a formal complaint on behalf of some five thousand cholera victims (on 3 November 2011) and the first response by the United Nations in the form of a letter signed by the UN Under Secretary General for Legal Affairs that deemed the complaint 'not receivable' because it was not of a 'private law character' since its consideration 'would necessarily preclude a review of political and policy matters'.[12] The UN's rejection of their claims led the Haitian petitioners to file a class action suit in US federal court that ultimately ruled that the United Nations was immune from suit under the Convention on Privileges and Immunities.[13]

This special rapporteur report is structured as a rigorously analytical brief. It lays out, first, the scientific evidence for UN liability; second, the legal flaws in UN determination that the claims were 'not receivable'; third, the wide-spread public and scholarly criticisms of UN actions to date; fourth, the applicable legal principles; and fifth, the reasons why UN arguments against accountability were (and remain) politically self-defeating. This is a lawyerly report that acknowledges nonetheless that legal arguments do not suffice.[14] It presents the UN's abdication of responsibility as moral and legal debacle that was, in addition, politically costly insofar as it threatens the organization's absolute immunity, encourages national courts to provide victims with access to a remedy, and threatens the viability of peacekeeping.[15] Alston's report-cum-brief gives a politically savvy explanation for the UN's posture, he suggests that the UN (and particularly its lawyers) were worried about setting an adverse legal precedent and overly solicitous to significant dues-paying states (like the United States).[16]

Alston's report on the human rights posture of the World Bank, pronouncing the Bank a 'human rights free zone', issued a year prior to the Haiti Cholera Report and of comparable length, shares many of the same structural characteristics.[17] Addressing a wide number of the Bank's operational policies, this report is a similarly lawyerly undertaking.

Michael N Barnett, 'How to Get Away with Cholera: The UN, Haiti, and International Law' (2016) 14 Perspectives on Politics 70.

[9] UN Doc A/71/367 (n 6) para 14.
[10] ibid para 14.
[11] ibid paras 17–28.
[12] ibid paras 28–31 (citing to the letter signed by Patricia O'Brien addressed to the director of the Institute for Justice and Democracy in Haiti dated 21 February 2013 and a similar letter, dated 5 July 2013, from O'Brien rejecting the request to review this finding and requesting mediation).
[13] ibid para 29, citing *Georges v United Nations* (n 8).
[14] ibid para 7.
[15] ibid paras 46–66.
[16] ibid paras 57–66.
[17] (Henceforth World Bank Report) Note by the Secretary General, 'Extereme Poverty and Human Rights' (2015) UN Doc A/70/274 *summary*, para 68; Philip Alston, 'The World Bank as a Human-Rights-Free Zone'

This special rapporteur report focuses on the chasm between the Bank's public relations efforts and its operational policies. Alston contends that while the Bank has rhetorically affirmed the links between human rights principles (such as gender equality) and development, its actual day to day operations, hemmed in by an ostensible prohibition against 'political' intervention, have ignored such links. As does his Haiti Cholera Report, this account takes aim at the Bank's lawyers' inconsistent interpretations and deployment of 'double standards' over time.[18] It canvasses successive General Counsel's revisitations of the prohibition in the Bank's charter against 'political' interventions—which have ranged from the view that the Bank is authorized to engage in political matters (including those involving human rights) so long as these have 'significant economic effects', to interpretations suggesting that the Bank can take any type of human rights into account so long as it these have some economic impact or relevance, to interpretations that bar anything other than purely 'economic' concerns.[19] Alston points out that the Bank's lawyers have, over time, authorized the Bank to engage in governance and rule of law matters dealing with the problems of corruption, money laundering, and terrorist financing. The Bank has also publicly asserted that 'development' is a broad concept that embraces social development, education, protection of global public goods, governance, and institutions. And yet, the Bank's lawyers have failed, he argues, to draw the connections between development and human rights. The result, he asserts, is that human rights are largely barred from the operational activities of the Bank, along with support for military and intelligence services.[20]

Alston's World Bank Report puts these flawed legal interpretations in a broader context. The Bank's aversion to human rights is not, he argues, simply the product of anachronistic, inconsistent, or misplaced legalism. It arises from an institutional culture dominated by economists who see rights as rigid, anti-market, and overly state-centric and who fear that a focus on rights will get in the way of their need to approve loans; by outdated ideas that human rights impose 'Western' values; and by exaggerated apprehensions that an emphasis on human rights will lead to the imposition of sanctions, turn the Bank into a human rights cop, or disadvantage the Bank relative to other lenders.[21]

As does his Haiti Cholera Report, Alston's World Bank Report makes the case that the Bank needs to become more receptive to human rights for pragmatic, instrumentalist reasons. Its tendency to treat human rights as if it were an 'infectious disease',[22] deprives the Bank from acting on issues essential to poverty eradication, renders it out of step with other major international organizations and with mainstream development theory, makes it more likely that the Bank's projects will lead to serious human rights violations and backlash, and denies the organization relevant information.[23] He contends that the Bank would be, in short, a better development institution if it backed the lip service it gives to human rights with action.

Unlike Alston's Haiti Cholera Report, which emphasizes the core need for accountability in a single instance of organization malfeasance, this more general examination of the Banks'

(2017) NYU University School of Law, Public Law & Legal Theory Research Paper Series Working Paper 17-50 <https://ssrn.com/abstract=3079899> accessed 10 September 2020.

[18] UN Doc A/70/274 (n 17) para 40 (describing the lawyers' interpretations as 'incoherent, counterproductive and unsustainable').

[19] ibid paras 6–11.

[20] ibid paras 12–20.

[21] ibid paras 34–51.

[22] ibid para 68.

[23] ibid paras 57–61.

policies relegates detailed discussion of 'accountability' to a letter referenced in its text, dated 12 December 2014, from twenty-eight special procedures mandate holders (including Alston).[24] The World Bank Report alludes to accountability as such only briefly, as when it enumerates the reasons Bank policies need to change and when Alston addresses the human rights gaps in the Bank's safeguards policies. As does the 12 December 2014 letter, Alston's report points out that while the Bank's safeguard policies express solicitude for the environment and the rights of indigenous peoples, they 'contain no explicit human rights policy'.[25] Alston's concern for accountability comes through in his report's concluding plea that the Bank use the language of human rights and not just surrogates like 'gender equality':

> Human rights provides a context and a detailed and balanced framework; it invokes the specific legal obligations that states have agreed upon in the various human rights treaties; it emphasizes that certain values are non-negotiable; it brings a degree of normative certainty; and it brings into the discussion the carefully negotiated elaborations of the meaning of specific rights that have emerged from decades of reflection, discussion and adjudication. Even more importantly, the language of rights recognizes the dignity and agency of individuals ... and human rights are inseparable from the notion of accountability. Where rights are ignored or violated, there must be accountability.[26]

Alston's Special Rapporteur report on the IMF, prepared pursuant to an HRC Resolution directing that a focus on that organization's impact on social protection is not as hard on that organization.[27] His IMF report does not, for example, describe that organization as a 'human rights free zone'. Nonetheless, common themes emerge, as does Alston's concern for organizational accountability. This report portrays the IMF (like the earlier reports did the United Nations and the Bank) as an institution whose progressive rhetoric does not match its on-the-ground operational efforts.[28]

The IMF Report mentions in passing the familiar critique that the IMF has long disregarded microeconomic 'social issues' by pursuing a macroeconomic 'pro-growth agenda' that for a time included structural adjustment policies consistent with versions of the Washington Consensus. Alston notes that despite the IMF's pro-development intentions, such policies may have immiserated millions in the world's poorest countries.[29] However, this 2018 report focuses not on the IMF's prior mistakes but on its current posture, namely its commitment since at least the 2007–2008 global economic crisis, to 'macro-criticality'. The IMF's new approach, Alston points out, would in principle permit consideration of a

[24] ibid para 33, fn 22 referring to the letter from twenty-eight special procedures mandates holders to the president of the World Bank, 12 December 2014. That letter focuses on the need for the Bank to embrace human rights in its safeguard policies. Philip Alston and others, 'UN Experts' Letter to World Bank President Jim Yong Kim' (December 2014) <https://sjc-cjs.org/wp-content/uploads/2014/12/UN-experts-letter-to-WB-Dec-2014.pdf> accessed 10 September 2020.

[25] ibid para 32.

[26] ibid para 65.

[27] (Henceforth IMF Report) UNHRC 'Report of the Special Rapporteur on Extreme Poverty and Human Rights' (8 May 2018) UN Doc A/HRC/38/33.

[28] ibid para 35. The IMF Report describes the IMF's preference for what it calls a 'social safety net' perspective on social protection as opposed to a human rights approach; the latter, which would incorporate principles like non-discrimination, gender equality, and social inclusion, 'offers elements of an accountability framework'. The Report argues that the IMF's 'social safety net' approach, by contrast, sees the need for such nets only as short-term fixes to mitigate the effects of fiscal adjustment, economic reforms, or external economic shocks.

[29] ibid para 2.

range of societal challenges, including social protection, inequality, gender equality, governance, and climate change.[30]

Alston's critique of the IMF's stance on human rights begins, as do his earlier reports, with criticism of its lawyers. Alston starts with a 2005 legal opinion by the IMF's then General Counsel, which had concluded that the organization, as a 'monetary' and not a 'development' agency, should focus on maintaining 'orderly exchange rates and a multilateral system of payments free of restrictions on current payments'.[31] As he does with respect to the United Nations' and the Bank's lawyers, Alston criticizes such 'formalism', noting the double standards suggested by the IMF's 2010 review of its mandate in the wake of the financial crisis, which had treated the Fund's Articles of Agreement as 'sufficiently flexible to accommodate major reforms'.[32] Alston agrees with this evolutive view of the IMF's Articles and not with a contemporaneous opinion issued by the IMF's lawyers that suggested that the organization was precluded from using its power for 'political objectives'.[33] Alston contrasts this cramped interpretation with the organization's actual operations. He contrasts the IMF's political will to act on a number of matters that have 'macro-critical' effects, such as corruption and military spending, with its lawyers' deployment of a 'human rights taboo' that forbids engagement on the basis that, for example, the organization is not a party to either the ICESCR or the ICCPR. Alston's report also criticizes other IMF policies—such as its willingness to target for reduction government benefits to the most vulnerable, its blinkered approaches to discouraging 'inefficient' government subsidies (as with respect to energy prices), its 'indicative targets' for social spending, and its failure to engage with other international organizations (eg the UN Conference on Sustainable Development or the ILO).[34]

The IMF Report also takes the IMF to task for its rhetorical stance. While Alston praises the IMF's comments on the need to address income and gender inequality, he criticizes the organization for 'air-brushing' human rights away even on these occasions. He points out that even when taking these progressive positions, the IMF fails to refer to states' obligations under the relevant human rights treaties, such as their duties under the Convention on the Elimination of All Forms of Discrimination Against Women (CEDAW).[35]

19.2 The Reports in Context: Accountability, Rule of Law, and Beyond

Alston's focus on organizational accountability reflects long-standing concerns among international lawyers. There is a considerable international law literature raising the titular question of this essay.[36] Even before UN system organizations expanded their mandates in the modern age, international lawyers worried about how or who would be authorized to bring these new potential lawmakers and law-enforcers to account. The three special rapporteurs under review here say little about whether or why international organizations within the UN system—namely interstate organizations established and subject to their own constituent

[30] ibid para 8.
[31] ibid para 12.
[32] ibid.
[33] ibid para 14.
[34] ibid paras 49-50.
[35] ibid para 30.
[36] For example, Mahnoush H Arsanjani, 'Claims Against International Organization: Quis Custodiet Isos Custodes' (1981) 7 Yale Journal of International Law 131.

instruments as well as relationship agreements with the central United Nations—are 'subject' to international human rights law. The most forthright effort to address this question occurs not in Alston's three reports but in a single paragraph in the joint letter issued by twenty-eight mandate holders directed at the president of the World Bank that is referenced in Alston's World Bank Report. That joint letter, co-signed by Alston, affirms that:

> Human rights are not merely a matter of sound policy, but of legal obligation. As an international organization with international legal personality, and as a UN specialized agency, the Bank is bound by obligations stemming not only from its Articles of Agreement, but also from human rights obligations arising under 'general rules of international law' and the UN Charter. Moreover, each of the 188 Member States of the World Bank has ratified at least one (and, in almost all cases, several) of the core international human rights treaties. Those States are also bound by human rights obligations stemming from other sources of international law. It is widely recognized that Member States should take their international human rights obligations into account when acting through an international organization such as the World Bank. States that borrow from the Bank also continue to be bound by their own international human rights obligations in the context of Bank-financed development projects and the Bank has a due diligence responsibility not to facilitate the violations of their human rights obligations, or to otherwise become complicit in such violations.[37]

While this statement does not identify precisely which international human rights obligations apply to international organizations as primary rules of obligation, it is compatible with the six most common arguments for finding that international organizations have a legal duty to abide by human rights violations and need to provide remedies when they breach such duties. These can be summarized as follows:

(1) Because, as international legal persons, international organizations have, like states, both rights and duties under international law and these include human rights duties imposed under their constituent instruments and any later treaties to which they have acceded, as well as rules under customary international law or general principles of law.
(2) Because, as the agents of entities bound by human rights, these organizational principles are not themselves exempt from the human rights duties imposed on the states that established them.
(3) Because, even if human rights duties were not initially imposed on these organizations, these have been accepted by the organizations themselves in terms of their subsequent practice.
(4) Because state members of these organizations cannot evade their human rights duties merely be establishing bodies to act collectively.[38]

[37] Alston and others, 'UN Experts' Letter to World Bank President' (n 24) 4 (footnotes omitted).
[38] ILC, 'Draft Articles on Responsibility of States for Internationally Wrongful *Acts*' (November 2001) UN Doc A/56/10 art 61. (Henceforth DARIO) (stating that a member of an international organization incurs international responsibility if it 'circumvents' its own international obligations by causing the organization to commit an act that if committed by the state would have constituted a breach of the obligation).

(5) Because, even if these organizations have acceded to no human rights obligations, they now have a duty, under evolving human rights law, not to facilitate the violation of those rights by states.
(6) Because human rights obligations, while once applicable by the terms of most human rights treaties only to states, have now evolved into obligations on certain non-state actors, including international organizations.[39]

All these contentions remain contestable. The ICJ's Reparation Opinion did not find, contrary to proposition 1, that the personhood enjoyed by the United Nations, or the duties associated with it, was identical to that of states. The ICJ said nothing about the nature of such duties or whether they included human rights and appeared to ground its specific findings in that instance on the object and purpose and functions accorded to the United Nations under its Charter.[40] Even if one assumes that organizations are analogous to agents (and are not eg closer to being the trustees of states),[41] it is controversial to pierce, as proposition 2 suggests, the organizational veil to impose member states' obligations onto them, particularly when the organizations are accorded powers/rights not generally given to individual states (such as the right/obligation to respond to threats to international peace and security, to respond to exchange rate fluctuations, or to engage in conditional assistance).[42] Proposition 3 may not surmount the problem that organizations are not parties to human rights treaties because, even if some international organizations have appeared to take human rights into account in their actions, it is not clear that, in these instances, the organizational practice was intended to constitute binding subsequent practice of the organization's charter instrument as a matter of treaty interpretation. Further, even if that were true and organizational practice exists showing that, for example, UN peacekeepers are now subject to international humanitarian law and perhaps human rights law because of practice backed by broad member acquiescence, that same institutional practice may also limit the available remedies should breach occur. If UN practice is that it only compensates for private law claims directed at peacekeepers and that the organization (or its lawyers) gets to decide what the definition of such claims are or that such claims can only be brought before Claims Settlement Commissions established when the United Nations and peacekeeping host states agree, that organizational practice may do little to enable accountability—as has been the case to date in the Haiti cholera case. Support for propositions 4, 5, and 6 remains similarly contestable, as is suggested by the meagre state or organizational practice cited in the ILC's commentaries in support of its Draft Articles of Responsibility of International Organizations.[43]

While Alston's three reports clearly imply that the United Nations, the World Bank, and the IMF are indeed subject to human rights obligations, his reports are circumspect on the

[39] ibid. While the DARIO, as adopted by the ILC, do not purport to address the primary rules of obligation that apply to international organizations, those secondary rules may presume that international organizations are subject to at least some human rights obligations on the basis of one or more of these six grounds.

[40] *Reparation for Injuries Suffered in the Service of the United Nations* (Advisory Opinion) 1949 <www.icj-cij.org/files/case-related/4/004-19490411-ADV-01-00-EN.pdf> accessed 10 September 2020, finding that the United Nations was entitled to pursue a claim against a state that had been implicated in the killing of a UN agent because this was functionally necessary to fulfil the United Nations' purposes.

[41] For Alston's own careful efforts to distinguish the two possibilities and their consequences, see, for example, Alston (n 2) 626–36.

[42] For example, Institut De Droit International, 'The Legal Consequences for Member States of the Non-Fulfillment by International Organizations of their Obligations toward Third Parties' (Session of Lisbonne, 1995) <www.idi-iil.org/app/uploads/2017/06/1995_lis_02_en.pdf> accessed 10 May 2021.

[43] ILC, 'Report of the International Law Commission on the Work of its 63rd Session' (9 November 2011) UN Doc A/66/10.

point. They do not attempt to explain why or to what extent this is the case.[44] Alston's reports do not discuss the aforementioned six rationales, variants on them, or possible counters. The IMF report, for example, identifies in a footnote criticisms of an IMF General Counsel's suggestion that the organization is not bound by human rights treaties but notes that 'this is not the occasion for a wide-ranging review of such matters which the IMF itself should undertake'.[45] Given Alston's refusal to countenance diplomatic politesse in these reports in other respects, this reticence to make definite legal findings probably reflects Alston's view of the functions of special rapporteurs.

As a scholar, Alston has argued that special rapporteurs fill several roles but they are neither jurisprudes nor judges. Special rapporteurs are 'front-line protection actors' engaged in the never-ending battle to make human rights real by protecting its victims;[46] 'interlocutors' who address those accused of violating human rights by engaging in critical fact-finding or 'communicators' of inconvenient truths. When specifically charged, they may also produce 'thematic' analyses of how organizational action matches up with human rights goals, such as social protection. But even if they do not engage in formal adjudication, special rapporteurs' proposed new international standards may still influence the subsequent interpretation of the law.[47]

As Special Rapporteur on Extreme Poverty and Human Rights, Alston has clearly adhered to his own recipe book. The three reports considered here go where the respective organizations fear to tread—but only up to a point. As an experienced human rights lawyer, Alston relies heavily on his legal training and his reports are, as noted, analytical briefs that express a definite point of view. But they do not purport to be binding legal judgments comparable to those issued by courts. In putting the interests of the persons adversely and directed affected at the forefront, the reports presume that the organizations seek to and need to comply with human rights, whether they are formally bound to do so under any single jurisprudential theory.

Consistent with Alston's view of the functions of special rapporteurs, the reports engage in detailed fact-finding that the organizations involved, through ignorance, malfeasance, or both, ignore. But these reports do not anticipate using a court of law, national or international law, to bring a legally binding action for damages owed to the human rights victims of any of the organizations involved as a result of the facts that the special rapporteur finds and the reports do not themselves purport to substitute for such a court. Indeed, even the Haiti Cholera Report, which in dealing with a specific claim seems most amenable to the issuance of a tort judgment does not conclude that the US court that heard the claims of Haitian cholera victims should pierce UN immunity in order to bring about accountability.[48] All three reports pursue, on the contrary, accountability through dialogue-cum-mobilization of shame. All three seek to achieve this goal by furthering a dialogue with the organizational officials involved and the states (and other civil society actors) that can influence them. The hope is that through this dialogue the relevant organizations, and their lawyers, will come to see human rights as friend not foe.

[44] UN Doc A/71/367 (n 6) para 69 for its part, says simply that the 'rule of law' requires that the United Nations comply with the status-of-forces agreement as well as 'fundamental human rights such as providing an effective remedy'.

[45] UN Doc A/HRC/38/33 (n 27) para 21.

[46] Alston (n 2) 571.

[47] ibid 572–78.

[48] Others have not been so reticent. For example, Kristen Boon, 'The United Nations as Good Samaritan: Immunity and Responsibility' (2015) 16(2) Chicago Journal of International Law 341 <https://chicagounbound.uchicago.edu/cjil/vol16/iss2/2>.

Alston's three reports convey the common message that such dialogues should not involve only the organizations' most powerful stakeholders, such as its principal funders. The reports encourage a broader dialogue on the view that anything less will short-change each organization and undermine its respective mandate. Each report argues that matters that seemingly have little to do with human rights—the need for organizational immunity in the case of the United Nations, the demand for apolitical development advice and projects, or operationalization of sound fiscal policies—are actually about human rights or at the very least have real human rights effects and would therefore benefit from a broader framing. Given Alston's specific mandate, all the reports understandably emphasize that the plight of the extreme poor are directly impacted by each organization's operational activities—and that such impact relates to the indivisible human rights obligations found in the ICESCR and the ICCPR.

Each report argues that what the organization's lawyers say matters and that 'sterile legalistic' arguments lead to human rights operational blindness. Each argues that such blindness is exacerbated by the blinkered expertise that accompanies professional mindsets. Expert-driven blindness is not limited to institutionally situated lawyers worried about setting adverse 'precedents'. It extends, in the cases of the Bank and the IMF, to economists who are more comfortable with 'science' than with messier notions of fairness or equity. All three reports fault professional elites for not taking into account how their professional expertise incorporates distinct values that protect the elites themselves at the expense of the most vulnerable. All three reports criticize the organizations for failing to consider the ethics of action; for ignoring the political economy of UN peacekeeping, development, or social protection; and for bypassing genuine engagement with actors with outsider views.

Although, as noted, Alston's three reports do not engage directly with the six rationales that might justify the human rights responsibilities of international organizations enumerated earlier, his reports are replete with reasons why it would be foolish to argue that such responsibilities do not apply to each organization or that somehow the organization is constitutionally barred from so finding. His special rapporteur reports suggest that those who resist the implication of the six rationales or who insist on parsing each of them to conclude that under positivist sources of international law international organizations bear no human rights responsibilities would be engaging in the very kind of sterile legalism that he is criticizing. But if readers of these reports draw this conclusion, the reports do not do it for them. Alston appears to assume that his role, as special rapporteur, is to persuade through pragmatic argument—but not to render, as would a judge, a top-down definitive legal ruling that could generate backlash.

This understanding of the role of special rapporteur is consistent with those who argue that the effectiveness of human rights norms can be understood as a form of 'experimentalist governance', namely iterative and broadly participatory processes involving states and non-state actors across a multilevel system that operate to implement shared commitments whose interpretation changes over time as a result of that same dialogic process.[49] Experimentalists argue that such processes—which in human rights regimes involve state reports and reactions to these by human rights treaty bodies, special rapporteurs, and other non-international organization actors such as NGOs—respond to the failures of 'command-and-control' or top-down regulatory efforts.[50] They also stress, as does Alston,

[49] For example, Grainne de Búrca, 'Human Rights Experimentalism' (2017) 111 American Journal of International Law 277.

[50] ibid 281.

'the importance of ensuring accountability through the regular provision of information and by means of an ongoing and transparent process of non-hierarchical review'.[51] Alston's three reports might be seen as supplying one of the feedback loops in experimentalist governance. As such their function is not to posit a definitive legal interpretation but to keep the interpretation of human rights 'open to reconsideration and revision [in] light of the information gained and lessons learned in the process of implementation'.[52] His information-generating reports might be seen as occasions for 'reflexivity' for the organizations and their stakeholders. Consistent with experimentalist goals, these reports appear to be structured as catalysts for reform. They seem intended to destabilize dysfunctional pre-existing legal interpretations without imposing rigid legal interpretations that may prove difficult to dislodge as circumstances change and as our understanding of what human dignity demands changes over time.[53]

Despite Alston's reluctance to engage with jurisprudential theory as a special rapporteur, his three reports are, of course, relevant to those interested in determining whether, as a formal legal matter, organizations are indeed subject to human rights. As Alston the scholar has acknowledged, special rapporteurs can be effective accountability mechanisms insofar as they exercise significant authority and persuade others of the validity of their underlying interpretations.[54] There is considerable evidence that this may have happened here. Alston's efforts on behalf of the victims of Haiti cholera—which extend far beyond the issuance of the single report discussed here—spurred the United Nations to issue the most detailed response to the complaint initially filed by the Haiti cholera victims, probably helped push the then-current UN Secretary General to provide a public apology to those victims, and continues to pressure the organization with respect to its evolving response to the disaster.[55] As Alston's IMF Report acknowledges, his prior report on the Bank drew considerable attention at the highest levels of that body and appears to have moved the Bank to take some of the recommendations in that report seriously.[56] It is too early to say whether his IMF report will have comparable effects. To the extent these reports, as intended, come to affect what these organizations do, they inspire the 'subsequent practices' and/or state practice that underlie a number of the six rationales for human rights duties noted earlier. Special rapporteurs like Alston undoubtedly aspire to have their soft law efforts become hard law through subsequent operational practice.

If the United Nations were ultimately to accept legal responsibility for Haiti cholera and to provide even a modest level of compensation to its victims, this would build on and solidify the organization's prior accountability precedents—as in the Congo case decades before. It would help to show that the United Nations is indeed accountable even for mass torts, despite its failures to establish Claims Commissions under peacekeeping or the limits on other adjudicative venues imposed by organizational immunity. To the extent internationally financial institutions accept that their mandates encompass human rights and need to address the human rights impact of their operations (as Alston's World Bank and IMF Reports urge), this would expand the meaning of those organizations' respective charters and administrative policies. And these changes would also potentially expand the scope of relevant human

[51] ibid 282–83.
[52] ibid 293.
[53] See generally ibid 311–12.
[54] Alston (n 2) 580.
[55] For example, Bruce Rashkow, 'Above The Law? Innovating Legal Response To Build A More Accountable U.N.: Where Is The U.N. Now?' (2017) 23(2) ILSA Journal of International & Comparative Law 345.
[56] UN Doc A/HRC/38/33 (n 27) para 10, fn 16.

rights treaties. It would expand what it means when states are told to 'respect and ensure' the rights contained in the ICCPR or to 'take steps' to advance the rights in the ICESCR.[57] More specifically, it would broaden what the latter instrument means when it instructs parties to 'recognize the right of everyone to an adequate standard of living for himself and his family'.[58] This is undoubtedly what Alston means when he says that special rapporteurs help build new understandings of the law.

Of course, the activity of special rapporteurs, like all those who seek to 'enforce' human rights, is not risk free. As Alston's IMF Report suggests, not all organizations (or states) take criticism well; some may simply reject critical human rights reports.[59] To the extent these reports—or parts of their recommendations for change—are not implemented or, after public consideration, are intentionally rejected by these organizations, that too may have an impact.[60] The more general point is that these reports—which have to be brief given the page limits their audiences expect—do not have to explicitly address the jurisprudential theories under which international organizations are subject to human rights to play a role in making these theories more (or less) plausible over time.

As a general matter, the three special rapporteur reports discussed here advance our understanding of how 'legal accountability' can be understood in the context of international organizations. The intense attention to 'accountability', has often generated more confusion than light. Like other related (and similarly lauded) goals such as achieving 'rule of law', accountability is often seen as a vague all-purpose solution to a wide number of contemporary anxieties. As do scholars like Richard Stewart, Special Rapporteur Alston seeks to bring some precision to the term.[61] Alston's three reports focus, as does Stewart's scholarship, on how best to 'remedy disregard'. As a scholar Alston argues that legal accountability requires (1) identifying who is responsible, (2) indicating to whom responsibility is owed, (3) stating what precisely is owed, (4) through what means, and (5) with what consequences.[62] Alston's three reports broadly follow this model.

Alston's Haiti Cholera Report, the only one focused on a concrete instance triggering legal accountability, accordingly argues that the United Nations (and not eg Nepal, which sent the peacekeepers to Haiti) is responsible; that this responsibility must include acceptance of legal responsibility by the United Nations, a formal apology to the Haiti cholera victims, meaningful process for the vindication of claims, and some forms of suitable redress (and not just the allocation of funds to build the country's infrastructure for clean water). That report also suggests that these remedies can emerge from arbitration or other forms of settlement that are attentive to the needs of victims. Finally, that report suggests the need for the

[57] International Covenant on Civil and Political Rights (adopted 16 December 1966, entered into force 23 March 1976) 999 UNTS 171 (ICCPR) art 2; International Covenant on Economic, Social and Cultural Rights (adopted 16 December 1966, entered into force 3 January 1976) 993 UNTS 3 (ICESCR) art 2.

[58] ibid art 11.

[59] UN Doc A/HRC/38/33 (n 27) para 10 (noting that the World Bank failed to facilitate meetings between the special rapporteur and the Bank's social protection experts perhaps in retaliation for Alston's World Bank Report).

[60] The same institutional progress that giveth can taketh away; experimentalist scholars accept that the same iterative processes that may expand the meaning of human rights over time may come to narrow them, for example, de Búrca (n 49) 296.

[61] Richard B Stewart, 'Remedying Disregard in Global Regulatory Governance: Accountability, Participation, and Responsiveness' (2014) 108 American Journal of International Law 211. Stewart argues that accountability is most needed to remedy the problem that the most powerful international regimes, such as those epitomized by UN peacekeeping and the actions of international financial institutions, tend to promote the objective of dominant states and economic actors and are inclined to disregard weaker groups and individuals; ibid 211.

[62] For example, Alston (n 2) 639–43.

UN to accept the legal principle that in the future comparable cases of mass torts should be treated by the UN as private claims eligible for similar treatment.

The three reports reflect the insight that in the international context what is required is a public evaluation of the power-wielder's conduct along with provision for an 'appropriate' remedy.[63] In a world where organizational 'accountability' is associated with a broad range of mechanisms—from ombudspersons to inspection panels—'legal' responsibility or accountability cannot be the exclusive prerogative of courts charged with issuing binding judgments.[64] Alston's reports reflect a highly pragmatic interpretation of 'legal accountability' befitting regimes where binding adjudicative awards containing full reparation remain exceptionally rare.

The suggested remedies contained in the Haiti Cholera Report heed Alston's warnings against legal formalism. His report suggests that remedies consistent with human rights law can and should be attentive to the financial and other practical constraints of the responsible entity; such remedies cannot involve the 'full' compensation that might be expected from, for example, a national court responding to tort claims between private parties. In the case of Haiti cholera, Alston anticipates that an effective remedy needs to take into account the triadic interests suggested by UN status-of-forces agreements—that is, remedies that, like those agreements, balance the interests of the organization, troop-contributing states, and the host states of the peacekeepers. He accepts that adequate reparation for the Haiti victims can consist of a lump sum settlement that would not undermine the financial viability of peacekeeping or of the United Nations as a whole.[65]

Alston's three reports should also be of interest to those who debate whether the most relevant analogy between international organizations and their members is that of principal-agent or principal-trustee. As would be suggested by his scholarship, Alston's prescriptions in these reports presume that the relationship between these organizations and their members is more akin to the latter.[66] His Haiti Cholera Report argues, in effect, that UN peacekeepers, UN investigating teams, and UN lawyers charged with examining the consequences of malfeasance resulting from peacekeeping, should not be seen as merely agents doing the will of states. The implication of his report is that UN peacekeepers are not sent to pursue the agenda of particular troop-contributing states or of significant funders of peacekeeping such as the United States, but of the international community as a whole. Consistent with this mandate, they are sent to protect vulnerable populations and must be accountable to them. Similarly, UN investigators and UN lawyers are not simply charged with protecting the finances of the organization or of the largest contributor to the UN budget, as would a mere agent. These organizational actors are charged with exercising some independent judgment and are most valuable to their 'principals' when they exercise that judgment. Neither should be penalized for rendering objective, if unwelcome, advice. Alston's reports see the relevant actors (including international organization-based lawyers and special rapporteurs like Alston himself) in each organization as trustees with responsibilities, including to

[63] For example, Stewart (n 61) 246–48.

[64] Cf Ruth W Grant and Robert O Keohane, 'Accountability and Abuses of Power in World Politics' (2005) 99 American Political Science Review 29 (describing seven mechanisms of accountability and limiting 'legal' accountability to the actions of courts); Mara Pillinger, Ian Hurd, and Michael N Barnett, 'How to Get Away with Cholera: The UN, Haiti, and International Law' (2016) 14 Perspectives on Politics 70 (blaming the UN stalemate with respect to respond to the Haiti cholera claims on 'legalism' insofar as it insists on accountability before a court since it 'forecloses non-legal modes of responsibility and accountability').

[65] UN Doc A/71/367 (n 6) 17–18.

[66] Alston (n 2) 634.

people adversely affected by their operational decisions. If he sees such organizational actors as 'agents' at all, they are agents of accountability.

Alston's three reports also provide some insight into another highly contested concept: the (international) rule of law. The literature on accountability is a pittance compared to that devoted to explicating what the (national) rule of law means, whether such a conception can be exported successfully to other nations, and whether there is any such thing as the 'international rule of law'. That vast literature cannot be surveyed here. Suffice to say that despite considerable attention to the 'rule of law' at the United Nations and particularly as embraced by UN peace operations, international lawyers continue to disagree over whether the rule of law has universally applicable content such that it can or should be successfully exported (as by UN peacekeepers or by the good governance efforts of international financial institutions) or whether the ideal of an 'international rule of law' is a viable concept.

These disagreements reflect, at least in part, divisions among legal philosophers who have defended 'thin' or 'thick' definitions of rule of law.[67] Advocates for a thin definition of rule of law commonly contend that it is satisfied by systems that respect certain procedural protections among parties such as evincing respect for the equality of arms. Critics of this view argue that the thin definition would be satisfied even by German law under Nazi rule, at least to the extent that law applied to all equally and that therefore the thin rule of law is a misnomer insofar as it really constitutes rule *by* law. Advocates of a thick definition argue that genuine rule of law systems require, in addition, the satisfaction of certain substantive standards of justice or fairness. In Lord Bingham's widely cited view, these would include respect for equality, publicity (ie accessible, intelligible, predictable law administered by courts), legally bound discretion, good faith exercise of power in accordance with the purpose for which powers were conferred, protection of fundamental human rights (including the rights to a fair trial, to liberty, security, and property), and access to other means to resolve civil disputes without prohibitive cost or delay.[68] Kofi Annan's enumeration of the characteristics of the rule of law is as 'thick' as Lord Bingham's:

> '[The rule of law] refers to a principle of governance in which all persons, institutions, and entities, public and private, including the State itself, are accountable to laws that are publicly promulgated, equally enforced and independently adjudicated, and which are consistent with international human rights norms and standards. It requires, as well, measures to ensure adherence to the principles of supremacy of law, equality before the law, accountability to the law, fairness in the application of the law, separation of powers, participation in decision-making, legal certainly, avoidance of arbitrariness and procedural and legal transparency.'[69]

[67] With respect to the (national) rule of law, the thin conception has been associated with the views of Joseph Raz, for example, Joseph Raz, 'The Rule of Law and its Virtue', in Joseph Raz (ed), *The Authority of Law: Essays on Law and Morality* (2nd edn, OUP 2009) 210–29 ; for one version of the 'thick' (or at least thicker conception) see, for example, Tom Bingham, *The Rule of Law* (Allen Lane 2010); debates over these rival definitions have included interlocutors concerned with whether it is a good idea to export either the thick or thin conceptions of the rule of law to others as part of legal reform efforts. For example, Ruti Teitel, 'Global Rule of Law: Universal and Particular' in András Sajó (ed), *Human Rights with Modesty: The Problem of Universalism* (M Nijhoff Publishers 2004) 231–47 criticizing the thick concept); Frank Upham, 'The Illusory Promise of the Rule of Law', in ibid 279–313 (criticizing the thin concept); for reflections of these debates within international law, see Robert McCorquodale, 'Defining the International Rule of Law: Defying Gravity?' (2016) 65(2) International and Comparative Law Quarterly 277; Simon Chesterman, 'An International Rule of Law?' (2008) 56 The American Journal of Comparative Law 331.

[68] Bingham (n 67).

[69] Report of the Secretary General, 'The Rule of Law and Transitional Justice in Conflict and Post-Conflict Societies' (2004) UN Doc S/2004/616 para 6.

The expansive characteristics of a thick rule of law predictably lead to complaints that these culturally pre-determined values are not necessarily universal and are not promising subjects for transnational export—or for successful application at the international level.[70]

Alston's three reports address the 'rule of law' only in passing but there are clear indications in all of them that their author subscribes to a relatively thick definition of the term. Of the three reports, the report on Haiti cholera has the most extensive passage on point. The reasons for a change of UN policy with respect to Haiti-type claims include, according to Alston:

> The rule of law. The Secretary-General and the Deputy Secretary-General have given strong voice to the resolutions of the General Assembly in which the Assembly underscored the central importance of respecting the rule of law. Yet, the approach of the United Nations in this case undermines the rule of law and diminishes the Organization's credibility as an advocate for its respect. By failing to take even minimal steps to hold itself accountable and compensate those affected, or even to explain the reasons for its refusal to do so, the United Nations replicates the very behavior it seeks to modify elsewhere. The rule of law requires that the United Nations abide by its treaty obligations, including those under the status-of-forces agreement, as well as fundamental human rights such as providing an effective remedy to those harmed by the Organization. It also requires that the Organization act consistently and respond in comparable fashion to all legitimate private law claims made against it. The United Nations should be leading by setting a good example.[71]

This statement affirms a thin conception of the rule of law insofar as it suggests that it is a violation of the rule of law to fail to follow the law. But Alston goes beyond that and appears to agree with Kofi Annan's thick definition. He suggests, as does the former Secretary General, that the international rule of law applies to all public institutions like the UN; that it necessarily requires accountability to law; that it needs to be consistent with fundamental human rights; and that it needs to avoid arbitrary or discriminatory application. Alston also seems to presume, in accord with Lord Bingham, that the rule of law embraces a number of qualities associated with the rule of law at the national level, namely what Bingham called equality, publicity, legally bound discretion, good faith exercise of powers conferred, and access to means for resolving civil disputes (or 'effective remedies'). To the extent Alston's prescriptions are followed, the resulting organizational practice will supply valuable ammunition to supporters of an exceptionally thick notion of the international (and perhaps national) rule of law.

But there are more subtle aspects to these reports insofar as the rule of law is concerned. In the rule of law statement just quoted, as well as in the other reports surveyed here, Alston is less interested in whether the rule of law in general contains one or more particular elements. His core argument is that the United Nations, the Bank, and the IMF each needs to adhere to a relatively thick conception of the rule of law because of those institutions' respective actions and statements. He is arguing that these organizations, prime movers of expansive conceptions of the rule of law in others and self-proclaimed adherents to human rights values and the 'rule of law', need themselves to adhere to these ideals because they have generated expectations that they will abide by what they are doing and saying. They need to respect the

[70] For example, José E Alvarez, 'International Organisations and the Rule of Law' (2016) 14 New Zealand Journal of Public and International Law 3.

[71] UN Doc A/71/367 (n 6) para 69.

rule of law because, in short, they have helped to define it and because they see themselves as helping to build it. Alston does not back this intuitively appealing argument with a formal legal argument. As usual, Alston, the non-judge, does not explain whether these organizations are bound to a relatively thick rule of law because, for example, they have made what amounts to binding unilateral commitments to that effect[72] or because 'their actions and even pronouncements are routinely treated as legally salient, even when they do not appear to be in binding form'[73] or because this is demanded by legal certainty, legitimate expectations, or for some other reason. The important point he is making, grounded in ideas of political economy and common sense, is that the credibility/legitimacy of these rule of law promoters is very much on the line should they violate the rule of law that they are seeking to enforce on others and that they claim to be upholding. These are distinct arguments for rule of law compliance by these organizations that have more to do with the reciprocity-respecting and good faith principles underlying *pacta sunt servanda* than with rival thick or thin conceptions of the rule of law.

Alston's reports also suggest that debates between those who disagree over whether the 'international rule of law' should emulate the characteristics associated with the national rule of law may be less important than is recognition that both international regimes and national legal systems need to deploy diverse tools to ensure the accountability of the powerful. Since national systems use their executive and legislative branches, and not only their courts to this end, it should not surprise us if international organizations need to employ a panoply of methods apart from formal adjudication. As suggested by these reports' prescriptions for change, those looking for rule of law mechanisms within international organizations (and among them) need to look for them in all kinds of places and among many actors. International organizations can draw inspiration from the rule of law mechanisms used in national systems but they are not limited to them and it is probably not wise to try to export national rule of law accountability methods to international organizations. Diplomatic (and not always fully transparent) approaches to accountability, for example, may be both necessary and more legitimate when it comes to international organizations. These reports also suggest that the goal of achieving 'international rule of law' should not be waylaid by the erroneous notion that fidelity to the rule of law is an either/or thing like pregnancy. Alston's pragmatic approach to accountability implies that the search for 'a' rule of law/accountability ideal may be the enemy of the good. His reports' incremental prescriptions for change reflect the insight that rule of law compliance is, at least at the international (if not the national) level, a matter of degree.[74] Finally, these reports' emphasis on organizational policies that have a serious adverse impact on individuals suggest that we ought to be most concerned about rule of law and individual accountability when international organizations' actions raise concerns comparable to those that arise between sovereigns and their subjects.[75]

Alston's three reports also appear to reject the notion, propounded by some legal positivists, that 'compliance' with international law is a simple matter of determining whether a state or an international organization abides by a pre-determined rule that is backed by some kind of sanction for disobedience. Alston's reports presume that international law is

[72] For example, *Legal Status of Eastern Greenland (Denmark v Norway)* PCIJ Rep Series A/B No 53; *Nuclear Tests Case (Australia v France)* [1974] ICP Rep 253, 267.

[73] For example, Monica Hakimi, 'The *Jus Ad Bellum* 's Regulatory Form' (2018) 112 American Journal of International Law 151, 165.

[74] See also McCorquodale (n 67) 304.

[75] For example, Alvarez 'International Organisations' (n 70) 21–22 (discussing Jeremy Waldron's comparisons of the relative powers of sovereign states versus international organizations with respect to rule of law concerns).

given effect in far more complex ways. His reports, which embody a fluid conception of how international law becomes more or less effective over time, reflect the insights of critics of 'compliance' such as Robert Howse and Ruti Teitel.[76] His reports on the Bank and the IMF, for example, presume that the benchmarks set by those organizations can affect the behaviour of private actors (such as those institutions' financial interlocutors); that pro-active efforts to change the interpretation of international law can change the context in which actors bargain or shift power from one set of actors (eg economists) to others (eg human rights lawyers); that cross-regime interactions among distinct international regimes can also alter the interpretations of both international and national law; that affecting what international organization lawyers say the law means can affect policymakers' views of the mandate of the organization or the constituencies to whom the international organization is accountable; and that institutional charters are best interpreted teleologically in light of social, political, and economic circumstances.[77] At the same time, Alston accepts that despite the multiple, sometimes political, avenues by which international law becomes effective, the use of legal language continues to matter.[78] Indeed, Alston's reports reflect a keen awareness that being seen as law-abiding is important to global organizations that appeal to and rely on universalist ideas.

Finally, the rapporteurs' reports discussed here evince strong views about the professional responsibilities of lawyers. This special rapporteur clearly expects more from organizational lawyers than legal interpretations that advance the perceived demands of clients. The reports' critiques of some of the lawyers' interpretations—whether of the definition of 'private law' claims or of 'political intervention'—reflect concerns that Alston the scholar has articulated. The reports critique legal interpretations by organizational insiders that reify, intentionally or not, the negative externalities of globalization.[79] They assert that some types of legal advice do not serve the long-term best interests of institutional clients. They imply that lawyers who tailor their advice to what they think the client wants to hear and not to what is the best interpretation of the law or who fail to warn clients about the social consequences of failing to follow that interpretation, engage in legal malpractice. These reports' critiques of legal formalism suggest that international organization lawyers' ethical responsibilities compel, as do many national professional codes of conduct, competent, objective, candid, and honest interpretations of the relevant law that include fulsome consideration of the moral, economic, social, and political context in which the lawyers' advice is sought and will be received.[80]

19.3 Conclusion

Philp Alston is of course not the only human rights scholar/activist attempting to be a guardian of our international guardians but his reports on three of those guardians, the

[76] For example, Robert Howse and Ruti Teitel, 'Beyond Compliance: Rethinking Why International Law Really Matters: Beyond Compliance' (2010) 1(2) Global Policy 127; Benedict Kingsbury, 'The Concept of Compliance as a Function of Competing Conceptions of International Law' (1998) 19 Michigan Journal of International Law 345.

[77] For example, Howse and Teitel (n 76) 127, 130–31.

[78] For example, ibid 133–34. This is why Alston affirms the importance of affirming human rights as such. See text at n 27.

[79] See generally Philip Alston, 'The Myopia of the Handmaidens: International Lawyers and Globalization' (1997) 3 European Journal of International Law 435.

[80] For example, José E Alvarez, 'Torturing the Law' (2006) 37 Case Western Reserve Journal of International Law 175, 221 (arguing that these standards were not satisfied by the legal memorandums authorizing the torture of terrorist suspects by Bush Administration lawyers).

United Nations, the World Bank, and the IMF, provide lessons for others. These special rapporteur reports take the words of institutionally based officials seriously. Alston urges these organizations to choose their words carefully and to rely expressly on human rights. He expects that when they generate expectations through their words that they will comply with the rule of law that they will follow through. He expects that what they claim to follow as a matter of public relations they will adhere to as a matter of operational policy.

In these special rapporteur reports, Alston uses international rules, particularly human rights norms, as agents of change and not as rules set in stone protecting the status quo because he sees them as the product of recursive interactions between legal and political actors. He accepts that the law can change as a result of critical engagements between organizational actors and special rapporteurs. Taking a page from Friedrich Kratochwill's notion of 'praxis', Alston's special rapporteur reports use practical reasoning and fact-finding to promote organizational change that will in turn affect subsequent reasoning within the organizations and changing conceptions of the law itself.[81] These reports evince hope that facts still matter and that the internalization of human rights values can occur even among experts hostile to them or organizational bureaucrats preoccupied with protecting their fiefdoms.

The three reports considered here respond to today's 'populist challenge to human rights' in the ways Alston himself has recommended. They appeal to instrumentalist, and not just legal arguments. They avoid the risks of undue (or 'sterile') legalism. They insist on accountability for human rights violations and they treat economic and social rights seriously.[82]

[81] See generally Friedrich V Kratochwil, *The Status of Law in World Society: Meditations on the Role and Rule of Law* (CUP 2014).

[82] For example, Philip Alston, 'The Populist Challenge to Human Rights' (2017) 9 Journal of Human Rights Practice 1.

20

The Persuasive Authority of Philip Alston's Work for Human Rights Regional Bodies

UN Reports, Statements, and General Comments do Matter

*Hélène Tigroudja**

20.1 Introduction

Professor Philip Alston has unparalleled knowledge and experience of UN human rights protection mechanisms: whether through his mandates as Special Rapporteur on Extrajudicial, Summary, and Arbitrary Executions[1] and Special Rapporteur on Extreme Poverty and Human Rights,[2] or in his capacity as a member and chairperson of the UN CESCR,[3] the treaty body monitoring the 1966 ICESCR. With these various strands of expertise, Alston has adopted—and is at the origin of—an extremely vast range of reports, declarations, statements, or general comments,[4] which constitute a rich source of *universal* human rights law, as highlighted in another chapter of this *Festschrift*. What is perhaps less visible is his contribution through his work as UN independent expert to *regional* human rights law, a contribution that is of varying nature and degree. The object of this chapter is to capture this contribution but also to go beyond it and share some reflections on the role that may be played by non-judicial human rights mechanisms and non-binding documents in the determination of individuals' human rights and the international obligations of states.

Beforehand, several issues must be underlined.

First, it is true that the proliferation of special procedures created by the former UN Human Rights Commission or the HRC that replaced it can make the UN human rights 'system' difficult to read, and the production of these bodies hardly accessible.[5] Moreover, internationalist lawyers acquainted with Prosper Weil would most probably consider that it contains no material to be studied since this work has nothing to do with *legal binding norms*. They would consider it as informative at best—on the state of human rights in a country, for example—but could in no way claim any place in the *international normative creation process*. The thematic report of a UN special rapporteur or a working group is obviously not binding; both the content (*negotium*) and the container (*instrumentum*) would be deprived

* I am deeply grateful to Ms Chloé Debord (AMU) for her editing work and to Professor Ludovic Hennebel (AMU) for his insightful and friendly comments.

[1] August 2004–July 2010.

[2] June 2014–May 2020.

[3] From 1987 to 1998, serving as the chairperson of the Committee from 1990 to 1998.

[4] General comments are adopted collectively by the CESCR and for the sake of my chapter, I am mentioning mainly the general comments for which Alston was rapporteur.

[5] As of 1 June 2021, there are forty-four thematic procedures and eleven country mandates.

Hélène Tigroudja, *The Persuasive Authority of Philip Alston's Work for Human Rights Regional Bodies* In: *The Struggle for Human Rights.* Edited by: Nehal Bhuta, Florian Hoffmann, Sarah Knuckey, Frédéric Mégret, and Margaret Satterthwaite, Oxford University Press.
 DOI: 10.1093/oso/9780198868064.003.0021

of any legal value or legal effect and, consequently, would be of no interest to the (serious and rigorous) lawyer.

It would be a mistake, however, to underestimate the importance of UN experts/bodies' production, which can take the form of thematic reports, reports following a state visit, communications, or declarations. Counterbalancing the strict positivist position, this chapter aims to demonstrate that international judicial and quasi-judicial practices go in the opposite direction. It does so by focusing on the experience of the ECtHR established by the ECHR of 4 November 1950 and the Inter-American Commission and Court on Human Rights in charge of the American Declaration of Human Rights and Duties of 1948 and the American Convention on Human Rights (ACHR) of 1969

The same applies to the general comments adopted by the UN treaty bodies. A general comment (or general recommendation as called by some treaty bodies)[6] allows a supervisory organ to specify the meaning of an article of the treaty or any other human right issue. This normative interpretation of the content and scope of a right or states' international obligations arises outside of any contentious claim. A general comment is therefore not a *judgment* with the authority of *res judicata* and unless it is considered that it merely reflects custom, it is difficult to oppose a general comment per se, that is, as an *instrument* to states parties to human rights treaties. However, underestimating its *legal* effects risks ignoring both what international public law is and how it is created. From this point of view, the role played by the general comments adopted by the CESCR when Alston was one of its members and then its president, in line with the shift launched by the Inter-American Court of Human Rights in its interpretation of the ACHR,[7] is undoubtedly one of the most striking illustrations not simply of the 'cross-fertilization' or migration of ideas, but more fundamentally of the normative power and persuasive authority that can be derived from a text that seems formally to be devoid of binding power.

It should also be added in the same breath that in the framework of special procedures and UN treaty bodies, not all work is equal and not all work is of the same quality and utility to victims, civil society, states, doctrinal reflection, or to the regional human rights bodies that wish to use it. Not all of it presents the same legal rigour, precision, and clarity in the information presented. More importantly, not all experts are nourished by a profound reflection about what they want to do with their normative project and, in particular, how they conceive the protected right or the values defended.[8] Nevertheless, as indicated earlier, the purpose of this chapter is to show how the work of a UN independent expert can have multiple effects and potentially contentious and normative consequences through the use made of that work by regional human rights bodies, provided that *the reports are sufficiently clear, precise, accessible, and rigorous.*

My reflection on this topic arose after reading a judgment delivered by the ECtHR—to which I will return later—where Alston's report on Romania—as Special Rapport on Extreme Poverty—was mentioned. The same report was further documented in the case-law of the Inter-American Commission and Court. My intention is not to present the practice of human rights organs by distinguishing them. Instead I will follow a relatively simple typology of the use made of Alston's reports, and the shades in the effects produced. As such,

[6] As the CERD and Committee on Elimination of Discrimination against Women (CEDAW).

[7] See sections 20.4 and 20.5 of this chapter.

[8] For reflections on the preparation of the 2018 UK mission, Philip Alston, Bassam Khawaja, and Rebecca Riddell, 'Much Ado about Poverty: The Role of a UN Special Rapporteur' (2019) 27 Journal of Poverty and Social Justice 423.

this chapter can be read in three different and complementary ways: in addition to paying tribute to a scholar and expert who has put his knowledge in the service of a holistic and humanist project, it also seeks to convince civil society actors, victims, and their defenders of the importance of making strategic use of the work of the special procedures as these can prove to be powerful tools for advancing the jurisdictional interpretation of rights and freedoms. Finally, the chapter aims to convince the human rights bodies themselves, and not only the regional bodies but also UN treaty bodies that can receive individual communications such as the Human Rights Committee, to use these reports to renew and refine their understanding of new human rights themes that are not covered by their original treaties.

The chapter's central contention is that under certain conditions of quality, rigour, and precision, the UN special procedures' reports reflect a peculiar approach or philosophy of human rights that may serve as a mean of *evolving* interpretation of human rights treaties. This is not just about explaining the technical and jurisprudential migration of ideas from the UN level to regional organs but to capture how Alston's normative human rights project as reflected in his reports and statements (section 20.2) have played and still play a procedural role and especially, in terms of evidence and substantiating a claim of violation before a judicial organ (section 20.3). I then seek to illustrate how a general comment may shape the interpretation provided by a regional tribunal of its binding treaty (section 20.4). Finally, in a more prospective tone, I will deal with the shift of paradigm launched by the Inter-American Court specifically based on CESCR's general comments (section 20.5).

20.2 Alston's Existentialist and Holistic Approach to Human Rights

Alston is not perceived nor read as a philosopher or legal theorist but as an international lawyer. He looks at the world, international society, and the human condition through legal analysis, schemes, concepts, and tools. It may therefore be odd to describe his normative project as an *existentialist* project in the philosophical sense of the term, that is, in the sense given to it by philosophers or thinkers such as Kierkegaard and Sartre. In philosophy, the existentialist project involves putting aside the metaphysics of Descartes in particular, which focused on the *essence* to situate the human being in his *existence*, and especially, in his relationship to temporality, to the moment, to the end and to the concrete. In the words of Sartre, at a conference in 1945 held in Paris: 'existence precedes essence' ('*l'existence précède l'essence*').[9] This well-known quote from existentialist thought can mean in substance that 'l'homme existe d'abord, se rencontre, surgit dans le monde, et qu'il se définit après. L'homme tel que le conçoit l'existentialiste, s'il n'est pas définissable, c'est qu'il n'est d'abord rien. *Il ne sera qu'ensuite, et il sera tel qu'il se sera fait. Ainsi, il n'y a pas de nature humaine, puisqu'il n'y a pas de Dieu pour le concevoir*'.[10]

Some of the existentialist authors—who, like Kierkegaard, refuted their qualification as 'philosophers' precisely because they rejected the abstraction, the construction of a system or concepts, and the metaphysics—focused on 'the question of *how to exist*, that is, the *choice*

[9] Jean-Paul Sartre, *L'existentialisme est un humanisme* (Gallimard 1996) 26.

[10] ibid 29 (emphasis added). The quote tentatively translates to: The existentialist believes that humans first exist, that they meet each other, that they arise in the world, and that they are defined afterwards. If the human being as conceived by the existentialist is not definable, it is because he is first of all nothing. He will only be afterwards, and he will be as he has been made. Thus, there is no human nature, since there is no God to conceive it.

of self as existing'. Existentialism emphasized the responsibility of the individual in becoming him or herself as well as towards others.[11] One of the common criticisms addressed to the existentialist project was its apparent pessimism, and its focus on the dark sides of human condition, such as the French naturalist Zola's sensitivity in literature.[12] However, as Sartre replied to these criticisms, what may be frightening is, on the contrary, the *optimistic* perception of human condition, based on freedom and the possibility of choice.[13]

It is obvious that the different branches and trends of existentialist approaches are much more complex than what is reflected in this over-simplistic presentation. But what may be taken from atheist existentialism are the key elements of *choice of existence, individual and collective responsibility*, and *individual freedom*. Having said that, what is the relation between Zola (naturalist), Sartre (existentialist), and an Australian UN expert (international lawyer)? By analysing Alston's reports, it is clear—at least through French eyes—that his thinking is existentialist in nature. This much appears from his work as a UN expert.

First, Alston adopts an existentialist posture. Indeed, he writes on the human condition and places himself at the heart of it, in its most concrete, tangible, and vulnerable form. The mandate of a special rapporteur implies direct contacts, discussions, and interactions with right-holders,[14] which is radically different from the position of an international human rights judge. This is apparent, for example, in his work as Special Rapporteur on Extreme Poverty,[15] and his adoption of a holistic and integral philosophy of human rights, that emphasizes *choice* and the *conditions of* individual freedom. These are clearly the values at the basis of Alston's project.[16]

To a large extent, the starting point of his approach is the deconstruction of the first sentence of Article 1 of the UDHR, which states that 'all human beings are born free and equal in dignity and rights'. In practice and concretely speaking, human beings are not born free and are not equal in dignity and rights, and much of Alston's work is devoted to determining *why* this is so and what can be done about it. Not only is his project existentialist but it is also *phenomenological*, in the sense that what seems to raise Alston's interest is to work on the conditions that will allow the individual to be in the world ('être au monde'). And because these individual conditions can be infinite and multidimensional—from the lack of access to menstrual products that hinder adolescent girls' schooling to inequalities, to the access to new technologies[17] or the effects of climate change[18]—the spectrum of his analyses is also constantly evolving. This is different from slow-motion collegial bodies such as the ECtHR, as I will detail further on.[19]

[11] ibid 30–31.
[12] ibid. 23–24.
[13] ibid 25.
[14] Alston, Khawaja, and Riddell (n 8) 2.
[15] Other chapters of this book are dedicated to Alston's doctrinal achievements. I will, however, not refer to this, for my contention is that an end of mission statement or thematic/country report may be read both as report and as a doctrinal piece on dignity, equality, and liberty.
[16] As expressed in his 2019 report on digital era, UNGA, 'Report of the Special Rapporteur on Extreme Poverty and Human Rights—Note by the Secretary-General' (2019) UN Doc A/74/48037 para 63.
[17] ibid, especially para 53 ff.
[18] UNHRC, 'Visit to the United Kingdom of Great Britain and Northern Ireland—Report of the Special Rapporteur on Extreme Poverty and Human Rights' (2019) UN Doc A/HRC/41/39; OHCHR, 'Statement by Professor Philip Alston, United Nations Special Rapporteur on Extreme Poverty and Human Rights, on His Visit to Malaysia' *UN News* (Kuala Lumpur, 23 August 2019) <www.ohchr.org/en/NewsEvents/Pages/DisplayNews.aspx?NewsID=24912&LangID=E> accessed 15 October 2020.
[19] Section 20.3 on European Court's 2018 decisions *FJM v UK* App no 76202/16 (ECtHR, 29 November 2018); *Poshteh v UK* App no 78375/17 (ECtHR, 20 December 2018).

This also makes it difficult to compare the way Alston thinks of human rights with the approach of another leading human rights expert such as Judge AA Cançado Trindade, who once put his theory of the new *Jus gentium* at the service of his mandate as judge and president of the Inter-American Court of Human Rights.[20] Cançado Trindade also denounces in his writings the 'contractual' and not 'communitarian' nature of markets and the fact that the latter 'live in the present, the moment, they lack intertemporal dimension'.[21] Nevertheless, the philosophy of Cançado Trindade is deeply metaphysical and religious and bases 'the Universality of International Law' on the 'Human conscience' and the '*recta ratio*'.[22] He has certainly used this metaphysics in his practice as a judge of the Inter-American Court and then of the ICJ to address technical issues such as provisional measures, jurisdiction *ratione temporis*, or the notion of '*dispute*' before the ICJ.[23] However, because his philosophy is metaphysical and seeks to extract the individual from his or her temporality,[24] it is very different from that of Alston, who on the contrary resituates the individual in this temporality and mortal condition.

When one reads the work of Alston as UN Special Rapporteur carefully, as varied as the themes may be, one realizes that there are in fact three strata that stand together, are complementary, and that resonate with this philosophy of choice and the conditions of individual freedom.

The first stratum is a priori the easiest to detect and capture. It consists in affirming the *indivisibility of human rights* and the *interdependence of state obligations*. It is well-known that many of Alston's doctrinal and expert work consists in affirming this indivisibility and its legal consequences, namely the justiciability of ESC rights for the interpretation of state obligations such as non-regressiveness or the need to implement rights considering available resources. His 2017 report to the General Assembly[25] and many General Comments of the CESCR for which Alston played a major role[26] are devoted to this topic.

But this statement is not only theoretical and conceptual. When the special rapporteur presented the *Statement* at the press conference held in Washington at the end of the US visit in December 2017,[27] he gave substance to what the indivisibility of rights and the interdependence of obligations might mean. Denouncing the absence of public toilets in most American cities or the lack of dental hygiene of people living in poverty—which prevents them from attending a job interview and reduces the chances of escaping the poverty spiral—is speaking of the *conditions of enjoyment and exercise* of Article 1 of the UDHR, which are not met for more than forty million people. Human rights can therefore only be conceived and applied in a *holistic and integral* way, in the sense that all the prerogatives recognized to the human being and all the principles underlying them—dignity, freedom, and

[20] Antônio Augusto Cançado Trindade, *International Law for Humankind: Towards a New Jus Gentium* (2nd edn, Martinus Nijhoff Publishers 2010) 726.

[21] ibid 28.

[22] ibid 141–45.

[23] For illustrations, see Antônio Augusto Cançado Trindade, *Judge Antônio A. Cançado Trindade. The Construction of a Humanized International Law: A Collection of Individual Opinions (2013–2016), Volume 3* (Brill Nijhoff 2017).

[24] Cançado Trindade, *International Law for Humankind* (n 20) 31 ff.

[25] UNGA 'Extreme Poverty and Human Rights—Note by the Secretary General' (2017) UN Doc A/72/502.

[26] In particular CESCR, 'General Comment No 3: The Nature of States Parties' Obligations (art 2, para 1 of the Covenant) (1990) UN Doc E/1991/23.

[27] OHCHR, 'Statement on Visit to the USA, by Professor Philip Alston, United Nations Special Rapporteur on Extreme Poverty and Human Rights' *UN News* (Washington, 15 December 2017) <https://www.ohchr.org/EN/NewsEvents/Pages/DisplayNews.aspx?NewsID=22533> accessed 11 September 2020.

equality—must be available at the *same time*. Without this, the 1948 universal project would lose its meaning.

The second *stratum*, which is perceptible in Alston's work and based on the previous stratum, is more precise for it focuses on the *socio-economic conditions* for the enjoyment and exercise of human rights. And this is undoubtedly one of the main contributions of his thinking to international human rights law. It would be simplistic to say that Alston is an expert on ESC rights. It seems to me that his project is much broader and more complex and consists in showing and capturing the importance of individual, national, and international socio-economic conditions, so that human rights are effective, whereas most thinkers, at least since the 'Siècle des Lumières', have focused their reflections on political conditions such as representative and parliamentary democracy and the rule of law. For Alston, the approach is somewhat different: not guaranteeing ESC rights weakens democracy.[28] And this element is fundamental and increasingly influential. As I will come back to in section 20.5, this paradigm is shaping in particular inter-American human rights law, under the influence of the general comments adopted by the CESCR when Alston was serving.

Here again, there is no need to immerse oneself in Alston's doctrinal writings to capture this second *stratum*. If we look back at the December 2017 *End of Mission Statement* and the 2018 report, we can see how it highlights the importance of working on the socio-economic conditions of human rights at different levels. At the *micro level*, first, the special rapporteur emphasizes in his analysis of poverty in the United States how the various characteristics of the human condition (age, gender, ethnic origin, health, disability, and so on) not only make the affirmation of Article 1 of the UDHR illusory from the point of view of equality and dignity but also make the very idea of seeking freedom extremely fragile. A child born into a poor family has very little chance of escaping the spiral and vicious circle of poverty, exclusion, and sociopolitical marginalization.[29] This statement is neither determinism nor fatalism or pessimism that would make any action to free from this condition useless. But it is a plea for a human rights approach free of any metaphysics and devoted to better making the project's realization possible.

However, individual (micro) conditions are closely linked to the socio-economic conditions of the state (macro) in which the people live. Thus, Alston's reports also highlight how policies or the absence of public actions in social, budgetary, fiscal, digital, or more narrowly economic and investment matters can allow individuals to move away from their initial condition or, vice versa, have the effect of keeping them in their situation of poverty, inequality, and deprivation of dignity. The criminal policy against homeless people in the United States,[30] the excesses of privatization in some sectors, the failures of the Universal Credit in the United Kingdom,[31] or the uncontrolled use of 'digital technologies in the welfare state'[32] are all obstacles to the effective realization of human rights. In other countries such as Chile, it is the very high economic inequalities that divide society that must be addressed if anti-poverty policies are to have a chance to prosper.[33] In Laos, international human rights

[28] UNHRC, 'Report of the Special Rapporteur on Extreme Poverty and Human Rights on his Mission to the United States of America' (2018) UN Doc A/HRC/38/33/Add.1, paras 18–24.

[29] ibid paras 37–41; UNHRC 'Report of the Special Rapporteur on Extreme Poverty and Human Rights on his Mission to Chile (2016) UN Doc A/HRC/32/31/Add.1, para 12.

[30] UN Doc A/HRC/38/33/Add.1 (n 28), paras 43–46.

[31] UNHRC 'Visit to the United Kingdom of Great Britain and Northern Ireland—Report of the Special Rapporteur on Extreme Poverty and Human Rights' (2019) UN Doc A/HRC/41/39/Add.1 para 44 ff.

More broadly on impact of privatization over enjoyment of human rights, see also UNGA 'Extreme Poverty and Human Rights—Note by the Secretary General' (2018) UN Doc A/73/396.

[32] UN Doc A/74/48037 (n 16) paras 4–5.

[33] UN Doc A/HRC/32/31/Add.1 (n 29) para 19.

obligations can only be respected if the state redirects a large number of policies, including taxation,[34] agrarian, and rural policies (those to do with water issues for instance)[35] as well as those related to foreign investment.[36] And in Malaysia poverty can simply not be addressed if the state authorities do not *measure* the phenomenon in a proper and transparent manner.[37]

These macroeconomic conditions of the state are themselves closely linked to the *international* framework in which it operates and to obligations that emanate from fields other than human rights (international monetary and financial obligations, respect for international investment law, etc). This dimension is also present in the special rapporteur's reports indirectly when he looks at the policies put in place in Laos, some of which have been endorsed or implemented by decisions of international financial and monetary institutions,[38] or more directly when he questions the applicability of human rights instruments, including the ICESCR, to the IMF and its *legal* responsibility in the event of violations of these rights as a result of the international plans imposed on states.[39]

Now—and this is the third and final layer of Alston's reports, which I believe goes to their very substance—what the analysis of socio-economic conditions at both individual and collective level reveals is a philosophy of choice and freedom. However, it is also one that invites us to rethink what the first sentence of Article 1 of the UDHR involves. By working on the concrete conditions in which an individual was born with all the characteristics that accompany him or her (gender, ethnic origin, migrant status, or situation of disability), Alston shows how the individual can, from an early age, be deprived of his or her choice to be free, dignified, and equal to others. And it is not surprising if in each of his thematic or visiting reports, he devotes a passage to child poverty.[40] The report adopted following the US visit is surely the most topical in this respect, as it denounces the idea that the poor are poor because they have *chosen* to be poor.[41] At the same time, by insisting on the role of the state and its multidimensional public policies, the special rapporteur demonstrates that maintaining a population in a situation of poverty or extreme poverty 'is a political choice'.[42]

And because Alston uses law as a tool to analyse the production of domestic and international societies, since this situation of human rights violations is the result of a *choice*, and therefore of a series of conscious or even deliberate actions, this must go hand-in-hand with the affirmation of *accountability*:[43] of the state for it remains the only sovereign power recognized in international law;[44] of international organizations and institutions when they more

[34] UNHRC 'Visit to the Lao People's Democratic Republic—Report of the Special Rapporteur on Extreme Poverty and Human Rights' (2019) UN Doc A/HRC/41/39/Add.2 paras 24–25.

[35] ibid paras 16, 29–38, 39–43.

[36] ibid paras 6, 15.

[37] OHCHR (n 18).

[38] UN Doc A/HRC/41/39/Add.2 (n 34) paras 6, 15.

[39] UNHRC 'Report of the Special Rapporteur on Extreme Poverty and Human Rights—Note by the Secretariat' (2018) UN Doc A/HRC/38/33; see Alston's reflections on the inadequacy of the method used to measure poverty or the "triumphalism" of the SDG in his final report as Special Rapporteur, UNHRC, 'The Parlous State of Poverty Eradication—Report of the Special Rapporteur on Extreme Poverty and Human Rights' (2020) A/HRC/44/40.

[40] For an illustration, see OHCHR (n 18).

[41] UN Doc A/HRC/38/33/Add.1 (n 28) para 13.

[42] ibid para 17.

[43] UNHRC, 'Report of the Special Rapporteur on Extreme Poverty and Human Rights on his Mission to China' (2017) UN DOC A/HRC/35/26/Add.2 para 66.

[44] ibid para 67; for the issue of accountability in the field of climate change, see UNHRC, 'Climate Change and Poverty—Report of the Special Rapporteur on Extreme Poverty and Human Rights' (2019) UN Doc A/HRC/41/39 para 72; in the field of extrajudicial killings, see UNGA 'Extrajudicial, Summary or Arbitrary Executions—Note by the Secretary General' (2006) UN Doc A/61/311 paras 30–64.

or less directly influence the choice of states;[45] and of the private sector[46] and foreign commercial companies that invest in states and can, through such investments, worsen the situation of populations.[47] But the problem Alston is raising awareness about—especially in a universal context of digitalization of social benefits—is 'a complete reversal of the traditional notion that the state should be accountable to the individual'.[48]

In short, in Alston's normative project, what matters is not the abstract and metaphysical affirmation of freedom, dignity, and equality that would be posed as a *given*. These are the conditions of self-realization in which the expert engages and that involve the individual as '*l'être qui a à être son être*' to use the famous Sartrian formula.[49] In the process, the role of the state as debtor of this substantial obligation to create the conditions for freedom, equality, and dignity was well as the responsibilities of the international community through its main institutions are highlighted. This is why I indicated in the introduction to this chapter that reading the *End of Mission Statement* of December 2017 is not simply reading a visit report: it shows Alston's views on the individual's relationship to the world, the society, and his or her human condition.

20.3 Special Rapporteur's Reports and General Comments' Role in the Individual Complaint Mechanisms before Regional Human Rights Organs

When read carefully, Alston's work as a UN expert does reflect a sophisticated philosophy that can influence regional human rights litigation, both in the European and inter-American context.[50] International human rights litigation is by its nature deeply unequal, since apart from very rare cases of inter-state litigation, it involves two parties of unequal power: the private person as the plaintiff and the state, which has allegedly violated its human rights obligations. In these circumstances, the question of fact-finding and evidence of violations is crucial, and it is at this stage that the work of the UN special procedures and treaty bodies can play an important role. Three examples from the use of Alston's work by the European Court and the Inter-American Commission and Court illustrate the litigation role of UN 'soft law' documents.

First, following his visit to Romania in 2015, the Special Rapporteur on Extreme Poverty adopted a report in which he devoted a substantial part of his findings to the situation of 'disabled' persons within the meaning of Romanian legislation, precisely to point out that the legislative definition of disability did not respect the 2006 UN CRPD.[51] He also denounced

[45] UN Doc A/HRC/38/33/Add.1 (n 28); in the specific context of Lao, see UN Doc A/HRC/41/39/Add.2 (n 34) paras 80, 82–85 on the role of IFIs.

[46] UN Doc A/74/48037 (n 16) paras 67 ff (on technology companies' resistance to take into account human rights in the digital sector).

[47] UN Doc A/HRC/41/39/Add.2 (n 34) para. 86.

[48] UN Doc A/74/48037 (n 16) paras 5, 50.

[49] Jean-Paul Sartre and Arlette Elkaïm-Sartre, *L' être et le néant: essai d'ontologie phénoménologique* (Corrected edn, Gallimard 2017).

[50] There are sometimes references to the work of special rapporteurs in decisions of the African Commission on Human and Peoples' Rights but, to my knowledge, they are relatively rare—the Commission cites other regional bodies more extensively. Nevertheless, in its decision *Noah Kazingachire, John Chitsenga, Elias Chemvura and Batanai Hadzisi (represented by Zimbabwe Human Rights NGO Forum) v Zimbabwe*, African Commission on Human and Peoples' Rights, Communication 295/04 (12 October 2013) <https://www.achpr.org/sessions/descions?id=237> on the right to life, it uses one of the reports of the special rapporteur that succeeded P Alston, C Heyns.

[51] UNHRC, 'Report of the Special Rapporteur on Extreme Poverty and Human Rights on his Mission to Romania—Note by the Secretariat' (2016) UN Doc A/HRC/32/31/Add.2.

that, from an early age, children with disabilities are placed in institutions,[52] excluded from school, or sent to schools with very low educational levels.[53] Once they become adults, they are often dependent on social assistance as they cannot find a job.[54] In addition, the report highlighted the use of institutionalization of adults with disabilities and the slow pace of implementation of the 'deinstitutionalization' strategy.[55]

This question of the deprivation of liberty of an adult for more than sixteen years based on a 'mental detention order'[56] is at the centre of the case of *N v Romania* examined by the ECtHR under Article 5 of the ECHR (conditions of deprivation of liberty). In assessing whether the detention of a person considered by the domestic authorities to be suffering from a mental illness was in accordance with the ECHR, the European Court first cited in the 'relevant international documents' included both the work of the Committee on the Rights of Persons with Disabilities[57] and the relevant parts of the abovementioned report on Romania of the special rapporteur.[58] As for the examination of the violation itself, the Court concluded as follows:

> according to the information available to the Court, it would appear that no thorough assessment has been carried out to date of the applicant's practical needs and the appropriate social protection measures. Furthermore, the action taken by the national authorities has been unproductive because of the lack of reception facilities. That *situation reflects realities in Romania which have already been described by the international organizations* [. . .]. Those factors are sufficient for the Court to conclude that the applicant's continued detention [. . .] was arbitrary under Article 5 § 1 (e) of the Convention.[59]

From the applicant's point of view, the use of the special rapporteur's findings has an obvious virtue: it does not exempt him from the burden of proof, but it relieves him from it; for the Court, which does not make frequent use of its investigative powers, it makes information available with an authoritative international stamp relating to the legislative and factual framework *independently of the parties to the proceedings*. The case also suggests the more systematic litigation role that universal special procedures before the European Court, as third parties, could play directly or indirectly (Article 36–2 of the ECHR). The practice is even more widespread in the inter-American proceeding: the Court may decide to hear UN special rapporteurs as witnesses or invite them to produce third-party interventions.[60]

For UN experts themselves, this allows their findings to produce significant contentious effects provided that the report is sufficiently accessible and disseminated. The quality of reports is also important. In the best of cases a sound report can lead to a finding that certain facts are '*de notoriété publique*', even though the European Court does not use this expression in the Romanian case. The 2017 judgment thus illustrates the fact that, in addition to the 'dialogue of judges' that may exist between human rights regional courts, a dialogue between courts and special procedures, which is more timid, difficult, and ad hoc, is emerging. Most of the time, this is for the benefit of the weak party to the proceedings (the individuals),

52 ibid paras 39–40.
53 ibid paras 41–43.
54 ibid para 44.
55 ibid paras 45–46.
56 *N v Romania* App no 59152/08 (ECtHR, 28 November 2017) para 16.
57 ibid paras 102–104.
58 ibid para 105.
59 ibid para 167 (emphasis added).
60 ibid, see illustrations in section 20.4.

the human rights bodies themselves, and a greater coherence in the determination of states' international obligations.[61]

Notwithstanding, there are limits to this process of drawing on reports. For example, the *End of Mission Statement* adopted in November 2018 at the end of Alston's visit to the United Kingdom failed to influence the position adopted by the European Court in cases concerning the right to housing of the most vulnerable. Indeed, two decisions of inadmissibility were adopted a few weeks apart, in the first case, concerning the state's obligations regarding housing in favour of a person suffering from mental disorders[62] and, in the second case, concerning the question of review of the refusal to allocate housing to an indigent person.[63] The almost simultaneous publication of the Special Rapporteur *Statement* and the two inadmissibility decisions of the European Court is instructive because it shows that two radically different approaches can emerge for the same state and for the same legal issue—housing obligations towards the most vulnerable people. Here the special rapporteur embraced the main poverty-related challenges in the United Kingdom and deplored the choice of the state to keep individuals in this situation contrary to its international obligations, while the European Court chose a sort of 'avoidance strategy' by declaring the applications inadmissible and therefore deciding not to rule on these issues.

While it may be objected that a UN special rapporteur is not in the same institutional position as a human rights court that renders decisions binding on states through a judicial procedure,[64] it will be seen later when examining the Inter-American Court that this objection does not hold. While maintaining a population in a situation of poverty and social exclusion is a choice, refusing to examine this situation on the merits is also a *choice of jurisprudential policy* that is in line with the European Court's inadmissibility decisions on the effects of austerity measures adopted by some states after the 2008 financial crisis.[65]

The other illustrations are taken from the inter-American bodies. They have been more willing to use the work of UN bodies, both as sources of information and to develop the factual framework of a case submitted to them. Two examples illustrate this use of the work of universal bodies in the course of litigation.[66]

[61] Under the condition that the ECtHR adopts a coherent and constant position on this 'external sources' referral practice. For the same country (Romania) and issues on education of children with disabilities, in another individual case, the applicant mentioned Alston's report of his 2015 visit as an element of context along with other UN materials but the Court did not refer to it and concluded that the access to school for a child with a physical disability was granted by the domestic authorities, *Stoian v Romania* App no 289/14 (ECtHR, 25 June 2019) para 82.

[62] *FJM v UK* (n 19).

[63] *Poshteh v UK* (n 19).

[64] On the specific position of a special rapporteur, see Alston, Khawaja, and Riddell (n 8) 1: 'Their principal focus is on analysing state policies and actions to assess whether governments are meeting their human rights obligations.'

[65] *Koufaki and Adedy v Greece* App no 57665/12 (ECtHR, 7 May 2013) para 37; *Da Conceiçao Mateus and Santos Januário v Portugal* App no 62235/12 (ECtHR, 8 October 2013); *Mamatas and Others v Greece* App nos 63066/14, 64297/14 and 66106/14 (EctHR, 21 July 2016) 84–120; *Mockiené v Lithuania* App no 75916/13 (EctHR, 4 July 2017) paras 43–49.

The same could also be said about new technologies topics: Alston disclosed his report to the UN General Assembly on October 2019, warning about the dangers raised by digital issues, but at the very same moment, the Grand Chamber of the European Court did adopt a judgment by fourteen votes to three in the case in *López Ribalda and Others v Spain* App nos 1874/13 and 8567/13 (EctHR, 17 October 2019) denying a violation of privacy (Article 8 of the CHR) in a case of video surveillance of employees.

[66] The Court does use also works of other special rapporteurs such as the former Special Rapporteur on Environment and Human Rights J Knox, *The Environment and Human Rights*, Advisory Opinion OC-23/17, Inter-American Court of Human Rights Series A No 23 (15 November 2017); the former Special Rapporteur on Torture and Other Cruel, Inhumane and Degrading Treatments J Mendez, Inter-American Court of Human Rights *Alvarado Espinoza et al v Mexico* (2018) Series C No 370 para 54; (extensively) the former Special Rapporteur on Contemporary Forms of Slavery G Shaninian , including its causes and consequences *Hacienda Brasil Verde Workers v Brazil* (Preliminary Objections, Merits, Reparations, and Costs) Inter-American Court of Human

The first example arises when the Inter-American Court is dealing with massive violations of the right to life as part of *structural* violence, such as the 2017 *Favela Nova Brasilia* case on police brutality.[67] In this instance, the extrajudicial execution of nearly thirty people by the police in the 1990s was denounced, these deaths having been justified by the state by claiming that victims resisted arrest ('actas de resistencia al arresto').[68] However, in order to examine both the general context of police violence in Brazil and the practice of justifying deaths by acts of resistance by those arrested, the Court adopted two reports prepared by Alston: one following his visit to Brazil and the other, a few months later, to follow up on the recommendations addressed to the state.[69] In both cases, the special rapporteur pointed out that 'killings by on-duty police' represented a significant proportion of murders in Brazil[70] and condemned the practice of the authorities to blame victims.[71] There was 'strong evidence that many of these killings were, in fact, unlawful killings, and that the practical effect of the "resistance" classification was to prejudice and limit objective follow-up inquiries into killings by police'.[72] He also noted in his visit report that the poorest neighbourhoods (*favelas*) also had the highest rates of lethal violence.[73]

In condemning Brazil in its 2017 judgment for the violation of judicial rights (Articles 8 and 25 of the ACHR) and the prohibition of ill-treatment (Article 5 of the ACHR), the Court extensively used Alston's report and adopted a similar position, except for a few points: on the one hand, the Court was limited by the date of the State's recognition of its contentious jurisdiction, and therefore lacked *ratione temporis* jurisdiction to examine the violations of the right to life (Article 4 of the ACHR).[74] On the other hand, and even if limited by its *temporal* jurisdiction, the Court's analysis of police violence went further than that of the special rapporteur since, in addition to targeting the poorest neighbourhoods, the Court gave special importance to the specific violence to which women are victims.[75]

The case therefore embodies the mutual beneficial influence that human rights bodies could obtain from working more closely together when confronted with similar issues: the Inter-American Court draws heavily on the findings of a UN expert, but deepens a dimension—in this case, the gender aspect—that was announced by Alston at the end of his mandate as a theme to be developed.[76] One

Rights Series C No 318 (20 October 2016); it also may happen that a special rapporteur is invited to testify before the Court, as the Special Rapporteur on Human Rights Defenders M Forst *Alvaro Espinoza* (n 67) para 59; Inter-American Court of Human Rights *Acosta Castellón et al v Nicaragua* (2017) Series C No 334 paras 7, 221; Or the former Special Rapporteur on the Right to Assembly and Association, *Mujeres victimas de tortura sexual en atenco v Mexico* Inter-American Court of Human Rights Series C No 371 (28 November 2018) paras 167–68, 172, 175, 240.

[67] *Favela Nova Brasília v Brazil* (Preliminary Objections, Merits, Reparations and Costs) Inter-American Court of Human Rights Series C No 333 (16 February 2017).

[68] ibid para 1.

[69] ibid paras 102, 108, 193; UNHRC 'Promotion and Protection of All Human Rights, Civil, Political, Economic, Social and Cultural Rights, Including the Right to Development—Report of the Special Rapporteur on Extrajudicial, Summary or Arbitrary Executions, Philip Alston, Addendum—Mission to Brazil' (2009) UN Doc A/HRC/11/2/Add.2; UNHRC 'Report of the Special Rapporteur on Extrajudicial, Summary or Arbitrary Executions, Philip Alston—Follow-up to Country Recommendations—Brazil' (2010) UN Doc A/HRC/14/24.Add.4).

[70] UN Doc A/HRC/11/2/Add.2 (n 70) para 9; UN Doc A/HRC/14/24.Add.4 (n 70) para 12.

[71] A/HRC/11/2/Add.2, 23 March 2009 (Mission to Brazil), para 11ff; A/HRC/14/24.Add.4, 28 May 2010 (Follow-up) para 13.

[72] A/HRC/11/2/Add.2 (n 70) para 12; A/HRC/14/24.Add.4 (n 70) para. 14.

[73] A/HRC/11/2/Add.2 (n 70) para 8 fn 10.

[74] *Favela Nova Brasilia* (n 68) paras 49–51.

[75] ibid paras 243–59.

[76] UN Doc A/HRC/14/24 (n 70) paras 62–63.

of his successors to the special rapporteur's mandate has partially taken over the issue.[77]

The second illustration of the litigation role that universal reports can play comes from the report adopted in October 2018 by the Inter-American Commission on Human Rights in the *José Isabel Salas et al v United States* case,[78] concerning the military operation *Just Cause* conducted in Panama in December 1989 by the US Army 'with the stated purpose of protecting the life of U.S. citizens, restoring democracy in Panama, asserting the State's rights to implement the Panama Canal Treaty and bring General Noriega to justice in the United States'.[79] In the petition submitted against the United States to the Commission in 1990,[80] many violations of the rights of nearly three hundred people were invoked (right to life, prohibition of ill-treatment, arbitrary detention, etc),[81] based in particular on the Charter of the Organization of American States, the 1948 American and Universal Declarations of Human Rights and international customary norms.[82] However, when examining allegations of destruction of property by the US Army during the attacks and the military occupation,[83] the Inter-American Commission drew substantially on the report of the technical assistance mission to Panama, which was carried out by the CESCR in 1995, to establish some of the facts.[84] This is a bit different from special rapporteurs' reports, in that the Committee's report was adopted in a collegial manner and that two other Committee members were sent to Panama to carry out this 'technical assistance' mission.[85]

Nevertheless, the 1995 report is interesting for at least three reasons. The first is that it prefigures Alston's practice of engaging in discussions on states' obligations for ESC rights where it is not 'natural' and therefore not expected, as in this factual and legal situation of military intervention and occupation.[86] In the early 1990s, the question of the relationship between human rights obligations and those due in time of armed conflicts or occupation was still not well-known—the ICJ's opinion on the legality of the threat and use of nuclear weapons partly dealing with this issue was rendered in 1996.[87] Moreover, the international case-law of human rights bodies on the destruction of property during an armed conflict

[77] UNHRC 'Report of the Special Rapporteur on Extrajudicial, Summary, or Arbitrary Executions on a Gender-Sensitive Approach to Arbitrary Killings—Note by the Secretariat' (2017) UN Doc A/HRC/35/23.

[78] Interam HR Report No 121/18. 5 October 2018. Box 10.573, OEA/Ser.L/V/II.169, Doc 138.

[79] ibid paras 104 ff.

[80] That is, almost thirty years before the adoption of the final report by the Commission.

[81] Inter-American Commission on Human Rights, Report No 121/18, Case 12,678, Merits, Paola del Rosario Albarracín Guzmán and relatives (5 October 2018) paras 6–35.

[82] It shall be reminded that the United States is not party to the ACHR but the Inter-American Commission may receive individual petitions based on the 1948 Declaration, which has been affirmed by the Inter-American Court as 'a source of international obligations' *Interpretation of the American Declaration of the Rights and Duties of Man within the Framework of Article 64 of the American Convention on Human Rights*, Advisory Opinion OC-10/89, Inter-American Court of Human Rights Series A No 10 (14 July 1989) para 45.

[83] Inter-American Commission on Human Rights, Report No 121/18 (n 82) para 271 ff.

[84] CESCR, 'Implementation of the International Covenant on Economic, Social and Cultural Rights—Report on the Technical Assistance Mission to Panama of the Committee on Economic, Social and Cultural Rights' (1995) UN Doc E/C.12/1995/8.

[85] For the negotiation with the government of Panama to organize this mission—the state firstly declined the Committee's offer of technical assistance 'this not being the most appropriate or convenient time to receive such advice' ibid paras 5 ff.

[86] ibid para 2.

[87] *Legality of the Threat or Use of Nuclear Weapons* (Advisory Opinion) 1996 <https://web.archive.org/web/20200809015312/https://www.icj-cij.org/files/case-related/95/095-19960708-ADV-01-00-EN.pdf> accessed 16 October 2020, p 226; For further legal developments, see *Legal Consequences of the Construction of a Wall in the Occupied Palestinian Territory* (Advisory Opinion) 2004 <https://www.icj-cij.org/en/case/131> accessed 16 October 2020, p 136.

was almost non-existent.[88] Therefore, the 1995 report of the Committee was at the *avant-garde* of the development of states' human rights obligations in periods of armed conflicts or military occupation, and especially when dealing with ESC rights aspects.

The second reason is that the 1995 report illustrates that the reports of UN treaty bodies can play a significant role in adjudicating individual petitions and helping to establish the factual framework, specifically in complex and disputed contexts where facts are controversial. In this case before the Inter-American Commission, it was used to establish the factual and legal framework in Panama at the end of the 1980s. Therefore, these works should be circulated and must be properly appreciated by the various actors of the international human rights mechanisms for the role they may have in the development of strategic litigation. Hence, the importance also for the experts who produce these reports to have a clear view of what their normative project is and of the effects, even if they are distant in time.

The last reason is more systemic. Cross-fertilization has mainly been identified and examined by the doctrine through the prism of international judicial interpretation, and I will give some illustrations later. Nevertheless, it is also clear that, beyond the differences in mandates and legal and procedural frameworks in which international human rights bodies operate, inter-systemic relations can be deeper and more varied. In some of the cases discussed in this section, they have become a piece of regional human rights litigation.

20.4 Special Rapporteur's Reports and General Comments as a Tool of Interpretation of Regional Human Rights Conventions

The earlier examples demonstrate what procedural role UN special procedures can play in regional human rights litigation. This section deals with more substantive aspects of that influence and will be shorter because, as already indicated, the cross-fertilization in the normative interpretation process is probably better known and has been more widely visited in this field. However, references to the work of a special rapporteur are a good indication not only of the credibility given by a regional body to a universal mechanism but also of the way in which a regional body conceives its own hermeneutics—more or less open or closed to external sources—and of its perception of itself as a finite and self-sufficient whole or as part of a larger *system*.

A greater openness has long been in evidence with the Inter-American Court of Human Rights, which has given an important place to the work of universal special procedures or treaty bodies. Even if voluntarist internationalists[89] or the states[90] may challenge these methods of interpretation of the Inter-American Court, which seem to depart from the *consent* of the state parties to the ACHR, it should be stressed that for the Court, the ultimate objective to which the interpreter must aspire is that of the *maximum effect of the American Convention*.[91] And if external sources, even non-binding ones such as reports of special

[88] For a first judgment on the topic, see *Dogan et al v Turkey* App nos 8803-8811/02, 8813/02 and 8815-8819/02 (ECtHR, 29 June 2004) para 135 ff.

[89] Gerald Neuman, 'Import, Export, and Regional Consent in the Inter-American Court of Human Rights' (2008) 19 European Journal of International Law 101.

[90] See the 11 April 2019 *Declaration on the Inter-American System of Human Rights*, sent to the Inter-American Commission by the governments of Argentina, Brazil, Chile, Colombia, and Paraguay and calling for the reinforcement of the subsidiarity principle, the recognition of a margin of appreciation in favour of states parties, and a restrictive interpretation of the sources of IHRL used by the Commission.

[91] For an illustration see *Muelle Flores v Peru* (Preliminary Objections, Merits, Reparations and Costs) Inter-American Court of Human Rights Series C No 375 (6 March 2019) paras 174–75.

rapporteurs and independent experts, must be used to do so, it considers this to be justified by her office.

Thus, when the Inter-American Court is confronted with cases of arbitrary deprivation of the right to life (Article 4 of the ACHR), which constitute an important part of its jurisprudence, it has relied on the conceptual and definitional framework established by Alston as Special Rapporteur on Extrajudicial Executions. It is therefore no longer only the factual information contained in the reports that is used by the Inter-American Tribunal as in the examples developed in section 20.3, but also the *substantive* analyses produced at the universal level.

In the case of *Zambrano Vélez et al v Ecuador*, which was tried in 2007, for example, the arbitrary execution by the security forces of persons during a police operation was denounced.[92] The president of the Republic had declared a state of emergency at the time of the events (1993), which the Court reviewed under Article 27 of the ACHR to determine whether the measures taken in this context of exception complied with Ecuador's treaty obligations.[93] On the merits and although the state had partially acknowledged its responsibility for the alleged violations,[94] the parties disagreed on the legal qualification of the deprivation of the right to life.[95] The Inter-American Court thus examined the allegations of arbitrary deprivation of life under Article 4 of the ACHR. To this end, the Court recalled the principles governing the use of lethal force—'exceptionality, necessity, proportionality and humanity'[96]—with special reference to the 'Report on the World Situation Respecting Extrajudicial, Summary, and Arbitrary Executions' presented by Alston in 2006.[97] Later in its judgment, the Tribunal borrowed a portion of the 2006 report that explained and justified the importance of procedural guarantees and the *due process of law* in protecting against arbitrary deprivations of the right to life.[98]

Nevertheless, it is above all the use made by the Inter-American Court of the very first General Comments of the CESCR that best reflects the way in which this *soft law* has been able to gradually, directly, and concretely influence the interpretation of state's international obligations by a regional Court. In this regard, it seems obvious that there is a clear link between the progressive evolution of the Inter-American Court towards an interpretation of the ACHR[99]—a treaty that initially protected only civil and political rights—that reveals the importance of *socio-economic conditions* in the enjoyment and exercise of those rights, and this same evolution, begun earlier and consequently more advanced at the universal level. This link is formally established in the jurisprudence of the Inter-American Court by the role played by the first General Comments of the CESCR in the interpretation of the 1969 ACHR. It is therefore worthwhile to give a brief overview of this development.

[92] *Zambrano Vélez et al v Ecuador* (Merits Reparations and Costs) Inter-American Court of Human Rights Series C No 166 (4 July 2007) paras 1–5, 73.
[93] ibid paras 42–71.
[94] ibid paras 8–11.
[95] ibid para 75.
[96] ibid paras 83–85.
[97] UNGA 'Extrajudicial, Summary or Arbitrary Executions—Note by the Secretary General' (2006) UN Doc A/61/311.
[98] *Zambrano Vélez* (n 93) para 90; The reference to Alston's Report, UN Doc A/61/311 (n 99) para 36.
[99] It has to be reminded that if the ACHR does not enshrine a list of ESC rights, the American Declaration on the Rights and Duties of Man adopted by the General Assembly of the OAS in May 1948 is based on the same *integral* philosophy that is contained in the UDHR adopted a couple of months after the American text. The American Declaration protects both civil and political rights and ESC rights as right to health (Article XI), right to education (Article XII), right to the benefits of culture (Article XIII), or the right to work (Article XIV) and to social security (Article XVI).

While the ACHR, like ECHR, protects mainly civil and political rights, it also contains a provision—Article 26 of the ACHR—which refers relatively vaguely to the ESC aspects of states' obligations. Nevertheless, given the way this clause was drafted, the Inter-American Court long ignored it, preferring to include the ESC rights in the substantive scope of the rights protected by the Convention as civil and political rights such as the right to life (Article 4), the right to personal integrity (Article 5), or special measures due to children (Article 19). However, to interpret these provisions and clarify states' obligations under the 1969 ACHR, which do not formally contain any guidance on the ESC rights, the Court used the first General Comments of the CESCR. For example, in the 2006 case of *Ximenes Lopes v Brazil*, which concerns the death in hospital of a young adult suffering from a mental illness, the Inter-American Court used the CESCR's General Comment No 5 both as 'evidence'[100] and as a direct source of interpretation,[101] to clarify two elements. First, it helped the Court draw a link between extreme poverty, the condition of a member of an indigenous community—as in this case—and the risks of suffering from mental illness.[102] It also clarified the nature of states' obligations, pointing out that there are not only negative but also positive obligations to ensure and guarantee human rights. To interpret the scope and content of these positive obligations under the right to life (Article 4 of the ACHR) and the right to personal integrity (Article 5 of the ACHR), the Inter-American Court thus used this General Comment as a means of interpretation.[103]

In another case on social security issues decided a few years later, the Court took from the Committee the principle of *progressiveness* in the realization of ESC rights and established it as consubstantial with the standards provided for in Article 34 of the Organization of American states Charter as well as with the general objective of ESC development enshrined in its preamble. It is clear for the Court that it would not be realistic to set out, in a legal rule, an outcome to be achieved *immediately*. However, as the CESCR pointed out in its General Comment No 3, which the Inter-American Court quoted extensively,[104] this does not mean that the provisions on ESC rights cannot serve as a basis for obligations to be implemented *immediately* and therefore for the recognition of subjective rights *immediately* due in favour of the individuals.[105]

In its subsequent case law, including the Peruvian judgments of 2017, when it took the step of recognizing a full and complete *justiciability* in favour of Article 26 of the ACHR,[106] the Inter-American Court referred, in particular, to the principle of interdependence and invisibility affirmed by the CESCR in its General Comment No 9 *on the domestic application of the Covenant*.[107] Finally, in 2018 the Court established the justiciability of the principle of progressiveness,[108] that is, the principle is not only used by the Court as a means

[100] *Ximenes-Lopes v Brazil* (Merits, Reparations and Costs) Inter-American Court of Human Rights Series C No 149 (4 July 2019) para 51.

[101] CESCR, 'General Comment No 5: Persons with Disabilities' (1994) UN Doc E/1995/22.

[102] *Ximenes-Lopes* (n 100) para 104.

[103] ibid para 9.

[104] *Acevedo Buendía et al v Peru* (Preliminary Objection, Merits, Reparations and Costs) Inter-American Court of Human Rights Series C No 198 (1 July 2009) para 102.

[105] About right to social security and referral to General Comment No 3 and No 19 (social security) adopted after Alston completed his mandate, see *Muelle Flores* (n 91).

[106] *Lagos del Campo v Peru* (Preliminary Objections, Merits, Reparations and Costs) Inter-American Court of Human Rights Series C No 340 (31 August 2017) para 141; Among others, see also on the recognition of the right to health as an autonomous right derived from Article 26 of the ACHR, *Cuscul Pivaral et al v Guatemala* (Preliminary Objection, Merits, Reparations and Costs) Inter-American Court of Human Rights Series C No 359 (23 August 2018) paras 98 ff.

[107] CESCR, 'Substantive Issues Arising in the Implementation of the International Covenant on Economic, Social and Cultural Rights' (1998) UN Doc E/C.12/1998/24 para 10.

[108] For extensive developments on states' ESC rights obligations derived from Article 26 of the ACHR read in light with General Comment of the UN Committee, see, for instance, *Indigenous Communities of the Lhaka Honhat (Our Land) Association v Argentina* (Merits, Reparations and Costs) Series C No 400 (6 February 2020) para 202 ff;

of interpretation of states' obligations in the economic and social field but may also be the *source of the commitment of international responsibility under the ACHR.*

There are several ways to analyse this migration of human rights ideas from the UN Committee to a regional court. From a pessimistic perspective, it can be noted that more than twenty years passed before the principle of interdependence of rights laid down by the first General Comments of the Committee was taken seriously by a body originally established to protect civil and political rights. Moreover, as the underdeveloped case law of the ECtHR on the subject illustrates, this movement towards the indivisibility of rights is still at an embryonic and fragile stage, including before the Inter-American Court of Human Rights.[109]

More optimistically, however, the indivisibility of rights has both benefited from a strengthening of the ICESCR monitoring mechanism through the adoption of an additional protocol allowing individuals to submit individual communications before the UN Committee[110]—already recommended by Alston at the 1993 Vienna Conference[111]—and from a still relative and imperfect incorporation into the substantive jurisdiction of certain bodies such as the Commission and the Inter-American Court. From this point of view, it should also be noted that during the preparatory work for Article 26 of the ACHR, the delegate of Chile expressed the wish that the provision should be modelled on Article 2 of the ICESCR, which would establish the 'cierta obligatoriedad juridica (hasta donde lo permite la naturaleza de estos derechos)'.[112] While this proposal was rejected, it is clear that through its interpretation of ACHR in the light of the work of CESCR, the Court has returned to the principle of original indivisibility common to both the universal and regional systems. Thus, it cannot be denied that considerable progress has been made in strengthening states' Parties obligations and individual rights in this field since Prosper Weil wrote in the early 1990s, taking the 1966 ICESCR as an illustration of a '*instrumentum* of dubious normative character'.[113]

20.5 Concluding Remarks—The Shift Towards a Socio-economic Paradigm of Human Rights?

If we analyse the evolution of the interpretation of the ECHR by the European Court and that of the ACHR by the inter-American bodies in a comparative way, it is clear that the movement towards the affirmation of the indivisibility of rights is not taking on the same magnitude—far from it. Admittedly, the ECtHR has handed down judgments on

Cuscul Pivaral (n 106) paras 146–47; *Poblete Vilches et al v Chile* (Merits, Reparations and Costs) Series C No 349 (8 March 2018) para 100 ff.

[109] The development of ESC rights based on the justiciability of Article 26 of the ACHR in the inter-American system is mainly attributable to President of the Court Judge Ferrer Mc-Gregor Poisot but, out of the seven judges of the Court, some totally disagree with this approach. See especially the partially dissenting opinion of Judge Sierra Porto in *Cuscul Pivaral* (n 106) and in *Poblete Vilches* (n 108): his dissent is not on the recognition of ESC rights as such but deals with the autonomy of Article 26 of the ACHR.

[110] Optional Protocol adopted in June 2008 and ratified by twenty-four states (date of reference: 1 November 2019).

[111] For the reference to and explanation of the *rationale* of the draft presented to the 1993 Vienna World Conference, see Philip Alston, 'Establishing a Right to Petition under the Covenant on Economic, Social and Cultural Rights' in Academy of European Law (ed), *The Protection of Human Rights in Europe* (M Nijhoff 1995), 107 ff.

[112] *Travaux préparatoires*, doc 7, 26 September 1969, 43, para 17.

[113] Prosper Weil, *Le Droit International En Quête De Son Identité: Cours Général De Droit International Public* (M Nijhoff 1992) 217.

environmental issues, access to social benefits without discrimination, non-discrimination on the grounds of illness, health care for people in detention, and the rights of people with disability. Any concern related to *social justice* is therefore not completely absent from the European case law, but its careful analysis shows that in reality most of the complaints related to poverty, social exclusion, the consequences of austerity measures, or access to housing for the most vulnerable people are rejected at the admissibility stage, as illustrated by the two British cases mentioned earlier in the chapter.[114]

Specifically, the example of the United Kingdom illustrates the failure of the European system *as a regional system for the protection of human rights*: indeed one of the first legal questions that arises when reading Alston's *End of Mission Statement* following his visit to the United Kingdom in November 2018 is why the dramatic situation described is not revealed nor addressed in the case law of the European Court, when many of the dysfunctions identified infringe civil and political rights that fall within the scope of ECHR (right to life, prohibition of ill-treatment, right to private and family life, or prohibition of discrimination based on social origin).

While the European human rights system is the most sophisticated—the jurisdiction of the ECtHR is mandatory and not optional as for the European Committee of Social Rights[115]—and the most richly endowed, why do we need to read the report of a UN expert to discover significant breaches of human rights for individuals under the jurisdiction of a European state? It may be understandable that UN reports analysing extreme poverty in Lao, Ghana,[116] China, or Saudi Arabia[117] reveal a less visible situation at the international level for the states mentioned are either not bound by regional mechanisms (Laos, China, and Saudi Arabia) or are bound by them, but the mechanisms in question, such as the African system, are hindered in their action (Ghana). In European law, on the other hand, one can only wonder about the gap between what is described in the visit report to the United Kingdom and what emerges from—or more surely is invisible in—the European case law.

The answer is relatively simple: the applications raising this type of complaint do not generally go beyond the admissibility stage as mentioned earlier,[118] and when they do get through this filter with success, such as the case before the Grand Chamber, *N v United Kingdom* of 2008 about the removal to Uganda of a woman suffering from AIDS, they lead the Court to reveal its approach to the 'implications of economic and social nature' of ECHR's rights,[119] as being the avoidance 'too great a burden on the Contracting States'.[120] To a large extent, the Alston UK report does not only speak to the shortcomings of the British authorities but also of the failures of the ECHR system and its Court to address properly the harshest consequences of neoliberalism of European states.

[114] *FJM* (n 19); *Poshteh* (n 19).

[115] Especially the United Kingdom has ratified the 1961 European Social Charter in July 1962 but not its 1996 revised version. More importantly, the United Kingdom has not accepted the collective complaint procedure before the European Committee on Social Rights.

[116] Ghana was visited by Alston in 2018. For the report, see UNHRC, 'Report of the Special Rapporteur on Extreme Poverty and Human Rights on his Mission to Ghana—Note by the Secretariat' (2018) UN Doc A/HRC/38/33/Add.2 paras 13–25 (extent of poverty).

[117] Saudi Arabia was visited by Alston in 2017. For the report, see UNHRC, 'Report of the Special Rapporteur on Extreme Poverty and Human Rights on his Mission to Saudi Arabia—Note by the Secretariat' (2017) UN Doc A/HRC/35/26/Add.3 paras 12–20 (poverty in Saudi Arabia).

[118] In addition to the abovementioned non-admissibility decisions, see also *O'Rourke v UK* App no 39022/97 (ECtHR, 26 June 2001); *Codona v UK* App No 485/05 (ECtHR, 7 February 2006); *Bah v UK* App no 56328/07 (ECtHR, 27 September 2011) para 40.

[119] *N v UK* App no 26565/05 (ECtHR, 27 May 2008) para 44 (case of deportation of a HIV-positive person to Uganda).

[120] ibid.

The position of the Inter-American Court has always been different. The San José Tribunal is more aware than its European counterpart of the extent to which serious economic and social inequalities cannot be separated from the protection of civil and political rights. In this regard, the Inter-American Court, with the help of the work of the UN CESCR, is building a jurisprudence based on the indivisibility and interdependence of rights and obligations as discussed in section 20.4, but more fundamentally. More importantly, it seems to be moving towards a paradigm shift in its analysis of the *socio-economic contexts* that have made possible serious and massive violations of civil and political rights, as well as the *consequences* that result from these violations.

With regards to contexts, the Inter-American Court is increasingly isolating the condition of economic vulnerability, or even of extreme poverty, as one of the essential factors that explains the pattern of violations of civil and political rights committed by the state. In its 2016 landmark ruling on slavery to which workers from northern Brazil have been reduced on plantations (Article 6 of the ACHR), the Court thoroughly analysed the structural discrimination to which these workers from the poorest regions of Brazil were subjected, accepted as such by a class-based society and not fought by the state.[121] In another judgment concerning illegal international adoptions in Guatemala, where many children were victims during the country's non-international armed conflict, the Court also attached importance to discrimination on the grounds of poverty of the families from whom these children were removed, concluding that there has been a *structural* violation of their rights.[122]

Both cases highlight that for the Court these persons were ill-treated by the authorities and the society as a whole partly because they belonged to the poorest populations. Not only were the violations they suffered not taken seriously by the state authorities but, moreover, they were *normalized* because they were based on a relationship of historical economic domination. On a continent that is known to be marked by a very large number of economic and social inequalities, the Inter-American Court has therefore decided to no longer ignore the socio-economic dimension of the enjoyment of all human rights, whereas until the end of 2010 this aspect was not particularly visible. The point here is for the Inter-American Court to go further than the affirmation of the indivisibility of rights and freedoms: in the manner of Alston, it too removes all metaphysics from its approach, adopting a concrete starting point, that of the conditions in which the person was born and concretely lives.

As for the consequences, the judge of the Inter-American Court Judge Ferrer Mc-Gregor Poisot has repeatedly invited the majority of the Court to analyse on the basis of Article 26 of the ACHR the violations of the *right to housing* that may result from serious civil and political rights violations committed during an armed conflict, as in Colombia.[123] The position of Mc-Gregor Poisot—not followed by his colleagues of the majority—means that in the context of violations of civil and political rights, the Court should also take into account the *economic* effects of the breaches. This not only at the stage of reparations, when it measures the material prejudice under Article 63-1 of the ACHR, but when it determines the wrongful acts of the state and the scope of its international responsibility. To this end, he

[121] *Hacienda Brasil Verde Workers v Brazil* (Preliminary Objections, Merits, Reparations and Costs) Inter-American Court of Human Rights Series C No 318 (20 October 2016) paras 334–41.

For another use of Alston's reports on poverty in a landmark judgment against Brazil, see also *Case of the Employees of the Fireworks Factory of Santo Antônio de Jesus v Brazil.* Preliminary Objections, Merits, Reparations and Costs. Judgment of 15 July 2020. Series C No. 407, esp. paras. 190 and f.

[122] *Ramírez Escobar et al v Guatemala* (Merits, Reparations and Costs) Inter-American Court of Human Rights Series C No 351 (9 March 2018) paras 278–93.

[123] See, for instance, his separate opinion in *Vereda La Esperanza v Colombia* (Preliminary Objections, Merits, Reparations, and Costs) Inter-American Court of Human Rights Series C No 341 (31 August 2017).

quotes extensively the CESCR's General Comment No 3 on the content of states' obligations and, although the majority of the Court does not currently follow it, it nevertheless illustrates the paradigm shift that the Court may follow in the future towards an *integral and holistic* approach to human rights.

As said in the introduction of this chapter, the interest for various human rights actors in reading and using special procedures' reports is obvious: it may be helpful for the individuals to substantiate a communication/application before a judicial or quasi-judicial body or to interpret a binding treaty. Beyond, the interest in reading Alston's reports is that they provide accurate, provoking, and profound thoughts on what international human rights law is, where we stand as international lawyers and members of the human rights community and more importantly what political, legal, and social steps still have to be taken in order to make Article 1 of the UDHR effective.

PART IV

HUMAN RIGHTS STRUGGLES

21

Dangerous Proportions

Means and Ends in Non-finite War

Nehal Bhuta and Rebecca Mignot-Mahdavi

21.1 Introduction

In his May 2010 report to the General Assembly, then Special Rapporteur on Extrajudicial, Summary, or Arbitrary Executions, Philip Alston, squarely placed the legality of the US practice of targeted killing of suspected terrorists on the agenda of the United Nations.[1] He noted that the lack of public acknowledgement of the very existence of the practice, and the absence of any public, reasoned, legal justification for the strikes, rendered the practice's legality under international law almost impossible to evaluate. He went on to observe that the available public statements concerning the legal bases for the strikes resulted in a 'highly problematic blurring and expansion of the boundaries of the applicable legal frameworks—human rights law, the laws of war, and the law applicable to the use of inter-state force . . . The result has been a *displacement of clear legal standards with a vaguely defined licence to kill, and the creation of a major accountability vacuum*' (para 3, emphasis added).

Alston's report goes on to develop a critique of states' policies and practices that is at once sober and challenging—he called upon states, in particular the United States, to publicly identify the rules of international law that they consider as providing a basis for any targeted killing they undertake. Alston's demand for clarification was partially pre-empted two months earlier by a speech to the American Society of International Law, by then State Department Legal Advisor Harold Koh.[2] Koh's speech was the first public articulation of some of the legal arguments underlying the US practice, and Alston's May 2010 report was followed by three other major speeches,[3] and, eventually, the public release of the so-called 'Playbook' for 'direct action against terrorist targets outside the United States and Areas of Active Hostilities'.[4]

[1] UNHRC, 'Report of the Special Rapporteur on Extrajudicial, Summary, or Arbitrary Executions, Philip Alston: Study on Targeted Killings' (28 May 2010) UN Doc A/HRC/14/24/Add.6.

[2] Harold Koh, 'The Obama Administration and International Law' (Annual Meeting of the American Society of International Law, Washington, 25 March 2010) <www.state.gov/s/l/releases/remarks/139119.htm> accessed 10 September 2020.

[3] Office of the Attorney General, 'Attorney General Eric Holder Speaks at Northwestern University School of Law' *US Department of Justice* (Washington, 5 March 2012) < www.justice.gov/opa/speech/attorney-general-eric-holder-speaks-northwestern-university-school-law> accessed 10 September 2020; John O Brennan, 'Remarks of John O. Brennan, Assistant to the President for Homeland Security and Counterterrorism, on Ensuring al-Qa'ida's Demise' (The White House Office of the Press Secretary, Washington, 29 June 2011) <https://obamawhitehouse.archives.gov/the-press-office/2011/06/29/remarks-john-o-brennan-assistant-president-homeland-security-and-counter> accessed 9 September 2020; Brian Egan, 'International Law, Legal Diplomacy, and the Counter-ISIL Campaign' (American Society of International Law, Washington, 1 April 2016) <https://www.lawfareblog.com/state-department-legal-adviser-brian-egans-speech-asil> accessed 9 September 2020.

[4] US President Barack Obama, 'Procedures for Approving Direct Action against Terrorist Targets Located Outside the United States and Areas of Active Hostilities' (2013) Presidential Policy Guidance <https://www.

Nehal Bhuta and Rebecca Mignot-Mahdavi, *Dangerous Proportions* In: *The Struggle for Human Rights.* Edited by: Nehal Bhuta, Florian Hoffmann, Sarah Knuckey, Frédéric Mégret, and Margaret Satterthwaite, Oxford University Press. © Nehal Bhuta and Rebecca Mignot-Mahdavi 2021. DOI: 10.1093/oso/9780198868064.003.0022

It cannot be known whether Alston's intervention had any impact on the extent and nature of US drone strikes. The strong upward trend in US drone strikes in Pakistan, Somalia, and Yemen, between 2009 and 2012, followed by a tapered decline in its use in some states (and a rise in others such as Libya)[5] suggests that even as his UN report focused attention sharply on the tactic, it was becoming thoroughly normalized as a means to pursue an extended military strategy against certain Islamist extremist armed groups. The endurance of the tactic, and its character as a permanent component of US counter-terrorism practices, was evident from 2010 onwards.[6] In a lengthy 2011 treatment of targeted killing by the CIA, after the end of his term as special rapporteur, Alston concluded that the tactic inhabited a legal 'greyhole', characterized by a lack of any real scrutiny of the legality of a strike and its targets.[7] He presciently observed that the institutionalization of the tactic as part of the US national security institutions, entrenched it within elaborate administrative routines and legal nomenclatures that provided a dense web of overlapping oversight *frameworks* without engendering any *real* accountability.[8] Among the challenges was the difficulty in concretely evaluating the determinate application of the governing international legal norms, in the absence of the possibility of assessing the factual claims said to satisfy the threshold conditions for the legality of the strike. Public information was scarce, and what was available easily muddied by denial and spin. The expansive role of intelligence agencies in leading the identification of terrorist threats, brought with it a wide cloak of secrecy over the essential judgments underpinning the decision to use force against individuals or groups in another state. The 'structural predisposition to secrecy on the part of intelligence officials' has only been strengthened by 'the heterogeneity and geographical spread of actual and potential terrorist groups, the reality of homegrown terror, and the potential for large-scale acts of terrorism'.[9] The basic applicable legal norms could be identified, but their concrete application to the *kinds of operations* that characterized US strikes rested not only upon forward-leaning interpretations of existing legal concepts, and sparse assurances about factual foundations, but also on a tendency to:

> lamely accept that there is insufficient information in the public domain to enable existing policies and practices to be meaningfully assessed against rule of law standards.... The default approach of presuming probity, good faith, constant self-discipline, and deference

justice.gov/oip/foia-library/procedures_for_approving_direct_action_against_terrorist_targets/download> accessed 4 November 2020.

[5] See data compiled by the New America Foundation Peter Bergen, David Sterman, and Melissa Salyk-Virk, 'America's Counterterrorism Wars' (New America 2020) <http://newamerica.org/international-security/reports/americas-counterterrorism-wars/> accessed 10 September 2020.

[6] Mark Mazzetti, *The Way of the Knife: The CIA, a Secret Army, and a War at the Ends of the Earth* (Penguin Books 2014); Charlie Savage, *Power Wars: The Relentless Rise of Presidential Authority and Secrecy* (Revised, First Back Bay Books trade paperback edn, Back Bay Books/ Little, Brown and Company 2017); Scott Shane, 'C.I.A. Is Disputed on Civilian Toll in Drone Strikes' *The New York Times* (11 August 2011) <https://www.nytimes.com/2011/08/12/world/asia/12drones.html> accessed 10 September 2020; Scott Shane, *Objective Troy: A Terrorist, a President, and the Rise of the Drone* (First paperback edn, Tim Duggan Books 2016); Greg Miller, Julie Tate, and Barton Gellman, 'Documents Reveal NSA's Extensive Involvement in Targeted Killing Program' *The Washington Post* (13 October 2016) <https://www.washingtonpost.com/world/national-security/documents-reveal-nsas-extensive-involvement-in-targeted-killing-program/2013/10/16/29775278-3674-11e3-8a0e-4e2cf80831fc_story.html> accessed 10 September 2020.

[7] Philip Alston, 'The CIA and Targeted Killing Beyond Borders' (2011) 2 Harvard National Security Law Journal 283.

[8] ibid 405–06.

[9] ibid 316.

> to formally accepted legal limits on the part of officials acting in secrecy undermines basic democratic principles, defies experience, and mocks the notion of human rights accountability.[10]

Alston's deep worries about the institutionalization of the tactic of targeting killing, and its corrosive consequences for any meaningful possibility of scrutinizing the legality of such strikes, proved far-sighted. While not cursed, Cassandra-like, to be disbelieved—Alston's forebodings have generated extensive public debate and halting attempts at the international level[11] to refute some of the international legal claims which underpin the tactic—the practice and attempts to justify it with respect to strikes on non-state armed groups have proliferated. Whereas under the Bush administration these legal arguments were made through non-public diplomatic representations,[12] after 2013 the claims were advanced publicly[13] and with a juris generative ambition to expand de jure the permissiveness of the legal regime governing the use of force. Western European states, such as France[14] and the United Kingdom,[15] have embraced and exercised the tactic of targeted killing, and (in the case of the United Kingdom) publicly endorsed the essential elements of the US legal justifications. In the United States, the Trump administration escalated drone strikes and kinetic strikes against Islamist groups in Somalia and Yemen, and reversed the downward trend in drone strikes in Pakistan. Small advances towards transparency and accountability, such as the annual report on civilian casualties mandated by President Obama, were scrapped, and policy constraints on strikes outside of areas of 'active hostilities' (in which US forces are already engaged in combat operations) were reportedly abolished.[16]

[10] ibid 299–300

[11] For example, the discussion by Dire Tladi, 'The Use of Force in Self-Defence Against Non-State Actors, Decline of Collective Security and the Rise of Unilateralism: Whither International Law?' in Mary Ellen O'Connell, Christian J Tams, and Dire Tladi (eds), *Self-Defence against Non-State Actors* (CUP 2019)<https://doi.org/10.1017/9781108120173> accessed 10 September 2020; Jutta Brunnée and Stephen J Toope, 'Self-Defence against Non-State Actors: Are Powerful States Willing but Unable to Change International Law?' (2018) 67 International and Comparative Law Quarterly 263.

[12] Wikileaks cables concerning arguments made in 2007–2008 by Bush administration international legal advisor John Bellinger, discussed in Victor Kattan, 'Furthering the "War on Terrorism" through International Law: How the United States and the United Kingdom Resurrected the Bush Doctrine on Using Preventive Military Force to Combat Terrorism' (2018) 5(1) Journal on the Use of Force and International Law 97.

[13] Daniel Bethlehem, 'Self-Defense Against an Imminent or Actual Armed Attack By Nonstate Actors' (2012) 106 American Journal of International Law 770; Right Honourable Jeremy Wright MP QC, 'The Modern Law of Self-Defense' (International Institute for Strategic Studies, London, 11 January 2017); Senator the Hon George Brandis QC, 'The Right of Self-Defence Against Imminent Armed Attack In International Law' (*EJIL: Talk!*, 25 May 2017) <https://www.ejiltalk.org/the-right-of-self-defence-against-imminent-armed-attack-in-international-law/> accessed 10 September 2020.

[14] Gérard Davet and Fabrice Lhomme, *Un Président Ne Devrait Pas Dire Ça...* (French and European Publications Inc 2016); Vincent Nouzille, *Erreurs Fatales: Comment Nos Présidents Ont Failli Face Au Terrorisme* (Fayard 2017); *loi* n° 2018-607 du 13 juillet 2018 relative à la programmation militaire pour les années 2019 à 2025 et portant diverses dispositions intéressant la défense [law n 2018-607, 13 July 2018, on military programming for 2019–2025 and establishing diverse provisions on defence].

[15] Ewen MacAskill and Richard Norton-Taylor, 'How UK Government Decided to Kill Reyaad Khan' *The Guardian* (8 September 2015) <https://www.theguardian.com/world/2015/sep/08/how-did-britain-decide-to-assassinate-uk-isis-fighter-reyaad-khan-drone-strike> accessed 10 September 2020; HC Deb 7 September 2015, vol 599, col 1; Foreign Affairs Select Committee, *Prime Minister David Cameron, Memorandum to the Foreign Affairs Select Committee, Prime Minister's Response to the Foreign Affairs Select Committee's Second Report of Session 2015–16: The Extension of Offensive British Military Operations to Syria* (HC 2015); Joint Committee on Human Rights, *The Government's policy on the use of drones for targeted killing, Second Report of Session* (HC, HL 2015–2016); UK Parliament Intelligence and Security Committee, *Report on UK Lethal Drone Strikes in Syria* (HC, HL 2017).

[16] Charlie Savage and Eric Schmitt, 'Trump Poised to Drop Some Limits on Drone Strikes and Commando Raids' *The New York Times* (21 September 2017) <https://www.nytimes.com/2017/09/21/us/politics/trump-drone-strikes-commando-raids-rules.html> accessed 10 September 2020: 'President Trump's top national

The 'vaguely defined licence to kill' that Alston grasped as so closely associated with the policy and practice of targeted killing, seems here to stay.[17] We do not argue in this chapter that this permissive framework for the extraterritorial use of force against individuals associated with non-state armed groups, is now *lex lata* or even *lege ferenda*. That is a question that cannot be settled easily, remains in flux, and may be susceptible to some containment if there is a concerted effort to refute it by other states using the fora provided by international organizations.[18] Rather, we take up Alston's intuition that the policy and practice of targeted killing, as part of a military strategy to combat Islamist extremist armed groups, is 'the ultimate asymmetrical weapon. The "battlefield" has been expanded exponentially in terms of both time and space. Individuals are no longer targeted solely on the basis of their status as combatants, but of their individual profiles.'[19] The tenacious re-articulation of relevant legal concepts from the jus ad bellum and the jus in bello, has fashioned a set of interconnected legal propositions that we call 'revisionist'. This revisionist framework—while not radically novel in terms of any single proposition or claim, as we will discuss in passing later—cumulatively engenders a highly permissive framework for the preventive, extraterritorial, use of lethal force against individuals and non-state groups, with a geographically and temporally expansive scope. This revisionist, 'asymmetricalized', jus ad bellum, is a modification full of consequences. It refashions legal rules resting on a presupposition of contained enmity between two legally equal public powers (states),[20] into a set of rules that are to govern the potentially unlimited hostility between, on the one side, recognized public powers (states), and on the other, networks of individuals characterized ultimately by their *potentially* dangerous characteristics and those of the human collectivity in which they are embedded.

In this chapter, we examine the revisionist framework and highlight its 'cascading' consequences on the conceptual content of foundational elements of the jus ad bellum, such as 'armed attack' and 'imminence'. We then turn to a less-examined question:[21] the revisionist framework's impact on the boundaries of the jus ad bellum concept of proportionality, and its traditionally understood function as a *limiting* or *constraining* concept within the argumentative space of force-justifying reasons afforded by the jus ad bellum legal framework. We consider how the 'determinate contentfulness' of the ad bellum concept of proportionality is

security advisers have proposed relaxing two rules, the officials said. First, the targets of kill missions by the military and the C.I.A., now generally limited to high-level militants deemed to pose a "continuing and imminent threat" to Americans, would be expanded to include foot-soldier jihadists with no special skills or leadership roles. And second, proposed drone attacks and raids would no longer undergo high-level vetting.... The policy paves the way for broader and more frequent operations against Al Qaeda, the Islamic State and other jihadists. It would also apply in countries where the United States has targeted Islamist militants outside of regular combat for years, including Yemen, Somalia and Libya, and would ease the way to expanding such gray-zone acts of sporadic warfare to elsewhere in Africa, Asia and the Middle East where terrorists operate'.

[17] Andris Banka and Adam Quinn, 'Killing Norms Softly: US Targeted Killing, Quasi-Secrecy and the Assassination Ban' (2018) 27(4) Security Studies 665.

[18] There is some evidence of initiatives of this kind, which remain tentative: see the Mexican initiative described by Pablo Arrocha Olabuenaga, 'The Time Has Come to Have a Conversation at the U.N. on Self-Defence' (*Just Security*, 13 April 2020) <https://www.justsecurity.org/69625/the-time-has-come-to-have-a-conversation-at-the-u-n-on-self-defence/> accessed 10 September 2020.

[19] Alston, 'CIA Beyond Borders' (n 7) 325.

[20] Pablo Kalmanovitz, *The Laws of War in International Thought* (OUP 2020).

[21] Ryan Goodman, 'The Obama Administration and Targeting "War-Sustaining" Objects in Noninternational Armed Conflict' (2016) 110 American Journal of International Law 663: 'Academic discussion has yet to grapple with some of the strongest and clearest evidence in support of the U.S. view on the legality of such targeting decisions. Indeed, intellectual resources may be better spent not on the question of whether such objects are legitimate military targets under the law of armed conflict, but on second-order questions, such as how to apply proportionality analysis and how to identify limiting principles to guard against unintentional slippery slopes.'

modified through the revision of concepts such as 'armed attack', 'imminence', and the slow death of the requirement of 'effective control' by the territorial state over a non-state armed group as part of the *conditionis rationae personae* for the use of force against that state. These conceptual revisions bring with them, we suggest, a reconfiguration of the structure of legal relationships presupposed by the jus ad bellum's concept of proportionality, and a new (in) determinacy that renders the concept more permissive than constraining. Indeed, 'proportionality' under the presuppositions of an asymmetrical relationship between recognized public powers and organized groups of hostile individuals, risks becoming a licence for an unending 'police action' in the territory of other states burdened by a limited territorial sovereignty. Such a concept of proportionality revives a limb of the jus ad bellum—the right to self-preservation—deemed to have atrophied, if not entirely disappeared, since 1945.

21.2 The Determinacy of Legal Concepts

As a preliminary to our argument, we first reflect on the idea of the 'determinacy' (or determinateness) of a legal concept, as this idea is important to our argument throughout this chapter. Robert Brandom's Hegelian account of the determinateness of legal concepts is germane to the argument we are trying to develop. Brandom's Hegelianism is described as 'neo-pragmatist', and he is perhaps now one of the best-known proponents of a pragmatist interpretation of German Idealism. The core of this account is an emphasis on the close interdependence between *reasoning* and *concept use*: the semantic and epistemic dimensions of thought and language are 'inextricably intertwined' such that the 'inferential relations sentences [and concepts] stand in to one another are an essential element of the *meanings* that they express'.[22] *Applying* a concept (such as 'red') is to paradigmatically describe how things are; understanding a concept is 'to practically master the *inferential* relations it stands in to other descriptions: its place in the space of reasons or implications'.[23] Inferential relations are logical relations of incompatibility (exclusion) and consequence (inclusion): the concept of copper as we define and use it (and the thought that 'A is copper'), is incompatible with the inference that A is an electrical insulator; but has as a logical consequence that A is an electrical conductor. On this account, the contentfulness of a concept (or a sentence using a concept) is derived from the inferential relations it stands in with other concepts: 'The space of reasons is the space of concepts'.[24]

Pragmatism[25] is broadly characterized by looking to uses or practices to understand the inferential relations that make up meaning (semantics) and content (truth-value). The conceptual content of acts, attitudes, and linguistic expressions is conferred by the 'role they play in the practices their subjects engage in'.[26] Conceptual content and the inferences it permits are a function of a linguistic community and its practices.[27] Reasoning in this account is discursive, rather than ontological, and concepts gain content through their inferential role (their function) in reasoning:

[22] Robert Brandom, *Reason in Philosophy: Animating Ideas* (Belknap Press of Harvard University Press 2013) 6.
[23] ibid 8.
[24] ibid 10.
[25] See discussion in Dina Emundts, 'Hegel as a Pragmatist' (2015) 23 British Journal for the History of Philosophy 611.
[26] Robert Brandom, *A Spirit of Trust: A Reading of Hegel's Phenomenology* (The Belknap Press of Harvard University Press 2019) 3.
[27] Brandom, *Reason in Philosophy* (n 22) 13.

> We undertake discursive commitments and responsibilities and what makes them discursive commitments and responsibilities is that they stand in *inferential* relations to one another: relations that codify what is a *reason* for what. Because our commitments are inferentially articulated, they are *conceptually* contentful.[28]

On this pragmatist view, determining what falls within the boundaries of a concept—and thus differentiating between a justified and unjustified application of the concept—is not fixed in some naturalistic way as though 'ideas just came with their contents . . . and it was up to the mind to apply them to find out what is true'.[29] The sense and reference of a concept are not completely and definitively settled in advance of applying the concept.[30] The determinateness of a concept, in the sense that the content of a concept and its justified or unjustified application can be reasoned to through its logical relations of incompatibility and consequence, is not a 'property' but a 'process':

> The [functional system which confers conceptual content] opens outwards from the cycle of perception, thought and intentional action on the part of individual subjects to the network of social practices those subjects engage in, and then further to include the diachronic dimension of those practices, both looking backward to their historical antecedents and looking forward to their future development.[31]

The content of concepts is, in the first moment of reflection on their application, a product of their antecedent history: the grasp of a concept is mastery of the use of a word,[32] where use in some sense stands in for the antecedently available applications of the concept as meaningful expressions. History—in the sense of 'the already-up-and-running communal linguistic practices into which I enter'[33]—gives us finite examples of how we make sense of a concept, by showing us how we have applied the concept in expressions that make judgments. When we use a concept, we understand (usually implicitly, but with the possibility of making explicit) what would be reasons for or against a particular application of that concept in a judgment, and what inferential consequences the application of that concept would have. But prior uses need not logically exhaust the potential applications of a concept, from a logical or semantic point of view; prior uses, endowed by history, do not 'determine the correctness of all possible future applications of a concept "like rails laid out to infinity"'.[34] In order for a concept to be contentful in a manner that is not limited to a collection of prior uses, they must be applied to novel circumstances (the present, which can resemble and differ from the past in an infinite number of respects) in order to develop and determine conceptual contents. The discursive processes and practices of concept application, in the form of judgments, is at once an application of pre-existing 'determinate' contents *and*, in this second moment, a process of revisiting and re-examining those contents in light of new possible determinations. The process of reconstructing a concept in this way, and thus revising its determinate contentfulness, is necessarily attended by a revision of *the inferential relations* in

[28] ibid 10.

[29] Robert Brandom, 'A Hegelian Model of Legal Concept Determination: The Normative Fine Structure of the Judges' Chain Novel' in Graham Hubbs and Douglas Lind (eds), *Pragmatism, Law, and Language* (Routledge 2014) 23.

[30] Brandom, *Reason in Philosophy* (n 22) 89.

[31] Brandom, *A Spirit of Trust* (n 26) 4.

[32] Sellars, quoted in Brandom, *Reason in Philosophy* (n 22) 72.

[33] ibid 73.

[34] Wittgenstein, quoted in Brandom, *Reason in Philosophy* (n 22) 90.

which it stands to other concepts and of the consequences of the application of the (revised) concept: on this pragmatic Hegelian model, all conceptual content is made through 'non-monotonic, seriously multi-premise material inferential and incompatibility relations, in the context of the realization ... that those relations depend on the whole context of collateral discursive commitments'.[35] Conceptual content is holistic, in the sense that 'the grasp of any conceptual contents requires grasp of many others, and or relations among them'.[36]

The reconstruction of a concept's content is always in some sense a 'petition for recognition', of a revised set of inferential and incompatibility relations and a whole set of collateral discursive commitments. This 'pragmatic order of explanation' of how the determinateness of a concept changes, looks to the process of applying concepts to novel particulars as a practical, constructive task—one that determines conceptual contents 'by *making it the case* that some applications are correct, by *taking it* to be the case that they are ... By investing one's authority in an application as being correct, one authorizes those who apply the concept to future cases to do so also. If they in turn recognize one in this specific respect, by acknowledging that authority, then a more determinate [or newly determined] norm has been socially instituted.'[37]

Conceptual content that is determinate, in this sense of bearing inferential relations of consequence and incompatibility, rests upon not only a history (in the sense used earlier) but also a relational substance: inferential relations presuppose logical relations, but logical necessity or possibility in this account rests upon practical attitudes made possible by recognitive relations that take place in history. Social substance—the substance of relationships between judging-and-acting subjects in actual communities of practices and institutions—conditions conceptual content, even as judging-and-acting subjects act upon and transform that substance through revising and reconstructing conceptual contents that reflected its history (and its possibilities) up to that moment.[38] These concepts have *force* in the sense that the determinate content of a concept that is used, 'settles just what one has made oneself responsible for in judging or intending, what norm one has bound oneself by, how *one has committed oneself to things being or being made to be*'.[39] Concepts both lead *and* lag the transformation of social substance, they both interpret *and* change the world.

This pragmatist semantic account of conceptual content, is, it should be noted, part of a complete theory of reasoning and knowing, extending to natural objects and natural science as much as social objects and social knowledges. But legal concepts are particularly amenable to this account, and Brandom himself has highlighted its application to thinking about the determinate content of legal concepts.[40] The determinateness of legal concepts matters because:

> The content of concepts affects what one is committed and entitled to by applying those concepts in judgment and argumentation ... For the idea that there is a difference between exercising normative authority by appeal to law and simply exercising power in its name depends on the possibility of distinguishing applications of the law that are rationally justifiable in virtue of the meanings of concepts that articulate the law and those that are not.[41]

[35] ibid 102.
[36] Brandom, *A Spirit of Trust* (n 26) 22.
[37] Brandom, *Reason in Philosophy* (n 22) 92–93.
[38] Brandom, *A Spirit of Trust* (n 26), 29.
[39] ibid 15.
[40] Brandom, 'A Hegelian Model of Legal Concept Determination' (n 29).
[41] ibid 19.

An applier of a legal concept (whether a judge or, as is more often the case in international law, a state advancing its considered legal view about its conduct or the conduct of another state) must begin with the existing contents of the concepts as derived from exemplary usages (case law, authoritative writings, codifications, digests of interpretations, etc), and proceed to decide *whether* the concept applies to the situation at hand, and *what* the application of the concept commits oneself to in terms of its material incompatibility exclusions and consequential inclusions.[42] In applying a concept to conduct at hand, the legal applier is responsible to the conceptual content expressed by the term, by being responsible to meanings available through the relevant exemplary usages; the applier of the concept must practically 'know their way about' the (holistic) space of possible applications and non-applications of the concept as it presents itself to them. This 'knowing one's way around' a space of reasons afforded by a concept, as already noted, is a discursive process that may entail *amplifying* certain inferential consequences of inclusion ('A is a logical consequence or extension of B') or *critically* distinguishing certain prior commitments as not essential or necessary or materially incompatible to the concept; in such a process, the application of the concept articulates and rearticulates 'what counts' as reasons for or against, or justifications for, the judgeable content of a concept; this is what renders the concept 'concrete' in the sense of having discernible boundaries of justified and unjustified application.

Brandom notes that the inferences that give reasons for and against the judgeable content of a legal concept will rarely if ever rest exclusively on formally, logically valid reasoning: The reasonableness of the inferences 'essentially depends on the contents of the non-logical concepts it involves ... [M]ost legal reasoning ... is probative [which means] that all the reasons considered are defeasible.... This defeasibility means that material inferences, including inferences that articulate legal concepts, unlike logical ones, are in general non-monotonic: a good inference can be turned into a bad one by adding further premises'.[43] Amplifying inclusive inferences and distinguishing incompatible ones in working through to the concrete content of a legal concept will depend on non-monotonic, multi-premise material inferential relations, and some practical sense of what materially good or materially bad inferences are within the whole context. The determinate contents of a legal concept depend on this practical sense of how to reason through its application; such reasoning-through at once rests on already-determined contents and boundaries endowed by history, and revises and reconstructs them to a new context in the present. The substance of this context is a social-historical one, on which the (new) determination of the content of concepts rests:

> [A] later recollective story [of a concept's content] ... may treat some quite different episodes as progressive and precedential, quite different material inferences as good, different constellations of claims as incompatible. The moment of *finding*, discovering how things already were, which shows up from the perspective of each recollective reconstruction of a tradition is balanced by the moment of *making* that shows up when a new constellation of commitments must be integrated, and a new recollectively instituted tradition discovered

[42] Brandom, *Reason in Philosophy* (n 22) 84.

[43] Brandom, 'A Hegelian Model of Legal Concept Determination' (n 29) 21: Non-monotonic logic covers a family of formal frameworks devised to capture and represent *defeasible inference*. Reasoners draw conclusions defeasibly when they reserve the right to retract them in the light of further information. Examples are numerous, reaching from inductive generalizations to reasoning to the best explanation to inferences on the basis of expert opinion, and so on. We find defeasible inferences in everyday reasoning, in expert reasoning (eg medical diagnosis), and in scientific reasoning; Christian Strasser and Aldo Antonelli, 'Non-Monotonic Logic', *The Stanford Encyclopedia of Philosophy* (Summer edn, Stanford University Press 2019) <https://plato.stanford.edu/entries/logic-nonmonotonic/#NonMonoLogiHumaReas> accessed 10 September 2020.

> to vindicate them ... The process of determining conceptual contents is characterized by discontinuities, caesurae, radical reassessment of old commitments, and the unravelling of previous progress. The open-endedness and determinability of conceptual contents lives in the space between successive recollective stories.[44]

In the following sections, we review the interconnected set of propositions that we call the revisionist framework. This framework, taken as a whole, is a diligent—if at times tenuous—attempt to give a new contentfulness to the relevant legal concepts. The concepts have been reworked in light of their historical endowment of available contents, to 'fit' a new reality and new constellation of security practices and routines, as well as new technologies that make those practices and routines possible. By being revised to fit this new assemblage, the reworked concepts also extend and unleash new kinds of action and presuppose a different substance of underlying practical engagements and relations. Specifically, we suggest that the presuppositions of the concepts shift from a largely horizontal relationship between two legally equal public powers, to a vertical relationship between public powers and networks of hostile individuals. In line with the implications of Brandom's theory of the determinateness of legal concepts, this altered set of presuppositions—'the whole context of collateral discursive commitments' upon which the contentfulness of concepts depends—brings with it a revised set of 'non-monotonic, seriously multi-premise material inferential and incompatibility relations' that not only portends new determinations of the concepts but also generates new inferences and incompatibility relations for adjacent or 'downstream' concepts (such as proportionality). The result is a holistic transformation of the relevant concepts, shifting considerably the scope and temporal extension of their application.

21.3 The Certainty of Old—Recollective Stories

In a recent short essay, Christian Tams noted that the use of force against non-state armed groups in the territory of another state, even where that state ('the territorial state') does not control or actively support the non-state armed group, was not unknown in state practice after 1945.[45] Drawing on Claus Kreß's doctoral dissertation,[46] Tams points to France's 1960 incursions into Tunisia to raid Front de Libérations Nationale (FLN) bases, during the FLN's armed conflict against France for the independence of Algeria. Similarly, India's use of force in Pakistani territory in 1948 relied on the justification of self-defence to attack against armed groups based in Pakistan that were launching raids into Kashmir. And Morocco pursued the Western Saharan national liberation movement's (Polisario's) armed forces into Algeria in 1979. These examples may be added to better-known instances where states claimed that international law accorded them a right to use force in the territory of another state, in order to attack non-state armed groups operating from the territory of that state, such as Israel's raids against fedayeen and Palestine Liberation Organization (PLO) bases in Jordan and Tunisia, apartheid South Africa's military campaigns against the African National Congress (ANC) in South Africa, and Portugal's incursions into Zambia, Senegal, and Guinea in its

[44] Brandom, *Reason in Philosophy* (n 22) 103.

[45] Christian J Tams, 'Embracing the Uncertainty of Old: Armed Attacks by Non-State Actors Prior to 9/11' (2017) 77 Zaörv 61.

[46] Claus Kreß, *Gewaltverbot und Selbstverteidigungsrecht nach der Satzung der Vereinten Nationen bei staatlicher Verwicklung in Gewaltakte Privater* (Duncker & Humblot 1995).

conflict with national liberation movements seeking to end Portuguese rule in Africa.[47] While the practice of Israel, South Africa, and Portugal was roundly condemned, the legal rationales offered for the criticism of their conduct related closely to the condemnation of occupation, apartheid, and colonialism, and the widespread sense that these states used of force in the pursuit of these ends;[48] there was 'very little opinio juris explicitly dismissing self-defence in response to armed bands per se. On the other hand … there was no genuine support for [these states'] self-defence argument'.[49]

Tams is right to suggest that our contemporary sense that the last twenty years has brought about an important revision or novel change in the application of the jus ad bellum rests on an exaggerated view of the certainty of the relevant concepts' application in the past: 'the "old days" when the law was certain'—in the sense of requiring a high threshold of effective control by the territorial state over the non-state armed group to give rise to a right to use force against the non-state group on the territorial state's territory—are in fact a repository of incomplete and partially determinate attempts to fix the meaning of concepts such as armed attack. The sense of certainty and clear contentfulness in the application of these concepts emerges, as Brandom's argument would suggest, through a moment of *recollection* that at once *found* the determinate content of armed attack and self-defence in the constellation of one set of available claims, and simultaneously *made* these claims into the essential content of the concepts. This process of determination renders other kinds of claims, *in retrospect*, clearly incompatible with the content of the concept; the concept's concreteness—the sense in which as matter of the logical application of the concept we can infer what is incompatible and what is a consequence of it—is always the result of one '*recollective story*' that stabilizes under the historical circumstances that make it seem necessary, inevitable, appropriate, or just.

In the 1963 book that would become a *locus classicus* of the 'restrictionist' interpretation of the use of force in the UN Charter, Ian Brownlie made an exhaustive argument for reading the UN Charter as reflecting and developing customary international law in a manner that restricted the permissible use of force to narrow readings of grounds found in the Charter (self-defence and Security Council authorization).[50] Of particular concern to Brownlie, writing in the aftermath of the Suez Crisis, was to refute the continued possibility of reliance of pre-Charter rights to use force under concepts such as the right to self-preservation, intervention, and necessity.[51] He complained that such doctrines were 'too vague and susceptible to selfish interpretation to provide a sufficient basis for a legal regime'[52]—intuitively grasping what amounts to Brandom's theoretical observation that legal concepts require determinate contentfulness (in the sense discussed earlier) if they are 'to serve as reasons justifying' the application of legal judgments and legal argumentation:

> The content of concepts affects what one is committed and entitled to by applying those concepts in judgment and argumentation. Some kinds of semantic indeterminateness of legal concepts would undercut the rational credentials of legal arguments and the normative authority of legal judgments. It is essential to the normative bindingness of applications

[47] Tom Ruys, *'Armed Attack' and Article 51 of the UN Charter: Evolutions in Customary Law and Practice* (CUP 2010) 399.
[48] ibid 403 ff.
[49] ibid 417.
[50] Ian Brownlie, *International Law and the Use of Force by States* (Clarendon Press/OUP 1963).
[51] ibid 47–48, 216.
[52] ibid 48.

> of legal concepts to particular cases that those are rationally licensed by laws articulating those concepts[53]

Crucial to Brownlie's self-described 'limitationist view' of how to understand concepts such as 'use of force' and 'armed attack' in the UN Charter are his efforts to demonstrate a break or caesura in the applied meanings (as discernible in state practice and opinio juris) between 1920 and 1945. These uses of relevant concepts marginalized certain available contents and privileged others, enabling Brownlie to maintain that the constellation of concepts determining the legality of the use of force by states had narrowed to 'self-defence'—as opposed to other available concepts such as self-preservation, necessity, intervention, or 'acts short of war'.[54] The latter concepts, in Brownlie's argument, lost their historical *semantic* connection with the content of the concept of self-defence, even as their status as lawful instruments of state policy was diminished (ultimately to vanishing point, in Brownlie's 'limitationist' claim).[55] Brownlie's endeavour to give determinate contentfulness to the concepts of 'use of force' and 'armed attack' after the UN Charter, was a recollective story in Brandom's sense: old commitments and premises in a web of material inferential relations of consequence and incompatibility are reassessed—critically rejected or distinguished as no longer warranted—and another set of multi-premise inferences and collateral discursive commitments engaged to make sense of the concepts. This recollective story is evident in the apotheosis of Brownlie's argument:

> Historically, the law [of self-defence] is bound up with the amorphous right of self-preservation ... [T]he state practice of the period before the advent of the League has a diffuse character which reflects the lack of legal regulation of the use of force in the nineteenth century.... The increasing acceptance by states in the period between 1920 and 1939 of the view that war or any use of force as an instrument of national policy was unlawful has resulted in the demise of the rights of self-help and of self-preservation. The right of self-preservation had always been capacious enough to justify action beyond what was necessary for the maintenance of the integrity of the territorial domain of the state. The legal developments of the period of the League had the result that, while the right of self-preservation no longer existed in its classical form, some of its content was preserved. This residual right was referred to as that of self-defence or legitimate defence. It was understood that this right ... was subject to objective and legal determination and that it was confined to reaction to immediate danger to the physical integrity of the state itself ... Unfortunately the acceptance of the existence of a right to self-defence which was essentially a legally defined right was not in fact accompanied by any precise definition of the content of the right.[56]

Brownlie understands his task as precisely to discern the 'objective and legal determination' of the content of the concept of self-defence, to reduce the risks of abusive auto-judgment that characterize what he deems to be indeterminate and subjective concepts such as self-preservation—even though from a genealogical perspective he accepts that self-defence is the offspring of a broader right of self-preservation. But Brownlie's premise is clear: legality

[53] Brandom, 'A Hegelian Model of Legal Concept Determination' (n 29) 20.
[54] Brownlie (n 50) chs 5, 11, 12.
[55] ibid especially chs 11–13.
[56] ibid 252.

demands objectively determinate concepts in the sense of concepts *capable* of engendering (material inferential) *reasons* for their application or non-application, where the validity conditions for these inferences can be adjudged by those agents to whom the reasons are offered. Objective determinacy means here intersubjective (between subjects) recognition of the grounds for the application for a concept and for the evaluation of the fulfilment of those grounds. In Brownlie's 'recollective story' it is an *argument against* the inferred legality of a purported rule, if it does not lend itself to 'objective determination' in the sense of its application being able to be judged intersubjectively by other members of the society of states; rules that permit extensive auto-determination threaten to revive the discredited (and, in Brownlie's view, now unlawful) right of self-preservation as a grounds for use of force, and thereby also imperil the essence of the constellation of rules *qua* legal regime. Thus, while very tentatively accepting the possibility of anticipatory self-defence, he observes:

> To permit anticipatory action may well be to accept a right which is wider than that of self-defence and akin to that of self-preservation. It is true that states must be accorded the right to decide on defensive necessity in the first instance but in making this *ex parte* decision *they should be inhibited by a rule which is related to facts which have objective characteristics* and not to mere estimates of intention [emphasis added].[57]

Brownlie places great weight on the principle of proportionality as giving some measure of objective content to uses of force that traverse the boundary between the concepts of self-defence and self-preservation. Proportionality 'may represent an attempt to create a necessary distinction between defence and self-help in reaction to a historical tendency to confuse them'.[58] Brownlie does not fully explain this intuition, but it seems to lie in the *logical* premise that in order to claim the proportionality of a use of force, a state must articulate sufficiently concrete ('unequivocal') facts concerning the nature of the threat faced to enable *other legal subjects* to judge the soundness of the application of the concept of self-defence (and as a corollary implication, that other legal subjects would not accept excessively vague or subjective accounts of the threat, leading at least to a kind of argumentative constraint on claims of anticipation).[59]

Brownlie's critical worry that anticipatory self-defence will become indistinguishable from self-help, relates also to *the kind of actor* he expects anticipation is most likely to be used against. He notes that, historically, anticipatory force was usually claimed against armed groups operating across the border in another state, and so formed part of a claim of self-help or self-preservation.[60] He does not rule out the use of force against armed groups a priori under the Charter concept of self-defence, but he insists that the nature of the threat must be amenable to the constraining logic, which he takes to be the essence of proportionality. This leads him to insert another condition before force can be used against armed groups: that these groups must in some way be the direct legal responsibility of the state from the territory of which they act.[61] Otherwise, the licence to use force against states on the grounds of 'indirect aggression' will be too conducive to auto-determination and so reintroduce self-help into the concept of self-defence.

[57] ibid 259–60.
[58] ibid 261.
[59] ibid 252.
[60] ibid 257.
[61] ibid 279–80.

The high threshold of attribution of an armed group's violence to a state—which Brownlie as counsel for Nicaragua convinced the ICJ to adopt in its landmark 1986 judgement—has its origins in this logic of prophylaxis against the risks of adventurous interventionism in the name of self-help. Brownlie appears to have concluded that the presence of hostile armed groups on the territory of another state, was shown by history to be too tempting and promiscuous a casus belli to persist unamended. Brownlie reaches for proportionality as a restraining concept against such temptations:

> It is possible in a very limited number of situations that force might be a proportionate reaction where there is unequivocal evidence of an intention to launch a devastating attack almost immediately. However ... to commit a state to an actual conflict when there is only circumstantial evidence of an impending attack would be to act in a manner that disregarded the requirement of proportionality.[62]

Using force against 'indirect aggression' by armed groups operating on the territory of another state 'cannot be derived from Article 51 if the requirement of proportionality is to be strictly observed'[63] *unless* the conduct of the armed groups is attributable to the state from the territory of which they act. The exact relation between proportionality and attribution is not made explicit here, but read as whole, his argument rests on an intuition that the symmetry of forms and statuses entailed in state-to-state interactions (even hostile ones) is in some sense a limiting one: states treating each other as enemies with equal rights, not as criminals or outlaws, is a constitutive element of the meaning of proportionality. An interstate legal regime governing the use of force rests on this presupposition of symmetry; to maintain it, actual hostilities between a state and a non-state armed group must nonetheless be incorporated or assimilated into this legal regime and its presuppositions, not stand outside it as a parallel legal regime. Such a parallel regime would revive the logic of self-preservation or self-help.

In the first twenty years after the UN Charter, the 'limitationist' view so trenchantly argued by Brownlie was not the only available content given to the concept of self-defence. Famously, Bowett maintained the pre-Charter rights, particularly relating to anticipatory self-defence,[64] continued in a broad form, and that force could be used in self-defence against armed groups even if they were not controlled by the state from which they operated. Bowett considered his view vindicated by practices such as the 1956 Israeli invasion of Sinai, the 1962–1963 Katanga intervention and the US blockade of Cuba.[65] The 'uncertainty of old' to which Tams refers, reflects the competing interpretive resources available to those endeavouring to discern the conceptual content of self-defence. This content is both 'found' *and* 'made', in the way that Brandom's theory helps us understand. And as Brandom's theory also entails, to grasp how the uncertainty of old became the *certainty* of old, viewed backwards from the uncertainty of the now, we must look for those contexts in which one possible recollective story crystallized as *the* determinate content of a concept.

While the *Nicaragua* decision is the visible apotheosis of this recollective story, its critical context seems to have been the strenuous effort by newly decolonized states from 1960

[62] ibid 259.
[63] ibid 279.
[64] DW Bowett, *Self-Defence in International Law* (Lawbook Exchange 2009).
[65] DW Bowett, 'International Law and the Use of Force by States. By Ian Brownlie' (1964) 13(3) International and Comparative Law Quarterly 1107.

to constrain the interventionist potential remaining within the concept of self-defence. The spectre haunting the right of self-preservation or self-help was not only 'auto-determination' of the contents of the concepts, but interventionism by stronger states in the name of essential interests.[66] Reflecting in 1962 on the 'contemporary attitudes of newly independent [recently decolonized] states toward the rules of international law',[67] Georges Abi-Saab noted that for decolonized states long subject to 'domination or intervention' by other states, 'sovereignty is a hard won prize of their long struggle for emancipation ... the doctrine of sovereignty is resorted to more readily by these countries to bar intervention by other states'.[68] Decolonized states' efforts to shape the content of international law unsurprisingly focused on UN fora 'where their voices can be heard and where they have scope for concerted action'.[69] The concern to constrain unilateral intervention, both military and non-military, by Western states, was framed by recent and ongoing wars of decolonization against colonial powers such as France, the United Kingdom, Portugal, South Africa, and the continuing practices of intervention in self-declared spheres of influence by Cold War rivals and former colonizing states (such as the Belgian intervention in the Congo).[70] At the same time, newly independent states sought to use the General Assembly to strengthen the content of sovereignty and non-intervention to exclude forms of political and economic coercion and more expansive justifications for the use of force, drafting, and passing a battery of resolutions whose titles displayed their normative ambitions: Declaration on the Granting of Independence to Colonial Countries and Peoples (1960);[71] Declaration on Permanent Sovereignty over Natural Resources (1962);[72] and Declaration on the Inadmissibility of Intervention in the Domestic Affairs of States and the Protection of their Independence and Sovereignty (1965).[73] In 1967 the General Assembly also voted to establish a Special Committee on the Definition of Aggression.[74] Commencing in 1963, the Special Committee on Principles of International Law Concerning Friendly Relations and Cooperation among States would meet in parallel to these developments, throughout the 1960s,[75] and draft the Declaration on Friendly Relations as an attempt to authoritatively state certain key principles of international law.[76] Taken as a whole, these texts reflect a 'revolutionary'[77] attempt by decolonizing states to recast, through General Assembly led processes, the content of constitutive norms of international law in a manner that articulated their concerns: reinforcing sovereign equality and discrediting foreign intervention, amplifying self-determination as an expression of sovereignty and national political and economic authority, and promoting a solidarist vision of cooperation between and on behalf of states that had come into being

[66] ILC, 'Addendum to the eighth report on State responsibility, by Mr. Roberto Ago' (29 February—19 June 1980) UN Doc A/CN.4/318/Add.5-7, for example, paras 14–15.

[67] Georges M Abi-Saab, 'The Newly Independent States and the Rules of International Law: An Outline Symposium: International Law Standards in an Era of Rapid Historical Change: Leading Article' (1962) 8 Howard Law Journal 95.

[68] ibid 103.

[69] ibid 98.

[70] Samuel Moyn and Umut Özsu, 'The Historical Origins and Setting of the Friendly Relations Declaration' in Jorge E Viñuales (ed), *The UN Friendly Relations Declaration at 50. An Assessment of the Fundamental Principles of International Law* (CUP 2020) 23–50.

[71] UNGA Res 1514 (XV) (14 December 1960).

[72] UNGA Res 1803 (XVII) (14 December 1962).

[73] UNGA Res 2131 (XX) (21 December 1965).

[74] UNGA Res 2330 (XXII) (18 December 1967).

[75] Established by UNGA Res 1966 (XVIII) (16 December 1963).

[76] Declaration on Principles of International Law Concerning Friendly Relations and Cooperation Among States, UNGA Res 2625 (XXV) (24 October 1970).

[77] Abi-Saab, 'The Newly Independent States' (n 67).

as representing peoples and territories previously dominated through colonialism and imperialism.[78]

The *Nicaragua* decision, although handed down in 1986, recorded the consequences of this decade-long effort at remaking the determinate content of the norms governing the use of force. A 'toilsome discussion'[79] took place throughout the 1960s, in the Special Committee on the Definition of Aggression and collaterally in the Special Committee on Friendly Relations, concerning the conditions under which incursions and hostilities by armed groups in a neighbouring territory could enliven the right to self-defence under the Charter. Ruys notes that this debate took place under the rubric of 'indirect aggression', with decolonized states, on the one hand, claiming the right to host or non-militarily support armed groups fighting in the name of self-determination and, on the other, maintaining that such support did not render assisting states liable to a lawful forcible response by those states fighting the armed groups, nor authorize direct intervention in the internal conflicts on newly decolonized states. For their part, key Western states (such as the United States), argued for a wider concept of anticipatory self-defence, and also maintained that the right to self-defence was activated by a broader category of conduct by the territorial state in respect of armed bands, including 'organizing', 'encouraging', 'assistance to', 'knowing acquiescence in', or 'lending support'.[80]

Ruys perceptively observes that both the final text of the 1970 Friendly Relations Declaration and the 1973 Definition of Aggression—both passed by the General Assembly after six or more years of negotiation within Special Committees—reflected a careful compromise between the Third World bloc (The Thirteen Powers) and the Western bloc (The Six Powers) over the meaning of Article 51. The result of this compromise was an acceptance, at that time, of 'the need for at least substantial involvement of the State and for the attacks themselves to be of a certain gravity', and 'the impression is that relatively minor forms of assistance, and a fortiori the tolerating of the group's presence within the State's territory may well constitute a breach of Article 2(4), but remain insufficient to justify an exercise of self-defence.... [I]t is moreover striking that even the Six-Power proposal never listed [tolerating a group's presence] as a form of indirect aggression (instead referring only to "organizing, supporting or directing")'.[81] *Nicaragua*'s holding on attribution and the enlivening of Article 51 in response to hostilities from an armed group in another state, faithfully reflected this negotiating history and compromise, and also 'the practice of states in preceding decades'.[82]

The certainty of old, it seems, was born not in 1945, or even in 1960, but in the two decades after the evanescent rise of the Third World bloc and its concerted pursuit of normative influence through the UN General Assembly and other multilateral fora in which the principle of sovereign equality secured a plurality or majority of voting power. This is by no means a story unique to the law on the use of force in the 1960s and 1970s,[83] and the particular conditions of Cold War super-power rivalry engendered a more accommodating posture by Western powers towards the non-aligned movement's UN agenda out of a concern that some newly decolonized states might gravitate more decisively into the Soviet sphere of

[78] Moyn and Özsu, 'The Historical Origins and Setting of the Friendly Relations Declaration' (n 70)
[79] Ruys (n 47) 389.
[80] ibid 368–99.
[81] ibid 389–90.
[82] ibid 418.
[83] For example, several case studies in Jochen von Bernstorff and Philipp Dann (eds), *The Battle for International Law: South-North Perspectives on the Decolonization Era* (1st edn, OUP 2019).

influence.[84] But even as the *Nicaragua* decision certified the birth of the certainty of old, it also began rapidly to enter its decrepitude. Alternative currents in the meaning of the concept of self-defence, while no longer widely advanced, continued to be available through the claims of some states, or through their practice. In 1986, US Secretary of State George Shultz elaborated on the 'Shultz doctrine' (first floated in 1984), in which the United States asserted the right under international law to:

> [capture] terrorists in international waters or airspace; [attack] them on the soil of other nations, even for the purpose of rescuing hostages; or [use] force against States that support, train, and harbor terrorists or guerrillas.... A nation attacked by terrorists is permitted to use force to prevent or preempt future attacks, to seize terrorists, or to rescue its citizens when no other means is available. The law requires that such actions be necessary and proportionate.[85]

Writing in 1989 in the *Israeli Yearbook of Human Rights*, eminent international lawyer Oscar Schacter acknowledged the limits placed by *Nicaragua* on claiming self-defence against terrorist groups without 'substantial' state support and involvement, but reached instead for a parallel principle, that of 'necessity' amounting to a form of forcible self-help to protect an essential interest.[86] The idea that necessity might persist as a basis to use force against non-state armed groups operating from the territory of another state, had been mooted by International Law Commission Special Rapporteur on State Responsibility (and later ICJ judge) Roberto Ago in his report of 1980.[87] Ago noted the shared lineage of necessity, the right of self-preservation, and the right of self-help;[88] while ruling out self-preservation and self-help as no longer available under the Charter, he left open the idea that a use of limited force against a non-state armed group not substantially supported by the territorial state, could at once violate Article 2(4) of the Charter *and yet* be excused as necessary, where that state was 'unwilling or unable' to contain the threat posed by the group. The characterization of the territorial state as 'unwilling or unable' as a test for justifying the use of force had no foundation in the law of self-defence and its special notion of necessity. Rather, unwillingness or inability of a state to meet its legal obligations (or protect the legally recognized interests of another state) was a legal reason to use force in the pre-Charter concepts of self-help and self-preservation.[89] Ago's report was highly suggestive of the desirability of retaining a general principle of necessity as an excuse for an unlawful use of force, distinct from self-defence (which rendered the use of force legal ab initio).[90] But the idea was not expressly endorsed in the ILC, nor was it taken up in subsequent reports of the ILC on state responsibility.

[84] This structuring condition of US–Soviet enmity was grasped by an early study of the rise of the New Nations in the United Nations. David Kay, *The New Nations in the United Nations, 1960–1967* (CUP 1970).

[85] George P Shultz, *Low-Intensity Warfare: The Challenge of Ambiguity* (US Dept of State, Bureau of Public Affairs, Office of Public Communication, Editorial Division 1986).

[86] Oscar Schacter, 'The Lawful Use of Force by a State against Terrorists in Another Country' (1989) 19 Israel Yearbook on Human Rights 229.

[87] Ago (n 66), paras 56–57.

[88] ibid paras 75–76, where Ago notes the numerous writers opposing the continued acceptance of a principle of necessity because of its historical relationship with rights of intervention.

[89] As Emile Simpson has shown decisively, the 'unable or unwilling' test that has now returned under the concept of self-defence has nothing to do with the law of neutrality (as claimed notably by Ashley Deeks in Ashley Deeks, '"Unwilling or Unable": Toward an Normative Framework for Extra-Territorial Self-Defense' (2011) 52 Virginia Journal of International Law 483) but in fact descends directly from the rights of self-preservation and forcible self-help; Emile Simpson, 'The Unwilling or Unable Test in the *Jus ad Bellum*: a Revisionist Historical Analysis' (2020, paper on file with authors).

[90] Ago (n 66) para 79.

21.4 The Revisionist Framework

What the Third World bloc (and Brownlie) sought to drive out the door, by reshaping self-defence to evacuate the residual content of rights of self-preservation and self-help, returned through the window afforded by the changing contexts of the use of force after 1989, and 2001. Stripped of the heated context of decolonization, and without the structuring enmity of the Cold War, territorial incursions to fight non-state armed groups were received with greater understanding—even if the precise legal bases of the actions were not approved explicitly.[91] Moreover, specific legal claims that were part-and-parcel of highly criticized uses of force against non-state armed groups between 1960 and 1990 (eg Israeli strikes against Palestinian guerrillas operating from Egypt and Jordan, and South African strikes against ANC guerrillas in neighbouring states),[92]—such as the 'pin-prick' theory of armed attack, and the notion that 'harbouring' or 'failing to control' an armed group rendered the host state liable to endure force being used against it—were much more readily accepted as assimilable to the rubric of self-defence, not outside it.[93] But a radicalization of these available threads of argument takes place after 11 September 2001, combining an interconnected set of propositions that, taken together, amount to a whole cloth, in an effort to remake the conceptual content of self-defence, at least as it applies to the use of force against non-state armed groups. We call this the revisionist framework, not because its content amounts to a complete break from past possibilities, but because it remakes the previously determined conceptual content of self-defence in a manner that takes 'quite different material inferences as good, different constellations of claims as incompatible'.[94] The determinate content of the concept is reshaped by an attempt to tell a different 'recollective story' that articulates, and also 'finds' already available, a new set of premises and reasons that appear to justify the application of the concept. The rapid refinement and deployment of the technology of armed drones did not cause this conceptual change, but smoothed the way for the possibility of certain kinds of actions in need of justification and rationalization.[95]

On 15 September 2001, then CIA director George Tenet proposed a plan to hunt and kill al-Qaeda members and associated forces without geographical limitation, and a widely drawn presidential authorization was issued to target and kill al-Qaeda leaders and to add to the list without further authorization.[96] The plan reversed a long-standing US policy that criticized targeted killings,[97] and also demanded forward-leaning legal arguments because 'there isn't a government on the planet that agrees with our legal rationale for these operations except for Afghanistan and maybe Israel'.[98] While not acknowledging the existence of a policy of targeted killing until 2010, the United States pursued a strategy of seeking behind-closed-doors diplomatic understanding for its legal rationale for targeted killing through

[91] See the examples discussed in Christian J Tams, 'The Use of Force against Terrorists' (2009) 20 European Journal of International Law 359, 379; Ruys (n 47) 431–33.

[92] ibid 168–70, 401–03, 420.

[93] Tams 'The Use of Force' (n 91) 382; Christian Tams and James Devaney, 'Jus ad bellum: Crossing Borders to Wage War against Individuals' in Steven J Barela (ed), *Legitimacy and Drones: Investigating the Legality, Morality and Efficacy of UCAVs* (Ashgate 2015) 25–47.

[94] Brandom, *Reason in Philosophy* (n 22) 103.

[95] Chris Woods, *Sudden Justice: America's Secret Drone Wars* (OUP 2015).

[96] See reporting sources helpfully collected and summarized in Banka and Quinn (n 17) 682–83.

[97] Mazzetti (n 6) ch 1.

[98] Former CIA and NSA Director, Michael Hayden, quoted in Doyle McManus, 'McManus: Who Reviews the US "Kill List"?' *Los Angeles Times* (22 March 2014) <https://www.latimes.com/opinion/opinion-la/la-oe-mcmanus-column-drones-and-the-law-20120205-column.html> accessed 10 September 2020, cited in Banka and Quinn (n 17) 696.

missions by the then US State Department Legal Adviser John Bellinger.[99] As Tams and others have noted, in the first decade after 11 September 2001, a wider range of states began to claim the right to respond to terrorist attacks with extraterritorial force, without meeting strong criticism.[100]

What we have called the revisionist framework is now relatively well-known, having moved gradually from the margins towards the mainstream of legal interpretation over the last nineteen years. It can be summarized in three propositions: (1) that non-state armed groups can commit armed attacks, enlivening the right to use force in self-defence against the non-state armed group on the territory of another state; even though (2) the territorial/host state does not effectively control the non-state armed group, but may have failed in its duties of due diligence in constraining the functioning of the group on its territory, due to connivance (unwillingness), negligence, or incapacity (inability) because its authority does not extend to those parts of the territory in which the armed group operates; and (3) the extent and nature of force used in self-defence must be necessary and proportionate to the nature of the threat posed by the armed group and individual members, but necessity and proportionality can have a concertina-like quality—at times focusing on the threat posed by particular individuals, and at other times encompassing the overall animus of the armed group, its hostile intentions, and its general capacity to continue to act.

A notable feature of the revisionist framework is its tendency to rely upon extensive or elongated versions of concepts within these three interconnected propositions. Thus, the 'armed attack' concept in the revisionist framework relies on the 'pin-prick' or 'accumulation of events' theory, whereby 'incidents that would in themselves merely constitute "less grave uses of force", can, when forming part of a chain of events, qualitatively transform into an "armed attack" triggering the right of self-defence'.[101] The 'pin-prick' theory is already notable for extending the temporal horizon of the evaluation of whether and when force is necessary to respond to an attack, engendering considerable uncertainty about how to determine how many small scale attacks or attempted attacks, over what period of time, could aggregate into an 'armed attack' such that the *risk of the next* pin-prick qualifies as an imminent or ongoing armed attack.[102] By reshaping the content of 'armed attack' along these lines, force that might previously be seen as unnecessary or disproportionate, or simply a reprisal against the *last* pin-prick, takes on the character of a defensive use of force to prevent the next needling blow. But the revisionist framework pushes the logic of the pin-prick theory even further: it asserts a right to use force in self-defence against a non-state armed group that has committed *or attempted to commit* several smaller attacks and has the *continuing intention and capacity* to do so. Claiming to reflect the practice of governments whom he had advised and with which he interacted over several years,[103] former UK Foreign and Commonwealth Legal Adviser Sir Daniel Bethlehem glossed the updated pin-prick theory in the following terms:

[99] See accounts of Bellinger's meetings with EU member state legal advisers, recorded in cables leaked by Wikileaks and discussed in Kattan (n 12) 119–22.

[100] Tams, 'The Use of Force' (n 91); Theresa Reinold, 'State Weakness, Irregular Warfare, and the Right to Self-Defense Post-9/11' (2011) 105 American Journal of International Law 244; Dustin A Lewis, Naz K Modirzadeh, and Gabriella Blum, 'Quantum of Silence: Inaction and Jus Ad Bellum' 61.

[101] Ruys (n 47) 168.

[102] Tams and Devaney (n 93) 41–42; Christian J Tams, 'The Necessity and Proportionaity of Anti-Terrorist Self-Defence' in Larissa van den Herik and Nico Schrijver (eds), *Counter-Terrorism Strategies in a Fragmented International Legal Order: Meeting the Challenges* (CUP 2013), 399–401.

[103] The so-called 'Bethlehem Principles' were cited with approval by Legal Advisers and Attorneys General from the United States, United Kingdom, and Australia. Egan (n 3); Wright (n 3); Brandis (n 3); French practice and official statements also reflect this. Former French President François Hollande, the then Prime Minister Manuel Valls, and Minister of Defense Jean-Yves le Drian also relied on a similar version of the right to self-defence for

> The term 'armed attack' includes both discrete attacks and a series of attacks that indicate a concerted pattern of continuing armed activity ... [A] series of attacks, whether imminent or actual, constitutes a concerted pattern of continuing armed activity ... [where] there is a reasonable and objective basis for concluding that those threatening or perpetrating such attacks are acting in concert ... Those acting in concert include those planning, threatening, and perpetrating armed attacks and those providing material support essential to those attacks, such that they can be said to be taking a direct part in those attacks.[104]

This version of the pin-prick theory extends both the *what* and the *who* that may be accumulated in order to reach the view that an armed attack is taking place or is about to be continued through another attempt. Planning, threatening, perpetrating, and providing material support for attacks or attempted attacks by persons 'acting in concert' can cumulate to tip over into an 'armed attack' for Article 51 purposes. The result is not a continuum (no acceleration or intensification is specifically required), but rather a Gestalt switch: depending on context and exigencies, and perhaps also the availability of an opportunity to strike, a collection of individual actors and contributing acts—plans, threats, preparations, as much as actual attacks or attempted attacks—may be qualified as an armed attack permitting the use of defensive force.

This revised content to the concept of armed attack, generates logical consequences for other concepts in the constellation that make up the law of self-defence, most dramatically for the concepts of imminence and of proportionality. Anticipatory uses of force never lost their controversial quality,[105] but even amongst those who maintained their legality, an imminent attack was, if not actually unfolding, discernible by a train of conduct that created the reasonable appearance that a specific attack was going to occur, and could not be averted except by a defensive use of force.[106] Echoing Brownlie, the Chatham House Principles of International Law on the Use of Force in Self-Defence[107] place anticipatory self-defence 'at

the strikes in Syria; Former Prime Minister Manuel Valls, '#Syrie: La France est en guerre contre le terrorisme, le djihadisme, l'islamisme radical. Ce sera long mais nous l'empoterons' (l'Assemblée Nationale, Paris 15 September 2015) <https://www.gouvernement.fr/syrie-la-france-est-en-guerre-contre-le-terrorisme-le-djihadisme-l-islamisme-radical-ce-sera-long-2873> accessed 10 September 2020; Jean-Marie Le Guen and Guillaume Durand, Interview with Former French Minister of Defense M Jean-Yves Le Drian (Radio Classique, 16 September 2015) <https://www.vie-publique.fr/discours/196393-interview-de-m-jean-marie-le-guen-secretaire-detat-aux-relations-avec> accessed 10 September 2020. They argued that it was legitimate for France to conduct strikes in Syria under the right of self-defence because of the attacks that are organized and perpetrated by ISIS members from Syria 'against France and other countries'. On 9 September 2015 France addressed a letter to the UN Security Council, stating that 'In accordance with Article 51 of the Charter of the United Nations, France has taken actions involving the participation of military aircraft in response to attacks carried out by ISIL from the territory of the Syrian Arab Republic'; S/2015/745 UNSC 'Identical letters dated 8 September 2015 from the Permanent Representative of France to the United Nations addressed to the Secretary-General and the President of the Security Council' (9 September 2015) UN Doc S/2015/745. In an interview of April 2018, President Macron justified the expansion of France's war against jihadist terrorist groups overseas to Syria, by emphasizing that 'in Syria, we wage war against IS, that is against the Islamist terrorist groups that had, I remind you, attacked our country, considering that it is in Raqqa that the November 2015 attacks were planned'; Mediapart, 'Macron, un an après: le grand entretien en intégralité' (15 April 2018) <www.youtube.com/watch?v=mt0as7x-kfs&t=964s> accessed 10 September 2020.

[104] Bethlehem, 'Self-Defense' (n 13) 6 (principles 4, 5 and 6).

[105] See the trenchant argument by Ruys that anticipatory self-defence was never accepted as a matter of practice and *opinio juris* before 2000: Ruys (n 47) 263–64.

[106] Noam Lubell, 'The Problem of Imminence in an Uncertain World' in Marc Weller, Alexia Solomou, and Jake William Rylatt (eds), *The Oxford Handbook of the Use of Force in International Law* (1st edn, OUP 2015) 607–719.

[107] Elizabeth Wilmshurst, 'The Chatham House Principles of International Law on the Use of Force in Self-Defence' (2006) 55(4) International and Comparative Law Quarterly 963.

the limits of an already exceptional category', and must be capable of 'objective assessment' through publicly demonstrable evidence.[108] But the extended pin-prick theory of armed attack just described elongates the concept of imminence both in a temporal sense and in the sense of causal proximity to an identifiable attack. In the Bethlehem Principles, an 'armed attack' is a state of affairs rather than an event, characterized by a widely drawn idea of a 'concerted pattern of continuing armed activity'. The agents who, through their actions, make up this concerted pattern, each in some way contribute to the ongoing state of affairs, and thus through their threats, plans, preparations, or material support take a direct part in the chain of events; at any moment in this chain, the next threat or preparatory act is a contribution to the continuance of the 'armed attack' as a state of affairs; so long as this concerted pattern of activity does not cease, 'imminence' seems a continuous rather than precipitative situation. As a fairly logical result of giving *this* content to the idea of armed attack, imminence no longer has any relationship to the identification of 'where an attack will take place' or 'the precise nature of an attack'.[109] Rather, 'imminence' comes to describe the threatening activities and propensities of individual actors participating in concert in the array of acts making up the pattern of continuing armed activity; *individuals*, rather than specific cross-border operations, become imminent threats, because they continually plan attacks and a government cannot be confident that a new attack is not about to take place. Part of the calculation of 'imminence' as a touchstone for defensive force becomes not the temporal and causal proximity of a specific attack, per se, but the potential loss of an opportunity to strike an individual whose intentions and propensities make them a threat.[110]

The result of this concept of imminence, is a radical subjectivization of what qualifies as an imminent threat, namely, it becomes a characteristic of *a subject*. But this makes 'objective determination' of the nature of the threat—already a fragile bulwark against auto-determination—all the more difficult. Information establishing the role played by individuals in terrorist networks will rely on human and signals intelligence to an overwhelming degree,[111] leaving very little 'evidence' to be shared in the public domain. An example of how the crucial question of imminence is almost impossible to evaluate because it rests on closely held judgments based on intelligence, is the review of the Reyaad Khan strike by the UK parliament's Intelligence and Security Committee (ISC). In its inquiry into the Royal Airforce's targeted killing of UK citizen Khan in Syria in August 2015, the ISC (composed of nine members of parliament from all parliamentary parties with security clearances necessary to oversee the UK intelligence agencies) sought to understand in what sense Khan constituted an 'imminent threat' requiring the use of force. In his explanation to parliament on 7 September 2015, then Prime Minister David Cameron had justified the strike as necessary and proportionate to the threat posed by Khan, an active and visible recruiter for the Islamic State in Syria and the Levant who, operating from Syria, was claimed to have been 'actively

[108] ibid 968.

[109] Bethlehem, 'Self-Defense' (n 13) principle 8. This is expressly endorsed by both Wright and Brandis, and also Egan (n 3); the 2011 DOJ White Paper approving the targeted killing of US citizen Anwar al-Awlaki in Yemen pre-dates the Bethlehem Principles, and the latter clearly echoes both the logic and content of the former; US Department of Justice, 'Lawfulness of a Lethal Operation Directed Against a U.S. Citizen Who Is a Senior Operational Leader of Al-Qa'ida or An Associated Force' Draft White Paper.

[110] ibid.

[111] For example, the discussion in 'The Drone Papers: Small Footprint Operations 2/13' <https://theintercept.com/document/2015/10/15/small-footprint-operations-2-13/#page-1> accessed 10 September 2020; 'The Drone Papers: Small Footprint Operations 5/13' <https://theintercept.com/document/2015/10/15/small-footprint-operations-5-13/#page-2> accessed 10 September 2020, showing heavy reliance on SIGINT for drone strikes in Somalia.

engaged in planning and directing imminent armed attacks against the United Kingdom'.[112] The ISC was given access to two intelligence assessments regarding Khan and twenty-five underlying reports, but not permitted access to targeting procedures and the submissions that were put to ministers about the intelligence assessments. The Committee noted that it was 'profoundly disappointing' not to have access to the case for the strike as it was put to ministers,[113] and concluded that while the intelligence assessments showed that Khan was a very serious threat to the United Kingdom, the ISC was unable to evaluate the conclusion that this threat amounted to an imminent 'armed attack'. The qualification of a threat as an armed attack, and its imminence, was decided by ministers, with support from the Attorney General. Without access to ministerial submissions, the Committee simply could not assess the process by which ministers concluded that the threat posed by Khan was to be equated with an armed attack by a state, or how that threat was deemed imminent.[114] Notably, however, the ISC was able to discern that a weighty consideration in the assessment of imminence was *not* intelligence about a *specific* future attack, but rather the fear that gaps in intelligence coverage might lead to an evolving plot going undetected and that intelligence agencies might lose 'sight' of Khan for a period.[115] Thus, it was considered that the only 'guarantee' of preventing rapidly unfolding *potential* future attacks, was to 'disrupt Khan himself'.[116]

This individualization of the imminent threat of armed attack expresses a different logic to that of interstate conflict. The revisionist jus ad bellum offers a framework for the continuous prevention of threats from networked individuals showing signs of continuing to intend to threaten, prepare, or support future attacks. This is akin to the exercise of a police power, with a posture of constant vigilance towards risks of harm emerging from the behavioural dispositions of individual members of a networked enemy group. One condition of possibility for this conceptual content of self-defence is a technological one: drone programmes and their associated surveillance and strike capacities.[117] Drones' capacities to loiter, gather large volumes of pattern of life data and signals intelligence, geolocate individuals at large distances, and strike intended targets in inaccessible places without being readily detected, are technological 'affordances' that enable an entire apparatus of intelligence collection, risk assessment, identification and location of specific individuals, and determination of opportunities to strike them—all constitutive elements, as we have seen, in a final judgment that an individual amounts to an imminent threat of armed attack who must be 'disrupted'.

As we have suggested, the 'limitationist' concepts of self-defence—the certainty of old—were part of a framework designed for interstate relations and aimed to reinforce the core principle of equal sovereignty. The conceptual content given to the prohibition on the use of force through the legal diplomacy of the newly decolonized states was a safeguard to territorial integrity, and rested on a basic premise about the nature and function of states as territorial public powers with a real or imputed supremacy over their peoples and territories: that time-limited defensive uses of force between states can be quickly subjected to peaceful forms of dispute resolution, where the underlying clash of interests leading to the outbreak of

[112] Prime Minister David Cameron, 'Oral Statement to Parliament: "Syria: refugees and counter-terrorism"' (UK parliament, London, 7 September 2015) <www.gov.uk/government/speeches/syria-refugees-and-counter-terrorism-prime-ministers-statement> accessed 10 September 2020.
[113] UK PISC (n 15) 2–3.
[114] ibid 10–11, 14–15.
[115] ibid 15.
[116] ibid 17.
[117] Jeremy Scahill and The Intercept, *The Assassination Complex: Inside the Government's Secret Drone Warfare Program* (Simon & Schuster 2017) 44.

conflict can be mediated or even adjudicated. Under the condition of the legal symmetry of states, each state's interests have in principle the possibility of being recognized, negotiated, and politically settled, as means of containing the use of force. It is in light of this logic that we might understand the strict conceptualizations of armed attack and imminent threat that have governed the 'limitationist' understanding of self-defence: states are not considered to have implacable and inevitable enmity towards each other (even if they are perpetual competitors or ideological enemies), but rather capable of changing their positions, even at the eleventh hour, in light of the changing constellation of forces being brought to bear upon them that may affect their understanding of their interests and how best to achieve them. As US Special Operations Command White Paper put it:

> There is an elegant simplicity inherent in nation-states.... There is a single, centralized entity with which to negotiate, and events can proceed at the pace of diplomacy. During the Cold War, even when nation-states made deliberate choices to engage in gray zone activities, US responses were still governed by the rules of state-to-state relations.[118]

As Brownlie's argument exemplified, legal exceptions to the prohibition on the use of force were conceptualized as capable of determinate all-things-considered judgments about the nature of the threat, its beginning, and its end. An important fulcrum in this judgment, and the crux of its limiting function, was the concept of proportionality. If the revisionist framework transforms the content of the concepts of self-defence into a kind of police power, exercised by states against individual members of a networked enemy group, what consequence does it have for the concept of proportionality? Discussions of the proportionality of a targeted killing tend to focus on the human and material toll of the specific strike, relative to the harm risked by failing to 'disrupt' the individual plotter.[119] But the notion of ad bellum proportionality is not limited to a weighing of harms caused by kinetic strikes; it is a judgment also about the temporal and spatial extent of force used, and implies consideration of the purpose or object of the use of force.[120] Depending on the nature of the harm experienced by the state subjected to the armed attack, and the likelihood of continuing or reoccurring attacks, the principle of proportionality is not reduced to a quantitative 'tit-for-tat' strike, but can include a more extensive use force in order to achieve the basic purpose of 'halting and repelling' the attack and preventing it from reoccurring.[121] But the mischief at which the application of the principle is aimed is the risk of over-application of force and escalation of conflict[122] —the principle of proportionality would not licence the destruction of another state's military capacity *in toto* or the overthrow of its government, except as an *in extremis* limit case[123] where the enmity between the states that are party to the conflict has become so absolute that neither can reasonably contemplate a negotiated settlement of the issues underlying hostilities. This limit case helps us grasp the logic of proportionality as presupposing, in all but extreme situations, that states—if far from inherently peace-loving—can be incentivized to the political settlement of underlying conflicts through a legal rule that

[118] US Special Operations Command, 'The Gray Zone' (2015) White Paper <www.soc.mil/SWCS/SWmag/archive/SW2804/GrayZone.pdf> accessed 4 November 2020.
[119] For example, the statement by David Cameron (n 112).
[120] David Kretzmer, 'The Inherent Right to Self-Defence and Proportionality in Jus Ad Bellum' (2013) 24 European Journal of International Law 235.
[121] Ago (n 66) para 121.
[122] Ruys (n 47) 114–25, 500–09.
[123] ibid 117; Judith Gardam, 'A Role for Proportionality in the War on Terror' (2015) 7 Nordic Journal of International Law 3, 16.

inhibits the pursuit of the total military defeat and incapacitation of the opposing public power. The concreteness of the concept of proportionality rests on this archetype of conflict between two legally symmetrical public powers.

Yet, individuals within a networked armed group that manifests the kind of continuous hostile intent and activity that, in the revisionist framework, falls within the concept of 'imminent armed attack', are not recognizable as public powers with a corporate 'right to exist'. Historically, most insurgent, anti-colonial, separatist or revolutionary groups claimed to be *public powers in waiting*, seeking to seize or claim a share of state power within a territory—and thus aspired to membership in the system of states and sought to assimilate to its logic.[124] This 'proto-state' quality enabled anti-colonial resistance movements, and some European states with recent experience of resistance to German occupation, to argue successfully for the partial extension of the statist concepts of the laws of war to conflicts between states and non-state groups in contexts of occupation and wars of liberation.[125] It also provided a set of modalities through which the conflicts could be concluded: negotiated power-sharing arrangements, peace agreements with provision for a decision on secession, or territorial compromise. Many jihadi groups engaged in civil wars against foreign-backed governments and continue to be 'centre-seeking' or 'secessionist' along these lines, in practice if not in rhetoric.[126] But some do not seek such an assimilation, and instead persist (at least at the level of ideology) in challenging the fundamental premises of an international society of states.[127] If religionist rebels do not 'seek to carve out a new, independent state that will receive international recognition', or 'capture the capital for the purpose of reclaiming the reins of government', but profess to want to remake the existing order into a religious one, then the political horizon for the conclusion of the military conflict recedes into a remote future: comprehensive defeat of the armed group or its (unlikely) final victory. Al-Qaeda and the Islamic State in Syria and the Levant have at specific moments in their development come close to a pure type of religionist rebel[128]—although no such movement remains unchanged through the vicissitudes of actual military engagement. The revisionist framework's notions of 'armed attack' and 'imminence' reify this pure type of religionist rebellion, expressing in legal-conceptual form the potentially unlimited relationship of enmity between the networked armed group and the state using force against them. But this reification transposes the concrete historical features of the armed group and its strategy, into an idealizing concept that can be applied prospectively to a wide range of circumstances.

Tams notes that one consequence of reliance upon the 'pin-prick' theory to trigger the use of force against non-state armed groups, is that states are 'not prevented from pursuing far-reaching aims going beyond the repulsion of ongoing, or prevention of imminent,

124 Tanisha M Fazal, 'Rebellion, War Aims and the Laws of War' (2017) 146 Daedalus 71, 76.

125 Boyd van Dijk, 'The Making of the Geneva Conventions. Decolonization, the Cold War, and the Birth of Humanitarian Law' (PhD thesis, European University Institute 2017); Fabian Klose, *Human Rights in the Shadow of Colonial Violence: The Wars of Independence in Kenya and Algeria* (1st edn, University of Pennsylvania Press 2013); Jessica Whyte, 'The "Dangerous Concept of the Just War": Decolonization, Wars of National Liberation, and the Additional Protocols to the Geneva Conventions' (2018) 9(3) Humanity: An International Journal of Human Rights, Humanitarianism, and Development 313.

126 Consider the recent tentative peace settlement with the Taliban in Afghanistan. Kalyvas notes that in 'many ways, jihadi rebel groups come across as rather undistinctive when compared to other rebel groups'. Stathis N Kalyvas, 'Jihadi Rebels in Civil War' (2018) 147(1) Daedalus 36, 37.

127 Fazal, 'Rebellion' (n 124); Tanisha M Fazal, 'Religionist Rebels and the Sovereignty of the Divine' (2018) 147 Daedalus 25.

128 For example, James P Piscatori and Amin Saikal, *Islam beyond Borders: The Umma in World Politics* (CUP 2019); Faisal Devji, *Landscapes of the Jihad: Militancy, Morality, Modernity* (Cornell University Press 2005); Faisal Devji, *The Terrorist in Search of Humanity: Militant Islam and Global Politics* (OUP 2009); Darryl Li, *The Universal Enemy: Jihad, Empire, and the Challenge of Solidarity* (Stanford University Press 2019).

attacks ... [T]he international community seems to have accepted that states are entitled to use self-defence as a means of severely weakening the terrorist organization'.[129] The result is that the 'ends' of anti-terrorist self-defence under the concept of proportionality become expansive and permissive, rather than restrictive and constraining. It rests on a state's own assessment as to when the risk posed by individual members of networked armed groups has been contained through military action and vigilance, an endpoint that is indeterminate and difficult to objectively qualify.[130]

This sense of indefiniteness is expressed in the policy documents of states that understand themselves to be fighting such a war. The 'Report on the Legal and Policy Framework Guiding the United States' Use of Military Force and Related National Security Operations', issued in the last days of the Obama Presidency, repeated President Obama's hope that 'this war, like all wars, must end', but maintains that 'Groups like Al-Qa'ida are unlikely to disarm and sign instruments of surrender ... [G]roups like Al-Qa'ida are also highly unlikely ever to denounce terrorism and violence and seek to address their perceived grievances through some form of reconciliation or participation in a political process'. The endpoint of anti-terrorist self-defence is thus concluded to be a situation in which:

> the United States will degrade and dismantle the operational capacity and supporting networks of terrorist organizations like Al-Qa'ida *to such an extent that they will no longer be able to attempt or launch a strategic attack against the United States*. At that point, there will no longer be an ongoing armed conflict between the United States and those forces ... Unfortunately, that day has not yet come.[131]

On the other side of the Atlantic, in France, a 2017 law on military programming defines the budgetary framework for the development of the conclusions of the 'Revue stratégique de défense et de sécurité nationale' (Strategic Review on Defence and National Security), which preceded and influenced the proposed law.[132] The Strategic Review insists that 'jihadist terrorism is going through a transformative phase that will not diminish its reach and the danger it represents for the forthcoming decade: the main jihadist organizations will decline in some areas, yet without disappearing, and their underpinning ideology will persist'. Indeed, thanks to their 'operational and ideological matrix, where the know-hows are transmitted from generation to generation', it further explains, 'the current jihadist organizations, Daech, Al-Qaeda and their several affiliates managed to adapt and mutate despite the setbacks they have suffered'. Against this background, French Ministry of Armed Forces Florence Parly explained that French troops should be deployed for as long as necessary, until terrorism as a whole is defeated and anywhere terrorist groups exist or emerge.[133] The

[129] Tams, 'Necessity and Proportionality' (n 102) 412–13.

[130] On the uncertainty concerning the appropriate legal position as to when ends of anti-terrorist self-defence are met, see Kretzmer, 'The Inherent Right to Self-Defense' (n 120); Rebecca Mignot-Mahdavi, 'Will the War on Terror Ever End?' (2019) Revue des droits de l'homme <http://journals.openedition.org/revdh/6269> accessed 10 September 2020; Dustin A Lewis, Naz K Modirzadeh, and Gabriella Blum, 'Quantum of Silence: Inaction and Jus Ad Bellum' (2019) Harvard Law School Program on International Law and Armed Conflict.

[131] President Barack Obama, 'Report on the Legal and Policy Frameworks Guiding the United States' Use of Military Force and Related National Security Operations' (The White House 2016), 11–12.

[132] Direction générale des relations internationales et de la stratégie, 'Revue stratégique: une analyse lucide et volontariste pour préparer la prochaine loi de programmation militaire' (*Ministère des Armées*, 12 April 2017) <https://www.defense.gouv.fr/dgris/presentation/evenements-archives/revue-strategique-de-defense-et-de-securite-nationale-2017> accessed 10 September 2020.

[133] Armelle Charrier, 'Florence Parly: "L'EI est d'ores et déjà en train de redéployer son action"' *France 24* (15 November 2017) <https://www.france24.com/fr/20171511-entretien-florence-parly-etat-islamique-terrorisme-barkhane-g5-sahel> accessed 10 September 2020.

report thus declares that 'deterrence remains the cornerstone of our military strategy' and that the significance of 'prevention' should be emphasized, in line with the 'global approach' adopted to face the threats.

The indefiniteness that comes with the revisionist framework is thus made somewhat explicit in the French justification of its military strategy and authorizing legal norms. The report to the new law insists that jihadist terrorism 'recomposes and extends itself to new regions of the world', being a 'complex and geographically dispersed' phenomenon.[134] Whoever poses a threat must be targeted and if the threat is posed by several individuals that increases through time it requires that enmity is extended to those individuals. This is true even if they act in the name of a terrorist group that did not exist when the conflict started. Such an approach is arguably inherent in the uncertainties related to the temporal delineation of conflicts. The objective of permanently addressing future threats before they fully materialize authorizes action against individuals who are not presently perpetrating hostile acts.

Proportionality under the jus ad bellum starts to take on qualities we would associate with the jus in bello. The test for what is proportionate is not what is proportionate to a concrete threat of a specific armed attack, but rather what level and extent of force is proportionate to the military incapacitation of the terrorist network *in toto*. The functional concept of proportionality relative to such an understanding of the enemy may often boil down to determining whether the targeted killing of individuals presenting signs of continuing armed activity (and thus posing a continuing imminent threat) is not excessive in light of the overall objectives of decapitating, demoralizing, intimidating, or disrupting the activities of the terrorist group. Because the pin-prick theory of armed attack, combined with the *characterological* approach to individual militants as 'imminent threats' until 'disrupted', creates a continuous state of imminence for as long as the armed group continues to function as such, the ad bellum concept of proportionality blurs with in bello considerations about how much force is functional to procure the submission of the enemy. In the course of conflict, the armed group can erode, split, and revert to sparse, low intensity military operations. The conditions that initially accumulated to amount to an 'armed attack' on the pin-prick theory may not be present throughout the conflict, but this rarely provides a clear-cut basis to determine the end of hostilities in the absence of some formal pact or agreement. This grey area concerning how to characterize the threat potential of the armed group contributes to a troubling sense of self-defence's indefiniteness.

21.5 Conclusion

The targeted killing of Iranian Revolutionary Guard Commander Qassem Soleimani was premised on the revisionist concept of imminent attack that had hitherto been restricted to non-state armed groups. When pressed on whether a specific attack planned by Soleimani had been disrupted by his killing, State Department officials in an anonymous briefing responded:[135]

[134] *Loi* n° 2018-607 (n 14) rapport annex. Annex appears at the end of the legislation (it should be noted that it also has legislative value) <www.legifrance.gouv.fr/affichTexte.do?cidTexte=JORFTEXT000037192797&dateTexte=20181122> accessed 10 September 2020.

[135] Office of the Spokesperson, 'Senior State Department Officials on the Situation in Iraq' (Special Briefing, 3 January 2020) <www.state.gov/senior-state-department-officials-on-the-situation-in-iraq/> accessed 10 September 2020.

QUESTION: The decision to take him out wasn't necessarily a way of removing this—[Senior State Department Official One], the threat that you were talking about in these different countries and these different facilities—but it's a way to mitigate it in the future? I'm just—

SENIOR STATE DEPARTMENT OFFICIAL THREE: It slows it down. It makes it less—

QUESTION: Since we don't know what the threat is—okay, that's what I was—

SENIOR STATE DEPARTMENT OFFICIAL THREE: It slows it down. It makes it less likely. It's shooting down Yamamoto in 1942. Jesus, do we have to explain why we do these things . . .

[. . .]

SENIOR STATE DEPARTMENT OFFICIAL THREE: I did this for two years in the Bush administration.

Assassinations are not allowed under law. Revenge killings, non-judicial executions are not. The criteria is do you have overwhelming evidence that somebody is going to launch a military or terrorist attack against you.

Check that box. The second one is do you have some legal means to, like, have this guy arrested by the Belgian authorities or something. Check that box because there's no way anybody was going to stop Qasem Soleimani in the places he was running around—Damascus, Beirut. And so, you take lethal action against him. *This is something that we have done many times over both Democratic and Republican administrations that I served in. It's the same criteria; it was applied in this case and all cases.*

The US government ultimately resiled from the claim that Soleimani was about to put in motion a particular plan to attack US personnel, stating to Congress that the attack was necessary to 'deter Iran from conducting or supporting further attacks on the United States forces and interests, to degrade Iran's and Qods Force-backed militias' ability to conduct attacks, and to end Iran's strategic escalation of attacks on, and threats to United States interests'.[136]

The risk of escalation inherent in the revisionist framework is evident, and the ease with which it 'crossed over' from a set of concepts reframed around conflicts with networked non-state armed groups, to being invoked in a conflict with a state that is ideological and power-political enemy, is ominous. Nonetheless, the attack on a leading Iranian military official also demonstrates the extent to which political and strategic considerations limited the military response from Iran to a 'proportionate' missile attack on several US military bases in Iraq. The legality of these missile strikes was doubtful, coming as they did several days after the US strike on Soleimani and in the absence of further US uses of force; the Iranian attacks had the characteristics of a (symbolic) reprisal.

But neither side claimed an ongoing right to degrade the other's military capacity in general; whatever the premises of the use of force on either side, the logic of proportionality entailed objective limitations on what could be justified through the concept. The objectivity of these limitations seems to us to be a feature of the *interstate* application of the concept; transposed to an asymmetric jus ad bellum—what we have called the revisionist framework—proportionality becomes a licence for temporally and geographically extensive uses of force. The conceptual contentfulness of the revisionist jus ad bellum is an attempt

[136] US Congress, 'Notice on The Legal And Policy Frameworks Guiding The United States' Use of Military Force And Related National Security Operations' (2020) <www.justsecurity.org/wp-content/uploads/2020/02/notice-on-the-legal-and-policy-frameworks-guiding-the-united-states-use-of-military-force-and-related-national-security-operations.pdf> accessed 10 September 2020.

to provide a recollective story that unravels the 'certainty of old' and, if not replace it, then restore to it certain conceptual possibilities that had been written out in a different historical context. Like any conceptual revision and innovation, it is also kind of world-making—restoring and amplifying some possible justified uses and consequently compatible actions, while muting or diminishing others. In the case of the revisionist framework, it appears to us to amplify an underlying strategic commitment to defeat a networked enemy militarily, in the sense of physical destruction and degradation of capacity. But as Emile Simpson recently observed, 'the brute force approach assumes a networked enemy can all be targeted in the first place. That is unlikely ... if the enemy is a globalized network. Rather it is a recipe for a forever war ... [in which] ... victory becomes a purely military concept without a political counterpart.'[137]

[137] Emilie Simpson, 'Clausewitz's Theory of War and Victory in Contemporary Conflict' (2017) 47(4) Parameters 7.

22

Human Rights 2030

Existential Challenges and a New Paradigm for the Human Rights Field

*César Rodríguez-Garavito**

22.1 Human Rights at a Crossroads

'We're like those dinosaurs happily roaming around, 65 million years ago, unaware of the meteorite coming their way.' This remark by a prominent human rights practitioner from Kenya has stayed in my mind since the day she shared it with me and the other participants in a workshop on the future of human rights in New Delhi in 2017. The risks for human rights have increased since then, as has the scientific evidence of the climate crisis and the onset of a sixth mass extinction of species—the first one caused by one of those species (us) and the first one since that meteorite wiped out dinosaurs from the face of the planet during the fifth extinction.[1]

I have little doubt that, if Philip Alston had been in attendance, he would have seized the opportunity of the dinosaur story to make a self-deprecating quip that would have filled the room with laughter. Characteristically, his comment would have also come with a healthy dose of provocation for all of us, urging us to raise our gaze and react to the existential threats to human rights looming on the horizon. He would have infused the conversation with a mix of hope and trepidation—the trademark tone of the effective calls to action he has made to the movement over the years, and of his innumerable contributions to human rights scholarship and practice.

Those calls and contributions have become even more relevant and timely, as practitioners and analysts have increasingly embarked on a series of soul-searching debates about the future of human rights. Indeed, uncertainty is the dominant mood in human rights circles these days. A growing body of scholarship debates foundational issues in the human rights movement,[2] and some wonder whether we have now entered its 'endtimes'.[3] Even before a global pandemic hit in early 2020, many advocacy organizations and activists around the world were sensing that the ground was shifting under their feet.

* Some sections of the chapter draw on blog posts I have published in *Open Global Rights* and my contribution to Conectas' *SUR International Journal of Human Rights* anniversary edition (vol 20). I am grateful to OGR and Conectas colleagues for comments, as well as for permission to reproduce those texts. I also gratefully acknowledge the generous and thoughtful comments by the editors of this volume, as well as all their wise and timely initiative to put together this *Festschrift* for Philip Alston.

[1] Elizabeth Kolbert, *The Sixth Extinction: An Unnatural History* (1st edn, Henry Holt and Company 2014).

[2] Alison Brysk, *The Future of Human Rights* (Polity Press 2018); Stephen Hopgood, Jack L Snyder, and Leslie Vinjamuri, *Human Rights Futures* (CUP 2017); Kathryn Sikkink, *Evidence for Hope: Making Human Rights Work in the 21st Century* (Princeton University Press 2017). For an overview of critical scholarship on human rights, see Malcolm Langford, 'Critiques of Human Rights' (2017) 14 Annual Review of Law and Social Science 69.

[3] Stephen Hopgood, *The Endtimes of Human Rights* (Cornell University Press 2013).

César Rodríguez-Garavito, *Human Rights 2030* In: *The Struggle for Human Rights.* Edited by: Nehal Bhuta, Florian Hoffmann, Sarah Knuckey, Frédéric Mégret, and Margaret Satterthwaite, Oxford University Press. © César Rodríguez-Garavito 2021. DOI: 10.1093/oso/9780198868064.003.0023

The proliferation and resilience of populist authoritarian governments and movements from the right and the left—from India to Venezuela, from Hungary to the Philippines, from the United States to Turkey, from the United Kingdom to Israel, from Australia to Nicaragua—amount to what Alston has called 'the populist challenge' to human rights, which embodies a powerful backlash against human rights norms, values, and narratives.[4] To analysts and activists already reeling from the turmoil associated with transformations such as technological disruption, climate change, and the fragmentation of global governance, the populist challenge had deepened the sense of uncertainty and even crisis well before the onset of the coronavirus pandemic.

In this chapter, I tease out the drivers and the competing readings of the current impasse in human rights, as well as what I see as some of the most promising ways out of it. Although I do not subscribe to the view that we are in the 'endtimes' of human rights, I posit that traditional strategies, narratives, and organizational forms are not always the best fit for the purpose of addressing the populist challenge and other structural shifts in geopolitics, technology, and ecology. My argument is that, although the field is not at a moment of terminal crisis, it is going through a period of profound transition, in which the paradigm of thought and practice that was developed in the seventy years since the adoption of the UDHR is increasingly at odds with the needs of the twenty-first century, to the point that a new paradigm is needed if human rights are to remain relevant and impactful by 2030 and beyond. As Yuval Harari noted in *21 Lessons for the 21st century*, 'while human rights movements have developed a very impressive arsenal of arguments and defence against religious biases and human tyrants, this arsenal hardly protects us against consumerist excesses and technological utopias'.[5] I would add that it hardly protects us against democratically elected autocrats, planetary risks such as global warming and pandemics, or digital megacorporations thriving on the accumulation and sale of personal data and the manipulation of human behaviour.

As Thomas Kuhn famously argued, a clear sign of a moment of transition between paradigms is the fact that fundamental questions are reopened for debate.[6] This is certainly the case in the human rights field, where practitioners and scholars alike are engaged in controversies over questions such as who counts as a member of the human rights movement, what the disciplinary bases of human rights knowledge should be, what strategies can be most efficacious in a multipolar and multimedia world, how to make the movement more inclusive and diverse, and what narratives and emotions should be prioritized in human rights messaging, among others. Important asymmetries—South versus North, elite versus grassroots, national versus global, white-led versus BIPOC-led organizations—are being openly discussed with the aim of overcoming such inequalities and strengthening the collective capacity of the movement.

The resulting uncertainty is an uncomfortable position for the human rights community, which has courageously confronted dictatorships, corporate abuse, socio-economic injustice, ethnocide, and environmental degradation for decades. Being left with more questions than answers is disconcerting for organizations and individuals that have come to be expected to provide clear-cut legal solutions to complex moral and political dilemmas.

Yet I believe we should welcome this discomfort. For transitions—between strategic models, intellectual frameworks, governance structures, technologies, or all of the

[4] Philip Alston, 'The Populist Challenge to Human Rights' (2017) 9 Journal of Human Rights Practice 1.
[5] Yuval Harari, *21 Lessons for the 21st Century* (Penguin Random House 2018) 215.
[6] Thomas S Kuhn (ed), *The Structure of Scientific Revolutioans* (3rd edn, University of Chicago Press 1996).

above—represent moments of creativity and innovation in social fields. In human rights circles, where we have erected such high organizational and ideational barriers that it has become difficult to be reflexive and self-critical, this raises an unprecedented opportunity to reconsider some of our core assumptions.

In order to contribute to this reflexive exercise, in this chapter I take a systems view of human rights. Instead of focusing on any given issue area or region, I take a step back and focus on features and challenges that cut across them. As the literature on social innovation has shown, this view entails understanding the system in which a given problem sits, and using the right tool to tackle the specific problem at hand.[7] This goes against the grain of the dominant paradigm of human rights advocacy, which has become fragmented into specialized issue areas and overly reliant on a limited tactical toolkit.

The remainder of the chapter is divided into three sections. First, in section 22.2, I offer a brief *diagnosis* of the factors driving the paradigmatic transition in human rights. In doing so, I investigate factors that are external to the field, as well as internal traits of human rights work that have contributed to strategic stagnation and a sense of crisis. Second, I discuss what I see as the main *readings* of the current moment in scholarly and advocacy circles in section 22.3. In addition to the 'endtimes' view, I characterize three alternative positions that I call business as usual, reflexive reconstruction, and constructive disruption. Finally, in section 22.4, from a perspective that combines reconstruction and disruption, I sketch a series of *responses* to the abovementioned challenges to human rights. Given my wish to prompt debate and action, and the fact that this essay is written in honour of Philip Alston, I will deliberately formulate my proposals as provocations—one of the genres that Alston has masterfully adapted to human rights scholarship and practice, and that has (depending on the occasion and purpose) inspired or jolted so many of us into action.

22.2 Between a Rock and a Hard Place: External and Internal Challenges to Human Rights

22.2.1 External Challenges

Human rights have been dislocated from the outside by epochal transformations in other fields that have profound consequences on human rights actors, frameworks, and strategies. I single out five main challenges of this type. The first one is the *geopolitical challenge*. The Euro-American world order inherited from the post-World War II period, which provided the geopolitical backbone for the globalization of human rights in the second half of the twentieth century, is no more. The initial death knell was sounded by the rise of the BRICS countries in the 2000s, which heralded a new era of multipolarity. As it turns out, all that remains of that acronym, in terms of realistic aspirations for global geopolitical power, is the 'C' for China. In the meantime, the Euro-American order imploded from within, after Brexit, Trump, and the rise of right-wing populism in Europe—with help from Russia, now relegated to the role of global disruptor. The result is a more fragmented and unpredictable international legal and political order, with no obvious consistent and principled government

[7] Susan Misra and Jamaica Maxwell, 'Three Keys to Unlocking Systems-Level Change' (2016) Stanford Social Innovation Review <https://ssir.org/articles/entry/three_keys_to_unlocking_systems_level_change> accessed 30 May 2021.

champions of human rights causes, and with global powers disinclined to put international human rights over their own sovereignty and narrowly defined national interest.

Second, the breakneck advance of information processing and telecommunications in the digital era presents a formidable *technological challenge* for human rights. While the story of the 2010s was about how the internet and social networks empowered and connected activists and social justice organizations across borders, the story of the dawn of the 2020s is about how those tools and other technologies such as AI are being used to collect unprecedented amounts of personal data, manipulate human behaviour, disrupt elections, and concentrate power in the hands of digital megacorporations and surveillance states. As Shoshana Zuboff has shown, the technologies and institutions of the new era of 'surveillance capitalism' fundamentally undermine the conditions for the exercise of basic rights, from privacy to autonomy to political participation.[8] Biotechnology, which enables wealthy individuals to purchase enhanced cognitive and physical capacities, raises an equally formidable challenge, as it threatens to crystallize and deepen the inequalities that are already tearing apart national polities and undermining human rights around the world.[9]

Third, the *political challenge* that populist authoritarianism presents to democracy and human rights is here to stay. Anchored as it is in long-term structural transformations—such as the abovementioned technological disruptions and increasing inequalities—its ascendancy is not a glitch in the trajectory of global liberalism.[10] As they polarize societies through a categorical moral division of the polity between 'us versus them', between the 'real people' and the rest, populists strike at the core belief of human rights in the equal dignity of all.[11] In doing so, they rely on the digital technologies (such as social media and messaging services) that were created to connect across group boundaries, and are now used to entrench tribal identities, be they ideological, ethnic, religious, nationalist, or otherwise. Since, as social psychology has shown, human beings tend to first belong and then believe,[12] the social tribes thus consolidated tend to operate as echo chambers, relatively impervious to the human rights truth-telling. This raises profound questions for the effectiveness of common human rights strategies of fact-finding and reporting.

Fourth, the climate and environmental crisis disrupts basic conditions of life on earth and thus those of human rights. This *ecological challenge* entered the mainstream in 2018–2019, as the reports of the UN expert panels on climate and biodiversity overlapped with the cascade of extreme weather events that scientists had been warning about for decades.[13] The advent of the Anthropocene, the geological era marked by the dominance (and potential annihilation) of the planet by the human species, was heralded by those early signs of the uninhabitable planet that future generations will inherit if drastic decarbonization measures are not urgently adopted to change the trajectory that is leading the planet to 1.5°C–2°C of warming by mid-century and 3°C –4°C by the end of the century.[14] The Anthropocene raises

[8] Shoshana Zuboff, *The Age of Surveillance Capitalism: The Fight for a Human Future at the New Frontier of Power* (1st edn, PublicAffairs 2019).

[9] Jamie Frederic Metzl, *Hacking Darwin: Genetic Engineering and the Future of Humanity* (Sourcebooks 2019).

[10] Yascha Mounk and Jordan Kyle, 'What Populists Do to Democracies' *The Atlantic* (2018) <www.theatlantic.com/ideas/archive/2018/12/hard-data-populism-bolsonaro-trump/578878/> accessed 6 August 2020.

[11] Jan-Werner Müller, *What is Populism?* (University of Pennsylvania Press 2016).

[12] Jonathan Haidt, *The Righteous Mind: Why Good People Are Divided by Politics and Religion* (Vintage Books 2013).

[13] Intergovernmental Panel on Climate Change, 'Special Report on Global Warming of 1.5°C' (IPCC 2018); Intergovernmental Science-Policy Platform on Biodiversity and Ecosystem Services, IPBES, 'Summary for Policymakers of the Global Assessment Report on Biodiversity and Ecosystem Services' (Zenodo 2019) <https://zenodo.org/record/3553579> accessed 8 August 2020.

[14] Bill McKibben, *Falter: Has the Human Game Begun to Play Itself Out?* (1st edn, Henry Holt and Company 2019).

existential challenges to human rights. It opens the gates to violations of human rights at an unprecedented scale, such as tens of millions of climate-induced deaths and waves of forced displacement that far surpass those caused by wars, and economic suffering much deeper and generalized than those associated with the Great Depression and financial crises.[15] In all of these respects, the coronavirus pandemic may be seen as a 'rehearsal' for the human rights impacts that worsening global warming will unleash in the coming years and decades if urgent and drastic action against it is not taken.[16] As Philip Alston argued in his role as UN Special Rapporteur on Extreme Poverty, 'tens of millions will be impoverished, leading to widespread displacement and hunger'.[17] What is more, the Anthropocene fundamentally questions human rights categories and concepts that have legitimized ecological harm, such as the denial of rights to future generations and nature.

Finally, increasing inequality poses a key *socio-economic challenge*. As Alston has argued, inequality is 'the antithesis of human rights',[18] as shown by rising income inequality in nearly all countries,[19] the fact that less than 1 per cent of the global population owns nearly half the world's wealth[20] and the reality (confirmed once more by the uneven effects of the coronavirus and powerfully exposed by the racial justice protests in mid-2020) that economic disadvantage is closely interrelated with other systems of oppression, from racism to patriarchy to discriminatory nationalism. Intersecting inequalities not only deepen the cleavages that underlie political polarization and populist backlash, but they also endow a small number of extraordinarily wealthy individuals and privileged sectors of society with an unprecedented power to shape human-rights-relevant institutions, rules, technologies, and decisions.

Taken separately, any of the structural drivers of change that I have singled out would entail deep transformations in the human rights field. Taken together, they amount to nothing short of an existential challenge to it. The simultaneity and the speed (as well as the interrelations among) those transformations have left human rights actors with a sense of disorientation and even crisis. Although, as we will see, some of those changes also offer opportunities that some individuals and organizations are seizing, the external challenges to human rights are indeed profound. And they are compounded by dilemmas coming from within the field, to which I now turn.

22.2.2 Internal Challenges

Although external challenges create serious risks for human rights, they also could have an unexpected positive effect: to push the human rights movement to carry out internal

[15] David Wallace-Wells, *The Uninhabitable Earth: Life after Warming* (1st edn, Tim Duggan Books 2019).

[16] Fraser Bryers, 'Bill McKibben—COVID-19 and Climate Change' <https://thetyee.ca/News/2020/04/20/Bill-McKibben-Talks-COVID-19-And-Climate-Change/> accessed 6 August 2020.

[17] OHCHR, 'UN Expert Condemns Failure to Address Impact of Climate Change on Poverty' *UN News* (Geneva, 25 June 2019) <https://www.ohchr.org/EN/NewsEvents/Pages/DisplayNews.aspx?NewsID=24735&LangID=E> accessed 6 August 2020.

[18] Philip Alston, 'Extreme Inequality as the Antithesis of Human Rights' (*OpenGlobalRights* 27 August 2015) <https://www.openglobalrights.org/extreme-inequality-as-the-antithesis-of-human-rights/> accessed 6 August 2020.

[19] Facundo Alvaredo and others, 'World Ineqality Report 2018' (World Inequality Database 2018) <https://wir2018.wid.world/files/download/wir2018-full-report-english.pdf> accessed 30 May 2021.

[20] Max Lawson and others, 'Public Good or Private Wealth?' (2019) Oxfam International <https://oxfamilibrary.openrepository.com/bitstream/handle/10546/620599/bp-public-good-or-private-wealth-210119-en.pdf> accessed 6 August 2020.

transformations in its architecture, tactics, and strategies that were imperative even before the onset of those transformations.

With the erosion of Euro-American hegemony in the 2010s, the conventional 'boomerang model' of human rights advocacy—which consisted in appealing to Washington, Geneva, or London so that governments of the global North would pressure their global South counterparts to comply with human rights—was already losing its effectiveness. Trump, the Brexiteers, and continental European populists further undermined the limited effectiveness and legitimacy of those strategies centred on the global North. Further, 'naming and shaming' delinquent states into compliance can no longer do the trick in a world where many leaders both in the North and the South are very happy to be named but shamelessly cover for each other.

The new context has put considerable pressure on the fault lines and blind spots of the contemporary architecture of the human rights field: the concentration of agenda-setting power and funds in international NGOs; the difficulties of international NGOs in collaborating on a level playing field with global South organizations; the insufficient connection between professional NGOs and social movements; and the inordinate dominance of specialized, law-centred narratives and strategies, which heavily limited the ability of the movement to connect with large sectors of the population and forge bridges with other movements.

Elsewhere, I have examined these and other internal weaknesses of the movement.[21] Here I want to stay at the higher level of analysis that I proposed for this chapter, one that takes a system view of human rights. From this perspective, I highlight five field-wide challenges for the movement. The first one is *fragmentation and lack of collaboration and learning across the field*. While collaboration has become a pervasive mode of operation in other circles, conventional funding and institutional models continue to encourage competition instead of collaboration among human rights organizations. For instance, while many academic disciplines have embraced co-authorship as the main form of knowledge production, far too many human rights organizations continue to individually pursue their own projects and publish solo-authored reports. The result is the suboptimal use of scarce resources, duplication of efforts, failure to capitalize on complementary skills and knowledge, and waste of precious opportunities for greater collective impact.

The second systemic limitation of the field is *strategic stagnation and limited innovation*. As in any well-established professional field, dominant human rights actors have become attached to the traditional strategies that have allowed them to win key victories for decades. They have thus been slow in responding to new challenges, and oftentimes lack the tools and incentives to innovate in order to remain impactful and relevant. The result is overreliance on conventional and increasingly ineffective strategies such as naming and shaming and traditional research, communications, and litigation. Despite the possibilities opened up by digital technologies and the insights provided by studies on effective communications and narratives, the mainstream toolkit of human rights continues to look more like a one-purpose hammer than like a versatile Swiss army knife.

Third, the human rights system is hampered by its *slowness and focus on the short term*. Over the last few decades, prominent human rights organizations have focused on *space* (as in Amnesty International's and Human Rights Watch's effort to decentralize their operations

[21] César Rodríguez-Garavito, 'The Future of Human Rights: From Gatekeeping to Symbiosis' (2014) 11 SUR International Journal of Human Rights <https://papers.ssrn.com/abstract=2553200> accessed 6 August 2020, from which this section is partially drawn.

across the globe). However, they and other actors in the field have yet to adjust their vision and use of *time* in responding to changes that now occur with exponentially higher velocity and thus demand urgency, in an age that has rightly been called 'The Great Acceleration'.[22] Moreover, while some of the existential threats to human rights stem from long-term, structural transformations (eg the erosion of democracy, the persistent trend towards rising inequality, and the heating of the planet), the vision of most human rights actors continues to focus on short-term, two- to five-year funding and operational cycles, and is focused on demonstrating 'impact' by showing success on low hanging fruit and near-term reforms. Given that the targets of human rights campaigns (from authoritarian governments to fossil fuel and social media corporations) tend to have much longer-term horizons, this is a systemic disadvantage that keeps human rights actors constantly on the defensive.

The success of populist and anti-rights movements and governments in gaining majority support has made visible another limitation of the human rights field, that is, its relatively *narrow membership and audience*. Specifically, it has shown that conventional human rights organizations and narratives—with their reliance on legal language and their larger membership in the global North—have failed to engage with and appeal to large sectors of the population, including the young and the 'persuadable middle' sectors in increasingly polarized societies.[23] Thus, human rights actors tend to paint themselves into a corner, where they appear as defenders of minority causes despite advancing causes that also benefit the majority of the population, such as protecting the socio-economic rights of the working class against austerity policies.

The final systemic weakness of the field that I wish to highlight is *unmanaged complexity*. As external challenges have multiplied, and as the number and interdependence of human rights issues and actors have increased, the field and the problems it tackles have become highly complex. In fact, some of the key contemporary challenges to human rights—from the erosion of civic space to global warming—fit the definition of a 'wicked problem', that is, one that is difficult to solve because of incomplete, contradictory, and changing requirements that are often hard to recognize.[24] Addressing complex problems in general, and wicked problems in particular, requires a systems view of the field, willingness to prioritize some issues over others, and openness to deconstructing complex problems and finding novel solutions to them. Predisposition for prioritization and systemic approaches is uncommon in human rights field, partly due to the fundamental moral commitment of the movement to the indivisibility and importance of all rights, and partly due to the abovementioned strategic stagnation. Thus, unmanaged complexity stands in the way of greater collective impact.[25]

These systemic challenges are not entirely new. They are the blind spots and accumulated liabilities of the traditional advocacy paradigm. Although many organizations and coalitions around the world are actively developing responses and solutions to the aforementioned challenges, the conventional paradigm continues to be dominant. Human rights activists and analysts should have mended these weaknesses in times of relative normality. Now we

[22] Gaia Vince, *Adventures in the Anthropocene: A Journey to the Heart of the Planet We Made* (Milkweed Editions 2015); Robert Macfarlane, 'Generation Anthropocene: How Humans Have Altered the Planet for Ever' *The Guardian* (1 April 2016) <https://www.theguardian.com/books/2016/apr/01/generation-anthropocene-altered-planet-for-ever> accessed 6 August 2020.

[23] Thomas Coombes, 'Hope, Not Fear: A New Model for Communicating Human Rights' (*Medium* 27 October 2019) <https://medium.com/@the_hope_guy/hope-not-fear-a-new-model-for-communicating-human-rights-d98c0d6bf57b> accessed 6 August 2020.

[24] David Epstein, *Range: Why Generalists Triumph in a Specialized World* (Riverhead Books 2019).

[25] Tim Wu, 'The Democrats' Complexity Problem' *The New York Times* (21 March 2019) <https://www.nytimes.com/2019/03/21/opinion/democrats-complexity.html> accessed 6 August 2020.

will have to do it in extraordinary times, when the old paradigm is no longer tenable, and a new paradigm has yet to emerge.

How do we make this transition? The answer depends partly on the interpretation of the current moment. As Kuhn showed, paradigmatic transitions are marked by heated debates among proponents of different readings of the state of the field. Thus, before offering some ideas about how to tackle internal and external challenges, I discuss the contending readings of the ongoing anxiety in human rights circles and make explicit the interpretation from which my proposals stem.

22.3 Crisis or Transition? Four Readings of the Human Rights Impasse

As in any debate, extreme views on the situation of human rights have elicited the most attention among practitioners and scholars. Less time and energy have been devoted to intermediate views that acknowledge the challenges while formulating pragmatic solutions to them. I seek to compensate for this bias by discussing jointly the more extreme readings of the situation—which I will call the 'endtimes' and the 'business as usual' views—and focusing on intermediate interpretations, which I will call 'reflexive reconstruction' and 'constructive disruption'.

22.3.1 Endtimes or Business as Usual?

The responses that many analysts and practitioners have offered tend to be grouped in two extremes: scepticism and defensiveness. The sceptics announce the 'endtimes' of the international project of human rights, based on a view that human rights were imposed by Euro-America. Given this view, the end of Pax Americana is also the end of the movement as we know it, as Stephen Hopgood has written.[26] His work is thought provoking and inexact in equal parts, and it forgets that this regime was built in part with the ideas and the pressure of states and movements of the global South, from those who created the American Declaration on the Rights and Duties of Man in 1948 to postcolonial nations that pushed for treaties against racial and religious discrimination in the sixties.[27]

Sceptics also rely on an incomplete reading of the global impact of the movement. For example, even if Samuel Moyn is right in claiming that the impact of international law on American human rights struggles (specifically on the civil rights cause) is negligible, generalizing to the rest of the world is empirically inaccurate.[28] It runs counter, for instance, to abundant evidence that the making and implementation of international norms such as those

[26] Hopgood, *The Endtimes of Human Rights* (n 3).

[27] Kathryn Sikkink, 'Latin America's Protagonist Role in Human Rights' 22 (2016) SUR International Journal of Human Rights 207; César Rodríguez-Garavito, 'Towards a Human Rights Ecosystem' in Doutje Lettinga and Lars van Troost (eds), *Debating the Endtimes of Human Rights* (Amnesty International 2014).

[28] Samuel Moyn, 'Trump and the Limits of Human Rights' (*openDemocracy* 14 November 2016) <https://www.opendemocracy.net/en/openglobalrights-openpage/trump-and-limits-of-human-rights/> accessed 6 August 2020. My response in this section is partially drawn from César Rodríguez-Garavito, 'Trump's Victory Could Push the Human Rights Movement to Transform' (*OpenGlobalRights* 10 December 2016) <https://www.openglobalrights.org/trump-victory-could-push-human-rights-movement-to-transform/> accessed 30 May 2021.

enshrined in the UN Durban Declaration or the Convention against Racial Discrimination—in combination with domestic political and legal mobilization—have made key contributions to advancing the cause of racial justice in different parts of the world.[29] More generally, Anglo-American sceptics tend to miss myriad processes of 'vernacularization' whereby international human rights have been incorporated into national constitutions, policies, court decisions, and social movements' frames and repertoires of contention.[30]

However, as noted, recognizing the history and accomplishments of the movement does not imply that the dominant tactics in human rights are without serious flaws. Nor does it imply that external and internal challenges can be satisfactorily tackled through a business-as-usual approach, one that doubles down on the tenets of the traditional paradigm. This traditional approach has been forcefully articulated by some pioneer advocates and defended by leading organizations like Human Rights Watch. Implicitly, it has also been embraced by many human rights players who continue to operate along the intellectual, organizational, and strategic lines of the second half of the twentieth century. Explicitly or implicitly, this reading assumes that there is nothing particularly new about the current moment, and that 'naming and shaming is still the human rights movement's best weapon'.[31]

Paradoxically, proponents of endtimes and business-as-usual views share strikingly similar conceptions of the history and architecture of the human rights field.[32] Although they are on opposite sides of the debate, they have in common an all too simplistic view of the actors, the content, and the strategies of the movement.

With regards to the *actors*, both paint a reductionist picture. Hopgood throws the first punch: 'Human Rights are a New York-Geneva-London-centered ideology focused on international law, criminal justice, and institutions of global governance. Human Rights are a product of the 1 per cent.'[33] Moyn's empirical analysis is largely focused on the global North, and his criticisms are almost invariably aimed at prominent international NGOs, as if they were a proxy for the movement as a whole,[34] as Gráinne de Burca and Julieta Lemaitre have convincingly argued.[35] In this regard, the sceptics embrace a Northern-centric view of the field that is similar to the most forceful defenders of the traditional paradigm. It is no coincidence that they all date back the origins of the human rights field to the 1970s (when Human Rights Watch and other professional international NGOs were established)[36] instead of the mid-1940s, when the foundational legal instruments (like the Universal Declaration and the

[29] Tianna S Paschel, *Becoming Black Political Subjects: Movements and Ethno-Racial Rights in Colombia and Brazil* (Princeton University Press 2017).

[30] Sally Engle Merry, *Human Rights and Gender Violence: Translating International Law into Local Justice* (University of Chicago Press 2006).

[31] Aryeh Neier, '"Naming and Shaming": Still the Human Rights Movement's Best Weapon' (*OpenGlobalRights* 11 July 2018) <www.openglobalrights.org/Naming-and-shaming-still-the-human-rights-movements-best-weapon/> accessed 8 August 2020.

[32] See César Rodríguez-Garavito, 'Against Reductionist Views of Human Rights' (*OpenGlobalRights* 30 July 2013) <www.opendemocracy.net/en/openglobalrights-openpage/against-reductionist-views-of-human-rights/> accessed 6 August 2020, from which this section is partly drawn.

[33] Stephen Hopgood, 'Human Rights: Past Their Sell-by Date' (*OpenGlobalRights* 18 June 2013) <www.openglobalrights.org/human-rights-past-their-sell-by-date/> accessed 8 August 2020.

[34] Samuel Moyn, *Not Enough: Human Rights in an Unequal World* (Belknap Press of Harvard University Press 2019); Samuel Moyn, 'How the Human Rights Movement Failed' *The New York Times* (23 April 2018) <https://www.nytimes.com/2018/04/23/opinion/human-rights-movement-failed.html> accessed 8 August 2020.

[35] Julieta Lemaitre, 'The View from Somewhere: On Samuel Moyn's Not Enough' (*LPE Project*, 9 July 2018) <https://lpeproject.org/blog/the-view-from-somewhere-on-samuel-moyns-not-enough/> accessed 6 August 2020; Grainne de Búrca, 'Shaming Human Rights' (NYU School of Law 2018) Jean Monnet Working Paper 2/18.

[36] Moyn, *Not Enough* (n 34); Aryeh Neier, *The International Human Rights Movement: A History* (Princeton University Press 2012).

American Convention) were adopted with the decisive participation of global South states and actors.[37]

Although sceptics like Hopgood are right to point out that the movement is profoundly unequal (organizations in the global North continue to have disproportionate power when it comes to setting the international agenda and receiving funding), in practice human rights actors are much more varied, and their relationships much more complicated, than what both critics and defenders of the traditional paradigm would suggest. The success of the language of human rights is such that it has been adopted by grassroots communities, social movements, networks of online activists, religious and professional organizations, scientific communities, and many other actors.

Instead of imposing on the whole movement a simplistic dichotomy such as Hopgood's contrast between elite, capital-letter Human Rights versus grassroots human rights players, what we need are useful concepts and strategies for a movement that is much more varied and dynamic than the one of past decades, and that needs to actively reframe and reimagine its mission and strategies if it is to be relevant and impactful under the radically new conditions of the twenty-first century. This is the view proposed by the readings of the current moment that take a middle road between scepticism and defensiveness.

22.3.2 Reflexive Reconstruction and Constructive Disruption

Since human rights practitioners and engaged academics cannot afford to rejoice in uncertainty or join the call for the demise of the movement, their responses oscillate between defensiveness and reconstruction. As noted, defensiveness tends to be the reaction of those who are highly invested in the conventional model of human rights advocacy. Reconstruction is the response of those who recognize internal and external challenges and yet believe that they do not represent the end of the human rights project, but rather the need for new ways of thinking about and practising them.

I distinguish two types of reconstructive views: reflexive reconstruction and constructive disruption. Reflexive reconstruction entails a careful inquiry into the movement's past and a critical examination of its present in order to distil lessons for the future. Scholars writing in this vein, such as Kathryn Sikkink, cogently question the inaccurate account of the history and the current moment of the movement embraced by sceptics and defenders alike.[38] They contest the historical account that locates the origin of the movement in the global North, as well as the empirical data used to support the premature announcement of the terminal failure of the human rights project. However, vindicating the movement's trajectory and achievements does not translate into complacency. For the same reflexive exercise brings to light the aforementioned challenges and internal fissures of the movement, which this view recognizes and proposes to tackle with a combination of time-honoured and new strategies. For instance, while Sikkink's work contests the notion that the populist challenge to human rights amounts to a global trend towards the closure of civil society spaces, it also highlights the need for new narratives and impact-oriented strategies that differ from those of the conventional human rights paradigm.

[37] Steven LB Jensen, *The Making of International Human Rights: The 1960s, Decolonization, and the Reconstruction of Global Values* (CUP 2017).

[38] Sikkink, *Evidence for Hope* (n 2).

Reflexive reconstruction is indeed much needed in human rights. My own work has been informed by this view.[39] However, I argue that it needs to be complemented by another, more urgent type of intermediate approach, which I call constructive disruption. This is so because the human rights movement has been sluggish in addressing the formidable challenges it faces. While increasingly ineffective, the inertia of the conventional paradigm of human rights advocacy continues to slow down internal transformation. For instance, an inordinate amount of time and energy in the emerging field of business and human rights has gone into debating contrasting approaches to the traditional task of standard setting. A myriad of organizations has heavily invested in the divisive debate between supporters of the UN Guiding Principles on Business and Human Rights and those who argue that real corporate accountability requires a binding UN treaty on the matter.[40] Meanwhile, not enough attention has been paid to ensuring that the existing standards are actually implemented to the benefit of workers, Indigenous people, and others whose rights have been violated by corporations.

Taking a cue from social innovation studies and initiatives in other fields (from health care to journalism to education[41]), what I propose is to undertake innovations that disrupt the dominant paradigm of human rights in ways that increase the collective capacity and impact of the movement. These constructive disruptions take the form of concrete initiatives that address systemic challenges in human rights and, if successful, have the potential to be scaled to the field level. As we will see in section 22.4, they consist of a wide variety of efforts, including novel interorganizational collaborations, new narratives, the expansion of the concept of rights holder, creative litigation and human rights education that expand the movement's toolkit and knowledge base, and so on. What they all have in common is a deliberate spirit of experimentation and willingness to learn from other fields, and even from failure.

This explicitly experimental approach is akin to the 'destabilizing' view of rights that Sabel and Simon proposed for litigation, in which rights are seen as means to disrupt power asymmetries and dysfunctional organizational arrangements that stand in the way of social justice.[42] As pragmatist and experimentalist social theory shows, this view of rights is particularly relevant under conditions of uncertainty like those of the current moment, in which traditional solutions are no longer effective and alternatives are not readily available.[43]

Given that the disruptive innovations that I have in mind have a (constructively) destabilizing purpose, and that they remain largely untested in the human rights field, I formulate them as provocations.

22.4 Disruptive Innovations: Towards a Human Rights Ecosystem

In line with reconstructive views, I have argued that instead of reinforcing the traditional boundaries of the field, human rights theory and practice must be expanded to include and

[39] Rodríguez-Garavito, 'The Future of Human Rights' (n 21).

[40] César A Rodríguez Garavito (ed), *Business and Human Rights: Beyond the End of the Beginning* (CUP 2017).

[41] Taz Hussein, Matt Plummer and Bill Breen, 'How Field Catalysts Galvanize Social Change' *Stanford Social Innovation Review* (2018) <https://ssir.org/articles/entry/field_catalysts> accessed 6 August 2020.

[42] Charles F Sabel and William H Simon, 'Destabilization Rights: How Public Law Litigation Succeeds' (2004) 117 Harvard Law Review 1015.

[43] Grainne de Búrca, 'Human Rights Experimentalism' (2017) 111 American Journal of International Law 277; Charles Sabel 'Dewey, Democracy, and Democratic Experimentalism' (2012) 9 Contemporary Pragmatism 35.

open spaces for new actors, themes, and strategies that have emerged in the last two decades. To capture and maximize this diversity, I have suggested that the field should be understood as an ecosystem, rather than as a unified movement or institutional architecture.[44]

As in any ecosystem, the strength of human rights will depend on symbiosis, that is, the interaction among its different actors, to the advantage of the latter and the broader cause they share. Collaboration and complementarity thus become even more important to the survival and thriving of the field as a whole.

Adaptation and learning will also be fundamental for the human rights ecosystem to thrive, as is the case in any system. As noted, this requires moving toward experimentalism. It also implies changes in the architecture of the movement, such that innovations can be nurtured and disseminated across it.

Transitioning from the current fragmentation and uncertainty to a human rights ecosystem will not happen spontaneously. It entails disruptive interventions in tactics, types of actors, narratives, and frames, among others. I single out three such interventions.

22.4.1 Collaborate, Collaborate, Collaborate

Given the prevalent mode of operation in the field, which encourages competition and dispersion of efforts and resources, human rights have yet to sufficiently enter the era of collaborative production. Collaboration has become predominant in other fields, from journalism to science to software development. A rich body of social science literature has shown that collaborative modes of production are needed to deal with the increasing complexity, volatility, and abundance of information in contemporary societies and systems of all kinds.[45]

I highlight two types of disruptions that can infuse and scale collaboration in human rights. My first suggestion is to develop more *collaborative platforms* of the type that professionals in other circles have built to exchange information and carry out joint actions. Specifically, human rights actors can get inspiration and concrete ideas from a neighbouring field—journalism. Under pressure from a failing business model, top journalistic outlets have responded with a new mantra that is thoroughly transposable to human rights: 'collaborate, collaborate, collaborate'.[46] One of the results in journalism has been sophisticated collaborative platforms and digital infrastructures such as those created by the International Consortium of Investigative Journalists, which have enabled hundreds of journalists from around the world to work jointly on massive investigative projects, such as the one that led to the revelations of the Panama Papers.

Here is the provocation: If journalists and media organizations—who have every incentive to scoop each other—have managed to coordinate efforts and pool resources to increase the collective impact of their work, why can't human rights actors? Although not with the frequency and systematicity of journalists, some civil society organizations do engage regularly in collaborative reports—for instance, when they constitute coalitions that work on a single

[44] César Rodríguez-Garavito, 'Human Rights: Gated Community or Ecosystem?' (*OpenGlobalRights*) <www.openglobalrights.org/cesar-rodríguez-garavito/> accessed 6 August 2020; Rodríguez-Garavito, 'The Future of Human Rights' (n 21).

[45] Yochai Benkler, 'Law, Innovation, and Collaboration in Networked Economy and Society' (2017) 13 Annual Review of Law and Social Science 231.

[46] Charles Lewis, 'The Future of Journalism in Three Words: Collaboration, Collaboration, Collaboration | Charles Lewis' *The Guardian* (18 April 2016) <www.theguardian.com/commentisfree/2016/apr/18/future-of-journalism-collaboration-panama-papers> accessed 6 August 2020.

report about a given country when the latter comes up for review before the UN Human Rights Council as part of the Universal Periodic Review system. Instead of publishing competing and redundant reports on an issue of interest to organizations in different parts of the world, would it not be more reasonable to do this more often and share scarce resources and maximize impact and attention by working collaboratively on a single investigation?

Collaboration does not always require building new platforms. In fact, human rights organizations could deepen and multiply joint initiatives without necessarily changing their institutional structures. They would, however, need to shift from a competitive culture to a collaborative one. This is the second route towards a more cooperative human rights ecosystem. All that it would take is for funders to systematically support collaboration and for NGOs to engage more frequently in collaborative efforts with other organizations, ideally through modes of cooperation that are more horizontal than the 'boomerang' model of the traditional advocacy paradigm. Under Euro-American hegemony, groups in the global South suffering under authoritarian regimes felt they had to appeal to northern NGOs in Washington, London, or Geneva. These northern advocates, in turn, pleaded, cajoled, and pressured northern governments and international organizations to get engaged. If successful, this human rights 'boomerang' eventually returned to its launching point in the form of northern political and economic pressure on southern authoritarian regimes. Although entrenching North–South asymmetries, this model led to key transnational victories, such as the campaigns against gross human rights violations by Latin American dictatorships in the 1970s and 1980s.

The boomerang is still widely used, but it clearly has diminishing returns. Thus, contemporary human rights actors are experimenting with less episodic, more horizontal collaborations. I distinguish three promising approaches, pursued by some international NGOs, virtual networks, and coalitions of national organizations. As for *international NGOs*, many are creating a stronger direct institutional presence in the global South, seeking new opportunities for policy influence, fundraising, constituency-building, and mobilizing popular enthusiasm. This new approach is evident in Amnesty's decade-long attempt to be 'closer to the ground', as well as Human Rights Watch's ongoing globalization process. In both cases, a classic, northern-based 'brand name' group is opening, or strengthening, offices in new centres of global and regional power, from New Delhi to Sao Paulo.

As in other globalized bureaucracies, however, these processes may lead to ultimate decision-making power remaining concentrated in the (northern) headquarters. Moreover, it may be the case that these and other international NGOs will tend to privilege collaboration within their globally dispersed organizational structure, rather than collaboration with local organizations.

A second promising approach to transnational collaboration is *global virtual networks*. Empowered by information and communications technologies, activists and online advocacy platforms like Change.org and Avaaz mobilize the power of decentralized crowds to put pressure on a variety of human rights targets, from states to corporations. This approach is also evident in the rapid, cross-border dissemination of pro-rights movements like the Occupy wave in the early 2010s, the younger generation's school strikes on climate change at the end of the decade, and the wave of protests against racial injustice that inaugurated the 2020s.

Although promoters of this model sometimes overplay its novelty, they rightly note that its power is 'open, participatory, and peer-driven'.[47] Bennett and Segerberg have cogently

[47] Jeremy Heimans and Henry Timms, 'Understanding "New Power"' (2014) *Harvard Business Review* <https://hbr.org/2014/12/understanding-new-power> accessed 6 August 2020.

dubbed this model 'connective action', in contrast to the traditional 'collective action' model of NGOs and other formal social change organizations.[48] Its strength lies in its ability to aggregate small contributions from around the world at dizzying speed, from local protests to donations in crowdfunding schemes to e-signatures in support of transnational petitions. Its weakness is the obverse of its highly disruptive and opportune power, that is, its difficulty to sustain collaboration over time and transform disruption into lasting influence, as evident in the fate of the Occupy movement.

Here is the provocation: What would it take for traditional human rights actors to collaborate more with connective action human rights players? How can the strengths of the two modes of mobilization be creatively combined?

Finally, a promising collaborative model is being built by *domestic organizations*. As global power becomes more multipolar, local NGOs are creating new coalitions focused on producing what I call 'multiple boomerangs'.[49] In this case, political pressure for human rights change comes from different geographic locations; and is simultaneously mobilized and directed towards multiple targets.

I witnessed this model at work in a successful coalition that Latin American NGOs forged to defend the Inter-American Human Rights Commission (IAHRC) when it came under attack from regional governments between 2011 and 2016. In this issue area, the United States was a major part of the problem; it had never ratified the Inter-American Convention on Human Rights, and its regional influence was in decline. As a result, lobbying US human rights groups, or appealing to the US government for pressure on Latin American governments, would have been ineffectual, even counterproductive.

Instead, Latin American NGOs developed a collaborative strategy centred on putting simultaneous pressure on their own governments to support the IAHRC. They also succeeded in inducing key governments such as Brazil to defend the IAHRC from attempts at stripping it of its key powers. A regional coalition of national human rights groups, lobbying their own governments and the region's emerging power, Brazil, got the job done.[50]

This was a South–South boomerang of domestic NGOs. But multiple South–North and North–North boomerangs are also arising. A telling example is the International Network of Civil Liberties Organizations (INCLO), a coalition of fifteen national NGOs from different regions of the world that produces comparative reports and coordinates domestic advocacy efforts undertaken by member organizations.

In light of the potential of this model both for impact and for instilling a collaborative mode of action, why not increase the use of multiple boomerangs? Why not activate some of the myriad human rights networks that rarely go into action mode, and turn them into action-oriented, collaborative coalitions that leverage multiple boomerangs?

[48] W Lance Bennett and Alexandra Segerberg, 'The Logic of Connective Action: Digital Media and the Personalization of Contentious Politics' (2012) 15 Information, Communication & Society 739.

[49] César Rodríguez-Garavito, 'Multiple Boomerangs: New Models of Global Human Rights Advocacy' (*openDemocracy* 21 January 2015) <www.opendemocracy.net/en/openglobalrights-openpage/multiple-boomerangs-new-models-of-global-human-rights-advoc/> accessed 6 August 2020, from which this section is partly drawn.

[50] Camila Barreto and others, *The Inter-American Human Rights System: Changing Times, Ongoing Challenges* (DPLF 2016).

22.4.2 'Timeful' Human Rights: Thinking Long Term, Responding in the Very Short Term

My next set of provocations is based on the following thesis: If the human rights movement hopes to have a future, it will have to take time seriously.

While the 1990s and 2000s were a period of concern about space, I believe that time will be the most important variable for human rights in the remainder of the century. Turn-of-the century globalization was a spatial phenomenon by definition: the expansion of markets across the world, the connection of the last corners of the globe to telecommunication networks, and the transnational rise of neoliberalism. Although the human rights movement was one of the sources of criticism and resistance against the inequities of globalization, it remained more focused on space than time. It focused on the global dissemination of human rights standards embodied in treaties and agreements, which became part of the language and common sense of global governance. Obsessed with going beyond the barriers of space, we put aside the concern about time, as if globalization was effectively the 'end of history' proclaimed by Fukuyama.

We now know this was a hasty diagnosis not only because nationalism is building up walls of hatred around the world, but also because our disdain for long-term thinking is taking its toll. If more evidence was needed that history did not end with the victory of liberalism and human rights, the populist-authoritarian wave is proof enough.

The time to cope with the climate crisis with conventional measures has also passed.[51] Generation Xers were a product of globalization and wasted the thirty crucial years we had to take gradual steps against global heating. Today generation Z teenagers go on school strikes to remind us of what scientists from the UN intergovernmental panel on climate change concluded: To avoid the most catastrophic climate change scenarios and the subsequent human rights crises, urgent measures that cut carbon emissions in half by 2030 at the latest are the only way out.[52]

Recovering time also means changing the way we think about it. When globalization was booming, the prevailing disciplines, from geography to political economy and international law, focused on space. Today it is necessary to learn from other fields that hold a fuller understanding of time, such as biology and geology, considering that they are more connected with temporal phenomena such as the evolution of earth and the species that live on it .

As geologist Marcia Bjornerud wrote, 'an acute consciousness of how the world is made by—indeed, made of—time', is what is required.[53] This vision means constructive disruptions based on 'timeful' (as opposed to timeless) ideas and proposals as beautifully expressed by Bjornerud.

I suggest two disruptive, 'timeful' ideas related to human rights. The first is to acknowledge the rights of future generations.[54] The UDHR falls short when it states that 'all human beings are born free and equal in dignity and rights'. The Declaration and international

[51] See César Rodríguez-Garavito (ed) *Litigating the Climate Crisis: How Human Rights, Courts and Legal Mobilization Can Bolster Climate Action* (Cambridge University Press forthcoming). See also César Rodríguez-Garavito, 'For Human Rights to Have a Future, We Must Consider Time,' (*OpenGlobalRights* 10 June 2019) <https://www.openglobalrights.org/for-human-rights-to-have-a-future-we-must-consider-time/> accessed 31 May 2021, from which this section is partly drawn.

[52] IPCC, 'Special Report on Global Warming of 1.5°C' (n 13).

[53] Marcia Bjornerud, *Timefulness: How Thinking like a Geologist Can Help Save the World* (Princeton University Press 2018).

[54] Bridget Lewis, 'The Rights of Future Generations within the Post-Paris Climate Regime' (2018) 7(1) Transnational Environmental Law 69.

human rights law writ large consider only present generations because the provisions do not prevent them from leaving an uninhabitable planet to future generations. A missing article in international law should state that 'every generation has an equal right to enjoy natural resources'.[55] The idea was already considered in non-binding instruments like the UNESCO Declaration of the Responsibilities of the Present Generations Toward Future Generations (1997). Now we have incontrovertible and detailed evidence about the looming human rights crisis that climate change would bring for future generations. Why not update the legal, strategic, and intellectual toolkit of human rights to fully incorporate consideration for the rights of future generations?

Another timeful proposal is the declaration of constitutional emergency to address the climate crisis and the consequent rights violations, just as emergencies are declared to allow for exceptional measures during economic crises or wars. Today we know that, unless we face climate change with the same urgency and scale that is required by a pandemic or a world war, global warming will cause an economic collapse much worse than the one caused by the coronavirus crisis and a death toll greater than that of both world wars combined.[56] If countries like England and Ireland declared in 2019 a constitutional emergency to face the effects of climate change and the massive loss of animals and plants, why not scale this initiative and other legal innovations to other countries, and to the regional and global levels? In addition to contributing to this type of initiative, human rights actors can help make them congruent with human rights norms, which populist authoritarian governments opportunistically suspend in times of constitutional emergencies, as shown by the way in which leaders in countries like Hungary and Brazil used the coronavirus pandemic as an excuse to pass anti-rights legislation.

These types of timeful ideas are supported by social movements with an acute awareness of time, such as the wave of student strikes for the rights of future generations, and the series of rallies led by organizations like 350.org and Extinction Rebellion protesting against inaction on climate change. While the former reminded us of the importance of long-term thinking, the later underlined short-term action.

The human rights movement can learn from these other movements. It must refine its long-term goals as well as its short-term response capacity. With regard to the first, thinking ahead of long-term trends is one of the blind spots of human rights players, like NGOs and philanthropic donors. We are habituated with one- to three-year planning and funding cycles, often failing to anticipate fundamental changes that require preparations now, but that will take place within ten to twenty years. An example is the deep changes in basic concepts and the practice of human rights that will come about because of new technologies, like AI and gene editing. If many of the targets of human rights advocacy—from fossil fuel companies to the military to AI corporations—operate with a multi-decade time horizon in mind, should human rights actors and funders not also develop a longer-term view and strategize in light of likely future scenarios?

At the same time, human rights players struggle to react with the necessary urgency in the short term. Mainstream organizations have been slow to respond to existential challenges, such as the dissemination of authoritarian populism or climate change, possibly as a result of the inertia of conventional strategies. For instance, the routine of state-centric advocacy

[55] George Monbiot, 'Capitalism Is Destroying the Earth. We Need a New Human Right for Future Generations' *The Guardian* (15 March 2019) <www.theguardian.com/commentisfree/2019/mar/15/capitalism-destroying-earth-human-right-climate-strike-children> accessed 8 August 2020.

[56] Wallace-Wells (n 15).

before intergovernmental institutions no longer suffices in a fast-paced world where some of the most serious threats to human rights do not come from states but from private corporations, whose social platforms can help destabilize electoral processes in a matter of days.

22.4.3 Learning from Other Fields: New Human Rights Narratives

Constructively disrupting human rights is most productive when it draws from a wide array of fields of research and practice, and from different forms of imagining the future. In addition to the types of knowledge that are familiar in human rights circles, such as law and the social sciences, this entails deploying the tools of a wide array of fields. In addition to those that I have alluded to throughout the chapter—such as journalism, futures thinking, social innovation, and design thinking—, this implies incorporating insights from studies on emotions, narratives, and the human mind. Disciplines like social psychology, neuroscience, and behavioural economics have made unprecedented progress in understanding the human mind in the last three decades, but many of their lessons have yet to be absorbed by human rights actors.

The good news is that a growing number of scholars and practitioners are practising human rights from these less well-travelled angles, explicitly engaging in forward-looking discussions on narratives and emotions. This is evident, for instance, in the *Open Global Rights* blog series for practitioners about emotions in general and hope in particular in human rights communications and messaging.[57]

Given the over-legalization of human rights in the traditional paradigm, actors in the field oftentimes lose sight of the moral nature of rights—and the fact that it was moral values that brought them to the field in the first place. More than a set of treaties or constitutional norms, human rights are moral claims about the intrinsic value of every human being. As Amartya Sen has written in criticizing the conventional, 'legally parasitic view of human rights', the latter must be seen as an approach to ethics, which stand in contrast, for instance, to utilitarianism.[58] Unlike the mode of reasoning that comes with the legally parasitic view of rights, engaging in such ethical debates entails taking seriously values and the strong personal emotions that they elicit.

Constructively disrupting the conventional paradigm entails putting the following question front and centre: If human rights are universal ethical claims and if their impact must be measured in our everyday life, what type of message can augment their efficacy, their emotional resonance among citizens? Considering the growing efficacy of populist-nationalist messages against human rights, the question is how to build narratives or counter-narratives that effectively influence public opinion and citizen perceptions about rights and about those who defend them. This includes contesting populists' 'us' versus 'them' discourses. Innovative organizations such as the Hungarian Civil Liberties Union are already experimenting with disruptive narratives that contest their government's nationalist framework, by choosing messages and frames that highlight the benefits of human rights for all Hungarians and associating national identity with respect for rights.[59]

[57] Thomas Coombes, 'Positive Narratives to Mobilize for Change' (*OpenGlobalRights*) <www.openglobalrights.org/positive-narratives/> accessed 8 August 2020.

[58] Amartya Sen, 'Human Rights and the Limits of Law' (2006) 27(6) Cardozo Law Review 2913–27.

[59] Stefánia Kapronczay and Anna Kertész, 'Dropping the Defense: Hopeful Stories Fight Stigma in Hungary' (*OpenGlobalRights* 24 August 2018) 57–70 <https://www.openglobalrights.org/dropping-the-defense-hopeful-stories-fight-stigma-in-hungary/> accessed 31 May 2021.

Both the theory and the practice of social movements provide useful elements for the task of reframing human rights. Studies in framing theory have shown how social changes depend on whether the activists who defend them manage to construct and reconstruct frames that give their movement an identity (*frame making*), so that they can have an echo with their audience (*frame resonance*) and so that they connect with discourses and agendas from other movements (*frame bridging*).[60]

In the face of the growing influence of anti-universal human rights political frames, these three tasks must be priorities for the human rights movement. There are promising examples of disruptive innovations in each one of them. With regard to *frame making*, indigenous peoples in the Americas have expanded the meaning and the impact of their right to be consulted about projects or laws that affect them. Initially, ILO Convention 169 conceived of consultation in liberal procedural terms and did not give indigenous peoples the power to veto actions that were harmful to their territories or culture. In practice, however, indigenous organizations and their allies have successfully promoted a more collective and substantive framing of that right, through narratives that also resonate with the environmental movement by connecting the protection of collective indigenous territories with the preservation of forests.[61]

Frame bridging is an equally important task. In order to counter and disrupt the trend towards increasing specialization and isolation of human rights, new narratives need to be developed that expand the resonance and constituency of human rights. For example, the values and emotions of millions around the world are inspired by religious creeds. In them, it is possible to find versions and interpretations that assert the intrinsic value of the human person in a way that has a strong affinity with the idea of dignity that underlies human rights. This is evident, for instance, in the encouraging convergence of human rights, environmental, and faith-based organizations around the climate crisis, through such coalitions as the Interfaith Rainforest Initiative.

Human rights actors cannot realistically expect their traditional frames and narratives to become universal moral common sense. If the past seven decades consisted fundamentally of constructing the contemporary human rights frame and translating it into norms and standards, the future will be more hybrid and will depend on human rights actors' capacity to appeal to broader constituencies and forge bridges with other frames of justice.

As Harari has provocatively put it, 'the only place rights exist is in the stories that humans tell each other. These stories were enshrined as self-evident dogma during the struggle against religious bigotry and autocratic governments … [This story] contributed to the happiness and welfare of humanity probably more than any other story. Yet it is still a dogma',— a story whose power depends on being credible and resonant to contemporary and future human beings in light of the radically new circumstances in which they must live.[62] To turn the provocation into a question: What new frames and narratives can make the human rights story credible and inspiring to anxious people, facing the prospect of an uninhabitable planet and technological dystopias?

[60] Robert D Benford and David A Snow, 'Framing Processes and Social Movements: An Overview and Assessment' (2000) 26 Annual Review of Sociology 611. See also César Rodríguez-Garavito, 'Reimagining Human Rights as a Frame of Justice' (*OpenGlobalRights* 28 September 2018) <https://www.openglobalrights.org/reimagining-human-rights-as-a-frame-of-justice/> accessed 31 May 2021, from which this section is partly drawn.

[61] César Rodríguez-Garavito, 'The Globalization of the Vernacular: Mobilizing, Resisting, and Transforming International Human Rights from Below', in Philip Alston (ed), *Festschirf for Sally Merry* (2021 forthcoming).

[62] Harari (n 5) 215.

22.5 Conclusions: Avoiding the Meteorite

In this chapter, I have argued that, while human rights are not in a state of crisis, they are undergoing a moment of transition that raises systemic challenges for the movement. Some challenges come from outside the field, such as technological disruption, populist authoritarianism, the climate crisis, rising inequality, and the end of the Euro-American order. Some others are intrinsic to the architecture and the modus operandi of the traditional paradigm of human rights advocacy, such as strategic stagnation, fragmentation, and competition, insufficient long-term vision, unmanaged complexity, and narrow membership and audiences.

I have argued that, although those challenges create an existential risk for the movement— they are indeed the meteorite in the firmament—, they do not necessarily spell the end of the human rights project. To avoid the collision, however, business as usual will not do. The traditional paradigm of human rights is plainly inadequate to deal with the simultaneity, the speed, and the depth of those challenges.

In order to contribute to a new paradigm of human rights for the next decade, I proposed ways out of the current impasse that draw on lessons from other fields, from journalism to public health to human-centred design, as well as from disciplines that human rights actors have yet to incorporate into their toolkit, from social psychology to geology to social innovation. My aim has been to flesh out an intermediate approach between despair and defensiveness, one that vindicates the rich history and continued value of the human rights project, while searching for and experimenting with new ideas and initiatives capable of disrupting the field's dysfunctionalities and finding solutions to its urgent problems.

To that end, I have suggested that we view the human rights field as an ecosystem, rather than as a hierarchy. In an increasingly complex and interdependent world, human rights strategies need to be informed by biology as much as by law and politics. They need to be more focused on symbiosis and much less on policing the current boundaries of human rights.

I proposed three types of disruptive interventions that could build up a human rights ecosystem: a more collaborative mode of operation, greater sense of time (both long term and short term), and heightened attention to narratives, emotions, and frames capable of connecting with larger constituencies and other social justice movements.

Constructing a human rights ecosystem is easier said than done. For international NGOs, this implies a difficult challenge: transitioning from the vertical and highly autonomous modus operandi that has allowed them to make key contributions, to a more horizontal model that would allow them to work with networks of diverse actors.[63] For domestic organizations, this entails pursuing strategies that allow such organizations to connect to one another and using new leverage points created by increased geopolitical multipolarity, as well as opening up to non-legal professionals, social movements, and online activists. For all actors in the field, this shift implies embracing an experimental approach based on a greater willingness to try new strategies, expand the repertoire of tactics, cultivate new organizational forms and funding models, and develop capabilities for and openness to learning and adjusting to rapidly changing circumstances.

[63] For a thoughtful discussion of this dilemma by a regional leader of Amnesty International, see Sarah Jackson, 'Toward Transformative Solidarity: Reflections from Amnesty International's Global Transition Program' (2020) 34 Emory International Law Review 705.

But we have no option if we are to avoid the fate of the dinosaurs, as Philip Alston probably would have quipped had he been present in that workshop on the future of human rights that I referenced in the introduction to this chapter. Characteristically, he would have said so with a stern face that insinuated an ironic smile. His humour would have invited us not to take ourselves too seriously, and thus to remain open to change. His seriousness would have reminded us that the future of human rights, perhaps even the future of the planet, hangs in the balance.

23
Praxis and the Critical International Human Rights Law Scholar

Obiora Chinedu Okafor

23.1 Introduction

The remarkably imaginative organizers of a 2016 academic conference held in Cairo, Egypt* focused the considerable energies of its participants on the broad thematic of 'praxis and the intellectual' or if you like, 'the role of the intellectual in the political and/or socio-economic struggles which go on beyond the academe'.[1] This is a thematic that some critical international law scholars,[2] for example, BS Chimni,[3] have for a long time identified as deserving of far more attention than it has received from similarly minded and oriented colleagues. Yet, to this day, the relationships among critical international human rights scholars (on the one hand) and politicians, diplomats, activists, civil servants, peasant movements, civil society, and so on (on the other hand) can still be said to be as important as they have been under-studied and under-enacted.[4]

Against this background, it is commendable that at least two of the sub-themes of this edited collection in Phillip Alston's honour, namely 'the activist struggle for human rights' and 'debates on the history, theory and politics of human rights', appear to call on us, as keen students of the discipline of international human rights law, to ponder and analyse the role(s) of the international human rights scholar in the kinds of praxis that go on beyond the boundaries of the academe; something that would help the gap just identified. In line with these two praxis-related sub-themes, this chapter will critically reflect on the role of the

* This chapter is adapted from my article 'Praxis and the International (Human Rights) Law Scholar: Toward the Intensification of TWAILian Dramaturgy', *Windsor Yearbook of Access to Justice 33*, 1–35, doi: http://dx.doi.org/10.2139/ssrn.3058117 © 2016, Obiora Chinedu Okafor.

I am grateful to Basema Al-Alawi, Okechukwu Effoduh, Serwaah Frimpong, John Mastrangelo, Olohirere Musa, and William Onyeaju, who are past or present students at the Osgoode Hall Law School, for their excellent research assistance in the preparation of this chapter. I should also especially thank Jeff Noonan, Sujith Xavier, Usha Natarajan, John Reynolds, and Hani Sayed for their comments and suggestions on the earlier version of the chapter.

[1] The organizers of that conference raised some of these questions in their 2014 'Call for Papers and Panel Proposals' (on file with the author); Amar Bhatia and others (eds), *Third World Approaches to International Law: On Praxis and the Intellectual* (Routledge 2017) 1.

[2] For a general sense of many of the key ideas defended by critical international human rights scholars, and thus of 'who they are', see Makau Mutua, *Human Rights: A Political and Cultural Critique* (University of Pennsylvania 2002); L Amede Obiora, 'Bridges and Barricades: Rethinking Polemics and Intransigence in the Campaign against Female Circumcision' (1997) 47 Case Western Reserve Journal of International Law 275; Shadrack Gutto, *Human and Peoples' Rights for the Oppressed* (Lund University Press 1993).

[3] Bhupinder Chimni, 'Third World Approaches to International Law: A Manifesto' in Antony Anghie and Bhupinder Chimni (eds), *The Third World and International Order: Law, Politics, and Globalization* (Martinus Nijhoff 2003) 48.

[4] The organizers raised some of these questions in the 'Call for Papers and Panel Proposals' (n 1); Bhatia and others (n 2).

Obiora Chinedu Okafor, *Praxis and the Critical International Human Rights Law Scholar* In: *The Struggle for Human Rights*. Edited by: Nehal Bhuta, Florian Hoffmann, Sarah Knuckey, Frédéric Mégret, and Margaret Satterthwaite, Oxford University Press. © Obiora Chinedu Okafor 2016. DOI: 10.1093/oso/9780198868064.003.0024

critical international human rights law scholar in the socio-economic and political struggles which take place outside the academe; focusing, for the most part, on our role as scholars in advancing struggles in favour of subaltern peoples from within or in concert with international institutions.

As such, the chapter is organized into seven segments, this introduction included. Section 23.2 examines the ideas and conceptions of praxis, to be clear from the outset as to the sense in which that key term is used in this chapter. The question of the ends or goals for which we do praxis is also discussed there. Section 23.3 focuses on a relatively brief analysis of some of the experiences that I have had as a critical international human rights law scholar who has also been closely engaged in some way with international institutions. Section 23.4 is devoted to a reflection on the promise of such close engagement, while section 23.5 focuses on the perils of engaging in this kind of praxis. Thereafter, the chapter ends in section 23.6 with some concluding remarks.

Before commencing the analytical exercise outlined, it must be intimated that it is a great honour and privilege to be able to offer the thoughts contained in this chapter in honour of Phillip Alston, whose 'vast contribution to the field of international human rights law'[5] and in particular whose highly insightful and impactful international human rights law praxis[6] is as impressive as it has been under-studied by fellow academics. Accordingly, the organizers of the conference that, in the more immediate, sired this edited collection must be commended for their insight and grit in putting it all together.

23.2 The Ideas and Conceptions of Praxis

As Mosco and a number of other scholars (such as Upendra Baxi) have noted, praxis is an idea with deep roots in the history of philosophy and one that has found several paths to social, political, and other studies, including through Marxian theory, the Frankfurt School of critical thought, and the 'action-research' tradition best embodied in sociology, and anticolonial scholarship.[7] Originating in the ancient Greek, it achieved some prominence in the work of Aristotle (who saw the goal of praxis as action).[8] Thereafter, it came to occupy a central place in the works of philosophers such as Hegel (who both separated and united praxis and theory), Kant (who saw full reason as the product of the unification of practical reason and theory), and Marx (who always insisted that philosophy be made practical).[9] Much later on, scholars of the Frankfurt School, especially Jurgen Habermas, treated the concept of social praxis as constituted by both work (ie purposive rational action) and communicative action (interaction).[10] And so there are more or less multiple and differing conceptions of praxis in the relevant literature sets.

[5] For example, Philip Alston and Ryan Goodman, *International Human Rights: Text and Materials* (OUP 2012); Philip Alston, 'Against a World Court for Human Rights' (2014) 28 Ethics & International Affairs 197; Philip Alston and Colin Gillespie, 'Global Human Rights Monitoring, New Technologies, and the Politics of Information' (2012) 23 European Journal of International Law 1089.

[6] For example, UNHRC 'Report of the Special Rapporteur on Extreme Poverty and Human Rights' (8 May 2018) UN Doc A/HRC/38/33.

[7] Vincent Mosco, *The Political Economy of Communication* (2nd edn, Sage 2009); Upendra Baxi, *The Future of Human Rights* (2nd edn, OUP 2006).

[8] Mosco (n 7).

[9] ibid 34–35.

[10] ibid 35; Jürgen Habermas and Thomas A McCarthy, *Legitimation Crisis* (Beacon Press 1975).

However, most of the contemporary usages of the term praxis embed deeply within them some notion of the inherent unity of thought and action, and of the 'inseparability of theory and practice'[11]—or at least of the critical desirability of such a unity and inseparability.[12] This is certainly the case with almost all Marxian and neo-Marxian approaches. Exemplifying this tradition, Claire Cutler pithily reminds us that 'the philosophy of praxis postulates the immanent unity of material and ideational conditions in a historical process of becoming'.[13] And Herbert Marcuse teaches us that to engage in praxis 'is not to thread on alien ground, external to the theory, for the theory itself is already a practical one; praxis does not only come at the end, but is already present in the beginning of the theory'.[14] In the same vein, Mosco has correctly noted that:

> Praxis guides a theory of knowledge to view knowing as the ongoing product of theory and practice. It rejects as partial those epistemologies which conclude that truth [or to put it more carefully, knowledge] can only result from contemplation. Rather it grows out of *the mutual constitution of conception and execution.*[15]

It is in this last sense of the mutual constitution of conception and execution, of the unity (or unification) of theory-imbued action and action-imbued theory, that the concept of praxis is used in this chapter. Some have even explained this concept as 'thoughtful doing'.[16]

Yet, whatever the sense in which the term praxis is understood and used, the critical question remains, praxis for what, and to what end? The relevant literature sets are heavily populated by left-leaning answers to this question. For example, Furman views praxis as involving the continual, dynamic interaction among knowledge acquisition, deep reflection, and action with the purpose of transformation and liberation in the service of social justice.[17] And Claire Cutler argues that the philosophy of praxis directs attention to identifying and transforming the social forces that give rise to laws that create and sustain a world characterized by increasing inequalities.[18] While critical international human rights law scholars will, of course, tend to identify with these progressive visions of the goals to which our own praxis ought to be directed, it is important to point out that the insights of scholars such as Antonio Gramsci and Upendra Baxi would suggest that praxis, on its own, and without more, might not be necessarily directed at attaining social justice ends. In this connection, Gramsci's famous warning about the dangers that can be posed by some organic intellectuals who are schooled in both theory and practice leaps quickly to mind.[19] And Baxi's mild anxiety about the critical difference between a politics *of* human rights and a politics *for* human rights is highly instructive.[20] For, if our praxis (as critical international human rights law scholars)

[11] Emmanuelle Jouannet, 'Koskenniemi: A Critical Introduction' in Martti Koskenniemi (ed), *The Politics of International Law* (Hart 2011) 3.

[12] Rebekah L Fox and Joshua J Frye, 'Tensions of Praxis: A New Taxonomy for Social Movements' (2010) 4 Environmental Communication 422; Stephen Kemmis, 'Research for Praxis: Knowing Doing' (2010) 18 Pedagogy, Culture & Society 9; Gail Furman, 'Social Justice Leadership as Praxis: Developing Capacities Through Preparation Programs' (2012) 48 Educational Administration Quarterly 191.

[13] Claire Cutler, 'Toward a Radical Political Economy Critique of Transnational Economic Law' in Susan Marks (ed), *International Law on the Left: Re-Examining Marxist Legacies* (CUP 2008) 216.

[14] ibid 219; Herbert Marcuse, *Studies in Critical Philosophy* (NLB 1972) 5..

[15] Mosco (n 7) 35 (emphasis added).

[16] Martha J Dede, 'The Praxis Journal: Integrating Theory and Practice' (2002) 8 Journal of Public Affairs Education 287.

[17] Furman (n 12).

[18] Cutler (n 13).

[19] Mosco (n 7) 36.

[20] Baxi (n 7) 83.

merely furthers the politics of human rights without the desired ideological moorings and underpinnings, how useful would it be from our perspective, and what would be the point, really?

And so, against this background, how should we think about critical international human rights law praxis? How might we enact such a critical praxis in pursuit of the kinds of global social justice goals that many of us desire and most of humanity definitely needs? I will begin my consideration of this question by reflecting in some depth (and within the bounds allowed by space) on my own experience of engaging in this kind of praxis within one international human rights body. I must note here that this exercise does not focus at all on my current praxis and service as the UN Independent Expert on Human Rights and International Solidarity.[21]

23.3 A Critical International Human Rights Law Scholar Partially Embeds at the United Nations

In 2011, I was elected by the UN HRC to membership in the UN Human Rights Council Advisory Committee (HRCAC).[22] The HRCAC is the principal subsidiary body of the Council and serves as its think tank. A year later, I was elected its vice-chairperson/rapporteur. I was re-elected to this body in 2014. Soon thereafter, I was elected and served as its chairperson. This body consists of eighteen human rights experts (mostly academics, but also a few judges, former diplomats, and practitioners).[23] In seeking election to the HRCAC, I had a reasonably well-developed sense of purpose. I saw my possible election to, and service on, that body as an opportunity to, as much as possible, enact a form of critical international human rights law praxis in that non-academic environment and within the bowels of relative power. I was aware of and inspired by the ideational and other kinds of impact that some other critical internationalists who had gone before me had made in the predecessor body to the committee I was asking to be elected to. That now defunct predecessor body was known as the UN Sub-Commission on the Promotion and Protection of Human Rights.[24] The widely disseminated and highly influential report written for that Sub-Commission by two of its former members, Joe Oloka-Onyango and Deepika Udagama, readily comes to mind.[25]

Nevertheless, I was also aware that the body that I was going to sit on was significantly weaker than its predecessor; and that it had been deliberately weakened (for different reasons in each case) by a previously unlikely grand coalition of Western and Global South states. For example, unlike its more powerful predecessor, the HRCAC cannot pass even a

[21] OHCHR, 'Independent Expert on Human Rights and International Solidarity' (*United Nations Human Rights Office of the High Commissioner*) <https://www.ohchr.org/en/issues/solidarity/pages/iesolidarityindex.aspx> accessed 7 November 2020.

[22] For more on this body, seeOHCHR, 'Advisory Committee' (*United Nations Human Rights Council*) <https://www.ohchr.org/EN/HRBodies/HRC/AdvisoryCommittee/Pages/HRCACIndex.aspx> accessed 7 November 2020.

[23] ibid.

[24] OHCHR, 'Sub-Commission on the Promotion and Protection of Human Rights' (*United Nations Human Rights Council*) <https://www.ohchr.org/EN/HRBodies/SC/Pages/SubCommission.aspx> accessed 7 November 2020.

[25] ECOSOC, 'The Realization of Economic, Social and Cultural Rights: Globalization and its Impact on the Full Enjoyment of Human Rights—Preliminary Report submitted by J Oloka-Onyango and Deepika Udagama, in accordance with Sub-Commission Resolution 1999/8)' (15 June 2000) UN Doc E/CN.4/Sub.2/2000/13, 13 <http://www1.umn.edu/humanrts/demo/Globalization_Oloka-Onyango,Udagama.pdf>.

mere resolution.[26] The HRCAC can only pass and make recommendations to the diplomats in the HRC who in turn ultimately report to politicians in their capitals.[27] And more importantly, while it can discuss any matter it wants to consider, the HRCAC cannot write a report on that matter, or make any recommendations in relation to it to the HRC, unless and until it is so authorized by the Council.[28] Against this background, I was and remain well aware of the fact that the opportunities for deploying my position on this body to make an appreciable critical/progressive impact on international human rights law and praxis were significantly circumscribed and necessarily limited. Even more significantly, I was certainly not naive as to the embedded and other limits of even the entire UN system (of which my own committee was only a small part), and of the formal texts we prepared and disseminated, in affecting the trajectory, orientation, and substance of international human rights law and action, what more the real politic of international relations and domestic behaviour. Such institutions and texts are after all almost always either relatively weak in the knees in the face of robust power,[29] or 'just words', which then require social mobilization and action to come alive![30]

Yet, I was also as aware—or at least I imagined—that there are always worthwhile spaces and opportunities to occupy and utilize within such institutions; spaces that would sometimes allow one to have significant effect on the debates and recommendations of the HRCAC itself and of more powerful organs within the United Nations (such as the HRC, the General Assembly, and even the Security Council). I was also aware that if one is insightful, creative, and effective enough, such spaces can be harnessed to yield even more significant dividend. After all, there were many states and other actors at the United Nations that, at least on a case-by-case basis, seemed to care for and push in favour of the kinds of issues I cared for and wanted to work in favour of as a critical international human rights law scholar. At the very least, I knew that my taking a seat as part of the African group on that body will have a valuable displacement effect on the large group of less critically minded professors, judges, and lawyers who tend to dominate the African international law scene. My taking a seat on the HRCAC meant one less such voice on that body. I also intended my membership of that body to have a kind of emplacement effect, in the sense that my presence on the HRCAC would—likely for the very first time—place my kind of critical international human rights law scholar firmly within the inner sanctums of that living organism and its habitat and allow our types of ideas and concerns to better percolate into that body and flow more fluidly in its veins. I saw myself as an agent for the infusion of as many critical international human rights law ideas as possible into the HRCAC, and through that body to the HRC, and beyond.

I soon came to realize that to be as effective as possible in achieving this goal I had to be clear enough from the outset as to what critical international human rights law praxis would require of me in this particular international institutional context, and in each scene of the many dramas that would continually unfold within it. I also had to ensure that my interventions were as technically competent and rigorous as possible (in order to keep the attention and even respect of one's colleagues, many of whom are among the brightest in the international law world). In this particular 'think thank' setting, the more rigorous and sounder

[26] UNHRC, 'Institution-building of the United Nations Human Rights Council' (18 June 2007) UN Doc A/HRC/RES5/1 paras 65–84.

[27] ibid.

[28] ibid.

[29] Obiora Okafor, 'Attainments, Eclipses and Disciplinary Renewal in International Human Rights Law: A Critical Overview' in James D Armstrong (ed), *Routledge Handbook of International Law* (1st paperback edn, Routledge 2011) 310–14.

[30] Joel Bakan, *Just Words: Constitutional Rights and Social Wrongs* (University of Toronto Press 1997) <https://www.degruyter.com/view/title/519460> accessed 9 November 2020.

one's contributions are, the more one's colleagues will respect them, and the greater one's chance of successfully infusing any ideas (critical or otherwise) into the body's deliberations and decisions. As importantly, I also realized that even the requisite technical international legal and policy-oriented competence, were on their own, hardly enough in this institutional and highly political environment. These were only the minimum one needed to possess to become effective. One also had to nimbly deploy diplomatic skills to get things done. And so my 'mission strategy' had both a substantive and stylistic component to it, and indeed, it had to.

To what extent did this mission strategy work over the six-year period I served on this particular UN body? To what degree were my goals for this iteration of my critical international human rights law praxis realized? And were these goals even realizable to begin with? Was I just a naive institutionalist and/or starry-eyed optimist? In the rest of this section, I will attempt to reflect briefly on this question in the context of the work that the HRCAC did during my time on it. First, let me point out that although all members have to, in the end, participate in the work of the HRCAC on each and every of the mandates given to that body by the HRC while he or she sits on that committee, a member tends to be more significantly involved in the discharge of the particular mandates in respect of which they are a member of the sub-group of the HRCAC constituted to take primary charge of that file. These are referred to as drafting groups. I should also note that such involvement ratchets up considerably if that member is elected the rapporteur (ie chief researcher/writer) of the relevant drafting group.

Secondly, it is important to note at the outset that of the fifteen or so mandates the HRCAC dealt with to a significant extent while I held a seat on that body,[31] I served on the drafting groups that primarily researched and prepared the reports of the HRCAC relating to at least nine.[32] Importantly, I served as the rapporteur of the drafting group on the practical ways and means of international cooperation in the field of human rights, drafted a significant portion of the report of the drafting group on human rights and unilateral coercive measures, and served as the chair of the drafting group on technical cooperation for the prevention of attacks against persons with albinism. I also served as the co-rapporteur of a report on the negative impact of illicit financial flows on the enjoyment of human rights. Thus, I had the greatest opportunity to shape the work and recommendations of the relevant drafting groups, and the HRCAC, in relation to the mandates on 'international cooperation' and 'illicit financial flows', in respect of which I served as the rapporteur or co-rapporteur, and prepared or co-prepared draft reports that were adopted by the entire HRCAC and forwarded to the HRC, where they were generally well received.[33]

[31] These are those on: human rights and international solidarity; enhancing international cooperation in the field of human rights; right to peace; promoting human rights and fundamental freedoms through a better understanding of the traditional values of human kind; human rights and issues related to terrorist hostage-taking; practical ways and means of enhancing international cooperation in the field of human rights; the negative impact of corruption on the enjoyment of all human rights; technical cooperation for the prevention of attacks against persons with albinism; human rights and unilateral coercive measures; local government and human rights; promoting human rights through sport and the Olympic ideal; and the protection of human rights in post-disaster/post-conflict situations. For detailed information on these mandates and the work/reports of the HRCAC on them, see OHCHR 'Advisory Council' (n 22).

[32] These are those concerning: international cooperation; right to peace; traditional values; terrorist hostage-taking; practical ways and means of international cooperation; the negative impact of corruption on the enjoyment of all human rights; albinism; and unilateral coercive measures. For detailed information on these mandates and the work/reports of the HRCAC on them, see ibid.

[33] UNHRC 'Preliminary Study on Enhancement of International Cooperation' (19 February 2014) UN Doc A/HRC/AC/12/CRP.2 (2014); UNHRC 'Draft Progress Report on the Research-based Study on the Impact of Flow of Funds of Illicit Origin and the Non-Repatriation Hereof to the Countries of Origin on the Enjoyment of Human Rights' (20–24 February 2017) UN Doc A/HRC/AC/18/CRP.3.

Due to space constraints, in the rest of this section, the details of my attempts to enact a critical international human rights praxis within the 'belly' of this UN body are illustrated by reference to two examples: one case in which I served as the rapporteur of the HRCAC's report, another case in which—though I did not serve in that leading role—I still had a more than averagely significant role in the preparation of the report.

23.3.1 Enacting Critical Praxis in Relation to the Mandate on 'International Cooperation'

With regard to the mandate of the HRCAC to prepare a study and offer research-based advise to the HRC on the practical ways and means of enhancing international cooperation in the field of human rights, I utilized the opportunity of my election as rapporteur of the drafting group of the HRCAC on this topic to ensure that the substance and tone of the report reflected as much as possible my critical international human rights law (especially Third World Approaches to International Law–TWAIL) orientation. Among other things, I and like-minded colleagues worked hard to ensure that the report highlighted the problematic ways in which international human rights discourse tended to function as a monologue rather than a real dialogue, and the need for it to become much more of a two-way traffic than it has hitherto been.[34] Along these lines, the report warned that 'the constructive dialogue that drives and reflects meaningful international cooperation is far less likely to occur unless it is based on the idea that human rights knowledge ought to circulate in a multi-directional way among the world's peoples'.[35] This aspect of the report thus spoke to the fact that the marginalization of third world voices has been a recurring decimal in critical international human rights (especially TWAIL) work. Secondly, in line with an earlier report on the subject, this report also highlighted the negative impact on international human rights cooperation of the selectivity that results from the 'logic of power'.[36] This is clearly a critical (and pro-TWAIL) thing to do. Thirdly, while urging the HRC to make greater effort to deepen civil society involvement in its work, the report pushed at the same time for the de-marginalization of third world social movements and NGOs and the de-centring of the Western NGOs who tend to dominate civil society space at the Council (including through the greater utilization of technology to bridge the physical and resource distance of these third world groups from the Geneva location of the Council's deliberations).[37] Clearly, this was also a critical international human rights law move. Fourthly, the report advised the HRC to show strong support for the ongoing push within sections of the United Nations to find ways of enhancing the effort to realize the right to development by holding development actors accountable while moving away as much as possible from the current 'charitable giving' framework of international development.[38] Again, this aspect of the report resonated with many critical scholars in the area; for despite some concerns for the particular ways in which it has been deployed by some states, the enhancement of the right to development is of course a long-standing critical TWAIL concern. Fifthly, in discussing the ways and means of augmenting the resources available to be deployed toward the enhancement of international

[34] ibid paras 5, 20–21.
[35] ibid paras 5, 20–21.
[36] ibid paras 5, 20–21.
[37] ibid paras 6–8.
[38] ibid paras 10–13.

human rights cooperation, the report highlighted the agency and capacity that already exists in the third world and the need to focus more on, utilize much more, and support far more robustly, such existing agency and capacity (eg through enhanced South–South cooperation). In particular the report highlighted the example of Nigeria's decades-old, but largely unacknowledged and unsung, Technical Aids Corps Scheme through which that country shares its massive human capital with other third world countries and peoples.[39] It was, in part, in these kinds of ways that the report *independently* provided technical legal and other justification, further voice, and a measure of legitimization to the concerns already expressed by many delegations in the Council (an added resource in their hands).[40] In this way did it also contribute to the process of the ongoing congealing of some of the positions that are justified by it. The adoption of the report by a very strong majority in the HRC is indicative of the strength and value of this ideational/practical contribution. All these pro-TWAIL, and thus critical, moves would not have of course been possible without the strong support of my colleagues on the HRCAC (including those that may not necessarily view themselves as critical scholars/practitioners) who were persuaded to unanimously adopt the report—albeit with minor modifications.

23.3.2 Enacting Critical Praxis in Relation to the Mandate on Unilateral Coercive Measures

Similarly, the mandate conferred on the HRCAC by the HRC to provide it with a research-based report and advise on the negative impact of unilateral coercive measures (UCMs) on the enjoyment of human rights and on mechanisms to assess such impact and promote accountability, provided another great opportunity to, at the very least, heighten the circulation and role of critical international human rights (especially TWAIL) thought, ideas, and strategies within both the HRCAC and the Council.[41] While I was not the rapporteur of this report, I served on its drafting group and worked closely with the rapporteur of the report—consulting with him frequently and in detail on all aspects of the report. I researched and provided him with a huge bibliography on the subject as well as a detailed summary of the contents of each bibliographic entry. In accordance with the agreed division of labour on the drafting group, I also wrote a key section of the draft report on the technical international legal and policy justifications for choosing one kind or set of mechanisms for assessing the impact of UCMs over the other.[42] And this portion of the report was adopted alongside other sections of the report by the drafting group, and later on by the entire HRCAC.[43] I also pre-presented this section of the report at a seminar on the same topic that was organized by the

[39] ibid paras 14–19.
[40] Martti Koskienniemi, 'The Place of Law in Collective Security' (1996) 17 Michigan Journal of International Law 455, at 478 (arguing that 'law's contribution . . . is not in the substantive responses it gives but in the process of justification that it imports into international policy and its assumption of responsibility for the policies chosen').
[41] For example, UNHRC 'Report of the Advisory Committee on its thirteenth session' (19 August 2014) UN Doc A/HRC/AC/13/2, 6.
[42] UNHRC 'Research-based Progress Report of the Human Rights Council Advisory Committee Containing Recommendations on Mechanisms to Assess the Negative Impact of Unilateral Coercive Measures on the Enjoyment of Human Rights and to Promote Accountability' (10 February 2015) UN Doc A/HRC/28/74 paras 43–58.
[43] UN Doc A/HRC/AC/13/2 (n 41) 6.

OHCHR.[44] In both cases, I made a strong technical international legal and policy argument for the appointment of a special rapporteur on the all-too-often negative impact of UCMs on the enjoyment of human rights; something that disproportionately and much more profoundly affects the lives of the nationals of the weaker third world states. Thus, the report, the section of it that I drafted, and my presentation at the OHCHR seminar,[45] provided what were seen by many as strong justification for the HRCAC and the HRC to act in the ways they eventually did. The HRCAC adopted the report with relatively minor modification.[46] For its own part, the HRC took the remarkable step of not waiting for the report itself to be formally submitted before acting on the HRCAC's eventual recommendation that it should appoint a special rapporteur on UCMs. The Council acted simply on the strength of the report of the proceedings of the OHCHR seminar at which I presented my ideas and policy advice. One can only surmise from these facts that the paper I presented at that seminar calling for precisely this step to be taken, played some justificatory role in the reaching of this decision. Lastly, regarding the HRCAC's report itself, my colleagues and I have been successful in making sure that it strongly recognizes the ways in which UCMs can and do undermine, at times quite profoundly, the basic human rights of targeted peoples, who are almost always third world peoples. To be clear, the reason I worked very hard to persuade my colleagues and the HRC that a special rapporteur on UCMs should be appointed was not because I felt that this act would somehow solve the problem of the negative impact of UCMs on the enjoyment of human rights by third world peoples. Rather, I worked hard toward this goal in order to expand the repertoire of resources available in the hands of a 'coalition of the willing' (states, activists, HRCAC members, etc) to struggle against this ill. A special rapporteur, such as the one charged with studying and acting on the UCMs issue, can only be a resource and is simply not a panacea.

On the whole, regarding this critical international human rights scholar's (admittedly partial) embedment within this one UN body in the goal of enacting a critical (especially TWAIL) praxis within that environment—it is fair to conclude that while no earth-shaking attainments have been realized, or could even have been reached, as a result of this particular set of manoeuvres, some modest but significant impact has nevertheless been made as a result, albeit within the narrow confines of the work of the HRCAC and the HRC. The ideational and practical orientation of those bodies has been affected to some extent by my sustained attempts, in close and necessary alliance with willing colleagues, to enact as effectively as is possible a form of critical praxis. As the ways of large organizations such as the UN are generally as slow as the tortoise crawls, it is as yet too early to fully assess the impact of this attempt to enact a critical international human rights law praxis. Yet, I am convinced that the HRCAC and the Council have profited in significant, if modest, measure from the enhanced circulation of critical ideas/justifications that I and others on the HRCAC have sometimes authored and disseminated. I am also convinced that even these modest successes would not have been possible, or would not have been as appreciable, without the deployed cocktail of rigorous technical international legal and policy argument, diplomatic

[44] Obiora Chinedu Okafor, 'Reflections on the Choice of Mechanism(s) for Assessing and/or Mitigating the Adverse Effects of Unilateral Coercive Measures on the Enjoyment of Human Rights' (Workshop on the adverse effects of unilateral coercive measures of the enjoyment of human rights, UN Office Geneva, May 2014).

[45] UNHRC, 'Proceedings of the Workshop on the Impact of the Application of Unilateral Coercive Measures on the Enjoyment of Human Rights by the Affected Populations, in particular their Socioeconomic Impact on Women and Children, in the States Targeted—Report of the Office of the United Nations High Commissioner for Human Rights' (10 July 2014) UN Doc A/HRC/27/32 paras 17–22.

[46] UN Doc A/HRC/AC/13/2 (n 41) 6.

manoeuvres, and critical knowledge/clarity/commitment that my like-minded colleagues and I brought to bear on our work within the HRCAC. It was also helpful that I was able to move as near-seamlessly and contemporaneously as I did between my job as a scholar/teacher and my more implementation-oriented and more practitioner-like role on the HRCAC. For, it is within the academe that one has the most space/time to think, dream, and hone ideas about our world.

23.4 The Promise of Close Engagement with International Institutions

23.4.1 The Strategic/Tactical Promise

A very important strategic/tactical promise of our close engagement with international institutions[47] and on-the-ground groups is that it will allow us a significantly better chance of bridging—as best we can—the 'two worlds'[48] in which critical international human rights law scholars (on the one hand) and diplomats, international/domestic civil servants, politicians, and activists (on the other hand) tend to inhabit. This divide appears to be mostly physical, but it is also a mental one, at least in the sense that very few of even those diplomats, international civil servants, activists, and so on who are in my experience anxious for, or would benefit from, our insights appear to even know about our ideas.[49] Bridging the divides that separate us from these actors will allow our ideas to flow more easily and robustly into the deepest recesses of the bodies and groups that we must influence much more in order to optimize our capacity to help effect the kinds of global/local social change we desire. If this kind of optimization is to be realized, critical international human rights law thinking and action needs to unite more fully with diplomatic/official action and thought. Nothing less than a partial bridging of habitats and mentalities is called for here.

Secondly, just as a partial embrace of diplomats/officials (ie of praxis beyond the academe) will help critical international human rights law scholars to more rapidly and robustly drive toward its end goals, our own intellectual skills and approaches will in the result enrich and help improve the very institutional praxis that we would have engaged. This point is so well acknowledged in the literature that it need not detain us here. Suffice it to state that intellectuals like us achieve this kind of enhancement effect by filling knowledge gaps within the relevant institutions, providing a more reflexive approach to their work, helping frame and name abuses, re-shaping existing movements, and even spurring new ones.[50]

[47] The phrase 'strategic/tactical' is used in this chapter so as to indicate the fact that some of the promises and perils discussed under that rubric are strategic (in the 'long term' and/or the 'structural' senses in which this term is used by Robert Knox) or tactical (in the sense in which the same author uses them) or both. As such, a detailed discussion of the distinctions between those two terms and the ways in which they have been used or abused in the scholarly literature are not warranted here. Robert Knox, 'Strategy and Tactics' in *Finnish Yearbook of International Law. Volume 21, 2010* (2013) 193.

[48] This idea is adapted from Lucie White's work on the two worlds in which women's lawyers and economic development bureaucrats appear to live in the Ghanaian context. Lucie White, 'Two Worlds of Ghanaian Cause Lawyers' in Austin Sarat and Stuart A Scheingold (eds), *Cause Lawyering and the State in a Global Era* (OUP 2001) 64.

[49] Saeid Mirzaei, 'Chair's Opening Remarks' (Annual CCIL Conference Panel, Ottawa, November 2013).

[50] For example, Steven Friedman, 'From Classroom to Class Struggle: Radical Academics and the Rebirth of Trade Unionism in the 1970s' (2014) 49 Journal of Asian and African Studies 526; Rachel Schurman and William Munro, 'Ideas, Thinkers, and Social Networks: The Process of Grievance Construction in the Anti-Genetic Engineering Movement' (2006) 1 Theory and Society 35; Obiora Okafor, *The African Human Rights System, Activist Forces and International Institutions* (2007).

Thirdly, becoming more embedded or engaging more closely with these diplomats/officials will afford the international (human rights) law scholar a greater chance of being able to generate, recognize, and seize the kind of teachable moments that can exert ideational and other influence on institutions and groups that often wield great political, social, and economic power in our world, and that tend to author or change policy/practice. Clearly, the ability to exert such influence will help improve our chances of more rapidly and robustly driving toward our own progressive goals. What could be more effective in this regard than us engaging as frequently as we can in 'pedagogies of the oppressed'[51] within the very bowels of institutional power, and having the very international high officials/diplomats/civil servants who control these bodies or groups learn to some extent from our work?

Fourthly, there is a sense in which enacting a form of critical international human rights law praxis beyond the academe by participating closely in the work of international institutions can result in our helping give birth to aspects of international human rights law itself. As Baxi teaches us, 'human rights values, standards, and norms are created by people's praxes of resistance and struggle'.[52] In the same vein, he has also correctly noted that 'the real birthplaces of human rights are far removed from the ornate norms of diplomatic conferences and are found, rather, in the actual sites (acts and feats) of resistance and struggle'.[53] Baxi's point here is not as much to exclude and devalue the 'birthing' of human rights texts that occurs in international institutions (bodies that remain as state-centric as ever) as it is to make clear that the praxis of the on-the-ground groups also matter as much (or even much more) in the relevant norm-generating processes. And so, close engagement with the work of international institutions (such as the HRC and the HRCAC), within which NGOs and social movements often struggle and matter, literarily allows international (human rights) law intellectuals like us to participate more actively in the creation or refinement of international human rights values, standards, norms, processes, and so on. The main benefit to us here is the much greater chance of exerting our influence on the DNA and character of the human rights offspring of these processes. Our deep participation in such a politics can matter, and matter quite significantly. For if law (the very law that we focus on and often accuse of responsibility for the suffering and disadvantage of all too many subalterns) is in reality congealed or legitimized politics, then deep participation in the politics of the institutions in which the processes of the congealing or legitimization of human rights politics into human rights law are enacted can matter.[54] This kind of deep participation will not, of course, totally change the world overnight, but it does have some potential to help change it significantly in our own time.

Fifthly, in engaging even more closely in the relevant international institutional environments, we have a greater chance of breathing life into our own critiques of international law and order, animating them into (non-academic) political action, and making them do the very jobs we want them to do for the subaltern. Since ideas play an important role in driving both the domestic and international systems,[55] we can in this way significantly enhance the

[51] Paulo Freire, *Pedagogy of the Oppressed* (2007).

[52] Baxi (n 7) 94.

[53] ibid.

[54] Burns Weston, 'The Role of Law in Promoting Peace and Violence: A Matter of Definition, Social Values and Responsibility' in Myres S McDougal, W Michael Reisman, and Burns H Weston (eds), *Toward World Order and Human Dignity: Essays in Honor of Myres S. McDougal* (Free Press 1976) 117; Thomas M Franck and Mark M Munansangu, *The New International Economic Order* (UNITAR 1982) <http://digitallibrary.un.org/record/28169> accessed 7 November 2020.

[55] Ibironke Odumosu, 'Challenges for the (Present/) Future of Third World Approaches to International Law' (2008) 10(4) International Community Law Review 467, 470.

chances of seeing our ideas markedly affect the praxis of the relevant international institutions, and through them the 'world out there'. However, it must be noted that as not all international institutions are the same, some may be more effectively subjected to critical international human rights law praxis than others. This could be because of the structures of such institutions. For example, the IMF and World Bank's voting arrangements and structures make them more resistant to the influence of the countries in which the vast majority of the world's subaltern live, than say the UN HRC.

Lastly, such close engagement and the outlined strategic/tactical benefits that it can generate also hold the promise of helping sustain the critical international human rights law 'movement' into the future. For, as Kenneth Karst once warned, 'a movement, even an intellectual movement, needs some sense of—well, movement. Otherwise it dissolves'.[56] The achievement of such a sense of movement can, of course, result from reaching almost all of a movement's possible goals and not just from negative stasis. Yet, in both cases the lesson would be the same. In any case, as critical international human rights law scholars are, at least in my view, nowhere near the realization of their overarching goal of achieving a global order that is much more favourable to the subaltern, we would do well to chew continually on Karst's insight.

23.4.2 The Conceptual/Theoretical Promise

In my own view, our close engagement with international institutions holds at least two broad types of conceptual/theoretical promise: we will be enabled to see in bolder relief and we will gain or renew certain theoretical insights. Examples of the latter are offered.

First, such close engagement will allow us to see in much bolder relief, in a kind of 'high definition', the details and contours of the many dramas, politics, manoeuvres, strategies, tactics, technologies, and so on that go on or are deployed within the very non-academic habitats within which world order is largely constructed, rejigged, or affected in some way. This can lead to an increase not just in the quantity of observed phenomena but also in the quality of our appreciation of what we do observe. There is a real difference between looking at the backyard of a house from space and looking at it while sitting right there. Most of what a researcher with an electron microscope can readily observe and factor into her theories, her counterpart who does not use such an instrument cannot usually observe or factor in. In the latter case, the world would more likely seem to be much freer from the blessings or plagues of micro-organisms than it would appear to be in the former situation. The latter researcher is not so much wrong as she is simply unable to observe. But her theory would nevertheless be relatively deficient. The former researcher is not so much right as she has just been enabled to observe. But her theory would still be relatively stronger than her counterpart's. Close engagement can therefore become the electron microscope or high-definition lens with which we as critical international human rights law scholars can become introduced to the tiny micro-dramas and nuances that together constitute the making and unmaking of international law and global order, and how they hang together to produce or unsettle certain processes or outcomes. As such, such close engagement holds the promise of allowing us to gain better or otherwise unavailable insights, and better explain our world. Our theory will become enhanced in the result (through the resulting processes of exemplification,

[56] Kenneth Karst, 'Integration Success Story: A Review of Three Recent Books on Critical Race Theory' (1996) 69 Southern California Law Review 1781, 1792.

complication, renewal, modification, or even partial or wholesale rejection). This point is not in the least contradicted by the fact that, as there is no radical separation between 'object' and 'subject', we are part of the terrain that we observe. Since there is no conflation as well between the two, there is still some zone in between; something to be regarded and examined.

Therefore, the second, related, conceptual/theoretical promise of such close engagement with international institutions is the probable harvest of new or even better insights that can, as a result, be gained for our own intellectual work. The examples that will be given of such insights work together to illustrate this point:

(1) As many members of the critical TWAIL 'school' or TWAILers (who themselves are critical international lawyers) have noted, since international law and order has not mostly given up its work in favour of power, domination, and imperialism,[57] and domination from past empires does not present itself in the same forms today,[58] a crucial TWAIL task is to focus on and better map/understand the specific and exact ways through which global power, domination, and imperialism are constituted, renewed, and circulated today.[59] This includes a focus on how TWAIL's goals can still be achieved even in these contexts. These critical tasks cannot be discharged effectively without more close engagement with the habitats in which these phenomena are largely produced and projected.

(2) Close TWAIL engagement can also lead one to realize that there need not be any radical or even significant separation between working in the academe and toiling in the trenches beyond the academic realm. For me, such close engagement has led to the realization that my work at the UN (at the time as an expert member of the HRCAC) has in fact been a largely seamless extension of my academic praxis. There has not for me been any sharp break between the two realms. Like a beach at high and low tide, the two jobs I do are—for the most part—two forms of the same reality.[60] Both jobs involve research, writing, dissemination, and formal/informal pedagogy. As I see it, a large swathe of the jobs or tasks that we, as critical international human rights law scholars might want to perform within or in relation to international bodies would involve some combination of these tasks. This is not always the case of course, but that has been my own experience. For, when I put on my UN hat, I do not therefore simply transform into a mere technician in the workshop of power. And when I put on my academic hat, I do not simply retransform into some kind of a purified thinker who reflects completely aside and apart from 'the world out there'.

(3) Another conceptual/theoretical insight that close engagement with international institutions has offered me is the realization that the 'internal perspective' on these bodies/groups (a la Koskenniemi) is neither the only perspective that I have nor the only one that I should have. I also possess, and should definitely possess, an 'external viewpoint' on these bodies. Both perspectives should and do work hand-in-hand for optimal insight to become possible. Neither a 'strictly internal perspective' (ie a comprehension of the situatedness of the relevant diplomats/officials as participants rather than observers in these bodies) nor a 'strictly external' one (ie attempting

[57] Antony Anghie, 'The Evolution of International Law: Colonial and Postcolonial Realities' (2006) 27 Third World Quarterly 739, 751.

[58] Michael Fakhri, 'Law as the Interplay of Ideas, Institutions, and Interests: Using Polyani (and Foucault) to Ask TWAIL Questions' (2008) 10 International Community Law Review 455, 456–57.

[59] Chimni 'Third World Approaches' (n 3) 48; Odumosu (n 55) 470; Fakhri (n 58) 456–57.

[60] Koskenniemi (n 40) 465.

to comprehend these bodies entirely from the outside) can suffice to lead us to the promised land![61] As such, as ethnography teaches us, it is of course possible to act as a participant/observer. In any case, this last posture better describes my experience engaging the United Nations from within. It is also an accurate description (though to a lesser extent) of my experience with engaging on-the-ground groups. Yet, it should be said that praxis beyond the academic terrain allows us to take better account of the 'internal perspective' on such bodies/groups without necessarily adopting such a perspective in a wholesale or non-reflexive way.[62]

(4) Being on the inside of, or engaging closely with, the relevant institutions can also enhance our critical international human rights law theory (and action) by revealing the precise locations and characters of the pressure points on which we must press our fingers to have a greater chance of getting the relevant 'machines' to work toward enacting the kinds of socio-legal change we desire. It can thus help reveal the identities and locations of the chinks in the armours of power, domination, and imperialism, so to speak. For instance, Koskenniemi's reflections on his time as the legal adviser of the Finnish delegation to the UN Security Council has taught us that international (human rights) lawyers tend to have a better chance of impacting the debate and decisions in such bodies when non-routine issues emerge, and that we are likely to exert far less influence when the political framework is already stable.[63] The critical international human rights law agenda and programme can benefit much from the teasing out and incorporation of these kinds of insights. Regarding Koskenniemi's present insight, this may, for instance, mean that we should target a good measure of their non-academic praxis toward the bodies and groups with important norm-creation roles (such as the HRC, HRCAC, WTO Appellate Body, and even international courts). It could also equip us better to engage other kinds of bodies more effectively.

(5) A closely related point is that close engagement will also allow us to see, or see more clearly, the exact and precise nature of the various spaces that are available or unavailable for *resistance*. As Rajagopal has correctly noted, international (human rights) law has at the very least been as historically hegemonic as it has been emancipatory.[64] This is a very important point. For example, we should not ignore the ways in which a third world coalition—however shifting its character and modest its attainments—more or less wields significant power at the HRC and in the HRCAC. Thus, the 'encadrement' of the diplomats who work in the relevant delegations to the HRC, and a similar process of socializing those who serve on the HRCAC, will be quite important if we seek to resist human rights texts and moves that are biased against subaltern peoples, or disadvantage them in any other way. And, in my experience, many such diplomats are already quite amenable and are ripe for encadrement. There are many simple ways to do so. For example, more of them need to be invited and attracted to critical international human rights law conferences; and more of us need to engage with them and feed them the literature and ideas we produce. For there is a relatively significant space within the bowels of international institutional power in which 'the rampant dis-regard of the lived experiences of Third World [and other subaltern] peoples'

61 Koskenniemi (n 60) 475..
62 Ibid.
63 Koskenniemi (n 40) 471 .
64 Balakrishnan Rajagopal, 'Counter-Hegemonic International Law: Rethinking Human Rights and Development as a Third World Strategy' (2006) 27 Third World Quarterly 767, 769–75.

that many of us have written about has a very good chance of not being replicated.[65] Speaking personally, it was through close engagement (my embedment within the HRCAC) that I came to realize just how much this particular institutional space is open to the enactment of a kind of critical international human rights law 'spring'.

(6) As importantly, engaging closely enough with the relevant institutions can also afford us certain insights that can help refine, and therefore enhance, our theories and understandings of 'essentialism' and its critiques. Essentialism is, without doubt, generally problematic as a conceptual and methodological approach to knowledge or to seeing the world. For example, as Baxi teaches us, 'essentialist constructions of the universal "human" fail to acknowledge cultural diversity' and 'the hegemonic conceptions of human rights allow little or no play for radical plurality'.[66] This understanding is almost canonical in many genres of critical international human rights law scholarship (including TWAIL)! Yet, as many of us realize, some critiques of essentialism have at times gone too far. For instance, as Baxi has queried, 'what is there to subvert if identities are all fluid and the subject is no more?'[67] More particularly, as Baxi has noted, close engagement with the 'actual human rights struggles' that play out within international bodies should lead us to acquire, exemplify, or renew much more complicated and less doctrinaire understandings of the question of essentialism.[68]

(7) Lastly under his head, it should be noted that by ensuring the enactment of our dramas of close engagement in ways that pay significantly more attention to what Eslava and Pahuja refer to as the non-typical international legal places that might at first glance appear unrelated to the international, important critical international human rights law insights can also be gained.[69] Clearly, at a minimum, this kind of expanded praxis will in turn enlarge our vistas even further and allow us to see 'new' things in these other 'material sites [such as in domestic administrative procedures] in which international disciplines are at work'—things that would otherwise be largely screened off from our views.[70] The accruable insights about the ways in which international law and institutions operate on the quotidian plane would have great potential to enrich our critical international human rights law theories. This is the last example of the ways in which close engagement with the relevant bodies/groups can lead us to acquire important insights.

[65] Pooja Parmar, 'TWAIL: An Epistemological Inquiry' (2008) 10 International Community Law Review 363; Rajagopal (n 64) 767, 769–75.

[66] Baxi (n 7) 142.

[67] ibid 152–53.

[68] ibid 152.

[69] Luis Eslava and Sundhya Pahuja, 'Between Resistance and Reform: TWAIL and the Universality of International Law' (2011) 3 Trade Law and Development 104, 109.

[70] ibid.

23.5 The Perils of Close Engagement with International Institutions

23.5.1 Strategic/Tactical Perils

First, one of the greatest strategic/tactical dangers of our close engagement with international institutions is that we can become consciously or unconsciously implicated in the production of outcomes (intended or unintended) that further undermine the status and conditions of third world societies and peoples. Gramsci had long theorized the role of the so-called organic intellectual in social relations.[71] The Gramscian conception of the organic intellectual provides a model of the intellectual schooled in both the theoretical tools of analysis and in practical political struggle and resistance.[72] All too often, these intellectuals help 'manufacture consent' to the hegemony of the ruling/dominant classes, groups, peoples, or states in the relevant society (domestic or international).[73] Their efforts are too often central to 'the absorption and assimilation of subordinate groups', and have an important legitimization function and effect.[74] For instance, as Claire Cutler has argued:

> In the content of the GATS, a fundamental transformation in the conceptualization of services was required in order to legitimate their commodification. This was achieved by lawyers, government officials, corporate actors and journalists who, as part of an epistemic community, functioned as organic intellectuals.[75]

There is, of course, no inevitability to this. For, the organic intellectual need not always play this kind of anti-subaltern role. He or she can in fact play the exact opposite role within the relevant contexts. Yet, the insidious danger here is that the very act of a critical international human rights law scholar's close engagement and participation in the discussions and processes that led to even a slightly or mildly anti-subaltern outcome may serve to legitimize those processes in the eyes of the outside world. Those processes may as a result appear fairer than they actually tend to be on the whole. Though clearly not an example that is on all fours here, the ways in which the participation of third world states in hegemonic UN organs like the Security Council lends a measure of legitimacy to that body is indicative here.

A related danger of our close engagement with the relevant bodies and groups is that we can become habituated over time to seeking the apparent middle ground (howsoever regressively that middle is constructed) in order to reach consensus and just get something done. In some sense, any form of 'progress' achieved in the non-academic terrain of praxis can begin to look acceptable enough, however far it remains from our legitimate expectations of the 'end-game', and however much it continues to disadvantage and immiserate the vast majority of the world's peoples. I should note that seeking the middle ground to get things done is not necessarily and always a bad thing. However, the danger here is that close engagement with those international institutions in which seeking some constructed middle ground is the norm, can function to habituate us to that approach. Here, the term 'habituation' is used in the sense in which Pierre Bourdieu theorized his concept of habitus; that is,

[71] Antonio Gramsci, *Selections from the Prison Notebooks of Antonio Gramsci* (Quintin Hoare and Geoffrey Nowell-Smith eds, 1st edn, International Publishers 1971) 5; Cutler (n 13) 217; Mosco (n 7) 36.
[72] ibid.
[73] ibid.
[74] Cutler (n 13) 217.
[75] ibid.

as a 'system of [acquiring] dispositions (lasting, acquired schemes of perception, thought and action'.[76] This kind of habituation can affect our imagination and skew our vision of what can be achieved and what is possible within the relevant institutional environments. As the horizon of the possible then shrinks before our eyes, so shall we begin to unconsciously self-censor in seeking to enact some form of critical international human rights law praxis within these bodies. As Bourdieu put it, one of the dangers of habitus is 'learning to want what conditions make possible and [learning] not to aspire to what is not available'.[77] Thus, in seeking to enact a form of critical international human rights law praxis within these bodies, we need to be alert to the insidious dangers of its possible 'training and socialization' effect on us.[78]

The related strategic/tactical danger in becoming habituated to seeking the constructed and often inadequate middle ground while struggling to enact a critical international human rights law praxis within international institutions is that we risk becoming the type of mild reformists who fill up the space for critical dissent that Chimni (adapting David Kennedy's work) has long warned against.[79] While mild reforms are often all that can result from the hardest of our pushes against the entrenched and powerful forces that disadvantage the subaltern, this should never become our main strategic ambition or role.

Another danger that is faced by an international human rights law scholar who closely engages with international institutions is that he or she can more easily place themself in positions where they are forced much more frequently to take simple concrete policy positions on rather complicated issues. Suddenly, mere 'on the one hand' and 'on the other hand' kinds of analysis are no longer available to them. For instance, the scholar may be forced in human rights or other fora to vote/speak for or against the UN-sanctioned limited intervention in Ghadafi's Libya or intervention within other third world countries (such as against ISIS in Iraq and Syria). If, as an international (human rights) law intellectual, one votes in favour of such interventions, one almost always legitimizes the maintenance or augmentation of great power hegemony and domination. If one votes against these actions, one will likely be widely regarded as insensitive to the masses of ordinary (usually third-world) civilians who are killed or otherwise harmed by powerful domestic and other elements in these states. Similarly, if one simply argues against the indictment of the sitting president of the Sudan by the ICC or that Court's then trial of the sitting president of Kenya, on the grounds that—inter alia—its geostationary orbit over only the African continent is excessively selective, one strongly risks being widely viewed as an opponent of attempts to end impunity for mass killings on that continent.[80] But if one supports these ICC trials, one legitimizes that Court's seemingly excessive and selective focus thus far on the weaker (African) states of the world (a situation that—though not entirely the ICC's fault—is most reminiscent of the colonial

[76] Pierre Bourdieu, 'The Force of Law: Toward a Sociology of the Juridical Field' (1987) 38 Hastings Law Journal 814; Richard Terdiman, 'Translator's Introduction: The Force of Law: Toward a Sociology of the Juridical Field' (1987) 38 Hastings Law Journal 805.

[77] Bourdieu (n 76); Terdiman (n 76).

[78] Basil Ugochukwu, 'Adjudicating Human Rights in Transitional Contexts: A Nigerian Case Study, 1999–2009' (DPhil thesis, Osgoode Hall Law School 2014) 81.

[79] Bhupinder Chimni, 'An Outline of a Marxist Course on Public International Law' in Susan Marks (ed), *International Law on the Left: Re-Examining Marxist Legacies* (CUP 2008) 54; David Kennedy, 'When Renewal Repeats: Thinking against the Box' (2000) 32 New York University Journal of International Law and Policy 372.

[80] Obiora Chinedu Okafor, 'The International Criminal Court as a "Transitional Justice" Mechanism in Africa: Some Critical Reflections' (2014) 9 International Journal of Transitional Justice 90; Obiora Chinedu Okafor and Uchechukwu Ngwaba, 'Between Tunnel Vision and a Sliding Scale: Power, Normativity and Justice in the Praxis of the International Criminal Court' (2015) 40 Africa Development 55. My own personal experience of engaging on this issue with a mass of bright, fervently pro-ICC, African activists at the Dakar meeting strongly supports this point.

era relations between Africa and the international system).[81] And so, strategic/tactical dangers loom either way. Of course, regarding each of these examples, one option is usually less acceptable than the other from a particular progressive perspective. But the complication is that even seasoned critical international human rights law scholars can sometimes disagree on which option better conforms to progressive goals. Thus, if we are to optimize the success of our non-academic praxis, we must sharpen our abilities to navigate these sorts of dangers in as nimble and effective a manner as possible. For instance, in my own experience, reminding the vast majority of human rights activists who tend to hold the ICC in a close, almost non-detachable, loving embrace that the critique of that Court's exclusive focus on Africans *can* at times be a call for more, and not less, prosecutions around the world, can blunt their criticisms. Another option for the international (human rights) law scholar who is engaged in such praxis is of course to abstain all the time from voting/speaking on such questions, but then they might as well stay away completely from close engagement with the relevant bodies/groups.

23.5.2 Conceptual/Theoretical Perils

Only three conceptual/theoretical dangers will be discussed here. First, one of the most important conceptual/theoretical dangers of our close engagement as critical international human rights law scholars with international institutions is that the habituation to seeking the middle ground that often comes with the territory can lead us to focus to excess on mild reformist goals, and that this mentality can ultimately seep into our academic work. This would definitely not be a good thing, given our primary roles as academics who are paid to push human society toward the as yet unimagined and unreal, and our pride of place as critical and progressive scholars who want to imagine and realize a different and more just world.

The process of engaging closely with the relevant international bodies can also lead us to lose our critical edge, and therefore our comparative advantage. It can have this effect by making us become too muddled, in the minutiae of the everyday work that the bodies we seek to closely engage do, to have enough time sit back and reflect as deeply and extensively as we are wont to do as academics. The resulting inability to see the big picture as clearly as before, to see beyond the immediate or the horizons that appear just a little ahead of us, may in turn hamper our abilities to play our proper role as critical intellectuals in as effective a manner as we could.

Lastly, a more widespread turn to praxis beyond the academe, and toward close engagement with international institutions, carries with it the theoretical/conceptual risk for us of succumbing or at least appearing to succumb to those who would, as much as possible, 'over-purify' professional disciplines such as ours, by purging them of what they see as way too much theorizing and far too little practical work. We risk giving the impression that all contemplation and the theories that result from such activity are somehow radically divorced from 'the real world'. We risk being sucked too deeply into the 'impact' frenzy that is currently sweeping through the academe. While I would strongly urge critical international human rights law scholars to turn as much as they can, and if they can, toward praxis in

[81] ibid.

various non-academic habitats, I also believe as strongly that we all need to stand on guard against this sort of danger of practical over-purification.

23.6 Conclusion: No Open, Sesame! Or Toward the Intensification of Critical International Human Rights Dramaturgy

In conclusion, it has been shown here that although, if praxis is conceived as the mutual constitution of conception and execution toward the goal of achieving progressive social change, critical international human rights law scholarship itself is already praxis, we have not—to date—paid as much attention as we ought to the imperative of enacting some form of praxis in the non-academic realm (including within or in relation to international institutions). The author's experience in undertaking such praxis within and in relation to international institutions (as basically a participant/observer) was offered as part of the 'raw material' from which to construct the chapter's arguments. Thereafter, the 'strategic/tactical' as well as 'theoretical/conceptual' promise and perils of such close engagement with such international bodies were discussed at some length.

In terms of the overarching argument of the paper, it is best to begin by harkening back to an iconic poem: one that speaks to the deep wisdom of a lot of African thought. As some of the lines of that poem, written by Chris Okigbo (one of the greatest poets of our time) go:

> And he said to the ram: Disarm
> And I said:
> Except by rooting,
> Who could pluck yam tubers from their base?[82]

A key lesson of this poem is that clearly, critical international human rights law scholars cannot simply command the ram (the global power matrixes) to 'disarm' and have it comply. We cannot just chant 'open sesame' and have the gates of power open to us so that our ideas can march through, settle in, and occupy international/transnational bodies.[83] As the poet sang, 'except by rooting who could pluck yam tubers from their base?'[84] While it may not be entirely correct to state, as Marx did in 1845, that 'the philosophers have *only* interpreted the world, in various ways; the point is to change it',[85] the point here is that some degree of effective and targeted praxis beyond our comfort zone within the academe seems nevertheless to be required.

Thus, in my own view, critical international human rights law scholars need to pay even more attention than we have to date, both in our academic contemplation/execution and in our other work, to theorizing and directly or indirectly affecting the ways in which intervention in the internationalist/transnational macro- and micro-dramas that are enacted in various non-academic, political, environments can be used to attain our short-, medium-, and long-term goals. As Marx admonishes us:

[82] Christopher Okigbo, *Collected Poems* (Heinemann 1986), 25.
[83] DL Ashliman, 'Ali Baba and the Forty Thieves from the 1001 Nights' (*University of Pittsburgh*, 3 February 2013) <http://www.pitt.edu/~dash/alibaba.html> accessed 7 November 2020.
[84] Okigbo (n 82) 25.
[85] Friedrich Engels and Karl Marx, *Ludwig Feuerbach and the End of Classical German Philosophy* (Progress Publishers 1969) 69–72.

> The chief defect of all hitherto existing materialism—that of Fuerbach included – is that the thing, reality, sensuousness, is conceived only in the form of the object or of contemplation, but not as sensuous human activity, practice, not subjectively. Hence, in contradistinction to materialism, the active side was developed abstractly by idealism—which, of course, does not know real, sensuous activity as such.[86]

While this turn toward what Marx refers to as 'sensuous human activity' and what we would rather describe as the enactment of 'praxis beyond the academe' will have merit in and of itself as a way of reinforcing our strategic craft and breathing life into our own alternative imaginaries of global order; as has been shown, it will also enrich our theoretical craft itself.

This will not necessarily mean a wholesale turn by all and sundry among the collegium of critical international human rights law scholars to international institutions, in the sense of most of us becoming embedded within or otherwise closely engaging those bodies. The dangers of close engagement that have been outlined in this paper, and the need to retain the 'external viewpoint', strongly suggest otherwise. What is more, we cannot be impervious to the fact that our positions as scholars, as members of the academe, allows us a space that is rather unique from which to think and speak more critically about these international institutions. What it does mean, however, is that while being as reflexive as possible, as many of us as are interested must strive, as best we can, to engage more closely with these bodies/groups, including in the mental as well as physical, locational sense. To do this effectively, nothing less than the intensification of critical international human rights law dramaturgy is required.

[86] Ibid, 72.

24

Should Human Rights Practice be Rights Based?

Sarah Knuckey and Margaret Satterthwaite

24.1 Introduction

Human rights scholars and organizations often call on governments to adopt 'human rights-based approaches' (HRBAs) to a vast array of policy areas and challenges, from climate change to housing, poverty, development, humanitarian response, and health policy.[*] HRBAs promote rights fulfilment as a core goal, call for the identification of rights and obligations along with their correlative rights-holders and duty-bearers, and advance the principles of participation, accountability, equality, and non-discrimination. Yet, curiously, human rights actors do not commonly describe their own human rights investigation and advocacy practice and methods as 'rights based'. Perhaps this is because it seems self-evident that human rights practice itself would be based in the human rights approach. Assessment of the entitlements of rights-holders and the obligations of duty-bearers is of course at the core of much human rights work. But rights-based approaches require much more than that. They advocate for work to recognize and promote the universality, indivisibility, and interdependence of rights, and to advance equality and non-discrimination. Importantly, HRBAs also seek to promote a way of working in which organizations are *accountable* to those most directly affected by human rights abuse and advocacy—rights-holders—and in which rights-holders and other key stakeholders *participate* in, own, and are *empowered* by the human rights work itself, rather than re-victimized, objectified, or marginalized. The approach aims to recognize, centre, and grow the agency and power of rights-holders over the conditions affecting their lives. However, especially on the HRBA process principles and rights-holder participation and empowerment goals, the human rights field far too often falls short, and some commonly used human rights advocacy practices undermine these ideals. Were HRBAs adopted by human rights organizations, the face of human rights advocacy would change—often dramatically—as rights-holders would be empowered to claim their own rights, becoming advocates themselves, and advocates not directly affected by the abuse would be re-cast in roles of support and solidarity.

In this chapter, we argue that the human rights-based approach has been exported to many fields without ever being sufficiently integrated within human rights advocacy practice. This assessment is offered in the spirit of 'introspection and openness': as both scholars and human rights practitioners, we agree with Philip Alston that the challenges facing human rights today require us to 'urgently rethink many of [our] assumptions, re-evaluate [our] strategies, and broaden [our] outreach, while not giving up on the basic principles'.[1] Indeed,

[*] The authors thank Ayesha Audu and Alexander Kristallis for their excellent research assistance. Margaret Satterthwaite gratefully acknowledges support from the Filomen D'Agostino Research Fund at New York University School of Law.

[1] Philip Alston, 'Human Rights under Siege: How to Respond to the Populist Threat Facing Human Rights' (2017) 25 SUR International Journal of Human Rights 267, 268.

Sarah Knuckey and Margaret Satterthwaite, *Should Human Rights Practice be Rights Based?* In: *The Struggle for Human Rights*. Edited by: Nehal Bhuta, Florian Hoffmann, Sarah Knuckey, Frédéric Mégret, and Margaret Satterthwaite, Oxford University Press. © Sarah Knuckey and Margaret Satterthwaite 2021. DOI: 10.1093/oso/9780198868064.003.0025

it is necessary to turn those principles back on ourselves, and to undertake a reckoning with whether human rights work is itself sufficiently rights based. Motivated by the leadership of rights-holders we have worked with and cognizant of the urgent need to end top-down approaches to human rights, we offer this chapter as an invitation to further discussion.

This chapter first briefly traces the development of the 'rights-based approach', explains its key principles, outlines its implementation in other fields of international practice, and sets out key critiques of the approach. We then examine the rights-based approach in human rights practice, focusing specifically on human rights work by outside advocates—that is, advocacy carried out by practitioners not based in the community experiencing the violations at issue.[2] We find that, although it is difficult to generalize across an enormous and heterogenous field, there is little formal, explicit use of the HRBA among human rights organizations. The substantive rights-based principles, including those related to the indivisibility, interrelatedness, and universality of rights, do receive broad commitment in the human rights field, and their implementation, while inconsistent, has significantly improved in practice over the past decades. However, through examining critical human rights scholarship and contemporary practice, we find that although human rights organizations have increasingly asserted their commitment to the process principles of participation, empowerment, and accountability, in practice the human rights field far too often fails to measure up. Even worse, common human rights research and advocacy approaches used by professionalized international and national NGOs not based in the communities where they work can actually disempower rights-holders and local advocates, produce and objectify victims, and be top-down and poorly accountable to those directly affected by abuse. Although there are many examples to the contrary—especially among grassroots organizations, newer organizations, feminist groups, and those based the global South—we argue that it is common in the human rights field for NGOs to fail to sufficiently adhere to foundational human rights principles in their own working methods. In so doing, their work can have the effect of reproducing unjust power hierarchies, and, where work involves northern NGO interventions in the global South, can also contribute to maintaining colonial northern advocate-as-saviour, southern rights-holder-as-victim frameworks.

We conclude with a challenge to those of us in the field and working as outside advocates to commit to a deeper exploration of what more active implementation of human rights-based approaches could look like, and a specific call to directly challenge the socio-economic and political structures that lead to human rights abuses and undermine the ability of rights-holders to claim their rights. We conclude with some questions that could guide human rights practitioners and scholars in examining the practices that may require reform, and to face the challenges inherent in using rights-based approaches.

24.2 Rights-based Approaches: Development, Principles, Implementation, and Critique

The rights-based approach is generally discussed in the context of efforts to bring human rights into the development and humanitarian fields, to mainstream human rights across the work of the United Nations, or to add a rights lens to work carried out in a range of areas

[2] See further Sarah Knuckey and others, 'Power in Human Rights Advocate and Rightsholder Relationships: Critiques, Reforms and Challenges' (2020) 30 Harvard Human Rights Journal 1 (discussing common harmful practices by outside advocates in relation to rightsholders).

from health to education. An extensive literature now exists explaining the framework, analysing the methods for integrating rights into diverse fields, and critiquing the adequacy of its implementation in practice. This section will first trace the development of the 'rights-based approach to development', and then consider its expansion to allied fields, such as humanitarian relief and health. The section then notes the broad application of HRBAs in more diverse fields. Finally, the section will end by considering some important critiques of HRBAs that are relevant to considering how to bring rights-based principles into human rights practice.

24.2.1 HRBAs: Development and Principles

'Human rights' and 'development' have generally advanced on parallel tracks and traditionally explained their goals differently: human rights sought the protection and fulfilment of the basic rights of each individual, while development was aimed at advancing the collective (economic) well-being of communities and nations. Human rights advocacy took new forms as states came together to create the UDHR and a series of international treaties that made states' treatment of those within their borders a matter of international concern—at least conceptually.[3] And as decolonization advanced after World War II, European states developed institutions to provide 'overseas aid' to newly independent states with the purported aim of helping former colonies launch themselves into the world order as modern states.[4] Under the surface of the different goals, there were of course other aims at work: the West championed a cramped and self-serving version of rights, critiquing the violation of civil and political rights in the East while downplaying socio-economic rights and ignoring rights infringements at home. Conversely, the Soviet bloc claimed to champion economic and social rights while rejecting criticism of their treatment of civil and political rights.[5] Government development agencies worked to ensure the countries they had previously controlled remained in their scope of influence and that they developed into states with economies compatible with the prevailing macroeconomic order.

Over time, the two fields grew toward each other: more and more, human rights were seen as encompassing wide-ranging social and economic rights that implicated the economic order and social institutions, while development was redefined as being aimed at 'human development', the expansion of individual agency and freedom.[6] The rapprochement was slow and sometimes halting, and its history is instructive for the human rights field, since it suggests reasons to both embrace and be wary of the rights-based approach. While the 1969 Declaration on Social Progress and Development asserted that 'Social progress and development shall be founded on respect for dignity and value of the human person, and shall ensure the promotion of human rights and social justice', this was still a fairly radical notion at the time.[7] In the 1970s development practice focused on basic needs and the eradication

[3] Paul Gready and Jonathan Ensor (eds), *Reinventing Development? Translating Rights-Based Approaches from Theory into Practice* (Zed Books 2005).

[4] ibid 14–20; Diana Mitlin and Sam Hickey, 'Introduction' in Samuel Hickey and Diana Mitlin (eds), *Rights-Based Approaches to Development: Exploring the Potential and Pitfalls* (Kumarian Press 2009) 6–9.

[5] Mary Robinson, 'Advancing Economic, Social, and Cultural Rights: The Way Forward' (2004) 26 Human Rights Quarterly 866.

[6] These concepts are often traced to the work of Amartya Sen, in emergent form in 1981, and in full articulation in 1999. Amartya Sen, *Poverty and Famines: An Essay on Entitlement and Deprivation* (Clarendon Press 1981); Amartya Sen, *Development as Freedom* (Anchor Books 2000).

[7] Gready and Ensor (n 3) 17.

of poverty as well as insisting on the participation of those whose development was being pursued.[8]

Through the 1972 UN Conference on Trade and Development, states in the global South asserted the right to development,[9] a right confirmed in 1977, when the UN Commission on Human Rights 'proclaim[ed]' its existence as well.[10] However, it was not until 1986 that this claim was codified in the UN Declaration on the Right to Development.[11] Development practice continued to focus on basic needs during this period, and human rights organizations appeared and expanded, still focused almost exclusively on civil and political rights. In the late 1980s, the failures of structural adjustment, the end of the Cold War, the emergence of an increasingly multipolar world, and a renewed interest in both sides of the human rights divide produced a convergence in which 'the threads of failing neo-liberalism, resurgent indivisibility, social movement activism and long-standing intellectual support combined to form a bond tying rights to development'.[12] In the post-colonial, post-structural adjustment era, states in the global South increasingly viewed international assistance as their right; in responding, northern donor states sought to hold their partners to standards of 'good governance' and democracy, increasingly seen as already guaranteed in human rights law.[13]

These reciprocal demands further solidified the bond between human rights and development. At the 1993 World Conference on Human Rights, states adopted a Declaration and Programme of Action that affirmed that development and human rights are 'interdependent and mutually reinforcing'.[14] Crucially, the Declaration also placed ESC rights on the same footing as civil and political rights. This explicit embrace of the interlinkages between rights and development allowed the process of integrating human rights into development programming to begin in earnest, as evidenced by the official statements emerging from later intergovernmental conferences, UN agency policies and practices, and cooperation among human rights and development NGOs.[15] During the decade that followed, the 'rights-based approach' to development was constructed as a specific method for advancing human development through reference to, and with the guidance of, substantive and procedural elements of international human rights law. By 1997, the UN Secretary General called on all agencies of the UN to mainstream human rights into their work.[16] UNICEF, which had been leading the pack on adopting the rights-based approach,[17] was soon joined by UNDP and OHCHR, which led the other agencies in advancing the embrace of rights-based approaches through training, policy papers, and guidance.[18] The appointment of an independent expert in 1998—and later, a Special Rapporteur—on extreme poverty and human rights, a post

[8] ibid 17–18.

[9] ibid 18.

[10] Philip Alston and Mary Robinson, 'The Challenges of Ensuring the Mutuality of Human Rights and Development Endeavours' in Philip Alston, Mary Robinson, and New York University (eds), *Human Rights and Development: Towards Mutual Reinforcement* (OUP 2005).

[11] Gready and Ensor (n 3) 18.

[12] ibid 21.

[13] ibid 47.

[14] UNGA, 'Vienna Declaration and Programme of Action' UN Doc A/CONF.157/23 para 8.

[15] Urban Jonsson, 'A Human Rights-Based Approach to Programming' in Gready and Ensor (n 3) 47; Mitlin and Hickey (n 4) 6. At the same time, human rights groups began to turn their gaze to the North, examining entrenched inequalities and discrimination, and applying human rights legal standards to states' international and extraterritorial activities.

[16] UNGA 'Report of the Secretary-General – Renewing the United Nations: A Programme for Reform' (1997) UN Doc A/51/950/Add.3.

[17] Alston and Robinson (n 10).

[18] Shannon Kindornay, James Ron, and Charli Carpenter, 'Rights-Based Approaches to Development: Implications for NGOs' (2012) 34 Human Rights Quarterly 472, 480.

Philip Alston holds at the time of writing, was also key to focusing international attention on and furthering analysis of development, poverty, and inequality as human rights issues.[19]

States also began to converge—at least conceptually—and in 2000 states promised in the Millennium Declaration to 'spare no effort to promote [...] respect for all internationally recognized human rights and fundamental freedoms, including the right to development'.[20] During this time, development NGOs such as Oxfam and CARE began to use the rights-based approach as well.[21] This work was catalysed not only by the separate advances in the human rights and development realms, but also by advocacy campaigns that united NGOs across the rights–development divide.[22]

Leading official development agencies adopted rights-based approaches in the early 2000s, with the UK's Department for International Development (DFID) and the Swedish International Development Agency (SIDA) in the lead,[23] and followed eventually by the then German Technical Cooperation Agency (GTZ) and the European Union's external cooperation efforts.[24] After several years of work on parallel tracks, UN agencies came together in 2003 to forge a 'Common Understanding of the Human Rights-Based Approach to Development Cooperation', formulated as follows:

> 1. All programmes of development cooperation, policies and technical assistance should further the realization of human rights as laid down in the Universal Declaration of Human Rights and other international human rights instruments.
> 2. Human rights standards contained in, and principles derived from, the Universal Declaration of Human Rights and other international human rights instruments guide all development cooperation and programming in all sectors and in all phases of the programming process.
> 3. Development cooperation contributes to the development of the capacities of 'duty-bearers' to meet their obligations and of 'rights-holders' to claim their rights.[25]

In practice, perhaps the most important part of the Common Understanding is its recitation of key principles drawn from human rights law, which are to guide programming:[26]

- *Universality and inalienability*: the concept that all human beings hold human rights that may not be taken away or surrendered. This principle is sourced to Article 1 of the UDHR and the preambles of the other major treaties.

[19] OHCHR, 'Special Rapporteur on Extreme Poverty and Human Rights' (*United Nations Human Rights Office of the High Comissioner*) <https://www.ohchr.org/en/issues/poverty/Pages/SRExtremePovertyIndex.aspx> accessed 29 September 2020.

[20] UNGA RES 55/2 (18 September 2000) UN Doc A/RES/55/2 para 22.

[21] For an overview, see Kindornay, Ron, and Carpenter (n 18).

[22] ibid 478 (internal citations omitted).

[23] ibid 480 (internal citations omitted); note that DFID no longer follows the RBA; Morten Broberg and Hans-Otto Sano, 'Strengths and Weaknesses in a Human Rights-Based Approach to International Development—an Analysis of a Rights-Based Approach to Development Assistance Based on Practical Experiences' (2018) 22 The International Journal of Human Rights, 664, 667.

[24] ibid 667.

[25] United Nations Development Group, 'The Human Rights Based Approach to Development Cooperation Towards a Common Understanding Among UN Agencies' <https://unsdg.un.org/sites/default/files/6959-The_Human_Rights_Based_Approach_to_Development_Cooperation_Towards_a_Common_Understanding_among_UN.pdf>.

[26] ibid.

- *Indivisibility*: the idea that all human rights are equally important and cannot be ranked or ignored. This concept undergirds the UDHR and was emphasized explicitly in the Vienna Declaration and Programme of Action.
- *Interdependence and interrelatedness*: the recognition that rights often rely upon each other for full enjoyment. This quality is inherent to human rights norms and was explicitly recognized in the Vienna Declaration and Programme of Action.
- *Equality and non-discrimination*: a bedrock principle of human rights law, included in the UDHR and every major human rights treaty.
- *Participation and inclusion*: the idea that 'Every person and all peoples are entitled to active, free and meaningful participation in, contribution to, and enjoyment of civil, economic, social, cultural and political development in which human rights and fundamental freedoms can be realized'.[27]
- *Accountability and rule of law*: the recognition that states are the primary duty-bearers under human rights law, that development efforts should strengthen the capacity of the state to fulfil this role, and that rights-holders can claim their rights and access redress when their rights are violated.

These principles, or some version of them, are the functional backbone of rights-based approaches as they are practised today, and they are seen as a succinct distillation of the core principles undergirding all human rights.[28] While most formulations include many of these elements, participation and non-discrimination are at the core of all.[29] Fifteen years after the Common Approach was created, the world has seen a 'cascade' of HRBA work; prominent development NGOs such as Save the Children and ActionAid have taken it on; and the official donor agencies of Denmark, Norway, Switzerland, and Finland have joined the earlier adopters in embracing HRBAs.[30]

What do these principles mean in practice, and have they made a difference? There is an extensive literature seeking to answer these questions. While it is beyond the scope of this chapter to provide a definitive answer to this question, the literature includes the following findings:

- Rights-based approaches are being combined with traditional service delivery by development actors. While HRBA practitioners try to avoid service delivery that displaces the role of the state, they have found that services are still badly needed to close deprivation gaps while the state gains capacity or redirects efforts to those who have been neglected through discrimination and marginalization. Further, development agencies can garner more engagement and participation for advocacy efforts when they have something concrete to offer.[31]
- Rights-based approaches have been especially promising in ensuring that the most marginalized sectors of the population can access their basic rights, such as health care, water, sanitation, and education.[32] The emphasis on non-discrimination and equality,

[27] ibid.
[28] Lauchlan T Munro, 'The "Human Rights-Based Approach to Programming": A Contradiction in Terms?' in Hickey and Mitlin (n 4) 189–91.
[29] Broberg and Sano (n 23) 665.
[30] Kindornay, Ron, and Carpenter (n 18) 481. (internal citations omitted).
[31] ibid 492–93 (internal citations omitted).
[32] Broberg and Sano (n 23) 672.

combined with legal empowerment related to economic and social rights has translated into improved access to rights.[33]

- Rights-based approaches have helped strengthen the capacity of governmental actors to fulfil their human rights duties, with rights standards serving as benchmarks against which to measure improvements in service delivery. HRBA principles have also been used to guide community participation in defining government strategies, ensuring those most affected have a seat at the decision-making table.[34]
- Despite these achievements, 'there is a wide gap between the conceptualization of the HRBA at the international level and its operationalization on the ground'.[35]

While the evidence is largely based on specific case studies or programme evaluations, many practitioners and scholars have concluded that HRBAs have been more effective in achieving the desired development outcomes, over all, than the needs-based approach that came before it.[36] Others do not go so far, but agree that the HRBAs have exerted important corrective influence by re-positioning development endeavours from the perspective of the rights-holder rather than the state and thus ensuring that *how* development is pursued is at least as important as the results achieved.[37]

24.2.2 The HRBA Expands its Reach

In addition to expanding across the development field, HRBAs have extended their reach, taking hold in the humanitarian, health, water and sanitation, and myriad other sectors. In the humanitarian sector, the rights-based approach developed in tandem with a broader concern about the accountability of humanitarian actors to disaster- and conflict-affected communities (who the sector referred to as 'beneficiaries'). Redefining beneficiaries as rights-holders was a crucial step in a transformation of the field following a series of humanitarian fiascos in the 1990s—specifically their implication in inadvertently assisting the rearming of Rwandan *génocidaires* following the genocide and their failure to protect civilians from massacre at Srebrenica in 1995.[38] As humanitarians redefined their relationship to those they served, they re-established the basis for their work as based in human rights. The sector undertook significant work to identify the rights of beneficiaries in human rights and humanitarian law, creating a 'Humanitarian Charter' in 2000 that drew on principles in human rights law, humanitarian law, and refugee law relevant to humanitarian assistance. The Charter recognized a right of disaster- and conflict-affected communities to access humanitarian assistance, and a duty in humanitarian actors to provide quality assistance according to principles such as non-discrimination.[39] One well-known expression of the sector's embrace of rights-based programming was the Sphere Project, which created a

[33] ibid 672–73.
[34] 'Mainstreaming Human Rights in Developing Policies and Programming: UNDP Experiences' (United Nations Development Programme 2012) <http://hrbaportal.org/wp-content/files/English_Web_draft6b1.pdf>.
[35] Tine Destrooper, 'Linking Discourse and Practice: The Human Rights-Based Approach to Development in the Village Assaini Program in the Kongo Central' (2016) 38 Human Rights Quarterly 787.
[36] Broberg and Sano (n 23) 674.
[37] Munro (n 28).
[38] For an overview of the relationship between these failures and the emergence of the rights-based approach in the humanitarian sector, see Margaret L Satterthwaite, 'Indicators in Crisis: Rights-Based Humanitarian Indicators in Post-Earthquake Haiti' (2011) 43 NYU Journal of International Law and Politics 865, 885–88.
[39] ibid 889–93.

Handbook for quality service provision based on intensive sector-wide consultations.[40] The Sphere Handbook set out the Humanitarian Charter and standards for quality assistance in numerous sectors, including water supply and sanitation, nutrition, food aid, shelter and site planning, and health services. As a review of an early edition of the Handbook explained:

> [T]he adoption of a rights-based approach to humanitarian assistance represents a fundamental and drastic revision of the philosophy underlying emergency relief that prevailed until [the Rwandan genocide in] 1994. For the Sphere Project, relief is not charity; it is not only the generous outpouring of support from goodhearted individuals and governments that is always welcome, but not always adequate or effective. Instead, the Sphere Project sees international disaster response as an obligation, incurred by those who can help, to ensure that the rights of affected individuals and populations are respected and accorded.[41]

A similar process was underway in allied fields. In relation to health, women's rights activism led to a victory when the International Conference on Population and Development in Cairo in 1994 adopted a Programme of Action that 'reflected a dramatic shift in public health from targeted policies based on demographic imperatives to policies based on reproductive rights'.[42] Another important wave of advocacy surrounded HIV/AIDS, where marginalized communities fought against the discriminatory treatment they experienced at the hands of health systems and medical providers. By the mid-1990s, antiretroviral therapy (ART) had become available, changing the life possibilities for those with HIV dramatically. However, ART was seen by the prevailing public health system as not cost-effective or feasible in low-resource settings. As Yamin and Constantin explain, 'international human rights norms and constitutional frameworks enabled activists to appropriate their human dignity' and 'empowered them to make claims for health benefits backed with the force of law', framing 'the demand for access to ART as a human right'.[43]

Successes like these were followed by advocacy campaigns to make clear that other crucial health issues were also human rights concerns, and to entrench normative standards into authoritative sources, such as General Comments from UN treaty bodies.[44] By the time of the Millennium Declaration and the roll-out of the MDGs, efforts were underway to transform the health sector using a rights-based approach. Though there was intense work by many to advance the health-related MDGs from a rights perspective, ultimately the technocratic approach embodied by the focus on goals, targets, and indicators shut down more transformational possibilities.[45] Despite this, advocates have created new possibilities in recent years by operationalizing rights-based approaches and demanding that it requires not only attention to the substantive norms of rights relevant to health but also shifts in power whereby rights-holders can enjoy full agency, dignity, and participation in decision-making

[40] The Sphere Handbook is now on its fourth edition. Sphere Project (ed), *The Sphere Handbook: Humanitarian Charter and Minimum Standards in Humanitarian Response* (4th edn, Sphere Association 2018).

[41] Marci Van Dyke and Ronald Waldman, 'The Sphere Project Evaluation Report' (Mailman School of Public Health: Centre for Global Health and Economic Development 2004). Subsequent editions of the Handbook integrated human rights guarantees more fully into the sectoral standards.

[42] Alicia Ely Yamin and Andrés Constantin, 'A Long and Winding Road: The Evolution of Applying Human Rights Frameworks to Health' (2018) 49 Georgetown Journal of International Law 191, 201.

[43] ibid 203 (citing and quoting Lisa Forman; internal quotation marks and citations omitted).

[44] ibid 191–239.

[45] ibid 214–16; Philip Alston suggests that the human rights and development fields failed to really engage with each other through the MDG process. Philip Alston, 'Ships Passing in the Night: The Current State of the Human Rights and Development Debate Seen through the Lens of the Millennium Development Goals' (2005) 27 Human Rights Quarterly 755.

concerning health services and systems.[46] These efforts have been reflected—at least to some degree—in the SDGs. As Winkler and Williams explain, the human rights community engaged intensively in the negotiation of the SDGs and the indicators used to track them. As a result, '[h]uman rights advocates achieved a lot in SDG negotiations: from the overall promise of 'leave no one behind', to references to human rights in the Declaration, to many of the targets which implicitly reflect human rights language'.[47] Whether these achievements are translating into improved rights on the ground is still an open question.

Efforts to advance rights-based approaches have grown and deepened over the past two decades. In the field of education, for example, rights-based approaches have drawn upon the right to education, as well as rights-based principles such as equality and non-discrimination to advance core concerns, including access to quality universal primary education[48] and against privatization.[49] In the field of climate change, human rights advocates and environmental advocates came together in 2019 to call for a rights-compliant movement for climate justice.[50] In debates about issues including arms control and tobacco regulation, rights-based approaches have been suggested as a way to reframe debates around rights-holders' freedom to live in security.[51] NGOs and UN human rights actors have also pushed rights-based approaches into intergovernmental strategies for state resilience,[52] migration policy,[53] housing policy,[54] and government responses to extreme

[46] Yamin and Constantin (n 42) 224–30; for a RBA to emergency and essential surgical care, see Kashmira S Chawla and others, 'Beyond a Moral Obligation: A Legal Framework for Emergency and Essential Surgical Care and Anesthesia' (2017) 41 World Journal of Surgery 1208.

[47] Inga T Winkler and Carmel Williams, 'The Sustainable Development Goals and Human Rights: A Critical Early Review' (2017) 21(8) The International Journal of Human Rights 1023, 1027.

[48] Leah K McMillan, 'What's in a Right? Two Variations for Interpreting the Right to Education' (2010) 56 International Review of Education 531.

[49] For example, The Abidjan Principles on the human rights obligations of states to provide public education and to regulate private involvement (2019), 'The Abidjan Principles' (2019) <https://static1.squarespace.com/static/5c2d081daf2096648cc801da/t/5d42ec41f9f33300011c16d1/1564666946331/Designed_Online+version_THE-ABIDJAN-PRINCIPLES_june2019.pdf> accessed 10 May 2021.

[50] 'Peoples' Summit on Climate, Rights and Human Survival' (People Summit Declaration) <https://www.climaterights4all.com/peoples-summit-on-climate-rights-and-human-survival/> accessed 27 September 2020. The Declaration was signed by more than two hundred environmental and human rights leaders; '200 Environmental and Human Rights Leaders Pledge to Tackle Climate Emergency Together' (Amnesty International 18 September 2019) <https://www.amnesty.org/en/latest/news/2019/09/200-environmental-and-human-rights-leaders-pledge-to-tackle-climate-emergency-together/> accessed 27 September 2020; in addition, a rights-based approach has been suggested as a way to reconcile possibly competing demands between those with rights to use ecologically fragile areas (such as indigenous peoples in the rainforest) and the desire to 'protect' those sites though heritage or other designations. For example, Josephine Gillespie, 'World Heritage Protection and the Human Right to Development: Reconciling Competing or Complimentary Narratives Using a Human Rights-Based Approach (HRBA)?' (2013) 5 Sustainability 3159.

[51] Daniel Mack, 'Small Arms, Big Violations' (2015) 12(22) SUR International Journal of Human Rights <https://sur.conectas.org/en/small-arms-big-violations/> accessed 27 September 2020 (arguing for a rights-based approach to small arms control); Carolyn Dresler and others, 'Human Rights-Based Approach to Tobacco Control' (2012) 21 Tobacco Control 208 (setting out the rationale for a rights-based approach to tobacco control); Asaf Bitton, 'Moving towards More Equitable and Integrated Approaches for Tobacco Control and Non-Communicable Diseases: Invited Commentary' (2012) 21 Tobacco Control 273 (arguing that using the rights-based approach will emphasize equity, access, and implementation of treatments and policies).

[52] Human Rights and Democracy Network, 'A Rights-Based Approach to Resilience: HRDN's Input to the EEAS and Commission Joint Communication on Resilience' <https://www.fidh.org/IMG/pdf/a-rights-based-approach-to-resilience.pdf> accessed 10 May 2021 (arguing that EU global strategy for state and social resilience should be grounded in a human rights-based approach, and should empower individuals as rights-bearers).

[53] FIDH and others, 'EU Migration: Time for an Ambitious Human Rights-Based Agenda' (International Federation for Human Rights 13 December 2017) <https://www.fidh.org/en/issues/migrants-rights/eu-migration-time-for-an-ambitious-human-rights-based-agenda> accessed 27 September 2020.

[54] UNGA 'Report of the Special Rapporteur on Adequate Housing as a Component of the Right to an Adequate Standard of Living, and on the Right to Non-Discrimination in this Context' UN DOC A/HRC/37/53 (2018) (outlining the key principles of a rights-based housing strategy).

poverty.[55] In Alston's work as the UN Special Rapporteur on Extreme Poverty, he has helped to promote rights-based approaches to poverty, including by pushing for the full recognition of ESC rights in government responses to poverty and through critiques of the World Bank's approach to human rights.[56]

24.2.3 Critiques of HRBAs

Alongside their embrace, rights-based approaches have been the subject of wide-ranging critique. Some of those critiques focus on implementation failures. Others suggest that HRBAs fail to achieve what they promise, or that there is insufficient evidence of impact. More searching critiques suggest that HRBAs can be implemented in a way that domesticates or de-fangs human rights. This section will briefly examine these critiques in an effort to excavate concerns that may be relevant to human rights advocacy as well.

Perhaps the most common concern about HRBAs is that they are just another development fad, to be added to other approaches that have come and gone.[57] Indeed, the development community has in many instances moved on to the next set of 'approaches', including an evidence-based approach, a results-based approach, and a value-for-money approach.[58] These critiques suggest that not much has really changed beyond the use of terminology.[59] For example, a primary school programme that was previously aimed at 'increasing school enrolment by the poor and reducing drop-out' might stay largely the same but be framed as aimed at 'achieving children's rights through universal, equal, and non-discriminatory primary school enrolment for all'.

Another set of concerns focuses on whether there is sufficient evidence to prove that HRBAs have had concrete impacts. For example, there has been debate over *how* to measure 'impact'—should practitioners count only development outcomes, such as improved health, or also 'rights' impacts, such as the ability of individuals to obtain healthcare as an entitlement?[60] Some studies have identified significant impacts from rights-based approaches.[61] These studies suggest that further evidence will be documented as methods are improved and more broadly assessed.

Some critiques focus on the difficulty of operationalizing HRBAs in practice. Writing in 2005, Philip Alston opined that the many HRBA frameworks, checklists, trainings, and

[55] 'UN Special Rapporteur on Extreme Poverty and Human Rights' (Center for Human Rights and Global Justice) <https://chrgj.org/focus-areas/extreme-poverty-human-rights-project/un-special-rapporteur-on-extreme-poverty-and-human-rights/> accessed 27 September 2020 ('Since he was appointed in June 2014, Professor Alston has stressed the importance of relying on a human rights based approach when confronting extreme poverty').

[56] UNGA 'Note by the Secretary General—Extreme Poverty and Human Rights' (2015) UN Doc A/70/274 (critiquing the World Bank's approach to human rights as 'incoherent, counterproductive and unsustainable'); UNHRC, 'Report of the Special Rapporteur on Extreme Poverty and Human Rights' (28 April 2016) UN Doc A/HRC/32/31 (explaining the importance of economic and social rights as human rights and outlining the recognition, institutionalization and accountability framework).

[57] Kindornay, Ron, and Carpenter (n 18) 474.

[58] Paul J Nelson and Ellen Dorsey, 'Who Practices Rights-Based Development? A Progress Report on Work at the Nexus of Human Rights and Development' (2018) 104 World Development 97, 101.

[59] Peter Uvin, *Human Rights and Development* (Kumarian Press 2004) 168 (discussing 'repackaging' of development assistance as RBA: 'Repackaging consists of the pleasant discovery that our development practice is actually, and has always been, a way of realizing human rights for millions of poor people').

[60] Paul Hunt, Alicia Ely Yamin, and Flavia Bustreo, 'Making the Case: What Is the Evidence of Impact of Applying Human Rights-Based Approaches to Health?' (2015) 17 Health and Human Rights 1.

[61] Perhaps the most important study of this kind is Flavia Bustreo, Paul Hunt, and World Health Organization, *Women's and Children's Health: Evidence of Impact of Human Rights* (World Health Organization 2013).

advisers had in fact offered 'little guidance in concrete situations' and tended to 'gloss over many of the complexities of real world decision making and trade-offs'.[62] In addition, HRBAs are sometimes seen as overly legalistic and complex in jargon and concept, ironically enhancing the power of human rights experts and disempowering regular people.[63]

Finally, deep concerns relate to the tensions inherent in HRBAs, and whether they have too often been implemented in ways that reinforce 'the epistemic and institutional power structures within each field, rather than exposing and subverting them'.[64] In the context of health, for example, Yamin and Cantor describe two contradictions:

> HRBAs to healthcare require subversions of power relations which lead systematically to patterns of ill-health among certain populations, yet also require working with and buy-in from those who have power—in governments, donor institutions and agencies. Second, human rights are set out as universal, deontological principles; yet in operationalizing them through HRBAs, trade-offs and deeply contextualized political realities necessarily enter the equation.[65]

These contradictions can be tackled, these authors suggest, by ensuring that programmes 'foster[] meaningfully participatory approaches', in which 'those who will be affected ... have meaningful voice', and that advocacy or programme conceptualization, strategy, implementation, and measurement all focus on this.[66] This also means tackling the inherently political issue of power.[67] In recent scholarship, Yamin has warned against HRBAs 'that may respond more to donor or government demands than ground-level social change', and which fail to 'transform the structural conditions that immiserate and sicken swathes of people across the globe'.[68] She stresses the importance of critical reflection on underlying premises, and of using human rights law to 'challenge larger governance models'.[69] Effective, rather than technocratic and depoliticized, rights-based approaches require focusing on 'people's appropriation of their agency',[70] and the empowerment of those marginalized and dominated, a process that involves 're-making the world'[71]—addressing the radical inequalities that are at the foundation of our international system.

24.3 HRBAs in the Human Rights Field

There is no formalized, coherent, and broadly discussed 'human rights rights-based approach' to human rights advocacy. In contrast to the vast literature describing, analysing, and

[62] Philip Alston, Ships Passing in the Night: The Current State of the Human Rights and Development Debate Seen Through the Lens of the Millennium Development Goals, 27:3 Human Rights Quarterly 755, 802 (2005).
[63] Munro (n 28) 196–201.
[64] Alicia Ely Yamin, 'Struggles for Human Rights in Health in an Age of Neoliberalism: From Civil Disobedience to Epistemic Disobedience' (2019) 11 Journal of Human Rights Practice 357.
[65] Alicia Ely Yamin and Rebecca Cantor, 'Between Insurrectional Discourse and Operational Guidance: Challenges and Dilemmas in Implementing Human Rights-Based Approaches to Health' (2014) 6 Journal of Human Rights Practice 451, 451.
[66] ibid 467.
[67] A similar argument is made in Munro (n 28) 225–27.
[68] Yamin (n 64) 4–5.
[69] ibid 5.
[70] ibid 4.
[71] Alicia Ely Yamin, 'Suffering and Powerlessness: The Significance of Promoting Participation in Rights-Based Approaches to Health' (2009) 11 Health and Human Rights 5, 17.

critiquing HRBAs in relation to diverse fields of practice, there is comparatively little scholarship discussing HRBAs within the human rights field itself.[72] Human rights advocates and scholars often call on governments and other actors to bring an HRBA into new areas of policy and practice: they use HRBA language in advocacy efforts to improve government responses to a vast array of problems, from climate change to housing.[73] Yet only a minority of human rights advocates and organizations describe their own practice as following a 'rights-based approach',[74] and the human rights field has no HRBA practice guides analogous to the guides for development and humanitarian agencies. Explicit rights-based approaches have a comparatively marginal role within the field of human rights practice, whether as a framework for assessing practice or a map to guide it forward.

While there is little *formal* use of HRBAs in human rights practice, examination of the language and practice of NGOs reveals a more complex picture. This section examines the status of HRBAs in the human rights field through an assessment of what human rights organizations say and do. This examination is necessarily incomplete, but it integrates a literature review, examples from the authors' own experience working with a range of groups, from large international NGOs to grassroots, community-based NGOs and movements, and a review of the websites and publications of a sample of human rights groups based in the global South selected because we expected they would be among the most progressive on the issues we examine in this chapter.[75] Overall, our experience is that relatively few human rights organizations use the term 'rights-based approaches' to describe their own methods and work. Although we do not make empirical claims about the entire field, our research and experience suggests that use of the HRBA also varies globally: in some regions, it seems to be used minimally or not at all; there appears to be greater use among African NGOs; and at large international NGOs, it is rare.[76] However, the rights-based principles that are

[72] For examples of human rights scholars and practitioners discussing HRBAs in the context of human rights practice, see: Margaret L Satterthwaite and Amanda M Klasing, 'A Rights-Based Approach to Research: Assessing the Right to Water in Haiti' in Elvira Beracochea, Corey Weinstein, and Dabney P Evans (eds), *Rights-Based Approaches to Public Health* (Springer 2011); Meena Jagannath, Nicole Phillips, and Jeena Shah, 'A Right-Based Approach to Lawyering: Legal Empowerment as an Alternative to Legal Aid in Post-Disaster Haiti' (2011) 10 Northwestern Journal of International Human Rights 6; Knuckey and others (n 2); for examples of scholars arguing that research on human rights issues should respect the HRBA, see Rhona Smith, 'Human Rights Based Approaches to Research' in Lee McConnell and Rhona KM Smith (eds), *Research Methods in Human Rights* (Routledge 2018); Anna Arstein-Kerslake, Piers Gooding, Sarah Mercer, Marlena Raymond, and Bernadette McSherry, 'Implementing a Participatory Human Rights-Based Research Methodology: The Unfitness to Plead Project' (2019) 11(3) Journal of Human Rights Practice 589.

[73] For example, FIDH and others (n 53); UN Doc A/HRC/37/53 (n 54).

[74] For rare examples, see 'Redress Is Seeking a Legal Advisor for a Project on Enforced Disappearance in Africa' (*Redress* 6 November 2018) <https://redress.org/news/legal-advisor-enforced-disappearance-in-africa/> accessed 28 September 2020 (describing a project as adopting a 'human rights-based and victim-centered approach to the challenge of enforced disappearance (ED) in Africa by developing African standards for the prevention of ED while empowering the families of victims of ED to pursue accountability').

[75] In research for this chapter, the authors examined the websites and publications of thirty-five human rights organizations based in the global South that indicated some commitment to ESC rights. This approach was chosen to ensure we captured the breadth of the human rights field (global South-based organizations were chosen to counter biases in academic research, which tends to privilege large organizations based in the global North), and with the expectation that organizations with a prominent commitment to indivisibility of rights (as represented by an embrace of ESC rights) might be especially likely to have integrated the full range of HRBA principles. In total, we examined the websites of thirty-five NGOs: eleven in Latin America and the Caribbean, nine in Asia, and fifteen in Sub-Saharan Africa, to determine whether they adopt the HRBA as a substantive and procedural matter. See further discussion, infra. This sample is in not representative of the field, and the websites may not reflect the work of organizations accurately or completely. Despite these limits, it is important to examine a broader set of examples than those that are typically discussed in the literature about human rights methods, advocacy, and NGOs.

[76] In the co-authors' experiences working around the world with diverse organizations and participating in frequent human rights workshops and conferences, HRBAs are rarely discussed *explicitly* in relation to NGOs' own practices. For example, the two most prominent international human rights organizations do not formally use the HRBA to frame their own research and advocacy methods. Of the thirty-five NGOs we examined for this chapter,

concerned with the substantive content of rights, including universality and inalienability, indivisibility, interdependence and interrelatedness, and equality and non-discrimination, have been taken on board by many human rights organizations in both rhetoric and practice the past several decades, although significant implementation concerns remain. On the other hand, the process-oriented HRBA principles of rights-holder participation and accountability have been less mainstreamed as values to be practised in advocacy across the entire human rights movement—though there are some important exceptions —and have, in some commonly observed NGO practices, been regularly violated.

24.3.1 The Substantive Focus of Human Rights Advocacy: Toward a Rights-based Transformation?

Human rights groups regularly state their core commitments to the universality, inalienability, indivisibility, interdependence, and interrelatedness of rights, and to equality and non-discrimination. The human rights movement has improved in concrete ways its implementation of these principles, even as weaknesses remain, such as in the implementation of social and economic rights, as Alston has forcefully argued.[77] Deficits in prior decades have been improved and many organizations now largely embrace the broad spectrum of economic, social, cultural, civil, and political rights—even though some specialize or focus on specific rights in their advocacy. The idea of non-discrimination and equality are rooted in human rights practice today in ways that was not true only twenty years ago. And universality—the idea that human rights apply to all human beings, and to all states—has also been taken to heart in new and deeply substantive ways in recent decades. Organizations are also increasingly recognizing and furthering understanding of the deep interdependence of all rights.

For the first several decades of the modern human rights movement, the concepts of universality and inalienability, indivisibility, interdependence, and interrelatedness, as well as equality and non-discrimination, were not well recognized and integrated into the actual practice of many NGOs, including some of the most powerful and influential.[78] This may seem counterintuitive, since advocacy for rights is inherently reflective of the content of rights. However, for many years following the birth of major international groups such as Amnesty International (in the 1960s) and Human Rights Watch (as the multiple 'Watch Committees' in the 1970s), the focus of much prominent human rights campaigning at the international level was largely on the civil and political rights of heterosexual cisgendered men.[79] As Philip Alston wrote in 1987, 'for a variety of historical, ideological, pragmatic,

we found that eleven used the term 'rights-based approach' to describe their mission, mandate, or a significant portion of their work. The term was in much more frequent use by the organizations based in Sub-Saharan Africa (eight of fifteen used the term or its relevant equivalent) than those based in Latin America (none used the term or its relevant equivalent) or Asia (three of nine used the term).

[77] Philip Alston, 'The Populist Challenge to Human Rights' (2017) 9 Journal of Human Rights Practice 1 (finding that 'mainstream human rights advocacy addresses economic and social rights issues in a tokenistic manner at best, and the issue of inequality almost not at all').

[78] UN Doc A/HRC/32/31 (n 56) para 11 (arguing forcefully that 'many of the most prominent' human rights organizations still treat economic and social rights as marginal).

[79] This is of course an oversimplification. But the focus of work by Amnesty International and Human Rights Watch in the 1970s and 1980s was on freedom from traditionally defined civil and political rights violations such as torture, detention on the basis of belief or conscience, and freedom of association. Although this focus on civil and political rights did not formally exclude women or LGBTI people, violations directed at these groups on the basis of sex, gender, and gender identity were not meaningfully addressed until the 1990s and 2000s. Philip Alston, Ryan

and other reasons, there remains a considerable reluctance on the part of many, if not most, human rights NGOs to become involved in' economic and social rights.[80] The methods used to research civil and political rights were insufficient for understanding the complex interrelatedness of the broader spectrum of human rights.[81] And the focus of much campaigning by these international groups (headquartered in and largely staffed by advocates from the global North) was on the global South, myopically seen as the locus of human rights violations, and in a way that served Western political and economic interests.[82]

As Alston has underscored, significant deficits remain in how many NGOs address economic and social rights.[83] For example, Alston's recent writings critique NGOs for failing to focus on the three 'essential elements of recognition, institutionalization, and accountability' of economic and social rights.[84] Yet, there is no question that NGO practice related to economic and social rights has radically changed in the last several decades. The human rights movement has formally embraced the full spectrum of human rights, and the practice of advocating for such rights has significantly expanded and improved: large INGOs and regional and national organizations work on all types of rights, and specialized organizations have formed to advance ESC rights in all regions of the world.[85]

The substantive elements of the rights-based approach can be seen not only in the embrace by international NGOs of economic and social rights, but also in the kind of work taken on by national human rights organizations across the globe. As Nelson and Dorsey note, human rights organizations are engaging in innovative advocacy to advance ESCR in the context of global injustice.[86] This work demonstrates an increasing embrace of the true indivisibility of human rights. The in-depth analysis of NGO websites and publications in different regions

Goodman, and Henry J Steiner, *International Human Rights: Text and Materials* (OUP 2013) 66–170 (women), 220–33 (sexual orientation and gender identity).

[80] Phillip Alston, 'Out of the Abyss: The Challenges Confronting the New U. N. Committee on Economic, Social and Cultural Rights' (1987) 9 Human Rights Quarterly 332, 372.

[81] Allison Corkery, 'Investigating Economic, Social, and Cultural Rights Violations' in Philip Alston and Sarah Knuckey (eds), *The Transformation of Human Rights Fact-Finding* (OUP 2016) 377 (exploring fact-finding methods used by human rights NGOs and finding that 'Although the human rights community generally recognizes that these preventable deprivations [of ESCR] need to be addressed, fact-finding methods have failed to evolve in response', internal citation omitted).

[82] Makau Mutua, 'Savages, Victims, and Saviors: The Metaphors of Human Rights' (2001) 42 Harvard International Law Review 201.

[83] Alston, 'The Populist Challenge to Human Rights' (n 77); 'Report of the Special Rapporteur on Extreme Poverty and Human Rights', UN Doc A/HRC/32/31 (n 56) para 11.

[84] Alston, 'The Populist Challenge' (n 77), 9.

[85] Human Rights Watch officially began doing some limited work on ESC rights in 1983, and Amnesty International adopted its 'full spectrum' approach in 2001. Alston, Goodman, and Steiner (n 79) 294; for examples of prominent NGO programming on economic and social rights, see: Amnesty International, 'Human Rights for Human Dignity' (Amnesty International) <https://www.amnesty.org/en/what-we-do/living-in-dignity/> accessed 29 September 2020; The Center for Economic and Social Rights, 'About Us' (Center for Economic and Social Rights) <https://www.cesr.org/> accessed 29 September 2020; 'Economic Justice' (Dejusticia) <https://www.dejusticia.org/en/issues/economic-justice/> accessed 29 September 2020; 'Economic and Social Justice' (Kenya Human Rights Commission) <https://www.khrc.or.ke/programmes/economic-and-social-justice.html> accessed 29 September 2020; organizations in all regions embrace ESC rights. Our examination of the websites of human rights organizations in Latin America, Asia, and Sub-Saharan African demonstrated that the embrace of these rights translated into concrete programming and reporting.

[86] Nelson and Dorsey (n 58),. In addition to the embrace of ESC rights, Nelson and Dorsey also find that human rights NGOs are increasingly focusing on new rights such as the right to free, prior, and informed consent (FPIC), a right that is crucial in the development context, since it recognizes communities' self-determination; ibid 104. While the results of the authors' in-depth assessment of NGO websites are not as striking concerning the issue of FPIC as they were for ESCRs, many of the NGOs examined for this chapter have worked specifically on FPIC. In Latin America and the Caribbean, for example, eleven of the sixteen NGOs examined had conducted work specifically advancing the right to FPIC in the face of development and commercial projects.

undertaken by the authors for this chapter confirmed that prominent NGOs in all thirty-five countries that addressed economic and social rights were not difficult to locate, and that many work on issues of global inequality. Global networks of NGOs focusing on ESC rights have also grown enormously in the past few decades.[87] These changes in the human rights movement mean that human rights organizations are 'consistently doing "rights-based development" on a significant scale'.[88] In other words, as development organizations have taken on a rights-based approach to their work, human rights organizations have taken on development and development-related rights in their work.

Human rights organizations have also improved their practice related to the universality of rights, and of equality and non-discrimination, recognizing and advocating for equality for women, LGBTQI people, people with disabilities, migrants, religious minorities, indigenous peoples, and those experiencing discrimination based on a wide variety of additional axes of identity. And human rights advocates recognize not only that individuals and communities in the global North experience human rights violations, but also that actors and institutions—especially powerful ones, such as those in the global North—violate rights through their extraterritorial actions across the world.[89]

Nelson and Dorsey also point to work on extraterritorial obligations (ETOs) as a crucial innovation by human rights organizations. This substantive area is important because it makes real the concept of universality—the idea that all humans have rights, regardless of where and who they are, and—in the case of ETOs—where and who the violator is.[90] Numerous NGOs in our assessment of websites included work on ETOs. For example, NGOs are engaged in advocacy within transnational development spaces such as REDD+ (the Forest Carbon Partnership Facility), through which they seek to ensure that human rights are guaranteed in the face of demands for developing countries to reduce carbon emissions,[91] as well as work to ensure the SDGs are implemented in a rights-based way.[92] International, regional, and national NGOs coordinate their work on ETOs through a dedicated global network.[93]

The work of some human rights organizations has begun to reflect a grounded understanding of—and an emphasis on the importance of—the interdependence of rights as well.

[87] For example, ESCR-Net, a global network of NGOs working on ESC rights, now has more than 230 organizational members. 'Our Members' (*ESCR-Net*) <https://www.escr-net.org/members> accessed 29 September 2020.

[88] Nelson and Dorsey (n 58).

[89] For example, the ETO Consortium was created in 2007 and has grown into 'a global network of over 140 CSOs and academics that seeks to create awareness on and advance the implementation of States' extraterritorial obligations'. 'The ETO Consortium' (ETOs) <https://www.etoconsortium.org/en/main-navigation/about-us/eto-consortium/> accessed 29 September 2020.

[90] Attention to extraterritorial obligations has also been important in other areas of human rights. For example, Philip Alston, in his role as UN Special Rapporteur on extrajudicial executions, led examination of the legal obligations of states operating armed drones and carrying out 'targeted killings' in the territories of other states. UNHRC, 'Report of the Special Rapporteur on extrajudicial, summary, or arbitrary executions, Philip Alston: Addendum—Study on Targeted Killings' (28 May 2010) UN Doc A/HRC/14/24/Add.6; UNHRC, 'General Comment No 36 (2018) on Article 6 of the International Covenant on Civil and Political Rights, on the Right to Life' (30 October 2018) UN Doc CCPR/C/GC/36 para 63.

[91] For example, the websites of the Aliansi Masyarakat Adat Nusantara (Indonesia) 'Profil Aliansi Masyarakat Adat Nusantara (AMAN)' (Aliansi Masyarakat Adat Nusantara) <http://www.aman.or.id/profil-aliansi-masyarakat-adat-nusantara/> accessed 29 September 2020; CEmSoJ (Nepal), 'Dialogue Seminar on Ensuring Communities' Rights in Nepal's REDD+ Process Organized' (Community Empowerment and Social Justice (CEmSoJ) Network 13 January 2017) <https://cemsoj.wordpress.com/2017/01/13/dialogue-seminar-on-ensuring-communities-rights-in-nepals-redd-process-organized/> accessed 29 September 2020.

[92] For example, The Post-2015 Human Rights Caucus, whose initial statement was signed by more than 350 organizations worldwide: 'The Post-2015 Human Rights Caucus' (CESR 5 September 2013) <https://www.cesr.org/post-2015-human-rights-caucus> accessed 29 September 2020.

[93] The ETO Network now has 140 NGO members (see n 89).

Examples of this stream of work can be found in endeavours calling attention to the human rights impacts of fiscal policy, especially austerity measures and taxation, where states may be tempted to trade one set of rights against another.[94] Other examples include studies that examine the interrelated nature of rights violations,[95] such as research examining how the violation of the rights to water and sanitation relate to violations of the right to security of the person, the right to dignity, or the right to equality.[96] Despite these growing streams of work, too little emphasis has been placed on constructing frameworks for fully understanding and assessing the interdependence of rights.[97] Here, Alston offers guidance: his latest work has demonstrated how a 'fully integrated approach' to the whole spectrum of rights—including true engagement with the issue of wealth and economic inequality—holds the key to making real rights-enhancing change in the global North as well as the global South.[98]

While there is still a great distance to travel, the human rights field appears to be moving in the right direction, increasingly embracing and implementing in practice the substantive HRBA principles of universality, indivisibility, equality, and non-discrimination.

24.3.2 The Process of Advocating for Human Rights: A Practice in Need of Further Reform and Mainstreaming

In addition to guiding which rights are advocated for, and which duty-bearers and rights-holders are included within advocacy work, HRBAs include important principles for the processes by which policies, programmes, and other work should be developed and undertaken, including *how* human rights organizations advocate for rights. However, the HRBA principles that are focused more on the processes by which human rights organizations conduct their advocacy, and particularly how organizations relate to rights-holders, have

[94] For example, 'Assessing Austerity: Monitoring the Human Rights Impacts of Fiscal Consolidation' (Center for Economic and Social Rights 2018) 28 (urging advocates to assess interdependence of rights by 'Identify[ing] how the civil and political rights context shapes the social, economic, political or cultural conditions that deprive people from power and voice regarding the definition of fiscal consolidation policies'); Philip Alston and Nikki Reisch (eds), *Tax, Inequality, and Human Rights* (OUP 2019) ('All rights cost money ... Taxes generate most of the revenue that states can use to protect and promote the rights of their populations'); David Stuckler and Sanjay Basu, *The Body Economic: Why Austerity Kills: Recessions, Budget Battles, and the Politics of Life and Death* (Basic Books 2013) (examining—though not using rights discourse—the health impacts of austerity policies).

[95] Johanne Bouchard and Patrice Meyer-Bisch, 'Intersectionality and Interdependence of Human Rights: Same or Different?' (2016) 16 The Equal Rights Review 186, 189 ('Our intuition was that it would probably be easier to demonstrate the interdependence of the violations of human rights rather than their positive interdependence').

[96] For example, Center for Human Rights and Global Justice and NYU School of Law, 'Yon Je Louvri: Reducing Vulnerability to Sexual Violence in Haiti's IDP Camps' (NYU School of Law 2012) (finding correlations between violations of the right to bodily integrity and the rights to food, water, and sanitation); Apoorva Jadhav, Abigail Weitzman, and Emily Smith-Greenaway, 'Household Sanitation Facilities and Women's Risk of Non-Partner Sexual Violence in India' (2016) 16 BMC Public Health 1139 (finding that 'women who use open defecation are twice as likely to face [non-partner sexual violence] as women with a household toilet'); Nupur Joshi, 'Low-Income Women's Right to Sanitation Services in City Public Spaces: A Study of Waste Picker Women in Pune' (2018) 30 Environment and Urbanization 249 (examining the consequences of women waste-pickers' lack of access to sanitation facilities on their income, health, and well-being).

[97] But see Bouchard and Meyer-Bisch (n 95).

[98] UNGA 'Extreme Poverty and Human Rights—Note by the Secretary-General' (2017) UN Doc A/72/502 ('(a) the poor experience violations of civil and political rights both disproportionately and differently from others; (b) their civil and political rights are more or less systematically neglected by mainstream human rights and development actors; (c) the resulting situation crucially and very problematically undermines the principle of the indivisibility of all human rights; and (d) both the human rights and the development communities need to make far-reaching changes in order to ensure that respect for and promotion of all of the human rights of those living in poverty are incorporated into their analytical frameworks, the methodologies they use and the programmes and policies they recommend').

generally entered less into the vernacular and practice of human rights than those related to the substance of the work.

Rights-holder participation and empowerment, in a limited sense, are part of much human rights advocacy. Rights-holders 'participate' in most human rights work in the sense that they are—at a minimum—often interviewed by advocates who are seeking their victim testimony. And insofar as rights-holders have been disempowered by human rights abuse, empowerment of rights-holders may also be the intended consequence of advocacy to end abuse or promote accountability, that is, their empowerment vis-à-vis the perpetrator state, individual, or corporation. While these are important processes and goals, the HRBA advances a much fuller understanding of these core concepts in relation to the work of advocacy itself.

Rights-based approaches see persons directly affected by abuse as rights-holders who are entitled to participate in processes and decisions that affect them, and not as mere 'victims' or objects of programmes or advocacy. Rights-holders are (and should be treated as) experts on their conditions, and their participation is essential to understanding social justice problems and reforms. Recognition of the importance of rights-holder participation has been core to the methodology of country fact-finding missions undertaken by Alston. In a recent article examining the country missions undertaken by the UN Special Rapporteur on Extreme Poverty, co-authors Philip Alston, Bassam Khawaja, and Rebecca Riddell explained that the 'single most important focus of any visit has to be on understanding the perspectives of the 'rights-holders', or those living in poverty'.[99] And critically, rights-holders are also agents of reform. Yamin and Cantor explain why participation is a 'crucial tenet' of HRBAs: 'it converts passive targets of policies and programmes into active agents and claims-holders with respect to their own well-being'.[100] Rights-based advocacy efforts focus on centring the interests and building the power of directly affected persons so that their capacities to influence the conditions affecting their lives are strengthened, and so that they are empowered to fight against abusive systems. Where rights-holders participate in and lead advocacy, it is more likely to effectively respond to their needs. Rights-based advocacy means that rights-holders are included in or lead the setting of agendas, participate in efforts to investigate and advocate against abuse, and are empowered—rather than constructed as victims in need of saving—through advocacy efforts.[101] As Alston, in his role as the UN Special Rapporteur on extreme poverty explained: 'the language of rights recognizes and insists on the dignity and agency of all individuals (regardless of race, gender, social status, age, disability or any other distinguishing factor) and it is intentionally empowering'.[102] Rights-based approaches also require NGOs to build processes to ensure that they are accountable directly to rights-holders, and not only to funders or other stakeholders in the human rights ecosystem.

There are numerous examples of activists around the world seeking to promote their own accountability to directly affected persons and to ensure the participation and empowerment of rights-holders in advocacy efforts, and of NGOs giving explicit priority to such aims in their mandates, working methods, or goals.[103] As expected based on our approach

[99] Philip Alston, Bassam Khawaja, and Rebecca Riddell, 'Much Ado about Poverty: The Role of a UN Special Rapporteur' (2019) 27 Journal of Poverty and Social Justice 423, 424.

[100] Yamin and Cantor (n 65) 467.

[101] For more on the concrete steps that NGOs do and can take to support rightsholder power, see Knuckey and others (n 2).

[102] UN Doc A/HRC/32/31 (n 56) para 8.

[103] For example, the work of Hakijami, a Kenyan NGO working with rightsholders 'to support them to claim their economic and socio-cultural rights' 'About Hakijamii' (Hakijamii) <https://www.hakijamii.com/?page_id=4630> accessed 29 September 2020; Ceasefire Center for Civilian Rights an NGO 'empowering civilians to monitor violations', 'Ceasefire | The Ceasefire Centre for Civilian Rights Is an International Initiative to Develop

to selecting NGOs to examine for this chapter, many of the thirty-five organizations in Asia, Latin America and the Caribbean, and Sub-Saharan Africa whose websites we examined included a clear commitment to rights-holder participation in their mandate, mission statement, or working methods. A smaller number appeared to actively use a participatory approach in their work, and it was difficult to obtain clarity for most organizations concerning whether or how they hold themselves accountable to rights-holders in a verifiable way.[104] In recent years, prominent international organizations have begun to learn from groups who have led rights-based methods, and have started to shift their language and practices.[105]

However, examples abound of human rights practice undertaken by outside advocates that excludes, marginalizes, or objectifies directly affected individuals and communities, or which is undertaken with minimal attention to how to promote deep rights-holder participation and empowerment. This is not only a question of poor implementation of accepted or professed rights-based values. Instead, doing work in a way that advances the agency of rights-holders has not been explicitly embraced as a shared value and goal across the entirety of the human rights field. Commonly employed and prominent NGO practices can undermine rights-based practice. This has not gone unnoticed. Many critiques of human rights practice share the concerns motivating the participation, accountability, and empowerment principles of the HRBA. A growing body of critical human rights scholarship has voiced significant concern about the tactics and methods employed by parts of the human rights field in its work with rights-holders and communities. Prominent critiques, made by scholars and practitioners alike, include the concerns that advocates approach rights-holders as 'victims' rather than agents of change, fail to promote accountability of advocates to rights-holders, and adopt decision-making processes, research priorities, investigative methods, and reporting formats that take inadequate account of rights-holder and local expertise and

Civilian-Led Monitoring of Violations of International Humanitarian Law or Human Rights' (Ceasfire Centre for Civilian Rights) <https://www.ceasefire.org/> accessed 29 September 2020; WITNESS, an NGO which works 'side-by-side with local communities to harness the power of video and technology in the fight for justice', 'Our Story' (Witness) <https://www.witness.org/about/our-story/> accessed 29 September 2020; MADRE, a feminist NGO which 'partners with grassroots women on the frontlines of war and disaster' at 'MADRE—Global Women's Rights' (MADRE) <https://www.madre.org/home> accessed 29 September 2020; NAMATI, a legal empowerment NGO which is working to build a 'global movement of grassroots legal advocates who help put the power of law in the hands of people' 'Namati' (Namati) <https://namati.org> accessed 29 September 2020; The Center for Economic and Social Rights 'About Us' (Center for Economic and Social Rights 6 August 2008) <https://www.cesr.org/about-us> accessed 29 September 2020 (supports 'efforts by civil society groups and affected communities to claim their economic and social rights. To this end, CESR is working in close collaboration with partners around the world to challenge the injustice of fiscal austerity and tax abuse').

104 NGOs were considered to use a participatory approach if the materials available on their website (statements of purpose or mission, annual reports, research reports, 'about' sections of websites, etc.) discussed active community involvement or decision-making in major NGO activities such as planning, programme implementation, research and reporting, and monitoring and evaluation. To research accountability, we looked for various accountability features, such as whether the NGO's website provided information about a specific mechanism holding the NGO accountable to communities (such as a complaint line or mechanism, as is common in the humanitarian field), or evidence of a practice of making in-depth information about the organization's work to advance the rights of the community directly available to communities.

105 Amnesty International now increasingly speaks of its efforts to 'empower' rights-holders, see 'Taking Injustice Personally: Our Goals 2016–2019' (Amnesty International 2016). One of Amnesty International's goals for 2016–2019 is to 'create a world' in which 'people know their rights and are empowered to claim them'), and to promote the participation of rightsholders in Amnesty International's work; 'Assessing Impact' (Amnesty International) <https://www.amnesty.org/en/about-us/how-were-run/assessing-impact/> accessed 29 September 2020; Human Rights Watch rarely uses similar language in its public materials, but has recently launched a 'partnership initiative' that seeks to 'directly enlist' affected communities 'Noted Kenyan Activist Launches Partnership Initiative' (Human Rights Watch 18 September 2018) <https://www.hrw.org/news/2018/09/20/noted-kenyan-activist-launches-partnership-initiative> accessed 29 September 2020.

priorities. Such practices are visible across the human rights movement, including at prominent, standard-setting organizations.

Much critical human rights scholarship has highlighted the ways advocates (especially those from international NGOs founded in the global North) have positioned themselves as 'saviors' to rescue 'victims' of human rights violations.[106] In this model of practice, advocates are the agents and decision-makers responsible for social justice efforts, and they can ignore or fail to support the efforts and empowerment of rights-holders themselves. Saviour advocates decide agendas, design campaigns, interview victims, and represent rights-holders in advocacy work. Human rights NGOs can produce victimhood when they publish photos of the 'downtrodden' and testimonies of suffering, and when their advocacy asks outside actors to 'save' the victims. It has been common, especially among larger international NGOs, to see human rights reports researched and prepared by outside advocates, describing in detail the suffering of victims, without even passing reference to the activism and agency of those most directly affected by the abuse—even when the rights-holders have been advocates themselves, as is often the case. Such advocacy can be 'voyeuristic', even 'pornographic', can reinforce global inequalities, and renders invisible rights-holder 'efforts to resist oppressive structures'.[107] It can disempower, make exotic, and essentialize persons harmed by human rights abuses.[108] While the representation—in visual imagery, human rights reports, legal briefs, and media work—of rights-holders as powerless 'victims' can be tactically useful to raise awareness of abuse and garner attention (to say nothing of raising funds), it can also undermine the agency of rights-holders[109] and local advocates, and can harm their 'independence [and] competence'.[110]

In viewing and representing rights-holders as victims, advocates can fail to take steps to support rights-holders' rights claims and advocacy for themselves; instead, following processes that increase the advocate's own voice and power at the expense of rights-holders'. In recent work, Alston has begun to critique this tradition of human rights advocacy. In his 2017 essay on 'The Populist Challenge to Human Rights', Alston calls on human rights scholars and practitioners to 'reflect on how better to ensure effective synergies between international and local human rights movements' by focusing more on supporting the capacities of experts and activists closest to the abuses.[111] In another article published in the

[106] Mutua (n 82); Lila Abu-Lughod, 'Do Muslim Women Really Need Saving? Anthropological Reflections on Cultural Relativism and Its Others' (2002) 104 American Anthropologist 783; David Kennedy, 'International Human Rights Movement: Part of the Problem? Boundaries in the Field of Human Rights' (2002) 15 Harvard Human Rights Journal 101; Dina Francesca Haynes, 'Client-Centered Human Rights Advocacy' 13 Clinical Law Review 379, 389–90.

[107] Jeena Shah, 'Rebellious Lawyering in Big Case Clinics' (2016) 23 Clinical Law Review 775, 791–92.

[108] Karen Engle, 'Female Subjects of Public International Law: Human Rights and the Exotic Other Female' (1991) 26 New England Law Review 1509; Tracy E Higgins, 'Anti-Essentialism, Relativism, and Human Rights' (1996) 19 Harvard Women's Law Journal 89; Ratna Kapur, 'The Tragedy of Victimization Rhetoric: Resurrecting the "Native" Subject in International/Post-Colonial Feminist Legal Politics' (2002) 15 Harvard Human Rights Journal 1; Alice M Miller, 'Sexuality, Violence against Women and Human Rights: Women Make Demands and Ladies Get Protection' (2004) 7 Health and Human Rights Journal 16; Karen Engle, 'Feminism and Its (DIS) Contents: Criminalizing Wartime Rape in Bosnia and Herzegovina' (2005) 99 American Journal of International Law 778; Ratna Kapur, 'Human Rights in the 21st Century: Taking a Walk on the Dark Side' (2006) 28 Sydney Law Review 665; Kamari Clarke, 'Constituting Terms for International Change: Reflecting on Strategies for Women's Rights' (2010) 104 American Society of International Law 561; Kate Cronin-Furman, Nimmi Gowrinathan, and Rafia Zakaria, 'Emissaries of Empowerment' (Colin School for Civic and Public Leadership, the City College of New York 2017).

[109] Christine Schwöbel-Patel, 'Spectacle in International Criminal Law: The Fundraising Image of Victimhood' (2016) 4 London Review of International Law 247; Daniel Joyce, 'Photography and the Image-Making of International Justice' (2010) 4 Law and Humanities 229, 239.

[110] Barbora Bukovská, 'Perpetrating Good: Unintended Consequences of International Human Rights Advocacy' (2008) 5 SUR International Journal of Human Rights 6, 8–10.

[111] Alston, 'The Populist Challenge to Human Rights' (n 77) 8–9.

same year, Alston noted that the practices can be extractive, and larger international NGOs can be particularly at fault for 'extracting information and leaving' instead of 'building or complementing national capacity'.[112]

Human rights scholars have identified common practices that fail to empower rights-holders, including advocates deciding to themselves speak to governments to make advocacy demands, or to testify about violations in international human rights fora, or to provide quotes to journalists in press coverage of the human rights issue, instead of supporting rights-holders to do so. Writing about litigation before regional human rights commissions, Crow has argued that victims can become dependent on lawyers, and their priorities may not necessarily be reflected in the legal strategy.[113] When advocates speak 'for victims', as Madlingozi argues, they can 'perpetuate[] their disempowerment' and enable 'relations of inferiority and superiority' to be reproduced through NGO practices.[114]

NGOs may also fail to set up processes to ensure that they are accountable to rights-holders. Human rights organizations often focus on accountability for human rights violations—the accountability of states, corporations, and individual perpetrators to victims of abuse. But a commitment and practice of accountability from *advocates to rights-holders* in human rights practice is often weak. Common NGO practices that undermine accountability occur when, for example, activists conduct interviews with rights-holders without full and meaningful informed consent, including for all the situations in which the testimony will be used, or when NGOs produce reports and conduct advocacy on issues without reporting back to rights-holders about the outputs or outcomes of the work. It is worth noting that it is not common—with a few high-profile exceptions, such as Amnesty International—for human rights organizations to construct accountability mechanisms such as grievance procedures or feedback hotlines for receiving external complaints about NGO practices.[115] While such measures may seem foreign and unnecessary to many human rights advocates, they are common among humanitarian and development organizations.[116] Indeed, Amnesty International is part of a well-known initiative among humanitarian and development organizations, Accountable Now, which requires member organizations to agree to a set of twelve 'Accountability Commitments' against which they publicly report on a yearly basis.[117] These commitments encompass transparency and accountability to

[112] Philip Alston, 'Human Rights under Siege: How to Respond to the Populist Threat Facing Human Rights' (2017) 25 SUR International Journal of Human Rights 1, 3.

[113] Melissa E Crow, 'From Dyad to Triad: Reconceptualizing the Lawyer-Client Relationship for Litigation in Regional Human Rights Commissions' (2005) 26 Michigan Journal of International Law 1096; Lucie White and Jeremy Perelman, 'Essay: Can Human Rights Practice Be a Critical Project—A View from the Ground' (2010) 44 Loyola of Los Angeles Law Review 157, 161.

[114] Tshepo Madlingozi, 'On Transitional Justice Entrepreneurs and the Production of Victims' (2010) 2 Journal of Human Rights Practice 208, 210–13; Carol Bettinger-Lopez and others, 'Redefining Human Rights Lawyering Through the Lens of Critical Theory: Lessons for Pedagogy and Practice' (2011) 18 Faculty Scholarship at Penn Law 337, 258; Ralph Wilde, 'Dilemmas in Promoting Global Economic Justice through Human Rights Law' in Nehal Bhuta (ed), *The Frontiers of Human Rights: Extraterritoriality and Its Challenges* (OUP 2016) (arguing that 'domination' can occur where advocates tell the stories of others); Hadas Ziv, '"Human Rights" Must Join Activists in Social Struggle' (*openDemocracy* 11 July 2013) <https://www.opendemocracy.net/en/openglobalrights-openpage/human-rights-must-join-activists-in-social-struggle/> accessed 29 September 2020 (critiquing NGO reporting *about* and advocacy *for* others).

[115] Amnesty International has a complaint form on its website, and complaints trigger a formal process. Amnesty International, '2018 Report to Accountable Now' (Accountable Now 2018) 19, 24–25 <https://accountablenow.org/wp-content/uploads/2020/01/2018-AI-Report-to-Accountable-Now-FINAL.pdf>.

[116] 'About Us' (*Accountable Now*) <https://accountablenow.org/about-us/> accessed 29 September 2020; 'About Sphere' (*Sphere*) <https://www.spherestandards.org/about/> accessed 29 September 2020; 'About Us' (*CHS Alliance*) <https://www.chsalliance.org/about/> accessed 29 September 2020.

[117] 'About Us' *(Accountable Now)* (n 116).

stakeholders, 'in particular the people (including future generations) whose rights we seek to protect and advance'.[118] Member organizations are expected to create mechanisms to translate these commitments into action.[119] Whether these forms of accountability are satisfying for rights-holders is an open question to which research should be directed. It may be more meaningful to instead ensure that human rights organizations work to develop deeper relationships of trust with rights-holders than to create potentially bureaucratic mechanisms for making complaints. Meaningful accountability is unlikely without more thoroughgoing shifts in the power structures of human rights advocacy itself.

Both scholars and practitioners have proposed ways to improve human rights practice, and many organizations, including some of those most subject to critique, have been seeking in recent years to shift their practices to be more participatory, accountable, and empowering. For example, Amnesty International has undertaken an extensive restructuring, from a single London headquarters office for research and strategy to a 'distributed system with organizational hubs dispersed across key regional capitals worldwide'.[120] Human Rights Watch has launched a new partnership initiative, with Maina Kiai, who co-founded the initiative, stating that 'lasting change in the struggle for basic rights and dignity can best be achieved by more directly enlisting those most affected'.[121] These changes can support efforts to improve human rights practice in line with rights-based principles. Rights-based methods have much in common with 'client-centred human rights lawyering', 'legal empowerment', 'victim-centred approaches', 'community lawyering', and 'radical lawyering', which all seek to partner with rights-holders and communities to support their empowerment.[122] In one of the few scholarly articles explicitly examining the HRBA in relation to human rights practice, Jagannath, Phillips, and Shah describe how a group of Haitian human rights lawyers practice legal empowerment, in contrast to 'traditional legal assistance to marginalized communities [which] tends to be top-down and exclusionary'.[123] They discuss human rights strategies that pair legal representation with 'broad-based organizing, giving communities the opportunity to learn their rights and assert themselves as rights-holders'.[124] For example, Haitian NGO

[118] 'Accountability Commitments' (*Accountable Now* 12 March 2020) <https://accountablenow.org/wp-content/uploads/2020/03/12Comm_Booklet_SCREEN.pdf> accessed 29 September 2020.

[119] ibid.

[120] Salil Shetty, 'Moving Amnesty Closer to the Ground is Necessary, Not Simple' (*openDemocracy* 20 January 2015) <https://www.opendemocracy.net/en/openglobalrights-openpage/moving-amnesty-closer-to-ground-is-necessary-not-simple/> accessed 29 September 2020.

[121] Human Rights Watch, 'Noted Kenyan Activist Launches Partnership Initiative' (n 105).

[122] For example, Benjamin Hoffman and Marissa Vahlsing, 'Collaborative Lawyering in Transnational Human Rights Advocacy' [2014] Clinical Law Review 255, 264–72 (advocates should work to establish a 'shared vision of justice' and a collaborative strategy with communities, building capacity where necessary to redress power imbalances that may undermine equal participation); Haynes (n 106) 381–82 (advocates should 'respect[]' and 'bolster[]' the agency of the victim 'in determining how or whether to address her human rights violation'); Shah (n 107) 793–94 ('rebellious lawyering' should see advocates working in '*meaningful collaboration and for the purpose of building power* within affected communities ... international advocates do not speak for local advocates, but local advocates speak their own truths in international fora').

[123] Jagannath, Phillips, and Shah (n 72) 8; for other examples of legal empowerment approaches, see Lorenzo Cotula, Thierry Berger, and International Institute for Environment and Development, *Improving Accountability in Agricultural Investments: Reflections from Legal Empowerment Initiatives in West Africa* (International Institute for Environment and Development 2017); Mustafa Mahmoud and Laura Goodwin, 'Community Facilitators in the Pursuit of Justice: Lessons from Jordan on Recruitment, Training & Data' (Namati 2018); Godfrey Massay, 'Pillars of the Community: How Trained Volunteers Defend Land Rights in Tanzania' (International Institute for Environment and Development 2016); 'Declaration of Villa Inflamable' (Namati 2017) <https://namati.org/network/justiciaparatodxs-english/> accessed 29 September 2020 (promising to 'work together with people and communities to put their rights in their hands, thereby promoting legal empowerment and strengthening processes for rights enforcement'); Lars Waldorf, 'Introduction: Legal Empowerment in Transitions' (2015) 19 International Journal of Human Rights 229.

[124] Jagannath, Phillips, and Shah (n 72) 9.

Bureau des Avocats Internationaux (BAI) engages 'grassroots coordinators', who work with local groups and the BAI lawyers to ensure that rights-holders have access to trainings about their rights and to support rights-holders to engage in advocacy themselves.[125] This helps rights-holders to understand and claim their own rights, bringing them in 'as partners in advocacy'.[126] The authors argue that:

> As opposed to viewing those communities as passive recipients of legal assistance, lawyers and legal advocates should employ a rights-based model that blends traditional litigation with broad-based organizing strategies to empower and mobilize communities to engage directly with the state and pursue their basic human rights.[127]

Working alongside their human rights colleagues, the authors of this chapter have attempted to embrace HRBAs in their scholarly writing[128] and implement them in their clinic-based human rights advocacy.[129] Finally, there is an emerging convergence between human rights advocacy and legal empowerment work. By centring the increased agency of rights-holders, legal empowerment strategies insist that *how* rights are protected matters as much as *whether* they are enforced or not.[130]

24.4 In Lieu of a Conclusion: Questions for Human Rights Organizations

The HRBA offers a powerful set of principles to guide and assess the substance and process of work undertaken to improve living conditions, justice, and rights. Fundamentally,

[125] ibid 10, 14, 16–17.
[126] ibid 14.
[127] ibid 18.
[128] For example, in a chapter examining rights-based human rights fact-finding, Satterthwaite and Klasing share the methods they used for an investigation of the right to water, setting out a process for centring rights-holders and elevating their voices. They worked to advance empowerment by ensuring that rights-holders were educated about their rights in the course of the research project, accountability through strong informed consent, and participation by involving rightsholders in 'the entire life cycle of a project—from needs assessment to implementation and evaluation'. Satterthwaite and Klasing (n 72) 143; Knuckey and others (n 2).
[129] For example, Columbia Law School Human Rights Clinic and Advanced Consortium on Cooperation, Conflict and Complexity, 'Red Water: Mining and the Right to Water in Porgera, Papua New Guinea' (Columbia University 2019) <https://web.law.columbia.edu/system/files/private_file/red-water-report-2019_1.pdf> accessed 10 May 2021 (describing the rights-based approach used); 'Human Rights in Haiti's Emerging Mining Sector' (Center for Human Rights and Global Justice) <https://chrgj.org/focus-areas/global-justice-clinic/preventing-violations-and-advancing-rights-in-haitis-emerging-mining-sector/> accessed 29 September 2020 (describing numerous activities GJC has carried out in collaboration with the Kolektif Jistis Min (Mining Justice Collective) in Haiti, aimed at empowering local communities to make informed decisions about potential mining activities). At times, implementing the HRBA means supporting partner organizations that take the leading role; South Rupununi District Council, 'Wapichan Environmental Monitoring Report' (2018) (report by indigenous partners of the NYU Global Justice Clinic in Guyana); Porgera Women's Right Watch and others, 'Disproportionate Impacts of Business Activities on Women: Lessons from Papua New Guinea to Inform Gender Guidance to the UN Guiding Principles on Business and Human Rights' (2018) (report by partners of the Columbia Human Rights Clinic); Collectif des Étudiants Musulmans Centrafricains, 'Submission to the UN Human Rights Council—31st Session of the Universal Periodic Review Working Group' (2018) Draft) (report by partners of the Columbia Human Rights Clinic).
[130] As Sukti Dhital writes, legal empowerment 'is a growing field of human rights practice, scholarship, and education' that strives 'to listen to the stories of communities affected by injustice, and to reverse the tide [of injustice] by strengthening the capacity of marginalized individuals to use the law to find solutions to their justice problems'. Sukti Dhital, 'Reimagining Justice: Human Rights through Legal Empowerment' (*OpenGlobalRights* 23 April 2018) <https://www.openglobalrights.org/Reimagining-justice-human-rights-through-legal-empowerment/?lang=English> accessed 29 September 2020.

the process principles are about centring rights-holders so that advocacy meets their needs and supports their agency and power. We believe it is time for the human rights community to turn the process principles of empowerment, participation, and accountability back on ourselves with significantly more rigour. Rather than standing outside these rights-based imperatives, self-examination might help us respond more meaningfully to the trenchant critiques of human rights practice that have stood unanswered for too long. For those activists and NGOs seeking to improve their practice using a rights-based approach, we offer here a set of starting questions to guide self-reflection on the participation, empowerment, and accountability principles:

Has your organization formally committed to using the principles of rights-holder participation, empowerment, and accountability to guide its work? Are the principles central to your organization's mandate and working methods?

Do advocates have organizational support to integrate these principles into every element of their work?

Does your organization adopt practices to promote accountability to rights-holders, including: meaningful informed consent processes; reporting back on findings, work undertaken, and outcomes; creating opportunities for feedback from, dialogue with, and response to complaints by, rights-holders?

How do rights-holders participate in your work and in advancing their rights? Do they play a role in influencing your organization's human rights priorities, strategies, and tactics? Are they consulted for their views, or do they have the power to decide on key issues? Does your organization help promote the conditions for effective participation, including through early consultation or joint decision-making, adequate timelines for meaningful engagement, and translation and funding where needed?

What is the role of rights-holders in any human rights investigation carried out by your organization? Are they merely 'victims' who provide testimony? Is the expertise and knowledge of rights-holders recognized, respected, and acknowledged in your investigations and reports? Does your organization carry out investigations in partnership with rights-holders, ensuring they are given credit for their work? Are methods transparently shared? Are the capacities of rights-holders to carry out investigations and understand and own the data relevant to their lives supported?

What roles do rights-holders play in your organization's advocacy? Does your organization 'represent' rights-holders in photographs, reports, or in advocacy, and if so, how is informed consent for these activities guaranteed? How are rights-holders represented, and what messages—intended and unintended—are conveyed in those representations? Does your organization support rights-holders to speak for themselves, to develop their advocacy skills, and to access advocacy platforms?

Does your organization evaluate whether rights-holders are empowered through their work with you? Does your relationship with rights-holders result in increased opportunities, skills, and knowledge among rights-holders? Are there situations in which your work could more usefully be directed to empowering rights-holders themselves to conduct research, design strategies, and carry out advocacy instead of doing the work within your organization? How does your organization examine whether its work is effectively crowding out the efforts of rights-holders?

Learning from critiques of the HRBA in other contexts, human rights advocates must also be careful not to implement HRBAs superficially, as a set of 'checklists', or to merely shift how work is described. It is essential to avoid a bureaucratic, technocratic approach. The principles capture a political vision and imperatives, and should be effected with purpose: to strengthen rights and empower those directly affected to claim their rights and to challenge abusive and unjust structures. Indeed, the work of truly transforming human rights work to make it more aligned with core rights principles will likely lead to thoroughgoing changes in the way many organizations work. Ultimately, we believe that asking searching questions of human rights practice and methods can open a door to transformative change that will place rights-holders truly at the centre of human rights advocacy.

25
Quite Enough (Still)
Human Rights in (Times of) Crisis

Florian Hoffmann

25.1 'You Learn to Know a Pilot in a Storm': Dealing with Human Rights in (Times of) Crisis

In one of the most recent iterations of his career-spanning engagement with the trickiest and most contested issues in and around (international) human rights,[1] Philip Alston has sought to take on both what he has termed the populist challenge to human rights and the new intellectual critiques that have emerged in the former's wake.[2] Hence, as many a time before, he has used his widely heard voice in academia, in the United Nations, and in the broader human rights community to argue against the detractors of human rights at a moment in world (and national) politics that he deems to be critical—both for human rights and for the plight of people across the globe. As usual, his tone has been measured, yet his argument clear cut and at times sharp; his perspective broad and non-sectarian, close to the legal mainstream while sensitive to its critique; yet always unforgiving of self-righteousness, complacency, or bad faith wherever detected. And, perhaps surprisingly for some, his vision has almost always been less orthodox and less predictable than might be expected from a heavyweight of the international human rights system. However, untypically for someone also known (and sometimes feared) for his glacial coolness and razor—sharp analysis (as well as his disarmingly dry sense of humour) vis-à-vis human rights violations and violators, there has been a tangible element of passion in this latest engagement that betrays a different dimension of concern. Indeed, in one well-publicised exchange on 'Human Rights in the Populist Era', he begins with the uncommonly bleak statement that 'the world as we in the human rights movement have known it in recent years is no longer'.[3] What is implied here is not just the nostalgia of someone who actively helped build that movement, nor the occasional professional gloom over the seemingly unsurmountable odds that anyone working in human rights continuously faces. It is a more fundamental disquiet about the present times, which are, as he concludes, 'extraordinarily dangerous [. . .] unprecedentedly so in my lifetime'.[4] For someone who to many of those who have worked with him has been as steady a rock in the structurally unsteady human rights sea as there may possibly be, this is quite an extraordinary statement.

Alston's primary focus here is of course the recent right populist turn in many places both the global North and South and the attendant espousal of a hard right political agenda that

[1] 'Gubernatorem in tempestate [in acie militem] intellegas', Lucius Annaeus Seneca and LD Reynolds, *L. Annaei Senecae Dialogorum Libri Duodecim* (E Typographeo Clarendoniano 1977).
[2] Philip Alston, 'The Populist Challenge to Human Rights' (2017) 9 Journal of Human Rights Practice 1.
[3] ibid 1.
[4] ibid 14.

Florian Hoffmann, *Quite Enough (Still)* In: *The Struggle for Human Rights.* Edited by: Nehal Bhuta, Florian Hoffmann, Sarah Knuckey, Frédéric Mégret, and Margaret Satterthwaite, Oxford University Press.
DOI: 10.1093/oso/9780198868064.003.0026

had long been thought consigned to the history books. The latter has not only unburied the most rabid forms of neo-nationalist, xenophobic, racist, anti-LGBTQ+, anti-poor (and in fact anti-everyone and everything deemed to be associated with the liberal centre, the left, or, indeed, the modern world) discourse, but it has also and often with particular verve scorned human rights and their defenders.[5]

However, perhaps even more detrimental than this political manoeuvring has been the cognitive onslaught against the very idea of human rights that the often neo- or para-fascist ideological templates of these political movements have produced.[6] For unlike openly autocratic regimes, the new populist configurations rely on significant electoral support for their position, and thus on a growing public acceptance of discourses and practices explicitly opposed to human rights and what they stand for.[7] The societies in which these movements have come to power or are growing in support therefore tend to be deeply divided, in some cases so much so that there is no longer any common ground upon which a shared basic consensus on the sort of society people wish to have could be built.[8] Certainly human rights or even just the fundamental recognition of equal human dignity seem no longer to provide such common ground and have instead become increasingly contested as ways to frame political, social, or economic issues.

However, the populist offensive against human rights is, arguably, only the tip of a much bigger iceberg of troubles for human rights and the human rights movement—a fact Alston has implicitly (and sometimes explicitly) acknowledged in many of his recent writings.[9] For in parallel to the rise of the populist right, a new round of intellectual critiques of rights has emerged over the past decade or so, a fact that is as overtly surprising as it is deeply symptomatic for the current conjuncture.[10] Ironically, these new critiques have mostly been

[5] Gerald L Neuman and Harvard Law School (eds), *Human Rights in a Time of Populism: Challenges and Responses* (CUP 2020); César Rodríguez-Garavito and Krizna Gomez (eds), *Rising to the Populist Challenge: A New Playbook for the Human Rights Field* (Dejujsticia 2018); Marcelo Alegre, 'Populism and Human Rights: Oil and Water?' (Sela Annual Conference, Athens GA, October 2016).

[6] This author is aware that the use of the term 'fascist' in connection with the contemporary turn to (right-wing) populism is both (somewhat) over-inflated and (therefore) highly contested. Broadly speaking, there seem to be two opposing schools of thought: one rejects the assimilation of contemporary forms of reactionary or authoritarian populism with the historical fascisms of Italian or German provenance on the grounds that the former allegedly does not fit all the characteristics of the latter and that their conflation therefore amounts to both misunderstanding the former and relativizing the latter; the other school of thought holds a wider conception of fascism in which structural similarities rather than historical context is deemed to determine an ideological framework's proximity to fascism; this author tends to the latter school, though would qualify the world views of these movements as neo—or para-fascist. Alston has, to this author's knowledge, not publicly opined on this. See, amongst an extensive literature, Enzo Traverso and Régis Meyran, *The New Faces of Fascism: Populism and the Far Right* (Verso 2019); Mabel Berezin, 'Fascism and Populism: Are They Useful Categories for Comparative Sociological Analysis?' (2019) 45 Annual Review of Sociology 345.

[7] Mark A Graber, 'Constitutional Democracy in Crisis?: The Right-Wing Populist Surge' <https://intr2dok.vifa-recht.de/receive/mir_mods_00003968> accessed 08 November 2020.

[8] For a seminal contribution here, see Wendy Brown, *Undoing the Demos: Neoliberalism's Stealth Revolution* (1st edn, Zone Books 2015); Thomas Carothers and Andrew O'Donohue (eds), *Democracies Divided: The Global Challenge of Political Polarization* (Brookings Institution Press 2019).

[9] Alston, 'The Populist Challenge' (n 2); Philip Alston, 'Reply to Dudai and Nagaraj' (2017) 9 Journal of Human Rights Practice 25; Philip Alston, 'Human Rights under Siege: How to Respond to the Populist Threat Facing Human Rights' (2017) 25 SUR International Journal of Human Rights 267; Alston's strongly—worded report, UNHRC, 'Report of the Special Rapporteur on Extreme Poverty and Human Rights—Note by the Secretariat' (28 April 2016) UN Doc A/HRC/32/31, 9.

[10] For an overview of some of the earlier (new) critiques, see Frédéric Mégret, 'Where Does the Critique of International Human Rights Stand? An Exploration in 18 Vignettes' in José María Beneyto and David Kennedy (eds), *New Approaches to International Law: The European and the American Experiences* (TMC Asser Press 2012); Malcolm Langford, 'Critiques of Human Rights' (2017) 14 Annual Review of Law and Social Science 69; see also, amongst many more, Samuel Moyn, *The Last Utopia: Human Rights in History* (Belknap Press of Harvard University Press 2012); Samuel Moyn, *Not Enough: Human Rights in an Unequal World* (Belknap Press of Harvard University Press 2019); Susan Marks, 'Human Rights and Root Causes' (2011) 74 The Modern Law

premised on the paradoxical affirmation that human rights are at once 'not enough' and 'too much'—they are, in other words, seen as too weak to address the root causes of the crisis, yet too strong in terms of the investment still placed in their promotion. Indeed, they have alongside similarly contested concepts—such as (representative) democracy, (neo)liberalism, or globalization—and in the unsavoury company of similarly tuned populist right critiques, come to be seen as primary symbols for what is wrong with today's world. This in itself should give reason for pause: Why rights and why now? How does the claim of powerlessness and irrelevance square with the significant intellectual investment made to debunk rights at a moment when political hostility to rights seems anyways to have reached a peak?[11] Indeed, many of the arguments made in this latest round of critiques seem not to be much more than re-enactments of the critical points already made during earlier periods.[12] It seems at times as if human rights in the abstract have been singled out as a cipher for a much more fundamental critique of the (neo)liberal world order or, indeed, of certain dominant readings of Western modernity as such.[13]

Several factors have, arguably, exacerbated this new debate: firstly, when these new critiques began to emerge around the publication of Samuel Moyn's influential *Last Utopia* in 2010, the human rights community had itself taken an inward turn; it was marked by a certain 'bubble think' with a growing emphasis on the technocratic aspects of human rights advocacy and an ever deeper focus on (state-level) policymaking and regulation.[14] This has meant that, until recently, the ensuing debate has mostly unfolded as a *dialogue de sourds* with each of the involved constituencies unwilling or unable to actually engage with each other's point of view. Hence, much of the populist militancy against human rights is largely oblivious of the real-life workings of national or international human rights systems, while the human rights community has so far mostly reacted to this challenge by simply proposing to do more of what it has always done. Likewise, few of the new (intellectual) critics of human rights have much footing in actual human rights work while coming, at times,

Review 57; Stefan-Ludwig Hoffmann, *Human Rights in the Twentieth Century* (CUP 2010); Walter Mignolo, *The Darker Side of Western Modernity: Global Futures, Decolonial Options* (Duke University Press 2011); Aakash Singh Rathore and Alex Cistelecan (eds), *Wronging Rights? Philosophical Challenges for Human Rights* (Routledge 2011); Susan Marks, 'Four Human Rights Myths' in David Kinley, Wojciech Sadurski, and Kevin Walton (eds), *Human Rights: Old Problems, New Possibilities* (Edward Elgar 2013); Robert Dickinson and others (eds), *Examining Critical Perspectives on Human Rights* (CUP 2012); Etienne Balibar, 'On the Politics of Human Rights: On the Politics of Human Rights: Etienne Balibar' (2013) 20 Constellations 18; José-Manuel Barreto (ed), *Human Rights from a Third World Perspective: Critique, History and International Law* (Cambridge Scholars Publishing 2013); Eric A Posner, *The Twilight of Human Rights Law* (OUP 2014); Stephen Hopgood, *The Endtimes of Human Rights* (Cornell University Press 2013); Nelson Maldonado-Torres, 'On the Coloniality of Human Rights' (2017) Revista Crítica de Ciências Sociais 117; Christoph Menke, *Critique of Rights* (Polity 2020).

[11] Grainne de Búrca, 'Shaming Human Rights' (NYU School of Law 2018) Jean Monnet Working Paper 2/18.

[12] For example, Anne Orford's successive contributions in Anne Orford, *Reading Humanitarian Intervention: Human Rights and the Use of Force in International Law* (CUP 2003) <https://doi.org/10.1017/CBO9780511494277> accessed 07 November 2020; and in Anne Orford, 'Beyond Harmonization: Trade, Human Rights and the Economy of Sacrifice' (2005) 18 Leiden Journal of International Law 179; and in Anne Orford (ed), *International Law and Its Others* (CUP 2009); in a similar vein and period, Wendy Brown, '"The Most We Can Hope For ...": Human Rights and the Politics of Fatalism' (2004) 103 South Atlantic Quarterly 451.

[13] Mignolo (n 10); Florian Hoffmann, 'Facing South: On the Significance of an/other Modernity in Comparative Constitutional Law' in Philipp Dann, Michael Riegner, and Maxim Bönnemann (eds), *The Global South and Comparative Constitutional Law* (OUP 2020) 41–67.

[14] For example, David Kennedy's well-known pieces:David Kennedy, 'The International Human Rights Movement: Part of the Problem? (Part 2)' (2001) 3 European Human Rights Law Review 245; David Kennedy, 'The International Human Rights Regime: Still Part of the Problem?' in Dickinson and others (n 10) 19–34; as well as Krizna Gomez, 'Why Do Progressive Movements Struggle to Answer Populists? Because They Are Technocrats' (*openDemocracy* 18 November 2019) <https://www.opendemocracy.net/en/frontline-insights/why-do-progressive-movements-struggle-answer-populists-because-they-are-technocrats/> accessed 07 November 2020.

uncomfortably close to the conclusions on human rights (defenders) drawn by populist politicians; conversely, besides trying to dig in its heels into an increasingly wobbly ground, the human rights community has not really sought to engage these new critiques on their own (intellectual) terms. Alston's uncharacteristically candid call for action must also be read as an attempt to wake the human rights community from a certain (self-content) lethargy. In doing so, he has, again, been an exception, as he has tended to think across and around these different bubbles with a view to understanding, rather than just reacting to the diverse challenges he has encountered—a stance that has, at times, confounded supporters and critics alike yet has given him a unique intellectual versatility for grasping the issues at hand. So here, too, he has argued that, on one hand, 'human rights proponents need to rethink many of their assumptions, re-evaluate their strategies, and broaden their outreach while [on the other hand] not giving up on the basic principles'.[15] The call is, hence, for a multi-front engagement with critique and against complacency, neither in despair nor in a spirit of 'business as usual'.

However, Alston's call to (intellectual and political) arms has also been seen in the context of one particular aspect of the current human rights crisis, namely its entanglement with the ongoing debate about the continued viability of the welfare state, or, more precisely, about the state's role in guaranteeing an adequate standard of living and an equitable distribution of basic goods such as health, food, water, housing, or education though a proactive economic and fiscal policy geared to these objectives. This is of course the realm of social and economic rights, long considered as 'second generation' (aka second class) and until relatively recently largely off the radar of the big human rights advocacy organizations, though the thematic area perhaps most closely associated with Alston ever since his entry into the world of international human rights protection. The passion with which he has led the current debate is, hence, not only due to a very real worry about the future of human rights, but it is, arguably, also linked to the fact that, as paradoxical as it may seem, social rights have been one primary target of the contemporary populist right. For they have come to be associated with classical welfare state entitlements and the rights-based social or transformative constitutionalism that has frequently emerged alongside it.[16] Although on the surface the populist right is all about economic nationalism and the preservation of the inherited privileges of its—however defined—core constituencies, and, hence, nominally against both political and economic liberalism, its actual economic agenda has almost always been subservient to the interests and premises of the neoliberal world order. Although it is debatable whether this apparently counterfactual alliance of (finance) capitalism and political nationalism is actually new or just newly transparent, on the ground it has meant that social rights have become primary targets that are associated with left welfare statism, developmentalism, and what would today be termed heterodox economic policies.[17] For the neoliberal right, the rights-based judicialization of social policies such as health, education, housing, food, or water and sanitation, as well as the parallel hardening of the international enforcement of

[15] Alston 'The Populist Challenge' (n 2) 2.

[16] Michaela Hailbronner, 'Transformative Constitutionalism: Not Only in the Global South' (2017) 65 The American Journal of Comparative Law 527; Günter Frankenberg, *Comparative Constitutional Studies: Between Magic and Deceit* (Edward Elger Publishing 2018); LaDawn Haglund and Robin Stryker (eds), *Closing the Rights Gap: From Human Rights to Social Transformation* (University of California Press 2015); Randall Peerenboom and Tom Ginsburg (eds), *Law and Development of Middle-Income Countries: Avoiding the Middle-Income Trap* (CUP 2014).

[17] Posner, *The Twighlight of Human Rights Law* (n 10); Gillian MacNaughton and Diane F Frey (eds), *Economic and Social Rights in a Neoliberal World* (Cambridge University Press 2018); Wendy Brown, *In the Ruins of Neoliberalism: The Rise of Antidemocratic Politics in the West* (CUP 2019).

social rights, present unwelcome obstacles to large-scale austerity programmes and 'anti-corruption' public sector reforms. To the populist right in turn they represent a universalist egalitarianism that stands in the way of its (more or less open) espousal of ethnocentric or class-based inequality and social stratification, of its agenda to criminalize poverty and 'the poor' and, generally, of its re-affirmation of the primacy of executive 'can do' politics over judicial or administrative 'meddling'.[18]

Against this backdrop, it is a deep irony, and one that has certainly not escaped Alston, that the latest round of intellectual human rights critiques has not only emerged roughly alongside the rise of the populist right, but also shares with the latter a particular antipathy for social rights, based, in essence, on the argument that they are either too powerful (for the right) or too powerless (for the left), or, curiously, simply irrelevant (for both) vis-à-vis the challenges of a (post-)neoliberal world. What these new intellectual critiques and the populist right's disdain for rights converge on is the common theme that rights advocacy is allegedly the game of a small cosmopolitan elite that represents, depending on where on the political spectrum the charge is made, either a neoliberal or a left-wing conspiracy to undermine national sovereignty and democratic politics. Typically, Alston has responded to this challenge by not directly responding to the fundamental critique but, instead, by drawing on his vast experience from the frontlines of both the international human rights system and the human rights field. He has thus highlighted the numerous instances in which rights have been used, by people 'on the ground' as much as in national and international institutional settings (not least tribunals), as one, or, sometimes, the only defence against the full-scale dismantling of welfare policies and a mutilation of the state into a rump permanently incapable of advancing egalitarian politics.[19] And he has not minced his words when calling out the nature of the problem, such as when he described:

> a world in which the richest 1% owns 48% of global wealth, and in which this imbalance continues to accelerate, is obscene. Radical inequality inevitably sustains extreme poverty just as surely as it sustains extreme wealth. And extreme poverty is best defined as a condition in which the vast majority of human rights cannot possibly be realized. In other words, inequality is not just as an economic issue, but also one of human rights.[20]

Yet, his vision has never been fundamentalist but rather pragmatic, with human rights always framed as a complementary means to advance human dignity through law, albeit a means still and quite uniquely endowed with both nearly universal symbolic currency and an evolved institutional infrastructure. Yet, as Alston's recent call has underlined, it is now more important than ever for the human rights community to engage openly and constructively with the (intellectual) critique if it is to forge an ever-stronger response to its real opponent, notably the populist right. For unlike the intellectual critiques, its agenda is to destroy the intellectual foundations not just of human rights but also of those alternative 'projects' that motivate the current critique of rights.

[18] For example, Brown, *In the Ruins of Neoliberalism* (n 17); Darren J O'Byrne, 'The Rise of Populism, the Demise of the Neoliberal and Neoconservative Globalist Projects, and the War on Human Rights' (2019) 9 International Critical Thought 254.

[19] While a point Alston has made throughout his career (and UN mandates), it is evidently particularly prominent in his current mandate on Extreme Poverty and Human Rights; an exemplary statement is Philip Alston, 'Extreme Inequality as the Antithesis of Human Rights' (*OpenGlobalRights* 27 August 2015) <https://www.openglobalrights.org/extreme-inequality-as-the-antithesis-of-human-rights/> accessed 07 November 2020.

[20] ibid.

25.2 Not Enough or Too Much: New Critiques of Human Rights in the Era of (Neoliberal) Populism

Both the latest round of intellectual critiques of human rights and the rise of the populist right—and its specific targeting of human rights—emerge in the context of a general social fallout generated by the neoliberal world order that has become increasingly manifest during the past decade or so.[21] Established legitimation narratives no longer work as the gap between what people perceive as reality—which has of course itself become a highly contested concept—and its 'official' image has become unbridgeable. Rising inequality, the precarization of labour, and the immiseration of growing sections of society, especially—but increasingly not only—in the global South, have led to massive disenchantment amongst those being -or feeling—left behind.[22] The consequent structural instability and social fragmentation has in turn led both to an ever more forceful policing of discontent by public authority and to a (right) populist turn based on old and new irredentist narratives.[23]

One backdrop to this development is the gradual transformation of the role of the state after World War II, from one geared to the provision of 'welfare' and 'development' driven by a broad (if often highly selective) egalitarian logic, to one largely limited to policing market functionality and insuring market failures, and therefore accepting of the social stratification produced (and required) by the market.[24] The contemporary state thus operates in a comparatively reduced policy space that structurally curtails its capacity to directly attend to the demands brought to it by its constituents, including in the area of social and economic policy.[25] Hence, while in Western constitutionalism's near dominant script, the state remains

[21] For example, William Davies, *The Limits of Neoliberalism: Authority, Sovereignty and the Logic of Competition* (Revised edn, Sage 2017).

[22] For example, Alston's strongly worded statement on austerity measures in Brazil: OHCHR, 'Brazil 20-Year Public Expenditure Cap Will Breach Human Rights, UN Expert Warns' (*UN News*, Geneva 9 December 2015) <https://www.ohchr.org/EN/NewsEvents/Pages/DisplayNews.aspx?NewsID=21006> accessed 07 November 2020; as well as his much-noted visits to the United States and the United Kingdom in his capacity as Special Rapporteur for Extreme Poverty and Human Rights; see OHCHR, 'Statement on Visit to the USA, by Professor Philip Alston, United Nations Special Rapporteur on Extreme Poverty and Human Rights' (*UN News*, Washington 15 December 2017) <https://www.ohchr.org/EN/NewsEvents/Pages/DisplayNews.aspx?NewsID=22533> accessed 11 September 2020; OHCHR, 'Statement on Visit to the United Kingdom, by Professor Philip Alston, United Nations Special Rapporteur on Extreme Poverty and Human Rights' (*UN News*, London 16 November 2018) <https://www.ohchr.org/en/NewsEvents/Pages/DisplayNews.aspx?NewsID=23881> accessed 11 September 2020.

[23] Jan Erik Grindheim, 'Why Right-Leaning Populism Has Grown in the Most Advanced Liberal Democracies of Europe' (2019) 90 The Political Quarterly 757.

[24] This is of course not to romanticize the classical welfare state not least as it is not necessarily associated with an egalitarian logic; there are many cases in which the real-life incarnations of these state models have preserved established social strata and have 'purchased' greater equality only at the cost of the purposive exclusion or minoritization of certain categories, such as women, 'minorities', or immigrants, or indeed of the global South (aka the third world); it is nonetheless the case that welfare states tended to actively seek to balance the interests of capital and labour within their jurisdictions and, at least under the specific conditions of post-war (Western) Europe and (North) America, were thereby able to prioritize redistributional policies that had social inclusionary and equality-enhancing effects; similarly, the classical developmental states of the South—especially the (so called) Asian Tigers; see, classically, TH Marshall, *Class, Citizenship and Social Development* (CUP 1950); Frank Nullmeier and Franz-Xaver Kaufmann, 'The Post-War Welfare State Development' in Francis G Castles and others, *The Oxford Handbook of the Welfare State* (OUP 2012) ch 6; Giandomenico Majone, 'The Regulatory State and Its Legitimacy Problems' (1999) 22 West European Politics 1; David Trubek, 'Developmental States and the Legal Order: Towards a New Political Economy of Development and Law' (2008) University of Wisconsin Legal Studies Research Paper 1075, <https://papers.ssrn.com/sol3/papers.cfm?abstract_id=1349163> accessed 07 November 2020.

[25] Florian Hoffmann, 'Revolution or Regression: Retracing the Turn to Rights in "Law and Development"' in Jarna Petman (ed), *Finnish Yearbook of International Law, Volume 23* (2016) 45–70.

the main duty bearer vis-à-vis its citizens, fulfilment of its concomitant obligations increasingly transcends its jurisdictional and fiscal remit.[26] Indeed, while 'on paper' states continue to be the sovereign monads of Vattelian international law, they have factually mutated into nodes within overlapping normative networks that can only fulfil their fundamental tasks collectively, in conjunction with other states, intermediated by international organizations or, indeed, alongside different types of non-state actors such as corporations or civil society organizations.[27] A further element of this transformation has been the growing juridification and, indeed, judicialization of politics under the auspices of an expansive rule of law and good governance agenda. Ever more aspects of national and international political life have become legalized and judicial bodies have (been) turned into core instruments for the disciplining of the domestic and international policy process.[28] This has in turn fostered the technocratization of democratic process and exacerbated the legitimacy gap that is at the base of the turn to the populist right.[29]

Human rights have been in the midst of these transformations and have variously been seen as either handmaidens of the neoliberal advance or as instruments of its containment, as productive of an unrealistic sense of (welfare) entitlement or as a necessary entrenchment thereof, as overstretching the fiscal capacity of individual states or as a privileged idiom to articulate and concretize human dignity in a post-national world. The increasing legalization of politics has exacerbated this ambivalence, as it has shifted rights to the centre of the policy process while simultaneously tightening the constraints under which governments must operate in order to fulfil the resulting obligations.[30]

Yet, while the growing ambivalence that surrounds rights discourse has certainly pierced the aura of self-evidence that surrounded it in the 1990s, rights remain, despite debate about their role and pedigree, a 'fact of the world' and still provide one of the principal frameworks for people on the ground to protest against real or perceived injustice and to demand minimally dignified living conditions.[31] Perhaps it is precisely this strange facticity of rights language in the face of not only their permanent violation but also continuous contestation that lies at the base of this latest round of critiques, all of which appear to be driven both by puzzlement over their strangely stubborn resilience as well as by irritation about the public attention they still draw, to the detriment of alternative 'projects'.[32] What is more, none of these critiques are entirely new, they are arguably merely the newest iteration of particular strands in the history of ideas about human rights and most directly succeed the previous round of debates that took place during the so called era of human rights triumphalism in

[26] For example, Hoffmann, 'Facing South' (n 13).

[27] This contention of course engages a large and diverse literature on the transformation of the state, state sovereignty, and the 'international', which cannot be reviewed here; in (international) law, relevant reflection includes,for example, Benedict Kingsbury, Nico Krisch, and Richard B Stewart, 'The Emergence of Global Administrative Law' (2005) 68 Law and Contemporary Problems 15; Andreas Fischer-Lescano and Gunther Teubner, 'Regime-Collisions: The Vain Search for Legal Unity in the Fragmentation of Global Law' (2004) 25 Michigan Journal of International Law 999.

[28] Ran Hirschl, 'The New Constitution and the Judicialization of Pure Politics Worldwide' (2006) 75, 721; Florian Hoffmann, 'The Future of Social Rights' in Nehal Bhuta (ed), *Human Rights in Transition – Between Past and Future* (2021, forthcoming).

[29] Alexander Somek and Michael A Wilkinson, 'Unpopular Sovereignty?' (2020) 83 The Modern Law Review 955; Michael A Wilkinson, 'Authoritarian Liberalism as Authoritarian Constitutionalism' (2018) LSE Legal Studies Working Paper No 18 <https://ssrn.com/abstract=3281320> accessed 07 November 2020.

[30] Hoffmann, 'The Future of Social Rights' (n 28).

[31] Eduardo Rabossi, 'La Teoría de Los Derechos Humanos Naturalizada' (1990) 5 Revista del Centro de Estudios Constitucionales 159.

[32] For an example of dimly concealed irritation, Kennedy (n 14), which, despite a gap of ten years, displays the same sense of exasperation with the international human rights movement.

the 1990s and early 2000s.[33] Some critics of the critics have in fact argued that most if not all substantive points about human rights have already been made during that period, which was dominated by debates about cultural relativism, liberal versus communitarian political theory, and the meaning and consequences of (neoliberal) globalization.[34] While this is broadly true, the circumstances in which human rights now operate and in relation to which the new critiques are made have become much more dramatic and therefore more revealing of the underlying issues faced by and held against human rights—a point that Alston has also made.[35] In addition, there have been a number of methodological shifts in relation to the earlier debates, most notably the mobilization of historiography as a tool to critically dissect the meaning of human rights over time as well as an attempt to measure and critically assess the empirical workings and effects of human rights.[36] These two methodological turns have raised the stakes of the debate and require a new level of response—with Alston having, again, been a pioneer within the human rights community in taking up this challenge.[37]

So what does the challenge consist of? One way of slotting these new critiques is in relation to the classical political categories of left, right, and centre, as per the respective positions assumed by their exponents or by the critical instruments employed. This is a common if contestable classification, as the meaning of the left–right spectrum has become (somewhat) fluid and as at least some of the critics have been loath to be identified with these traditional political positionalities—a certain irony given that all critiques contend in one way or another that human rights stand in the way of dealing politically with what, in their view, is fundamentally political. Yet, for all the deficiencies of the left–right spectrum, it is, arguably, still relevant not only to understand what human rights are intellectually up against but also to where these positions stand vis-à-vis the parallel (right) populist programme.[38]

[33] For example, Susan Marks, 'The End of History? Reflections on Some International Legal Theses' (1997) 8 European Journal of International Law 449.

[34] Some of the most discussed critical engagements were, ironically, published as part of the Oxford Amnesty Lecture series; for example, Barbara Johnson (ed), *Freedom and Interpretation: The Oxford Amnesty Lectures, 1992* (BasicBooks 1993); Stephen Shute, *On Human Rights: The Oxford Amnesty Lectures* (Susan Hurley ed, Basic Books 1993); Olwen H Hufton, *Historical Change and Human Rights: The Oxford Amnesty Lectures* (Basic Books 1995); Matthew J Gibney (ed), *Globalizing Rights: The Oxford Amnesty Lectures 1999* (OUP 2003); Nicholas Owen (ed), *Human Rights, Human Wrongs: The Oxford Amnesty Lectures, 2001* (OUP 2003); Tony Evans (ed), *Human Rights Fifty Years on: A Reappraisal* (MUP 1998).

[35] Alston, 'The Populist Challenge' (n 2) 1.

[36] On the historiographical turn in human rights, Samuel Moyn, *Human Rights and the Uses of History* (Verso 2014); Jan Eckel, 'Human Rights and Decolonization: New Perspectives and Open Questions' (2010) 1 Humanity 111; Jenny S Martinez, *The Slave Trade and the Origins of International Human Rights Law* (OUP 2014); Roland Burke, *Decolonization and the Evolution of International Human Rights* (University of Pennsylvania Press 2013); Daniel R Maul, *Human Rights, Development and Decolonization: The International Labour Organization, 1940–70* (Palgrave Macmillan 2012); Fabian Klose, *Human Rights in the Shadow of Colonial Violence: The Wars of Independence in Kenya and Algeria* (1st edn, University of Pennsylvania Press 2013); Steven LB Jensen, *The Making of International Human Rights: The 1960s, Decolonization, and the Reconstruction of Global Values* (2016); for the empirical turn in human rights, Philip Alston and Colin Gillespie, 'Global Human Rights Monitoring, New Technologies, and the Politics of Information' (2012) 23 European Journal of International Law 1089; AnnJanette Rosga and Margaret L Satterthwaite, 'The Trust in Indicators: Measuring Human Rights' [2008] Berkley Journal of International Law <http://www.ssrn.com/abstract=1298540> accessed 10 November 2020; Debora Valentina Malito, Gaby Umbach, and Nehal Bhuta (eds), *The Palgrave Handbook of Indicators in Global Governance* (Palgrave Macmillan 2017); Kevin Davis and others (eds), *Governance by Indicators: Global Power through Quantification and Rankings* (OUP 2012); Todd Landman and Edzia Carvalho, *Measuring Human Rights* (Routledge 2010).

[37] For instance, his engagements with, on one hand, human rights historiography in Philip Alston, 'Does the Past Matter? On the Origins of Human Rights' (2013) 126 Harvard Law Review 2043; and, on the other hand, empirical human rights research such as in Alston and Gillespie (n 36); or in Philip Alston, 'Towards a Human Rights Accountability Index' (2000) 1 Journal of Human Development 249.

[38] It is, arguably, also the most—and perhaps the only—concrete way to distinguish these various positions at this moment, as the (taxonomically) more relevant question of their epistemic pedigree and vision is not addressed in sufficient detail (in these critiques). While this deeper engagement needs, thus, yet to be had, both on part of the

The rights–critical spectrum can hence be seen as being made up of, firstly, a right critique that takes issue either with the universalism and egalitarianism of human rights as entitlements meant to be held by everyone equally, individually and in abstraction from any form of collective identity; or with their (legal or moral) trumping of the 'objective' requirements of social (self-)organization through market mechanisms within a capitalist framework. Of these two seemingly incompatible—though, arguably, deeply entangled[39]—views, the former can be broadly associated with the populist, the latter with the neoliberal right. It is the neoliberal right critique that has gained particular intellectual currency through the likes of Eric Posner and others working in the wake of the 'law and economics' movement.[40] It argues, *in nuce*, that rights—in particular when they come in the form of constitutionally entrenched or internationally positivized and fully justiciable social and economic rights that mandate minimum levels of social protection—are impediments to the efficient allocation of scarce resources through market mechanisms and, as such, distort the formation of the 'just market value' of such basic goods such as health care, education, housing, or food, water, and sanitation. In this vein, rights are seen as standing in the way of austerity measures required to correct (allegedly) inefficient welfare policies that purport to provide these goods through redistributive schemes. Posner's rights critique is embedded in a wider diatribe against international law, which he sees as a similarly distortive attempt to establish an international rule of law despite the absence of a world state.[41]

Next, a new centrist critique has been dominated by the revisionist human rights historiography around Samuel Moyn that sees as 'the most troubling shortcoming of the contemporary attempt to give human rights a history [... the distortion of] the past to suit the present'.[42] As an antidote, this new revisionism has contested the semantic unity of what has been called human rights and has, instead, advocated a 'discontinuist' reading of the various events around which the human rights narrative has been constructed.[43] The overarching point has been that the politics surrounding the progressive legalization of (international) human rights reveals their fundamentally epiphenomenal character as ideological constructs legitimating and naturalizing (great) power politics—a perspective that does not, however, much transcend the long-held premises of classical (political) realism. Moyn in particular has notoriously proposed to divide the post-World War II timeline of international human rights into two fundamentally distinct semantic phases, with the former ranging from their inception in the 1940s to just after the decolonization period in the 1960s, and which engages rights language in order to express claims for national sovereignty in the context of Third World emancipation; and the latter, as of the 1970s to the contemporary period, in which rights are re-signified as a simultaneously anti-sovereigntist and anti-communist cosmopolitan project meant to substitute (real-existing) socialism as the primary ideal for emancipatory politics.[44] This later project, however, is, to Moyn, entirely utopian, driven by

critics and on part of their critics, the left-centre-right taxonomy shall here be used for heuristic purposes and very much in (invisible) quotes.

[39] Brown, *In the Ruins of Neoliberalism* (n 17).
[40] Posner, *The Twilight of Human Rights Law* (n 10).
[41] Eric A Posner, *The Perils of Global Legalism* (University of Chicago Press 2009).
[42] Moyn, *Human Rights and the Uses of* History (n 36) 13.
[43] See further, Florian Hoffmann and Bethania Assy, '(De)Colonizing Human Rights' in Jochen von Bernstorff and Philipp Dann (eds), *The Battle for International Law: South-North Perspectives on the Decolonization Era* (OUP 2020) 198–215.
[44] Moyn, *The Last Utopia* (n 10) 120ff.

(Northern) liberal elites and therefore 'not enough' when it comes to taming the neoliberal beast.[45]

To Moyn, human rights (in their post-1970s connotation) suffer from the crucial blind spot of (in)equality, as they allegedly neither articulate an egalitarian utopia nor are capable of serving as instruments against inequality.[46] By exclusively focussing on floors of protection rather than on any ceiling, they actually end up doing part of neoliberalism's dirty work of maintaining the lowest strata of society just around subsistence level while removing any cap on how far upward stratification can go. Hence, insofar as human rights merely imply formal status equality and not distributive equality, they are, in this view, unsuitable as instruments against the neoliberal social fallout. Yet, while Moyn's contentions on human rights and (in)equality mimic the classical Marxist critique of rights (on which more will follow), he appears not to be prepared to actually engage in Marxist analysis. Instead, he eschews consistency in order to occupy a middle-of-the-road whereby rights are meant to be neither all bad nor enough to address the structural problems of contemporary societies. But he largely refrains from taking an explicit position in the ongoing discussion on the roots causes of these problems and skirts question of alternatives.[47]

Lastly, a set of what could, broadly, be termed new left critiques tend to see human rights as an ideological configuration that distorts our understanding of social reality.[48] More specifically, they claim that human rights do not seek to address social ills, such as different forms of violence, oppression, or exploitation by state and non-state actors, discrimination, inequality, immiseration, and, generally, the denial or curtailment of human dignity, on a structural level but merely individually and piecemeal. As such they are taken to help maintain these causes (cumulatively 'the system') intact or even aid their proliferation and they obscure and obstruct more effective ways of addressing them. Insofar as human rights substitute genuinely political action—which is here often understood as involving the open struggle over (material or immaterial) distributional schemes—with a (legally) formalized and individualized approach to merely the symptoms produced by these underlying causes, they effectively de-politicize or even naturalize the latter and thereby contribute to their continuity and reproduction. They are, hence, seen as essentially system stabilizing and retrogressive.

This broad bottom line forms the intersection of a host of otherwise distinct but often cross-referenced left critical projects that have emerged or re-emerged during the past decade or so. The specific genealogies and assumptions of these critical theories cannot be sketched here, but their central theme is, arguably, already set out in Marx's triple critique of rights. To him, they, firstly, articulate a fundamentally anti-social, atomistic, and purely self-interested conception of human nature; secondly, they are co-constitutive—as supposedly 'equal' property rights—of the commodity form and thus act as central elements of the capitalist reproduction regime; and, thirdly, they are ideological smokescreens that cloak the inherent inequality of commodity exchange through the mirage of equal rights.[49] Many, but not all, of the new left critiques are explicitly or implicitly premised on this contention and

[45] Moyn, *Not Enough* (n 10).
[46] ibid.
[47] ibid.
[48] See the rights-critical literature listed in (n 10); in particular, Balibar (n 10); Barreto (n 10); Dickinson and others (n 10); Hopgood (n 10); Maldonado-Torres (n 10); Menke (n 10); Marks (n 10); Mignolo (n 10); Rathore and Cistelecan (n 10).
[49] Darren J O'Byrne, 'Marxism and Human Rights: New Thoughts on an Old Debate' (2019) 23 International Journal of Human Rights 639.

they have, consequently, framed rights as 'part of the problem' of capitalism (aka the neoliberal world order) rather than as a solution.[50]

In essence, these rights-critical perspectives have transposed the Marxian baseline into different theoretical keys, so that the ideological cloaking function of rights vis-à-vis class difference in Marx is turned into one in relation to race, women, gender, or coloniality/subalternity. The critical algorithm is, however, the same, namely that rights help paint over and are thereby implicated in the exclusion, exploitation, or elimination of certain categories of humans. This process is seen as not accidental but constitutive of modern/Western (aka capitalist, racist, gendered, or imperialist/neo-colonialist) societies and cannot, as the logic of rights presumes, be addressed through the very state apparatus—as the primary addressee of rights claims—that is itself a product of and necessary element in capitalist reproduction. To be sure, like Marx himself, many of these critiques acknowledge a positive role for rights in particular moments or in relation to specific issues, or at least as a tactical device to advance specific progressive causes; yet they would insist that the problematic aspects of rights prevail and that, therefore, an investment in rights as a politically relevant form of struggle is misplaced.[51]

In sum, then, human rights are too much for the right critique and too little for the centrist and left critiques. To be sure, none of these intellectual interventions should, prima facie, be thrown in with the unqualified rumblings of the populist right. These are, ultimately, attempts at a good faith engagement with what, from their perspective, has been an overly dominant discourse and attached professional community.[52] Yet, the political empowerment of the populist right, and the centrality the critique of human rights plays in its rhetorical strategy, makes this crunch time for human rights—a time, in other words, in which even the critique within the confines of intellectual debate is not politically innocent but has to account for the consequences of the vision it enounces. Likewise, the defence of human rights has to engage with these alternative visions and make its case beyond the mere reiteration of the self-evidence of the existing framework. As Alston put it with characteristic frankness, 'human rights proponents need to urgently rethink many of their assumptions, re-evaluate their strategies, and broaden their outreach, while not giving up on the basic principles'.[53] This is, arguably, at the heart of Alston's dual injunction against both the new critics and the established human rights community, lest both sides end up unwittingly playing the game of the populist right.

25.3 Beyond 'Straw Rights': Some Initial Responses to the Intellectual Critique(s)

In order not to play that game and reduce human rights to a mere cipher, the critique must be taken seriously and the case for human rights must be built in response to it. This evidently much larger endeavour can only be outlined here. It must begin with a (preliminary) assessment of the critical angles sketched earlier in order to frame the types of responses required; starting with the (neoliberal) right critique, it is, on a base level, perhaps the most

[50] See, again, Kennedy (n 14).
[51] Grietje Baars, *The Corporation, Law and Capitalism: A Radical Perspective on the Role of Law in the Global Political Economy* (2019), at 378.
[52] David Kennedy, *A World of Struggle: How Power, Law, and Expertise Shape Global Political Economy* (Princeton University Press 2016).
[53] Alston, 'Human Rights under Siege' (n 9).

straightforward to respond to as it actually takes human rights quite seriously. Indeed, it considers the proliferation of rights and their (increasing) enforcement through judicial or quasi-judicial bodies to be potentially perilous to the functioning of a capitalist market economy.[54] The neoclassical framing of capitalism that underlies this reading is notoriously premised on the ideal of a largely unimpeded market logic as the fundamental principle behind a resource efficient social order. Human rights, alongside redistributive welfare policies and, generally, all state intervention beyond the maintenance of market functionality are here seen as potentially detrimental to that order and therefore as dangerous. While the guaranteeing of basic civil rights in the domestic sphere is taken to be required in order to allow for rational agents to operate 'freely' and therefore efficiently, rights activism that is capable of distorting the outcomes of 'free' market exchange is clearly as bad inspired by what one of this vision's doyen's has notoriously termed a mirage, notably social justice and the egalitarian ideals attached to it.[55] Hence, contrary to the left and centrist critiques, the neoliberal perspective has no difficulties with associating rights with equality and, indeed, it disdains them for precisely their egalitarian impulse that contradicts the vertical differentiation that the logic of capitalism requires. Even though Posner and others have couched their treatises in the language of ideology, critique in order to expose rights as the plaything of left liberals and closet socialists, rights do not really play an ideological function in this framework. On the contrary, to the neoliberal critique, they are pretty much doing what they advertise, which, in turn, essentially corresponds to what most in the human rights community think they should be doing. This is, incidentally—or maybe not so incidentally—, as true for the neoliberal as it is for the populist right critique as both are inconvenienced by what they see as the excessive and excessively successful use of rights to promote what are to them all the wrong causes—amongst which are (redistributive) public policies to guarantee universal access to minimum welfare standards premised on the equal dignity of all, including non-nationals. The fact that these two 'rights' both associate rights and their defenders with these causes obviates the need for further response.

The centrist critique, in contrast to the (neoliberal) right critique, does treat human rights as an ideological construct, and thus as both epiphenomenal and ephemeral, but does not frame this contention as a formal ideology critique; instead it mobilizes the purported objectivity of historical fact to make its case (of sorts) against human rights. A replique to it will, hence, involve an engagement with the historiographical premises under which the revisionist historians operate, an endeavour to which Alston has himself contributed with his seminal review *Does the Past Matter? On the Origins of Human Rights*.[56] There he unmasks the revisionists' portrayal of the human rights movement as following a crudely anachronistic 'linear progress narrative' as a straw person image that side-lines the real questions about historiographical method that underlie the revisionist argument. For that argument, in essence, contends that the question of whether, or not, the concept of human rights is semantically continuous over time and whether, or not, its use by different actors at particular moments only serves the ideological cloaking of ulterior motives is one of mere historical fact; hence, whoever musters the more accurate historical evidence, which of course the revisionists claim to have been doing, is bound to 'win' the debate.

[54] Posner, *The Twilight of Human Rights Law* (n 10).
[55] Friedrich A von Hayek and Friedrich August Hayek, *Law, Legislation and Liberty, Volume 2: The Mirage of Social Justice* (University of Chicago Press 1978).
[56] Alston, 'Does the Past Matter ? On the Origins of Human Rights' (n 37).

This, however, as Alston points out, is a ruefully under-complex treatment of the historiographical challenge at hand. Indeed, it fails to respond to a series of methodological questions that inform the way in which human rights can be reconstructed historically. As he puts it:

> Moyn heavily discounts the significance of the ebb and flow of rights discourse across the centuries, and of the often long and bitter struggles that have helped to shape today's complex and multifaceted human rights endeavors. By doing so, he is able to conjure up a parody of the human rights movement with shallow and unconvincing roots, defined almost exclusively from an America-centric vantage point, and sure to be swept away by the emergence of an international order no longer dominated by the West. Such a vision might explain what some consider to be the parlous situation of human rights in certain advanced democracies, but it does little to help us understand why, for example, one of the most vibrant human rights cultures in the world today is to be found in India.[57]

To respond to the latter, it would be necessary to first reflect on some of the foundational questions of historiographical method: Is it, for instance, synchronic context or diachronic reception that bestow ideas such as human rights with meaning at any one point of time? Are ideas articulations of fundamental propositions, timeless *philosophemes* that occur in different guises throughout concrete history, or are they, instead, *epistemes* that emerge from the material and linguistic conditions of their societal context;[58] or are they instantiations of the intentions of their articulators who think within specific discursive practices;[59] or is the meaning of human rights really a combination of all of these? And how are ideas transmitted across time, how is the relationship between author and reader, removed in time and by hermeneutic horizon, conceived?[60] If the revisionist charge against progress narratives has correctly pointed to the latter's anachronistic use of historical evidence, the revisionists have not really provided a more complex and self-reflective historiography either. Instead, they have tended to style the debate as one over the correct reading of historical fact rather than assuming what it really is, notably an exchange over incommensurate metatheoretical positions on the history of the idea of human rights.

Hence, where progress historiography seeks to inductively (re)construct causal connections between different event contexts (aka periods) to establish the cross-temporal meaning of human rights, the revisionist approach starts from a particular premise about that meaning and then proceeds to find its articulation in a specific event context. In other words, the former approach seeks to establish meaning from presumed facts, the latter the facts from presumed meaning.[61] It is, however, these presumptions that represent the open flank of either approach. For if the progress narrative's quest for cross temporal meaning carries the inherent risk of over-interpretation and anachronism, then the revisionists are bound to base the plausibility of their narrower definition on diffuse assumptions about general

[57] ibid 2081.

[58] For example, Donald R Kelley, 'What Is Happening to the History of Ideas?' (1990) 51 Journal of the History of Ideas 3; Reinhart Koselleck, *Vergangene Zukunft: Zur Semantik Geschichtl. Zeiten* (Suhrkamp 1979) 130; as well as, generally, Leonard Krieger, *Time's Reasons: Philosophies of History Old and New* (University of Chicago Press 1989).

[59] Quentin Skinner, 'Meaning and Understanding in the History of Ideas' (1969) 8 History and Theory 3, 35.

[60] Melvin Richter, 'Reconstructing the History of Political Languages: Pocock, Skinner, and the Geschichtliche Grundbegriffe' (1990) 29 History and Theory 38; Hans-Georg Gadamer, *Truth and Method* (2nd edn, Continuum 2004).

[61] Hoffmann and Assy (n 43) 205.

intellectual history.[62] The historiographical debate on its own will thus remain inherently inconclusive as each of the two positions is marked by what could be termed a hermeneutic 'problem of induction'—that is, within a certain set of premises, no amount of additional evidence will corroborate the correctness of these premises vis-à-vis their opposite, but will tend to merely reinforce them.[63] This leads to an incremental closure of the epistemic horizon and to increasing incommensurability vis-à-vis alternative interpretations. The only unequivocal fact that materializes from this debate is that human rights emerged in the 1940s from earlier incarnations as a powerful signifier that, because of its very conceptual openness and semantic indeterminacy, has engaged people's imagination all through to the 1970s and on to the contemporary period. This, then, represents their conceptual continuity, despite and because of their discontinuous use in different contexts and periods.

History alone will not therefore resolve the question of whether human rights are, can, or should be relevant to transformative social change in general, and to advancing equality in particular. The question of whether human rights as they are used by, amongst others, the human rights community as of the 1970s are actually the same thing as the rights that commanded at least some sustained attention during, say, the post-World War II or decolonization periods; or whether those rights are in turn recognizable re-incarnations of their use in the anti-slavery or women's suffrage movements in the nineteenth century, or, indeed, of national bills of rights as of the eighteenth century, needs to be reformulated.[64] The real question is, arguably, neither whether the conceptual continuity of human rights can ultimately be demonstrated nor whether their use in these different instances can be shown to have been 'authentic' by some semantic standard or to have merely been 'ideological'; the real question is how human rights have acquired such power of signification over time and beyond any semantic coherence or political salience. The answer to this question lies, arguably, not only in the archives but also in the multifaceted practices associated with rights discourse, from its 'colloquial' use to articulate injustice and demand accountability, via its continued appearance as a form of political protest and militancy, to the complex dynamics of rights-based litigation and its repercussions. Hence, the meaning of rights and their specific relevance at any one moment cannot primarily be determined by their genealogy -and some pre-determined functionality associated therewith—but it rather resides in their evolution over time. The latter is driven not by a uniform and hermetic human rights movement but decentrally by all those using rights across a diversity of contexts and by the emergence of various (intended and non-intended) consequences thereof.

Indeed, the left critique, arguably, also suffers from this genealogical bias, as it tends to derive the meaning and role of rights from premises about their origins and base function rather than from an engagement with 'rights-in-practice'. Hence, their focus is on the ideology

[62] See, inter alia, Samuel Moyn and Andrew Sartori, 'Approaches to Global Intellectual History' in Samuel Moyn and Andrew Sartori (eds), *Global Intellectual History* (CUP 2015) 3–30.

[63] This involves a large and multifacetted discussion on the historiography of ideas and historical method that cannot be easily be summed up; see, generally again Richter (n 60); Aviezer Tucker, *A Companion to the Philosophy of History and Historiography* (2011) part II; as well as recent discussion in international legal history, such as Rose Parfitt, *The Process of International Legal Reproduction* (2017); Anne Orford, 'International Law and the Limits of History' in Wouter Werner, Marieke De Hoon, and Alex Galán (eds), *The Law of International Lawyers: Reading Martti Koskenniemi* (2017) 297–320.

[64] See, inter alia, Alston 'Does the Past Matter? (n 37); Alston and Gillespie (n 36); Alston, 'Towards a Human Rights Accountability Index' (n 37); Micheline Ishay, *The History of Human Rights: From Ancient Times to the Globalization Era* (University of California Press 2009); Lynn Hunt, *Inventing Human Rights: A History* (First published as a Norton paperback, WW Norton 2008); Peter N Stearns, *Human Rights in World History* (Routledge 2012); Paul Gordon Lauren, *The Evolution of International Human Rights: Visions Seen* (3rd edn, University of Pennsylvania Press 2011).

critique of right by which their ideological function must be exposed and (thereby) transcended. As argued earlier, while the particular critical vectors employed to this end are diverse, they all broadly follow the framework set out in Marx's critique of rights in capitalism and therefore tend to reconstruct rights in relation to premises about their genesis rather than through an analysis of the real-life practices they underwrite. This would seem to make the Marxist account of rights prone to deductive over-interpretation in the sense that the factual workings and effects of rights 'out there' are exclusively deduced from premises about their function in the political economy of capitalism. While this conforms with the historical materialist method, it risks an under-complex account of the 'real' life of rights (under capitalism). For rights activism is not static but highly time-dynamic, involving elements—people, institutions, legal frameworks—that, over time, generate effects that generate further effects and so on. In the language of systems theory, which also owes some debts to Marx, 'rights-in-practice', produce systemic recursivity, self-reflexivity, and, more often than not, nonlinear consequences.[65] The state is here a test tube in which the different and decentrally generated impulses from the different uses of human rights are mixed together to produce uncertain and often unstable outcomes. While some of these impulses may well be generated by corporate actors seeking value maximization—much in the way already understood by Marx—many actually come from the smallest units of agency, notably people, who nearly always resort to (legal) rights as a last resort to try to resist the concrete instantiations of an ever-advancing commodification process.

To be sure, this is not a romantic story of 'little people' (eg Galanter's 'have-nots') going against the 'big bad state' or 'big bad companies' (the 'haves') through human rights upheld by heroic courts, because the results of rights-driven judicialization are neither uniform nor uniformly in favour of the 'have-nots'.[66] Fundamentally, their repercussions over time grow less transparent as complexity augments. Yet that is the point: not that 'rights-in-practice' may (also) be enactments of neoliberal-capitalist ideology but that they are capable of irritating 'the system' despite and beyond their ideological function. Concretely, rights irritate Marx's 'law of value' in capitalism in two ways: they produce a certain form of (legal) uncertainty against capital's requirement of a certain form of legal certainty and they can, momentarily though, over time, cumulatively, impact on the amount of extractable surplus value in particular sectors, forcing capital to adapt in unplanned ways. This dual irritation, generated from within 'the system' itself and regardless of its concrete consequences at any one point of time, produces subversive—and potentially emancipatory—dysfunctionalities. Marx himself recognized the self-subversive potential of capitalism though neither he nor his followers, nor anyone else, have so far been able pinpoint exactly how this process unfolds: whether it is only self-conscious struggle or also the more diffuse and complex interaction of emergent properties, including—but not limited to—those that are generated by the long term and indirect consequences of rights-based activism.

[65] See, inter alia, Günther Teubner, 'Counter-Rights: On the Trans-Subjective Potential of Subjective Rights' in Poul F Kjaer, *Law of Political Economy* (2019) 372–93.

[66] See, classically Marc Galanter, 'Why the "Haves" Come out Ahead: Speculations on the Limits of Legal Change' (1974) 9 *Law and Society Review* 95–160, doi: 10.2307/3053023; Doutje Lettinga and Lars van Troost, *Can Human Rights Bring Social Justice?* (2015); Alicia E Yamin and Siri Gloppen, *Litigating Health Rights: Can Courts Bring More Justice to Health?* (2011); Octávio Ferraz, 'Harming the Poor through Social Rights Litigation: Lessons from Brazil', (2010) 89 *Texas Law Review* 1643, at 1667.

25.4 Quite Necessary (Still): Human Rights in an Unequal World

Ultimately, all three intellectual critiques as well as their distorted reflection in the populist right's histrionics, might be due to a deeper frustration with the world that has been emerging over the past decades. Frustration tends to derive from two sources, one pointing to the past and the disappointed expectations of how differently that world could, should, or might have emerged from an earlier vantage point; the other to the future and a sense of despondency over the often seemingly unsurmountable odds involved in actually changing the world to align with those expectations. Where these critiques of course differ is about what the expectations and the odds for realizing them are. For the neoliberal (right) critique it seems to be a world without redistributive welfarism and the gradualist egalitarianism associated with it, a vision that, at least for its critics, is plainly on course to being achieved but which, for its proponents, is apparently still being challenged by the, to them, irritating recurrence of such macroeconomic challenges as financial crises, climate change, pandemics, as well as political claims for social justice underwritten, inter alia, by rights-based social constitutionalism.[67] By (unsurprising) contrast, the right's frustration is the left's (and also centrist's) hope, namely the achievement of social justice through equality, broadly understood as encompassing both status and distributional equality and, concomitantly, the eventual elimination of exploitation and discrimination. If, as especially Moyn argues, this vision, was already only insufficiently realized during the West's post-war welfarist consensus—not least on account of its asymmetric application both within and in relation to the global South—the rise of neoclassical economics and neoliberal governance as of the late 1970s has systematically undermined egalitarian politics and marginalized equality as a political objective. Indeed, the apparent fall in interstate inequality over the past decade, largely due to the rise of China and other emerging economies, seems to have been bought through a rise in intrastate inequality the world over.[68] From this vantage point, inequality is not only an essential denial of social justice but also a root cause for the (re-)emergence of the populist right and the breakdown of neoliberal governance.[69] Yet, to these critics, it has largely been excised from mainstream political discourse and has been replaced by a fragmented and depoliticized focus on 'the poor', on vulnerable groups, and on mere survival sufficiency. Human rights are, as was seen, alleged to being key instruments through which this replacement is realized.[70] They are therefore seen as part of the odds that frustrate the achievement of equality by impeding its return to the centre of political struggle.

Unlike the right critique (whether neoliberal or populist), this cannot but resonate within the human rights community as, arguably, a majority of its self-conscious adherents would identify with the overall aim of social justice and equality. It must therefore be open to engage in critical self-reflection on whether the human rights optic might inadvertently have been drawing attention away from neoliberalism's underlying distributional scheme by narrowing in on specific issues and on partial and minimum remedies.[71] It has also to openly query whether and to what extent human rights activism, not least in and through

[67] Frankenberg (n 16) 101.

[68] See, inter alia, François Bourguignon, *The Globalization of Inequality* (Thomas Scott-Railton tr, Princeton University Press 2015).

[69] Gaby Oré Aguilar and Ignacio Saiz, 'Introducing the Debate on Economic Inequality: Can Human Rights Make a Difference?' (*openDemocracy* 27 October 2015) <https://www.opendemocracy.net/en/openglobalrights-openpage/introducing-debate-on-economic-inequality-can-human-ri/> accessed 07 November 2020.

[70] Moyn, *Not Enough* (n 11) 212ff.

[71] See Kennedy (n 52), chs 6, 7.

the courts, might impede potentially more effective and macro-level collective political action, ranging from traditional party electoral politics, via collective (economic) interest representation through trade unions and similar, to broader and often transnational social movements.[72] However, while such querying might provide a more nuanced view of human rights as a means to the end of equality, it will not reveal a fundamental divergence with that end. For anyone as immersed in the real-life human rights community as Alston is, the idea that the latter would espouse inequality as a positive good or happily tolerate it as the inevitable cost of the freedom of a few is spurious. Most contemporary human rights defenders would see themselves as committed to equality every bit as much as their critics, though would understand their human rights activism as a relevant and, indeed, indispensable element of this commitment. While there are, as Alston clearly pinpoints, some in that community who seem to have blind faith in the universal self-sufficiency of human rights, there are many others who hold a more realistic view of rights-in-practice and their place in the bigger scheme of things—with Alston and his unrelenting (self-)irony and disdain for any form of human rights romanticism being, again, the case in point here. Hence, and crucially, where these views and those of the critics differ is not in the commitment to equality but in the assessment of the stakes involved in a transformative politics towards equality. For if the point of the (left and centrist) critics merely was to recuperate equality as a central theme of progressive politics, then their primary focus on human rights and human rights defenders would seem diversionary; even if the critics' handmaiden contention was all there was to human rights, it would still be perplexing why the handmaiden rather than her lady (aka neoliberalism or capitalism) should be picked out for particular censure. After all, and as the neoliberal rights critique plainly demonstrates, the defenders of the dominant political economy are not at all keen on human rights, especially in the comprehensive package in which they are framed today.

Yet, beyond mere rhetoric, when it comes to assessing the long-term impact of human rights as measured against concrete alternative approaches, the jury is still very much out. The test the critics have imposed upon themselves requires them to show that, on one hand, such alternative approaches promise to generate a much stronger transformative energy than human rights have been able to; and, on the other hand, that these alternatives are actively impeded in their emergence by human rights (activism). Both of these conditions express legitimate concerns and call for serious engagement on part of the human rights community, a point Alston has, as was seen, repeatedly made when, for instance, he clearly acknowledges the 'importance of reflecting on the deeper values underpinning human rights' and alerts that we must not merely 'assume that the mere invocation of the latter is sufficient to capture the deeper essence of the enterprise in which we are engaged'.[73] However, if human rights defenders have—in fact for quite some time—been called upon to critically examine their practices, to conjecture their long-term impact, and to cultivate a big-picture vision of their activities, their critics, too, must heed the call to ground their argument in a concrete and plausible outline of social transformation without human rights.[74] That alternative transformational strategies and pathways exist few would doubt. In fact, many human

[72] ME Glasius, 'Economic and social rights and social justice movements: some courtship, no marriage, no children yet' in Ida Lintel, Antoine C Buyse, and Brianne McGonigle Leyh (eds), *Defending Human Rights: Tools for Social Justice: Volume in Honour of Fried van Hoof on the Occasion of His Valedictory Lecture and the 30th Anniversary of the Netherlands Institute of Human Rights* (Intersentia 2012) 127–42.

[73] Alston, 'Reply to Dudai and Nagaraj' (n 9).

[74] See for an early sum up of the self-critique, Florian Hoffmann, 'Shooting in the Dark: Reflections Towards a Pragmatic Theory of Human Rights (Activism)' (2006) 41 Texas International Law Journal 403; and matured by Sarah Knuckey and Margaret Satterthwaite in Chapter 24 in this volume.

rights defenders actively participate in or are at least sympathetic to such strategies, which range from the conventional means of political participation provided in (liberal) democracies, via experimental forms of alternative living, and to more radical and anti-systemic protest movements. Indeed, contrary to their portrayal by Moyn, most people who talk and practice human rights do not do so as a comprehensive political ideology exclusive of other political ideologies or hermetically associated with just one political ideology (liberalism); instead they see human rights as one instrument amongst others to articulate a broad band of political visions grounded in much more complex ideological frameworks. That rights-oriented argument is so (relatively) prevalent in political discourse can thus be read in quite the opposite way from what the critics claim: not that it is a sign of the crowding out of alternative projects but of the frequent use of rights as an articulation of precisely such alternative or transformational projects. Indeed, few, if any human rights defenders would consider their advocacy of, say, economic and social rights as self-sufficient and exclusive of parallel engagements on other fronts. While a human rights optic may place a particular spin on the means a transformational politics can take, the political visions behind rights advocacy are, arguably, as widely open and can be as radically transformational as any alternative framework.

However, against such objections, the critics have tended to build up a dramatic contrast between, on one hand, a professionalized, managerialist, and elite human rights expertocracy (which, in this cliché image, also tends to be from the global North, white, male, Euroamerican(ized), middle class, and, generally, heteronormative); and, on the other hand, those 'others' who are (primarily) the victims of human rights violations and subjects of that human rights expertocracy, subaltern, voiceless, often poor(er), overdetermined, and epistemically (re)colonized, as well as frequently in or from the global South and outside of the dominant identarian traits characteristic of the expert class.[75] Needless to say, as a central figure in the international human rights movement—and hence as part of that expertocracy—Alston has had to weather this storm, too, which, by his own account, has at times felt like an additional crosswind in already exceedingly rough seas.[76] However, the devil lies again in the detail here, as a critically self-reflective human rights community must, in principle, be open to being examined in terms of its makeup and functional logic and how the former impact on its relationship to those it purports to aid and protect. Yet, while it is important, indeed, indispensable, to spell out the deep structure, blind spots and dark sides of the epistemic community that pervades professional human rights advocacy, the critics commit a category mistake when they single out the human rights community as a major 'part of the problem' or, indeed, as a problem as such.

For what is really meant by this critique is not some problem but rather the deep structure of late (capitalist) modernity itself, a deep structure that afflicts (nearly) everyone everywhere and that determines both the immanent horizon of our knowledge and the threshold for social change. The great achievement of critical thought has not been to overcome this deep structure but to make it explicit and to enjoin us to face up to what modernity really

[75] Accounts in this vein range from Matti Koskenniemi, 'The Effect of Rights on Political Culture' in Philip Alston, Mara R Bustelo, and James Heenan (eds), *The EU and Human Rights* (OUP 1999) 99–116; Matti Koskenniemi, 'Human Rights Mainstreaming as a Strategy for Institutional Power' (2010) 1 Humanity: An International Journal of Human Rights, Humanitarianism, and Development 47; Kennedy, 'The International Human Rights Movement' (n 14); Kennedy, 'The International Human Rights Regime' (n 14); to Julia Juaréz Krabbe, *Race, Rights, and Rebels: Alternatives to Rights and Development from the Global South* (Rowman & Littlefield 2015).

[76] For example, his public lecture at the London School of Economics (LSE), Alston, 'The Populist Challenge to Human Rights' (9 December 2016) <https://www.youtube.com/watch?v=kAy4RUPVA2w&t=4266s> accessed 07 November 2020.

always was, notably a deeply ambivalent, hybrid, complex, and contingent message that is very different from the clichéd image enshrined in the *Western* progress narrative.[77] Two contentions follow from this in relation to the human rights community: firstly, that the tendency towards professionalization, managerialism, and, generally, the 'will to power' through knowledge is not particular to the human rights community but is inherent to all modern social formations, including those that pursue alternative ways of social transformation. Yet, this modern mode of governmentality is not a hermetic but highly dynamic and often nonlinear process that continuously generates new emergent properties that can be system stabilizing but also transgressive and transformational. No amount of (human rights) managerialism can overcome this fundamental contingency, but neither can a self-conscious 'counter-disciplinarity' that rejects all knowledge regimes.[78]

The second contention is that the reality of the human rights community is much more diverse than the caricature dichotomy of elite experts versus victimized subaltern 'others' allows for; human rights agency is distributed much more diffusely and is highly dynamic over time; there are clearly power asymmetries and epistemic hegemonies, but they unfold through complex processes of interaction and are continuously manipulated, subverted, side-lined, and re-signified by those stylized by the critics to be merely on the receiving end of the human rights industry.[79] Indeed, the claim of a hegemonic and potentially epistemicidal human rights expertocracy seems to problematically assume that those subjected to it have no meaningful agency (epistemic or otherwise) of their own and are merely under the sway of false consciousness—an assumption that would fly in the face of the express intent of the critics. Indeed, anyone who has experienced the deeply committed yet highly diverse forms of human rights advocacy in some parts of the global South and the fundamental importance accorded to rights by people up against seemingly insurmountable odds could not but give the lie to any such claim.

In the end, the reality of human rights is simply more complex and less determined than either the true believers or their critics are prepared to admit.[80] Fortunately, that complexity is now beginning to be explored both in the incipient turn to ethnography in international legal scholarship and in the growing field of empirical studies of human rights.[81] What emerges from these explorations is that human rights remain the discourse of choice for most people in most places when it comes to framing claims for fundamental human dignity and social justice, but that this framing is only the beginning of a dynamic process that, especially when it becomes institutionalized—for instance in courts—produces diverse

[77] Historically, this argument can be seen to have unfolded between Max Horkheimer, Theodor W Adorno, and Gunzelin Schmid Noerr, *Dialectic of Enlightenment: Philosophical Fragments* (Stanford University Press 2002) and Michel Foucault's 'Governmentality' (eg in Graham Burchell, Colin Gordon, and Peter Miller (eds), *The Foucault Effect: Studies in Governmentality* (University of Chicago Press 1991)); Florian Hoffmann, 'Discourse' in Jean D'Aspremont and Sahib Singh (eds), *Concepts for International Law: Contributions to Disciplinary Thought* (Edward Elgar 2019).

[78] Martti Koskenniemi, 'Law, Teleology and International Relations: An Essay in Counterdisciplinarity' (2012) 26 International Relations 3.

[79] Hoffmann, 'Facing South' (n 13).

[80] For the true believer category, see Makau w Mutua, 'The Ideology of Human Rights' (1996) 36 Virginia Journal of International Law 589.

[81] For the ethnographic turn, see Fleur Johns, *Non-Legality in International Law: Unruly Law* (CUP 2013); Luis Eslava and Sundhya Pahuja, 'Beyond the (Post)Colonial: TWAIL and the Everyday Life of International Law' (2012) 45 Journal of Law and Politics in Africa, Asia and Latin America 195; Luis Eslava, *Local Space, Global Life: The Everyday Operation of International Law and Development* (CUP 2015); for the empirical turn, see again the literature in (n 36); Kevin L Cope, Cosette D Creamer, and Mila Versteeg, 'Empirical Studies of Human Rights Law' (2019) 15 Annual Review of Law and Social Science 155; Gregory Shaffer and Tom Ginsburg, 'The Empirical Turn in International Legal Scholarship' (2012) 106 American Journal of International Law 1.

outcomes over time. Whether these outcomes are taken to be progressive (aka transformational/advancing social justice and equality) or regressive depends, in part, on the criteria used to measure progress and on the particular point in time at which this measurement is taken. Should the impact of rights, for instance, be measured by their symbolic or material empowerment of injusticed individuals and groups,[82] or by their effect on poverty reduction,[83] or in terms of their effect on distributional (social) justice?[84] And is it sufficient to just look at their short-term direct effects (or lack thereof), or should longer-term and indirect effects also be considered? And how ought these criteria and the respective spatial and temporal cut off points be chosen?

Perhaps, overall, the way ahead is to adopt a *long-duree* systemic perspective and look at rights as a form of decentralized social accountability that generates long-term repercussions and irritations. These can and do produce progressive outcomes at particular moments, but they can and do also provoke backlash and regression. Indeed, in part the populist right's obsessive bashing of rights is, arguably, just such a backlash. But, from a systemic point of view, this is not the end of the story and it will itself produce counter reactions that will mobilize human rights as one among several means to (re)claim equality and to articulate solidarity in a frequently counterfactual and always subversive insistence on human dignity in the face of its denial. Like few others, Philip Alston has been part of this endeavour and his continuing presence gives us hope that this storm, too, can be weathered.

[82] João Biehl and others, 'Judicialisation of the Right to Health in Brazil' (2009) 373 The Lancet 2182.
[83] Daniel M Brinks and Varun Gauri, 'The Law's Majestic Equality? The Distributive Impact of Judicializing Social and Economic Rights' (2014) 12 Perspectives on Politics 375.
[84] Ferraz (n 64).

26

Alston in Alabama

Towards a Theory of Praxis in International Human Rights

Frédéric Mégret

26.1 Introduction

In 2017, Philip Alston made a visit as UN Special Rapporteur on Extreme Poverty and Human Rights to the United States. On that occasion, he visited California, Alabama, Georgia, Puerto Rico, West Virginia, and Washington DC. In Alabama, Alston witnessed open sewage. The visit was notable for many things, but perhaps mostly for its aesthetics and symbolism. Here was a UN rapporteur flashing a light on perhaps a relatively unexpected area, in the midst of (still) the richest country in the world. On videos, Alston appeared both empathetic and imperial, often in the posture of being shown around by his hosts of the day and not mincing his words when facing the camera to communicate a message about how evidently he felt the United States was failing its international human rights obligations.

There was, it seems, much to relish about that moment, a sense of speaking truth to power, of bringing human rights where it hurt (the powerful) most, of a renewed sense of the thickness of the human rights project and its ability to deal with a range of social issues. In many ways, this was international human rights law as it was meant to be: on the ground and concrete, yet also luminous and animated by the highest concern for the dignity of human beings. The ability to connect sanitation needs to a global project of human rights was, in short, nothing short of irresistible. Briefly, the world seemed to enjoy a fleeting moment of unity in its condemnation of poverty in Alabama. This is a victory not to be shunned, I suppose, and one that made a compelling narrative.

At the same time, and even as I cheered on the side-lines, a part of me felt that sense of victory was not entirely warranted, and that perhaps this otherwise edifying spectacle came at a cost, or at least was more complicated than its performance suggested. This is not just because obviously not everyone was basking in the moment and that the US government was livid at what it considered a largely unjustified attack—if anything, as I will suggest, that rather cemented the success of the mission. Instead, I felt enjoying the moment as a sympathetic observer involved a guilty pleasure of sorts, like taking advantage of something you cannot really afford: perhaps the *frisson* of having someone say more or less exactly what you think from a position of authority but in a context where it is not clear that this authority can be sustained.

I happened to broadly agree with the tenor of what Alston said and I was certainly glad that someone in his position—a UN special rapporteur no less—was given a pulpit to say it. But I wasn't sure that the pulpit could carry the message. By what performative magic, for example, did what Alston might have said in one of his articles as a scholar—no doubt

Frédéric Mégret, *Alston in Alabama* In: *The Struggle for Human Rights.* Edited by: Nehal Bhuta, Florian Hoffmann, Sarah Knuckey, Frédéric Mégret, and Margaret Satterthwaite, Oxford University Press. © Frédéric Mégret 2021. DOI: 10.1093/oso/9780198868064.003.0027

fascinating—turn into something even somewhat authoritative merely by virtue of him now giving it the imprimatur of the United Nations? And at any rate, I thought, we were probably fooling ourselves. The world was not united in its condemnation of poverty in Alabama, or only in the most abstract terms. The world, for the most part, did not care, or only in the most superficial way, and human rights had done very little to correct the situation.

This led me to the question that is the focus of this chapter, namely what exactly is it that we are cheering when we applaud Alston in Alabama? Why is Alston's performance, understood here as emblematic of the broader aesthetics of international human rights law, both appealing and problematic? To explore this and in doing so, I want to go beyond an exploration of human rights or human rights law per se to engage the nature of what I understand to be a human rights *praxis*. What is it that Alston was *doing* in Alabama? How does it shed light on a certain way of being in the world *through* human rights? Can the *praxis* of human rights as a form of political action help us escape the limitations of human rights as a political idea? And should it give us reason to hope or to despair of the role of rights?

I seek to offer a subtle answer to those questions by focusing on one narrow instance where they can be seen to be put in play. The practice of human rights as a specific field of inquiry has become a motif of significant interest over the last decade in ways that stand to fundamentally enrich our understanding of what is involved.[1] In this chapter, I move beyond a social scientific or socio-legal concept of legal practice to more specifically examine its normative status. In particular I seek to shed light on the intersection of law promotion and legal activism that is the trademark of most special rapporteurships at the United Nations.

Praxis is a distinct tradition of conceptual and philosophical inquiry, one that is less interested in ideas and in being than in *doing*, even though it arguably can only address the question of doing through the ideas through which praxis manifests itself. It is also a tradition which is less interested in asking ontological questions (such as 'Is international law really law?' or 'Do human rights really exist?') or equally unanswerable instrumental or functional questions ('Do human rights really work?' or 'Are they a good idea?'). Instead, it asks the question: What should one do in the world and how should one do it? Praxis focuses on the experiential nature of learning rather than knowledge as a systemic conceptual construction. It blurs, in fact, the line between knowing and doing, bringing attention to the extent to which all knowledge is embodied in certain forms of action.

Note that I do not ask the question of 'What should one do?' in the quasi-religious meaning of what is virtuous to do. I have no doubt that there is an ethical dimension to human rights work, but nor do I think such work is propelled merely by a moral imperative. Human rights practitioners—I think—do not only engage in their trade out of a quasi-religious fervour about the idea of rights but because they see rights as a potent discourse to change the world for the better. The fate of human rights depends on whether human rights actually achieve something, rather than whether they 'exist'. This is important: despite all the mystical and naturalist origins of human rights, today that origin provides little more than a certain nostalgic allure to what is otherwise a thoroughly pragmatic endeavour. Human rights praxis, in short, is a praxis that is in fact aware that it is principally a praxis, even if not always self-reflectively.

I examine the praxis of human rights, simultaneously, with a certain wariness about the retreat to pragmatism. One cannot simply escape the dilemmas of the ideologies we have produced by pretending that they are not there and simply 'getting on with things'. There

[1] For a useful recent synthesis of what the field of research on 'human rights practice' entails, see Ron Dudai, 'The Study of Human Rights Practice: State of the Art' (2019) 11 Journal of Human Rights Practice 273.

cannot be a philosophy of action that is not based on a philosophy of knowledge and values. The praxis of human rights may on some level be at least as fraught as the theory of human rights. However, I also want to suggest that there is a peculiar dignity to action, and the choices it forces us to make in the course of doing. Human rights praxis is characterized by encounter (with others, with situations) and therefore an invitation to open oneself up to the diversity of the real, to the fact that things up close are never quite what they seem from afar. As a praxis, international human rights law is riddled with ethical traps that constantly threaten to engulf its spokespersons but from which they can also emerge victorious in the moment. As such, I suggest it is worth highlighting praxis as an irreducible dimension that is, if not redeeming, at least inherently worthy.

The emphasis on praxis also suggests, more intimately, an emphasis on *embodying* the idea of rights rather than merely reflecting on or acting upon it. That is, incidentally, an apt metaphor to think about Alston's career, a career spent going back and forth between the *vita activa* and the *vita contemplativa*. Indeed, it is one of the specificities of international human rights law that it has often relied precisely on that sort of professional trajectory (Nigel Rodley, Françoise Hampson, Adama Dieng, Antonio Cassese, Juan Mendez, Olivier de Schutter, etc) as if over time the human rights movement also produced a particular socio-professional ideal-type. The basic intuition is that people are not just slaves to ideas but are agents who constantly produce, enrich, modify, push back against, and transcend the projects in their care.

To embody an idea, for sure, is to shape oneself—one's mind and body—to fit that idea, or at least one's idea of that idea. It is to *be* what one does. If Alston had tattoos, they might profess his undying professional devotion for human rights, although what shape those tattoos would take is open to question. To embody an idea is not to escape its contradictions and limitations, but to live them. But precisely also because it is to embody and not merely to be a repository, to do human rights is not so much to *have* a tattoo—perhaps as a slightly embarrassing reminder of some old flame—but to *be* the tattoo, the mark of human rights.

Of course, there is only so much one can step out of oneself to reinvent oneself as a standard bearer for a certain cause. Moreover, how one will be understood in the moment is beyond the individual: Alston the person does not have a monopoly on Alston the signifier. One senses that Alston might be received differently by different people: perhaps as the bearer of good news, perhaps as the bearer of bad news; perhaps as a neutral Oracle for human rights, perhaps as a rude interferer in domestic affairs; perhaps as a figure of dignity, perhaps as hegemonic white masculine presence. On one level there is not much that Alston can do about how he is perceived; on another level, there is everything that Alston can do about what he decides to be, at least as a rapporteur. On that front, the way one shapes the role can make a world of difference; perhaps the difference between kitsch and authenticity.

I do not mean this in the trivial sense that special rapporteurs can be more or less crass or graceful—that is banal and there have been superlative and abyssal special rapporteurs. Rather, I mean it in the deeper sense that praxis can, however temporarily, dissolve polarities, exploit contradictions and belie expectations to do good in the world. That good then becomes not necessarily the good of human rights—any more than we would primarily credit the English language for the good things that some anglophones do—but nor of course would it be possible without English. To take an image: we recognize Shakespeare's genius as his own; English does not spring to life to become Shakespearian English without the creativity of Shakespeare to bring out its virtualities; but nor of course is that Shakespearian genius without debt to English as a language. In short, English is not exactly unconnected—to say the least—to the great cultural forms produced in the English language. The same language spoken by different persons can be the closest thing to approximating a universal, or an obscure and obfuscating dialect.

As will be argued, praxis does not inevitably redeem some of the flaws inherent in the human rights project, but it can show it under a more productive light than that shone by its critics. The praxis of human rights is often richer, more searching, and inspired than the bare idea of human rights. It often acknowledges, if implicitly, the flaws and contradictions inherent in the project. It thrives on the idea of human rights but is also, in the best of cases, better—more graceful, more inspired, more attuned—than the idea itself. It elevates the cause. At the same time, the practice of human rights suggests that the idea of human rights is also much more fragile, dependent as it is on a range of very concrete performances.

I use the episode of Alston in Alabama to throw light on how a theory of praxis can help us make sense of two major critiques that have been addressed at the international human rights movement over the past few decades (themselves variants of critiques that have been around for much longer). These have destabilized the human rights movement (perhaps more than it cares to admit), largely because they were broadly sympathetic critiques (although they were not always understood as such). The critiques are interesting because, I suspect, they work at cross-purposes, potentially creating an almost impossible trap. The critiques are: first, that human rights seeks to have it both ways, claiming to be beyond politics whilst engaging in politics (Koskenniemi);[2] second, that specifically when it comes to economic issues, human rights does not have much to say that is of substance to address the major global economic issue of the day, notably inequality (Moyn).[3]

Rather than addressing these critiques on their own terms and in line with the emphasis on praxis, I investigate how Alston's visit to Alabama can be understood as both vulnerable to and a response to them. The idea is partly that the critique has always been already internalized in the practice of human rights, that it constantly shapes what human rights practitioners do. This does not necessarily save the praxis of human rights from the critique of human rights because as will be seen there may be limits to how far one may modify human rights through praxis without simultaneously undermining some central claims made in the name of the human rights project; but it does offer an opportunity for creative resolutions of the contradictions within the moment that occasionally resurrects the promise of human rights. The point, then, is neither to refute or abound in the direction of those critiques, all of which are very well taken just as they are limited by some of their assumptions. Rather, it is to identify a distinct space for praxis within and amongst those critiques: vulnerable to them just as they are, to a limited extent, vulnerable to it. In the process, the chapter will propose a moderate defence of the genre of special rapporteurship that is often subtly denigrated as not directly productive of positive international law but which, I will suggest, also, precisely because of its fluidity, better allows human rights a breathing space.[4]

[2] Martti Koskenniemi, 'The Effect of Rights on Political Culture' in Philip Alston (ed), *The EU and Human Rights* (OUP 1999).
[3] Samuel Moyn, *Not Enough: Human Rights in an Unequal World* (Harvard University Press 2018).
[4] For a somewhat similar approach, see Joanna Naples-Mitchell, 'Perspectives of UN Special Rapporteurs on Their Role: Inherent Tensions and Unique Contributions to Human Rights' (2011) 15 The International Journal of Human Rights 232.

26.2 Doing Politics Without Doing Politics: On 'Cheating' and the Constitution of Authority

Alston in Alabama speaks from the authority of human rights. Were it not for that authority, Alston would merely be Alston, one smart and committed human being among many smart and committed human beings. His mandate, in other terms, is decisive in transforming mere words into symbolic capital. But what is the nature of that authority, and do we have reason to defer to it? How are 'ideas' transformed into authority, and why should we take that process seriously?

There has long been a genre of scepticism about human rights that is wary of its ability to make grand claims about politics from the safety of rights discourse. Martti Koskenniemi in particular has long criticized human rights for impossibly prioritizing rights over the good and in the process foregrounding only a particular conception of the good; for maintaining the status quo through banal and technocratic monopolization of rights; and for failing, in the end, to convey any experience of pain or injustice. In particular Koskenniemi has argued (in a collection edited, as it happens, by Alston), that:

> rights-rhetoric is not as powerful as it claims to be. It does not hold a coherent set of normative demands that could be resorted to in the administration of society. To the contrary, despite its claim for value-neutrality, rights-rhetoric is constantly reduced to conflicting and contested arguments about the political good.[5]

As a result of pretending that things are, however, otherwise, human rights law often institutionalizes a political culture of 'bad faith', one that seeks to make entirely political points whilst pretending to be outside of politics. This is a damning and influential critique that was, it should be said, quite focused on the European judicial system. How does it fare in the context of Alston's excursion as a rapporteur in the southern United States, which is of course quite a different exercise from the mainstreaming of human rights at the United Nations[6] or the day-to-day administration of human rights justice at the ECtHR? Is human rights law 'as powerful as it claims to be', and what happens if is not?

At the heart of Koskenniemi's critique is a sense that human rights organs proceed from a sense of inherited authority that allows them to gloss over the profound contradictions and indeterminacy of human rights. One might happen to agree with Alston, but the question is whether his is a message that can be delivered from a position of authority rather than merely a position of faith; whether it is, moreover, a message that can convince and perhaps compel others than those already converted. There are many people claiming that inequality is wrong. In the end, the question is why should one take Alston's word for it that poverty arises in Alabama as a result of certain social and political dysfunctions in the United States? Why should we listen to 'Philip' rather than 'Bernie' or 'Elizabeth', for example?

The answer would have to be something like: Although Alston does not have four decades of experience in state and federal US politics trying to push a socialist or social-democratic agenda, although or perhaps precisely because he was never elected, he has at least been put in the position he is in to speak for human rights. But what does it mean to speak for human rights? To begin with, it is worth noting the main claim to authority of Philip's reports about

[5] Koskenniemi (n 2) 133.

[6] Martti Koskenniemi, 'Human Rights Mainstreaming as a Strategy for Institutional Power' (2010) 1 Humanity: An International Journal of Human Rights, Humanitarianism, and Development 47.

poverty is not what they say; it is that it is him who says them in his quality as special rapporteur. After all, the discourse on radical inequality is simply a widespread left critique. Human rights certainly have no monopoly over indignation about poverty. Moreover, even rights discourse about poverty comes in many forms, some of which are barely distinguishable from the general political conversation about poverty and some of which are no doubt quite different from Alston's version of it. Erase the document reference number and Alston's report becomes just one among a great many documents deploring poverty in the name of human rights. The point of the report is purely performative.

Immediately though, this will seem to restate the problem. What is that performativity and why should we take it seriously? Simply because a document has a UN number does not make it authoritative; in fact, we may have all kinds of reasons to be wary of reports that bear the UN imprimatur. The obvious route for international lawyers is to remind us that the underlying treaties are binding and that the special rapporteurs are merely a binding prolongation of such treaties. But the question of the binding character of special rapporteurs' pronouncements, even more than that of treaty bodies, remains contentious.[7] For hard-nosed positivists, this will simply seem like an argument that cannot be won on its own ground. A special rapporteur does not have the means of such ambition and, indeed, at best his or her work is understood as authoritative.

But I would go further: Even if it could be argued that a special rapporteur's pronouncements were binding—that Alston's word, in short, was as good as, say, the ECtHR's—my suspicion is that this would not alleviate the suspicion of intellectual fraud implicit in Koskenniemi's critique. The claim about the binding character of human rights rapporteurship from a positive law point of view might in fact weaken Alston's authority, either by stretching credulity or by cheapening the source of his true authority, such as it may be. This is because hanging the fate of human rights onto a legal commitment was always a perilous gambit, where the force of human rights has traditionally been found to lie in the fact that they would be binding *even* if states did not formally subscribe to them. And it is because to persistently invoke the law against states who are speaking politics is to risk looking strangely disconnected, perhaps even naive.

It is here that a theory of the praxis of human rights—a praxis freed from fragile and pompous claims about the binding character of international human rights law—may help reconceptualize our understanding of Alston's *actual* authority. Rather than try to assimilate special rapporteurs to treaty bodies or courts, the point may be to fully engage the idiosyncrasy of what it means to be a special rapporteur. As a reminder, a special rapporteur is an *independent* expert: working, as it were, at the United Nations' behest but in their own name, even as they may claim to speak for some broader constituency. It is worth foregrounding the intense peculiarity of the position of authority represented by a special rapporteur. In the Weberian sociology of the state, an international human rights rapporteur is neither here nor there, and not just because he or she exists in a supranational arena that was not Weber's focus. They are something of a free-wheeling, unknown entity: not sufficiently embedded in the system to be a technocrat; yet not so inspiring as to be a charismatic leader.

But perhaps this is precisely the cue for someone like Alston to forge a path towards his own authority, an authority that is less the authority of human rights as idea or law, and more the precarious authority of a particular individual, thrust in a particular role at a particular

[7] Surya P Subedi and others, 'The Role of the Special Rapporteurs of the United Nations Human Rights Council in the Development and Promotion of International Human Rights Norms' (2011) 15 The International Journal of Human Rights 155. See Chapter 20 in this volume by Hélène Trigoudja for a more optimistic assessment.

moment—an authority, in short, that is more constructed and performed than merely derived and received. It may be that the authority of a special rapporteur lies precisely in his or her ability to not fall into the jargonic know-it-all of global human rights talk—to resurrect the possibility of a politics of the human that is not entirely naturalist nor instrumental; a politics in fact that belies the occasionally well-taken Koskenniemian wariness with what human rights tend to become, and in the process of producing an aesthetic that both conjures up and exorcises the worst fears about human rights. As he steps into—in his case—the well-worn shoes of special rapporteur, Alston arguably makes a triple claim to authority that goes to the very heart of his position.

First and at least implicitly, he makes a point about expertise. Expertise is a highly coded term within the international human rights world. For example, 'political' bodies (the HRC) are contrasted with 'expert' bodies (the treaty-monitoring mechanisms). Expertise directly points to a legal-technocratic form of legitimacy. In the context of a special rapporteurship, Alston could be understood as saying something like: 'If I am a special rapporteur, I must know what I am talking about.' Indeed, the human rights expert 'knows a lot' about human rights and their content. Part of the performance of some rapporteurs is making it clear that they know a lot, both about the facts and the law. I certainly do not think Alston is cheating in embodying that claim; the problem is what kind of authority knowing a great deal about human rights provides. There are a lot of people who know a lot about human rights, including those who violate them or those who study them from the Ivory Tower, who we would not necessarily consider as having any particular authority to speak about them.

Second, Alston can of course rely on his mandate. Expertise is just a convenient short hand, but really what is at stake is a particular kind of 'authorized expertise'. 'Authority comes from the fact that I was invested with it', seems to be the elegantly circular claim. Throw in a bit of media confusion, however, and before you know it Alston is presented as a 'UN official' on TV shows, endowing him with the full strength of the organization rather than his sole expertise, possibly to the actual UN officials' chagrin (this is clearly a confusion that would have arisen despite Alston of course). This is fine as far as it goes, and no one is claiming that Alston was improperly made a special rapporteur. But the authority of the mandate is too circular and too formalistic. It allows one to print letterhead with the name 'special rapporteur', but it does not in and of itself confer any deep authority to act and be heard except through possibly referring back to the expert claim. The United Nations might have had all kinds of bad political reasons for nominating someone as special rapporteur. No one is fooled.

Third, the authority of the special rapporteurship might be a function of the fact that Alston is only in the United States, as it were, at that country's invitation. The claim is something along the lines of: 'I am only there by virtue of the treaties you yourself ratified'. It is subtly different from merely claiming that the treaties are binding; a more pointed and personalized reference to the notion that, whatever contingent opposition the United States may manifest to the visit, it occurs against the background of that state's hypothetically stated commitment to international human rights. Per Alston's US report:

> Successive administrations, including the current one, have determinedly rejected the idea that economic and social rights are full-fledged human rights, *despite their clear recognition not only in key treaties that the United States has ratified, such as the Convention on the Elimination of All Forms of Racial Discrimination, but also in the Universal Declaration of*

> *Human Rights, which the United States has long insisted other countries must respect.* But denial does not eliminate responsibility, nor does it negate obligations.[8]

This is a powerful claim, again, but it only goes so far in the face of persistent denials by the host state that the rapporteur's visit is useful or welcome. States will disagree about how much authority they intended to give away to rapporteurs; they will disagree that rapporteurs paying them a visit is a good use of scarce resources; they will accuse the rapporteur of doing someone's bidding. One is probably better off not reminding states at every turn that a special rapporteur's mandate is law and invitation based, lest they be tempted to rescind that invitation.

In this context, my contention is that it is inevitable that sooner or later one will retreat to a position that invokes the authority of human rights per se, as the ultima ratio of what one does. Ultimately it is the force of rights rather than the force of law that stands as the ultimate default line. This is quite clear in Alston's approach. Yet this is a tricky point to make because we are not sure what kind of authority speaking in the name of human rights confers. It is here that the praxis of human rights might alleviate these tensions somewhat, especially a praxis that is closely attuned to both the pitfalls of the language that it uses (and therefore does not succumb to it) and the potentialities of its environment. Philip achieves this in a variety of ways. First, and rather than just the force of law itself, Alston invokes an implicit communitarian standard. He points out that:

> In practice, the United States is alone among developed countries in insisting that, while human rights are of fundamental importance, they do not include rights that guard against dying of hunger, dying from a lack of access to affordable health care or growing up in a context of total deprivation.[9]

'You are alone', Alston seems to say, and this cannot be right, especially when it comes to rights. This is of course not full proof: The United States might, alone, be right in not considering that economic rights are real rights. The authority of the international community majority may not exactly do wonders with a country imbued by its sense of self-determining exceptionalism. In fact, many more states and their leaders might think exactly the same thing as the United States even though they went ahead with the ratification of treaties that seemingly say the contrary, but which they then barely took seriously. Rhetorically isolating the United States in this way, though, even if it means making the most of what may be a paper-thin formal consensus, at least helps Alston position himself as speaking for a better, more universal version of human rights.

A second strategy involves building authority from the ground up by relinquishing the international-majority argument and, instead, seeking to hold the target state to its own standards. For Alston:

> Since the US has refused to recognize economic and social rights agreed by most other states (except for the right to education in state constitutions), the primary focus of the present report is on those civil and political rights reflected in the US Bill of Rights and in the International Covenant on Civil and Political Rights which the US has ratified.[10]

[8] Philip Alston, 'Statement on Visit to the USA, by Professor Philip Alston, United Nations Special Rapporteur on Extreme Poverty and Human Rights' OHCHR (Washington 15 December 2017) para 8.

[9] ibid para 8.

[10] ibid para 9.

This shows remarkable adaptability: not quite stooping to a country's low but processing one's review of it through some of its own categories. As it happens, for Alston there is a connection between the economic and social neglect of one's population and the undermining of American constitutional 'sacred cows': 'The foundation stone of American society is democracy, but it is being steadily undermined.'

A third and somewhat perilous strategy involves drawing on the 'facts'. Of course, we know that the facts do not quite speak for themselves and hardly select themselves, but they speak to something that is less easily refutable. Even if we do not agree about their exact legal characterization, a rapporteur might at least shed light on a situation that is intuitively, viscerally even, deplorable. But perhaps more than the facts, Alston seeks to invoke the victims as they have conveyed facts to him. Facts are transformed by the fact that they come from victims, for which Alston presents himself as merely a messenger. This is perhaps one of the most compelling twists in the life of a rapporteur: the sort of self-effacement that comes from presenting oneself (and, presumably, thinking of oneself) as 'merely the messenger'.

Ultimately, there is more to the performance of good rapporteurship, even beyond the appeal to human rights, something in the nature of a moral quality that shines through (or not) in the denunciation of injustice. In Alston's case, it is a sense of cold indignation and even anger. These reflect not just the injustice of the situation but also the betrayal (of one's peoples), the incoherence (of claiming to abide by certain standards and not doing so), and the inequity (that so much wealth could achieve so little). The case for law violation clearly takes second place to a more 'sentimental' performance. Alston re-subjectifies the reaction to what he sees. This is interesting because there is no obvious reason why one should treat Alston's moral indignation, genuine as it may be, more seriously than any other (we live, after all, in an age of constant indignation), except perhaps that it is a channelled indignation that, in a flash, transcends its author and is expressed in the collective name of all those who share it. In that respect, the role of the special rapporteur, their specific authority, is less to authoritatively interpret international human rights law than it is to express a residual sense of revulsion at raw inequity that is largely pre-legal.

26.3 Poverty, Economic Inequality, and International Human Rights Law's Lack of Substance

The problem, however, is that what enhances the special rapporteur's authority, what elevates his or her function, may be what weakens their policy relevance. We can all agree that the lack of sewage is awful, but we do not agree about what the causes are and how to remedy the situation. The purity of indignation and the specificity of recommendations about how to solve the problem are inversely correlated. At worst, the condemnation may make the problem harder to solve. To solicit indignation, the special rapporteur might be required to abstract violations from their cause, to make them appear as a uniquely, perhaps even evil by design, when they may only be the result of immensely complex structural policies. Moreover, in designating the government, as it is often only natural for a UN rapporteur to do, he or she may further obfuscate responsibilities, including of corporations but perhaps most notably of capitalism itself. The resulting report may end up relatively unhelpful because it is embedded in international legal discourse as much as it is about human rights. It may as a result be compelled to focus narrowly on the state, which is not always primarily responsible for economic and social rights violations.

Indeed, I wonder if those relishing the moment of Alston's presence in Alabama (among which I include myself) do not risk mistaking their particular social-democratic ethos with the universalism of human rights; and whether, in doing so, they don't risk forgetting that it is hardly as if neoliberalism, including its most aggressive libertarian forms, does not have its own human rights apostles; or indeed as if the international human rights movement cannot be suspected of at least the occasional complicity with neoliberal modes of thought.[11] Of course, one can always claim that theirs is not the true or proper understanding of human rights but as soon as one gets embroiled in such arguments (as we, no doubt, should), then one can no longer claim the high ground of a dominant universal human rights standpoint. One will either invoke a consensus view about human rights that, it turns out, has never existed except in the echo chamber of a particular human rights technocracy, or one will reveal human rights as little better than what they seek to transcend, a political mud fight with no end in sight.

This is the heart of Sam Moyn's well known critique of the overarching investment in rights and in particular minimal subsistence at the expense of social justice. In *Not Enough*, Moyn argues extensively that human rights have proved inadequate to the task of reducing inequality as the primary political problem of our age.[12] He faults the human rights movement in particular for having become a sort of tepid and polite advocacy group that merely prolongs the status quo in a context of cruel inequality. Others have taken issue with Moyn's lack of interest in the actual praxis of human rights and the fact that he artificially separates the movement's focus on status on the one hand and economic justice on the other.[13] There is plenty of evidence that at least part of the human rights movement has been very interested in the problem of inequality.[14] But if Moyn's book had been more fully versed in the multifarious ways in which the international human rights discourse does engage issues of economic welfare, would he not still have had a point, albeit a more appropriately nuanced one? Surely the idea that international human rights discourse has emphasized sufficiency over equality is broadly reflective of the claims made on behalf of a minimum core of economic and social rights. It reflects a real unease within the human rights movement when it comes to critiquing particular social regimes as opposed to their results.

In the end though the interesting question is less who said what and whether the 'international human rights movement' is to blame than whether, assuming the lack of focus on inequality is a reasonable point to make about the recent mainstream history of human rights, this signals something inherent or merely contingent about human rights. Part of the problem here may be the definition of what counts as the international human rights movement or even thinking in terms of a movement, with its connotation of homogeneous impetus. Maybe international human rights law is better understood as a field of contestation over the very meaning of human rights where, to be sure, over time certain meanings become dominant, but where such meanings remain contested and contestable, as fundamentally rooted in ethical and political questioning.

[11] Jessica Whyte, *The Morals of the Market: Human Rights and the Rise of Neoliberalism* (Verso Books 2019).

[12] Moyn (n 3).

[13] Gráinne de Búrca, 'Not Enough: Human Rights in an Unequal World' (2018) 16 International Journal of Constitutional Law 1347.

[14] Gillian MacNaughton and Diane F Frey, *Economic and Social Rights in a Neoliberal World* (CUP 2018); Madeline Baer, *Stemming the Tide: Human Rights and Water Policy in a Neoliberal World* (OUP 2017); Karen Ann Faulk, *In the Wake of Neoliberalism: Citizenship and Human Rights in Argentina* (Stanford University Press 2012); Manfred Nowak, *Human Rights Or Global Capitalism: The Limits of Privatization* (University of Pennsylvania Press 2017).

Here again, the praxis of international human rights offers no easy resolution, although it does offer possible paths to addressing these critiques. The critique cannot be made to magically fizzle away because a UN special rapporteur, whether they want to or not, is embedded in a particular human rights discourse that makes the highlighting of inequality problematic. One can of course utter the word 'inequality' (words are cheap) but the question is whether one can do so whilst still claiming the authority of human rights and not be seen as merely slipping in one's political agenda in the process, a clandestine stowaway on a ship that is unreceptive. Human rights rapporteurs may be on the strongest grounds when they merely deplore violations that are fairly easy to ascertain. Persons have been thrown to jail, tortured, or, indeed, blatantly denied food or water. Such is the appeal of apparently raw facts and the testimony of those who convey them, even when it comes to persons' economic condition: there in the slum, we recognize the unmistakable stench of injustice, even if we cannot agree how it came about, who is to blame, or what to do about it.

Perhaps our quite wide revulsion at what we see (or are made to see) and our sense that it is an unfortunate situation unites us briefly in our belief in human rights and their potential for critique: this is not what we signed up for. Human rights law, then, may not be able to pick between socialism or the free market, or even have much of an intrinsic understanding of why poverty happens, but it can at least tell abject poverty when it sees it. That is not nothing, but nor is it a particularly impressive feat: many other value systems can and have been indignant about radical poverty. It is not obvious that we need human rights to tell us that poverty is shocking or that what made the project appealing to its supporters can survive being thinned out in this way. Moreover, the critique of human rights is only so strong as what it has in front of it: formidable vis-à-vis the cartoonesque tyrant but more ill-at-ease when faced with complex questions of distributive justice.

However, the praxis of human rights rapporteurships does suggest ways in which it may depart from the script that has been written for them, in the creativity of the moment as it were. The act of reporting on poverty from a human rights angle can be an opportunity to play with the limits of the discourse and perhaps transcend it. It is useful in that respect to again pay attention to some of the rhetorical strategies that Alston as a special rapporteur deploys to make his case. To begin with, Alston, for all his boldness in both decrying poverty and pointing out how it persists, does predictably fall just short of prescribing economic policy. Indeed, not overstepping the boundaries of one's authority may be seen as the very essence of authority, as a discipline of restraint. The one thing that Alston tries not to do, although one senses he would like to at times, is to suggest how exactly one should go about remedying all these things. Instead, perhaps prudently, he reformulates US poverty as a case of lack of political will rather than of difficulties in coming up with the optimal policy mix:

> There is no magic recipe for eliminating extreme poverty, and each level of government must make its own good-faith decisions. At the end of the day, however, particularly in a rich country like the United States, the persistence of extreme poverty is a political choice made by those in power. With political will, it could readily be eliminated.[15]

This both recognizes that Alston does not have the final answer, yet that he can still fault the United States for not doing enough. Note that there may be much more value in that raw moral claim and what it constructs than appears at first. Sceptics emphasize the difficulty

[15] Alston, 'Statement' (n 8) para 17.

of politics and the intractability of economic problems; but in doing so, they always seem to proceed from the assumption of a benevolent sovereign, struggling to deliver the goods. But why should we have any reason to think that this is the starting point in economic and social terms any more than it is in civil and political terms, when so much evidence points not only to the benign neglect but even the malign oppression of the poor? The US may be as good a place to start as any on that score, exposing its flagrantly unequal and racialized politics to the gaze of an outside observer.

Still, this is a bold claim and one whose tenor was not missed by the United States, which in response vociferously insisted that:

> Accusations that the United States shows 'contempt and hatred' for the poor, including accusations of a criminal justice system designed to keep low income persons in poverty while generating public revenue, are inaccurate, inflammatory, and irresponsible.[16]

Moreover, the accusation of lack of political will raises interesting questions. Where does political will come from? Who exercises agency? Did not the American electorate choose leaders whose record in fighting poverty was well known? Is the issue one of the dysfunction of democracy? Of oppressive minorities? Is it Alston's will that Americans 'will' a different society or his diagnosis that they did and were lied to? What if American citizens, including the poor, had voted, behind a veil of relative ignorance, for a system of lottery that would make the 1 per cent extremely rich and the rest poor? What of self-determination? I do not take a position on these issues here so much as I want to note that the critique of poverty can be simultaneously a critique of both the dysfunctions and the functioning of democracy.

It is at this stage that the praxis of human rights is drawn out, as it were, to transcend the bare moral denunciation of outcomes to engage in a critique of the material and political conditions of poverty. In fact, Alston's visits to the United States and United Kingdom and ensuing reports may partly belie Moyn's claim about obliviousness to inequality, putting that question right front and centre, and making a strong connection between inequality and poverty (one expects not prompted by Moyn's critique, although one cannot be sure!). Certainly, Alston did not mince his words upon returning (as it were) from his US country visit:

> The United States has the highest rate of income inequality among Western countries. The $1.5 trillion in tax cuts in December 2017 overwhelmingly benefited the wealthy and worsened inequality. The consequences of neglecting poverty and promoting inequality are clear. The United States has one of the highest poverty and inequality levels among the OECD countries.[17] (. . .) [N]ew policies: (a) provide unprecedentedly high tax breaks and financial windfalls to the very wealthy and the largest corporations; (b) pay for these partly by reducing welfare benefits for the poor; (. . .) The share of the top 1 per cent of the population in the United States has grown steadily in recent years.[18]

Elsewhere, Alston points out that:

[16] US Mission Geneva, 'Country Concerned Statement in Response to SR Alston's Country Report on the United States' US Mission to International Organizations in Geneva (Geneva, 22 June 2018) <www.geneva.usmission.gov/2018/06/22/country-concerned-statement-in-response-to-sr-alstons-country-report-on-the-united-states/> accessed 16 July 2020.

[17] UNGA, 'Report of the Special Rapporteur on Extreme Poverty and Human Rights' (2018) UN DOC A/HRC/38/33/Add.1 [5].

[18] ibid [5].

> High child and youth poverty rates perpetuate the intergenerational transmission of poverty very effectively, and ensure that the American dream is rapidly becoming the American illusion. The equality of opportunity, which is so prized in theory, is in practice a myth, especially for minorities and women, but also for many middle-class White workers.[19]

Again, the emphasis is on the United States as an outlier ('The infant mortality rate, at 5.8 deaths per 1,000 live births, is almost 50 per cent higher than the OECD average of 3.9'), on things that the government itself is aware are problematic (pointing out the existence of 'federally designated 'dental professional shortage areas'), or on the United States falling short of its own ideals. But Alston goes further, specifically pointing out that 'What is known, from long experience and in the light of the Government's human rights obligations, is that there are indispensable ingredients for a set of policies designed to eliminate poverty.' A list follows of certainly not particularly objectionable but also quite specific ingredients ('democratic decision-making, full employment policies, social protection for the vulnerable, a fair and effective justice system, gender and racial equality, respect for human dignity, responsible fiscal policies and environmental justice'). The list steers quite clearly short of explicitly endorsing distributive policies or economic policies. It is almost as if, on the cusp of doing so, Alston held back, certainly one suspects not because he thought that such policies are inappropriate, but because he may have sensed that this could backfire.

Still, this is language that goes significantly beyond deploring an outcome, into the fraught terrain of means. The irony may be that just as Moyn's book was coming out, Alston was pushing the envelope in terms of what could be said from within his function about why rights violations occurred in the first place. Here is a special rapporteur going beyond the clinical diagnosis of rights violations to indict an entire system. This is not unheard of in human rights reports, but nor is it really business as usual.

The problem is that critiquing inequality or privatization as a source of poverty (and not just poverty) gets Alston very close to the essence of politics. But it is that obvious (except to those who already believe it) that it is 'known' that certain things need to be done to eliminate poverty? Is Alston not dangerously at risk of overextending himself in his specific role as a special rapporteur? Or does he only do so at the risk of vague generalities? How does the ability to condemn radical poverty, such as it may be, equip Alston to diagnose poverty and condemn inequality? The point is not that he is necessarily wrong; I happen to agree, as do many people, that is not the point. The report is tightly written and constitutes a useful summary of a particular critique of poverty in the United States. But the causes of US poverty are surely remarkably complex. How likely is it that a well-written but ultimately quite panoramic indictment could go to the bottom of them and not end up just representing the well-informed, sensible view of, ultimately, a particular individual, embedded in a certain left-of-centre liberal ethos?

An interesting postscript to this sortie is Alston's subsequent report on the United Kingdom and his taking on of the problem of privatization, a problem that many would recognize is crucial to questions of economic welfare and the rise of inequality, but which by and large the international human rights machinery has steered clear from. In that report, Alston is forced to recognize that 'Existing human rights accountability mechanisms are clearly inadequate for dealing with the challenges presented by large-scale and widespread

[19] ibid [10].

privatization. Human rights proponents need to fundamentally reconsider their approach.'[20] Here then is a special rapporteur at the pinnacle of the human rights system recognizing that the problem might not just be with states but with the approach of the international human rights movement.

Also, remember that one does not get rewarded for preaching to the choir. Making those who happen to think that inequality breeds poverty happy does not equal proving that inequality breeds poverty. Alston is the champion of many people in the United States, the United Kingdom, and elsewhere, but it seems more interesting to understand under what conditions he might convince those who happen not to think that inequality is the cause of poverty—who think in fact that inequality is a formidable engine of competition and the overall lifting of the tide. Maybe those are few and far between, but the claim that trickle-down economics or some version of it is not actually genuinely believed by some is not plausible, and in fact dangerously conspiratorial. In its response to Alston's country report the United States in fact emphasized the importance of supply-side economics, noting that 'Sadly, Mr. Alston's report does not give due credit to current policies enacted by this administration to spur economic growth and the prosperity it brings for all Americans.'[21]

And this of course leaves out the left of the centre-left, those who will think that the kind of tepid denunciation that human rights produce will never go far enough. Forget about economic and social rights! Tell us about class struggle! White domination and racial oppression! Decolonizing capitalism! Alston can maybe hint at these themes but even if he is sympathetic, is hamstrung by his role within the system. To step too much out of the bonds of conventional expertise (eg à la Jean Ziegler)[22] would be quixotic and counterproductive. Human rights must, in the end, remain in the realm of generality or appear as incarnating merely 'the human rights party'. That is not a trick that can be pulled off, as the audience, whether it be on the right or on the left, would immediately call the bluff, the smuggling of politics into rights.

The economic and social terrain therefore tends to draw the special rapporteur into the open, into a place where his hard-won authority may not withstand the contestability of the claims made in its name. There is a mismatch in particular between the foundation of that authority (international law) in the best of cases and the sort of arguments that would need to be made to structurally tackle poverty (economic, social, and political arguments). There are limits, in other words, to how much the authority of the expert international lawyer can translate into the expertise of the social and economic reformist, not to mention the revolutionary.

26.4 Conclusion: Human Rights Are What We Make of Them?

In the end, whether Alston in Alabama 'pulls it off' is open to question. What pulling it off in this context means remains a puzzling question, itself shaped by practice. Is it getting attention for the cause? Is it expressing something even if it leads to no change? It is sticking

[20] UNGA 'Report of the Special Rapporteur on extreme poverty and human rights' (2019) UN DOC A/73/396 [26].

[21] US Mission Geneva (n 16).

[22] Jean Ziegler wrote some of the most evidently political reports on the 'right to food' and proved a relatively controversial figure in his days as special rapporteur. See UNHRC 'Report of the Special Rapporteur on the Right to Food' (2008) UN Doc A/HRC/7/5.

it to the man? Is it developing the law in new and insightful ways? Is it connecting to people on the ground? What emerges is an image of a praxis that may be significantly better than a critique targeted at a stultified, somewhat straw-manish version of human rights; but also a praxis that is not as free of complication as it is often imagined to be by those fully invested in the discourse of human rights. The critique is often right but only in a general way, as capturing a certain sentiment about what could be wrong with human rights.

The structure of international human rights law—under one light at least, technocratic, monolithic, and consensual—has helped the critique make a series of points that are quite devastating. But the critique is also only so strong because what it imagines to have in front of itself is weak and predictable. International human rights, no doubt, can be this poor version of itself that sceptics like to scorn. But its very indeterminacy creates opportunities—in the moment—for the nimble interpreter of human rights to not be where he or she is expected; to be, perhaps, where he or she is the least expected. The critique, in such circumstances, seems to miss its mark because suddenly it faces a praxis that is at once more fluid and robust than it expected. At the same time, the contortions that someone like Alston needs to make to respond to the implicit critique also put it in a place that is vulnerable. What he gains in substance, he risks losing in authority; what he gains in authority, he loses in substance. This is a hard circle to square in the best of circumstances.

A theory of the praxis of international human rights law, of doing human rights, is one that focuses on the sense of opportunity and indecision offered up by the world. There is no immanent nature to human rights or obvious policy prescriptions that flow from them. There is only an endless and dauting sense of opportunity provided by particular moments within which human rights can, briefly, be made sense of because they raise the right questions in the right place at the right moment. The question that 'Alston in Alabama' raises is: How might one use one's mandate to effectuate change here and now, given the cards one has been dealt? Alston's particular intervention is one way in which one might make sense of a mandate, at the intersection of law and politics; it bears his style and his imprimatur; it auto-corrects for some known biases of human rights; it struggles with some of its limitations; and it finds creative ways to occasionally belie the sceptics.

A few things do emerge from what might be a theory of the (best) praxis of international human rights law. First, is a key element of choice and timing. Was it a good idea to organize this visit and at this time? It was, arguably, the moment to talk about privatization, for example, or the moment to bring the fight to populist politics, although some will think that it was too little too late. Second, an element of authenticity. Is a special rapporteur speaking law to the state or are they using the law to translate claims made by actual people based on their own, irreducible version of events? Are they reaching behind the jargon, maybe, to recover something more basic, like a sense of indignation? Third, an element of situationality. One cannot but note, for example, that Alston is, simultaneously and unusually for a special rapporteur, living within although not from the country in which he speaks. He is thus both an insider and an outsider on a great many different levels. The question is what it does for the human rights project to 'break ranks' with the comforts of privilege.

What stands out, in the end, is a certain performativity of human rights. The visit is the message, as it were, and what matters is what it conveys far beyond the report itself. For example, merely in meeting certain unprivileged groups, the special rapporteur further constitutes them as interlocutors, and therefore as subjects. In adopting a listening composure, the rapporteur suggests that victims of human rights are not merely conduits to make a claim on the world stage but ends in themselves. What is striking about Alston's visit to Alabama, moreover, is how it seems destined to speak truth to power; to refuse the exoticizing thrust of human rights by bringing the fight to the heart of the hegemon.

One is reminded of another influential critique of human rights, one that this short chapter cannot do full justice to. In a sizzling piece written more than two decades ago, Makau Mutua indicted the human rights movement for its saviour complex.[23] That critique, again, is only so strong as what it finds in its way. It is brilliant when human rights are used as a bully pulpit to lecture the third world, as no doubt they often have been. It is less powerful and too broad when human rights happen to be mobilized in the global South to force social change or when they are used to challenge the hegemon from within. The critique does not necessarily fall flat: one might still hold Alston's (reconstructed) antipodean white masculinity against him as itself a signifier (perhaps of privilege, of access). By the same token, his willingness to use his position to defend the poorest among the poor, victims no doubt of systemic racism as well as poverty, speaks to a sense of human solidarity that is perhaps the human rights movement's most unsung but highest virtue.

It is almost as if Alston, a veteran of international human rights causes only too aware of the pitfalls of human rights action, were systematically engaged in what one might call a sort of 'methodological offsetting'—the technique by which one consciously and deliberately compensates for the known negative effects of one's activity, just as one might offset one's carbon emissions as one was engaging in a particularly carbon-intensive moment.

What all of this points to, in the end, is that whatever good may come out of this particular visit to Alabama need not be chalked up entirely to the international human rights movement as such or, indeed, to Alston himself. Of course, this is a temptation, just as it will be tempting to dissociate oneself from purported human rights talk that one disagrees with (states invoking the 'right to security' to put in place repressive policies, or individuals invoking 'freedom of religion' to refuse to serve same sex couples). But there is a risk of confusion. Human rights are not so much the cause of that moment than, at best, the language in which it expresses itself. This rather relativizes the status of human rights and shows how they must be secondary to a broader politics of the good. It should also relativize the calls announcing human rights' demise or calling us to give up on them, because there are no 'human rights' waiting to be given up on, only performances of human rights waiting to be engaged in (or not) and which we may simply decide to leave to others, who we have reason to think may take them in all the wrong directions.

So are human rights really what one makes of them, much more than what they make of us? This is an eminently complex question, but one thing at least seems certain. The more the individuality of the human rights practitioner shines through, the more it is precisely that that we will applaud or condemn, rather than 'human rights' in any general sense. Applauding the individual is of course trivial on one level: individual merit has relatively little to do with producing the sort of effects we should hope for human rights in the world. It may even feed into a cultish veneration that ought to have little to do with human rights. And just as one should resist unduly praising the human rights project for the great deeds of a few individuals, one should resist excessively condemning the human project for the bad or limited things occasionally done in its name. At the same time, in applauding the individual we may merely be applauding a particularly edifying example of political responsibility in the face of an uncertain world. Ultimately, what we applaud is less human rights per se than a particularly savvy use of the politics that human rights make possible.

[23] Makau Mutua, 'Savages, Victims, and Saviors: The Metaphor of Human Rights' (2001) 42 Harvard International Law Journal 201.

The politics involved is perhaps, at heart, a politics of persuasion, artfully mixing attempts at seduction and admonition. Alston does take his state interlocutors seriously, refusing to give up on them. He appeals to their better selves even as he may privately be highly doubtful of their good faith. Doing so creates the conditions for dialogue and, perhaps, more importantly, respect. If the better selves are nowhere to be found, of course, the effect of suasion may be limited. Indeed, the limit of a politics of human rights rapporteurship may, in the end, lie in its politeness, its hesitancy towards all-out confrontation. Compared to more conventional political struggles, human rights, in their wholesome embrace, lack a sense of an enemy where we have reason to think that nothing keeps political movements going like enemies. The engine of the *gilets jaunes* is as much hatred for elites as it is a form of distributive justice—and it is certainly not human rights. But Alston is probably only too aware that going after enemies could collapse the project into a crude form of politics and in the end do away with what makes human rights special as that-political-discourse-that-claims-it-is-not-a-political-discourse.

One interesting irony, at any rate, is that being a special rapporteur may well provide more opportunities for a rich and grounded praxis of human rights than, for example, a conventional judicial appointment. This goes against the positivist grain that sees special rapporteurs as somewhat down the food chain in terms of bindingness and even authoritativeness. By contrast, it may be that the nimbleness afforded by the position, the fact that it is relatively unshackled from procedural or even substantive constraint, means that it is more likely, all other things being equal, to reconnect with some of the foundational energy of human rights. That it does so at the cost of being less binding and authoritative, then, may be a small price to pay to periodically breathe life into the project.

Index

For the benefit of digital users, indexed terms that span two pages (e.g., 52–53) may, on occasion, appear on only one of those pages.